THE BRITISH MUSEUM

ENCYCLOPEDIA

OF

# Native
# North
# America

# THE BRITISH MUSEUM

## ENCYCLOPEDIA

### OF

# Native
# North
# America

## RAYNA GREEN

WITH

MELANIE FERNANDEZ

INDIANA UNIVERSITY PRESS

BLOOMINGTON AND INDIANAPOLIS

First published in 1999 in the United Kingdom
by British Museum Press, a division of
The British Museum Company Ltd
46 Bloomsbury Street, London WC1 3QQ

and in the United States by
Indiana University Press, 601 North Morton Street,
Bloomington, Indiana 47404-3797

Manufactured in China

Library of Congress Cataloging-in-Publication Data

A catalog record for this book is available from
the Library of Congress.

ISBN 0-253-33597-3 (cloth)
ISBN 0-253-21339-8 (paper)


1  2  3  4  5   03  02  01  00  99

*Cover*: A Southern Cheyenne man, 'Little Hand', photographed by
D.I. Gill in 1909. National Anthropological Archives, Smithsonian
Institution, Washington DC; a young Plains pow wow dancer.
© Tony Stone Images; a buffalo hide painted in 1992 by Dennis
Fox, Jr. (Mandan, Hidatsa and Sioux). National Museum of
American History, Smithsonian Institution, courtesy of the artist.

*Half title*: Portrait of Scott Bear Don't Walk (Crow and Salish), a
writer and Rhodes Scholar, at an honouring ceremony given him
on his return from Oxford University in 1996. Courtesy of Marjorie
Bear Don't Walk (Salish-Chippewa).

*page vii*: Iroquois embroidered burden strap. © The British Museum.

# Contents

Using this book — vii

Maps of First Nations and Culture Areas — viii

Introduction — 1

**The Encyclopedia** — **2**

Information sources — 183

Picture credits — 186

Quotation acknowledgements — 193

Authors' acknowledgements — 200

General Index — 201

Index of Individuals — 210

## Using this book

The main entries are in A-Z order.

Often more than one version of a Native North American word exists and people may say or write it differently in different languages. In that case, the word is placed in the A-Z entries in its most widely known form, with the variations given. For example, if you look up the **Ojibwa** entry you will also see Anishinabe/Chippewa/Nipissing/Mississauga.

If you are in any doubt where to find something in the A-Z section, you can look it up in the indexes on pages 201–213 .

In the encyclopaedia entries, if a word is shown in **bold type** that means it has an entry of its own that you can look up.

Use the indexes on pages 201–213 to find names, places and things that do not have a main entry of their own.

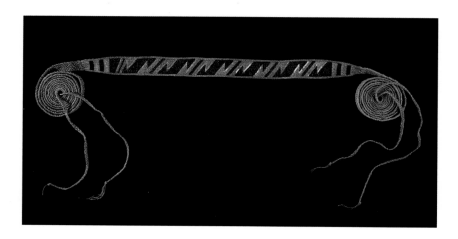

The First Nations

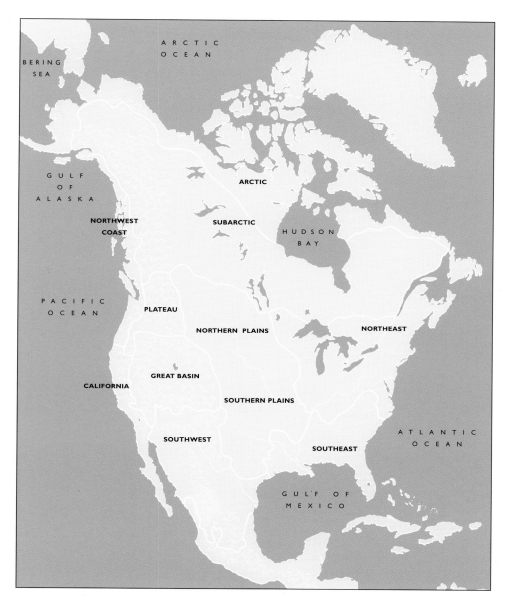

ARCTIC
OCEAN

BERING
SEA

GULF
OF
ALASKA

ARCTIC

NORTHWEST
COAST

SUBARCTIC

HUDSON
BAY

PACIFIC
OCEAN

PLATEAU

NORTHERN PLAINS

NORTHEAST

GREAT BASIN

CALIFORNIA

SOUTHERN PLAINS

ATLANTIC
OCEAN

SOUTHWEST

SOUTHEAST

GULF OF
MEXICO

Culture Areas

# Introduction

This book is an introduction to Native North American history and culture. It does not deal with the ancient people of North America or with the indigenous peoples of South America, but with the peoples inhabiting what became Canada and the United States from about 1,000 AD. In this book, we can give descriptions of only a very few of the over 300 tribal peoples of North America as well as fragments of their histories, religions, art, languages and individual lives, but it does offer some introduction to the peoples, issues and ideas (past and present) that make up Native North American history and culture.

This introduction to Indian history comes as much through pictures and objects as through the words of native people. It represents a simple map of the history – a visual history – of Native North America. The objects, paintings and photographs show much that is painful as well as beautiful; they mean to make a reader want to go further than the pages of this book in order to understand how much more there is to know in that history.

# A

## Abenaki

The name Abenaki refers to the 'People of the Dawn Land', a number of **Algonquian**-speaking peoples (including Pennacook, Penobscot, Sokokis, Pigwacket, Norridgewock, Kennebec, Androscoggin and Wawenock). They lived in the area from the state of Maine to the state of Vermont, then on to the Canadian Northeast. As part of the 17th- and 18th-century Wabenaki Alliance, which included other groups from the Maritime Provinces and the American Northeast Coast, they were large in number and influential. The Abenakis in the West grew **maize** in the Champlain Valley. Those in the East were expert hunters, **basket**makers and **fish**erpeople, centred around Mount Katahdin. They were among the first Natives to experience the devastation of epidemic **disease** such as smallpox in the 17th century and also among the first to convert to **Christianity**.

When their homelands were shattered as the French and the **British** battled for control of their lands, most Abenakis moved toward French-speaking European communities. The Seven Years War (1756–63) caused most Abenakis to lose virtually everything. The Penobscot remained fairly stable in Maine, although many of their lands and rights were removed. Most Abenakis 'went underground', appearing to be assimilated (see **acculturation**) as French-American basketmakers and woodsmen.

Today, Penobscots (and their Passamaquoddy neighbours) still live in Maine. They successfully sued the US government for payments for land taken in violation of the Indian Trade and Non-Intercourse Act of 1789. Odanak Abenakis in Québec, where the Abenaki language still survives, are recognized as **status** Indians by the Canadian and Québecois government. Abenakis in Vermont still lack recognition by the US government, although they are trying to restore their recognition internally and externally as a viable Native community.[1]

## Acoma Pueblo

Acoma Pueblo houses one of the oldest continually occupied sites in North America, in the East of New Mexico. The group of people who live here speak Keresan. Acoma (a name which is related to the people's long occupation of the place) is one of several pueblos (towns) situated on the Rio Grande River. It is linked in culture and language with the other villages of Cochiti and Laguna. Like most of the living pueblos in New Mexico, Acoma has a combination of a traditional religious government and a modern elected **tribal government**. The group has recovered about 500,000 of the several million acres of **land** it originally held when the Spanish arrived in 1539. The tribe runs a large tourism business with its spectacular setting, ancient structures and a thriving and respected tradition of **pottery** making.

## Acculturation, assimilation, adaptation

The word 'acculturation' is used to describe how people undergo great changes and adapt when another culture is introduced to them or forced on them. Thus, the Native, indigenous and aboriginal Indians acculturated to the culture of the Europeans, becoming more like them in the process. An Indian who adopted Western dress and manners, learned English, French or Spanish, adopted Western **agricultural** methods, intermarried with whites, went to school and church, and apparently abandoned Native territory and detectable 'Indian' ways of behaving would be said to be acculturated into white society. The US and Canadian governments, **missionaries** and others tried to enact the 19th-century policy of '**civilization**', to force Indians into a European, American and **Christian** culture. What many saw as successful acculturation of Indians may often have been creative and clever adaptations to Western standards on a surface level in order to survive.

**Mi'kmaq** in Nova Scotia on the most Eastern Coast of North America, were among the first Native peoples to meet Europeans. **Inuit** peoples in the far West of North America were among the last to meet Europeans. In both cases, they began to use

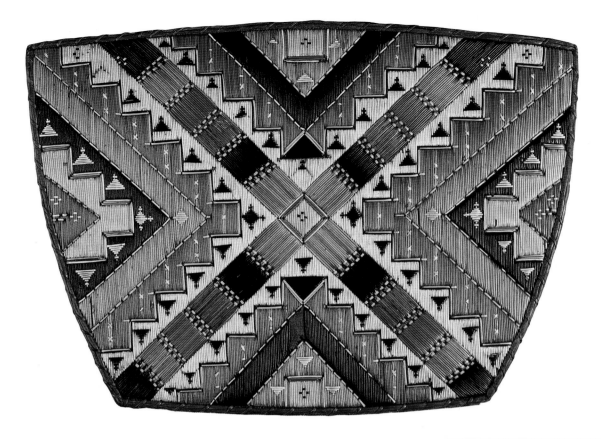

**1 Above** An 18th-century **Mi'kmaq** chair seat made from dyed porcupine quills.

Native materials, designs and techniques to produce objects of European form and function. This suggests an immediate understanding of a new 'market' and shows the flexibility and creativity of Native **art** and behaviour. The Indians who made these new objects had not become like white people, they had just adapted in order to survive.

For some people the only 'real' Indian is a 'traditional Indian' – clad in buffalo robes, adorned with feathers, astride a horse – the classic Hollywood stereotype. This buckskin image of the Plains Indian is indeed part of my history, but so too are suit-wearing tribal leaders. So-called Indian aficionados don't seem too happy about the suit-wearing type. They are often disappointed to learn that

**2 Below** An early 20th-century **Inuit** ivory cribbage board.

Indians wear [ordinary] clothes and that sometimes they dress more like cowboys than Indians. They are not too pleased when they learn that the majority of Indian people identify themselves as Christians… though this certainly doesn't preclude participation in Native religions. Fact is, Indians live in a multi-racial, multi-ethnic world just like everyone else in this country. They've always made alliances, intermarried, and borrowed ideas and technology from other people. This can be a productive process, a source of great vitality and innovation. Indian history didn't end in 1800. Indian cultures aren't some sort of museum piece that are frozen in time, preserved under glass. They evolve, grow and continually try to renew themselves.
*Mark Trahant, Shoshone-Bannock journalist*

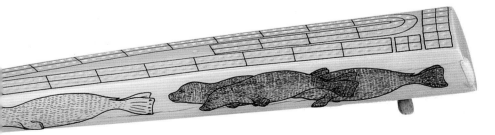

**3**

**3 Above** Santa Clara Pueblo, in northern New Mexico, 1900. Adobe formed most of the houses and outbuildings and all of the bread ovens. In the beehive-shaped ovens, called 'horno' and based on a Spanish design from North Africa, people baked using the wheat introduced into Indian Country by the Spanish. The wood fire made in the horno is allowed to burn up. The wood and its ash are scraped out, and the dough is put in to bake in the heat held in the mud of the high domed oven. Women in Pueblo villages bake hundreds of loaves for feast days.

## Adobe

Adobe is the Spanish word meaning a clay used for building. The insulating power of adobe – cool in the summer and warm in the winter – is remarkable. It makes a perfect modern building material, and is still used by Hispanics and Indians in the American Southwest. The clay bricks enabled people to build huge communities with bigger, more durable and restorable buildings. Pecos, Puyé, Pueblo Bonito and Chaco Canyon, which, at their peak, were home to thousands of people, still stand today as proof of the strength, adaptability and environmental soundness of adobe and show the people's close ties with this extraordinary building material.

The word for clay in Tewa, the language of some Northern Pueblo people who live in the Upper Rio Grande Valley, is *nung*; a word for people is also *nung*. To Pueblo people, humans are clay, mud and earth. People needed clay for shelter and for storage and cooking vessels.

The adobe structures flowed out of the earth and it was often difficult to see where the ground stopped and the structures began…. As we are synonymous with and born of the earth, so we are made of the same stuff as our houses.
*Rina Swentzell, Santa Clara Pueblo landscape historian*

## Africans, African-Americans and Indians

Africans have been in the Americas since Europeans arrived in the late 15th century. One of the first recorded encounters between Native people and Africans was in 1540. It was between the A:*shiwi* or **Zuni** and a North African Spaniard or 'Moor' called Estevanico or Esteban, who represented the Spanish in their explorations into the Southwest. They met and fought at a village called Hawikuh, where the Zuni killed Estevanico and others who had threatened them and demanded tributes for the Spanish King. Other Natives first met Africans and people of African descent in the Caribbean, where Spanish and Portuguese brought them as slaves.

Early colonists in the Caribbean and on the American Continent tried to enslave Indians, forcing them to work the sugar and maize plantations alongside Africans. Many free blacks worked on the whaling ships operating from the New England Coast and they worked alongside Native **Algonquian** peoples from the area. They intermixed with those peoples, creating the mixed-blood, tri-racial **populations** of coastal Indian peoples in the Northeast, such as Narragansetts, Pequots and Shinnecocks.

Slaves often ran away from their masters, fleeing to friendly Indian towns. Several Northern tribes, such as the Tuscaroras who had moved from the South in the 18th century, helped runaway slaves escape to Canada. Some of these escaped slaves stayed, intermarrying with tribal men and women. **Intermarriage** and interbreeding occurred regularly between runaway and freed Africans and Indians, as it did between whites, Indians and blacks. Some **Northwest Coastal** peoples held slaves who never rose beyond slavery. Other tribes in the Southwest had forms of slavery – more like an agreed contract over a number of years – that would absorb slaves (Indian, white or African) into the community when their period of slavery was over. For some tribal peoples, such as **Creeks**, **Seminoles** and Choctaws, interrelationships were common and there were even recognized groups of African-Indians, such as the Black Seminoles.

For **Cherokees**, however, slavery remained of the kind familiar in the American South. The Cherokee Constitution of 1835 forbade intermarriage between Cherokees and Africans. In 1835, over 1,500 slaves lived in the Cherokee Nation, the property of a few wealthy Cherokees. Planters, such as the Vanns who owned over 100 slaves according to the 1835 Cherokee Census, used slave labour to cultivate crops and work as servants. Cherokees took slaves with them to the West during **Removal**. After the **Civil War**, the Cherokees extended 'all the rights of Native Cherokees' to some 2,500 former slaves (thereafter called 'Freedmen'). Cherokees established separate schools for Freedmen, who could also claim 160 acres of Cherokee land. Some tribes never did grant full tribal membership to Freedmen, unlike the Seminoles, who even made elected slots for them in its tribal government.

Before the **Civil War** (1861–65), many blacks moved west, some as traders in the Rocky Mountains, others as members of the US Army, sent to pacify the Indians and ensure that tribal lands were taken, often at gunpoint. These men became known as 'Buffalo Soldiers'. The opening of Indian Territory to settlers, some of them blacks, created greater divisions because some of the land **allotted** to blacks was land removed from Indians. At **schools** such as Hampton Institute, founded in order to educate blacks and Indians, their education was separate. The founding fathers feared the 'race mixing' that inevitably would and did happen when they were put together.[2]

## Agriculture and farming

One of the great misunderstandings about American Indians is that they were all hunters and gatherers before European **contact**. By 2,000 BC, Indians in the Andes, Mexico and the American Southwest domesticated at least four major Native **food** plants. For over 10,000 years, indigenous women in the Northeast, the Southeast and the Central Plains and men in the Southwest had been developing plant breeding. They had selected and refined useful plants, such as **maize**, **beans** and **squash**, and had domesticated some wild varieties. Using a mixture of communal and individual land ownership and use, Natives had adapted farming techniques to the environment and climate.[3] Many tribes cultivated and farmed the majority of their foods and readily shared this knowledge with the European newcomers. Indians of North and South America domesticated six of the world's 13 major food plants (maize, brown beans, peanuts, potatoes, cassava and sweet potatoes).

**T**he Plant People were put here for us. The sky is the one who does the planting… . He moves clouds… male rain… female rain and dark mists over the plants, and they grow… . They are our food and our medicine and the medicine for our livestock. From the Plant People we have Iináájí Azeé – the medicines of the Life Way… .
*George Blueeyes, Navajo storyteller and teacher*

For centuries most Native people lived well on some combination of farming, gathering, hunting and fishing. Their agricultural systems – both in terms of production and the distribution of goods – were deeply connected with their spiritual belief, ceremony and with social relationships. For example, among the Iroquois, the tribes of the Southeast and the Mandan, Hidatsa and Arikara of the Northern Plains, the products of agricultural labour were the women's to trade and distribute.

The European systems of agriculture were introduced into a world where many Native peoples had been farmers for centuries. When the US and Canadian governments tried to 'civilize' the Indians they saw as 'Savage' hunters' by converting them to farmers, they disrupted Native systems and ideas and changed forever those spiritual, social and economic relationships so carefully constructed over thousands of years.

On the often unarable, water-starved reservation lands, men who could not and did not know how to farm were encouraged or forced to do so, while women (who had been the farmers and distributors of agricultural goods) were supposed to learn the 'domestic arts' of European women and leave the land. However, many could not meet their needs for food and cash income on these lands. They were dependent on the rations given by the government in treaty payments that were often inadequate or even denied.

You ask me to plough the ground! Shall I take a knife and tear my mother's bosom? Then when I die she will not take me to her bosom to rest. You ask me to dig for stone! Shall I dig under her skin for her bones. Then when I die I cannot enter her body to be born again. You ask me to make hay and sell it, and be rich like white men! But dare I cut off my mother's hair? *Smohalla, the* Wanapum *prophet, c. 1880*

I was now seventeen years old… and got very much interested in farming…. Gradually I forgot my earnest promise to my father, that I would some day suffer in a Sun Dance, and became quite reconciled to the government's orders. *Goodbird, Hidatsa, 1913*

**4 Below** Dakota (**Sioux**) schoolboys with watermelons they grew at Lower Cut Meat Creek Indian Day School, Rosebud Reservation, South Dakota, c. 1895–99. The Indian **schools** taught European-style agriculture and students grew unfamiliar crops using unfamiliar farming methods.

**A**s time went by… Pueblos began to gradually move away from farming the land, and as a result many of the lands became fallow, as one generation succeeded the next. There was less and less emphasis on farming, and more and more emphasis on arts and crafts.
*Gregory Cajete, Santa Clara Pueblo educator*

Later, when Europeans had introduced new animals and plants into the Americas, women once again became the centre of the new plant and animal **economies**. Women were responsible for sheep in the Southwest, pigs and fruit orchards in the Southeast and Southwest, and cattle in the Northeast. Some Indian men, such as Crows and Shoshone, took more to cattle and **horse** ranching than to farming. A few tribal people have, in the last 10 years, revitalized Native agricultural methods, attempting once again to raise Native varieties of maize, beans, squash and **tobacco**. They are also bringing back **buffalo** to the grasslands.

## Alaska Native Claims Settlement Act (ANCSA) of 1971

This land settlement awarded $962.5 million in compensation and ownership of 44 million acres of land to Natives of Alaska (United States). Although most settlements of land claims made the point that it was land, not monetary compensation, that mattered, many did involve financial payments and a system of settling such compensations that can now only be regarded, like **treaties**, as insufficient in comparison to what was given up.

The effect of the ANCSA, which established 13 Native corporations in place of tribal membership, will be the end of Native **status**. The ANCSA, in effect, extinguished aboriginal title to the land. Native children born after the ANCSA, unlike their parents and grandparents, were not granted automatic membership and shares in the corporations. People afraid of losing ancestral lands started a tribal movement to have changes made to the ANCSA and to re-establish the languages, **ceremonies**, traditional forms of government and the **subsistence economies** based on **hunting** and **fishing**.

**N**ative land is now a corporate asset.
*Justice Thomas Berger, 1985*

## Alaska Purchase

In 1867, the United States bought the rights to Alaska from Russia. The Russians had first begun colonizing in the **Aleutian** Islands via **fur traders** and **hunters** in the mid 18th century. They had **Christianized** many Yup'ik, Tlingit and Aleut peoples from the Aleutian Islands to the area known as Prince William Sound. Nevertheless, the Alaska Purchase from Russia brought an entirely new set of colonial values and efforts into an already devastated world.

**H**e said… he's here to talk about ANCSA (the Alaskan Native Claims Settlement Act) … They might not like what he has to say but what he says comes from the heart… . He said that the Russians did not live here… because the Russians were not born here, and they did not own this land, that it was illegal for them to sell it… . The Russians sold it like they owned it and ignored the real owners… the ancestors who originally owned it, way before recorded time.
*Peter Waska, Yup'ik, at a land conference*

## Alcohol, alcohol abuse

Very few indigenous communities – and none in the Eastern Americas – made any fermented substance at all before the arrival of the Europeans, but Indian alcohol use and abuse became a serious problem in the 17th century. The enormous American alcohol **trade** developed on the back of the slave trade and sugar cultivation in the Caribbean. It was as important an economic factor in the Americas as the **fur trade** and the **maize** and **tobacco** trade in the 17th and 18th centuries. At a time when most North Americans drank daily amounts of alcohol unthinkable today, alcohol was used as enticement, as pay and as a weapon against Indians whose goods, lands and rights were wanted by the government and private business alike. The short- and long-term disastrous effects of alcohol abuse were clear to both Indians and non-Indians and led to a never-ending debate on the supply of alcohol to Indian areas. The alcohol trade brought a direct and forceful response from many Indians and from whites associated with them. Others supported the trade, seeing the benefits it brought them in obtaining land, goods and the utter demoralization of Indian communities.

**5 Above** This buckskin banner, made c. 1900 by the women of the Women's **Christian** Temperance Union from the Warm Springs Indian **Reservation** in Oregon, is white to signify 'social purity'. On the banner, the women raise the Indian tomahawk and the hatchet of the temperance reformer, Carry Nation, against the enemy alcohol. They use the symbol of the pipe (well-known to whites) to show the alliance of their cause with that of others. The 'Don't Tread on Me' snake of the American Revolutionary motto may represent the healing snake of **Salish creation stories**. The beaded flowers – the most common symbol on Plateau and Great Basin **beadwork** – probably represent the flowers of the camas root, one of the most important ceremonial and food plants of the Wasco and Salish peoples.

Although statistics on modern alcohol abuse by Indians do not differ much from those of other people in their areas, the stigma and consequences of alcohol abuse still deeply affects Indian communities more negatively than others. A substantial movement in Indian Country – a new temperance movement – has recommended and achieved sobriety. Associated with women's suffrage, the 19th-century temperance movement was a part of the reform movement in America that demanded justice for American Indians.

By the turn of the century, many Indian women had joined the temperance movement. Susan LaFlesche (1865–1915), an Omaha and the first Native woman to become a doctor, was a notable activist for Indian rights. With her sister Susette (1854–1903) and other relatives, she lobbied for the banning of alcohol on **reservations** and for health reforms. Realizing that alcohol was a means of making Indians sign over their lands and goods, she fought against the corruption of the government and its laws that tried to make Indian people dependent and demoralized.[4]

## Algonquin/Algonquian

With the exception of the **Iroquois**, Algonquian-speaking groups populate Northeastern America. These communities in Canada are dominated by two language groups (**Ojibwa** and **Cree**) and one dialect referred to as Oji-Cree. They occupy a large area known as the Eastern Woodlands. This diverse environment has forests, lakes and rivers, cold winters and short summers and an abundance of game, **fish**, berries and **wild rice**. The Northern communities live in small independent groups, such as the Saulteaux, Ottawa, Mississauga, Algonquin and Nipissing. The Cree, Montagnais and Naskapi are also from the same linguistic groups, but see themselves as separate political groups.

## Aleut/Alutiit/Alutiiq

The Russians called the Native residents of the Aleutian Islands, Kodiak Island, the Alaska and Kenai peninsulas and Prince William Sound Aleut or Aliut. These peoples were Sasignan/Unangan and Suqpiaq/Alutiiq peoples, related to Yup'ik of Western Alaska and Inupiaq of **Arctic** Alaska. By 1900,

**6 Above** Susan LaFlesche and some members of her family, c. 1880.

There has been much speculation on why Indians abused alcohol, including ideas about genetic susceptibilities, Indians' belief in the power of alcohol to produce **dreams** and visions, and the Europeans' part in the social and mental degradation that came with alcohol and its abuse.

Handsome Lake declared alcohol the greatest source of sin… . Alcohol was the biggest force of sin in changing the lives of the Native people.
*Reg Henry, Cayuga faithkeeper, Six Nations Reserve*

**disease**, environmental disasters (such as earthquakes, tsunami and later oil spills) and political upheaval as a result of the Russian colonization reduced the once large population of sea-going, **hunting** and **fishing** people. The presence of the Russian Orthodox Church and Russian customs and language is still felt in these areas. The United States re-colonized this area and its people after the **Alaska Purchase**, forcing them to adapt to a new culture for a second time. Many still speak Russian, English and the Alutiiq or Suk language, although that language may be more endangered than the other two. Although the Alutiiq way of life has suffered greatly from the environmental and cultural changes forced upon it, there have been recent attempts to revitalize its culture and its **subsistence economy**.[5]

## Allotment, General Allotment Act/Dawes Act

The period of allotment, under the General Allotment Act or Dawes Act of 1887, brought economic and cultural disaster. With **Removal**, many Indians, such as the Choctaw, had been given the chance of choosing allotment within the lands they had given up. They would then become citizens where they were instead of moving west. Under the Dawes Act, Indians received certificates entitling them to a land allotment. They had a period of 25 years to learn how to run a business and how to **farm**; after which time the land was to be given to them. Allotment was part of the assimilation policy (see **acculturation**), and it was assumed that all Indians would take to farming. Indian agents denied rations and other payments set out in the **treaties** to Indians who did not work their allotments. Much land could not be farmed and many more acres were lost through the then-legal sale of individual lands. Indian landholdings were reduced to one-third of their former size (from 138 million acres in 1887 to 48 million by 1934).

The US government mixed the issue of **citizenship** with allotment – issuing patents-in-fee (deeds of ownership) and American citizenship to Indians (usually mixed bloods) who they believed were 'competent' and holding lands in trust for those they considered 'incompetent'. In this way, the **Cherokees** received only 110 acres each in 1902 and so were no longer able to hold land

in common as they traditionally did or to continue as an independent nation. Although many wanted to oppose allotment and keep their own government and identity, wealthy Cherokees, railways and mining companies and homesteaders (who went west to settle) argued for it. The Cherokee Republic and its institutions formally ended when Oklahoma became a state in 1907. The state fell under the control of white homesteaders, who outnumbered the Indians seven to one. Two-thirds of the Indians lost the small allotments given to them within 20 years, due to an inability to pay taxes, the pressures to sell to whites or outright fraud. Cherokees could obtain homesteads as well as their allotments. They could not sell their allotted land without permission. Many traditional Cherokees, such as those of the Keetoowah Society, refused to have anything to do with allotment or the soon-to-be-formed state of Oklahoma. Redbird Smith, the Keetoowah leader at that time, and Eufaula Harjo, a **Creek**, founded the Four Mothers Society to resist allotment and to support continued communal ownership of property and the preservation of traditional ways.

## American Indian Religious Freedom Act of 1978

This Act was meant to counteract the long history of official and unofficial hostilities against American Indian religions and religious practice. It was intended to protect the religious rights of American Indians and remove 'unnecessary impediments to Indian access to sacred sites'. However, the Act was intentionally vague and had no provisions on how to enforce it, and so has achieved little.

The first colonists in North America regarded Native religious beliefs and practices as barbarous. **Missionaries** and government leaders adopted policies that would change what they saw as the Indians' 'savage' ways through schooling, conversion to **Christianity**, and the banning of Native **ceremony**, dress, medical practices and language. There was even violence toward Native religious ceremonies and expression. Indian religious and ceremonial objects were taken to museums and Indians were forced from their lands of origin and sacred places.

The government, missionaries, industries and **tourists** have intruded on **sacred sites**

**7 Right** A sign posted on one of the *kivas* (ceremonial dwellings) at San Ildefonso Pueblo warns visitors not to intrude into sacred space.

**8 Above** During feast days, Santa Clara Pueblo posts regulations suggesting appropriate conduct for visitors. Tribal police and members of the *kivas* enforce good behaviour. In charge of them is the War Captain, who traditionally used to deal with enemies and who now deals with the world outside the Pueblo.

and religious rites of Native peoples. Tribes try to restrain people and organizations from violating traditional ceremonial grounds, such as **stomp dance** grounds or ancient places for prayer or rituals. For example, in 1906, the US Forest Service took over Taos Blue Lake, the sacred waterspring of the Taos Pueblo people, and made it a part of the newly developed Kit Carson National Forest. For 65 years, the people of Taos tried to regain their sacred site. In 1970, they succeeded and now manage it as a preservation site where they

can go to practise their sacred ceremonies without disruption.

From the beginning of time the Pueblo of Taos and its people and the elders before them, they were using this place known as Blue Lake area. And for a religious purpose. Man should have a privacy… to do their own talking to the Great Spirit.
*Paul Bernal, Taos religious leader,* 1990

Pueblo people believe it is their obligation to share their **food**, their prayers and their **dances** with all those who come to the pueblos (towns). Yet so many interested non-Indians visit pueblos on ceremonial days that they trample villages. In many places, such as Taos Pueblo, tourists have invaded sacred places, such as the *kivas*, essentially contaminating holy space. In 1990, the Zuni Council closed Shalako, one of their winter ceremonies, to all outsiders, as tourists had continued to violate its sanctity with photography, film and tape recording. The pueblos have special procedures to restrain people during feast days, for example parking rules and restricted access to old or fragile structures. Tribal police and, during ceremonial times, sacred **clowns** keep people from disrupting ceremonies and from being disrespectful to the private lives of residents and to religious sites.

## Apache

Apaches, all Athapaskan-speaking peoples, are composed of several quite diverse groups who live in the Southwestern United States. Plains Apaches encountered the Spanish in the 16th century. They adapted to **horses** immediately and expanded over the Southern Plains. By the mid 18th century, Plains Apaches formed in three groups (Jicarillas, Lipans and Mescaleros), who traded with Mexicans and spoke Spanish. Most Mescaleros were imprisoned with **Navajos** by the US Army at Bosque Redondo (see **Long Walk of the Navajo**) in 1868, but escaped in 1873. The US Army imprisoned Kiowa-Apaches with **Geronimo** and the Chiricahuas at Fort Sill, Oklahoma. Jicarillas and Mescaleros were separated when sent to **reservations**. Following their imprisonment, most Chiricahuas joined the Lipans and Mescaleros in their New Mexico reservation, but some stayed at Fort Sill in Oklahoma where they remain today. Eventually, both Jicarilla and Mescalero reorganized themselves and tried to restore their culture. They became ranchers and now operate a successful tourism business.

Western Apaches lived for a long time in Arizona before the Spanish occupation in 16th century. The White Mountain and San Carlos Apache belong to the **Athabaskan**-speaking family related to **Navajo**. They are **agricultural** peoples from the uplands, and their main spiritual connections are with mountain spirits or Crown **dancers** (*gaan*) who return from the mountains during puberty **ceremonies** for the purpose of healing. Although heavily **missionized**, much of Apache traditional spiritual practice – centred on women's puberty ceremonies in this **matrilineal** group – persists. White Mountain has many natural resources, while the high desert San Carlos has a long history of hostile relations with the US government and heavy environmental exploitation with logging, **dams** and mineral extraction.

## Architecture

Chickee (**Seminole**), hogan (**Navajo**), wickiup (**Apache**), roundhouse, tipi (Plains tribes), longhouse (**Iroquois** and **Northwest Coastal** peoples), arbor/ramada (many Southwestern, Southern Plains people), plank house (California people), pit house (California), **adobe** (Pueblos), earth lodge (Pawnee, Mandan/Hidatsa), igloo (**Inuit**), wigwam (**Ojibwa**), sweathouse/sweatlodge (many Native people).

North American Indians developed hundreds of types of permanent and temporary, domestic, communal, ceremonial and public buildings. Climate, technologies and materials influenced the way they built. Seminoles in the hot, wet areas of Florida made chickees open to the air on all sides. Inuit igloos, made of snow blocks, offer maximum insulation from the cold and wind.

In addition, Indians' social, religious and political structure as a people, together with their beliefs about their origins and their philosophy on life, affected the kinds of structures they built and used. The Pawnees' beliefs about their relationship with the celestial universe caused them to build homes that opened out and were directed at the skies for observation. An understanding of the importance of human relationships led

the **Iroquois** and **Tlingit** to build structures that could contain an entire **clan**. Long-held religious and social traditions of where people lived and whose family controlled property caused some peoples (for example Navajos, Apaches and Crows) to have women build and control the use of a house. Hidatsa/Mandan women built the earth lodges and their daughters inherited them. The lodge was home to all these women, their children, husbands and brothers

W e thought an earth lodge was alive and had a spirit like a human body, and that its front was like a face, with the door for a mouth.
*Maxiwidiac/Buffalo Bird Woman, Hidatsa, 1921*

Many forces altered traditional forms of architecture, including **Removal** from traditional lands and the assault on religious and cultural lifestyles. **Traders**, white farmers and persons new to Indian lands constructed new buildings such as churches, schools, military and government buildings. People often combined traditional forms of architecture with the new forms. **Cherokees** and **Senecas**, for example, who had always built structures for the storage of **maize**, began to build maize cribs that were more like those of their Scots-Irish neighbours.[6]

**9 Above** This engraving shows a **Creek** house in 1791, by this stage essentially a log cabin much like those of white neighbours.

**10 Above** The **Tlingit** Whale House of Kluckwan Village (built in 1835) was an enormous structure for the time. Fifteen metres wide and deep, built of cedar and spruce planks, the simple external structure with its deeply pitched and peaked roof housed elaborate and beautifully carved house poles (see **house posts**), a cedar plank ceremonial screen and carvings of the Tlingit religious universe. This winter house, built to represent the title and crests of a particular family, was home to that family's ceremonies and **potlatches** and could accommodate its own **clan** and others during those formal events.

**11 Right** These Inuit ivory snow knives are for carving snow to make it into structures such as igloos. They are simple but versatile tools for such complex architectural ideas.

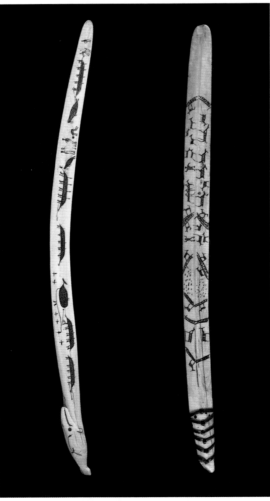

There are new buildings in Indian Country. Some repeat old forms and are used ceremonially, ritually and in remembrance, including tipis put up for special annual gatherings (such as the Crow Fair and the Anadarko Fair for Kiowas and Comanches). Mass public housing was built on **reservations** by the US Office of Housing and Urban Development, the **Bureau of Indian Affairs**, and the Department of Indian Affairs (Canada). Other structures are by an entirely new generation of Indian architects who use traditional forms, materials, processes and ideas to inspire new architecture in the building of Native schools, museums and other public buildings.

**14 Above** The Canadian Museum of Civilization, designed by Douglas Cardinal, **Blackfeet/Métis** architect. Douglas Cardinal was born in Calgary, Alberta and grew up in the prairie town of Red Deer. He opened his own firm in 1964, and his first contract, an Indian church, won him national recognition. He explored his native heritage, asking the council of elders for advice on his projects. Cardinal has developed a powerful and distinctive style, influenced by the curving, natural forms in the geography of his Alberta homeland. This museum was his first major commission and the first major building in Canada designed completely on computer.

**12 Left** In 1994 Dixon Palmer, Kiowa from Oklahoma, designed and painted this canvas tipi in the style of tipis made by his family. It is typical of those now made and used for ceremonial and social gatherings rather than to be lived in by Kiowas. It has **buffalo** on the body with the stars of the winter night sky on the top. Day is represented on the right side, near the doorway which always faces east, and the red line represents living things.

**13 Above** Santa Clara Pueblo built a new housing development in 1992, with the help of the US government. Tribal members previously unable to live in the town because they had no houses or because they could not live in or mend the older traditional **adobe** buildings they had inherited from their families, can now live in these new houses. Although, occasionally, traditional architectural styles are imitated, most Indian housing facilities have actually disrupted traditional social patterns, such as **matrilocal** residence (living with the mother's side of the family).

## Arctic

Above latitude line 66° 30° North, millions of square miles of land and sea make up the Arctic Circle. In this vast area, the sun does not appear in mid winter or set in mid summer. In the Arctic there are hundreds of species of animals such as caribou, **whale**, moose, seal, polar **bear** and a wide variety of birds. Average winter temperatures are -24 to -26 °C. In this environment, north of the tree line, the **Inuit** live in the Arctic tundra. They have adapted to life in this inhospitable climate by using the environment well. Inuit in the Arctic Circle have linguistic and cultural similarities with other circumpolar groups, such as the Inupiaq of Northern Alaska and Inuit of Greenland. In the Eastern and Southern sub-Arctic live the **Cree**, Naskapi and Montagnais, called Innu in Labrador. In the Western sub-Arctic, the Yukon and the Northwest Territories live the Dené.

## Art

Most traditional Native art forms had an established function in cultural life. No-one hung a painting on a wall or mounted a **sculpture** on a pedestal just to admire, instead almost everything that was made for daily life was decorated in some way. Art was part of daily life – in **food** preparation, spirituality, language, teaching, philosophy, **agriculture** and much more.

Indian people have no word for art. Art is a part of life, like hunting, fishing, growing food, marrying and having children. This is an art in the broadest sense… an object of daily usefulness, to be admired, respected, appreciated and used, the expression thereby nurturing the needs of both body and soul, thereby giving meaning to everything.
*Mary Lou Fox Radulovitch, Ojibwe Cultural Foundation*

Where the environment allowed more leisure time, as in the case of the **Northwest Coast** and Eastern Woodlands, objects were more highly decorated. In the mid 1800s, when European art materials became available and Native artists began to copy European painting techniques, much changed. Some of the old 'craft' disappeared entirely. Some arts failed, then returned; others never went away.

Indian people still make musical instruments for **dances** and for **ceremonies** (including ribbon shirts, Gourd Dance **blankets**, dance sticks, **flutes**, bone breastplates, **beaded** hair ties and buckskin dresses). Some of the old **basket** and **pottery** styles have been revived and the new painting and **sculpture** has evolved into a living, breathing art.

When some Kiowa, Comanche, Cheyenne and Arapaho warriors were taken to Fort Marion in Florida from jails in Oklahoma, after the terrible wars that would bring the end of the world as they once knew it, the last thing they might have imagined from their own and tribal tragedy was the beginning of contemporary American Indian art. From the ledger drawings that, like Bear's Heart's, mourned the past life, to the new **dream** vision paintings produced by Kiowas, new art forms were born. Awa Tsireh's remembrances translated into canvas, paper and chalk, recalled old stories. Out of old rocks and the paintings on them, from the landscape itself, Bob Haozous' sculptural forms took life. Horace Poolaw's **photographs** documented the Kiowa world of the 1930s that no-one else was interested in.

By the time he was a young man, my father had got enough of farming. He wanted to be an artist, a painter…. At some point he moved out of that old world of the Kiowas.
*Scott Momaday, Kiowa writer*

Shelley Niro's photographs of an unexpectedly comic and crazy **Iroquois** country insist that we pay attention to its heartless history. Nora Naranjo Morse's clay sculptures transport old clay pottery to a new world, while Lil Pitt in the state of Oregon gives us Africa and Japan out of clay masks that remember the **Salish** past.

The 20th century saw the emergence of a lively contemporary Native art movement. Internationally renowned artists in visual arts, **literature**, dance, theatre, **music** and crafts have combined traditional and contemporary influences in a new creative voice which is informed by Native issues, histories and stories. Art schools, such as the Centre for Indigenous Theatre in Toronto and the Institute of American Indian Art in Santa Fe, specialize in teaching skills and creating work with Native skills and ideas. Communities rich with artisans working in beadwork, quilting, carving, dance and storytelling keep communities culturally alive.[7]

It is this blessing of being able to make things that reconstruct my life, that gives me the knowledge to restore myself. The things I saw – the collaborative living structures, the places of worship and feasts, the outfits of antiquity, the buckskin garments, the beaded objects, the woven baskets for subsistence, the cradleboards for protection, the feathers of prayer, the couriers to a higher thought. They were made, traded and collected by great-grandparents and by living relatives, and I saw that they loved deeply. These messages – the beaded birds, horses, trees, stars and geometric abstractions – are like prayer, a prayer for our present worlds to know again the root connection to our existence.
*Elizabeth Woody, Navajo, Wasco, and Warm Springs artist and writer*

## Athabaskan/Athapaskan

The Athabaskan-speaking peoples in Alaska include the Tanaina (Dena'ina), Kutchin (Gwitch'in), Holikachuck, Koyukon, Tanana, Upper Tanana, Tanacross, Upper Kuskokwim, Han and Ingalik (Deg Het'an). Most live in remote villages where people alternate a few mainstream jobs in the community with seasonal **hunting** and **fishing**. They have traditional forms of government along with new government under the **Alaska Native**

15 Left An Athabaskan/
Gwitch'in/Kutchin chief's
moosehide jacket, with
**beaver** fur, **beadwork**,
caribou tufted flowers and
moose antler buttons,
made by Dixie Alexander
in 1997 for an exhibition
in Washington on the
cultural and
environmental impact of
the Alaska pipeline. A
chief's jacket was made
especially for wearing to
**potlatches** or other
special occasions. This
one has particular
touches that are
meaningful to Native
peoples in the North.
The beaded **wolf**, lynx,
**rabbit** tracks and
ptarmigan trails, like
animal tracks in the
snow, 'bring men
good luck when
they go trapping',
Dixie told curators at the
National Museum of
American History, 'so
they'll bring back lots of
**food** and furs and good
stories to share'.

# Awl

An awl might represent the work of women in
Indian Country, just as a **bow and arrow**
might the work of men. Indians gladly
accepted the **metal** awl tips, fixed into wood,
bone, antler or horn handles, that came with
the **traders** from Europe. Native women
everywhere used awls to punch holes in
hides, wood and **bark**, so that they could join
or decorate those hides and utensils with
**beads** and quills. They used them to tighten
a **basket** weave. Men usually made the
handles for them. A young girl might receive
her first awl at the time of her first
menstruation and she could then practice her
**quillwork**. Women on the Northern Plains
carried their awls, their most treasured tool,
in small rawhide or beautifully beaded and
decorated cases, usually on their belts.

Men, too, used awls, to make
and repair some of the things
for which they were
responsible. Jim Northrup, an
Anishinabe writer and
humorist, calls the awl an
Indian cordless drill.[8]

**16 Left** A mid 19th-century
bone or elkhorn handled
Omaha or Otoe awl with
iron tip. A Lakota woman,
Blue Whirlwind, told an
historian that Lakota women
kept a record of their
accomplishments on the
elkhorn handles of their
awls. Black dots would
represent tanned robes, red
dots ten tanned hides or
one tipi. An etched circle at
the bottom of the handle
could represent 100 robes
or 10 tipis.[9]

**Claims Settlement Act** and elected
governments administered through the
**Bureau of Indian Affairs**. The **Alaska
Purchase**, the Yukon River Gold Rush (*c.*
1890), the intrusions of Russian traders and
missionaries into Athabaskan territories in
the 19th century and the building of the
Alaska pipeline in the 20th century had far-
reaching consequences for these and other
peoples in Alaska. Some land and cultural
revitalization has occurred through the Alaska
Native Claims Settlement Act and through
strong campaigning for Native **subsistence**.

Navajos, Apaches and some other smaller
groups in Canada share an Athabaskan
language with the Alaskan peoples.

# B

## Baby carrier

Many Native peoples used baby carriers or cradleboards. They were made of wood, reed and hide, and some had hide or cloth covers. Some people carried babies for the entire first year of their lives, so baby carriers had to be strong and comfortable for the carrier and the baby. The carriers held the babies securely, perhaps strapped to a woman's back while she worked, leaving her hands free. Some could be leaned up against trees or supports, and others could be strapped to **horses**. **Inuit** women carried their babies in the hoods of special **parkas** called *amauti*.

Baby carrier decorations of carvings, **beads** and embroidery symbolized protection as well as being entertaining for the child. Today, decorated traditional baby carriers and carrier covers are made for show pieces and for special **gifts** to the parents and child, although they no longer have the widespread practical uses they once had. Modern manufactured baby carriers used worldwide by non-Indians are similar to the ideas and designs of Indian baby carriers.

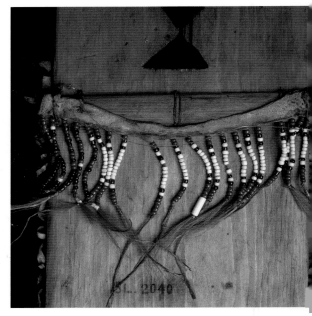

**18 Above** Detail from an early Cree cradleboard from Hudson Bay, decorated with beads and quills.

**17 Right** This 19th-century wooden Mohawk cradleboard, with an elaborately carved back and simple head piece and footrest, is from the St Regis area, on the border between Canada and the United States. The baby was bound to the board by a cover (missing) and a tumpline or burden strap.

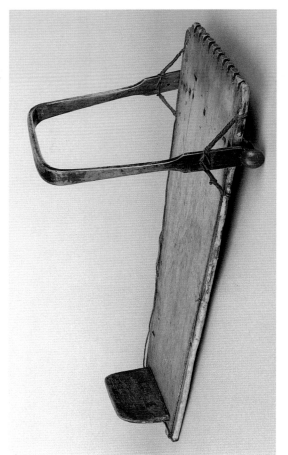

**19 Right** Horace Poolaw, a Kiowa **photographer**, took this picture of Lizzie Little Joe in Oklahoma in 1955. Wearing high-heeled shoes along with her traditional dress and the **elk** tooth decorated baby carrier, Mrs Little Joe embodied the ways in which Indian people merged the new Western ideas with traditional Indian ways.

**M**y mother used to tell me that when I was still a baby in the cradle, she would strap my cradle to her saddle and drive a herd of ponies across the prairies, sometimes all day long.
*Arapaho woman*, c. 1930

## Bandolier bag

Native peoples made all sorts of strapped bags, pouches and purses to carry tools, personal effects, cosmetics, plants, hunting and gathering tools and shot for rifles. Originally, they made bags from hide and decorated them with quills, shells, **feathers**, bone and animal hair. Following **contact** with European **traders**, bags were also made from trade cloth, trade **beads** and woven cloth. Some people developed very elaborate bandolier bags, so called because the straps went across the chest like a band. Most Southeastern bandolier bags hung from fingerwoven sashes, but the Choctaws, Alibamu and Koasati (Coushatta) often used belts from red trade cloth with the older white seed bead designs. Some men wore two belts or sashes, crossed over each side.

These bags often held ammunition and military and hunting equipment. Men later valued these bags as ceremonial or formal wear, even when they had no practical use anymore, and they can be seen today as part of **dance** costumes.

**20 Above** That the Choctaw men were wearing these bandoliers (minus the bags that usually accompanied them) with **feathered** hats in 1908, along with their Western-style, rural American clothing, shows how much the Choctaws had resisted the assimilation efforts directed toward them and their fellow Southeastern Native peoples (see **acculturation**). Note the **stickball** sticks in the hands of the man to the right. The Mississippi Choctaws, having resisted **Removal**, retained their language, traditional **foods** and **agricultural** lifestyle as well as the **music**, **dance** and **games** of their ceremonial life, even though they appeared to be 'Christianized' on the surface.[10]

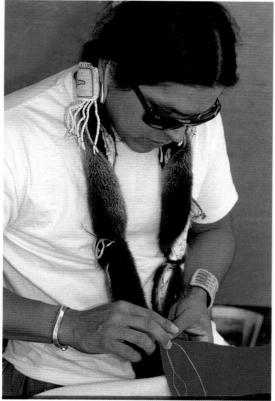

**21** and **22 Above** Ken Taylor, **Creek** and **Cherokee**, in 1992 making the 19th-century Southeastern-style bandolier bag (**top**). Ken reproduces old clothing styles that he studies in museum collections. The bag he is making won a prize for traditional costume at the prestigious annual Indian Market in New Mexico. It has white seed **beadwork** in Mississippian-period designs on flannel or red **trade** cloth.

## Bark

Bark was one of the main materials used by Indians to make clothes, utensils, **transport** and housing. The skills involved in transforming tree bark into fibre that could be woven into cloaks or bent into a waterproof frame are complex. On the **Northwest Coast**, Native peoples made cedar bark into clothing and, in the area of the Great Lakes and the **Algonquin** Northeast, birchbark was used to make house walls, cooking vessels, **baskets** and **boats**. Birchbark was an invaluable material because it was thin, tough and waterproof, and Indians learned to manipulate it with steam, sap and ingenuity. Perhaps the most skilful use of bark was the birchbark canoe, an engineering innovation so perfect that it remains unchanged from its original design.

They always respect the birchbark… when you go you respect the trees because they make big canoes out of it …. It's based on respect for the birch, because you can make sutures out of it, sleds and lots of good out of it.
*Belle Deacon, Athabaskan basketmaker*

**23 Left** A 1940s replica of an 18th-century Mohawk-style birchbark pail used for collecting maple sap. For centuries, Indians in the Northeast exploited the maple tree each year, drawing sap and making sugar from it.

**24 Above** A very early **Beothuk** *Guin-ya-butt*, which means 'water **basket**' or bucket, made from birchbark and sewn roots.

25 **Above** This Nuu-chah-nulth/ Nootka cedar bark, nettle fibre and goat hair cloak was brought back to England by Captain James Cook from his third voyage in 1776–80 to the **Northwest Coast** of America.

26 **Below** Nuu-chah-nulth/ Nootka people used this walrus bone or ivory tool to beat the cedar bark so that it could be spun and woven into material for clothing.

## Basket, basketmaking

Native peoples have woven baskets from plant materials such as vine, tree **bark**, branches, wood strips and grasses for more than 10,000 years. Basketry is one of the oldest and most widespread forms of work done by Native peoples and shows the most diverse use of materials, tools, shapes and forms of any craft. Ancient people used baskets, along with **pottery**, as their main utensils. Basket-weaving techniques were used to make **food** containers, storage containers for plants for **medicines**, mats, **fish** traps, clothes (such as **footwear**, **headgear** and cloaks), small water **dams**, animal pens and housing. Some baskets are so finely made that they are watertight; others so strong that they can be used for cooking. Even when made for the most basic of uses, Indians decorated their baskets. The three

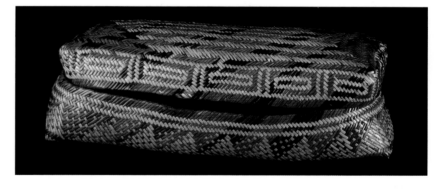

27 **Above** This 18th-century **Cherokee** lidded basket (*talusa*) is from South Carolina. It is plaited from river cane and dyed in natural dyes, which were probably made from pokeberries (*tsayatika*) or mulberries (for red/blue/purple), sumac (*kalogwa*) or walnut (*sedi*) (for black) and bloodroot (*gigage unastetsi*) or coreopsis flowers (for yellow). It is one of the two oldest known surviving Cherokee doubleweave baskets, brought to Sir Hans Sloane in 1725 by the colonial **British** Governor, Sir Francis Nicholson of South Carolina.

major techniques used in Native basketry are plaiting (**Cherokee**), coiling and sewing (Hopi) and twining (Hupa/**Yurok**/Karok).

Basketmaking – like weaving and pottery – is deeply connected to ceremonial and ritual life. It is taken very seriously because ancient stories associated it with the very origins of life. The way the materials are gathered and how the baskets are given and used are also very important. The techniques for gathering and preparing materials followed the seasons. The construction and design of the baskets were often accompanied by ritual, song and prayer. The **Inuit**, for instance, have many songs associated with gathering grasses. Yuroks credit rattlesnakes with being the first basketweavers, so they pray before they go into woods, hoping rattlesnakes will leave the fields. If a snake is seen leaving the fields, it is a sign that it has given permission to use the materials.[11] The **Navajo** have ceremonial

28 **Left** At San Juan Pueblo, in New Mexico, the ceremonial aspects of baskets can be seen in the Basket Dance. This **dance**, also performed at Santa Clara Pueblo and at Hopi, is connected to the **agricultural** cycle of life and women and their fertility. An equal number of men and women dance. During the dance, the women strike the baskets (female) with a wood rasp (male).

wedding baskets, and the religious rules about making these baskets are so strict that many Navajos have stopped making them, leaving the business of wedding basket manufacture to Paiutes, Utes and Hopis.

**S**ometimes I get sad because today we do not have very many old weavers left... . I get... upset when I hear people say that weaving is a dying art... that nobody is doing it... I'm doing it... I know... there are others... going to carry on that wisdom and that knowledge.
*Susan Billy, Pomo basket weaver, in 1994*

Basketmaking had economic significance for every Native group, whether or not they made them. Indians who made baskets always used them as a desirable trading item with other tribes and, eventually, in the Northeast, Great Lakes, the Great Basin and the Southwest as a trading item with Europeans. Indian baskets, made by men and women, also became a major part of the tourist trade. At Niagara Falls, Wisconsin Dells and the along the coast of Maine, **Mohawks**, **Senecas**, **Abenakis** and **Ojibwas** sold baskets to visitors. Some of those – such as the Adirondack pack basket, fish creels, Victorian sewing baskets and egg baskets – became the standard forms by which other baskets were known and judged.

Museums and private collectors acquired Indian baskets during the 19th century, particularly the complex and refined baskets of California, the Great Basin and Southwestern peoples.

**T**he earth is shaking From our beating the basket drums.
*A Tewa song from the Basket Dance*

Now, where some Indians rarely make and need practical baskets for use in their communities, they make them for an external **art** market. Basketmaking materials, from often non-renewable resources, are threatened everywhere, and some suffer from pollution and environmental damage. Competition from low-cost baskets from Asia and Africa makes basket production for a commercial market unattractive. However, for as long as people need and want ceremonial baskets, basketmaking will continue in Native communities.

Most Southeastern Native peoples used river cane and rush, found in and near the waterways of the South, to make mats for ceremonial uses, and to make bedding, flooring, seating, lining walls, ceilings and containers. They stopped making many of the mats when they changed their houses to the log cabins and frame structures of white men. Their uses of baskets also changed. Baskets for gathering medicinal plants became egg or sewing baskets, also used by their white neighbours.

After **Removal**, Oklahoma **Cherokees** no longer had river cane (*ihya*) available to them and used oak (*tala*), hickory (*sohi*) and honeysuckle. For the Cherokees, then in North Carolina, river cane became scarce, threatened by extensive roadbuilding along old waterways and damage caused by carbon monoxide from cars. Both Eastern and Western Cherokee women have revived basketmaking, more for the tourist market and art market than for their own use, but also because basketmaking reflects a pride in maintaining ancient traditions. Where they can find river cane, Cherokee weavers still make doubleweave baskets.

**M**y grandmother made baskets. When I was a little girl, I would go with her down in Southeastern Oklahoma to gather dye plants and buckbrush and honeysuckle... . I hated gathering black walnuts because they would stain my hands and clothes with a sticky black substance, and because they were hard to crack and eat. But... the pokeberries were juicy and fat and I loved the purple stain they made on everything. If we were gathering honeysuckle, I would help strip it of leaves and twigs, coil it in a circle for storing and carrying, then later strip off the bark after it was soaked and boiled... . My grandmother later in her life took the Baptist church very seriously and she stopped making medicines because the preachers told her it was heathen nonsense. So she didn't make medicine for her arthritis, which made her hands hurt, and she stopped making baskets.
*Rayna Green, Cherokee folklorist*

## Beads, beadwork

Before **contact** with Europeans, Indians used beads made of clay, **quills**, **shells**, horn, **feathers**, ivory, bone and some **metal** (copper or lead) for ornamentation and design. When Europeans brought glass beads to the Americas, Native peoples adopted them immediately and they became a major part of the **trade** between Indians and Europeans. Indians used beads on clothing, implements, household goods and **horse** equipment. Beading societies replaced and supplemented the old women's quilling societies as women's trade networks elaborated on the beadwork traditions. Women of the Plains and the Plateau tribes specialized in beadwork. They used their skills to create elaborate and complex floral and geometric designs or beaded designs on cylindrical objects using the so-called 'peyote' stitch. Indians have used traditional techniques and designs to transform commercially manufactured objects and Western objects.

**A**nt was a very clever young man who wished to marry the daughter of a great chief. The latter told Ant he could not marry his daughter until he performed a difficult task. At that time, beads were scattered all over the earth, and the chief asked Ant to gather them all up, heaping each colour in a pile by itself. This seemed impossible to Ant, and he went to his Grandmother, Short-Tailed Mouse, for advice. She told him how to do it; so he accomplished his task, and won the girl. He heaped the beads in seven piles – red ones in the first, then blue, white, black, yellow, green, and bone beads in the seventh. After this, his father-in-law used beads on his clothes, and other people began to do the same.
*A Salish story*

**O**ld One gave four bundles to a man who had treated him kindly. He gave the man a bundle each of porcupine quills, red headed woodpecker scalps, eagle tail feather and dentalium shells, telling the man that people had not valued these things before, but would value and use them from that time forward.
*A Salish story*

Since Indians started using European glass and ceramic beads (mostly from Italy and Czechoslovakia), they have been beading items of clothing and tools. In the 19th and 20th centuries, Plains Indians beaded doctor's bags and stethoscope ear pieces, ladies' shoes and evening bags as gift or

**29 Above** Nettie Watt (**Seneca**) made this early 20th-century style of shopping basket in 1985. She could make many of the older style baskets, such as a basket for washing hominy (hulled **maize**), rarely used nowadays. Most baskets like this one are made for a different market. The old shapes and forms have changed to fit more modern uses and decorative ideas.

presentation pieces for special friends. Nowadays, Indians bead everyday items of clothing (such as denim jackets) and presentation pieces (such as academic/graduation gowns). In some instances, expert beadworkers choose difficult objects, such as a mayonnaise jar or a pair of athletic shoes, to demonstrate their skills.

**30 Below** A 19th-century Dakota **Sioux** beaded vest. The beaded images, almost like ledger drawings, show an Indian warrior battling another Indian warrior and a Cavalry soldier.

**31 Right** A Plateau beaded vase, c. 1987. Great beadworkers attempt beaded objects like this one to show off their skills in an extremely difficult piece.

## Beans

Native peoples developed many varieties of beans. They provide humans with one of the major sources of vegetable-based protein and amino acids. Like other legumes, beans return more nitrogen to the soil than they take out. Thus, they replenish the soil with nutrients removed by other crops, such as **maize**. Many can withstand heat, drought and disease, and can be grown in conditions that would starve other similarly nutritious and high yielding **food** crops. Throughout the Indian Country, they are intercropped (grown together) with maize and **squash** to meet most of the nutritional needs of the people who grow them. Along with maize and squash, they are sacred food for Indians and form the 'Three Sisters' of **Iroquois** religious belief.

Taken from wild seeds in Europe and the Americas, beans have been cultivated for 8,000–10,000 years by Native Americans. By 1,000 AD maize, beans and squash were among the most important food plants in North America. Bean seeds were also traded from the Southwest to Mexico. Many Indians annually cultivated at least five varieties. Some villages may have held more than 15 different varieties in their seed stocks, planting them and replenishing them each year. The **Iroquois** once grew over 60 varieties of beans. Indians have continued to grow some of the varieties most important to them. Native farmers and environmental biologists interested in the preservation of old species and varieties, have cultivated some of the beans, once gathered wild, such as the tepary (*phaseolus acutifolius*).

The tepary is well suited to its Native high desert where the growing conditions are hard. Tepary beans need less water and attract fewer pests than other types of beans. Until recently, teparies were used as a staple food by many Southwestern tribes, such as the Yuma, Tohono O'odham and **Zuni**. They are high in fibre and protein, and are rich in iron and calcium. They become even more nutritious when grown under desert conditions, because the amount of protein they contain increases in dry climates. Although extensive cultivation of tepary beans ceased among most Southwestern tribes at the beginning of the 20th century, current research indicates that by returning to a more traditional diet of high fibre and slowly digested tepary beans (as opposed to rapidly digested pinto beans) Southwestern Indians may be able to reverse the rise in diabetes.

**S**o that is why the white tepary bean is the child of the Desert People. It was born here and endures dryness. When it doesn't rain enough, the white bean still comes up. The Desert People will always eat it and live here. The Milky Way is said to be the white bean. He lives clear across the sky. Beans grow in abundance and we see them scattered across the sky.
*Sand Papago story*

## Bear

The bear – polar, brown, black, Kodiak and grizzly – is one of the most revered animals among Native peoples, along with salmon, **eagle**, **coyote**, **raven** and **buffalo**. For many Native peoples, the bear was a symbol and a source of power, wisdom and **medicine**, often taking human form. Sometimes the bear can have dangerous powers. At such times bears and bear power are to be avoided. The bear was often a **clan** animal, so there are many stories of bears in their human and bear form, and pictures of bears and bear paws (as well as actual fur and claws) are common on clothing and pots. **Navajos** believe that Changing Woman gave them the bear for protection, and bear imagery appears in their songs and **art**. On the Northern Plains, a bear 'Cult' existed among the **Blackfeet** and Assiniboine, giving men a special power to heal and the medicine power for war. Men of this group wore bear claw necklaces, carried bear shields and used knives set in bear jaw handles.

**32 Below** Marjorie Bear Don't Walk, a **Salish**-Chippewa designer, made this beaded bear claw necklace for her friend Rayna Green in 1994, telling her of the need for the ancient power and protection associated with the bear. Marjorie's brother obtained the bear claws and she did the **beadwork** onto them, stringing them onto old brass **trade** beads.

**33 Left** A bear-headed rattle from the **Northwest Coast.**

**34 Below** A bear paw is a common symbol on Santa Clara **pottery**. It is used on this blackware water jar (c. 1920) by the famous potter Margaret Tafoya. The bear represents good fortune to Santa Clara people; an old story tells of how the bear helped them find water during a drought.

## Beothuk

In about 1,000 BC, the Beothuks of the East Coast of the United States and Canada (now Newfoundland and Labrador) may have been among the first Natives to encounter Viking sailors. When Europeans arrived, the Beothuks, weakened by **disease** and famine, battled with the French **fishermen** and settlers over resources. They are among the first groups to have had bounties placed on their scalps by governments. French and **British** settlers and fishermen drove the Beothuks into further starvation and isolation, ultimately into virtual extinction. Although some Beothuk descendants may have joined with traditional friends, such as the Montagnais in Labrador, the last identifiable Beothuk, a woman named Nancy Shanawdithit, died in 1829. They are thought to have been the first to be known by Europeans as 'Red Indians', because they used red ochre on their bodies and clothing, although the term was later generalized to other Indians.

**35 Above** A **Haida** carved wooden **food** bowl inlaid with mother of pearl and haliotes **shell**. The bowl is in the form of an animal with some features of a beaver and its tail, but with an **eagle** and human face that forms the handle. It is highly polished from the oils of **fish** (eulachon) and sea mammals served in it. Bowls like this were greatly valued and used for feasts and ceremonial occasions that required the lavish hospitality of chiefs and their clans. The greater the carving on the food bowls, the higher the status of the chief giving the feast.

## Beaver

In many tribes there are **clans** associated with beavers. The beaver was, for many peoples, a major source of food, fur and **medicine**. Beaver and deer were the main animals in the **fur trade**. Beaver hides were sent to make the **headgear** fashionable in Europe at the time. Those hides were certainly the most important currency in the 18th-century **Iroquois**-European trade. The **British** and French fought fiercely all over northeastern North America for the beaver trade, securing Indian allies and **hunters** in a competitive war that almost wiped out the beaver, as well as the deer, in the Southeast.

Too great is what you are doing our chief.
Who equals our chief?
He is giving feasts to the whole world.
*Tlingit potlatch song*

**36 Right** A Beothuk bone/antler comb, possibly an amulet.

**37 Below** This fringe may have been part of the rectangular cloak, sometimes with a deep collar, worn by Beothuk men and women. Little of Beothuk culture survived their disappearance; a few pieces exist in the British Museum in London.

## Bering Strait Theory

Since the mid 19th century, scholars have believed that the peoples called 'Indians' came to the Americas 12,000–60,000 years ago, over a land bridge formed during periods of glaciation. That land bridge (called the 'Bering Strait') stretched between the continents of America and Russia, in Siberia (or Beringia). Animals of the last Ice Age and then humans travelled across it over many thousands of years, coming in small groups to settle in the northern reaches of the Americas. According to the theory, they then travelled south, and many thousands of years later, around 300 BC, a new migration crossed the Bering Sea in **boats**. The different migrations might explain the many different **language** families and patterns of settlement of the highly diverse Native population of North America.

Although there is very little scientific evidence to dispute this theory, there is also very little to prove it, only the genetic and skeletal similarities of the Natives of Siberia, Asia and Native North America. Although continuing evidence suggests that Indians have been in North America for more than 20,000 years, most Native people would challenge the Bering Strait Theory. Each Native group has its own theory and origin/**creation story** about its beginnings, attached to the places which it finds sacred and significant.

## Blackfoot, Blackfeet

The powerful Blackfoot Confederacy (Blackfoot in Canada, Blackfeet in the United States) was composed of the Blackfoot, Blood, Piegan and allied Gros Ventre. At the height of their power, the Blackfoot held vast areas from North Saskatchewan to the Missouri River, covering much of the modern states of Alberta and Montana. This area was short-grass high plains and they hunted in the foothills of the Rocky Mountains. Pressure from the **Cree** pushed them south until the Blackfoot were on the Bow River and the Blood and Piegan/Pigunni in southernmost Alberta and later Montana.

Originally, the Plains **Cree**, **Ojibwa** and Assiniboine were on friendly terms with the Blackfoot Confederacy, joining together to drive the Kutenai, who were trying to encroach on **buffalo** hunting, out of Southern Alberta. Disputes over **horses** caused the Gros Ventre to break with the Confederacy. At the beginning of the 19th century, the Cree and Assiniboine moved onto Blackfoot land and hostilities began. This warfare continued until the **reservation** period in 1870.

The Blackfoot were nomadic people, who travelled over great distances to hunt, trade and fight. After the decline of the buffalo due to overhunting by Europeans, the Blackfoot were obliged to sign **Treaty** Number 7 in 1877 and eventually to move onto reservations. Today, the Blackfoot occupy a reservation along the Bow River, the Blood south on a reservation near the Belly River, and the northern Piegan have a small reservation near the Blood. The Southern Piegan occupy the Blackfeet Reservation in Northern Montana, bordering the massive Glacier National Park. The Sarcee took land near Calgary.

Modern Blackfeet in Montana have lost millions of acres of land due to **allotment**, land leasing and government mismanagement, although stockraising and small enterprise, along with tribally controlled education, have given them back some measure of control over their lives.

## Blankets

Until **contact**, Indians wore robes of animal fur, hide and **feathers** for warmth and cover. A few peoples in the Northwest and Southwest had woven materials. When the Europeans arrived, especially in the 18th century, woven wool and cloth blankets became the major item for the Indian trade. The Hudson's Bay Company blankets, for example, set the standards for the trade **economy**. A blanket which had four or five woven marks on it indicated that it was worth four or five **beaver** or deer skins. Particular blankets, associated with particular companies, were sought after at different times.

The private Pendleton Company made other types of blankets that, like some Hudson's Bay blankets, are still in use and still immensely popular with Indians. Some Pendleton patterns were heavily influenced by Spanish designs; others adopted **Navajo**, then Great Basin and Plains designs. One of the most important patterns is the 'Chief Joseph Pattern' – named after Chief Joseph (1840–1904), the Nez Perce leader who led his people into exile escaping the US Army.

Indian women developed uses for blankets other than just as cloaks and

**38 Below** Rayna Green wears a modern capote coat, made in 1992 from a new Hudson's Bay blanket by Marjorie Bear Don't Walk, a **Salish**/Chippewa designer. This red blanket coat is typical of the coats that **hunters**, trappers and **traders** wore in the 19th-century Canadian West during the **fur trade**. It has four black 'points', showing it is worth four **beavers**.

padding. They cut them up to make baby blankets, bags, pouches and leggings. Blankets (mostly Pendletons and Hudson's Bays), shawls (adapted from the Spanish) and quilts were used for **dance** and for **diplomatic** and ceremonial **gifts**.

We welcome our children with a handmade quilt or small Pendleton blankets as we wrap them in our prayers…. For a couple's marriage, we share wisdom and a feast that includes cornmeal mush. To honour the occasion, the woman's body is draped with a Pendleton shawl, the man's with a Pendleton robe. As we move into old age, we pay tribute to the spirit world with ceremony, prayers and gifts. Often we bury our people with their special possessions and beautiful Pendleton blankets.
*Rain Parrish, Navajo artist, 1997*

A blanket is an extension of an Indian man's status and feelings. In the past, an Indian man judged wealth and status in numbers of horses. Today, trade blankets are like horses were in past times… if a man's daughter is chosen to be a princess for a gathering… he shows his appreciation by giving blankets to the people who bestowed this honour on his daughter…. When a man receives a blanket as a gift from a special person… he will consider this blanket above all other blankets…. A blanket is the most prized gift and it is given for special reasons… to express appreciation to someone who has come from afar to attend the dances… to a person or a family who has shown kindness in hard times or in times of sorrow over a lost loved one… to acknowledge someone for their [work]… giving the gift is important… receiving a blanket is another show of acceptance.
*Bob Block, Osage, 1997*

## Boats

Three basic types of canoes were used by Indians. The first was the elm, birch**bark** or animal hide covered wooden frame used in the Northeast and Great Lakes. The second was the whole log dugout used in the Northwest, where people hunted large mammals on the open sea. The third was the plank canoe from Northern California. Some **Northwest Coastal** peoples recently brought back the construction of plank and dugout canoes in order to restore the ceremonial life connected with the boats, hunting and seagoing.

Canoes, dugouts and kayaks (and their larger relative, the *umiak*) were associated with war and hunting, and so with survival and danger. This meant that building and navigating them were processes filled with ritual, **ceremony**, songs, prayers and charms. Those who made these vehicles were highly skilled, and able to follow the rituals needed to complete the work to make a boat both technically and spiritually good.[12]

Native people developed types of boats other than the canoe. Typical in the Northern Plains was a kind of skin boat called the bullboat. Mandan and Hidatsa people used these to navigate rivers and streams. Animal (including **buffalo** bull) hide covered a rounded frame, made of bent wood like the top of their earth lodges. Although these bullboats were not as easy to manoeuvre as the kayak or canoe, they did provide basic water-going transport for land-based people who needed to **transport** small loads.

My family made these travels in sealskin boats, which were wooden frames covered with sealskins. They used to be called the women's boats because they were sewn by the women.
*Pitseolak, an Inuit artist*

**39 Above** A model of an *umiak*, an **Inuit** boat for several people.

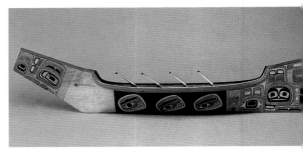

**40 Above** A model of a carved dugout ocean-going **Haida** canoe, used for hunting, trade and ceremonial purposes. These excellent, sculptured canoes hold from two to twenty people.

# Boudinot, Elias

Elias Boudinot (c. 1804–39) was the first American Indian editor and publisher. He was originally called Buck Watie (born *Galagina*), and was the brother of the famed **Cherokee** Confederate General Stand Watie. He began his literary career as a Bible translator for the **missionary**, Samuel Worcester. Sent to a Moravian mission **school** by his family when he was a small boy and tutored by a white minister, Reverend Boudinot, Watie took the name Boudinot in the man's honour. When he entered theological college in the East, he fell in love with a white woman, and in marrying her, caused protest even from the **Christian** whites who supported Indian causes. He went home to Georgia, and from 1828 to 1832, he published the *Cherokee Phoenix*, the first Indian newspaper. The newspaper – devoted to Cherokee culture, history and politics – was printed in New Echota, Georgia in the Cherokee syllabary (a set of characters representing syllables), developed by **Sequoyah**, and in English. The *Phoenix* printed the laws of the Cherokee Nation, local, national and international news, scripture, editorials and advertisements. It inspired generations of tribal and Indian newspapers and magazines. After **Removal** and Boudinot's death, the *Phoenix* ceased to operate. The newspaper, revived as the *Cherokee Advocate*, was published again in Indian Territory by the Cherokees in 1844–1906 and again today by the Cherokee Nation of Oklahoma.

To obtain a correct and complete knowledge of these people, there must first exist a vehicle of Indian intelligence…. Will not a paper published in Indian Country… have the desired effect? I do not say Indians… may exhibit specimens of their intellectual efforts, of their eloquence, of their moral, civil and physical advancement, which will do quite as much to remove prejudice and to give profitable information.
*Elias Boudinot, 1826*

Boudinot, his brother Watie, his uncle (The Ridge) and others who were involved in the Removal Party insisted that Cherokee's safety lay in a move to Indian Territory. This was a feeling not shared by others in the Cherokee Nation. The **Treaty** Party was in favour of negotiation with government on Removal, but the elected government of John Ross forbade any debate on the topic. In 1828 Boudinot and others illegally signed the Treaty of New Echota with the US government, agreeing to Removal and the confiscation of Cherokee lands in Georgia. Cherokees exacted the law of blood revenge on Boudinot and the other Treaty signers, such as Boudinot's uncle, assassinating them in Indian Territory after Removal.

You must not remain longer in your contact with the Whites. Sure safety lies in isolation. Fly – fly for your lives.
*Elias Boudinot on the subject of Removal*

41 **Above** The front page of the Cherokee *Phoenix* on 4 June 1828.

## Bow and arrow

A highly efficient tool for hunting and self-defence, the bow and arrow epitomizes the skills of the Indian male. Bows and arrows are some of humankind's oldest tools (the oldest in North America dates to roughly 19,000 BC). Unlike arrowheads, they show very little variation in form, although much variation in material, decoration and accompanying carrying cases. Indian bows and arrows are forms of bent and straightened hardwoods, and whether small (for birds) or large (for animals and humans), they are ingenious devices. Like the 'atlatl' (the ancient object used to propel spears), they increase the force of the projectile. Making and using these devices was an essential and highly valued skill among men. As early colonists discovered to their surprise, a man using a bow and arrow could easily outfire a man using the awkward, heavy, long rifles first brought by Europeans to the Americas.

**42 Below** This Omaha bow and arrows with quiver is made of Osage orange or bois'd'arc wood, and the quiver is made of mountain lion skin. It was probably collected by Duke Friederich Paul Wilhelm of Wurtemburg on his voyage to North America in 1823.

**43 Right** The making of both a straight-sided and bentwood box is one of the most difficult tasks for a woodworker. That challenge was more than met by the skilled woodcarvers on the **Northwest Coast**. This grooved, steamed, bent and carved **Tlingit** bentwood 'box of treasures' stored crest hats and clan regalia that kept and told the history of the clan.[13]

## Box of treasures

**Northwest Coastal** peoples often carved and painted boxes which represented the **clan** histories, maps, laws, genealogies, symbols, **name**, origins, social ranks and duties (*ada'ox*). These boxes were brought out at important occasions when the history and laws of the people were recited. In 1997 in a ruling for the clan houses of the Gitksan and Wet'suwet'en nations, the Supreme Court of Canada decreed that the laws and testimonies described in such ways had standing in courts when considering the settlements of aboriginal titles. When, in the court, the hereditary chiefs 'opened their bent-cedar boxes', according to their tradition, their 'box was full'.

**44 Right** On the Northwest Coast, high-ranking Tlingit men, the hereditary chiefs of their clans, wore these crest hats (*at.oow*) at feasts and **potlatches**. The hats are skilfully made with intricate twining of spruce roots and are painted in the traditional colours of red, black and blue. Some believed that each of the cylinders on top of the hat represented a potlatch given by the owner. Others believe that the number of cylinders is associated with a particular crest fixed long ago. Similar hats were worn by and made for Pacific Eskimo, Chugatch and Koniaq men, probably received in trade with Tlingit.[14]

## Brant, Joseph

Joseph Brant (Thayendanega) (c. 1742–1807) was, like **Red Jacket**, a powerful non-hereditary chief of the **Iroquois** Confederacy. He favoured alliances with Europeans instead of war. His grandfather was among the four Indian 'kings' who visited Queen Anne's Court in London in 1710. Joseph and his sister, **Mary (Molly) Brant**, were among the most influential Iroquois of the 18th century. They were comfortable in both **Mohawk** and English societies. Yet to some Iroquois, they were traitors because of their affiliations with the **British**. As his sister was the common-law wife of Sir William Johnson, the Commander of British Colonial Indian Affairs in the North (New York and Canada), Brant was able to negotiate a favourable arrangement for his people at the Albany Congress of 1754. However, when his British alliances proved treacherous and then too dangerous for his defeated people after the American War of Independence, he was forced to lead an exodus of Mohawks, **Senecas** and **Cayugas** into Canada in 1784. The descendants of those people now live on the Six Nations Reserve in Canada.

**45 Above** A 1786 painting, *Joseph Brant, Mohawk Indian,* by Gilbert Stuart, who was known for his portraits of men such as George Washington. Notice Brant's silver gorget given to him by his **British** allies, and the **trade** silver brooches worn on his very Iroquoian headpiece and European-style collar. Brooches like these and, later, Iroquois-made brooches, had symbols of **clans** and European church and social groups, such as the masons.

## Brant, Mary/Molly

Mary Brant, or Molly as she was called, was the sister of **Joseph Brant**. She was highly placed politically in the **Iroquois** nations because she was a **clan** mother. As the common-law wife of Sir William Johnson, Commander of **British** Colonial Indian Affairs, she had a powerful influence on Iroquois affairs. Nevertheless, although several portraits and mementoes of Joseph Brant have been preserved, no object commemorating Molly Brant's place in history has surfaced.

In 1762, *Kanadiohora*, a **Seneca**, told Sir William Johnson that he was to come and speak to the Council, at the request of the women. However, Johnson was opposed to both men and women attending the Council meetings with the British. He insisted that only the chiefs should come, as with British practice. *Kanadiohora* said, 'It was always the Custom for them to be present at Such Occasions (being of Much Estimation Amongst Us, in that we proceed from them and they provide our Warriors with Provisions when they go abroad), they were therefore Resolved to come down.'[15] It is ironic that Johnson should have been the one to disrupt the traditional power of the women, as, by marrying Molly Brant, he had benefited greatly from the relationship and access to influence brought by his own wife.

> **O**ur Ancestors considered it a great Transgression to reject the Council of their Women, particularly the female Governesses. Our Ancestors considered them Mistresses of the soil. Our Ancestors said who bring us forth, who cultivate our Lands, who Kindles our Fires and boils our Pots, but the Women, they are the Life of the Nation.
> *Domine Pater or Good Peter, a Seneca-Cayuga orator,* 1788

## British, The

When the British founded what became the first permanent settlement in North America at Jamestown, Virginia, in 1607, they were one of the first groups of colonists to encounter and displace Indians in the Americas. They engaged in **wars** and battles with the other settlers, and with the support of various Indian groups, they gained or kept **land** and power in the former Indian territories. However, in general, like the French and

Dutch, they tried to play one Native alliance off another in cycles of **treaty** making, mutual aid, **trade** and peacemaking. Most tribes supported the British in the American War of Independence of 1775 (the Revolutionary War), as the American rebels clearly represented the interests of encroaching settlers. After the American defeat of the British, such support resulted in no **status** for Indian allies of the British in the Treaty of Paris of 1783.

The Crown had official Indian policies administered through the colonial government, such as that run by Sir William Johnson in the 18th century. In New England, the Southeast and the Mid Atlantic, British military, religious and commercial interests had different relationships with various Indian groups and with other European groups, depending on their negotiations over Indian lands with commercial potential (such as for **tobacco** and **maize**). Through the Hudson's Bay Company, the British (English, Scots and Irish) established trading posts and trading relationships with Indians who brought **furs**.

The **Royal Proclamation** of 1763 and the Indian Acts of 1868–1969 established in Canada the equivalent of the US **Bureau of Indian Affairs**, called the Department of Indian Affairs, creating an administrative office for the Crown's relationships with Indians. These Acts also created boundaries for colonies, establishing the incongruities typical of the US relationships with Indians, pushing Indians onto lands then taken by whites. In Canada, the British government (like its US cousin) had decided in 1830 to set aside lands where Indians could be '**Christian**ized' and '**civilized**', and had entered into **treaties** with tribes in exchange for the hand-over of lands. In return, the tribes were guaranteed reserve lands, annual payments, education and other services.

**47 Left** Different kinds of **gift**s were exchanged between allies or those hoping to make **diplomatic** and military alliances. The British, Dutch and, later, 'Americans' liked the presentation tomahawks and silver gorgets (the tomahawk being emblematic of the Indian **wars** in North America). This 18th-century pipe tomahawk, made for **Joseph Brant**, but never given to him after he escaped to Canada, is engraved with a typical scene in which an Indian is tomahawking an enemy, with the other side showing the common engraving of two hands shaking in peace and friendship.

**46 Above** The **Iroquois** valued silver as a symbol of spiritual purity, strength and prestige. They adopted the art of silversmithing and the giving of silver **gifts** from the Europeans. Settlers and diplomats presented gorgets like this one to Indians as a sign of respect, as evidence of the wealth of white colonists and to encourage **trade** and friendship. This gorget is engraved with a British coat of arms and bears the mark of Dutch silversmith Barent Ten Eyck of Albany, New York. It is inscribed with the name 'Daniel Cryn' and dated 1755. It is possibly related to the family 'Kryn', Mohawks of Caughnawaga, a **mission** at Sault-Ste Marie.

## Buffalo

The animal ancestors of the buffalo (called *bison bison* or the 'American bison') have lived since the second Ice Age. These huge mammals lived on the vast grasslands of the American Plains and Midwestern Prairies, although some smaller types inhabited the Appalachians hills, the grasslands in the Southwest and the desert of the Sonora. Indians from these areas always had a special relationship with the buffalo which, before the arrivals of Europeans and their **horses** and guns, formed a major part of their spiritual and day-to-day life.

Buffalo were hunted by Indians. Their meat was used as **food**, their hides were

*Bears Heart. Cheyenne*

used as clothing and housing, and their bones were made into tools. The hides were also used as canvases on which the Indians painted their personal and tribal histories. Some paintings on the hides, called Winter Counts, were an attempt to record the events and significant moments of each calendar. Others, made by individuals, painted a history symbolic of significant events in their lives.

The near extinction of the buffalo on the Plains of North America, slaughtered by American and Canadian hide hunters at the end of the 19th century, came to symbolize the probable disappearance of Indians. By 1880, the Canadian Prairies were empty of buffalo. The **Sioux wars** came as a direct result of hunters and the military separating Indians from, and starving them of, their major resource. The United States and Canada enacted laws and regulations that further separated Indians from the buffalo. The military protected the **traders**, **hunters** and cattle ranchers. Hunters who formerly only took winter long-haired buffalo for their hides, throwing the meat away, developed a

**48 Above** In the late 19th century, imprisoned Indians and Indians sent to boarding **schools** began drawing pictures of their lives and histories on paper given them by their captors. A Cheyenne named Bear's Heart made this 'ledger' drawing of men hunting buffalo and men and women in tipis.

method of processing short-haired animals. The resulting slaughter was immense. Then hunters bought buffalo guns, rifles that could kill the animals at some distance. The buffalo all but disappeared. Once the Indians had been placed on **reservations**, the new cattle industry grew, with its profits coming from cheap or free Indian lands and sales of new range-bred cattle to the government to feed then-starving tribes.

However, cattle could not replace the buffalo in the ceremonial life of the people. The Sioux continued to tell the story of White Buffalo Calf Woman who brought the 'Way of the **Pipe**' and Truth to the people. They believed she would return when the tribes drove out the whites and returned to their old ways. *Wovoka*, the Paiute prophet, said that the buffalo would return if the people performed the **Ghost Dance**. The buffalo spirit was the source of warrior bravery and even the **Cherokees** and the Pueblos, who lost access to buffalo long before their brothers on the Plains, kept songs, **dances** and masks of this important animal.

Although the tribes were never able to restore life on the Plains and although they shifted their attentions to beef for everyday **food** and to deer or **elk** meat and their skins when they could get them, they never forgot the buffalo. Buffalo remains the ceremonial food and buffalo imagery continues to dominate **art**. Recently, Indian people, environmentalists and ranchers have revived buffalo raising. Tribes have worked together to bring buffalo to Indian Country and to restore grasslands and prairies devastated by drought and huge agricultural development.

**49 Below** This watercolour, *Buffalo Dancers, c.* 1925, is by Awa Tsireh (Alphonse Roybal), a Pueblo artist. Pueblos still perform annual Buffalo Dances, symbolic of the times when buffalo were important to them, and they would exchange valued goods with buffalo hunting Comanche **traders**.

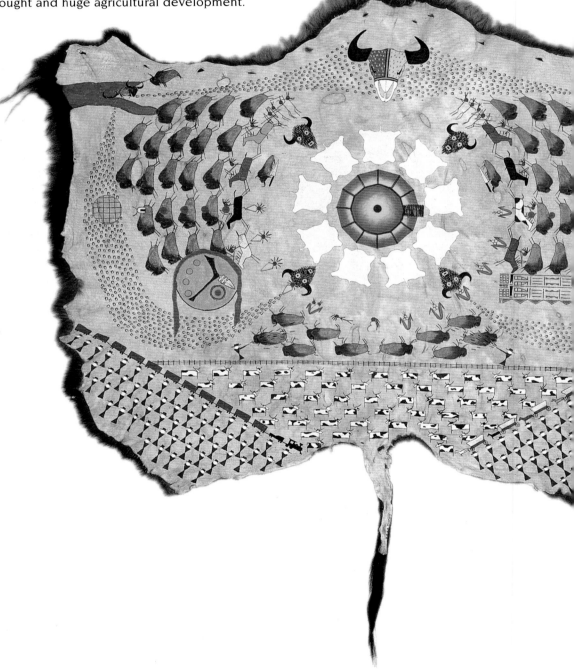

**50 Below** Dennis Fox, Jr. (Mandan, Hidatsa and **Sioux**) painted this hide of a young buffalo in 1992. On it, he tells his version of Hidatsa history. Fox shows the changes with the coming of the railroads, **missionaries** and cavalry, the change from the buffalo to cattle, and the change from growing **maize** to a dependency on goods bought from stores and **traders**.

51 **Right** Anna Old Elk, a young Crow and **Sioux** Indian, wears Dennis Fox's painted buffalo hide to show the way such hides – painted and perhaps **quilled** – would have been worn by Plains Indians in the 19th century.

# Bureau of Indian Affairs

The US War Department created the Office of Indian Trade in 1806 to manage the relationships between the government and the Indians. The Office had dealt particularly with **land**, **treaties** and the 'Indian trade'. The Bureau of Indian Affairs (BIA) was created in 1849, primarily to oversee treaty negotiations, and moved from the War Department to the US Department of Interior. After the **Civil War**, the BIA handed over much of its authority to Indian agents and, sometimes, to **missions** and churches. The Indian agents distributed rations and goods, managed **schools** and supervised lands under treaty agreements. They also supervised **allotment** from the 1880s until the early 1900s. Essentially, they stripped any remaining power from the **tribal governments** and leaders.

In 1934, a new Commissioner of the BIA, an anthropologist called John Collier, helped halt the government's official policy of **Christianization** and 'assimilation' (see **acculturation**) and initiated reforms in tribal government that still remain controversial. Despite Collier's reforms, however, the BIA

managed to supervise the **termination** of 100 tribes during the 1950s.

Today, the BIA has four main functions: education, services to **reservations** (such as housing, roadbuilding and the management of natural resources), economic development and BIA operations. The BIA operates tribal schools, hospitals and clinics, and is meant to protect Native American land and resources. Increasingly, it is supposed to support tribes in taking responsibility for the administration of the government's programmes and services of benefit to Indians.

Indians have a complex relationship with the BIA and, indeed, with the US government. Indians in the 1960s used to say that BIA meant 'Bosses Indians Around'. Indians accuse the BIA and the Department of Interior of corruption, inefficiency, wastefulness and bureaucracy. However, the BIA represents the carrying out of the government's promises to Indians through treaties, the so-called 'trust relationship'; so, for many Indians, the BIA and reservations may be the only visible symbol left of that continued relationship.

So far, the self-determination policy can only be judged a limited success. BIA administration trust responsibility, and budget control continue to severely constrain tribal governments and Indian reservations communities. Despite continuing tribal efforts to decentralize BIA administrative and budgetary powers, the BIA will most likely remain a major force in Indian affairs… well into the next century.

*Duane Champagne, Turtle Mountain Chippewa scholar*

## Calendars and time

In the Americas before the coming of Europeans, each group kept their own calendar with their own systems for marking the passage of time and the seasons. The Maya and Aztec referred to years simply as specific annual periods based on their complex calendric system. Most calendric systems in Native North America were based on solar (sun) or lunar (moon) and stellar (star-based) observation and systems to predict their seasonal round of **hunting**, **farming** and **ceremonial** life. Calendars and astronomical observation are linked. Indian people took note of and recorded (by word of mouth or in pictures) happenings on Earth and in the skies. Pictorial stories, called Winter Counts, were painted on animal hide or paper by tribal historians on the Plains. These were historical records of important events and changes in the lives of groups and individuals. These included astronomical and celestial events (such as eclipses, meteor showers, earthquakes and floods), the battles and deeds of warriors, events such as the time when the Pawnees stole many Lakota **horses**, the deaths of important people, the coming of smallpox and measles epidemics, and even important mythological events (such as the bringing of the **buffalo** and the **pipe** by White Buffalo Calf Woman).

Indians had many ways of keeping and telling time, and marking events. Calendar sticks of all sorts were common. Before the Pueblo Revolt, runners took a deerskin strap with knots tied in it to each of the pueblos (towns), telling them to untie one knot each day, and the last knot would be the day to begin the resistance to the Spanish.[16]

**52 Above** In this photograph of 1921, Joseph Head (Pima) holds a calendar stick made from the ribs of a saguaro cactus. The stick's markings begin with 'the night the stars fell', noting an 1833 meteor shower visible in the Southwestern desert.

January was *Wicogandu*, Centre Moon (also Big Moon)... February was *Amhanska*, Long Dry Moon... March was *Wicinstayazan*, Sore Eye Moon... (snow blindness was common)... April, *Tabehatawi*, Frog's Moon... May, *Induwiga*, Idle Moon... June, *Waweqosmewi*, Full Leaf Moon... July, *Wasasa*, Red Berries Moon... August, *Capsapsaba*, Black Cherries Moon (Chokecherries)... September, *Wahpegiwi*, Yellow Leaf Moon... October, *Anukope*, Joins Both Sides (the middle)... November, *Cuhotgawi*, Frost Moon... December, *Wicogandu-sungagu*, Centre Moon's Younger Brother.... Old men kept account of the days in a moon by notching on their pipe cleaners, one notch for a day. These pipe cleaners were made from a small willow branch the size of a pencil and about a foot long. A row of notches the length of a pipe cleaner would constitute a moon period, or a month.... One of these sticks notched down four sides counted four months, and three fully notched sticks made a full year.
*James Larpenteur Long, Assiniboine*

Ultimately, Indians were forced to work and live to the Western clock. The **school** bell, the **mission** bell, the **Christian** calendar, the watch and the train schedule all altered the way in which Indians had measured time and the periods of their lives.

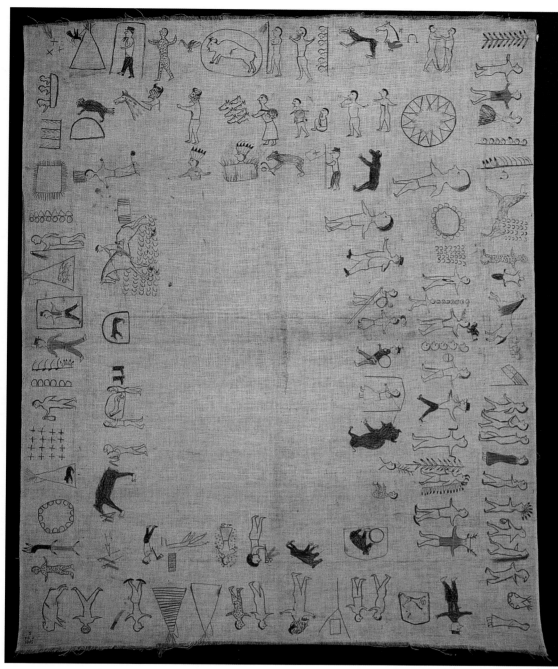

**53 Above** A Winter Count, painted onto hide.

## Canadian Indian Act of 1867

Many **treaties** were negotiated in Canada after the **Royal Proclamation** in 1763. Native groups worked hard to obtain fair agreements for their lands and to retain certain basic rights. The government saw its role as to protect, **civilize** and gradually move Native people into the mainstream society. The **British** North America Act (now known as the Constitution Act of 1867), which formed Canada, gave the Canadian government responsibility for Indians. The Indian Act of 1867 put them in a different legal category from all other Canadians. This division was meant to further the federal assimilation policy (see **acculturation**), but instead restricted Native people and isolated them.

Women who married non-Native men were removed from Indian **status** (recognition as Indians by the government). Men who did the same did not lose their status and the non-Native wives of Native men automatically became Native. Anyone who obtained a university degree or a profession was automatically removed from status and Native men and women could give up their status for lump sum payments of money. The Act banned many **ceremonies**, such as the Plains **Sun Dance** and the **Northwest Coast potlatch**, and gave the

The train was called the Chili Line… people kept time by the whistle because… the one that came from the North always came by about the same time. So when people were out in the fields working, they went by the whistle… well, people didn't have wristwatches and they went by the line of the sun and their shadows, just knowing that it's noontime and time to go home. But anyway, they changed from the shadow to the sound of the whistle.
*Esther/Estefanita Martinez, San Juan Pueblo*

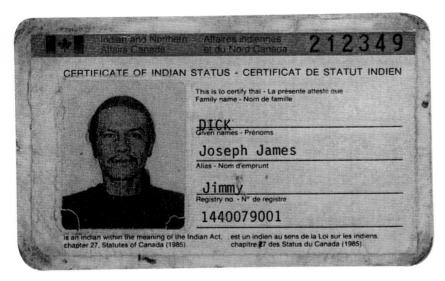

Indian and Northern Affairs Canada — Affaires indiennes et du Nord Canada

212349

**CERTIFICATE OF INDIAN STATUS · CERTIFICAT DE STATUT INDIEN**

This is to certify that - La présente atteste que
Family name - Nom de famille

DICK
Given names - Prénoms

Joseph James
Alias - Nom d'emprunt

Jimmy
Registry no. - N° de registre

1440079001

is an indian within the meaning of the Indian Act, chapter 27, Statutes of Canada (1985).    est un indien au sens de la Loi sur les indiens, chapitre 27 des Status du Canada (1985).

**54 Above** This Canadian Indian **status** or band card identifies a person from the Moose Factory Reserve. Unlike Certificates of Degree of Indian Blood (CDIB's) or tribal enrolment cards in the United States, Canadian Indian status cards do not show blood quantum (see page 40).

Indian agents complete control over **reservations**. In 1951 revisions to the Act reduced government powers and dropped the ban on ceremonies. In 1960, voting rights were granted to Native people and it was possible for them to obtain Canadian **citizenship**.

In 1969, the Canadian government proposed sweeping changes to the Indian Act and the way in which Native relationships with the government were structured. The Indian Act continues to prohibit First Nations from ownership of the reservations, rights to resources and personal property. Taxes cannot be collected on reservations or on band properties. People who live or work on reservations do not pay any taxes, whereas off-reserve employment is taxed. Some recent negotiations have allowed for transfer of some responsibilities to First Nations communities and some bands now have control over their own finances, education and social programmes. A few bands have also recently negotiated self-government (**self-determination** in the United States) agreements which give them more control over their lands and resources.

> Let no-one forget it… we are a people with special rights guaranteed to us by promises and treaties. We do not beg for these rights, nor do we thank you… because we paid for them… and God help us the price we paid was exorbitant.
>
> *Chief Dan George, Squamish Nation*

Following changes to the Act in 1985, any

woman who lost status through the Act's original provisions can now regain it without marrying another Native. In the future, two Native parents will be able to pass on their status. A child with one Native parent will be considered Native, but will not be able to pass on status to his or her children. By late 1994, approximately 93,000 people had obtained status under this Act.

## Cayuga

This Nation of the **Iroquois** Confederacy originally lived on the shores of the Cayuga Lake in Western New York State. Their name means, 'the place where locusts were taken out'. The community has four **clans** and ten delegates in the Grand Council of the Haudenosaunee. After the American Revolution, large parts of the tribe were removed to Canada and scattered to Ohio, Oklahoma and Wisconsin. Cayugas also joined with **Senecas** on the Cattaraugus and Allegany **reservations**. They began official land claims for their original homelands in the late 1970s and are still negotiating them in the late 1990s. Today, gaming provides huge revenue to a number of Cayuga communities.

## Ceremony

All Native people, indeed all peoples everywhere in the world, engage in some forms of ceremonial life. Whether based in an organized, written and 'official' religious philosophy (such as Judaism, Islam, **Christianity** or Buddhism) or in less organized spiritual beliefs, every culture has means of religious observation structured in a ceremonial way.

Ceremonies are characterized by the participation of special people and/or special roles played by people who otherwise lead ordinary lives. These people wear special clothing, offer special prayers and perform **dances**, songs and acts (rites or rituals) as part of the ceremony. For most Native people, ceremony was a part of daily life – from the daily prayers and songs at dawn or sunset to the elaborate rituals surrounding healing, **hunting** or **war**. Ceremonies ensured that things would go well, by restoring balance and harmony in relationships. Some ceremonies or rituals were given to the people in their origin stories (or myths). These important stories about their past

**55 Above** A common Pueblo way to store ceremonial or **dance** clothing was on a pine pole. This one – provided by a Santa Clara Pueblo man – hung in the house from the ceiling. The evergreen pine is important, and evergreens are used as part of a dancer's ceremonial costumes. On the pole hangs a Pendleton **blanket** shawl, a woman's back shawl (*aahi*); **turtle-shell** rattles (*oku*); a man's **rain** sash/belt (*se'yen*); a **Navajo**-style woven belt (*se'yen*); a girl's black *manta* (dress) from San Ildefonso Pueblo; a woman's embroidered *sega* (dress) made by Janice Baca, Santa Clara Pueblo; a man's shell **bandolier** (*ove*), worn across the chest; a boy's kilt (*waage*) made by Janice Baca; a man's fox skin (Dee Khowaa), and a man's skunk fur anklets (*saa*). The year-round presence of ceremonial clothing reminds family members of their ceremonial responsibilities.

described certain songs, clothes or objects (often thought to be prayers in a material form). The sandpaintings made by **Navajo** singers (*hataali*), the Hopi **Bean** Dance, Longhouse singings and sitting at the **drum** were all given to people by specific characters or figures (human, animal or spirit) in their stories.

Some **games** and dances once served important ceremonial functions, often built around the calendar, as prayers to the gods. They expressed the hope for fertility, for **rain**, for giving and prolonging life or for healing. They also provided entertainment and a chance for people to display physical powers. **Iroquois**, **Ojibwa**, **Cherokee** and Muskogean peoples (**Creeks** and **Seminoles**) played lacrosse and **stickball**, not only as a form of mock war, but also as a healing ritual.

C ome and be blessed, come to the people of the village and let them give you thanks. They will feed your spirits with corn meal and sing their songs of love for you.
The people will wear the costumes of ceremonial, and their women will shower blessings upon you.
*San Juan Pueblo song*

T he Holy People gave us this earth to live on. That is Hozhoni, or beauty, which the Diné are required to live by. When something goes wrong… the effort to achieve beauty is destroyed. We… have a… Ceremony to make things right.
*Jesse Biakeddy, Big Mountain Navajo*

## Cherokee

The Cherokee (*Tsalagi*), who also called themselves The Real People (*Aniyunwiya*), had been living in the Southern Appalachian region for centuries when they began to have frequent **contact** with **explorers** from other continents in the early 1700s. The arrival of outsiders, particularly Anglo-Americans, brought dramatic changes to their way of life. Early in the 1700s, the Cherokee started using guns rather than **bows and arrows** to **hunt** large animals. As the men became skilled with guns and traps and killed more deer, they traded in deerskins for European goods, such as **metal** hoes, knives, axes, copper kettles, cloth and **blankets** and more guns and ammunition. This brought more European goods into Cherokee daily life and depleted the hunting grounds. Now hunters had to travel farther and stay away longer in search of deer. Women, the **farmers** in Cherokee life, took time away from the fields to prepare hides for the **trade**. Like the men, their traditional areas of power, authority and skill were undermined. However, with the goods came the newcomers' greed for **land**, and Cherokees took up arms in defence of their homelands.

By the 1790s, the Cherokees were plagued by **war** with frontier Anglo-Americans, extreme poverty and severe **food** shortages. They realized that they could not preserve their Nation by war and decided instead to make peace. The US government encouraged Cherokees to farm in the Anglo-American style, with its unfamiliar values of individual effort and profit. In return, the government promised full and equal **citizenship** to Cherokees and other American Indians.

In the face of cultural and political war, some Cherokees clung to their ancient traditions. Others adopted **Christianity**, European-style **farming** and other aspects of white culture. To drive the Cherokees from their Southeastern homeland, the majority of US policymakers and most citizens ignored the Cherokees' rights, guaranteed in **treaties**, US law and court decisions, to remain on their land. Cherokees and other Southeastern Indians became a main target of **Removal**. In 1838, the Administration run by Andrew Jackson brutally tore most of them from their homelands and sent them to Indian Territory.

God is dissatisfied that you are receiving the white people in your land without any distinction. You yourselves see that your hunting is gone – you are planting the corn [maize] of the white people – go and sell that back to them and plant Indian corn and pound it in the manner of your forefathers; do away with the mills. The Mother of the Nation has forsaken you because all her bones are being broken through the grinding [of the mills]. She will return to you, however, if you put the white people out of the land and return to your former manner of life. You yourselves can see that the white people are entirely different beings from us; we are made of red clay; they out of white sand. You may keep good neighbourly relations with them.
*Vision experienced by three Cherokees*, 1811

The lands in question belong to Georgia. She must and will have them.
*Resolution of the Georgia Legislature, December* 1827

The Cherokees have been stripped of every attribute of freedom and eligibility for legal self-defence… . We are denationalized! We are disenfranchised!… . We are deprived of membership in the human family! We have neither land, nor home, nor resting-place, that can be called our own.
*John Ross in a letter to the* US *Congress*, 1835

The Cherokee's Removal became known as the Trail of Tears. The Cherokee, Choctaw, Chickasaw, **Creek**, **Seminole** and numbers of other Midwestern and Eastern tribes (such as the Delaware, Sac and Fox, Miami and

Cayuga) were promised protection in their own Indian Territory once removed from their traditional homelands, but they did not receive it. Further attacks by the US Army, **missionaries**, agents and **traders** made Indian separation impossible. The **Civil War**, **allotment** and the disbanding of Indian Territory in 1906 further damaged Cherokee **sovereignty**.

About 1,100 Cherokees managed to avoid Removal, and most settled in North Carolina. As they lived on non-tribal lands outside the main Cherokee Nation, they were not taken by the US Army. Few wanted to assimilate into Anglo-American society, and their remote mountainous locations limited contact with outsiders. Change came gradually to the Eastern Band of Cherokee Indians, but traditional beliefs, pastimes and lifestyles endured. Some Eastern Cherokees had to develop new skills for living near non-Indian groups.

After the **Civil War**, the government forced them the state to acknowledge them as permanent citizens and they were brought under the laws of the state of North Carolina in 1889. Most moved to the officially recognized area of Qualla Boundary. The land there is held in trust by the US government and cannot be transferred out to anyone other than tribal members. Today, most of their **economy** has been based on **tourism** to this beautiful Appalachian mountain area.

The 17,500 member Cherokee Nation of Oklahoma (*Tsalagi Ayili*), the largest Indian tribe in the United States, resides not on a reservation, but in a legal service area in the former Indian Territory. Membership is composed of the surviving original enrolees of the tribe under the Dawes Act (see **allotment**) Census of 1906 and their descendants. Its members occupy a considerable portion of land in Northeastern Oklahoma, spread over 14 counties.
The Nation runs a successful business, and is one of the most financially secure and growing economies in Indian Country. It is one of the tribes which has self-government (see **self-determination**) under the new structures approved by the United States, and the tribe controls and administers its own health, education, social and legal services, as well as its own courts and tax systems.

## Christianity

Converting the Natives of North America to Christianity was a major goal of the European colonists. **Missionaries**, soldiers and colonists all targeted Natives. In a different way to the political and military pacification, which inevitably involved brutality and physical extermination, Christian pacification (Catholic and Protestant) was meant to exterminate Native values, and social and religious systems.

For many Native people, the conquest was so devastating that they accepted the strength of their conquerors. Perhaps they thought they could achieve some of that power if they followed the strangers' ways.

discarding their previous ways of worship and belief. Others, such as the Pueblo people, managed to absorb aspects of Christianity into their traditional and ancient religious beliefs and practices. Many others took their traditional lifestyles underground, into the *kivas* and into their houses where the priests and ministers would not see them.

**57 Above** Mose Sanders, Joanne McLemore, Joanne Fourkiller, Louise Dreadfulwater and Georgia Glass, members of a Cherokee Baptist choir, sing Christian hymns in the **Cherokee language**. Many of their songs are Cherokee in origin, such as 'One Drop of Blood' and 'Orphan Child', both said to be written on the Trail of Tears. Others, such as 'Amazing Grace', are Protestant songs. Ironically, Cherokee Christian churches helped maintain Cherokee culture by preserving the language, in the Bibles, sermons, prayers, songs and lessons written and given in the Cherokee language.

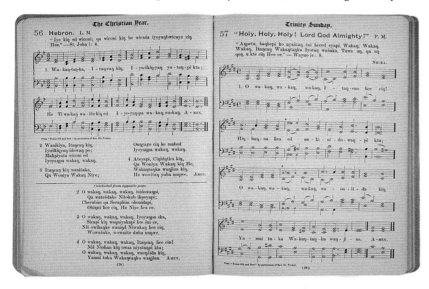

**56 Above** Hymns in the Lakota **language** from *Okodakiciye-Wakan Odowan Qa Okna Ahiyayapi Kta Ho Kin* (Hymnal With Tunes and Chants According to the Use of the Protestant Episcopal Church in the Missions Among the Dakotas), 1931.

In addition, Native religious belief was often incredibly flexible and open, allowing for many different ways of being and thinking. Native people could not conceive that a religion would demand that they cast aside their previous gods, spirits, beliefs and practices. Yet, little by little, Native beliefs and practices were eroded. **Schools** were established to teach Indians to read English (in order to read the Bible). Missionaries often made their first task the translation of the Bible into Native **languages**. However, many did not accept early attempts to Christianize them. 'Well, it seems to be a good book', Cherokee Chief Yonaguska is said to have remarked after hearing a reading of the Gospel of Matthew. 'Strange that the white people are not better, after having had it so long.'

Some Native people adopted Christianity,

**58 Right** This cope made in 1985 for the priest at St Joseph's **Apache** Mission Church in New Mexico, pictures a *gaan* or Mountain Spirit, a Mescalero Apache masked **dancer** with traditional symbols of magic, authority and power. The swords and crosses are symbolic of the healing powers of traditional Apache religion combined with Christianity. The crowns represent mescal, the cactus, from which the Mescalero Apaches derived their Spanish name.

**59 Right** The title page of an 1860 **Cherokee** Bible. The Reverend Samuel Worcester, a minister to the Cherokees and **Elias Boudinot**, translated the Old and New Testaments into Cherokee in 1825.

ᏔᎵ ᎣᏍᏛ ᎤᎭᎨᏓᎵ

ᎠᎴᎣᏆᏎ ᏔᏍᏗᎵ ᏂᎤ ᏍᎦᏃ ᎣᎢᎵᏍ.

ᏗᏎᏈᏫᏗ ᎠᏊᎢ ᏗᎲᎦᎴᎣᎴᎢᎪᏴ ᎤᎤᏔᎢᎡ
ᏧᎰᎭᎠ ᏗᎲᎩᏴᎳᎣᎤᎠ.

ᏳᏎ̈Ᏼ ᏗᏍᎦᏴᎤᎤᎠ.

NEW·YORK:
AMERICAN BIBLE SOCIETY,
INSTITUTED IN THE YEAR MDCCCXVI.
[Cherokee 12mo.]   1860.

**60 Right** This model of a common Pueblo Catholic household shrine reflects the mix of ancient Pueblo and Christian practices. On the shrine stands a *retablo* or painted wood panel of saints, an ear of corn and a clay covered gourd, taken from the last feast day **dances**. These rest on a Hopi style woman's dress (*sega*), made by Jessie Overstreet of Isleta Pueblo, along with a commercial statue of Santa Clara, their patron saint, a cross, a rosary, votive candles and another *retablo* of El Santo Niño de Atocha. In addition, there is a statue of *Kateri Tekakwitha*, a **Mohawk** woman, one of the first North Americans declared Blessed by the Catholic Church.

# Citizenship, tribal

Indians in the United States and Canada dispute issues of tribal citizenship more than issues of US or Canadian citizenship. Citizenship, in the case of Natives, is almost the same as identity. Long-standing ideas about gender, marriage, race, blood and ethnicity govern ideas about tribal identity.

Canadians have endured massive disputes over who can and cannot be identified as **status** Indians. In the last 20 years there have been strong debates over the means of determining status through the provisions of the **Canadian Indian Act**. In the United States, the Supreme Court has upheld the notion that tribes are free to determine their own membership. Much of the dispute over tribal membership or status came about because of forced changes in attitude to and treatment of women, marriage and race.

Since the Indian censuses of the 19th century, taken in order to make **Removal** easier, the US government classified Indians according to their blood quantum (degree of Indian blood), rather than by general lines of ancestral descent. After Removal, tribal citizenship or enrolment was carefully documented to establish the right of individuals to remain on tribal lands and to share in payments and other benefits guaranteed by **treaties**. The first blood quantum standards were set under the Dawes Act (see **allotment**), to determine who was eligible to receive land. Tribes, forced to list their members, designated those of 'one-half or more Indian blood'. During the **allotment** period, so many did not qualify for enrolment under the blood quantum standards accepted by the tribes that the lands eventually passed out of Indian hands. Since then, the government has raised and occasionally lowered blood quantum standards to control who is eligible for land, housing, healthcare, education and all those benefits guaranteed by treaty.

Today, tribes can set standards for enrolment into the tribe that are governed by lines of ancestral descent along with blood quantum. Multi-tribal intermarriage for over a century has virtually ensured the birth of people who cannot meet minimum blood quantum standards. A person can be a 'full-blooded Indian', that is have eight-eighths Indian blood, but still not be enrollable in X tribe if the tribe's and the government's standard holds enrolment to those with one-quarter and over blood quantum. If a man who is one-quarter Potowatomie and enrolled there, one-quarter Pawnee, one-quarter Shawnee and one-quarter Otoe marries a woman one-quarter Choctaw, one-quarter **Creek** and one-half **Cherokee** (but not descended from someone on the Dawes Act Rolls), their child would be 'full-blooded', but not enrollable in any of the seven tribes.

In the Cherokee Nation of Oklahoma, for example, only those who can trace their descendency to Dawes Act Enrolees of 1906 can be enrolled, regardless of their blood quantum. In other tribes, enrolees can come only from persons who have one-quarter or more blood descended from someone living on the **reservation**. In others, someone who can prove one-quarter blood descended from an enrolled father or enrolled mother (*Onondaga*) may be enrolled.

**S**et the blood quantum (standard); hold it to a rigid definition of Indians, let intermarriage proceed as it had for centuries, and eventually, Indians will be defined out of existence. When that happens, the federal government will be freed of its persistent 'Indian problem'.
*Patricia Limerick, historian, 1987*

## Citizenship, US and Canadian

The right to vote in public elections, to hold public office and to participate in some public welfare programmes is restricted to those who hold US citizenship, although most other political and legal rights are guaranteed to all. American Indians were not citizens of the United States until after the Indian Citizenship Act was passed in 1924. A few had previously become citizens by joining the military in the First World War or by applying to the federal courts for citizenship (if they were living in one of the territories that were not yet states). Many Indians who signed treaties and gave up their lands became state citizens, but they lost their tribal citizenship in the process. Some tribal and very traditional peoples regarded US and state citizenship as negative, unnecessary or secondary to their tribal citizenship. The 1924 Act guaranteed citizenship to all born within US territory, without affecting tribal citizenship. Today then, Indians may hold both tribal and US citizenship.

Canadian Indians in tribes that had negotiated treaties with the United States could hold joint US/Canadian citizenship and/or cross the border without a passport (according to the **Jay Treaty**). Canadian Indians, however, were not granted voting rights and Canadian citizenship until 1960.

## 'Civilization' policy

In the latter part of the 18th century, the US government introduced its 'civilization' policy for Indians. This was followed in the 19th century by an assimilation policy (see **acculturation**). The thought was that the so-called 'Indian problem' would go away when Indians ceased to act like Indians.

**Missionaries**, often working with the government, urged Natives to give up their 'savage' practices. After many Indians were **reservationized**, the government banned **ceremonies**, songs and **dances** and forced them to wear 'citizen clothes'.[17] Often they put traditional and ceremonial dress in **museums**.

Children were taken away to boarding **schools**, splitting families up even further. Young **Sioux** girls married white men and never came home or returned as white women, no longer Sioux in behaviour or **language**. Old people, once respected for their wisdom and guidance in traditional Sioux culture, were rejected, and the **medicines** and skills they had known so well were condemned as savage silliness.

Many **Cherokee** families adopted almost the entire way of life of white Southerners around them. Some joined the plantation **economy** of the American South and became wealthy. Many more accepted some things such as log houses and **metal** tools, but rejected **Christianity** and the English language. Others reacted to change by returning to traditional practices. Most Cherokees were **farmers**, supplementing their meagre livelihood by **hunting**, **fishing** and gathering. Like their ancestors, they cultivated Native **maize**, **beans** and pumpkins (see **squash**) on small garden plots. Now, with the aid of shallow draft ploughs and steel hoes introduced by Europeans, they were encouraged to farm. Many adopted new plants (such as wheat and potatoes) and used **horses** for ploughing, hauling and riding. They earned a small cash income from the sale of surplus livestock and forest products to American markets, and their household implements included some Anglo-American goods alongside traditional Cherokee items.

## Civil War, American

Many tribes were drawn into the American Civil War (1861–65). The Civil War, or the War Between the States, affected issues over **Removal** and slavery among Southeastern tribal members. Though Eastern tribes generally fought for the Union, many of the tribes in Indian Territory signed alliance **treaties** with the Confederacy. The Confederacy promised to follow former treaty obligations, protect tribes from invasion and invite Indian representatives to the Confederate Congress. In return, tribes would defend themselves. Many favoured neutrality, but they were caught between the Confederacy and nations who were not neutral.

During the war, **Cherokee** lands, for example, were ravaged both by Union troops and pro-Union Indians. The Cherokees in Indian Territory had just recovered from Removal and the Trail of Tears when the Civil War struck and tore them apart once more. As the war in the East escalated, the federal government abandoned its promise to protect Indians in Indian Territory. Guerrilla bands on both sides stalked the area and raided communities. Old divisions among the Cherokees were once again inflamed. Many Cherokees were forced into Confederate regiments. Thousands of Cherokee civilians fled to Kansas and Missouri, and others to Texas. By the end of the Civil War, more than 7,000 Cherokees had died, many had been made homeless, one-third of the women had been widowed and one-quarter of the children had been orphaned.

**M**y father was neutral and did not want to go away; he did not believe in fighting [but] father was forced into the Southern Army. At the time they took father away, there were no other families left in the country. [We tried] to stay as near to father as we could... but in a short time the war became so fierce that mother realized that we must get out of the country or be killed.
*Betsy Thornton, Cherokee*

After the end of the war and the defeat of the Confederacy, there was turmoil in the former Union and Confederate areas in Indian Territory, with great destruction of Indian property and economic disaster. The Union government punished those who had joined the Confederacy with new treaties that forced them to give up more land.[18]

## Clans

Although not all Indians organize themselves into clans, for those who do, clans describe a system of relationships, government and behaviour that teaches humans their place among plants, animals and fellow human beings. In the Anishinabe world view, for example, the clans have certain responsibilities. Some may be responsible for the water, for the earth and the places under the earth. For other peoples, the clans have responsibilities for human experiences, such as healing, singing and **ceremonial** life.

**M**y clan is Bitter Water [*Tó dich'ii'nii*]. I am Bitter Water... My connection to the land, to creation, to religion, is directly connected with the beginning: Bitter Water Clan created through the Holy People by Changing Woman.
*Luci Tapahonso, Navajo poet*

Organization by clan – by family relationships either through the maternal or paternal line of the family and clan outmarriage (between members of different clans) – had a practical origin and nature. Ancient peoples appear to have understood how marriage and relationships out of one's own group can be politically and economically useful. Furthermore, early people must have begun to recognize the problems associated with **intermarriage** within a family, and cross-clan marriage helped to prevent genetically transmitted **diseases**.

Indians followed their clan relationships in many ways. For the female-centred **Iroquois** and **Cherokee**, every clan had a clan mother. These clan mothers 'raised up' or deposed the men who carried out the day-to-day government. They traced inheritance of personal common property and the right to hold office through the female line. Women joined men in Council and represented children as well. Mothers of those killed in battle and the clan mothers had control over the fate of prisoners, and could intervene in the path of **war** and peace itself. They also had authority over how the products of their work and the work of the men (including **food**

**61 Above** A painting, *The Iroquois Tree of Peace*, by Oren Lyons (**Onondaga**), c. 1970. The Great Law of Peace was proclaimed by *Deganawida*, the Peacemaker. The law established the **Iroquois** Confederacy and set out the principles by which the five nations were to co-operate and live. The Law and the religious authority bound in it are symbolized by the white pine growing in the earth on Grandmother Turtle's back. Animals that represent most of the maternal family clans are grouped around the tree. The clans shown here are Heron, **Eagle**, Eel, **Beaver**, Wolf, **Bear**, **Turtle**, Snipe, Hawk and Deer. With its four white roots of peace extending north, south, east and west, the pine draws the people together at its base.

many cases, these symbols, such as the carved heads of birds, animals or fish, are not only clan animals, but the animals to be hunted or those with spiritual power.

*A*h-ji-jawk (Crane), Mahng (Loon), Gi-goon (Fish), Muk'wa (Bear), Wa-bi-zha-shi (Martin), Wa-wa-shesh-she (Deer), Be-nays' (Bird). The seven original clans o-do-i-daym'-i-wug (clans) of the Anishinabe.
*Eddie Benton-Banai, Anishinabe teacher*

*T*he Seven Cherokee (Ani Yunwiya) clans: Deer (Ani Awi), Long Hair Clan (Ani Gilohi), Paint Clan (Ani Asuwisga or Disuhwisdi), Wolf Clan (Ani Waya), Wild Potato Clan (Ani Nunaanisaquali), Bird Clan (Ani Jisgwa), Blue Clan (Ani Sagonige). *From oral tradition*

## Clowns

A considerable number of Native peoples have a role in their **ceremonies** for characters that might be called clowns.

In some pueblos, clown societies are attached to *kivas*, with clowns initiated very young and committed to the role of sacred clown for life. In Hopiland, sacred clowns (*tsuskut*) arrive during the **katsina dances**. Initiates are often made members of the Clown Society just a few days before a dance by the sponsor of a dance or by a *katsina* group. Clowning is religious duty. Clowns teach people to laugh, look and learn. They perform satirical and disrespectful songs. They are instructed to sing, and warrior *katsinas* torture them, drench them with water, whip them, then give them **gifts** of **food**.

The clowns at Zuni perform in the plaza during the season. Wearing Clown University sweatshirts, they play basketball and imitate a Plains Indian **pow wow** dance. They also mimic popular political figures. The clowns in Zuni, called mudheads (*koyemshi*), have conflicting qualities – they are both serious and comic, respectful and disrespectful. They represent the chaos that can come to life if prayer, ritual and respect are not observed by everyone.

Western **Apaches** at White Mountain, for example, practice their spiritual connections to the mountains through the Clown or *gaan* (mountain spirit) Dance. Those spirits drive away evil. During the times of the dance, clowns enter the community with a wand that represents **rain**, thunder and lightning, and a

and other resources) were distributed.

As cross-clan marriage was needed, and in order to recognize the clan relationships in political, social and ceremonial contexts, Native peoples made images of clan symbols on ceremonial objects (such as **headdresses**), instruments (such as **rattles** and **drums**) and in **architecture** and **sculpture** (such as the totem or house poles of Northwest peoples). Many everyday tools and utensils (such as spoons, combs, weapons and **fishing** and **hunting** lures) also show clan symbols. In

**62 Right** Lois Gutierrez de la Cruz and her sisters (Gloria Garcia and Thelma Talachy from Santa Clara and Pojoaque Pueblos) make **pottery**. Lois and her sisters' work explores common themes in Pueblo philosophy and ritual practice. Here, the traditional clowns, called *kossa* in the Tewa language, gamble, read upside down, wear cowboy hats and sunglasses and eat their traditional **food** of watermelon. On the water jar itself, the world is upside down, even though the jar's steps to heaven are the right way up.

**63 Below** A photograph by Owen Seumptewa, a Hopi photographer, of a young clown from Hopiland, who is painted in traditional white and black stripes of clay and wearing his cap of **maize** husks.

noise instrument (bullroarer) that represents the winds. The clowns and *gaans* appear at sunrise and during ceremonies, including girls' puberty ceremonies.

Clowning can be fun, but it is sacred too. Clowns and *gaans* are sacred. They have the power to cure.
*Edgar Perry, White Mountain Apache*

# Contact

In 1492, an Italian **explorer** called Christoforo Columbo (Christopher Columbus), who was working for the government of Spain and looking for a route to Asia and the 'Indies', came across a small island in the Caribbean he called 'San Salvador'. That voyage and his two subsequent trips to this 'New World' began the encounter between Native peoples and Europeans that reshaped the history of the world. The residents of what Columbus thought were the Indies became 'Indians' or 'Indios' (which means 'In God' or 'Of God' in Spanish). A wave of exploration and conquest began in the newly found 'Americas'. In the 10th–15th centuries, the Norse from Iceland arrived in what became Nova Scotia and met the **Beothuks**. Later they travelled to Greenland, encountering **Inuit**/Eskimo. In the 15th century, they became involved in **trade** disputes which led to violence and to their departure. People in the far **Arctic** and Northeast, then those of the Southwest and Southeast, were the first to experience contact with Europeans. Then from 1540 in the Southwest and 1607 in the Northeast, the strangers from Europe once again entered Indian land.

The European invasion of North and South America started enormous biological and cultural change, sometimes referred to as the 'Columbian exchange'. Plants, animals and **diseases** were passed back and forth between the Americas and Europe, and on to Africa and Asia, altering life on all the continents. Religion went only one way, from Europe to the Americas. This exchange deeply affected the indigenous population, the 'Indians' 'discovered' by Columbus. Many of the first Native peoples experienced contact with Europeans before they ever encountered an actual European person. Diseases such as smallpox and tuberculosis travelled north from South America and the Caribbean and killed many thousands. Whole communities were devastated by these new diseases to which Native peoples had no resistance. Many tribal groups were entirely wiped out. In the first 200 years of the European occupation of North America, it is estimated that between 8 and 20 million Native people died.

Suddenly, peoples new to the Native world appeared, demanding **land**, demanding that they abandon their traditional religions, demanding their **food** and goods, even demanding their labour and their loyalty. Although Indians resisted these demands, the effect on the people and communities was devastating. Native people must have felt that their own gods and spirits were weak against the extraordinary powers of these people with weapons (guns and germs) that killed at a distance.

Columbus made three voyages to the Americas, confining his explorations to the Caribbean. He died a bankrupt and bitter man. During the anniversary 500th year of his voyages in 1992, the man and the results of his explorations were criticized by Indian, **African**-American and Hispanic artists, scholars, **political activists** and writers.

**Corn**, see **Maize**

**64 Right** A jacket or shirt patch, issued by the American Indian Movement in 1992 on the anniversary of the Columbian 'discovery' of America. The picture is of one of Columbus' ships from his first voyage (the *Niña*, the *Pinta* or the *Santa Maria*) with the international symbol for 'No' or 'Off' through it.

**65 Right** This Zuni pot, *c.* 1700, is from Hawikuh, a town occupied by Zuni at the time of the Spanish invasion. It was the site of a struggle in July 1540 between Spanish soldiers under Francisco Vasquez de Coronado and the Zuni. The Spanish, seeking Cibolá, the 'Seven Cities of Gold' (which did not exist), interrupted religious **ceremonies** and a battle followed. The town was abandoned after the **Pueblo Revolt** of 1680. Zunis **traded** with many people at this time and, when the area was later excavated by archaeologists, much **pottery** was found there.

**66 Above** Jaune Quick-to-See Smith, a **Salish** artist, offered her 1992 version of 1492 in this pastel. Modelled on sets of paper **dolls** for children combined with references to the 'Barbie' doll, the costumes of Smith's Ken and Barbie Plenty Horses portray the history introduced by **schools**, priests, **disease** and economic powerlessness.

# BUFFALO BILL'S WILD WEST
## AND CONGRESS OF ROUGH RIDERS OF THE WORLD.

## WILD RIVALRIES OF SAVAGE, BARBAROUS AND CIVILIZED RACES.

**67 Above** The poster for the 1890 Buffalo Bill's Wild West Show, portraying the 'Wild Rivalries of Savage, Barbarous and Civilized Races'.

### 'Cowboys and Indians'

The 1890 Buffalo Bill's Wild West Show set the stage for the powerful image of 'cowboys' and 'Indians' which was then played out in films, television and folk mythology throughout the next century. Bill Cody was a cattle herder, wagon driver, fur trapper, miner and Pony Express Rider before he became an Indian Scout for the US Army. He developed the Wild West Show 'to give a realistic entertainment of wild life on the Plains' and to earn money in the show business he had come to enjoy. **Reservationized** Indians defeated in the Plains Wars joined in the fantasy of the Wild West Show. They included Pawnees such as Knife Chief and Young Chief and Lakota such as **Sitting Bull**, American Horse and Long Wolf (who died in England and whose body was returned to his family in

1997). Cody, Indians, cowboys and *vaqueros* (Mexican cowboys) toured the United States and Europe, appeared in England and met the Queen. In the show, Indians rode, shot and attacked wagon trains, the Mail Riders and the cowboys.

This fantasy continued in the children's game of 'cowboys and Indians', which is still played by millions of children in the Americas and in Europe. It requires a toy tomahawk and **feathered** headband for the 'Indians' and a hat and toy gun for the 'cowboys'. Rather than the existing vocabulary for Indians' roles (brave, squaw, etc.), there are gestures and pidgin-English words. In the game, the 'Indians' 'walk Indian file', they howl and yell, putting their flattened palm repeatedly against their pursed mouths in an imitation of the shrill, ritual 'lu-lu' of Plains women or the battle cry of men. They greet each other with the upraised right forearm, saying 'how' in a misunderstanding of the Lakota greeting '*hau kola*' or 'greetings, brother'.

The 'Indians' 'creep up' on the 'cowboys', who do not use such sly behaviour. This part of the game is left over from the shock that the **British** and French troops suffered when Indians would attack from the shadows rather than lining up and marching straight towards the enemy in one line, as 17th- and 18th-century European warfare demanded. In the game, the 'Indians' are allowed to 'run wild' and shout, whereas the 'cowboys' must behave scrupulously, staying silent and calm.

## Cowboys, Indian

Despite the images from the Wild West Shows and films, Indians have always been 'cowboys'. Plains and Great Basin Indians were the ultimate 'cowboys'. They were noted for their horsemanship from the moment the **horse** came to Indian Country, . Many, such as the Nez Perce, bred and trained horses. The agile and intelligent Appaloosa (or 'paint pony') became highly favoured as 'cow ponies' by cattlemen and Indians alike. Indians were often hired as cowhands by stock and cattle companies, and, after **reservationization** they were given cattle as part of the **treaty** payments and raised cattle themselves.

Ranching, although difficult on their small **allotted** lands, allowed many of the former **buffalo** people to continue their traditional collective practices of getting and using meat. Today, many tribal peoples on the Plains and in the West have remained cattlemen and some are raising buffalo again. In addition, Indians have taken to the American rodeo, demonstrating their continued excellence in horsemanship and cowboying skills. Indian rodeo, particularly among **Navajos** and other Western tribes, is a big business as well as a pastime.

**68 Above** Champion rodeo bull rider J.P. Paddock, a **Navajo** from Winslow, Arizona.

**69 Left** A watercolour of 1940, *Bronco Busting*, by Ma Pe Wi (Velinos Herrera), a Pueblo artist.

## Coyote

Known to non-Indian ranchers and **farmers** as a nuisance and a predator that steals eggs, lambs and calves, Coyote is something quite different to Indians. He is a creator in the lives and legends of many Native peoples, including the **Navajo**, Karuk, Spokane (*Spilyé*) and Tohono O'odham. Navajo elders, for example, say that *Ma'ii*, the trickster Coyote, hastily tossed the stars into the heavens. He has many names, according to the different people, and is bumbling, clever, foolish, greedy and lustful. He is a creator, but he is also destructive – a type of reverse role model for good behaviour. He has powers of transformation and is like other 'tricksters', such as Spider (**Sioux**/*Iktomi*), **Raven**, Crow and **Rabbit**, who lie and steal their way through life. Stories about him make people laugh, as do the actions of ceremonial **clowns**, but they also make them take note about how to behave in relationships with others.

**70 Above** Harry Fonseca, a Maidu artist, produced a series of paintings in the 1980s built around the exploits of a very modern Coyote. In the best known of this series, called *Portrait of the Artist As A Young Coyote*, Coyote is a very American Uncle Sam, 'shuffling off to Buffalo' (an old vaudeville dance routine).

> **C**oyote was given some good corn [maize] seed after the fall [autumn] harvest, but instead of saving it for the next planting, he ate nearly all of it. When the summer rains finally came, he had forgotten to prepare some good land. He finally just threw the seeds along the bad ground around a wash. Then Coyote slept through the growing season. He didn't learn the right songs to sing to the corn when it did come up. Knowing that he had to sing something to make it grow, he just made up a song. It was terrible. The corn grew anyway. But it didn't grow up to be corn, because it never heard the corn's songs. In a poor place like the rough edge of a wash, only another kind of plant would grow. The plant grew up to be *Ban Wiw-ga*, Coyote's Tobacco (wild tobacco).
> *Story recorded by Juan Delores, Papago, c. 1911*

## Creation stories/origin tales

Every cultural group in the world has origin or creation stories about how the world came into being and about how people were created.

Some of those stories are made 'official' in written texts – the Book of Genesis in the Old Testament, the Ramayana and the Koran tell Jews and **Christians**, Hindus and Muslims how they, their world and their religion came to be. Other creation stories were passed by word of mouth, only written down at the end of the 19th century or even unwritten to the present day.

Such stories appear in song, **dance**, **art** and **ceremonial** drama.

> **L**izard said, 'I'm going to make human beings.' Coyote told Lizard, 'Oh, don't do that. [They will just fall to arguing and cause trouble.]' But Lizard said, 'I'm going to do that.'
> *Lizard, His Song, sung by Nancy Richardson, Karuk teacher*

These stories not only tell *how* things came to be the way they are (why women are priests and why the possum's tail is bare), but *why* things are the way they are (because *Iyetiko* was angry with the men for their drunkenness and **gambling** and because **Coyote** was angry with the village when they would not let him marry a beautiful woman). These tales often tell how people came to live in a certain place, making them important in establishing their ownership of the land. They describe many kinds of creators (spirits, ancient animal and human ancestors) and the relationships between people, animals, plants and spirits in the natural universe.

> **W**e do not like our stories referred to as myths; this is because our sense of who we are and our world view are wrapped up in these stories. Even clothing, tools, baskets… so important in everyday life have direct links to the stories of the people.
> *Dale Curtis Miles, San Carlos Apache*

The way in which people see the roles of men and women in their culture can come from the roles that men and women had in the origin stories of their people. For many Indian people, the origin of their people stems from a woman or a female spirit. Unlike the Judeo-Christian tradition in which there is one God and he is male, many Native peoples insist that the spirit or process of their creation comes from the female and from more than one being.

Many people believe that female spirits are central to everyday life and to ceremonial life. **Cherokees**, for example, say they came from the breast of Corn Mother (*Selu*), who died so that **maize** would spring from her body and give life to the people. The **Iroquois** believe they were born from the mud on the back of the Earth, known as Grandmother **Turtle**. Apaches believe that they are descendants of Child of the Water, a male child of White-Painted Woman, who kept the child safe to slay all the monsters and make the world safe for The People. For the **Sioux**, White-Buffalo Calf Woman gave the people the 'Gift of the **Pipe** and Truth'. The first mothers of all the Tewa Pueblo people were called Blue Corn Woman, Summer Mother, White Corn Maiden and the Winter Mother.

Once all living things were in the womb of Mother Earth. Corn Mother caused all things to have life and start to move toward the surface of the Earth. With Corn Mother's help, the people were born onto the surface of the Earth, but because the people did not know how to care for themselves, they started to wander… . Finally the Arikara came to a beautiful land where they found everything they needed to live. A woman of great beauty came to them and the Arikara recognized her as Corn Mother. She stayed with them for many years and taught them how to live and work on the Earth and how to pray. When she died, Corn Mother left the people a corn plant as a reminder that her spirit would always guide and care for them. The Arikara say that the beautiful place where they learned to live was the valley of the Loup River in Kansas.

*An Arikara story*

## Cree

Cree occupied lands in what is now Canada surrounding James Bay and the Western shores of Hudson Bay north almost to Churchill River, where they bordered the **Inuit**. Their territory extended as far west as Lake Winnipeg and as far south as Lake Nipigon. During the **fur trade** period, after the Cree had obtained guns through trade on Hudson Bay, they increased their territory. Profits from the fur trade lured them to expand far west, eventually occupying the south of the Western sub-Arctic as far as the Peace River in Alberta. Many groups pushed out onto the Plains, allying with the Assiniboine against their enemies and adapting to life as Plains **buffalo** hunters.

By the 19th century, Cree speakers with nine different dialects occupied the largest area of any Canadian Native group, stretching from Labrador to the Rockies. The Cree hunted moose, caribou, **bear**, **beaver** and waterfowl. Birch**bark** canoes, sleds, snowshoes and toboggans were used for travel. They lived in conical wigwams, often covered with caribou or moose hides. They wore tanned hides with **quills** and later **beads** and colourful threads in floral designs.

Three to five families travelled together as a hunting group and larger groups gathered at one location during the summer months, generally near water. Men were the hunters, while women trapped smaller game and **fish**. Women collected firewood, cooked, prepared hides and made and mended clothing. To the Cree, hunting was religious activity and they believed that animals could only be killed by following the proper ceremonies.

Cree culture was similar to that of the **Ojibwa** to the near south and, as the fur trade expanded, many Cree and Ojibwa communities joined in hunting and trapping groups. Today some communities are known as 'Oji-Cree'. More isolated communities to the north are often located at the sites of former trading posts. These communities are mostly Native, but many have Euro-Canadian administrators, teachers, **missionaries**, merchants and medical personnel. The government of the communities or 'bands' shifted from the traditional informal methods to an elected chief and councillors. On many reserves, the band government is the major employer of those working in construction, logging, **tourism**, guiding and commercial fishing. Rather than having to attend residential **schools** in the South, many communities are now taking control of their own education through distance learning, technology or the construction of local schools. Trading posts have remained central to the communities and are now retail stores. Unemployment is high and bands are always exploring economic development projects.

The introduction of Euro-Canadian culture changed Native life. Rifles and steel traps replaced traditional methods. Like the Inuit, the Cree use motor **boats**, snowmobiles and aeroplanes for travel. Many communities are accessible only by air travel. However, some families still go to the bush to hunt, trap and fish for part of the year. In areas such as James Bay, there are still many hunters. Parents often withdraw their children from school in order to teach them the 'bush skills' they need to survive as a Cree.

Throughout Manitoba and Ontario, Cree have surrendered most of their land through **treaties**. In Québec and Labrador, Natives did not sign away their lands. Finally in 1975, the governments of Canada and Québec and the Cree and Inuit of James Bay signed the first **land claims** agreement in modern Canadian history (after the 1867 Canadian Confederation). In return for the surrender of lands, the Cree and Inuit received $225 million, as well as ownership of the lands around their communities and exclusive hunting, fishing and trapping rights over a much larger area.

## Creek/Muscogee

More widely known as Creeks, the Muscogee people, Natives of the Southeast, had no single name for themselves and no single political organization at the time of **contact** with the Europeans. They held 50–80 towns, with at least 20 ethnic groups speaking different **languages**. After settling in Alabama and Georgia, the villages banded together in a loose Confederacy based on a common language. The prospect of war with Europeans and the need to protect their boundaries brought Creeks into a tighter group. However, individual towns could reject the decisions of the regional Confederacies. During the American Revolution, the groups made the decision to remain neutral, but a number of Creek towns allied themselves with the **British**. The Treaty of Paris in 1783 put the Confederacy within the boundaries of the newly created United States. The Muscogee worked to protect their territory and culture. The **Red Stick Wars** evolved out of their attempts to protect themselves against constant invasions.

Alexander McGillivray, son of a Scots trader and a Native and French mother, was probably the best-known Creek leader of the 18th century. He was called Great Beloved Man (*Isti atcagagi thlucco*) by his fellow Koasati Creeks. This educated man from the Wind Clan focused on forging alliances between various Creek groups and the British, and later the Spanish. He pushed for towns to develop a unified foreign policy. His leadership helped to form a Council, culminating in the 1790 Treaty of New York in which the United States pledged to protect the Confederacy from outside settlement and compensated the Creek for their loyalty. The loyalty did not last for long when the Creek realized that the government was allowing settlers into the state of Georgia.

During the 1820s, the leaders reluctantly realized that absolute resistance was impossible. In 1832, they signed a **treaty** outlining the terms for **Removal**. Most Creek emigrated west, but a few remained in Alabama. A new Council was created to act on behalf of all towns and a new entity, called the Muskogee Nation, was created. The unity was short lived as the **Civil War** erupted and old loyalties and tensions surfaced. After the War, rival groups were able to bridge their differences and to unite again. Some Creeks remained in Alabama, where their **land** was turned over to sharecroppers (who didn't own the land, but who worked for farmers for a share of the income from the crops). In 1963 the remnant of these groups organized themselves as a tribe once more, and in 1980 the United States accepted them as the Poarch Creek.

In 1899, the Dawes Commission began to allot to individuals land that was once communal. Resigned, most Creeks accepted it. In 1934, the Indian Reorganization Act halted the allotment policy and the tribe was able to gain more recognition. In 1972, the tribe gained full control again and became a **sovereign** nation even though it didn't have a communal land base. The present capital of the Muskogee Nation is Okmulgee in Oklahoma. Businesses there include casinos as well as services for the local community. Despite 300 years of conquest, many customs remain and district representatives still meet in Council to handle tribal affairs. Creek still attend ceremonial stomp **dances**, hold the **Green Corn Ceremony** and identify themselves by town affiliations. Families gather, fast and play **stickball** and speak the Muskogee **language**.

# Dams

Issues concerning Indian lands – of **water**, **fishing** and **hunting rights**, mineral exploitation and land-based economic development – have always been at the forefront of any debate involving Indians. Colonization, **disease**, **Removal** and urban **relocation** programmes have caused many Indian peoples to move.

Much Indian **land** was redistributed due to **reservationization** and **allotment** and this caused much cultural loss. The building of dams and reservoirs on Indian lands in North and South America – usually in order to provide water and electrical power for non-Indians – had a similar effect.

There is no tribal area unaffected by dams. Virtually all areas have seen the relocation of thousands of people and the destruction of traditional fishing, hunting and plant-gathering grounds. Even the dead have undergone Removal. For example, the grave of Cornplanter (the great **Seneca** leader and brother of the prophet **Handsome Lake**) was moved when Kinzua Dam covered the traditional land of the Seneca in the states of Pennsylvania and New York. George Gillette, the Chairman of the Mandan-Hidatsa-Arikara tribe at Fort Berthold, North Dakota, wept as an agreement negotiated by the **Bureau of Indian Affairs** was signed which would move his people off their land to make way for Garrison Dam. The people of Fort Berthold are still struggling for compensation from the US government for what was promised them 55 years ago when they allowed the dam to be sited in their territories.

Cochiti Dam was built by the US Army Corps of Engineers in the 1960s in order to provide water for recreation and **maize farming** in the dry New Mexico highlands. However, the dam has leaked, causing the area to become wetlands, and the proposed income from tourism has never materialized.

Cochitis want the dam removed so that the lands can be converted back to farming. They achieved a partial legal solution in 1990 by having Congress forbid the construction of hydro projects using the Cochiti Dam.

**Cree** land claims and unresolved treaty issues came to a head in 1971, when Québec launched a massive hydro-electric project, which blocked and diverted the rivers flowing to James Bay. The **Cree** temporarily halted the project, which threatened to flood their traditional hunting and fishing areas and relocate several villages. More recently, the Cree of James Bay, under the leadership of Grand Chief Matthew Coon-Come, have been fighting a new hydro-electric project by Hydro Québec. The Cree wouldn't allow a repeat of the environmental damage caused by the first hydro project in the 1970s. Through local, national and international pressure, they gained support from powerful environmental groups. After New York State and a number of other large consumer said that they would not buy power from the new hydro site on Cree lands, Hydro Québec cancelled the project.

**71 Above** Seferina Ortiz made figures in the style of 19th-century humorous Cochiti **pottery** 'Monos' or 'Men' (sheriffs, priests and **cowboys**). She started making these 'bathing beauties' in the early 1970s, after thousands of outsiders came to the recreational lake formed from Cochiti Dam. 'We never saw these things before', she said, when she saw the tourists in their bathing suits.

STOP JAMES BAY II

**VOICE FROM THE WISE:**
THE LAND IS, AND HAS BEEN FOR THOUSANDS OF YEARS, THE ECONOMIC BASE OF MY PEOPLE. LEFT ALONE FOR ANOTHER THOUSAND YEARS, WE WOULD STILL SURVIVE!
–JOHN PETAGUMSKUM
CREE ELDER OF WHAPMAGOOSTUI

**72 Above** A Canadian Indian sweatshirt, c. 1995, which tells people to 'Stop James Bay', the hydro-electric project sponsored by the Québecois government and opposed by the **Cree** and **Inuit** peoples of the Northwest Territories.

## Dance

In Native cultures, the art of dance, like song, is connected to **ceremony**, ritual and prayer. Dance is usually an expression of the relationships between people, animals and the spirits of the world. Particular dances (and dance clothing) came to people in **dreams** and visions (for example the Kiowa **Ghost Dance** and the jingle dress). Most North American Indian dancing has a religious and seasonal meaning (for example the Crow Sun Dance, the Pueblo Corn Dances and **Cherokee** and **Creek stomp dances**). In the traditional Plains 'straight' dance, men wear undyed **feathers** and animal parts and imitate the movements of animals and birds.

Some dance is social, rather than religious. 'Good time' dances and songs, mostly expressed in round dance in North America, were used in courting or celebrating the company of other Indian people. Although much Native dancing was originally specific to particular tribes, it has developed into intertribal, social or **pow wow** dancing that is often for display and competition (for example 'fancy' dancing and hoop dances).

T he Creator again sent someone from his heavenly domain to restore peace and love amongst his Native people… . This was the second religious reform among us Iroquois… . To restore peace he made the Natives more aware of our Creator; he taught them to appreciate most everything that was created for us… through ceremonies that mostly consisted of dancing… . These ceremonies were continuous from when the air is warmed in the spring until the air grew cold in the fall from frost. It was a continuous event of thanksgiving dancing.

*Reg Henry, Cayuga faithkeeper, Six Nations Reserve*

## Department of Indian Affairs, Canada

Amendments to the Indian Act in 1880 formally established the Department of Indian Affairs (DIA) as the Canadian government agency responsible for all recognized '**status**' or registered Indians. The DIA was to carry out the Indian Act's policy of assimilation (see **acculturation**). It controlled all aspects of Native life, including **agriculture**, government, education, religion and travel on and off the reserves.

Over the years, there have been many amendments to the Indian Act and the DIA.

Today the DIA works towards handing over the responsibilities of education and social services to the communities themselves. Some think that the Canadian government is off-loading responsibility for Natives without formally recognizing their aboriginal rights or methods of **self-government**. The Canadian government set up a Royal Commission in 1992 to study aboriginal issues. One of its recommendations was for major changes to the role of DIA.

## Diplomacy

Indian tribes have been sending specially appointed persons to represent them and their interests to government officials in England, France and the United States for four centuries. In turn, they have received political delegations representing those countries. Diplomatic **gifts**, such as pipe tomahawks and presentation tomahawks, trade medals, **blankets**, strings and belts of **wampum** and silver gorgets are evidence of diplomatic efforts between Indians and whites.

When Thomas Jefferson was President of the United States, he sent a number of Peace Medals to be presented to Indian 'chiefs' by the members of the Lewis and Clark expedition to the West. M. Lewis and W. Clark told the tribes that 'a great chief of the 17 great nations of America' had replaced the French and Spanish in the West and that he had adopted them all as his children. They said, 'When you accept his **flag** and medal, you accept therewith his hand of friendship, which will never be withdrawn from your nation as long as you continue to follow the councils which he may command his chiefs to give to you.'

Indians who have Peace Medals passed down to them continue to wear them on ceremonial occasions because they represent the government's promises of peace and friendship.

From the period of **Removal** to the present day, tribal delegations have travelled to Washington, D.C., to take their concerns, pleas, questions and gifts to the Great Father. The National Archives and the White House collections are rich with objects presented by Indians to officials. Similarly, tribal peoples still display and wear items given in diplomatic meetings between their ancestors and government officials.

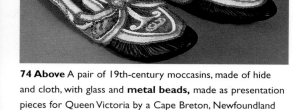

**74 Above** A pair of 19th-century moccasins, made of hide and cloth, with glass and **metal beads,** made as presentation pieces for Queen Victoria by a Cape Breton, Newfoundland **Mi'kmaq** woman, *Whycocomaughh*.

**73 Above** Four members of a **Mohawk** delegation were painted by John Verelst in portraits commissioned by Queen Anne during their diplomatic visit in 1710. In one painting, Brant (*Sa Ga Yeath Qua Pieth Tow*), the grandfather of **Joseph Brant**, wears a scarlet cloak, white cloth shirt, quill-decorated black-dyed moccasins, a powder horn and a burden strap belt. He has a series of blue tattoos over his face and body. The **bear** in the background indicates Brant's **clan**.

**75 Above** Lewis and Clark presented this medal to an Osage chief. It has the bust of Jefferson on one side and the clasped hands of friendship beneath the crossed **pipe** and tomahawk. It was passed down through the generations to Chief Henry Lookout, and loaned to and then sold to the Smithsonian Institution by his heirs.

**76 Left** These moccasins are in the British Museum's collections, and are believed to have been given by one of the four **Mohawks** who went on a diplomatic mission to England in 1710.

**53**

**77 Above** A delegation of Southern Cheyenne and Arapaho men in Washington, D.C., Smithsonian Institution, 1899. Left to right, front row: Lame Man, Yellow Eyes, Henry Roman Nose, Turkey Legs, He Bear, Little Chief or White Spoon, Yellow Bear and Little Man (all Cheyenne). Left to right, middle row: Black Coyote (Arapaho), Andrew John (**Seneca**), Leonard Tyler (Cheyenne) and Phillip Cook (Cheyenne). Left to right, back row: Cleaver Warden Victory (Arapaho), Bird Chief, Sr (Arapaho), Grant Left Hand (Arapaho), Jesse Bent (Arapaho) and Robert Burns (Cheyenne).

## Disease

The introduction of diseases such as smallpox and cholera after European contact in the 16th and 17th centuries caused a massive decline in the Indian **population**. These diseases spread widely and from 1500 to 1800 the death toll was close to 10 million. Wars, **Removal**, migration, loss of **hunting** and **fishing** lands, and a complete change of diet caused further illness. Loss of traditional **food** resources and increasing environmental and industrial pollution caused yet more hazards. By 1900, the 'Myth of the Vanishing Indian' was a near reality. Infectious diseases that came under control for other Americans by 1900 were still common in Indian populations by the mid century. Even in 1980, Indians were still three times more likely to die or be ill with diseases such as tuberculosis and adult-onset diabetes than the majority of the population.

## Dog

Dogs were the earliest domesticated animals and have lived in relationship to Indians (like their relatives **wolves** and **coyotes**) for centuries. Some Natives (**Apaches**, for example) used large dogs as pack animals, before there were **horses**, donkeys and mules in Indian Country. Many Plains women (such as Hidatsas and Mandans) used dogs, hitched to travois, to haul wood and smaller loads. The most well-known use of dogs is the Eskimo sled dogs. These dogs are specially bred and trained to travel long distances and pull sleds or toboggans heavy with **fishing** and **hunting** equipment, **food** and clothing. The Inuit development of work dogs is so much admired that Alaskans have developed dog sled racing and breeding into a competitive **sport**.

Many Indians considered dogs close relatives and involved them in ceremonies or

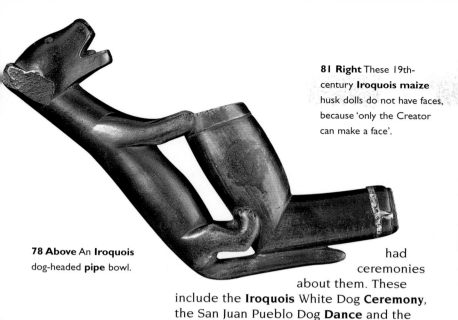

**78 Above** An **Iroquois** dog-headed **pipe** bowl.

**81 Right** These 19th-century **Iroquois maize** husk dolls do not have faces, because 'only the Creator can make a face'.

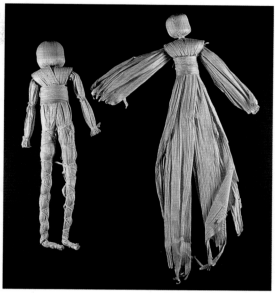

had ceremonies about them. These include the **Iroquois** White Dog **Ceremony**, the San Juan Pueblo Dog **Dance** and the Grass Dance (a dance with many meanings shared by several Northern Plains peoples). The **Sioux** still eat dog after the ceremonies associated with vision-seeking and healing.

**79 Below** A 'mother' *katsina* doll, *Hahay'i*.

## Dolls

For most Native peoples dolls are made mainly for children's play. Yet the dolls' dress was also important because dolls were meant to teach children their roles in society and ceremonies. Some were used by adults and children in ceremonial and ritual ways. *Katsinas* at the Bean **Dance** (*Powamu*) or at the Home Dance (*Niman*), give *katsina* dolls. *Katsina* dolls, which are made from

**80 Below** Rovena Abrams (**Seneca**) made these **maize** husk dolls in 1985, dressing them in the style of late 18th-century Senecas. From the dolls' necklaces, we can tell that they belong to the **Turtle Clan**, and so are probably related, perhaps brother and sister. Nowadays, presentation pieces can be very elaborate.

cottonwood roots painted and decorated with **feathers**, teach young girls about being Hopi. They are like prayers for water, as cottonwoods only root in wet areas and seek water. Although girls are still given dolls, today artists produce them for the commercial market as well for the traditional uses in the community.[19]

A female infant always receives a flat Ha'hay'i (*wuuti*) as her first *katsina* doll. A new bride is also presented one on the occasion of the *Niman* ritual. This doll she slides down her body... for the purpose of bearing many children.
*Noq pu' manawya tihut susmooti makiwe', pam it hahay'it putsqatihut mooti makiwngwu. Pu' i' naat pu' löökökqa aapiy nimantikive piw put makiwe', pu'pam put naapa siroknangwu, pam hapi ti'o'yniqey oovi.*
Michael Lomatuway'ma, Hopi teacher

**82 Left** Owen Seumptewa, a Hopi photographer, took this picture of a Hopi girl with a *katsina* doll she had just received during a Home **Dance**.

## Dreams

Many Indians value dreams greatly and believe that actions and behaviours can be accounted for by dreams. People may make certain designs on clothing, make objects a certain shape and paint them a certain colour, go hunting for particular animals, sing, **dance** or make **medicine** all because of dreams and visions.

In dreams we have learned how everything given to us is to be used; how the rice is harvested and the animals hunted. So that we would learn all the crafts, once a pair of humans was taken from the earth and brought to a place where they learned everything that the Indians know, even how you follow the |dictates| of dreams and honour the spirits.
*Bill Johnson, Nett Lake Ojibwa, 1947*

I am a medicine man because a dream told me to be one… you become a *pejuta wicasa*, a medicine man and a healer, because a dream tells you to do this.
*John Fire Lame Deer, Lakota medicine man, 1972*

## Drums

Many Indians believe that drums are alive and have a body. The drum is a heart, a heartbeat. Drums breathe, as do **rattles**. Among the Anishinabe, for example, drums may be referred to as Grandfather or Little Boy. The drum speaks, and must be cared for by a drumkeeper, whose life is devoted to caring for that drum.[20]

About the Penobscot drum. They accompany their songs with drums. I asked the origin of this drum, and the old man told me that perhaps someone had dreamed that it was a good thing to have and thus it had come into use.
*LeJeune, 1634*

He says that drum… it's living. The drum, he said, is just like you… . That drum is a human being too… . Cause the Creator gave that to our people when the earth was new.
*Tom Porter, Akwesasne Mohawk sub-chief and Longhouse speaker, 1980*

**Iroquois**, **Navajo**, **Cherokee**, **Creek** and **Apache** people play small water drums, as do members of the Native American Church (or Peyote Way). A water drum is a small drum filled to various levels with water, which changes the tone. Navajos use water drums for social **dance** songs in the Enemy Way **Ceremony**. Cherokees use them for **stomp dances** and the Anishinabe for Midéwiwin ceremonies. It is common among **Inuit** and **Northwest Coastal** peoples and among peoples in the Great Basin and Plateau areas of the United States for both men and women to play hand drums in **gambling**, stick and bone or hand **games**.

Anishinabe/**Ojibwe** peoples used hand drums called **dream** drums, and the visions of men and women often determined the way that the drum was made or decorated. The colours, the types of hides and the way the drum is wrapped all have meaning.

Many say that the Grass or Omaha Dance came from the dream vision of a young Sioux woman, Wananikwe or an Anishinabe woman. A spirit came to her and said, 'Go at once to your people and tell them to stop their war and become friends with the white man. Do you see the sky, how it is round?… . Go then, and tell your friends to make a circle on the ground just like the round sky. Call that holy ground. Go there, and with a big drum in the centre, sing and dance and pray to me…. . You will have one heart'.
*Eddie Benton-Banai, Anishinabe, 1984*

In the regions of the Plains and Great Lakes women generally have not sat at the 'big' drum or the medicine drum. Women, as Sissy Goodhouse(a Lakota singer) would say, are in the Third Circle (the *wiclagata*) behind the men. Their voices 'second' and join the men's. In the Southern Plains, women who stand behind the drum or 'sing behind' (second) are often called 'chorus girls'. Changes are underway, however, particularly in the Northern Plains, with more women 'sitting at the drum' or being 'called to the drum' in the way that men have been.

I have always looked after the drum; that is probably why they chose me to be drumkeeper. I felt the drum should not be alone. I felt that someone should look after it. I had to learn more about it… . The drum and I are not apart. We are one. When that drum beats, I beat, my heart goes the same way the drum goes… It just draws you.
*Margaret Paul, Maliseet drumkeeper*

**83 Below** Thunderbirds fly on this early 19th-century Plains hand drum, perhaps because playing the drum calls the thunder and lightning. Many Native peoples feel that thunder is connected with the bringing and taking away of life. For Crows, the lightning flies out of the thunderbird's eyes and **rain** comes when it flaps its wings. On the Plains, thunderbirds are *wakinyan* or 'sacred flying ones'. For **Cherokees**, thunder is a friend, having warned them of and defended them against evil. **Ojibwe** and Kwakwaka'wakw people believe that the old and wise thunderbirds bring messages to humans.

**84 Above** In this photograph taken in Washington, D.C., in 1978, Matilda Mitchell, Nettie Showaway and Sylvia Wallulatum from the Warm Springs Reservation in Oregon sing and play the hand drums common in their region.

**85 Above** A group of **Navajo** singers from Chinle, Arizona, the 'Sweethearts of Navajoland', sing and play the water drum.

**86 Right** Chief Charles Shunatona (Pawnee), Leroy Two Hatchet (Kiowa), John Fitzpatrick (Crow), Jay Hill (**Seneca**), Dick Baker (Lakota **Sioux**) and Kirby Kimball (Ponca) sit at the big drum (**pow wow** or 'fun' drum) singing an intertribal round dance song in Washington, D.C., in 1989.

# E

## Eagle and eagle feathers

The eagle is a significant animal to Indians, who revere him as a messenger and an advisor. The eagle is the bravest of the birds, a living symbol of a warrior, that possesses special powers of sight. Eagles can transform into humans at will and bring their messages to humans. For **Iroquois**, he might be the Dew Eagle or thunderbird, always seen on top of the Tree of Peace. For the Maidu and Anishinabe, he is a messenger of the Creator. The Eagle **clans** in the Southwest are responsible for the sky.

**87 Above** In this watercolour by *Awa Tsireh* (Alphonse Roybal) of 1920, Eagle Dancers from San Ildefonso Pueblo perform one of the dances which, like the **Buffalo** and the Deer Dances of the Pueblos, honours and calls the spirit of the animal represented.

Eagle feathers are used in the most sacred and most important **ceremonies**. In the Southeast, eagle feather fans and wands were used in ceremonies. The **Cherokee** Eagle (*awoh'li*) **Dance**, which is no longer performed, had eagle feathers as its central symbol. Eagle feathers are worked into **headdresses** of all kinds, most notably the well-known Plains headdresses.

Eagle feathers are given to those who have brought honour to the people, for example in war, and bring with them much respect. In ceremonial dance, for example, only a warrior (or veteran) can retrieve a dropped feather; no-one else may touch it.

The United States adopted the eagle, probably derived from both Iroquoian and German ideas of him, as a symbol of democracy and union. The American eagle appears on **flags** and official symbols of the United States from the 18th century onward. Often he is holding the arrows representing unbroken unity in one talon – a symbol known to the Iroquois.

**88 Right** A 19th-century Plains **quillwork** and eagle feather fan. Fans can be made of an entire wing of a bird.

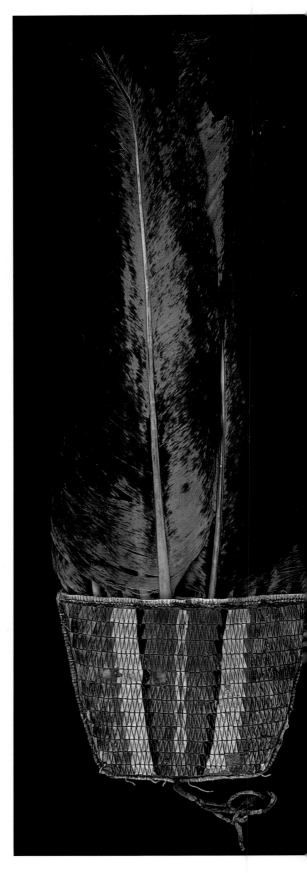

## Economies and economic change

There were many types of aboriginal economies. Each was based on the tribe's cultural, political and religious understanding and use of land, water and other natural resources for obtaining **food**, clothing and shelter. There were simple resource-based economies which involved using local resources by **hunting** and gathering (**subsistence**). Some peoples had more elaborate and complex systems which involved the mutual and often disputed exchange of goods and use of territories between peoples. Groups such as the Pueblos, for example, exchanged goods in trade, sometimes across long distances. Other groups, such as the **Ojibwa**, exchanged agreements for the use of lands, animals and waters understood to be other's territories.

Many internal tribal economies had different systems of distributing goods within their own communities. For example, **Cherokee** and **Iroquois** women controlled the lands on which crops were grown and the distribution of cultivated plant foods.

Wealth has always been measured in different ways by different peoples. For some, the accumulation of goods and land measured wealth. For others (such as the Plains and **Northwest Coastal** peoples), wealth was measured by how much one accumulated in order to give it away. For some, it was the manner in which someone redistributed his wealth rather than in the way he accumulated it that mattered. For others, it was what kinds of goods he accumulated or what value was attached to those goods. A woman's worth might have been measured in how many **horses** it took to persuade her father to allow a suitor to marry his daughter. Status, too, may have been measured by another, less material standard. 'I have always been a poor man',

**89 Above** In Northern California, many tribal peoples used these carved and decorated 'purses' made of elkhorn (antler) for carrying the strings of dentalium **shells** that they referred to as 'Indian money'. Like **wampum**, abalone, conch and other shells, dentalia were a highly valued in trade.

**90 Right** This beaded Indian chequebook cover symbolizes well the change from a barter to a cash and credit economy. It was made in the 1990s by an **Ojibwa beadworker** and sold through a tribal craft shop. It acknowledges the presence of a world of banks and paper money in Indian Country and shows their desire to remain Indian by Indianizing Western objects and Western ideas.

a **Navajo** man told an anthropologist. 'I do not know a single song.'

The coming of Europeans changed forever the internal economies of tribal peoples. The first changes came because of the different understandings held by Europeans and Indians about land ownership, the accumulation of wealth and the benefits of exchanging of goods. Then came the cash economy, which changed the lives of everyone, including the white men.

We know not what to think of the French. Why… did the French come into our country?… . They asked for land of us because their country was too little for all the men that were in it. We told them that they might take land where they pleased, there was enough for them and for us; that it was good the same sun should enlighten us both, and that we would give them our provisions, assist them to build, and to labour in their fields. We have done so, is this not true? What occasion then did we have for Frenchmen? Before they came, did we not live better than they do, seeing we deprive ourselves of a part of our corn [maize], our game and fish to give a part to them? In what respect, then, had we occasion for them? Was it for their guns? The bows and arrows which we used were sufficient to make us live well. Was it for their white, blue and red blankets? We can do well enough with buffalo skins, which are warmer; our women wrought feather blankets for the winter, and mulberry mantles for the summer; which were not so beautiful; but our women were more laborious and less vain than they are now. In fine, before the arrival of the French, we lived like men who can be satisfied with what they have; whereas that this day, we are like slaves, who are not suffered to do as they please.
*Stung Serpent, Natchez, c. 1720*

**91 Above** A Crow dress with elk tooth decoration.

## Elk

For Indians, the elk was the symbol of fertility and long life. The elk provided **food** and highly valued and durable hide. In addition, the distinctive bugling songs of the spring courtships between male and female elk gave Plains peoples the rich gift of the societies of elk **dreamers** and elk dreamer songs. Elk tooth decoration on clothing was common on the Plains, such items being given as prestigious **gifts** to young women and girls in particular. The two elk teeth that came with each animal were highly valued as trade items, and were even swapped for **horses**. The dentalium **shell**, known as 'Indian money' in the Northwest was often substituted for the scarce elk teeth, and California Natives kept dentalium in elkhorn purses.

> Two teeth remain after everything else has crumbled to dust… and for that reason the elk tooth has become a symbol of long life… . When a child is born… an elk tooth is given to the child if the parent can afford the gift.
> *Okute, Lakota elk dreamer, early 20th century*

## Explorers

From representatives of Spain, Italy and France in 1,500 AD to scouts for petrochemical companies in 1980, 'explorers' travelled to Indian Country in search of gold, goods, minerals, lands and souls. Columbus is perhaps the most famous of the explorers of the North American continent, but debates continue about who was the first to reach its shores. In the centuries after Columbus came a flood of soldiers, **hunters**, adventurers and scholars. Spanish, **British**, French, Portuguese, German and 'Americans' all sought something from the Indians.

Explorers – individuals and those representing governments and businesses – staked out the areas of New France, New Spain, New England, Nieuw Amsterdam, the Northwest Passage and the Pacific Coast. Captain John Smith, Sir Walter Raleigh, Jacques Cartier, Samuel de Champlain, Hernando DeSoto, Captain James Cook, and Lewis and Clark were all explorers, as were lesser known men, such as Karl Bodmer (the painter), Prince Maximillian of Wied, Prince Paul of Wurtemburg, the Marquis of Lorne, Edward Curtis (the photographer), Herman Schweitzer of the Fred Harvey Company. There were also 19th century anthropologists who travelled the North American continent and the South Pacific and the Caribbean making pictures of Indians, hunting animals and collecting Indian goods.

# F

## Feathers

Native peoples valued every usable part of indigenous plants and animals, but they always considered some parts more important and more symbolic than others. Indians used bird feathers of all kinds, and virtually every Native group of people recognized certain birds, even mythological birds such as thunderbirds that gave **food**, clothing, power, wisdom, **medicine** and spiritual protection. **Eagle** feathers have always been the most revered among Native peoples, but feathers of woodpecker, wild turkey, flamingo, macaw, parrot and prairie chicken have held special meaning for specific people.

People used feathers in prayer and ritual objects, for example in **headgear** and in ceremonial **dance** clothing. Particular feathers had significance for particular deeds, events or types of people. The kinds of feathers people held or wore, or the way in which they wore them, might define their status – social, political or religious. Thus, the number of feathers and the way in which they were worn on an **Iroquois** man's headdress (*gustoweh*) indicated whether he was **Mohawk**, **Seneca** or **Onondaga**.

**Artists** now replicate feathers in clay, paint and **metal**, because their presence still sends prayers up to the spirits and ancestors. Sculptors carve feathers into **masks**, wooden boxes and house poles (see **house posts**) in the **Northwest Coast** to represent important **clan** animals (such as the **Raven**).

Feathers, like some hides, remain part of wide-spread **trade** among Indians. The need for feathers was multiplied by the 19th- and 20th-century fashion for exotic feathers. They led to a number of bird species, such as flamingos and egrets, becoming endangered. Eventually, restrictions against bird hunting and feather gathering were introduced. In the latter part of the 20th century, Indian religious practices involving the use of feathers of endangered species caused renewed conflict between Indians and the government.

**M**y children, my children,
The wind makes the head-feathers sing.
The wind makes the head-feathers sing.
*Arapaho/Inuna-Ina Ghost Dance Song*

**92 Left** A late 19th century Crow feather bonnet.

## Federally recognized tribes and status Indians

In the United States, certain groups of Native people (or 'nations' of tribes) negotiated their relationships with the US government, and thus their official existence, through **treaties**. These nations have what is referred to as 'federal recognition' by the US government and are guaranteed certain rights. However, numerous tribal peoples do not now have federal recognition. These are peoples who did not negotiate treaties with the United States, those who were in relationships with colonial powers (such as Russia or Mexico) before their lands were annexed or taken over by the United States, and those who were terminated as **tribal governments** by the United States (Modocs, for example). Some have been recognized by states as Indian tribes. Others have attempted and occasionally succeeded (Pequots, for example) in gaining recognition or in regaining it after termination by the United States (such as the Menominees). Issues surrounding who does and who does not have federal recognition (and the benefits that come to those who do via the **Bureau of Indian Affairs**) have caused an ongoing debate and continued test cases before the courts. The **Lumbee** of North Carolina, for example, recognized by their state of North Carolina, continue to seek recognition before the US government.

In Canada, tribal groups are said to have 'status', rather than 'recognition'. Others are 'non-status', that is they are not acknowledged by the **Department of Indian Affairs** in Canada for the purposes of government and rights. **Inuits**, for example, are recognized as Indians, and Canada has federal responsibility for them, but they do not have status under the **Canadian Indian Act** and do not have reserves. **Métis** are not status Indians, but are included as a political group in important discussions. Canada, unlike the United States, does not have an official category, other than state recognition, for non-status, unrecognized tribes or for individuals who are not or cannot be enrolled in a federally recognized/status tribe.

## Fish and fishing

In the Northwest and in Southern Alaska, **salmon** and the other fish that swim in the big rivers are the source of life. Life revolves around fishing, whether in freshwater or saltwater. For **Arctic** peoples, the primary **food** sources are sea mammals and fish, for example the Arctic char, herring, lamprey eels, blackfish, tomcod, sculpin and salmon. The culture built around fish and fishing can be seen in the people's **dance**, ritual, song and **ceremony**. The fish and sea mammals feed them, and their **clan** and family spirits guide and define people's relationships.

In the Great Lakes, **hunting** and fishing, combined with the traditional gathering of **wild rice**, form the basis of social activity and **subsistence** living. The building of giant **dams**, the shifting of rivers, the pollution of streams and oceans and over-fishing brought great change to fish resources in the Northwest, Arctic and Great Lakes. Whereas some rivers were once alive with five varieties of fish (including salmon) in the Northwest, now just one variety is common. Sportfishing and **sport** fishermen, even Japanese industrial claims on fishing resources, have reduced the number of salmon available for Native peoples. Legal disputes challenging the Indians' rights to fish in once tribal waterways and to use traditional practices (such as gillnetting and spearfishing) have eroded Native spiritual and legal claims on those resources.

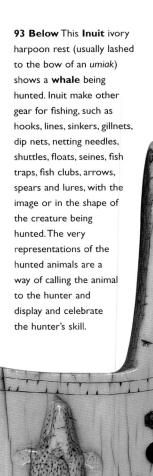

93 **Below** This **Inuit** ivory harpoon rest (usually lashed to the bow of an *umiak*) shows a **whale** being hunted. Inuit make other gear for fishing, such as hooks, lines, sinkers, gillnets, dip nets, netting needles, shuttles, floats, seines, fish traps, fish clubs, arrows, spears and lures, with the image or in the shape of the creature being hunted. The very representations of the hunted animals are a way of calling the animal to the hunter and display and celebrate the hunter's skill.

94 **Below** Sam Jones, a **Yurok** canoe-maker and traditional fisherman, made this cedar fish net needle in 1976. Used to catch freshwater **salmon** in Northern California, gillnets used by tribal peoples have caused enormous dispute and challenges in the courts to tribal **fishing rights** in the Northwest.

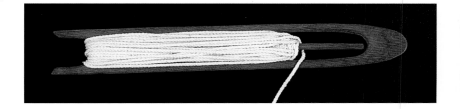

**95 Left** An ivory **Inuit** toggle, used to secure and mark the depth of line let out. It may have been used for hunting and/or fishing lines. The toggle, in the shape of a pair of breeches, has a human face carved on one side.

## Fishing rights

In 1859, a treaty with the Yakama guaranteed the Northwestern tribes 50 percent of the catch from waters where they had traditionally fished. For years, they fished in off-reservation fishing grounds using gillnets in the **salmon**-rich streams, a practice forbidden to non-Indian fishermen. However, the enormous increase in the Pacific Northwest in commercial and **sport** fishing and the increased pressure on US fishing grounds from Japanese and Russians in the 1970s, was indirect competition for the Indian fishermen (who mostly fished for **subsistence**). Commercial fish wheels, which blocked rivers and funnelled fish to commercial **boats**, effectively stopped Indian fishermen from receiving any of the catch.

Despite the **treaty** provisions, hostilities increased during the late 1960s. Eventually, the government, acting on behalf of the tribes, took their case to the courts where, according the 'Boldt Decision', the tribes were found to have a greater and prior right to the catch than the non-Indian citizens of the territory. Indians have fought to protect the guarantees of resources – water, game and fish – laid down in the treaties. The fishing rights wars have provoked occasionally violent battles in Montana,

**96 Below** Traditional gillnet fishing in the Upper Skagit River, Washington, 1920.

Wisconsin, Minnesota and Michigan, between Indians and the white groups who protest against Indians' reserved rights.

**A**t this time our people are fighting to preserve their last treaty right – the right to fish… . Fishing is part of our art form and religion and diet, and the entire culture is based around it… . Our people have fought a legal battle for more than 49 years… . Our source (the salmon) is being depleted… . Finally, we said this is enough.
*Ramona Bennett, chairwoman of Puyallup (Washington State) and Indian rights activist*

**T**he privilege of hunting, fishing and gathering the wild rice, upon the lands, rivers and the lakes included in the territory ceded, is guaranteed to the Indians, during the pleasure of the President of the United States.
*1837 Treaty with the Chippewa, Article 5*

**97 Below** Lac Courte Oreilles tribal members spearing walleye on Round Lake in Sawyer Country, Wisconsin, in April 1998. Non-Indian sportfishermen oppose Indian **treaty** spearfishing. Some hold signs up at the lakefronts during the season that say 'Save a walleye, Spear an Indian.'

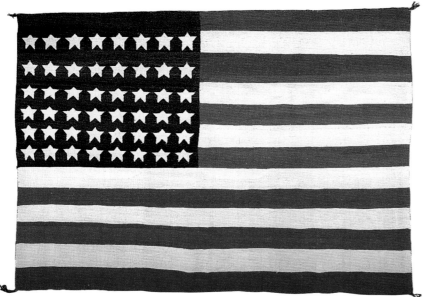

**98 Above** This **Navajo** weaving of 1920 was made by Nez Baza in honour of her son who served in the US Army during the First World War. It has 48 stars to represent the 48 states of the United States (Alaska and Hawaii were not states in 1920). When her son returned alive, she gave the rug in gratitude to the Indian school at Shiprock, New Mexico. The school raffled it off and the person who won it gave it to the Indian Commissioner, Cato Sells. Sells then passed it to the US National Museum (the Smithsonian Institution), where it remains in the flag collections of the National Museum of American History.

**99 Right** A Winnebago beaded **bandolier** bag.

# Flag, American

Almost all Native peoples use the US flag, particularly on the Plains and in the Southwest, where the flag appears on clothing, in weavings and in representations of all kinds.

The Lakota were finally seduced, forced into and relegated to reservations in the late 1880s. During this time, the US flag started to appear in Lakota art and design in clothing and regalia… . History shows that a conquered people will adapt something, a symbol or some material representation, from their captors to maintain a sense of being or identity that helps them survive. I believe the Lakota people adopted the US flag as such a symbol because within the Lakota culture, the flag carries a far different meaning than that of patriotism… . In war times, flags captured by the Lakota were used as prizes of war. Some were donned as clothing to show off the prize, symbolic of bravery and glory. Many geometric configurations of the flag crept into the material culture and were expressed artistically in many mediums, especially in beadwork, quiltwork, porcupine quillwork, carvings, clothing and dance regalia… . The flag enjoys widespread utilization as a symbol to show beauty and attractiveness, to lend meaning to the warrior tradition, and more importantly, as a reminder of the relationship between the Lakota and American people… . Through the flag, the individual warrior is honoured, recognized and memorialized; it symbolizes the prowess of the individual warrior, not patriotism.

*Howard Bad Hand, Lakota singer*

**100 Left** A **British**-style police whistle, **bead**ed in a peyote stitch with a US flag design. 'Fancy' dancers often use modern whistles instead of those of bird bone or **eagle** bone used by veterans and 'straight' **dancers**. The flag design is often used to honour veterans.

*T*unkasilayapi tawapaha kin oihanke sni naji ktelo,
*Iyohlate oyate kin wicicagin ktaca, lecamun*
The flag of the United States will fly forever.
Under it the people will grow and prosper.
Therefore have I done this [fought for my country].
*A Lakota flag song*

## Flute

Many Native peoples play some form of flute made of reeds or wood. The flute is one of the few non-percussive Native musical instruments. On the Plains, for **Sioux** and Anishinabe alike, the flute was a courting instrument played by a young man trying to impress a young woman. Birds and bird song were connected with flutes, and the courting 'dances' of birds were imitated by Indians in **dances** and songs.

Young Indian musicians have taken up the flute again as a performance instrument, and have developed both the flutes and the music played on them. Recordings of Native flute music have become very popular.

Some young women have taken up the Plains courting flute and others (including **Navajo**, **Apache** and Pueblo) compose new songs using the Indian flute (which has a different number of stops to the European flute, and is made of wood and played differently). One singer has even adapted flute songs for the voice, and others have transposed flute music for the piano and synthesizer.

**101 Below** A Plains-style cedar flute with six stops, decorated with hide ties.

**102 Right** Charles Shunatona, a traditional (not elected) chief of the Pawnee, plays a Plains-style red cedar courting flute, c. 1990.

In an **Ojibwa** love charm song, sung by Georgia Wettlin-Larsen (Assiniboine), a love-struck Ojibwa woman tries to get her beloved to take notice of her, but she tries and fails three times. Heartbroken, she asks her grandmother for advice: 'What do we have that equals the power of the flute?' Her grandmother tells her of the love charm songs, that, when sung, will cause the person you desire to fall in love with you. The song says, 'Truly, I am arrayed like the roses, and as beautiful as they'.[21]

## Food

*T*his man wanted to benefit his people, so he said, 'I am going to be a palm tree.' So he stood up very straight and very strong and very powerful, and soon the bark of the tree began to grow around him... . The meat of the fruit was not very large, but it was sweet like honey, and was enjoyed by everybody – animals and birds too. The people carried the seed to their homes and palm trees grew from this seed in many places. The palm trees in every place came from the first palm tree, but, like the people who change in customs and language, the palms often were somewhat different... all, every one of them, came from this first palm tree, the man who wanted to benefit his people.
*Francisco Patencio, Cahuilla*

To talk of American Indian foods and cookery means, in one way, to talk of food and cooking traditions based solely in the natural universe. Things were gathered from the ground, trees and bushes, plants, fresh and salt waters, desert sands, mountain forests and animals. To talk of American Indian food and cooking is also to talk of dynamic and tragic change, of creative adaptation, like that of Indian people themselves. Long ago, there was **bear** and **buffalo**, seal, **salmon** and oyster, cactus fruit and **wild rice**, hickory nut and prairie turnip. There was **maize** from Corn Mother, which together with **beans** and **squash**, became what the **Iroquois** call the 'Three Sisters'. Now there is beef and pork, wheat flour and sugar, cheese, watermelon, red peppers, lemons, coffee and gelatine. Once, there was food eaten raw, smoked, dried and boiled. Now foods are fried, baked and microwaved. The people still **hunt**, **farm** and gather, but they also get cheese and beans from the Indian agency. Like other Americans, they hunt and gather in supermarkets.

They also call us Sand Root Crushers. It must be true. We do dig the sweet potato-like plants with long roots. It is very good and sweet. We eat many different plants. The mesquite beans we pound and make a drink out of it. The desert asparagus [broomrape] that grows in the soft banks of the arroyo…. We eat fish from the ocean…. Sometimes we come [to the Picantes] to gather cactus fruit and deer.
*Molly Jim Orozco, Sand Papago/Tohono O'odham*

Ceremonial foods have remained important. Every morning in the Southwest, someone throws maize pollen into the wind and prays for the renewal of life. In the Northwest, someone fills the hole made when the camas root or bitterroot is dug with **tobacco**, and offers a prayer and thanks for its gift. Certain things are still eaten in certain seasons only by certain people. Everything is shared with

Before we eat whatever we grow, we feed the Spirit World… we have to feed the Spirit World first, and then we eat. Sometimes we forget, but then the old-timers remind us…. They take a little pinch of the food and throw it to the four winds – so that the Spirit World will have the same food that we are having here on Earth. And since the Spirits help to raise the food, it possesses great powers to heal the body and mind.
*Pablita Velarde, Santa Clara Pueblo artist*

For the Plains peoples, **buffalo**, deer and **elk** were their primary animal relatives and the source of life, supplemented in the Northwest by the abundance of gathered plants, such as berries, nuts and tubers. Buffalo and deer (meat and hides) were a major commodity for **trade** between Indian peoples and later with Europeans. Maize too became a cash crop for Indians, although it caused wars when Indian stores were taken or destroyed by the Europeans. Other crops and resources are used by Indians for cash income as well as for food, such as fish in the Great Lakes and Northwest, wild rice in the Great Lakes, ginseng in the Southeast, mutton in the Southwest, and sea mammals and fish in Alaska and Canada.

**103 Right** Made in the mid 19th century, in the 18th-century style, this bowl most probably was used to let dough rise. By the mid 18th century, Senecas were growing wheat and were already used to European-style leavened wheat breads.

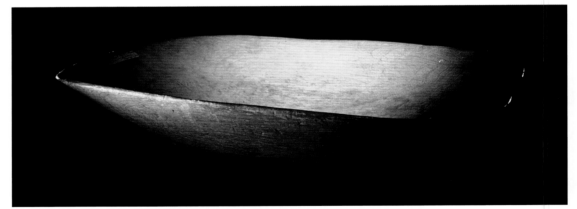

family, with neighbours, with new friends. Now, as in the past, how much food there might be is less important than sharing whatever there is with, as the Lakota prayer says, 'all our relations'. Thus, food is central to being Indian and to life itself. For **subsistence**-based peoples, the animals they hunt and the things they find in the lands they inhabit provide food, clothing, tools, fuels and **medicines** – all that is needed for life to go on.

By the fires that night/we feasted… grease was beautiful/oozing/dripping and running down our chins/brown hands shining and running with grease./We talk of it when we see each other far from home./Remember the marrow/sweet in the bones/we grabbed for them like candy./Good/Gooooood/Good Grease.
*Mary Tallmountain, Athabaskan poet*

Some foods now closely linked with Indian peoples (for example frybread) and sometimes used in **ceremonies** come totally from European food sources. Wheat-based breadstuffs, such as bannock and scones, eaten by Canadian Indian peoples, are Scottish in origin. They were adapted by Native peoples who were colonized by Scots immigrants who came for the **fur trade**. On the Plains, a stew made from beef and Asian rice is a staple of everyday **Sioux** life. In the 16th century the Spanish introduced the pig to the Southeast and Northeast, and the sheep to the Southwest. These and other introductions into the diet, such as sugar and dairy products, have been welcomed and widely used, but they have not come without serious consequences for health and nutrition.

staple of the **Ojibwa** diet. Indians in rice-growing areas have turned some into cash crops. In the 1980s, some Pueblos turned to blue corn harvest and product manufacture. Northwest tribes process some fish for a gourmet market. Some tribes have brought back buffalo ranching. On the whole, however, tribal peoples have rarely been able to capitalize on those markets; inevitably, they are exploited by non-Indian interests.

In the Southwest, Northwest and Great Lakes, in particular, there are enormous efforts to prevent further economic, environmental and socio-cultural assaults on traditional foods and land where food is gathered or grown. Tribal peoples are buying back their **lands**, reintroducing traditional

**104 Above** Mary and George McGeshick **(Ojibwa)** parching wild rice in their rice camp on the Wisconsin-Michigan border in 1986. In the background, their canoe, in which they have gathered or 'knocked' rice, is filled with drying rice.

For the restoration and preservation of **ceremonial** foods and of the ways of life centred around traditional **agriculture** and subsistence, Native peoples everywhere are trying to save or support traditional foods, forms of gathering, preserving and growing. Some supplies have been considerably diminished and have had to be replaced by others. Other foods are so scarce that they have been reduced to occasional ceremonial or special use. Wild rice, however, remains a

animals and plants and teaching older and environmentally sound agricultural methods. Others are cleaning up contaminated land and water resources and attempting to halt development or further erosion of water and land resources. Tribes have, with the help of specialists such as plant ecologists, hydrologists, ethnobotanists, fisheries biologists, foresters and agronomists (some of whom are now Indian) started to protect their resources from further loss.

**105 Above** Agnes Vanderburg, a **Salish** elder, roasting camas root at her cultural camp on the Flathead reservation in Montana. The camas root is a sweet, starchy, nutritious tuber related to the lily. It is gathered in the regions of the Plateau and Northwest. Wheat **farming** diminished camas root fields in the Northwest, but elders help to restore camas fields by reintroducing traditional gathering, food preparation and food-related ritual

If it is not the roots, it is the berries, if not the berries,
then Medicine, something for the house,
sweet Cedar, Fir, Sage, or Juniper that beckons the industrious.
Gathering, the women are vessels holding vessels,
the roundness of our humanity.
*Elizabeth Woody, Warms Springs/Navajo poet and artist, 1996*

## Footwear

Moccasin (*maskisina*) is an **Algonquin** word adopted into English and, since the 18th century, used to describe hide footgear for all tribes. Although most Natives used animal hides to make footwear similar to the **beaded**, **quilled** and embroidered moccasins used by Eastern Woodlands peoples, not all Native footgear was *maskisina*. In the Northwest and the **Arctic**, Natives made boots of seal fur or caribou hide to keep out ice, snow and water.

**106 Above** Beaded trainers made in 1990 by Cecelia Firethunder, a Lakota Sioux **beadworker**. Like the beaded baseball caps, lipstick holders and bingo markers that Indians all over North America have been making for the last 15 years or more, beaded athletic shoes tell a story of change and persistence in Indian Country.

## Fur trade

Furs and hides were an important commodity for Indians – domestically and as trade items. When the Europeans arrived, they wanted to exploit the rich North American natural resources. The first demand was for **beaver** fur and deer hide. Later, fancy furs such as sable, otter and ermine became important too. These were exchanged for **metal** tools, cloth and other items. Initially, all furs were obtained from Native hunters through the long-established Native trade networks and alliances. However, Europeans eager to obtain furs started to by-pass this established system. This competition caused great disruptions in traditional alliances and damaged the traditional **economies** and cultures of Native groups. They were used to hunting for **subsistence**, and now had to compete for alliance with the European traders. Their economy was being transformed from one based on subsistence to one based on the need for European goods. Traditional territories and alliances were destroyed as groups warred among themselves for access to trading relationships.

As the fur trade expanded and pitted the French against the British in a search for more products, tribal rivalries became more intense as groups struggled to maintain dominance in the trade. Charles II of England granted the Hudson Bay Company (HBC) Charter in 1670, opening a huge area of the sub-Arctic up to the fur trade, which it controlled until after the Canadian Confederation of 1867.

The French sent **explorers, missionaries** and **traders** into the Western lands and expansion continued in the 18th century. They built trading posts and intermarried with Native women. White trappers competed with Native ones, but did not respect the unwritten rules that stated what could not be killed (namely, pregnant and young animals). During the 19th century, over-hunting greatly reduced wildlife. By 1840, raccoons and **buffalo** had replaced the beaver trade in the West and many species (for example sea otters on the coast and deer in the Southeast) were hunted to near extinction.

The fur trade with whites increased women's work, because they alone had the skill to tan the hides of deer, **elk** and buffalo. It might be true that the degradation which whites believed they saw among the Plains women was due to the increased burdens upon the women from the excessive demands of the fur trade. This was a disaster for both the women and the animals the trade slaughtered. It might even have been that some Indians' systems of multiple wives that so repelled whites may have increased as a result of the fur trade as so many more hands were required to prepare the food and hides when tribes entered a market economy.

Russians colonizing Alaska took **Aleut** slaves to work on **boats** hunting **whale**, walrus, otter and seal. Pacific Coast Native groups competed with the European trappers for goods. The Gold Rush of 1849 expanded settlements and forced local economies to change. Trading posts were closed and sold. The mid 19th century saw reductions in Native land holdings and the fur trade spread far north. By the 20th century **farming** had expanded, but the demand for fur continued and the railway now made **transportation** of goods easy. Many species were depleted, but Native groups continued to trap selectively which kept the populations viable.

Environmental groups, especially in Europe, kept up a strong anti-fur campaign through the 1980s and 1990s, which reduced the demand for fur products in Europe and prices dropped rapidly. In 1980, the HBC sold its stores in the North and in 1957 the New York factory of the American Fur Company closed. Generations of Native trappers found their economic bases severely threatened. Joined by non-Native trappers who harvest seals and the fur industry, Native trappers and political organizations mounted a major campaign of their own explaining humane trapping and the necessity of culling herds. In the mid 1990s, the Native fur industry seems to be making a slow come-back.

**107 Above** Moccasins from many tribal cultures. From left to right: **Inuit**, Nava, Kansa, Woods **Cree**, Tuscarora, **Sioux**, Alaskan (sic.), Chippewa, Shawnee, Cree, Kiowa, Arapaho, Kiowa, Sioux/Dakota, Slavey, Arapaho, Arapaho, Comanche, Montagnais/Naskapi, Tohono O'odham, Oneida, Nez Perce, Chamula, Cree, Eastern Sioux/Dakota, Comanche, Eastern Sioux, Shoshone, **Algonquian**, Cheyenne, Arapaho and Blood.

# G

## Gambling

Gambling games or betting games have been common among Indians for centuries. Whether **games** of skill or chance, these competitive and often intertribal gambling games (called stick, hand or moccasin games) remain popular today, although rarely with the type of high stakes such as **horses** which used to be common in the 19th century. Plains Indians (Crows, Cheyennes and Kiowas for example), Great Basin Indians (Luiseños and Cahuillas for example) and Northwest peoples (at Warm Springs) still participate in gaming and gambling.

A rich song tradition accompanies most hand or **stickball** games. There were also magic songs associated with the games, as there were for **Cherokee**, **Creek** and Choctaw stickball. There are traditional gambling songs for the hand, stick or bone games. Among **Northwest Coastal** and Great Basin peoples, Ute, **Salish** and Kootenai, people sing in hand games as parts of a team, as lead singers. In Southern California, Natives sing for their gambling game *peon*. For Anishinabe, songs that came from **dreams** and visions, accompanied by a **drum**, caused people to bet which of two moccasins a marked object had been hidden under.

**T**he Osage play a traditional hand game with sticks. The object of the game is to guess who has a small item in their hand. Every time you guess correctly, you get a stick. You must win six sticks to win the game. In the old days, the singers sang hand-game songs while the game was played. At the end of each game, they would sing a Round Dance song. All the ladies would get up and put their shawls on and dance to the music. Then they would sit down and sing a giveaway song. They would pass out gourds to the people who would stand and shake the gourds. After that, people would put a donation up on the table. They still play hand games today at Gray Horse… . They raise funds with the money gathered at the games. Years ago, the winner would get a pig or a horse. Now, the players put money or groceries on each side of the game.
*Abe Conklin, Ponca*

Churches brought the game of bingo to Indians on the **reservations**, and it became so popular that many tribes used it as a money-making enterprise in the late 20th century. Small-stakes gambling came to be an important part of cash income on small reservations, just as it has for Catholic churches, volunteer firemen and social clubs such as the Masons.

**I** only have two dollars, but I'm going to bingo anyway.
*eskanyeh songverse by Hubert Buck, Seneca, sung by his daughters Sadie and Betsy Buck*

**108 Below** Osage handgame, with beaded tin can **rattle**.

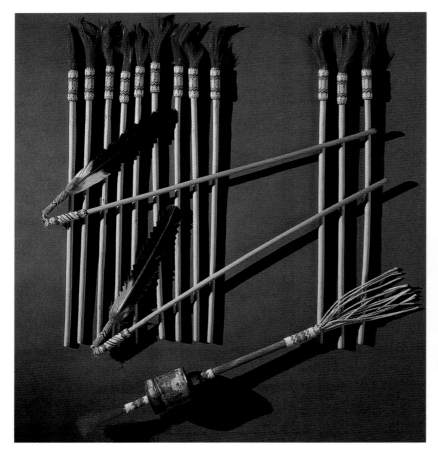

**109 Left** A **beaded** bingo dauber.

**110 Right** A Pueblo needlepoint bingo bag. Some Indian people who gamble in small-stakes bingo have transferred many Native beliefs and behaviours to modern gambling and 'Indianize' gambling accessories.

However, the development of high-stakes Las Vegas style casinos as a form of economic development came to be a focus of the debate over Indian **sovereignty**. Over 100 tribes now have some form of gambling on reservation, and although practised by only 20 or so tribes, high-stakes gambling has increasingly proved to be both an economic boon and a hotly debated political and cultural issue for Native peoples. The tribes remain in constant battle with the US government and the states over attempts to control gambling on the reservations. They insisted that their ability to do what they wish on tribal lands is an issue of sovereignty.

## Games and sports

Like all people, Indian adults and children played and still play many games and sports. Much sport was connected to ceremonial and ritual life, even to **war** in a symbolic way. Running was common to many tribal peoples. Although most Native running is ritual – as in the running that **Navajo** and **Apache** young women do during their puberty **ceremonies** – it has become a well-developed modern sport among Pueblos, Navajos and Apaches.

▐▐▐ **Above** An aerial photo of the largest and most lucrative Indian casino, Foxwoods, at the Pequot Nation in Connecticut.

**Y**ou boys should go out and run. So you will be swift in time of war. You girls, you should grind the corn. So you will feed the men and they will fight the enemy. And you should practice running. So, in time of war, you may save your lives.
*Maria Chona, Tohono O'odham, 1934*

Some games were not only tests of physical skill or endurance, but also of mental agility. Vi Hilbert, a Lushootseed linguist, remembers that her family liked challenge or competition singing.

112 **Right** Two Inuit women – Madeline Allagariuk and Phoebe Atagotaaluk – throat singing. They learnt this traditional form of song from their grandmother. Men and women on the **Northwest Coast, Inuit** and other **Arctic** peoples engage in competition singing. Inuit think of throat singing as a kind of game, the object being to outlast the other singer before giving way to laughter.

113 **Above** These sticks are for the **Ojibwa** ball game, which is similar to lacrosse.

114 **Right** Tohono O'odham women play a stickball game called *tóka*, a game in which there are two balls.

115 **Right** In many places in the **Arctic, Inuit** children and adults (here probably Chukchi) play kickball games. Sometimes they used decorated and moss-filled balls made of hide. Some of these games are similar to a modern game called hackeysack, in which the object is to keep a small leather or cloth ball in the air, solely by kicking it.[22]

Many Natives (including the **Cherokee**, Navajo, **Ojibwa** and Tohono O'odham) have some form of **stickball**, that is a game involving a ball hit with or thrown by pouched or curved sticks. The stickball game called lacrosse, played by **Iroquoian** and **Algonquin** peoples across the Northeast, is the most famous, having made its way into the mainstream of international sport.

Although Native peoples still play traditional sports and games, many also play mainstream sports they have learnt at school, such as basketball and American football. American football had its major development at Carlisle Indian School, by a coach named Pop Warner whose best-known player was the Sac and Fox athlete, Jim Thorpe.

**117 Left** New York and Canadian **Iroquois** still play an old winter competitive sport called snowsnake, in which players throw a long carved wooden pole down a long trough carved in the snow.

**116 Above** Kahnawake Lacrosse Club in Montreal, in 1867.

**118 Below** **Inuit** athletes compete in the neck pull. It is played competitively at the Eskimo Olympics. In the neck pull, competitors cannot use their hands and arms, and the object is to pull the other competitor off balance.

## Geronimo (Goyathlay)

119 **Right** Most photographs of Geronimo show him as a fierce **Apache** warrior, armed and on horseback. Others, taken during his captivity, show him as a performer and a 'star', riding around in a Cadillac. Geronimo held authority over the Chiricahua band partly because of his status as a medicine man. In this photograph, he appears with the **headdress** that identifies him as a medicine man.

To non-Indians, there is perhaps no figure as famous (or infamous) as the Chiricahua **Apache** war chief Geronimo (*Goyathlay*). His raids on white settlers and his battles against the US Cavalry are legendary. Equally legendary are his refusal to accept **reservationization**, his final surrender in 1886 and his imprisonment. Less well-known are the roots of his and his people's hostility towards and resistance to Mexican and US troops who slaughtered, pursued, starved and dispossessed several groups of Apaches with which Geronimo was associated. Having been captured, arrested and imprisoned, Geronimo and his people (including a large number of Apache scouts who had worked for the US government for years) finally surrendered and were exiled to Florida, where many died. Another forced journey took the Apache prisoners, their

wives and families to Alabama, then to Fort Sill, Oklahoma, with only 400 survivors.

He was, according to those who knew him at Fort Sill, proud of the watermelons he learned to grow and the cattle he raised. He loved attending the fairs at which he was paraded by government soldiers. He joined the Dutch Reform Church, later being expelled for **gambling**. He died in 1909, far from the territory and people that he had so vigorously defended. He remains a legend and a symbol to Indians and whites of the conflicts between them.

When they were released in 1913, some Apaches went to the Mescalero Reservation in New Mexico and others, Geronimo's Chiricahuas, stayed in Oklahoma where their descendants live today.

## Ghost Dance

Tribal peoples across the Northern and Southern Plains adopted the Ghost Dance, a religious belief and practice based on prophecy by a Paiute man called *Wovoka* (Jack Wilson). He said that the people's belief could drive the white man from the West and cause the **buffalo** to return. He told how he had ascended to Heaven in a **dream** and had seen Indians living peacefully forever. He claimed that living Indians could have this paradise if they performed this dance and returned to their traditional ways. The **Sioux** changed this peaceful message to one that insisted that a messiah would make whites disappear and the buffalo return. That messiah assured the white bullets would not penetrate the special shirts (painted with figures of the moon, stars and buffalo) and dresses that the people wore when performing this dance and when fighting. The Sioux **Sitting Bull** (*Tatanka Yotanka*) became the leader for this new faith among his people.

Thus, the Ghost Dance was part of the battle to keep Indian lands and lifestyles, against the onslaught of **Christianity** and the extermination of Native religious belief. The government and the whites who saw such tribal religious behaviour were afraid of its consequences and fought back. This ended in the arrest and murder of Sitting Bull, and the massacres of Sioux men, women and children at **Wounded Knee**. The government outlawed the Ghost Dance in 1923, afraid that it would rejuvenate Indian nations and cause **war**.

**120 Left** A Ghost Dance shirt.

**121 Below** This white buckskin dress of about 1890 was worn by a Kiowa woman who participated in the Kiowa version of the Ghost Dance. It bears simple colours and a moon and stars design. According to the visionary instructions given about how Ghost Dance garments should be made, there are no ornaments on the dress.

The whole world is coming.
A nation is coming, a nation is coming.
The eagle has brought the message to the tribe.
The father says so, the father says so.
Over the whole earth they are coming.
The buffalo are coming, the buffalo are coming.
The crow has brought the message to the tribe.
The father says so, the father says so.
*Ghost Dance song believed to be sung by Kicking Bear, the Minneconjou Sioux leader*

My children, my children
It is I who wear the morning star on my head
says the father, says the father.
*Ghost Dance song*

## Gifts and giveaways

Gift giving and gift exchange among many Native peoples was a complex matter. It was influenced by the status of the giver and the receiver, the value of the goods given or exchanged, and whether a gift was expected in return. Among tribal peoples in North America, gift giving and exchange involved a huge set of mostly unspoken relationships.

Everyone had to share **food**, although the way it was shared was based on the status of the people. In the Plains tribes, women might give decorated clothes, robes, shirts and leggings – all made with great skill. Men might be obliged to give **horses** they had brought, traded or stolen. Everyone gave and still gives **blankets** and, in some areas, quilts. Whereas once parfleches filled with clothing and other goods were given away, today people fill plastic laundry hampers with lengths of cloth, dishcloths and towels to give away. In the pueblos, when children take part in their first ceremonial **dance**, their families throw sweets, fruit and bags of food to the people watching the dances.

Europeans and Indians had very different ideas about the giving and receiving of gifts and what that exchange meant. This caused misunderstandings about the implications and obligations of the exchange, which led to conflict between the two parties. Whites used the term 'Indian givers' as an insulting way of describing what the Indians expected in this two-way relationship of gift giving. The one area in which gift giving and receiving seemed to be fairly well understood was that of **diplomatic** gift exchange.

Gift giving brought honour and respect to

the giver, making the person who received the gift obliged to the giver. An anthropologist tells the story of a Hidatsa woman who gained retribution on a man who had annoyed her by giving him a beautiful **quilled** shirt and pair of leggings; in return he had to give her a **horse**.[23]

The quilt ceremony is about honouring people. 'When you are honoured, you know you are held in high esteem by the family', says *Spike Big Horn.*

**122 Above** Basketball Star Quilt, made in 1996 by Rae Jean Walking Eagle (Assiniboine/Sioux) for a high school basketball tournament giveaway. Star (or morning star) designs in particular are used in the Northern Plains on quilts made for honouring ceremonies.

When a veteran returned from **war**, he and his relatives gave gifts to honour those who had supported him. This was later transferred to other moments of achievement, such as graduation from school. A first ceremonial dance, a marriage or a basketball tournament might all require a giveaway, a kind of official public offering of gifts made by the people in the Northern and Southern Plains. In much of Indian Country, the honoured person or family and friends acting behalf of him or her, give gifts, rather than receiving them as in European societies.

Families pile up blankets, cloth, shawls and jewellery in order to show their support for a loved one in this way. In a baby naming **ceremony** or when someone is being given a traditional name, a Lakota family gives goods in honour of the person whose name is used.[24] For some people, giveaways are associated with the death of a family member. The relatives of a dead person might want to give away goods belonging to that person, either at a memorial feast a year after the death or after the services for the dead. See also **potlatch**.

At times, the Giving Away is hard, but also
is an honour
for the treasured, or Giving Away when we are so Full,
the Harvest is the memory of the Living.
*Elizabeth Woody, Wasco/Warm Springs/Navajo poet*

Come  This is a give-away poem
I cannot go home
until you have taken everything & the basket which held it
When my hands are empty
I will be full
*Chrystos, Menominee poet, 1988*

## Green Corn Ceremony

Several Southeastern Indian peoples (for example Choctaw, Yuchi and **Creek/Seminole**) hold an annual Green Corn Ceremony. Although there are frequent **stomp dances**, this is the main religious ceremony of the year for these peoples. It is an annual gathering of traditional peoples at which much of political, social and religious importance takes place. They hold ceremonies on traditional grounds kept for this purpose and the rituals are important for the ongoing life of the people. Although each of these tribes celebrate Green Corn in different ways, for all of them it is a time of healing, forgiveness and of reconciliation. Before the Green Corn Dance, no-one can eat **maize**. Afterwards, maize is eaten to show how it is a symbol of continued life and good for the people. Several Creek, Seminole and Choctaw Green Corn sacred ceremonial grounds throughout the South are now threatened by development. The tribes are struggling to hold onto them because of their significance in the life-renewal ceremonies of their people.

## Haida

The Haida, **Tlingit** and Tsimshian are the three language groups that occupy the rugged islands off the **Northwest Coast**. Separated into two clans, the **eagle** and the **raven**, they trace descent through the female line. They travelled great distances in large carved dugout canoes, which were highly prized by other groups for **trade**. **Fishing** for **salmon**, halibut and sea mammals was the main **economy** of these people. Today fishing fleets can still be found in many coastal communities. Men fish and build **boats**, while women work in canneries. More recently, logging has become important and a number of bands have formed logging co-operatives. Although tourism has increased, unemployment has forced many to leave the **reservation** and go to the cities in search of work. Along with economic development issues, **land claims** and campaigns against logging and clear-cutting continue to be the central issue of the Haida and other communities on the Northwest Coast.

The Haida were master carvers and were highly acclaimed for their **art** that depicted animals or images from myths. They carved fine figures in wood, bone and horn; spoons, bowls and other domestic objects; wooden **sculptures**; and massive crest, 'totem' or house poles. Their important architectural achievements could be seen in their large cedar houses with carved support posts.

The Haida system of **potlatch** laid down a structure of social hierarchy based on both hereditary status and acquired wealth. It also reinforced a system of redistribution of wealth within the community.

## Handsome Lake

The **Seneca** Handsome Lake was the brother of the traditional leader, Cornplanter and a hereditary chief of the **Iroquois** Confederacy. In 1799 he founded the modern Longhouse religion. His rise as a prophet began with a series of visions. Messengers from the Creator instructed him to tell the people to restore and keep their traditional **ceremonies**, to give up alcohol, sexual promiscuity, wife-beating, quarrelling and **gambling**. Instead the people were to start social reform among families and to oppose further European intrusions on their land and culture. His gospel, drawn from ancient Iroquois religious ideas and practices, was

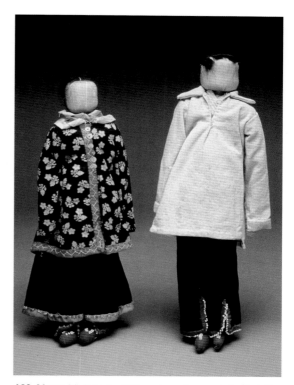

**123 Above** Made in the 20th century, these corn husk **dolls** show construction and clothing typical of the 18th century. They are plainly clothed, like followers of Handsome Lake during the Longhouse festivals of the early 1800s. The male doll wears a white cotton shirt, black beaded leggings and brown cloth moccasins. The female doll wears a calico tunic, a black skirt with glass **beads** on the hem and leggings of blue strouding (woven wool cloth) beaded at the bottom.

reinforced in part by similar **Christian** beliefs and customs and by the Iroquois' traditional faith in prophecy. Handsome Lake died in 1815 at Onondaga in New York. By the 1850s, his gospel had spread widely and the new rituals had become part of Iroquois religious custom. The moral code spread quickly and restored a ceremonial cycle whose survival today continues to make the Iroquois a distinct political and ethnic group.

The women faithkeepers asked Handsome Lake's grandson, James Johnson, to help set down his grandfather's teachings. James Johnson and Ely S. Parker (a Seneca scholar) finally recorded Handsome Lake's words in 1845. These teachings are often known as the 'Code of Handsome Lake', and are called the Good Message (*Gawi'yo*) by Longhouse people. The Seneca are the 'firekeepers' of the Longhouse religion. To this day they visit reservations to preach the Good Message of Handsome Lake.

This is from an English version of Part B of the Good Message of Handsome Lake:

It was the original intention of our Maker,
that all our feasts of thanksgiving should be
seasoned with the flesh of wild animals.

But we are surrounded by pale-faces, and in a short time
the woods will all be removed.
Then there will be no more game for the Indian to use
in his feasts.

The four Messengers [who appeared to Handsome Lake] said, in
consequence of this, that we might use the flesh of domestic animals. This will not be wrong.

The pale-faces are pressing you on every side.

You must therefore live as they do.

How far you can do so without sin, I will now tell you.

You may grow cattle, and build yourselves warm and comfortable
dwelling-houses.

This is not sin; and it is all that you can safely adopt of the
customs of the pale-faces.

You cannot live as they do.

Thus they said.

Continue to listen: It has pleased our Creator to set apart as
our Life, the Three Sisters [maize, beans and squash]. For this special favour, let us ever be thankful.

When you have gathered in your harvest, let the people assemble,
and hold a general thanksgiving for so great a good. In this way you will show your obedience to the will and
pleasure of your Creator.

Thus they said.

*Reg Henry, Cayuga faithkeeper*

## Headgear and headdresses

Native headgear shows much more diversity and variation from group to group than **footwear**. This might be because headgear is usually non-essential and can be adapted to style, fashion, climate, environment and culture. Headgear is associated with **ceremony**, and often shows status, achievement and relationship. In this way it says much more about the culture than footwear. Some men's headgear identified the

man's role or rank in society and told of his actions and achievements, for example in **feathers** fixed to the headpiece. Other headgear might have been practical, perhaps decorative, but designed for daily wear.

Headgear used in ceremonies was thought of as special, almost sacred, and only to be handled or worn by people who had the right to do so. The Pueblo women wore painted *tablita* during certain **dances** and the Goose Society headdress was worn by Hidatsa women. In the Plateau region of North America hats made of hemp (or jute) and beargrass had designs woven into the cap and shell, with feather and **bead** attachments. Women wore these caps during the Longhouse religious rituals and ceremonies connected to root digging, weaving them like the root bags into which they gathered the roots. Nowadays, some women might wear them for **pow wow** dancing, although traditional religious people believe they should only wear them for traditional root feast activities. The wearing of one today designates someone honoured for her knowledge of the traditional skills and ceremonies. Many caps worn today are old ones, passed down by relatives; but in California the caps are being made anew by **basketmakers** among the **Yurok** and Karok women whose traditions demand them.

I have been learning to weave root bags... .
My teacher told me as we sat twining, 'We are
making beautiful houses for our little sisters.' I...
asked, 'Who are our little sisters? 'The roots –
*pia-xi, khoush, sowit-k, wak amu*', she answered.
*Elizabeth Woody, Wasco, Warm Springs and Navajo poet*

Women and men in the Northeast often copied European hats, 'Indianizing' them to suit their own purposes. In the 18th century, **Iroquois** women favoured plaid wool Glengarry caps, the common hat worn by Scots military men. Often mistakenly called 'Princesses' by Europeans, young Indian women wore a type of crown, often **beaded** or decorated with silver and ribbons, when they represented their tribe in public events of the late 19th and 20th centuries. In the 18th and 19th centuries, **Cherokee** men, such as **Sequoyah**, often wore a kind of wrapped trade cloth turban, sometimes decorated with the **feathers** of flamingos, spoonbills and red-tailed hawks.

**124 Above** A
Tsististas/Cheyenne feather
bonnet of the 19th century.

**125 Above** This commercially made baseball cap was **beaded** by Arvo Mikkanen, a lawyer and tribal judge of the Comanche Nation of Oklahoma. Modern Native peoples, like their predecessors, show their tribal affiliation or identity on all sorts of objects. These include car bumper stickers ('I'm Comanche Indian and proud of it'), T-shirts ('Don't Worry, Be Hopi'), hats and badges. Baseball caps have been popular with Indian men since the late 19th century.

**126 Below** A **Mi'kmaq** 19th-century women's headdress, made of velvet and **beads**. The shape may be derived from 18th-century French women's headdresses.

headdress made of deer hair or the soft, long belly hair of the porcupine which gave the same look. It became an important hair style to wear with the **pow wow** fancy dance outfits in the 20th century.

## Horses

Horses, first called 'sky (or holy) dogs', revolutionized the **economy** of the Plains. They came to be a measure of value, as deer and deerskins had been before them. Plains **economic** exchange was worked out according to how many horses some goods, prospective marriage partners and services were worth.

The decoration of horse equipment in Plains cultures, with ornamented saddles, and **beaded** and carved bridles, shields, swords and lance scabbards, shows how important the horse was in the Plains world. Plains Indians (such as the **Sioux**) painted and gave spiritual protection to horses before battle just as they did to human warriors. Crows (a so-called 'horse culture') are well known for the number and quality of their horses, and for the decoration of horse equipment for war, show and presentation.

Beaded headbands, worn by **Algonquin** women and men, were mistakenly thought by whites to be headgear worn by all Indians. Indians in films, for example, commonly wear either beaded headbands or Plains 'war bonnets', no matter what tribe or kind of person they are supposed to represent.

Much headgear was also closely associated with hairstyles. Indian men from many tribes shaved their heads on the sides and wore their hair down the centre made to stand up straight. This famous 'Mohawk' hair style was popular among many Indians in the Northeast in the 18th century and again with young people in Europe and the United States from the 1970s (so-called 'punks'). Later, some tribal peoples stopped wearing their own hair shaved on the sides and 'roached' up the centre, instead wearing a

**127 Left** This Otoe roach spreader, c. 1820–25, is made of **elk** antler with a **buffalo** head design. It helped to hold apart the 'porky' or deer hair roach on the man's headpiece. **Feathers** – an **eagle** feather perhaps if the person had the right to wear one – were placed in the holder on the top of the roach spreader, between the fringes of animal hair.

**128 Below** A late 19th-century **beaded Blackfoot** man's 'pad' saddle. Women made the highly valued Blackfoot saddles, for their own families and for **trade**. As in other horse cultures, men's saddles were different to women's saddles and their horse equipment and horses had different decoration.

Crows still feature mounted horse parades at their annual celebration and gathering, the Crow Fair, but now also decorate and use cars in the way they did horses.[25]

Some peoples, such as the Nez Perce, developed specific pony breeds (Appaloosas or 'paint ponies') which, to the present day, are very valuable in the horse and cattle business. Crow, **Blackfeet**, the Nez Perce and Kiowas were called the 'Lords of the Plains', because of their command of the horse. These tribes, along with the **Navajos**, developed the tradition of the Indian **cowboys**, cattle raising and the rodeo after **reservationization** and their days of riding the Plains were restrained.[26]

**129 Below** Coastal **Salish** house posts.

130 Kwakwaka'wakw house in Vancouver, c. 1900.

## House posts

House posts are often mistakenly referred to as 'totem poles' by non-Indians. They appear inside and outside the dwellings and gathering places of people on the **Northwest Coast**. The rights to have these sometimes elaborately carved posts were first acquired by supernatural heroes in legends. The rights were inherited – along with feast dishes – by **clan** chiefs and aristocratic families. The posts display the crests of chiefs and their families, and tell the stories of how they were acquired and the deeds of their supernatural ancestors.[27]

## Humour

Native humour appears in traditional stories and creation tales and in **ceremonies** and rituals. Storytellers detail the outrageous and socially unacceptable deeds of animal trickster figures such as **Coyote**, **Rabbit**, Crow and **Turtle**. Sacred **clown** figures, *katsinas*, and animal **dancers** act out humorous dramas before an audience that learns good behaviour by laughing at bad behaviour.

There has always been intertribal joking, usually about the strange habits and customs of the other tribes. Like all peoples, Indians joke about **food**, especially if their foods are strange or forbidden to other peoples. The largest group of jokes told by Indians across the country revolve around **Sioux** and **dog** eating. Although many tribal peoples all over the world eat dog, and, in fact, many (such as the Plains tribes) only eat it ceremonially, the dog's place as a domestic pet for Europeans has made people feel uneasy about eating it. For Indians, teasing Sioux about dog-eating amounts to a national sport. At a **pow wow**, some **Ojibwa** sing a mock 'honouring' song called 'How Much is that Doggy in the Window?' to their long-time traditional Sioux enemies. The Sioux retaliate by singing a song called 'Here Comes Peter Cottontail' to their Ojibwa enemy-neighbours, who are known as 'rabbit-chokers' because of their fondness for rabbit.

Finally, there is Indian humour that involves joking about white people. Artists and potters, at Cochiti Pueblo for example, make humorous **sculptures** of foolish figures from their own communities and of sheriffs, priests, **cowboys** and the white people who have come to their world. (See page 51.) Tales from the 18th century onwards record jokes that pass back and forth between these different peoples with different sets of rules about how to behave.

## Hunting

Hunting and **fishing** provided the **food**, clothes and shelter for Native peoples, and continue to provide it for some. Although the significance of hunting, as opposed to **agriculture**, has probably been overestimated for some Indians, some Native peoples in the **Arctic** and Northwest Territories and Plains rely almost solely on hunting for their provisions. Before the **fur trade** disrupted traditional hunting, it was an activity characterized by ritual practice and by a huge variety of tools and weapons.

People on the West Coast of Vancouver Island, Nuu-chah-nulth/Nootka, Makah and some **Inuit** hunted **whales**. Whale hunting needed hunting and leadership skills, the wealth to buy and keep a craft and crew, and the religious knowledge to follow the many ritual and religious practices necessary for whale hunting. The role was very well respected in the community. The hats they wore (decorated with scenes of whale hunting and ivory, bone, **shell** and **feather** ornaments) sheltered the heads of men, reduced glare on the open sea and were a sign of the prestige and position of those allowed to wear them.

**132 Below** A Nuu-chah-nulth club of whalebone, c. 1778, from Vancouver Island. Before **bows**, arrows and guns, clubs were used for hunting, for war and for rituals in the **potlatch**.

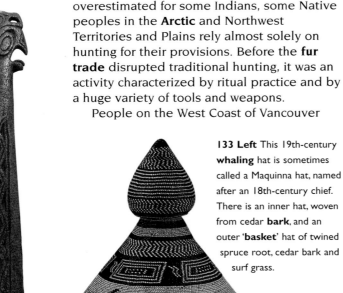

**133 Left** This 19th-century **whaling** hat is sometimes called a Maquinna hat, named after an 18th-century chief. There is an inner hat, woven from cedar **bark**, and an outer '**basket**' hat of twined spruce root, cedar bark and surf grass.

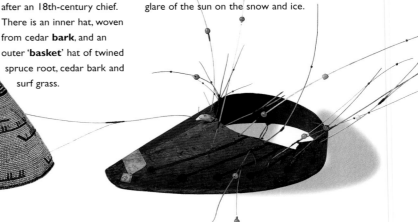

**134 Below** This Alutiiq/**Aleut** bentwood hunter's visor is decorated with bone and **feathered** objects that bring good fortune in hunting. It shields the hunter's eyes from the glare of the sun on the snow and ice.

## Indian Territory

The notion of an 'Indian Country' to which tribes would be removed arose with the Louisiana Purchase of 1803. The idea was to have new lands to exchange for Indian Eastern lands, and the country immediately west of Missouri and Arkansas came to be that 'Indian Territory' in about 1830. Treaties with the tribes removed from the Southeast stipulated that their new lands would never be included in any state or territory, and 'the Indian Territory' would never endure white settlement.

The so-called 'Five Civilized Tribes' (**Cherokee**, Choctaw, Chickasaw, **Seminole** and **Creek**) were removed there, while other removed tribes were put in 'Kansas Territory' just north of Indian Territory. After the **Civil War**, the US government cancelled all of the **treaties** with tribes in the area, reduced their lands again and opened them up to other tribes. The Cheyenne, Arapaho, Caddo, Comanche, Wichita, Kickapoo, Otoe, Missouri, Shawnee, Eastern Shawnee, Modoc, Pawnee, Tonkawa, Kaw, Osage, Peoria, Potawatomi, Iowa, Sac and Fox, and Wyandot were moved from other territories and resettled there after 1866. Indian Territory then covered much of the present-day state of Oklahoma.

In 1889, the government opened up lands to non-Indian settlement, to allot Indian lands not from the Five Civilized Tribes under the Dawes General **Allotment** Act, and sell 'surplus' (unallotted) lands to whites. A plea from the Five Civilized Tribes to create the state of Sequoyah failed in Congress in 1905. The creation of the new state of Oklahoma in 1906 cancelled all agreements with tribes for the preservation of Indian Territory, Kansas Territory and Oklahoma Territory.

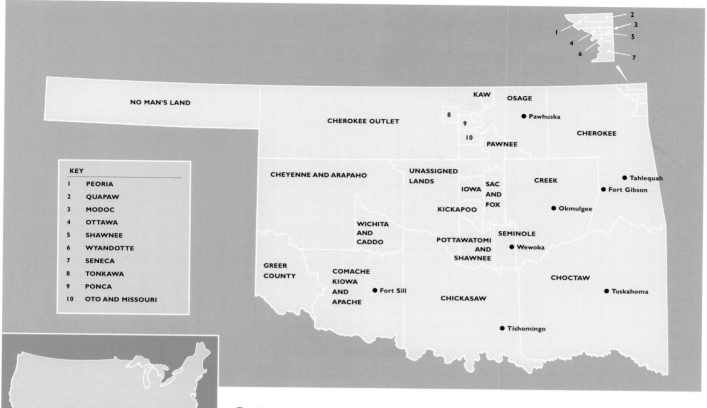

KEY

| | |
|---|---|
| 1 | PEORIA |
| 2 | QUAPAW |
| 3 | MODOC |
| 4 | OTTAWA |
| 5 | SHAWNEE |
| 6 | WYANDOTTE |
| 7 | SENECA |
| 8 | TONKAWA |
| 9 | PONCA |
| 10 | OTO AND MISSOURI |

**135 Above** Indian Territory, 1886-1889.

## Intermarriage

The Native peoples of North America intermarried with one another for centuries before Europeans, **Africans** and others arrived in North America. However, it was the invasion of North America and the intermarriage and sexual relations with non-Indians that created an enormous mixed-blood population – Indian, European and African – that began to change the political and cultural landscape of North America. Some thought that such interaction was predictable and desirable. Others thought it was disastrous, but inevitable. Europeans applied many different theories of race and culture to the different mixes of people developing in the 'New World', even though they themselves were composed of just such mixed populations.

The day will soon come when you will unite yourselves with us, join in our great councils, and form a people with us, and we shall all be Americans; you will mix with us by marriage; your blood will run in our veins and will spread with us over this great continent.
*Thomas Jefferson to the Indians in the West in 1808*

European men mostly saw Indian women as sexual partners. Whether by force, with consent or to create political alliances, European men and Native women began to have sexual relations, creating the first of a new group of mixed-blood peoples. Such alliances, whether temporary or permanent, changed forever the terms under which Native peoples existed and survived.

According to the customs of many Native peoples, adult women were free to form sexual alliances with anyone they chose; marriage being a different category of behaviour. In matriarchal societies, children belonged entirely to women, as did the property and distribution of resources gained from **agricultural** or **hunting** land. Indian men would abide by the rules concerning women. So if the couple separated, the man would leave with only that which belonged to him when he arrived. If an Indian woman formed an alliance with a European man by choice, she would have had every reason to imagine that her rules would be followed. Europeans, however, often held different notions about inheritance, especially concerning children.

Just as European ideas about property, leadership and government differed greatly from the Native ideas, so did the alliances between men and women. European men often married or formed alliances with Indian women of status (the sister of a leader, for example) so that they could then – according to their understanding of inheritance – secure a right to her property as well as access to the friendship of her male relatives. In a way, such actions acknowledged the importance of women. In the European mind, this alliance gave the male control of the property and of the children born from the relationship.

Conflict over the interpretation of different practices was inevitable. With European laws imposed on them, the Indians lost out and women's status was undermined. As late as the early 20th century, when oil was discovered in Oklahoma, it was common practice for white men to marry into high status female-centred Indian families. Under common property laws, they would then inherit the wealth which would have been reserved for the woman's family (under Osage practice, for example). In a number of famous instances in Oklahoma, men murdered Indian women so that husbands could inherit their wealth. So it was that women's high status was sometimes used as a way of removing Indian property and altering the position of women.

Moreover, people of mixed race (Indian, white and, in some instances, African) were thought of and treated differently than their supposedly 'full-blooded' relatives (Indian, African or white). In some instances, when their bloodlines included white genes, their status was raised. In others their mixed bloodlines caused them to lose status. Some used terms such as 'squawmen' for men who had sexual relationships with Indian women and 'half breed' became a negative term. Others thought that mixed bloods were the key to the 'civilization' of the Indian. In Canada, certain people of mixed Indian and European descent were called **Métis**. They have no formal **status** in Canada, but are recognized in the political process. In the USA, there is no formal recognition for a 'mixed-blood' tribe. Each tribal group treats mixed bloods differently, measuring the blood quantum of each part of an individual's genealogy and granting status/enrolment in the group based on that quantum (see page 40) and other forms of ancestral descent.

## Inuit/Inupiaq

The Inuit are made up of several distinct groups: the MacKenzie Delta Inuit of the Western Canadian **Arctic** and the Yukon coast; the Central Inuit made up of the Copper,

Netsilik, Iglulik and Baffinland groups who occupy much of the Canadian Arctic from Victoria Island and Coppermine River in the west to Baffin Island in the East; the Caribou Inuit of the Hudson Bay interior; and the Inuit of Northern Québec and Labrador.

The Inuit **hunted** sea mammals with harpoons in kayaks or *umiaks*. On land, caribou was the most important prey. The Inuit lived almost completely on animal meat (which they ate raw), but also gathered berries and bird eggs. Sea mammal blubber provided an important source of nutrition as well as oil for lamps and heat.

Social groups varied with the seasons. Several families, generally related through the males, remained together throughout most of the year. Hunters shared the kills among the group of families. When **food** was abundant, larger social groups of 100 or more formed. Women were skilled in preparing winter clothing from caribou hides and spent much of their time repairing or preparing garments. Various pastimes were also part of community life. During the winter, groups held many festivals at which people played **drums** and **danced**. In some communities women performed throat singing. **Games** such as the cup and pin or string figures were also popular, as was storytelling.

**Contact** between the Inuit and Europeans goes back to the Norse settlements of Greenland and takes the form of both battles and **trade**. **Fishermen** and **whalers** of several European nations were working off the Labrador coast after 1500 and probably came into contact with Inuit. The earliest continuous contact began in Labrador where Moravian **missionaries** helped the British governor of Newfoundland to negotiate peace with the Inuit in 1765. They then began establishing missions, near which the Inuit began to settle. **Explorers** did not reach the Arctic and the Central Inuit until the 19th century. Early contact was brief and mostly for trade as the explorers were still looking for the Northwest Passage (a seaway from the Atlantic into the Pacific north of North America). Then commercial whaling started along Baffin Bay and Hudson Bay. This brought the Inuit and European whalers into close contact and a few worked on whaling **boats**. After using up the Alaskan reserves, American whalers moved into Canadian waters by 1890. There they wintered near the MacKenzie Delta Inuit, bringing **alcohol** and **disease**.

The whaling and **fur trade** era took its toll on the Inuit. Alcohol abuse, infant mortality, tuberculosis and other health problems brought some groups close to extinction. The Canadian government did little to help the Inuit and left them in the hands of the missionaries. By the 1950s, the Canadian government became more active in the Inuit communities, and took over services provided by missionaries, fur traders or police. The government built **schools**, encouraging settlement in permanent communities. Inuit abandoned their hunting camps and nomadic lifestyles for the lure of this subsidized housing and other services. Life has changed greatly for the Inuit, with modern technology replacing traditional Inuit ways. Snowmobiles replaced **dog** sleds, boats and motors replaced kayaks and air **transport** links Northern communities. Unemployment is high and jobs are seasonal. Some families still try to live off the land or return to the land for part of the year, hoping to retain or regain something of a traditional **subsistence**, land-based lifestyle.[28] Only in recent years have Inuit been able to demand control over their lives.

In 1991, approximately 30,000 people identified themselves as Inuit and 19,000 as partially Inuit. The Inuit remain a majority population throughout their traditional land. Taught in schools, Inuktitut is still the **language** of the Arctic. It has two written forms, one using syllabics and the other using Roman alphabet. The Inuit Broadcasting Corporation produces newspapers, radio and television. **Land claims** settlements have given Inuit some measure of **self-government** and **economic** status. The Northwest Territories have now been split in two to create a self-governing Inuit homeland of **Nunavut** in the Eastern Arctic. This territory has status similar to that of a province in Canada.

**T**his land of ours is a good land and it is big, but to us Inuit it is very small. There is not much room. It is our own land and the animals are our own, and we used to be free to kill them because they were our animals. We cannot live anywhere else, we cannot drink any other water. We cannot travel by dog-teams in any other place but our land.
*Innakatsik, Baker Lake, 1989*

## Invention and innovation

Every culture has within it forces for change, innovation and invention, as well as the forces for resistance to change. Moreover, each has different levels of tolerance for such change. Both internal forces (such as the death of leaders and the appearance of prophets) and external events (such as war, famine and drought) push change, as do external forces such as **war**. Certain individuals and groups, moved by personal or practical needs, create the objects, the ideas or the events that start change. Some changes come from a need to solve problems, such as a **hunter**'s need to reduce glare in the **Arctic**. Other changes come from an individual's desire to do something new, or different, such as **Sequoyah**'s development of a written **language** for the **Cherokee** or the artist's need to change a traditional design. New technologies (for example guns or motorized vehicles) cause people to respond with further innovations. Natives have produced their share of inventions and changes.

**136 Below** Wood goggles, the first 'sunglasses', created by the **Inuit** to shade **hunter**'s eyes from the sun's glare on the ice.

**137 Below** The canoe and the kayak remain models of invention. Their basic structural forms were so perfect that they have never changed, even when the materials for building them (wood, hide and **bark**) were modernized (fibreglass). Kayaks, like this one from King Island, Alaska, remain enormously popular, although used more for **sport** by non-Indians than for **hunting** and **fishing**.

**A**t first, I made Klikitat cedar root baskets using only the traditional mountain designs with horses or people in between…. Next I took an idea from the coastal baskets, putting an edging of animals around the top … with a black line above and below…. I moved from the old traditional designs to putting what I wanted on a basket… I began to use scissors instead of the knife my teacher used.
*Nettie Jackson, 1992*

138 **Above** In 1871, some of the hereditary chiefs of the *Haudenosaunee* (once 50 in number) gathered to recite the laws of the Confederacy, using the **wampum** belts that remind them of the history and the structure of the people. From right to left: Joseph Snow (**Onondaga**), George Martin Johnson (**Mohawk**), John Buck (Onondaga), John Smoke Johnson (wampum keeper and Mohawk), Isaac Hill (speaker and Onondaga) and Seneca Johnson (**Seneca**).

# Iroquois Confederacy

The Iroquois Confederacy – sometimes referred to as the League of the Iroquois – was the political group formed by six nations, together called the Iroquois. The Iroquois call themselves *Haudenosaunee* ('people of the longhouse'). This is taken from the custom of building permanent towns with communal houses and ceremonial buildings called 'longhouses'. The members of the Confederacy saw themselves as a family with 'one body, one mind, one heart'. They shared religious and cultural beliefs and they acted as a single group in **trade**, **war**, peace and **treaties**.

The exact date that the Confederacy was founded is unknown, but by 1600, it comprised five separate nations: the **Seneca**, **Mohawk**, **Oneida**, **Onondaga** and **Cayuga**. Their original homeland is in New York State and Ohio, but all groups are now found in communities in Canada as well. By 1720, Tuscarora had joined the five nations, forced in defeat by Southern colonists and other Indians to migrate from North Carolina. *Deganawida* (the Peacemaker), a Huron prophet, came to end years of war and bloodshed among the individual nations. In 1799, a Seneca prophet called **Handsome Lake** travelled through the Iroquois territory in an attempt to restore traditional religious practice and to encourage the leaders of the various Iroquois nations to work together to replace violence with positive actions. He enlisted the assistance of the Onondaga Chief, Hiawatha, to spread his Great Law of Peace. The Nations came together into a Confederacy or League and structured themselves like the upper and lower house of some parliamentary systems. Governed by a Council of 50 chiefs (*sachems*), the League holds its main Council Fire (meeting place) at Onondaga. When a Chief dies, the senior woman in his **clan**, the clan mother, has the responsibility of choosing his successor, who governs (like his predecessor, whose name he inherits) until his death or removal by the clan mother.

The Confederacy supported trade, negotiated agreements and settled disputes among the six nations as well as with European colonists and other Indian nations. When the American colonies tried to unite during their war with Britain, some thought that the Confederacy might be a partial model for the new US government. During the American Revolution the Iroquois Grand Council declared neutrality. However, many Iroquois aligned themselves with the **British**. After the war, the state of New York took most of the Iroquois land. **Joseph Brant**, a British loyalist, negotiated lands in Canada as a result of the Iroquois participation in the war. In the 1840s, the Oneida were resettled to land in Wisconsin and in Ontario, Canada. The Grand Council again formed at Onondaga, New York, adding a new Council at Grand River, Ontario.

On many occasions the US and Canadian governments tried to break the power of the traditional Confederacy Council and install an elected system. In 1924 on the Grand River, Six Nation Reserve, the Canadian Royal Canadian Mounted Police arrested all the Confederacy chiefs and arranged elections. In 1959 the chiefs attempted to overthrow the elected government, but were arrested. Although an elected band council is still in place, the traditional Confederacy chiefs continue to hold Councils and discuss the business of the community. Today modern communities split their religious life between **Christianity** and the traditional Longhouse religion following the teachings of Handsome Lake.

Iroquois have always said that they are a sovereign nation and oppose many of the policies of the Canadian and US governments and the Indian Act. Traditionalists also believe that Iroquois should not participate in Canadian or US politics and oppose voting in elections and military service as a threat to their **sovereignty**. In the 1920s, the Six Nations Reserve issued its own passport and currently competes internationally in lacrosse.

## Jay Treaty of 1794

The Jay Treaty granted Indians free passage between Canada and the United States. This was of particular importance to Iroquois because once the United States and Canada had been established, their peoples were split across the borders. Both nations had difficulty respecting the Treaty. For years, the **Iroquois Confederacy** held annual border crossing events in defiance of the violations of their **sovereignty**, finally forcing the US government to honour the Treaty in 1928.[29]

**139 Right** Rick Glazer Danay, a **Mohawk** artist, produced this work, *Mohawk Lunch Pail*, as a comment on Mohawk/**Iroquois** bicultural and binational identity. The Mohawk eats a good lunch (on the New York side), composed of a Canadian Moosehead beer. He is half Canadian and half American, he is half free and half captive, he is half high steel ironworker and half culturally 'Mohawk'. He is able to cross the US-Canadian border freely because of the Jay Treaty, whereas his ancestors were driven across that border because of their loyalty to the **British** during the Revolutionary War.

## Treaty of Amity, Commerce and Navigation, 1794

His Britannic Majesty and the United States of America, being desirous, by a treaty of amity, commerce and navigation, to terminate their difference in such a manner, as, without reference to the merits of their respective complaints and pretensions, may be the best calculated to produce mutual satisfaction and good understanding; and also to regulate the commerce and navigation between their respective countries, territories and people, in such a manner as to render the same reciprocally beneficial and satisfactory; they have, respectively, named their Plenipotentiaries, and given them full powers to treat of, and conclude the said treaty, that is to say:

Who have agreed on and concluded the following articles:

### Article I

There shall be a firm, inviolable and universal peace, and a true and sincere friendship between His Britannic Majesty, his heirs and successors, and the United States of America; and between their respective countries, territories, cities, towns and people of every degree, without exception of persons or places.

### Article III

It is agreed that it shall at all times be free to His Majesty's subjects, and to the citizens of the United States, and also to the Indians dwelling on either side of the said boundary line, freely to pass and repass by land or inland navigation, into the respective territories and countries of the two parties, on the continent of America (the country within the limits of the Hudson's Bay Company only excepted) and to navigate all the lakes, rivers and waters thereof, and freely to carry on trade and commerce with each other.

No duty of entry shall ever be levied by either party on peltries [hides] brought by land or inland navigation into the said territories respectively, nor shall the Indians passing or repassing with their own proper goods and effects of whatever nature, pay for the same any impost or duty whatever. But goods in bales, or other large packages, unusual among Indians, shall not be considered as goods belonging *bona fide* to Indians.

In faith whereof we, the undersigned Ministers Plenipotentiary of His Majesty the King of Great Britain and the United States of America, have signed this present treaty, and have caused to be affixed thereto the seal of our arms.

Done at London this 19th day of November, one thousand seven hundred and ninety-four.

(Seal) Greenville

(Seal) John Jay

## Katsinas

For six months of the year, from February (with the Bean **Dance**, called *Powamu*) to July (with the Home Dance called N*iman*), the *katsinas* come from their home in the San Francisco mountains and stay in Hopiland, dancing in the plazas and teaching the children the Hopi way. They come from Katsina Village in the sky with other *katsinas*, the Council of the Gods, to bring messages from and take them to the gods.

There are over three 300 *kacinam* in Hopiland. These masked spirits come in the winter to Hopiland to chastise and reward the people, to teach the Hopi ways, to make the crops grow by bringing **rain** and to accompany the Cloud People to the *mesas*. In their dances, a form of prayer, they bring the families, **clans** and villages together. Sometimes they bring presents, sometimes they behave in a frightening way. Often they behave like the **clowns**, misbehaving and acting in strange and wonderful ways – making fun of people, rolling in the dirt and worse.

Hopis don't worship *katsinas*. *Katsinas* are intermediaries between the Creator and humankind. They deliver the blessings of life – health and happiness and hope. *Katsinas* provide living examples of how life is conducted.
*Ramson Lomatewama, Hopi educator and poet*

## Land

Despite their diversity, American Indians eventually shared a common experience. Their lives changed forever following the arrival of Europeans, as Indian land became American land.

Indians and non-Indians had different understandings of the land and their place on it. These include issues of 'ownership', the ways in which land is used, issues of control, the sacred nature of some land and the **Removal** from homelands.

The Great Being... gave us this land, but the white people seem to want to drive us from it.
*Attakullakulla (Little Carpenter), Cherokee, 1769*

Question: What did Indians call America before Columbus came?
Answer: Home!
*Indian joke*

The Rio Grande Valley is high and dry, laced with a few streams that carry precious water from the mountains that surround it. To the Pueblos who believe they have been here since they emerged from the *sipapu*, a hole in the ground, to the centre of the Earth – the centre which each of them inhabits now and forever, this land was sacred space, an indivisible entity of earth, plants, animals, humans and spirits. Spaniards saw a conquerable human and material resource which would enrich the Spanish Empire, individual men and the Holy Catholic Church through Christian conversion. Later immigrants saw a land of marketable, but unexploited commodities, human and material, as beautiful and unpopulated landscape.
*Simon Ortiz, Acoma Pueblo poet*

In our language, our name is *q'idicca?atx* (pronounced kwadich cha'ak) This means the 'People who Live Among the Rocks and the Seagulls'.... Our stories say that we have lived here since the beginning of time. We have always been whale hunters and fishermen.... Our people learned to make a living from the sea and to respect the power of the ocean and its inhabitants.
*Greig Arnold, Makah carver, 1997*

Native people throughout the Americas have always had an intimate relationship with their lands and with the places from which they come which give them nourishment, which give them life, which give them identity.... For Native American people, art and the ways in which they made a living from their lands, whether it was farming or hunting and gathering or fishing, and the expressions of various kinds of ritual and ceremonial ways of being, are all an integrated whole, which in a sense are reflection of a spiritual ecology... in which Native people throughout the Americas understood the relationship and expressed the relationship to their land and their place.

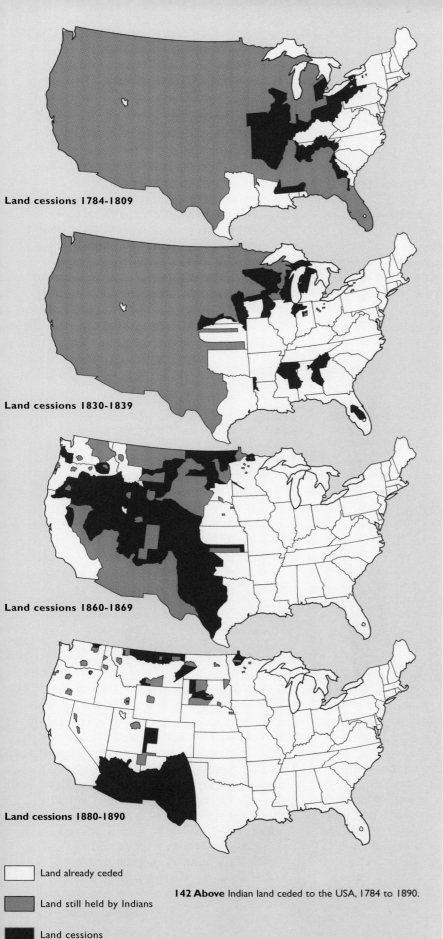

**Land cessions 1784-1809**

**Land cessions 1830-1839**

**Land cessions 1860-1869**

**Land cessions 1880-1890**

Land already ceded

Land still held by Indians

Land cessions

**142 Above** Indian land ceded to the USA, 1784 to 1890.

Through time, of course, and especially with the first contact with Europeans, this way of understanding, this way of relationship, changes sometimes dramatically.
*Greg Cajete, Santa Clara Pueblo educator, 1995*

It is important and a special thing to be an Indian. Being an Indian means being able to understand and live with this world in a very special way. It means living with the land, with the animals, with the birds and fish, as though they were your brothers and sisters. It means saying the land is an old friend and an old friend your father knew, your people always have known… we see our land as much, much more than the white man sees it. To the Indian people our land really is our life.
*Richard Nerysoo, Fort McPherson*

## Land claims

In the United States, the Indian Claims Commission, established in 1946 to settle land claims that could previously only be settled by Congress, could award only a limited amount of money to tribes whose claims were successful. Until 1978, when the Commission's work ended, it came to be seen as a way of extinguishing aboriginal title. Many land claims that followed the break-up of Indians lands according to the General Allotment Act (see **allotment**) remain unsettled, as do the **reservation** rights to **hunt**, **fish** and use resources. The inability of most tribes to settle their land claims shows the difficulties of taking land claims to court when such claims are against non-Indians.

However, the courts have settled a few claims in favour of tribes. The US Supreme Court found that the State of Maine violated the Indian Trade and Intercourse (Non-Intercourse) Act of 1790, which forbade the acquisition of Indian land by non-Indians without the approval of Congress. States, not Congress, took Mashpee, Penobscot and Passamaquoddy lands. As a result of the court's finding, the Penobscot and Passamaquoddy received a US$81.5 million settlement which enabled them to buy lands and develop **economic** structures for their futures.

The **Bureau of Indian Affairs** leased much of the remaining land held by Indians for 99 years at favourable lease rates to non-Indian businesses, ranchers, hoteliers and domestic residents. As these leases came up for renewal from the 1960s to the 1980s, newly reinvigorated tribes have refused to renew them or have renegotiated them for better financial and legal terms. Thus, Native nations in Palm Springs (California) and Salamanca (New York) have held up property sales and exchanges for years until they have received more favourable leases on lands that belong to them.

Although the government, states and business have tried to resolve land claims cases by making compensation payments to tribes, some tribes have refused to take money in return for land. The **Sioux** case for the Black Hills, their sacred Paha Sapa, is one example. When gold was discovered in the Black Hills of South Dakota in 1871, the federal government tried to buy the land from the Great Sioux Nation, but the nation refused money for the land it believed to be sacred. The government broke the Treaty of Fort Laramie, removing the Black Hills from the nation's land settlement, but continuing to offer money as payment. The Sioux have refused it to date.

In Canada, there are two types of land claims. The first are 'comprehensive claims' based on aboriginal title, where the title to the land has never been removed. The second are 'specific claims', where the title is in dispute. The cornerstone of the legal argument for comprehensive claims is the **Royal Proclamation** of 1763. Where no formal **treaties** exist between Native bands and **British** and Canadian governments in most of Northern Québec, the Northwest Territories and most of British Columbia, groups claim that they never surrendered their lands. They claim land rights because they occupied Canada before the Europeans. The Indian Act made it illegal to raise money to pursue land claims until 1951, when the Act was amended. In 1973, the Supreme Court of Canada agreed that aboriginal rights did exist, and the long, slow process of negotiating settlements began. There were millions of dollars at stake as Native groups sought rights to resources as well as land.

The first claim settled was with the **Cree** in northern Québec. It was very controversial because it involved the development of a huge hydro-electric project. Later, groups in British Columbia, the Northwest Territories and the Yukon filed claims. The British Columbia claim by the Gitxsan-Wet'suwet'en

people (settled recently), is seen as a landmark decision. This is not only because it recognizes aboriginal title, but also because it affirms that the title must be upheld and protected under the Constitution. It states that the First Nations' spoken history is acceptable evidence and is as important as written legal records of the past.

Before the 20th century, about half of Canada's Native bands had signed treaties that surrendered certain rights in exchange for promised lands, money and other guarantees. Since the 1970s, Native groups have launched hundreds of specific claims over treaties. A number of groups have become frustrated that the government has been slow to settle these claims and have become militant, protesting with marches, and road and rail blockades. The most dramatic confrontation over a land claim was near the town of **Oka** in Québec in 1990. Heavily armed **Mohawks** blockaded the town in protest over a proposed golf course that would disrupt some of their **sacred lands**.

## Languages

Before **contact**, Indian languages were as diverse and numerous as the tribes themselves. Many Native people spoke several languages, including sign and **trade** languages, which they used when communicating with other tribes.

**Missionaries** and the government led a cultural assault on Native languages, forbidding the speaking of those languages in **schools** and even on the **reservations**. For a few peoples, such as the **Cherokee**, development of a written language (**Sequoyan**), was combined with the rare support of the Church in using the tribal language in a religious context, in order to keep the language alive. Language was usually the main target for those who wished Indians to 'assimilate' and be 'civilized'.

Many languages, such as those spoken by Timuacan peoples in the Floridas, died with their people in the latter part of the 17th century. Most coastal **Algonquian**, California Indian languages and those from Oregon (Wappo, Yuki, Chimariko, Shasta, Takelma, Kalapuya, Coos, Chumash, Costanoan, Esselen, Siuslaw and Yana) cannot be restored, because there are no Native speakers remaining. In many places, only a few Native speakers of a language are alive.

At the beginning of the 20th century, most Indians spoke a tribal language and English was their second language. At the turn of the century, over 300 languages were spoken by Indians. In the last years of the 20th century, the only languages used by over 50,000 speakers are **Navajo** and **Ojibwa**.[30]

The introduction of a new people, a new culture, changed their whole outlook on life… . Handsome Lake predicted… that this new culture would introduce their language which in time will completely erase our own Native language from our minds.
This will be the last of Natives as a people.
*Reg Henry, Cayuga faithkeeper, 1990*

Linguists predict that Yup'ik Eskimo, Cherokee, Choctaw, Mikasuki, Cocopah, Keresan (Santo Domingo, Jemez), Havasupai-Walapai-Yavapai, Hopi, Tohono O'odham, Yaqui, Navajo, Mescalero, **Apache**, Tiwa, Western Apache, Yaqui and **Zuni** in the United States, and **Cree** and Ojibwa in Canada can survive into the 21st century.[31]

Most tribal peoples are making major efforts to revive and support their languages, because they know that tribal language – in the words of the Cherokee Language and Culture Preservation Bill – is the 'single most important attribute of cultural persistence'. Many tribes have language committees, cultural preservation offices, dictionary and language projects, and projects for the introduction and use of languages in schools. Now there are a number of professionally trained Native linguists and many others committed to the preservation and survival of Native language.

A few tribes besides the Cherokee have written languages. Almost everyone is aware that both new and traditional forms of language are passed on through the processes of song, story and **dance**.

The Mesquakie language, our ways, our religion are woven into one… . With another language, we cannot perform our religion.
*Don Wanatee, Mesquakie, 1969*

My parents are traditional, and I grew up with ceremonies and chants. I'd speak Navajo in front of a lot of friends at school, and they referred to us as 'sheep-camp girls'. What

stays with me is a saying, 'Don't ever be afraid of having an accent. It just means you are worth two people.'
*Susan Baldwin, Dilkon, Arizona, c. 1992*

## Literature

Although some Native peoples recorded their stories in pictures of various kinds before Europeans came to the Americas, most storytelling was by word of mouth (the oral tradition). Dramatic performance in **ceremonies** and in storytelling was the main body of literature for every tribe, although the styles, content and contexts for those performances varied from group to group. Indians have been writing in English, Spanish and French, but primarily in English, since the early days of the **missionary** invasion in the 18th century. From that time, Indians began writing down the stories that had remained only in memory and verbal form. They also began writing in a European way. From **Elias Boudinot** onward, many Native journalists documented the lives, histories and stories of Indians in the United States and Canada. Samuel Occam (1723–92), a Mohegan Methodist missionary, first published sermons on the conditions of Indian life in 1722. From the mid 19th century, Native writers such as Charles Eastman, **Sioux**; Humishuma (Chrystal Quintasket), Okanogan (1888–1934); John Joseph Mathews, Osage (1894–1979); and John Rollin Ridge, **Cherokee** (1827–69), have brought a rich body of written literature to the American public in the form of autobiography, novels, poetry and humour. They have also turned material from the oral tradition into an accessible written form for an Indian and non-Indian audience. Native writers of the 20th century, such as Will Rogers, Cherokee (1879–1935); N. Scott Momaday, Kiowa; Leslie Silko, Laguna Pueblo (born 1948); James Welch, **Blackfoot**/Gros Ventre (born 1940); and Louise Erdrich, **Ojibwe** (born 1954), have gained worldwide audiences and literary awards for their work.[32]

Emily Pauline Johnson was born on the Six Nations Reserve near Brantford, Ontario. She was the daughter of a hereditary **Mohawk** Chief *Teyonnhehkewea* and an English woman. Johnson assumed her great-grandfather's Confederacy title and signed all of her poems largely on Indian themes. She retired from performing and settled in Vancouver in 1909, collaborating there with Joe Capilano, a Squamish Chief she had met in London. Her work with him led to the much acclaimed *Legends of Vancouver* (1911). In 1912, she published *Flint and Feather*. She died of cancer in 1913. Johnson was the first Indian woman to publish books of poetry and collections of short fiction, and one of the first writers to explore the theme of mixed-blood Indians and their search for identity and place.

Joy Harjo, a member of the Muskogee tribe, was born in Oklahoma in 1951 and raised in New Mexico. She has written several books of poetry, including her award-winning *In Mad Love and War*, *The Woman Who Fell from the Sky* and *She Had Some Horses*. Most recently, she edited a new anthology of work by Native women, *Reinventing the Enemy's Language*. She has taught creative writing at several universities. Whilst a student at the Institute of American Indian Arts in Santa Fe, she discovered the value of poetry at a time when Indian politics were changing. At the heart of Harjo's poetry is compassion, grace and, in her own words, the need to express 'how justice can appear in the world despite forces of confusion and destruction'. These same ideas are important to her band 'Poetic Justice'. She is very inspired by the musical work of Jim Pepper, a Kaw jazzman, and she puts her words to a mix of jazz, blues and traditional music.

The music that speaks for us is a blend of influences that speak of community, love for people, for all creatures, for this crazy beautiful history and the need to sing with and of the sacred. These musics are our respective tribal musics… born of the indomitable spirit of a tribal people in a colonized land, a music born of the need to sing by African peoples in this country, a revolutionary movement of predominately African sources influenced by Europe and the Southern tribes; and rock and blues, musics cradled in the South that speak of our need to move with heart and soul through this land, this spiral of life. We are forged by this dance for justice and the absolute need to sing.

*Joy Harjo, Muskogee poet and musician*

141 **Above** Joy Harjo, Muskogee poet and musician.

'E. Pauline Johnson' and '*Tekahionwake*'. Often billed as the 'Indian Princess', Johnson performed part of her programme in fringed buckskin. In 1894, she travelled to London to give recitals and published her first book of poetry, *The White Wampum* (1895), based

142 **Right** Tomson Highway,
**Cree** playwright, in 1995.

battle marked the end of freedom for the Northern Plains Indians and became a symbol for both Indians and whites of how far apart they were. New myths about the cavalry, Sitting Bull, Crazy Horse, Custer and Buffalo Bill all came from this incident.

The victors could hardly have predicted what followed: Crazy Horse's assassination, the Wild West Show stardom (and later murder) of Sitting Bull, the **allotment** of the Indian lands under the Dawes Act and the final killing of the Minneconjou Sioux over the **Ghost Dance** resistance of 1890.

For both whites and Indians, Little Big Horn remains a significant battleground. The site lies on a Crow reservation and is part of the US National Park system. It was called the Custer National Monument until 1990. Indians everywhere petitioned for a name change to the 'Little Bighorn National Monument'. Everyone wants the story told the way they remember it. The Little Bighorn River still flows with blood.

Tomson Highway, a **Cree** from Northern Manitoba, is the eleventh of 12 children. He earned two undergraduate degrees in music and one in English and is a gifted pianist. A Native theatre group in Toronto performed his 1986 play, *The Rez Sisters*. His sequel, entitled *Dry Lips Oughta Move to Kapuskasing*, was an immediate hit and won the Canadian Dora Mavor Moore award for Best New Play. His work captures the humour and reality of Native life on the reserve.

## Little Bighorn

Known to whites as 'Custer's Last Stand', the battle of the Little Bighorn in 1876 was the dramatic beginning of the end for the Indian Wars of the Plains and the final closing of the reservations. The trail that led to the Little Bighorn included the Fort Laramie Treaty in 1851, which established tribal boundaries in the Northern Plains, the 1864 massacre of Cheyenne at Sand Creek by the US Army, the 1868 Treaty establishing the Great **Sioux** Reservation, and the discovery of gold in the South Dakota Black Hills in 1875. **Sitting Bull** and Crazy Horse, leaders of different Sioux peoples, were doomed to battle General George Armstrong Custer in the last fight against **reservationization**. The Sioux and Cheyenne outmanned and outgunned Custer's cavalry and his Crow allies, but this

**M**y friend, I do not blame you for this. had I listened to you this trouble would not have happened to me. Sometimes my young men would attack the Indians who were their enemies and took their ponies. They did it in return.

We had buffalo for food, and their hides for clothing and our tipis. We preferred hunting to a life of idleness on the reservations, where we were driven against our will. At times we did not have enough to eat, and we were not allowed to leave the reservation to hunt.

We preferred our own way of living. We were no expense to the government then. All we wanted was peace and to be left alone. Soldiers were sent out in the winter, who destroyed our villages. Then Long Hair [Custer] came in the same way. They say we massacred him, but he would have done the same to us had we not defended ourselves and fought to the last. Our impulse was to escape with our squaws and papooses, but we were so hemmed in we had to fight.

After that I went up on the Tongue River and lived in peace. But the government would not let me alone… I came here with the agent to talk with the Big White Chief, but was not given a chance. They tried to confine me. I tried to escape and a soldier (a Sioux) ran his bayonet into me.

*Crazy Horse, on his deathbed, to Agent Jesse Lee, 1877*

## Long Walk of the Navajo, The/Bosque Redondo

In 1864, more than 8,000 **Navajos** and 400 Mescalero **Apaches** (long enemies of the Navajo even though they shared a common Athapaskan language) were held at Bosque Redondo, a reservation in Eastern New Mexico. They had been marched there by Kit Carson and Union military forces in the Southwest. Bosque Redondo proved to be the Navajo equivalent of the Trail of Tears. The Long Walk, a forced migration, was the tragic end of a long and bloody conflict between Navajos and others for control of the lands and minerals in Navajo country. Bosque Redondo proved a disaster. As many as 2,000 died, suffering **disease** and winters with little housing, clothing or **food**. A few thousand Navajos escaped the round-up. Eventually, these remaining people and the Navajos at Bosque Redondo pleaded for their return rather than exile to **reservations** far from their homeland. Mescaleros fled Bosque Redondo in 1865. In 1868, the remaining Navajos were allowed to begin the slow march home to rebuild their lives.

**T**he mourning of our women makes the tears roll down into my moustache.... I want to go and see my own country.
*Barboncito, Navajo war leader, 1868*

## Lumbee

Lumbees, who now number more than 40,000 people, are the largest non-**federally recognized** group of Indian people in the United States. With much controversy over their origins as a people and their identity as Indians, their history remains muddied. For at least two centuries, the ancestors of Lumbee people – named after the Lumber River that flows through the area in which they live – have resided in North Carolina. According to their spoken stories, they have several possibilities of origin: as **Algonquian** peoples who lived in coastal North Carolina and merged with the descendants of the so-called Lost Colony of Roanoke; as Siouan or Cheraw or other tribal remnant peoples who fled the **disease** and encroachments that accompanied white settlement; or as mixtures of the two groups named above. What is certain is that, whoever they were as Indians, they mixed and **intermarried** in their North Carolina setting, with whites and with **Africans** after the 1700s. Whatever Native languages they spoke and whatever Native lifestyles they led, they had merged with those of the people with whom they intermarried. Still, they remained separate from white communities, and were always treated and recognized as non-whites. Known for their resistance to racism, they organized a massive protest against the Ku Klux Klan in 1858, driving the Klan out of Robeson County.

In the 20th century, they were known as Croatan, **Cherokee** and the 'Indians of Robeson County'. In 1953 they took the name Lumbee, and have since worked hard for the education of their people as well as for federal recognition that so far has been denied them. In many ways, the Lumbees are typical of a number of communities, largely on the East Coast of North America (such as the Wampanoags in Massachusetts and the **Abenakis** in Vermont) who have persistently claimed Indian histories and connections, but who, for the most part, have been denied federal recognition and federal services.

## Maize

Maize (called 'corn' in the United States) is cultivated from the area south of Chile in South America, north to Montreal in Canada.

It is grown in both high and in low altitudes, in wet and dry climates, on high plateaus and in tropical forests. Its grains vary in size. The stalks can be 1–3.5 m high and the ears 12–15 cm long. Wild maize has been dated to 80,000 BC, long before human inhabitation. Domesticated in Mexico, maize (*zea maize*) was introduced to the American Southwest at least 6,000 years ago. Along with **beans** and **squash**, it is the most important **food** plant of Native peoples in the Americas and one of the three most important grains in the world.

In the 17th and 18th centuries, 'Indian maize' was one of the major export crops of North America, and remains a major grain in world **trade**. Even now, ecologists and agricultural specialists insist that we have much to learn from both the cultivation and preservation methods of so many varieties of maize by Native peoples.

Most Native peoples intercrop, that is plant other species along with maize. When maize is interplanted with beans or other legumes, its stalks provide support to the climbing bean vines. The legumes also add nitrogen to the soil. Almost all Indian farmers plant in hills. Low-growing crops, such as squashes and pumpkins, can be interplanted between the hills, thus choking out the weeds. It also, as is often the case in Mexico and Central and South America, allows edible green crops, called *quelites*, to thrive.

Each Native group adapted maize to suit its agricultural needs. A Hopi blue maize is adapted to deep seeded planting in hilled sand conditions. In Hopi country, the sand stays moist at a depth of 20–30 cm. The Hopi maize has a root and shoot elongation much tougher and faster growing than other varieties. Locally cultivated plants are distinctive plant populations adapted over centuries to specific climates and soils and selected to fit certain conditions.

**143** A ladle (c. 1850) used by Seminole for stirring and eating *sofky*, a hominy soup made by Muskogean people.

The culinary preferences of particular cultures have favoured the forms, tastes and colours of some plants over others. Hopi maize is red, white, blue and yellow as a result of selective growing. Blue, red, white, yellow and black varieties mirror the sacred colours of the universe.

There are six colours of corn: yellow, white, blue, black, red and speckled. And each colour stands for a direction: north, south, east, and west, up and down… . White is for the East, where the sun rises, and the blue is for the West. In a **ceremony**, when they're about to blow tobacco smoke and incense to the six directions, they sing the song of corn and growth, and here is one:

  Ha-o, my mother, ha-o, my mother,
  Due west, blue corn ear, my mother,
  Due eastward, blooming blue-bird flower,
  Decorate our faces, bless us with flowers.
  Thus being face-decorated,
  Being blessed with flowers,
  We shall be delighted, we shall be delighted.
  Ha-o, my mother, ha-o, my mother.
  Due east, white corn ear, my mother,
  Due south, red corn ear,
  Due northward, blooming maiden blossom,
  Due above, black corn ear, my mother.
  Due downward, blooming sunflower,
  Due below, sweet corn ear, my mother,
  Due upward, blooming, all kinds of flowers.
*Agnes Dill, Isleta Pueblo*

By 1500, the Iroquois had flints, dents, popcorns and sweetcorns, and grew several varieties of each. In the Northeast, archaeological evidence shows that enough maize could be stored to feed thousands of people for over a year. The tribes went to war when the **British** and Spanish destroyed or confiscated corn stores. The British succeeded in weakening the **Iroquois** who fought for the American side in the Revolutionary War by burning their maize stores. Maize remains central in Iroquois life today as it was in the 18th century. Whereas women had the primary responsibility for all cultivation until the mid 18th century, now both men and women tend the fields. Iroquois people still cultivate many old varieties of maize and store it in a traditional manner (in braids) after harvest. Foods made from maize remain important in the ceremonial and daily diet, and Iroquois still make objects from the husks such as **dolls** and **masks**.

In the Southwest, Southeast and Northeast, maize is the main religious and ceremonial symbol. Cornmeal accompanies prayers made to the spirits. **Dances** and prayers for healing take place around it and it appears in **art** and stories.

One **Navajo** story says that the wind created people from two perfect white and yellow ears of maize. Among the Pueblos of the Southwest, a baby's naming ceremony is accompanied by maize pollen scattered over the ground, thrown to the air and rubbed into

**144 Below** Maize from Ramos Oyenque's fields at San Juan Pueblo.

the hair. Some of the **katsinas** bring and give corn. A young **Apache** girl, in her puberty ceremony, is covered in cornmeal. The Iroquois have an important ceremony for Green Corn, which, as in the Southeast, reconciles all bad feelings between people.

Corn is the basic ingredient that all of us, as Indian people, believe in. We use it in our ceremonies; we use it for subsistence; we use it to feed our animals. So the corn plays a very significant role in our daily lives. We start with it, we end up with it… . We give thanks to the Creator for providing this to us. Corn… we use in our songs, we use in our dances, we use in the daily life of all of us.
*Walter Dasheno, Governor, Santa Clara Pueblo, 1995*

But for me, I cannot forget our old ways. Often in summer I rise at daybreak and steal out to the cornfields, and as I hoe the corn I sing to it, as we did when I was young. No-one cares for our corn songs now.
*Maxiwidiac or Buffalo Bird Woman, Hidatsa, 1921*

I start planting, helping my father, when I was about 12 years old… my father… always tell me, 'You better do it right now, because Mother Nature is right there looking at you, so you'd better talk to Mother Nature so she can give you some food, some good vegetable… . He said someday when you become a farmer, be sure and get up early in the morning, about 4:30. If you plant corn in the field, come down and talk to them. Talk to all little spirit around there, so they can hear you talk your Indian language. Talk to them in Indian and pray and say your Indian prayer early in the morning.' So that's why we always have a good crop.
*Ramos Oyenque, San Juan Pueblo, 1995*

Before I go out into my field, I sing a song … . My cornfield has a prayer… . I offer corn pollen to Mother Earth… . I use Corn Pollen to communicate with the Holy People. She gives me dried cornhusk so people can smoke tobacco at ceremonies… . I also grow corn so my family eats roasted corn, kneel-down bread or mutton stew with corn.
*Jesse Biakeddy, Navajo, Big Mountain, Arizona*

**145 Left** A Navajo maize farmer in Canyon de Chelley, Arizona.

**146 Above** This modern version of the Corn Mother was made by Pablita Abeyta (*Tah-nez-bah*), a Navajo ceramic sculptor. Many native people, including Hopi, Cherokee and Arikara, believe in a Corn Mother who gave birth to them and made the land that provides for them. The extensive and continued use of Corn Mother's image on ceremonial clothing, in ceremonies themselves, in prayers, songs and dances reminds us that the crop remains important to Native people.

**147 Above** Onondaga women in the 18th and 19th centuries used a double-headed stick to pound and grind shelled, dried maize in a wooden mortar, such as this. Cherokee, Creek, Choctaw and Seminole women used similar pounders, usually made from the hard and durable hickory tree.

## Masks

All over the world, people hold **ceremonies** and ritual **dances** for healing, for **war** or peace, for hunting and **fishing**, and for weddings, births and funerals. Masked characters join in these dances. Humans take on the roles of the animals or spirits that must be called upon or driven out in order to put things right. Although not all Indians use masked ritual dramas, many do. For those people, the masks themselves become part of their spiritual and cultural heritage, living things that must be handled with respect and care.

Seneca societies used **medicine** masks, carved from a living tree, along with **drums**, snapping **turtle rattles**, canes, songs, dances and plant medicines in healing ceremonies. To many **Iroquois**, masks are among the most sacred of objects, inappropriate for display in a **museum** or in a book. Some Iroquois continue to use masks in the practice of the Longhouse religion. The **Cherokees** made carved wooden masks, called 'booger masks' by the first anthropologists who studied them, to embody the spirits who came to frighten, heal and instruct during Cherokee ceremonies. However, Cherokees today do not use these masks, although they still refer in story, song and ritual to some of the creatures (such as **buffalo**) and spirits that the masks represent.

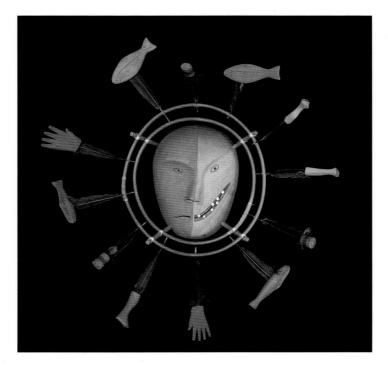

**Inuit** and tribal peoples from the **Northwest Coast**, **Navajos** and **Apaches** use masks in their religious and social rituals. On the Northwest Coast, the Canadian government recently returned to the Kwakwaka'wakw many masks it had taken away when it banned the **potlatch**.[33]

**148 Left** This Nunivak mask from the **Inuit** of the Bering Sea was probably worn at feasts. In the mask, the human spirit and animal spirit (*inua*) merge and reverse themselves, surrounded by the **fish**, **whales** and tools that characterize the **hunter's** world.

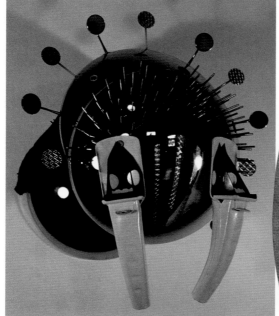

**149 Right** This Punk Walrus Mask/Spirit (*Pooka Timerik Inua*), c. 1987, was made by Larry Beck, a Yup'ik artist. Beck's masks, made of 'found' materials, bring to life animals from his **Arctic** world, with their *inua* (spirit) intact.

I'm an Eskimo, but I'm also a 20th-century American… my found materials come from junk yards, trash cans [bins] and industrial waste facilities, since the ancient beaches where my ancestors found driftwood and washed up debris from shipwrecks are no longer available to me… even though I use Baby Moon hubcaps, pop rivets, snow tires, Teflon spatulas, dental pick mirrors and stuff to make my spirits… because, below these relics of your world, reside the old forces familiar to the *inua*. *Larry Beck, Yup'ik artist*

**151 Above** Bella Coola sun mask.

The *matachinas* (masked) dance, brought to the Americas by the Spanish, may have been taught to Indians as a way of making them accept the power and rule of Spain and of **Christianity**. Indians in Mexico and in New Mexico have turned the dance into a drama about the encounter between them. Usually danced on Christmas Day, it features the masked M*onarcha* (King), two *abuelos* (grandfathers), a bull and an unmasked young girl, who represents M*alinche* (the Spanish name for the conqueror Cortez's Indian mistress and translator). The young

**150 Right** Lillian Pitt, from the Warm Springs/Wasco people of Oregon, makes modern masks. This one is constructed with the Japanese *raku* method of ceramic firing. Pitt creates spirit masks from the stories and legends of her tribal past and from the physical characteristics associated with **Inuit** and Yup'ik masks.

girl represents innocence and goodness. The *abuelos* function as **clowns**, dancing among the other characters, keeping order and teasing the **tourists** in the audience. They also symbolically kill and castrate the bull, which represents Spain and evil. Some say they learned the dance from Moctezuma, the last Aztec emperor. In some pueblos, it is very 'Indianized', with the dancers wearing Pueblo ceremonial costumes and dancing to drums. In others, it is very Hispanic and Catholic, with *Malinche* wearing a white communion dress and dancing to fiddle music.

## Matrilineality and matrilocality

Unlike the patrilineal Anglo-American society, in which women and children took the name of their husbands and fathers, some Native people, such as the **Cherokee**, were matrilineal. Cherokees received their **clan** affiliation (**Wolf**, Paint, Blue, Wild Potato, etc.) from their mothers, and considered a person's only blood relatives to be those on the mother's side. This matrilineal kinship played a part in the status of women in Cherokee society. Men in matrilocal societies went to live in the homes of their wives, and a mother and her family had sole authority in raising children. Many Native peoples (such as **Iroquois** and **Navajo**) had matrilineal societies until the **Christian** and European laws of property and male descent were forced on them.

**B**y the time Napi came over to this side of the ocean, the Creator had already made more people. But the women couldn't get along with the men, so Napi sent them away in different groups. Not long after, he got together with the chief of the women so that they could decide about some important things. The chief of the women told Napi that he could make the first decision, as long as she could have the final word; the old people say that ever since then it has been this way between men and women. Napi decides many things for the men and women, and the chief of the women countermands him, making women have better skills than the men. Then she decides that men and women will live together after Napi put them apart. Now at that time men were living real pitiful lives. The clothes they were wearing were made from stiff furs and hides. They couldn't make moccasins or lodges and they couldn't even keep themselves clean. They were nearly starved. They were very anxious to join the women.
*Beverley Hungry Wolf, a Blackfeet writer, in her version of a creation story, 1980*

Although matrilineality was predominant in Indian societies, some tribal peoples were male-centred. These tribes had male gods, spirits and origin stories (see **creation stories**), and had government, inheritance and residence patterns determined by the male line of descent.

## Medicine

Medicine is the English word by which Indian traditional healing – mental, spiritual (religious) and physical – became known. Native medical practice and scientific knowledge, based on plants, is connected to and even inseparable from spiritual healing. American Indians were skilled at using plants for medicinal purposes. Their knowledge of plants' different properties gave them a pharmacy of cough, cold and fever remedies, laxatives, emetics, antiseptics and pain killers. Research on a number of these plants now verifies their traditional Indian uses. American Indians were not only aware of the medicinal properties of a plant's roots, leaves, **bark**, berries and flowers, but also of how the properties of one plant enhanced the properties of another. Thus, they frequently made medicines of combined ingredients. Indians knew which plants could be eaten raw and which had first to be prepared in such a way as to reduce the plant's natural poisons. They knew how mature or how young a plant should be to be effective. They understood the dosages needed and they always ensured that a plant was not harvested in a way that would interfere with its own future propagation.

One plant used by many Native peoples for different purposes was May apple (*Podophyllum peltatum*). Many tribes used the plant as a laxative, an emetic and remedy against intestinal worms. The Penobscots of New England prepared a May apple ointment to use as a treatment for warts and skin cancer. In 1820, it was added to the United States *Pharmacopoeia*, an official registry of medicinal substances. May apple is also still used in several commercially prepared laxatives and for skin problems. Researchers believe it be to effective against some tumours and cancers.

## Medicine bag, medicine bundle

Medicine bags and bundles have always fascinated non-Indians (although only a few Native cultures possess and use them) and so **museums** have often collected them. Medicine bags and bundles carry the tools and objects needed to protect an individual or a group. The bag or bundle and what it contains might come from a **dream** or vision, from a protective spirit or from someone or something with power. It could be filled with items of importance to the individual who carries it, for example special stones, parts of animals, **feathers** and painted objects. Like crosses to **Christian**s, these objects (often called fetishes, charms or amulets) have special meaning and special protective powers to those who believe in them.

Anyone might carry a bag, but bundles are usually carried by someone who has been specially chosen to do so, either by a medicine man or by the previous bundle carrier. As bundles are sacred, they are brought out only occasionally and in a ceremonial context. They cannot be opened by anyone not responsible for them. They can only be seen by those participating in a traditional religious **ceremony**. Many peoples, such as the **Navajo**, have begun to recover bundles and objects (*jish*) used for healing which were taken from them. On their return, they have either been dismantled and destroyed, because they have been away from the medicine people for such a long time that they are contaminated, or they are 'reconsecrated' and used once again by those who understand their uses and powers.

## Medicine men and women

The term 'medicine man' covers a wide variety of people who, in different tribes take care of the physical and spiritual welfare of their people.

The much used, often misused, terms of 'shamans' and 'medicine men' have different names in different cultures, but the term 'Indian doctor' in English covers most of them and their practices.

Medicine men and women carry the sacred knowledge and history of their people. They know the stories, songs, **dances**, **ceremonies** and rituals connected with the origin of humans, plants and animals, and their relationships. They understand the forces in the universe that can cause illness and disharmony and those that can heal and restore peace. Many believe that **Coyote**, the trickster, was the first doctor and that he created them.

Not all medicine people look after and heal the body, not all look after and heal the mind and spirit, but all know that body, mind and spirit are connected. Each of their particular practices are built on that understanding. Some specialize in particular conditions and problems, others specialize in diagnosis. Some **Navajo** *hataali* (singers) know only specific rituals for certain kinds of healing. After the problem has been diagnosed, by a hand trembler or a crystal singer for example, a person would go to a certain *hataali* who would conduct the 'sing' appropriate to that problem. In the Lakota way, some healers would conduct certain ceremonies because spiritual illness had manifested itself in a physical way. Others would be more like a minister, rabbi or priest, constantly overseeing the spiritual health of his or her people.

Among the Natives of California and the Navajo of the Southwest, some of the most respected medicine people were women. Changing Woman, the 'mother' of the Navajo People in their origin stories, gave them many ceremonies and stories for healing. She was herself a medicine woman. A girl usually begins to learn medicine from her grandmother at an early age. The Navajo women, who were weavers, had extensive knowledge of plants and the properties of many plants that are dyes. They also know the specific songs and ceremonies that will heal. Women may hold **medicine bundles** and special objects (*jish*) for healing. They may be herbalists themselves or be helpers or apprentices to others. They may be diagnosticians, working out what is wrong with a patient and what ceremony and procedure will provide the cure.

Of course, as with all cultures who practice or believe in traditional spiritual and physical medicine, there can be a 'dark side' to the practice of that medicine. The knowledge of the forces that affect the body and mind can be used for evil purposes, and Indian cultures do have sorcerers (so-called 'witch doctors' or 'magicians') who do not use their knowledge for good. Most groups forbid gaining and using such knowledge for evil and have stories that tell of the punishments for such practice.

## Metal/metalwork, minerals and metallurgy

Before the arrival of the Europeans and their industries, Native peoples extracted minerals and worked metals of all sorts. Copper was abundant all over North America, and may have been used as early as 3,000 BC. In the Southeast, Adena and Hopewell peoples (sometimes called Moundbuilders) made copper into jewellery, including spiral-shaped earspools, gorgets (breastplates or neckpieces) and bracelets, **beads** and tools (**fish** hooks and axe heads). Copper appeared on **pottery**, together with **shell**s and mica. Ancient people mined copper from surface mines or gathered it from rivers and hammered it, probably using heat in the process. In the North, near Lake Superior, copper and lead mining was common. In British Columbia, Alaska (on the Copper River) and the Yukon gold, silver, copper and lead did not require smelting. Cold-worked copper existed widely in Tsimshian Territory, with beads and bracelets found there as early as 500 BC. Copper proved to be an important material in the Northwest tribes, in the manufacture of coppers for the **potlatch** and for the display of wealth.[34]

In the Southeast, the Pueblos mined lead and, like their neighbours to the South in Mexico, used lead as pigment for fired pottery. However, this was not a healthy practice as the pottery leaked lead into the diet. The Spanish commandeered their lead mines to make bullets, and the Pueblos abandoned lead paints and took to vegetable-based pigments for their pottery. In this way, they produced the extraordinary pigments and painting styles distinctive to Pueblo clayware. Indians traded with Europeans for valuable iron goods, and scavenged metals from trade **boats** and expeditions. They remade metal goods such as gunstock, pots and tacks into items for their own use (see **recycled materials**).

**153 Above** Indians smelted and forged copper, but others hammered, engraved and cut copper. Most often it was used for tools and weapons, but sometimes also for decorative work. Copper knives, like these, were made before worked iron and were an important **trade** item.

**101**

**154 Below** An early 20th-century **Navajo** ring and necklace. Navajos took the tools and techniques of Spanish silverwork and turned them into a uniquely Navajo **trade**. This was made possible by the silver and turquoise mines in the Southwest. The designs and symbols used were important to Navajos, such as the **squash** blossom and the *naja* or inverted rainbow seen in this necklace.

Native silver (mined or melted down from coins) was an important commodity. It was valued in the same way that gold was by the Europeans. Indians in the Southwest learned the metal stamping and casting techniques of the Mexicans and developed silverwork into a major **art**form and **trade** that continues today. In the Northeast, too, silverwork was used in trade and presentation. Indians combined traditional designs with European techniques and styles to create brooches, gorgets and other items. The Indians in the Southern Plains and Southeast became expert at a form of metalwork with German silver, or nickel silver, an alloy of zinc, copper and nickel, using it to make objects associated with the **Native American Church**.

## Métis

The Métis were a distinct society that emerged in the 19th century in Western and Northern Canada. They are of mixed Native and European heritage. The word Métis comes from the French use of the Latin *miscere*, meaning 'to mix'. Much of this population is French-speaking. The rise and spread of the **fur trade** in the Hudson Bay and the St Lawrence trading systems in the Canadian Northwest began this population, usually born to Native mothers and Scots, French or English fathers.

Métis cultural roots rest near the Red and Assiniboine Rivers (Winnipeg today). **Buffalo hunting** and trapping were central to their identity. A distinctive clothing style evolved, mixing European and Native heritages.

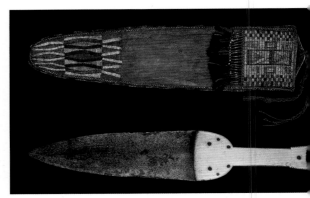

**155 Above** Métis loomweavers made detailed and complex objects, using the tiny **quills** that other Indians found hard to use with Native tools. This knife sheath, with loomed quills laid onto a buckskin frame, was probably made in about 1860 for a Sheffield knife traded to Métis for furs.

Men wore a long hooded coat (*capote*) with a brightly coloured sash or belt, trousers and moccasins. Women wore European dresses, with shawls or **blankets** covering their head and shoulders, with moccasins. The red sash (*ceinture de fleché* or *L'Assomption* sash), which was adopted from the French and worn by many Indians from the fur trade era onwards, is an important symbol to Métis. Women were skilled **beadworkers** and they decorated moccasins, pouches and other items with floral designs. Fiddle **music** and step **dancing** became popular, a legacy of French and Scots heritage that remains important today in Métis communities.

In 1812 and again in the 1860s, the Métis found their way of life threatened. This was due to an influx of settlers onto lands given

**156 Right** An photograph of Louis Reil, the Métis leader, taken in 1868.

**157 Below** Maxim Marion, a Métis guide, is typical of mixed-blood children who became both a source of dispute and a bridge between their relatives. These children were 'between two worlds'. They understood the cultures of both their mother and their father and so became translators, guides and negotiators. This picture dates from 1872.

in 1812 and 1869 by the Hudson Bay Company to Scots settlers, 'the new Canadian government'. Métis communities turned to **farming** as the buffalo and other wildlife were hunted. They demanded **land rights** along the Red River in Alberta, a movement of 1885 known as the Northwest Rebellion.

It was during this period that Louis Reil emerged as a community leader in Alberta. He was educated in Montreal and was fluent in French, English and **Cree**. The Saskatchewan River Métis leader Gabriel Dumont called on the Red River leader Louis Reil to help in the land struggles. This uprising in 1870 forced

Reil into exile. Negotiations on Manitoba's entry into the Canadian Confederation called for an amnesty for all Métis involved in the rebellion. Even though he was exiled and so could not take up his seat, Reil was three times elected to the Parliament in Ottawa. Reil returned to Red River in 1885, seized a church and again proclaimed a provisional government. They demanded the right to govern themselves as well as to be represented in the Canadian Parliament.

After many months of skirmish, the Métis lost the rebellion at the Battle of Batoche. Dumont fled to the United States and worked in Buffalo Bill's Wild West Show (see **'Cowboys and Indians'**). Louis Reil surrendered and the government hanged him. Canada has recognized the importance of Louis Reil in the struggle for nationhood. His statue was recently erected in front of the Alberta Parliament buildings in Winnipeg, and the Canadian government apologized in 1998 for hanging him.

In 1991 approximately 75,000 people identified themselves as Métis, but it still remains unclear who should be considered Métis. Many people who are simply a mix of European and Native have begun to call themselves Métis, but they may not necessarily share the cultural heritage of the historical group. This definition can create tensions. A number of Métis organizations came together to define Métis as 'an aboriginal person who self-identifies as Métis and is a descendant of those Métis who were entitled to land grants or scrip under the provision of the Manitoba Act of 1870 of the Dominion Land Act'. In 1984, the Métis were officially included as a community in the Canadian Constitution.

Although there may be many people in the United States who are relatives of the Canadian Métis – usually referring to so-called 'landless Chippewa' in Montana and to the **reservation**-based Turtle Mountain Chippewa in North Dakota – the term still has little 'official', even unofficial, meaning in the United States.[35]

## Mi'kmaq/MicMac

The Mi'kmaq homelands lie on the East Coast of North America. The Mi'kmaq are closely related to neighbouring Malecite/ Maliseet, but are a more coastal people. In a Mi'kmaq **creation story**, Glooscap, the Mi'kmaq trickster/creator, transformed animals into their present shapes and taught humans how to make tools.

In the winter small groups of related families would gather. In the summer larger groups met, living in portable **bark**-covered wigwams. The sea was important for food and **transport**. Mi'kmaq made birchbark canoes, snowshoes and sleds like the other Algonquian peoples in the Northeast. They wore highly decorated hide clothing with dyed **quillwork**. After **contact** with Europeans, they used cloth decorated in a distinctive Mi'kmaq style with **beads**, ribbons and embroidery. The women's traditional high peaked caps of beaded and embroidered dark cloth (adapted from French women's clothing of the 17th century) and the adoption of Gaelic-influenced fiddle **music** and **dancing** show the considerable French influences on Mi'kmaq culture.

Each chief (*sagamore*) in the Mi'kmaq tribes held power over the group. In the 17th century a *sagamore* called Membertou recorded the first contact with the **explorer** Jacques Cartier in 1534. Intensive French colonization began in the early 17th century and the Mi'kmaq became French allies and partners in the **fur trade**. Their associations with the French drew them into conflict with the British and their **Iroquois** allies. Disputes between the British and French came to a temporary halt with the Treaty of Utrecht in 1713, and the French gained temporary control over Atlantic Canada. Tensions brought about the formation of the Wabenaki Confederacy, an alliance of Northeastern Algonkians, Mi'kmaq, Maliseet, Passamaquoddy, Penobscot and **Abenaki**. The **British** signed **treaties** with the Mi'kmaq in 1752; these formed the basis for the **Royal Proclamation** of 1763. Settlers poured into Mi'kmaq country and the Mi'kmaq lost much of their land, their role in the fur trade and their population due to **disease**.

Today 27 bands of Mi'kmaq live in three Maritime Provinces, in Québec and in Newfoundland. Their treaties have stood the test of time and Mi'kmaq traditional **hunting** and **fishing** rights have been protected by the Supreme Court of Canada. Many communities today are involved in the lumber industry, fishing, lobster trapping and the crafts industry. However, unemployment is still high on reserves and many people have moved to cities for work.

Politically very active, the Mi'kmaq created the Union of New Brunswick Indians and the Union of Nova Scotia Indians to help settle **land claims**. Today the Council acts as the political and religious leadership for the community.

## Missions/missionaries

Missions and missionaries, Catholic and Protestant, became one of the main and effective tools of the conquest of the Indians. From 1524, when the Spanish **explorer** Cortés first introduced missionization as a way to conquer Mexico, to the present day, when vast efforts continue in the Southwest to missionize the **Navajo** and Hopi, missionary activity has always accompanied the dismantling of traditional Indian society. The missionization of Indians, in South and North America, was thought of as pacification – peaceful conversion – as it was not supposed to need **war** in order for it to succeed. Often, however, Spanish efforts at conversion led to military action.

**158 Left** An 18th-century **trade** silver cross, probably brought by French Catholic brothers from France and given to **Mohawks** in Canada.

Many missionaries in Indian Country had military back-up, although missionaries and military men often felt that they were at odds with each others' methods and goals. In many instances, however, missionary zeal to convert and civilize Indians interfered with military and civilian force. This was the case of the Moravian, Baptist and Methodist

**159 Right** James Luna, a Luiseño (named after San Luis/Saint Louis) or 'Mission' Indian and artist from California, often explores aspects of Indian history. In *California Mission Daze*, he creates a graveyard. This is much as he imagines those graveyards next to the missions created by the friars for those Indians who died during their service to the missions.

**160 Below** California 'Mission' Indians, who were superb **basketmakers**, made this woven hat, with crosses woven into the basketry in the style of the hats of Spanish friars.

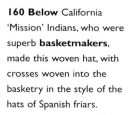

missionary stand against the Jackson administration and the state of Georgia in the issue of **Cherokee Removal**. Reverend Samuel Worcester was imprisoned by the state of Georgia for his acts in defence of the Cherokees. He insisted that **Christian** pacification was already working and he took cases to the Supreme Court to prove that point.

The people who came here with us have done grave injury to the Natives of this land. This brought great discredit to our teaching, for [the Indians] said that if we who are Christians caused so much harm, why should they become Christians?
*Fray (Friar) Francisco de Zamora, 1601*

An Indian listened to a long missionary sermon about Heaven and Hell and finally said to him, 'Pastor, when you die, will you go to Heaven?' And the minister said, 'Absolutely, I will go to Heaven'. And the Indian said, 'Well, if you are going to Heaven, then I believe I will go to Hell.'
*An old story that Indians like to tell*

Even before the Spanish established a permanent settlement in the Rio Grande Valley, between 1598 and 1680, Franciscan friars were sent to convert Indians. Their missions forced a different social order on the people and made them abandon their old way of life. They destroyed religious objects and shrines sacred to the Indians. Although there were laws to protect the Indians, missionaries and the colonists who followed them demanded labour and tributes from them in the form of **food** and **blankets**. The Pueblos resisted these efforts to change their lives, even taking to war in 1680 (the Pueblo Revolt) and driving the friars and the Spanish armies out of the Pueblo world, only to have them reintroduced 13 years later.

The Franciscan, Junipero Serra, went into California in 1769 with troops from the Vice-Regency of Spain. He built a mission system that depended on Indian labour and Indian lands. In the South and in the rich coastal areas of California, Indians were forced to support the military encampments, missions and towns developed by the Spanish. The Spanish and, later, the Mexicans moved Indians to villages near the towns and missions to continue their labour for the 'cross and the crown' and to work for the new generations of ranchers and businesspeople.

## Mohawk

The Mohawk occupied Eastern New York and were the most easterly nation of the **Iroquois Confederacy**. Their original name means 'people of the flint'. The Dutch and British called them 'Mohawk', meaning 'man eaters'. In the Confederacy Council, Mohawks are one of the three elder brothers along with **Seneca** and **Onondaga**. They have nine chiefs. They led the move to create the Confederacy and they remain dominant in Iroquois **diplomacy**.

As with all Iroquois nations, the Mohawk are **matrilineal**, with a life based on **agriculture**. They were among the first Iroquois nations to come into **contact** with Europeans. By allying themselves with Europeans, especially the Dutch, they could control access to **trade** routes. Mohawk communities adopted many of the the Huron and Neutral nations, which were dying out from **war** and **disease**. In the 18th century many Mohawks were converted to Catholicism by French Jesuit missionaries called 'black-robes'.

The British tried to win Mohawk support. During the American Revolution the Confederacy Council voted to remain neutral, however many tribes took sides in the conflict that tore the Confederacy apart. When the **British** lost the war, the Mohawks were forced out of the Mohawk Valley and followed **Joseph Brant** to negotiated lands in Ontario. Other Mohawks fled to Montreal, later settling at Tyendinaga, Oka and at Akwesasne. In 1993, a small group relocated back to the Mohawk Valley in New York State.

A century ago, Mohawk men found a niche as high steel construction workers and can be found working on large projects in the United States and Canada.

## Museums

The history of Indians and the history of museums are almost inseparable. The first museums in North America (Peale's Cabinet of Curiosities in Baltimore and the Smithsonian Institution) and in Britain (the Ashmolean) were built around their display of ancient artefacts gathered by naturalists and **explorers** on their travels. The earliest museums considered Indians to be part of the natural universe. They displayed geological specimens, animals, plants, Indian artefacts and skeletal remains. The presence and evidence of ancient people in North America intrigued and baffled early scientists or 'naturalists', and they collected specimens of all known species to study.

Explorers, artists and military men also collected objects **traded**, given by Indians or taken by force. In addition, **missionaries**, who urged Indians to give up the objects associated with a pagan culture, piled up collections of Indian artefacts.

Displayed first in private exhibitions, whether in the Great Houses of Britain or in Thomas Jefferson's Monticello, these objects then found their way into newly developed museums. Only in the late 19th century did the collection of American Indian objects become deliberate, and then associated with the archaeologists, anthropologists and private collectors such as General Pitt-Rivers, George Gustav Heye and Prince Maximillian von Wied. The Peabody in Boston, the American Museum of Natural History in New York, the Pitt-Rivers in Oxford, the Volkerkunde in Vienna, the museum at Cambridge University and the Carnegie in Pittsburgh, the Royal Ontario Museum and the Canadian Museum of Civilization all joined the Smithsonian and the British Museum as places where one would find Indians and all with which they were associated. These places became, alongside universities, centres for research on indigenous peoples of the world. Many places built their reputations on their displays of and research on Indians. The museum associated with the University of California at Berkeley even put an actual Indian on display when it 'collected' I*shi*, the 'last' Yahi Indian in California.

In the 20th century Native peoples began to question the ethics of collecting and displaying human ancestral remains, asking for their return to Indians. People all over the world then began to call for the return of objects obtained by **war** or force as well as the objects that represented important cultural and religious property. Thus, Indians

**161 Above Cree** from Hudson Bay made this set of nesting **birchbark baskets** decorated with porcupine **quills**. In the early 19th century an **exploring** sailor, Captain Middleton, acquired them. He inscribed them to 'Miss Nellie Middleton', but gave them instead to Sir Hans Sloane, the man whose collection established the foundation for the British Museum in London.

**162 Right** An early bone spoon (1702) from New England, from the collection of Sir Hans Sloane.

and museum curators, acknowledging that museums can return something – both materially and intellectually – to Indian Country. Some people have undertaken professional training in the last 15 years so that they can interpret and preserve Native history and cultural materials from a Native point of view.

Many museums in Britain, Canada and the United States now work closely with Native scholars, both academic and community-

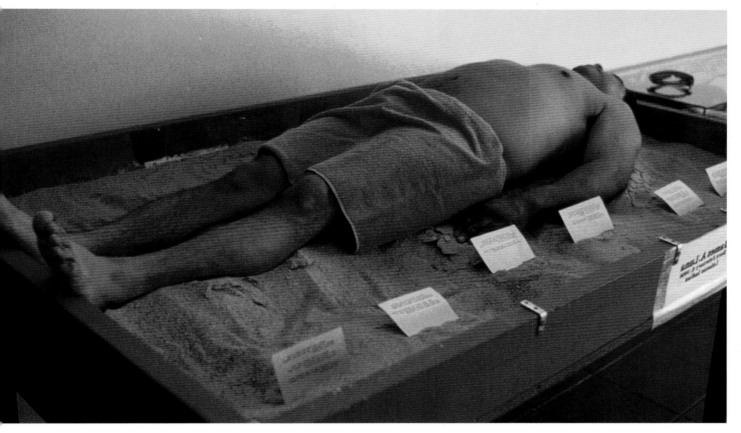

**163 Above** James Luna, in his 1987 performance theatre work, *The Artefact Piece*, makes himself into an object in a museum case. Around him are personal artefacts, such as his diploma, tapes from his music collection and family photographs. Commenting on non-Indians' obsession with dead Indians, Luna's work is about the relationships between Indians, Indian **'art'** and museums.

in the United States encouraged the Native American Graves and Repatriation Act 1990 to be passed by Congress, so that they might recover both their sacred and culturally important objects from museums.

Indians in many areas have now established museum-like institutions (cultural resource centres) which better fit their notions of what a cultural store should be. These are places where Native people interpret their lives and histories for an Indian and non-Indian audience. Many Native peoples now work closely with anthropologists, archaeologists, historians

based, to share materials and to produce exhibitions and programmes that reflect a new understanding of Indian life and history.

The British Museum's Ethnography Department collaborated with **Inuit** in the development of an exhibition 'The Living **Arctic**' in 1987. The Smithsonian's new museum, the National Museum of the American Indian, is curated largely by Natives. It promises to offer a partnership between Indians and museums that will reflect new ways of working and thinking about Native peoples.[36]

# Music

The way the Indian people, long ago, made their songs was by looking at what the Great Spirit gave them to understand in their minds… to make songs out of what they saw. Like the leaves when the wind blows, they're shaking; they make a little noise. That's how they got the idea to put bells on their legs. And sometimes you see a fowl, like an eagle, an owl, a chickenhawk. The Indian people looked at them, the way they'd sway their wings, how they'd go down and up. That's how they'd make the pitch of their songs… and everything they'd see; when they looked at the sky, the clouds, they'd make songs out of those… . And they'd think that there's kind of a holy spirit going round, and that's how they'd make their songs.

*Fred Benjamin, a Mille Lacs Ojibwe elder,* 1984

Indian music, like Indian **dance**, is connected to specific tribal traditions, usually religious. Music accompanied **ceremonies**, **games**, stories and dance. Tribal groups developed musical forms very specific to them, modified and adopted from other groups (Indian and non-Indian) with whom they had **contact**, **trade**, **intermarriage** and even **war**. The distinctive regional and tribal styles exist and thrive, along with more '**pan-Indian**' and intertribal music, such as **pow wow** war dance songs.

Whenever corn [maize] is being ground, there are certain things that go with it, and so the woman never tires out in grinding corn. She can grind it for three or four hours straight, because while she grinds, the men come and sing. And in the grinding songs they tell you almost what to do. And you have to grind to the beat, to the rhythm of the songs… . And in the singing, it tells you to keep grinding, and you grind in rhythm. It's a beautiful song. I think it's all in Laguna.

*Agnes Dill, Isleta Pueblo*

Most Native peoples sing Protestant and Catholic hymns and gospel music in the various Indian **languages**. There are special tribal versions of mainstream songs, such as 'Amazing Grace'. **Mi'kmaq**, **Métis**, **Creeks**, **Cherokees** and **Ojibwa** adopted fiddle music from French, Scottish and Irish traditions. They even took the Gaelic styles of step dancing from those traditions. In the Southwest and California, Mexican Indian and Spanish music from 19th-century Mexico influenced and merged with some California Indian music.

Indian professional musicians have mixed European and Indian styles of music and instruments, incorporating rock and roll, rhythm and blues, jazz, reggae, folk and even classical music. Guitars, synthesizers and keyboards, in addition to the horns and strings adopted in the 19th century, supplement **drums**, **rattles** and **flutes**.

'Traditional' Native music has experienced a revival. Modern Native music, meant to appeal to a non-Indian audience too, has also grown. There are Native recording companies and Native radio stations. Indian musical events, such as pow wows, are likely to feature everything from flute players to blues singers along with different styles of traditional tribal dance music.

We make all our own songs. The songs just come to you. You have to wait for them. We practice and teach each other. Our songs are in Cree and the other ladies are real good. They learn to sing the songs in Cree and we sing some songs in Nakota.

*Celina Jones, Cree, leader of the Crying Woman drum group, Fort Belknap, Montana*

When the dance is over, Sweetheart, I will take you home, in my one-eyed [one headlight] Ford.
…
I'm from Oklahoma, Got no-one to call my own, So, I come here looking for you, *heya.*
…
I don't care if you're married, I'll get you anyway.
…
BIA, I ain't your Indian anymore, So farewell, goodbye to you, *heya.*
*Oklahoma-style intertribal social dance songs, sung in English, called 'Forty-Nine's'*

## Names

Names given to the indigenous peoples of the Americas, at various places and times, by specific groups of people:
aboriginal/aborigine, Amerindian, *barbaros* (Spanish for 'barbarous'), First Americans, First Nations, Indian, indigenous, *indios* (Spanish for 'in or with God'), Native American, Original, redskins, savage/*sauvage*.

I'm just glad Columbus wasn't looking for Turkey!
*Indian car sticker*, c. 1975

Names given to some specific Indian peoples or types of people, often generally applied to any male, female or child:
brave, buck, Chief, King, maiden, papoose, Princess, squaw, Queen.

Names translated from French or Spanish, or in English about misunderstood or caricatured physical characteristics or relationships:
**Blackfeet/Blackfoot**, Flatheads, Gros Ventres (French for 'big bellies'), Nez Perce (French for 'pierced noses'), peaux rouge (French for 'red skin'), redskin.

Names given to **sports** teams and mascots in the United States:
Braves/Chief Noc-A-Homa, Chief Wahoo, Indians, Little Red, Redskins, Savages, Seminoles/Sammy Seminole.

Names given to specific groups of indigenous people, alongside the names those people called and call themselves:
**Aleut** – Alutiiq, Unangan, Suqpiaq, Sasignan
**Cherokee** – Tsa-la-gi – Aniyunwiya
Cheyenne – Tsististas
Chippewa – **Ojibwa**/Ojibwe – Anishinabe, Shinnob (Ojibwe slang)
Crow – Absaroke
Huron – Wyandotte – Wendat
**Iroquois** – Hodenosaunee
**Navajo** – Diné
Nootka – Nuu-chah-nulth
Petun – Tiontati
Pojoaque Pueblo – Po'sua'geh (Spanish for 'town dwellers'), San Juan Pueblo – Oke Okweenge, Santa Clara – Kha'po
Winnebago – Ho-Chunk.

In Canada, the current official term for specific tribal peoples recognized by the Canadian government is 'First Nations'. This term acknowledges the **sovereign status** of the Native people and the nation-to-nation relationship of the Native peoples, their governments and the national governments of the countries. Much like any **diplomatic** acknowledgement of one country to another, France to England for example, 'First Nations' suggests that these people were 'first' on the land that was once all theirs. This means that these nations enjoy equal status. In everyday speech about Native peoples, Canadians tend to use the words 'Native', 'aboriginal' and 'First Nations'.

In the United States, the current 'official' term for North American indigenous people is 'Native American'. First developed out of a concern that 'Indian' was inappropriate, the term 'Native American' allowed people to avoid specifying 'North American Indians, Aleuts and Eskimos' (the three distinct groups that were formerly classed together under the word 'Indian'). However, in official regulations and law the term 'Native American' now applies to all government-recognized 'Indians' as well as to Native Hawaiians. Most American Indians prefer to refer to their tribal names, using the general term 'Indian' and, more rarely, 'Native American' in everyday speech.

Names in North America that come from Indian sources:
Alabama – Alibamu
Alaska – Alutiiq or **Inuit**
Illinois – Illini
kayak – Inuit
Massachusetts, Michigan, moccasin, racoon, **squash**, pecan, toboggan, caucus, chipmunk, moose – Algonkian
Nebraska – Sioux or Otoe
Oklahoma – Choctaw for 'red people'
Ohio – Iroquois
Tallahassee – Muskogee for 'old town'
Tennessee – Cherokee/*tanasi*.

Words from other Native languages became part of the standard US vocabulary as early as the 18th century. Most of these words remained as neutral descriptive words. For example the Algonquian 'moccasin' came to mean any style of Indian hide shoe and 'papoose' became a way of describing a baby or any Indian baby no matter what the tribe. However, the word 'squaw', which was an Algonquian word that meant 'a married or distinguished woman', came to have a negative meaning as an insult to Indian women. In the 19th century, there were two very separate images of Indian women common among non-Indians. The first was that Indian women were violent, degraded and filthy creatures, who were brutal to captives. The second was that Indian women were beautiful and pure princesses, like **Pocahontas**, who were kind to whites. These romantic ideals often had the fair-skinned Princess suffer a tragic death, separated from her usually white lover by a cruel world. Sadly, the once honourable Algonquian word 'squaw', widely adopted to apply to non-Algonquian Native women, remains a term of derision for Native women.

## Native American Church and the 'peyote' religion

Native religious practices, whether ancient or new, always aroused suspicion and fear in non-Indians. **Missionaries** and military leaders saw it as a form of resistance as well as 'savagery'. From the **Handsome Lake**/Longhouse religion of the **Iroquois** to that preached by the Shawnee Prophet, from the **Dream Dance** of the **Algonquian** peoples to the **Ghost Dance** of the Plains, religious belief inspired Indians to fight and resist white encroachment on their **land** and on their lives. No religious movement inspired more negative reaction from whites than the Peyote Way.

Peyotism is a religious practice in which the hallucinogenic cactus is used to bring on dreams and visions. It started in Mexico and spread to the Mescalero **Apaches**, Comanches, Caddoes and Kiowas in the mid 19th century. By the late 19th century, thousands of Winnebagos, Menominees, Pawnees, Cheyennes, Arapahos and Shoshones had converted to peyotism. In the mid 20th century, more than 80 tribes were involved in some sort of peyotism. In 1944, to survive opposition to it, followers of the Peyote Way developed the practice into a formal religion called the Native American Church. They stated their need to protect their sacrament, peyote, in the same way that the use of sacramental wine was protected under the First Amendment to the US

Constitution. The multi-tribal officials of the Native American Church tried to put themselves and their religion under the protection of the US government by incorporating the Native American Church in the state of Oklahoma.

Several tribal governments passed regulations prohibiting the use of peyote, as did states and territories. Peyotists and tribal nationalists joined together to protect their Constitutional rights to the freedom of religion. The fight of the Native American Church for survival led to increased lobbying for political rights of all sorts. In 1964, the California Supreme Court upheld peyotism, a decision that was seen as a victory for religious freedom. Despite their religious practices being legal, members of the Native American Church remain stigmatized in US society, and are often denied jobs by public institutions, such as state governments and schools.

**164 Right** Members of the Native American Church put images of 'peyote' or 'water birds', and other ritual images of the Native American Church, on jewellery such as these German silver earrings and on **drums**. Connected with the cleansing power of water in prayer, the birds act as spirits to convey prayers and visions.

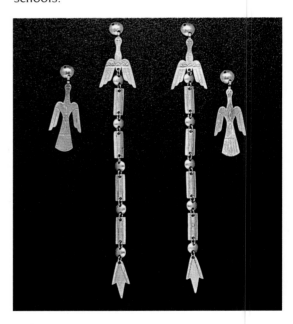

## Navajo

Navajo, Diné or 'The People', believe the Holy People created them and placed them on Earth. They emerged through a reed, having journeyed through the underworlds (the Black World, the Blue World and the Yellow World). Finally they came to the present world (*Dinétah*) in Northwest New Mexico. The 'Holy People' served as disciples to Mother Earth by taking the form of wind, **rain**, thunder, lightning and snow. They defined the Navajo homeland by designating the Four Sacred Mountains – Sierra Blanca Peak to the east (Colorado), Mount Taylor to the south (New Mexico), San Francisco Peaks to the west (Arizona) and the La Platas to the north (Colorado). *Shii'kayah* ('my home') is what the Navajos call this landscape of valleys, plains, *mesas* (hills) and mountains.

Now the largest American Indian tribe in the United States, the modern Navajo Nation has shaped itself through three centuries of changing relationships with their Pueblo neighbours. War with the Spanish, and, later, the United States, forced education, religious change and **relocation**. Most Navajos now live as part of large extended families. Although jobs for wages are the main source of income, most families still **farm**, keep livestock, weave and make jewellery. The Navajo Nation has its own **sovereign tribal government** recognized by the Treaty of Bosque Redondo (see the **Long Walk**), made with the United States in 1868. It operates its own **schools**, police and courts, a tribal college system, industries and businesses, spread over Arizona and New Mexico.

**A**s humans, we are part of Mother Earth. Animals and insects emerged through the four worlds from the pit of the earth. The Holy People created First Man and First Woman, who gave flesh to the Navajo people. We are told our legs are made from earth, our midsection is from water, our lungs from air, and our head is made out of heat and it is placed close to the Father Sun. We are known as the On-Earth Holy People. For that reason, our skin is brown like the earth. A child has certain similarities to the Mother.
*Bennie Silversmith, medicine man and herbalist, Pine Springs, Arizona*

Navajos have been subjected to strict government policies on land and land use. They still object to the policy of forced stock reduction due to overgrazing in the 1930s and 1950s. They believe that a reduction in the number of sheep causes the rains and vegetation to diminish. In addition, many Navajo were relocated in the 1950s to traditional Hopi lands by the government. This was encouraged by the large mining companies that wanted access to the emptied lands. They joined the Navajos who had been living on lands partitioned to the Hopi Reservation when it was formed in 1882.

Each tribe believes the land has always been theirs. From 1930, the Hopi government tried to recover those lands where Navajos were living – even though they had been designated a 'joint use' area. The government split the jointly used lands into equal parts and forced 8,000 Navajos to relocate.

**T**o the federal government, there is the written law…. For centuries, to us, the law is what is out here… the law of Mother Earth. The Holy People placed us here as a people and we abide by their instructions. When you live in harmony with the land, no-one fights, no-one argues and everyone is happy. That is *hozhone*. But when people begin to argue and fight, the Wind People report to the Holy People of our discontent, That's when rain is withheld…. I think Mother Earth hears about this dispute and doesn't appreciate it. We don't get as much rain as we once did.
*Jesse Biakeddy, Big Mountain*

## Northwest Coast

The area generally called the Northwest Coast is made up of rainforests that follow the Pacific shore from Southeast Alaska to Northwest California. Native cultures in these areas have access to rich resources from the sea and forests. Coastal groups also extend inland up the major rivers. A variety of **languages** and customs exist among communities, but they share a similar cultural pattern. In this region, 17 languages were once spoken. In the north are the **Haida** and Tsimshian (divided into three languages) and the Tlingit of Alaska. In the central region are the Kwakwaka'wakw (three languages), Nuu-chah-nulth (two languages) and Bella Coola (a Northern group of **Salish** speakers). In the Southern area are the speakers of six related languages called 'Coast Salish'.

The sea provides **salmon**, clams, sea lions and seals. Large cedar trees are used to build houses and for carving. There are complex political structures, with chiefdoms and inherited classes of nobility and commoners. Their lavish **ceremonial** life included huge feasts to show status, distribution of goods and **dancing**. Since the end of suppression in the Northwest – during which the government removed ceremonial regalia and banned the **potlatch** and traditional **subsistence** methods – a cultural resurgence is taking place, with **art** traditions noted worldwide.

Fishing and some logging continue to be the main **economies** of the area and **land claims** remain one of the key issues affecting Northwest Coastal groups. The entry of British Columbia into the Canadian Confederation in 1871 shifted responsibility for Natives to the Canadian government. The Nishga and Gitsan-Wet'suwet'en took their land claims cases to the Supreme Court of Canada. In 1997, the Court decided that they had aboriginal title to the land and that history passed by word of mouth could be used as evidence. In addition, the **Haida** and Nuu-chah-nulth have led highly publicized demonstrations protesting against logging in their traditional territory. Northwest Coast groups are also active in national debates on constitutional issues and **self-determination** issues in Canada. The Sechelt, a Coastal Salish group, negotiated their own self-government agreement with the Canadian government. They are now free to develop their lands as they wish because they are exempted from the Indian Act. The government has also transferred ownership of the reserve lands to the band.

**165 Below** Nunavut, the Inuit homeland, created in 1999.

## Nunavut

In 1999, the **Inuit** homeland of Nunavut ('Our Land' in the Inuktitut language) came into existence. The Inuit of the Western **Arctic** signed an agreement in 1984, surrendering their aboriginal title (ancient right to the land) in exchange for US$445 million in compensation and title to 770,000 square miles. The agreement gives the Inuit rights to the resources below the surface of the Arctic as well as **hunting** and **fishing** rights. The lands formerly known as the Northwest Territories are now split in two, separating Inuit from the Dené, **Métis** and settlers. This division creates an Inuit majority homeland with political and economic **sovereignty** similar to other Canadian provinces. The split is costly as no political, social or economic structure existed in the territory and has to be created from scratch. Although at the beginning, the territory is 95 percent dependent on the rest of Canada for maintenance, there are plans to develop the **economy**. The new capital is in Iqaluit, a community of 3,552 people.

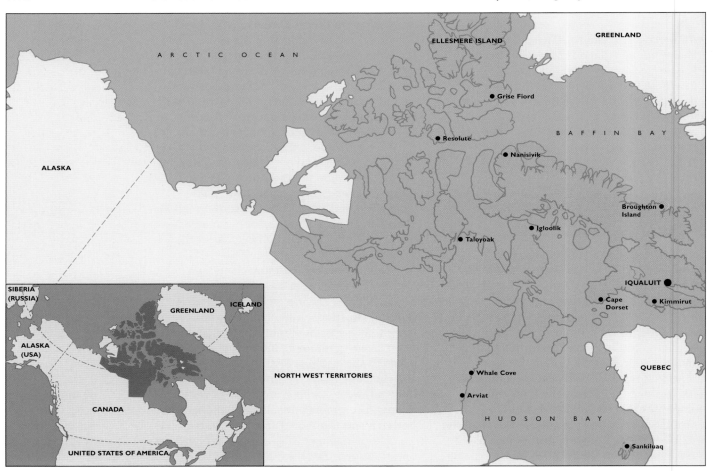

## Ojibwa/Anishinabe/ Chippewa/Saulteaux/ Nipissing/Mississauga

The early homeland of the Ojibwa was along the Northern shores of Lake Huron and Lake Superior. The major **fishing** and cultural centre was located at Sault St Marie. Their territory then extended dramatically and some moved southeast into the **Iroquois** lands of Southern Ontario. Others pushed west to Wisconsin and Minnesota, displacing the Dakota people.

The **fur trade** lured many groups far north and west in search of new trap lines (the areas and technologies for trapping fur-bearing animals) and some even spread onto the Plains. The Ojibwa groups then adapted to their new environments and cultural differences emerged between groups. The Ottawa (Odawa), whose lifestyle and language were virtually the same as the neighbouring Ojibwa and Potawatomi people of Lake Michigan, occupied much of the Northern shore of Georgian Bay as well as the Bruce Peninsula bordering on the Huron and Petun people. The three groups remained allied in a loose Confederacy known as the Council of Three Fires.

When Europeans arrived, many separate groups gradually became known collectively as the Ojibwa. Although the groups did not have a common national identity, a cultural and national identity is forming today in Canada under the term 'Anishinabe (Original) Nation' for all groups speaking the Ojibwa **language**. Linguists class the Ojibwa, Ottawa and Algonquian into a single language group with numerous dialects. In Canada, the **Cree** are also almost indistinguishable from the northern Ojibwa and many communities today are considered Oji-Cree, having members from both groups.

Intermarriage and common cultural traditions link these communities. Each community had its own chief and hunting territory. Bands stayed in family hunting units for much of the year, assembling in great numbers only during late spring and summer. The patrilineal society, divided into **clans**, had an informal leadership, with chiefs holding power by virtue of skill in **hunting**, **warfare** and medicine. By the mid 17th century, the fur trade took over the **subsistence** lifestyle, based on hunting, **fishing**, the tapping of maple sap for sugar

and the harvesting of berries and **wild rice**.

Traditionally, Ojibwa made birch**bark** canoes to travel rivers and lakes. In the winter, people travelled by snowshoe and sled. Ojibwa wigwams, both temporary and portable, reflected their mobility. They used dome-shaped structures with layers of birchbark and moss as insulation. By the 19th century, tipis covered in birchbark became popular. Women made winter clothing from tanned hides of moose and deer and hats and mittens lined with **beaver** or **rabbit** fur. Clothes were decorated with dyed porcupine **quills** and, when traders arrived with **beads**, with elaborate beaded patterns.

Large summer camps allowed for feasting, **dancing**, lacrosse playing, **gambling** and for young people to meet and arrange marriages. Storytelling was also an important pastime with tales of supernatural beings such as Nanabush (the terrifying Windigo, a giant with a hunger for human flesh), the thunderbirds (that controlled the weather) and the Mishipisu (a large water serpent). They believed that every object or animal possessed a spirit (*manitou*) and offerings such as tobacco had to be given to calm them. The ultimate and most sacred force was the *Kitchi Manitou* (the Great Spirit), often identified as the sun. Widely respected for their spiritual power, many asked the Ojibwa to cure illness and provide charms for hunting. They developed a formal organization of shamans (Indian doctors or healers) called 'Midéwiwin' or the Grand Medicine Society. Its primary purpose was to heal, but it became the main expression of the Ojibwa religion.

Today, Ojibwa people struggle to protect hunting and fishing rights and to settle **land claims** issues. Casinos are also rapidly changing the life on many **reservations**.

## Oka

After the Europeans' arrival, the strategic position of the town of Oka (close to where the Ottawa and St Lawrence Rivers cross) helped the **Iroquois** to control the **fur trade**. However, in 1717, the King of France granted the lands to a **missionary** group, the Seminary of St Sulpice. Although many **Mohawk** peoples were converted to Catholicism and taken to the mission, other Mohawk people already lived in the area and challenged the mission's ownership of the

# Oneida

Living between the **Mohawk** and **Onondaga** Nations are the Oneida. Their original name means 'people of the standing stone'. They have nine chiefs represented in the Confederacy Council and are the 'Younger Brothers' along with the **Cayugas**. Together with the Tuscaroras, they sided with the colonists in the American Revolution, playing key roles in guaranteeing victory on behalf of the Americans and enduring terrible loss of life in the process. The 1784 Treaty of Fort Stanwix was to have guaranteed them lands in exchange for their loyalty. However, New York State ignored this treaty and the Oneida steadily lost land. Most were removed to either Wisconsin or Ontario, although some remain in New York.

Throughout constant change and **Removal**, the Oneida have struggled to preserve their **language** and their cycle of Longhouse **ceremonies**. Today casinos provide important sources of income and employment for the Wisconsin Oneida.

# Onondaga

The Onondaga Nation ('People of the Hills') occupies the geographic centre of the **Iroquois Confederacy**. Within their communities, all nine **clans** are found. The Onondaga were among the strongest voices supporting a position of neutrality during the American Revolution. They were attacked by the revolutionary forces whose leaders assumed they were supporting the **British**. After the war, they entered into **treaties** with New York State that gave them lands near Syracuse, New York, while some members relocated to the Grand River in Canada. The Onondaga continue to host meetings of the Confederacy and act as 'fire keepers' who keep the symbolic Council fire burning.

The Onondaga have long rejected attempts to install an elected government and instead have kept their traditional systems. Since the 1960s they have also been a major force in the fight for **sovereignty** and have challenged military service and other government and state controls over them, their land and their religious life. Since 1994, they have refused any state or government grants of money which they believe would compromise their independence and sovereignty. They have launched **land claims** to regain their original territory.

**166 Above** In 1990, Alice Olsen Williams (Anishinabe) of Curved Lake, Ontario, made this quilt called *The Tree of Peace Saves the Earth*. The quilt uses pictures from a traditional **Iroquois** story with a new image of the Oka dispute. The Tree of Peace, emerging from the mud on the back of Grandmother Turtle (Earth) and spreading its White Roots of Peace among the nations, shoots up through the Canadian Parliament building. Beneath the tree, **war** clubs are buried. On top, the **eagle's** heart is a circle with the Four Directions and colours, a symbol often used by US and Canadian Indian political activists.

Oka lands. In 1841, the Canadian government confirmed that the land belonged to the religious order, but the right of Native people to live on the land was never disputed. This conflict arose again in 1881. Some Mohawk families moved to Gibson, Ontario; others decided to stay. In 1912, the Judicial Council decided that the land belonged entirely to the Seminary.

The Mohawks of Kanesatake (Oka) and two other Mohawk communities repeatedly made **land claims**, stating that they had first rights to significant areas of land. The most fierce conflict over this land erupted on 11 March 1990, over the plans to expand Oka's golf course onto land considered a sacred religious burial site. Mohawks and other Natives erected a road blockade. The Québec Provincial Police were summoned to tear it down, and a police officer was shot and killed. Although the siege ended after 78 days, the land issue at Oka still remains unresolved to the satisfaction of both communities.

## Pan-Indianism

Indians had been meeting and mixing with one another for centuries before **contact** with Europeans. Many developed mutually understood **languages**, such as **trade** languages and sign language, to communicate with each other. They shared and traded songs, **dances** and stories. Different groups formed alliances and friendships. Some eventually lived and merged with each other, having been driven from their homes by famine, **disease**, drought and **war**. When **schooling** was made compulsory in the late 18th century and when various groups were forced together through imprisonment, **Removal** and **reservationization**, a type of forced intertribalism became common.

New types of 'Indian' behaviour emerged. Indian peoples who were once very different began to adopt each other's vocabularies (like the so-called meaningless sounds and words of **pow wow** songs), clothing styles (such as ribbon shirts), **foods** (such as frybread) and even jokes. This common behaviour is often called 'pan-Indianism'. It has often been used in an insulting way to describe actions, social styles and language that is not particular to one tribe, but which is mixed. It has been applied to people who do not speak their tribal languages and who were raised not with a specific culture (such as Otoe, **Navajo** or Karok), but as 'Indians' – vaguely Siouan or Plains in cultural style (those being the dominant styles in pan-Indianism). However, instead of weakening specific tribal cultures, these these new intertribal behaviours have often brought Indians together, and given them a strong unified voice on political issues.

## Parka

'Parka' is the general **Inuit**/Inupiaq name for an overcoat. It is used in English to describe a hooded coat now made in cotton and synthetic materials as well as the traditional hide, and worn by Inuit of the **Arctic** and non-Indians. Although styles of parkas differ in the various areas of Canada, Greenland and the United States, they are important among all the Inuit. Parkas are necessary for survival in the Arctic and making them, even the new 'show' parkas, exemplifies a woman's role and her skills as a seamstress. The demand for 'fancy' parkas from the oil and communications line workers from the United States and Europe, who went to the Arctic in the 1950s, helped to rejuvenate nearly abandoned skills. Some styles of parkas embody a woman's role as giver of life, with the apron flap (*kiniq*) as a symbol of childbirth. The long back tail represents animals, the Inuit source of fur, oil, hide, bones and meat. The carrying pouch (*amauti*) works like a **baby carrier**, but is built into the garment.

**167 Left** A Copper **Inuit** woman's parka and pants. Copper Inuit live in the far west of the Canadian **Arctic**, in the Northwest Territories, now the independent province of Nunavut. In world of tundra, forest tundra, fresh water lakes and rivers and ocean, people use the rich animal life of musk ox, caribou, seal, mink, squirrel, wolverine, **wolf** and freshwater **fish** to support their needs for **food**, clothing and shelter. For clothing nowadays, Copper Eskimos also use **dog** skins, commercially tanned hides and imitation fur.

How sweet he is when he smiles
With two teeth like a little walrus.
Ah, I like my little one to be heavy
And my hood to be full.
A *Thule Inuit lullaby*

**168 Right** Nora Ann Rexford-Leavitt, Inupiaq, from Barrow, Alaska, made this new woman's fancy parka in 1997. Made from wolf, wolverine, muskrat and calfskin, the **wolf** ruff helps protect the face from the cold **Arctic** wind. Wolf and wolverine furs do not ice up with condensation from breath.[37]

**169 Below** This waterproof **Aleut** gut parka was made by cleaning yards of intestine (perhaps walrus), drying and bleaching it, cutting it into strips and sewing it together with sinew. Aleut **medicine** men and dancers in **ceremonies** may have worn them. They are sometimes worn on St Laurence Island to honour the walrus god, the master of the sea. They are often decorated with **feathers** and animal/bird parts.[38]

# Photography

American Indians are among the most photographed peoples of the world. From the time photography was invented in the mid 19th century, people built their artistic reputations on their pictures of Indians. Men such as Edward Curtis began, like the painters before and after them, to document and stage a beautiful world that they believed was on the verge of extinction. Their photographs continue to offer a portrait of Indians that most people (including many Native people) use to define the 19th-century and present-day Indian world.

Native peoples' attitudes to the camera were complex. Many believed it to be a powerful magical 'soul-stealer' from which they must hide. Others saw it as an intruder in their ceremonial, family and community life. Others would come to be grateful for its record of their ancestors and hang those pictures on their walls. Later in the 20th century, many banned the camera and outside photographers from their villages, their **ceremonies** and their private lives.

Since the early part of the 20th century, the number of Native photographers has grown. Some, out of a passionate interest in their own communities, document the daily lives of their people. One such photographer was Horace Poolaw (1906–84), a Kiowa, who was an aerial photographer in the **Second World War**. When he returned home, he wanted to show life as the Kiowas, Comanches, **Apaches** and Delawares in Southwestern Oklahoma were living it in those times – as a remarkable mixture of old and new, traditional and progressive, **Christian** and pagan, and **farmers** and horsemen. From the memorial feast at the Rainy Mountain Baptist Church to Lizzie Little Joe with her high heels and **baby carrier**; from Poolaw and his friends in the nose cone of a B-52 bomber to his Mexican captive grandmother, the best **beadworker** in the town; from the beef jerky drying at one families' butchering site to the parade featuring three Kiowa Princesses, Poolaw made an enormous record of the changes and character of the world he understood.

Some took pictures of the world as outsiders. Others made their pictures a commentary (often humorous) on the history and politics of Indian life and on the history of photographing Indians.[39]

**170 Right** *Watcheye II: Mary Matinaas* (1996) is a silver print by Greg Staats, a **Mohawk** and professional photographer, who was born in 1963 on the Six Nations Reserve in Southwestern Ontario. Staats' work includes portraits, especially of elders, who he sees as a 'living history; a link with the past and into the future'.

**171 Below** *The Iroquois is a Matriarchal Society* by Shelley Niro, a **Mohawk**. Her work explores issues of identity, stereotypes, history and the environment through the use of humour. She shows the contrast between the idea of the **Iroquois** as a matriarchal (see **matrilineality**) society and this Iroquois woman under her hair dryer.

**172 Above** Kiowa Group in American Indian Exposition Parade, Anadarko, taken in 1941 by Horace Poolaw.

## Pipes

Most Native peoples engaged in some form of smoking for ritual, **diplomatic** and social purposes. Consequently, pipe-making and the accessories associated with pipes developed into an important artform.

On the Northern Plains, many peoples used pipes, usually made of wood with a stone bowl. Smoking the pipe, whether alone or with several people, was a means of seeking assistance from spirits and the **tobacco** used was a form of prayer or way of communicating with those spirits. Many peoples used the **medicine** pipe in healing. Europeans mistakenly called all pipes 'peace pipes' because Indians would use the smoking of the pipe, passed among groups of men in discussion, as a symbol of good feeling between the parties.[40]

I watched the old Sioux men carve and learned from them. The quarry is sacred ground. I make my offerings before I go. Back at my home, I say a prayer with the stone. The Sioux have always carved. In earlier times, a holy woman gave us the pipe, with instructions as to how we should live; the pipe has meaning to our people today. The pipe provides guidance, shows us a way of life. When we travel, we place the pipe on the dashboard of our car, and they watch over us.
*Amos Owen, Dakota elder*

The Lakota considered smoking with others a way of affirming the truth and believed that the 'Way of the Pipe' was given to them by White Buffalo Calf Woman.

Then she gave something to the chief, and it was a pipe with a bison [buffalo] calf carved on one side to mean the earth that bears and feeds us, and with twelve eagle feathers hanging from the stem to mean the sky and the twelve moons, and these were tied with a grass that never breaks. 'Behold!', she said. 'With this you shall multiply and be a good nation. Nothing but good shall come from it.' Then she sang again and went out of the teepee, and as people watched her going, suddenly it was a white bison galloping away and snorting, and soon it was gone.
*Black Elk* (c. 1863–1950), *Lakota medicine man*

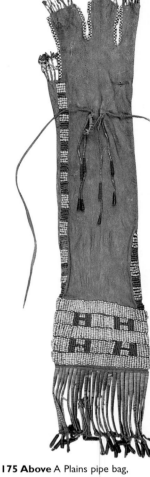

**173 Below** An **Ojibwa** pipe and bowl.

**174 Below** An early **Mi'kmaq** stone pipe bowl.

**175 Above** A Plains pipe bag, shown from the back, where it can be tied to a belt.

The Lakota had men called pipe carriers, who carried the pipes used only in **ceremonies** in highly decorated **beaded**, **quilled** and painted pipe bags. These bags also held tobacco and various small tools associated with smoking and cleaning the pipe. The stem and the fragile bowl are kept separately and joined only when they are used in ceremonies.

**176 Right** The classic and best-known image of Pocahontas in the court dress, fashionable hat and ruff of Elizabethan England. Like two other images of Pocahontas, a popular engraving of *Pocahontas Saving Captain John Smith* and the painting *The Baptism of Pocahontas*, this one has no basis in reality as no-one made portraits of her from life.

*Ætatis suæ 21. Aº. 1616.*

Matoaks als Rebecka daughter to the mighty Prince Powhatan Emperour of Attanoughkomouck als Virginia converted and baptized in the Christian faith, and Wife to the wor.ᵗˡᵉ Mʳ Tho: Rolff.

## Pocahontas

Pocahontas, or *Matoaka*, was born in about 1595, the young daughter of the leader of several **Algonquian** tribes in Southeast Virginia. When the **British** came to her country in 1619, she became a figure in 'American' legend, known less for her real role in history than for her symbolic role representing the relationships between the new colonists and Indians. Few facts are known about her. Captured by the British visitors in order to force land agreements with her father and his tribesmen, she was eventually married to a colonist, John Rolfe, in order to forge an alliance between the British and the Indians. She travelled to England with Rolfe. She was baptized as a **Christian**, presented in the Court of Elizabeth I, had a son, caught smallpox and died in England in about 1617.

Captain John Smith's version of Pocahontas' story in his *Generall Historie of Virginie* of 1624 tells of a girl smitten with Englishmen, who intervenes in Smith's

**177 Right** In 1997 Murv Jacob, a **Cherokee** artist and illustrator, took the standard painting of Pocahontas in her Elizabethan clothing, and restored her in his fantasy painting to a true daughter of the Southeast. Still in her English and **Christian** clothes, she now appears on the arm of **Rabbit** (the trickster hero of Southeastern Indians), instead of with John Rolfe or John Smith. Jacob has darkened her skin and made her features more Indian. Rabbit wears his traditional 16th-century style Cherokee clothes, including his **dance** apron and engraved gorget made from freshwater pink mussel **shell**.

execution by throwing herself between him and her father's tomahawk. Her father, the Powhatan, is forced to make peace with the Englishmen. Pocahontas marries John Rolfe, goes to England and becomes a Christian.

An Indian, specifically an Algonquian, version of the story presents a very different picture. In that version, Powhatan chooses John Smith to be adopted in a ritual way into his family. As a woman of some status, the daughter of the tribe's leader would have acted as his 'mother' so that he could be reborn, after his ritual death, as one of the tribe. At that time, Algonquian, **Iroquoian** and **Cherokee** people honoured the wishes of women with respect to the fate of captives. Women could determine whether captives would live or die. Captives chosen to live could be adopted as a son or daughter by a childless woman or one who had lost a child

to **disease** or **war**. Whatever the case, the adoption **ceremony** often involved symbolic death and rebirth. That is what happened to John Smith. Rather than Pocahontas betraying her own people, as Smith portrayed it, she was attempting to make him become one of them. This would have forced the British and the Indians to cease competition and behave like relatives toward one another, with mutual responsibilities and obligations.

The story of Pocahontas as told by John Smith, in school books, in hundreds of paintings and pictures, and recently by the Disney Corporation in a 1997 film, is very nearly an American **creation** or **origin story**. The story of Pocahontas made legitimate the European presence and the mixing of European and Indian heritage. Pocahontas makes the colonists (and so the takeover of Indian lands) welcome.[41]

## Political activism, 1880–1980

Indians engaged in political action from their first **contact** with Europeans. Indians have always tried to intervene in the political decisions that affected them, by actual physical resistance in the first few hundred years, by **diplomacy** in the 19th century and by intellectual resistance and reform in the early 20th century. Writers, doctors, lawyers, social workers and politicians have followed and replaced the **war** chiefs as the defenders of Native rights.

Members of the Omaha LaFlesche family – Susan (a doctor), Suzette (a journalist) and Francis (a scholar) – put their talents to use in influencing the outcome of the 1879 court decision over *Standing Bear v. General George Crook*. When the Ponca people were removed from their Nebraska homelands, reformers were sure that the Omahas would be the next to follow them. When Standing Bear and other Poncas tried to return home, they were arrested. The LaFlesche family and other activists backed the Ponca cause. The *Standing Bear* case went to court and proved to be one of the most significant legal decisions in civil rights law for Indians, as it established that an Indian is a person before the law and has the right to seek legal redress before the court.

At the start of the 20th century, a group of Indian activists, including Carlos Montezuma and Charles Eastman, organized the Society of American Indians (SAI). These educated people gathered to lobby for Indian **self-determination**. Gertrude Simmons Bonnin (*Zitkala-sa*) (1876–1938), a Yankton **Sioux** woman, joined them in their cause. She helped organize the modern Indian reform and **pan-Indian** movement and began taking an active role in the SAI's business. Eventually, she moved to Washington, D.C., where she wrote works supporting Indian **citizenship**, and **land** and **water rights**. In 1926, she formed the National Congress of American Indians, which is still a major Indian lobbying group, and became its President with her husband as Secretary.

In the mid 20th century – after the devastating period of **reservationization** – activism once again took shape. In November 1969, a small group of Indian activists and students, later joined by another 100, went to the abandoned, former prison island of

**178 Above** The famed photographer Gertrude Kasebier took this photograph of young Gertrude Simmons Bonnin (*Zitkala-sa*), a classically trained violist, in 1898. Bonnin often wore traditional Native dress when she lectured.

Alcatraz, demanding that it be given over to Indians by the government. Alcatraz was occupied by Indian groups for over two years, and it became a national focal point for the issues of Indian political and cultural nationalism. Ultimately, the courts refused to uphold their claims, and the last remaining occupiers were removed by force.

During the same period, the American Indian Movement (AIM) grew from the civil rights movements of the 1960s (including the blacks, Hispanics, women and anti-war protests). Members of the AIM took up Native issues such as education, self-government (see **self-determination**), oppression, poverty, religious freedom and the control of natural resources. The emergence of pan-Indian activism and even the militancy of groups such as the National Indian Youth Council, Indians of All Tribes and the AIM drew urban Indians and reservation-based Indians together in a new kind of nationalism. They were determined to protect their land and identity.

Some political protests were dangerous. In Wisconsin, Oregon, Washington, South Dakota, the District of Columbia and Québec, Canada, Native men and women faced government agents, the National Guard, the Royal Canadian Mounted Police, SWAT teams of police and armed non-Indian civilians in numerous disputes. The most prominent of the AIM protests were the 1972 March on Washington (known as the Trail of Broken Treaties Caravan or The Longest Walk), the occupation of the BIA Offices in 1972 and the 1973 occupation of **Wounded Knee** on the Pine Ridge **Sioux** Reservation.[42]

The last 30 years have seen debates over Indian rights to use methods of **hunting** and **fishing** (for example spear fishing and gillnetting) which are not forbidden for non-Indians, religious rights and the government's intervention in or neglect of Indian affairs. Essentially, the women and men who fought these battles have been fighting for the preservation of their heritage and traditions.

Just as the **Second World War** produced a new and invigorated leadership, such movements and actions rallied national support around Indian issues and created yet new leaders and generations of Indian activists to campaign for Indian causes. Activist movements also helped increase the numbers of Indian lawyers and other professionals. Thus, the battles were moved from the barricades and marches to the courts and educational institutions.

## Population

Estimates of Indians in America (north of Mexico) before European **contact** range from 1 million to 18 million. It is probably somewhere in between, perhaps under 8 million.

During the first contact in 1500 and 1900, the Indian population declined heavily. Devastation, such as **disease** and **war**, took the Indian population from 500 distinct groups of people to 300 **federally recognized** tribes (some incredibly small in number), many unrecognized peoples and as many **urban Indians** in just over two centuries.

Many questions remain unanswered. How many Indians were there in North America or South America at the point of first contact with Europeans? How did Indians come to be in North and South America? How many Indians died from disease, war, famine and **Removal**? How many Indians were **reservationized** and how many existed in North America at the turn of the 20th century? How many Indians exist now?

There is much research on the population before Columbus. The people who study populations, the history of diseases, economics, archaeology, social history and political history all have different ways and reasons for counting Indians. To determine how many Indians were at any given place at any given time, who lived, who died and how, scholars have analysed information from Indian winter counts and government censuses during Removal. They have studied grave sites following smallpox epidemics, court records, voting behaviour, land records and employment statistics.

In 1900, there were about 400,000 Indians counted in both the United States and Canada. Most scholars and government officials predicted the extinction of Indians. However, from that time, Native populations started a slight recovery, and the estimates of the numbers of North American Indians, **Inuit**, **Aleut** and **Métis** (in Canada) range widely over the next three-quarters of a century. The 1990 US census counted 1.95 million Indians; a little over half of those who called themselves Indians were enrolled members of federally recognized tribes. Even the federally recognized population has grown as the Indian birth rate rises regularly. The next census in the year 2000 anticipates 2 million Indians. However, the Native population in the United States and Canada is tiny compared with other ethnic groups. Many problems (mostly because of old ideas about race and ethnicity, and the Native resistance to counting by governments) make it difficult to know just how many Native people there are in North America.

## Potlatch

Gift giving has always been an important aspect of Indian culture. In the Pacific Northwest of the United States and Canada, it is known as potlatch. **Haida**, Makah, Kwakwaka'wakw, Nuu-chah-nulth, **Tlingit** and Tsimshian communities participated in potlatches. The gifts included **blankets**, furs

## Pottery

Pottery, like **basketry**, is one of the oldest and most widespread of Native crafts, which is connected to the very source of life. The Pueblo pottery is a good example of the world of Indian pottery. The Tewa word for clay, *nung*, is the same as the word for people. For the Pueblos, people are clay (see **adobe**), and thus making pottery from Mother Clay is a sacred act. Gathering clay and making a dish is intimately connected with and must be accompanied by prayers and good thoughts for the well-being of the world, just like **dances** and songs. Over the centuries, before **contact** with Europeans, Pueblos and others made pottery for everyday use, for storing water and cooking food. They, like other peoples who made pottery, traded their pottery with other tribes for goods – hides, **feathers**, **shells**, minerals such as turquoise, dyes, **horses** and food.

When the Spaniards came, they demanded from the people pottery to match their needs – flat dishes, smaller water jars, cups, soup plates and dough bowls for the raised wheat breads introduced into the Pueblo world. So the Pueblos began to make a great range of pottery goods to meet those needs. In the late 19th and 20th centuries, new demands from new markets and a shift from a trade to a cash **economy** changed the objects produced. **Tourists** wanted less expensive objects, so potters made small animal figures, matched sets of dishes modelled after china, representations of trains and candlesticks.

**180 Above** A bowl from the excavated Hopi village of Sityatki, *c.* 1600.

As the Spanish had commandeered Pueblo lead mines, they went from using mineral-based paints to the vegetable paints for which they are now well known. They used the manures of the newly introduced sheep, cattle and **horses** to create new, black polished ware.

and skins, jewellery, money and, in the 20th century, appliances. Native people on the **Northwest Coast** made 'coppers' for use in the potlatch. The coppers, which had names, were large **metal** shield-like pieces passed down to male relatives, distributed, traded for blankets or broken down during potlatches. Coppers were often carved, painted or hammered into traditional designs that reflected the **clan**, family crests and historic stories of the persons giving or breaking the copper. In a way, they reflected the giver's honour and wealth. Today artists made small coppers as jewellery, decorations and as reproductions for **tourists**.

The potlatch kept the community hierarchy and allowed individuals to gather wealth and move up in status. It was an important system of redistribution. Hosts would give away most, if not all, of their material goods to show good will to the rest of the community and to keep or gain status.

Laws in Canada (in 1884) and the United States (in the early 20th century) banned the potlatch to control Indians and reduce traditional systems of tribal government. After decades of repression, the potlatch was allowed in the United States in 1934 with the Indian Reorganization Act and in Canada in 1951 with the revised Indian Act. The potlatch remains central to community life.

**123**

**181 Above** A bowl made by Nampeyo (1860–1947) of Hano, a Hopi-Tewa woman who created what **art** historians would later call the Sityatki Revival of Hopi pottery. Inspired by seeing the excavated potteries found accidentally by Hopis and then later by archaeologists in the 1890s, Nampeyo, with her husband, began to reconstruct old traditional forms not produced for centuries among the Hopi. Her old and new designs revised and preserved the symbols of her people's culture. The work of Nampeyo and another Pueblo woman from San Ildefonso called Maria Martinez aroused much interest in Pueblo pottery. They inspired many others to revive traditional forms while contributing enormously to the **economic** survival of their people.

Although pottery was made mostly for the tourism and **art** market, it was still used within communities and for **ceremonies**. Many potters and ceramic sculptors have returned to a more traditional way of making pottery, reviving the prayers and the rituals needed to accompany the process.

> *Nan chu Kweejo,*
> *na ho uvi whageh oe powa,*
> *du huu joni heda di aweh joni*
> *hey bo hanbo di koe gi un muu.*
> *Wayhaa ha yun maa bo,*
> *we un tsi maai pi.*
> Clay Mother,
> I have come to the centre of
> your abode, feed me and clothe me
> and in the end you will absorb me
> into your centre.
> However far you travel,
> do not go crying.
> *Nora Naranjo-Morse's version, learned from her mother,*
> *of a prayer Pueblos offer to Clay Mother*

**W**henever you … get the pottery clay, you take your cornmeal (for prayers). You can't go to Mother Clay without the cornmeal and ask her permission to touch her. Talk to [her]. She… will hear your word and she will answer your prayer.
*Margaret Tafoya, Santa Clara Pueblo*

**182 Above** The Hopi potter, Nampeyo of Hano.

**183 Above** Russell Sanchez, a potter from San Ildefonso Pueblo takes issue with the motto of the state of New Mexico ('Land of Enchantment') in his jar, 'Land of Entrapment'. The water jar (*olla*) was imported by the Spanish. This one portrays three figures on crosses in a glazed area. The lip or centre of the jar goes back to the centre or navel of Mother Earth (the *sipapu*), 'where we all belong in the end', according to Russell. Russell comes from near the Los Alamos Nuclear Laboratory that developed the atomic bomb, and his art often records how Mother Earth has suffered.

## Pow wow

The term 'pow wow', **Algonquian** in origin, meant a person of power, perhaps a '**medicine** man' or a gathering for healing **ceremonies**. It has now come to mean an organized gathering of tribal people where friendships are renewed and **dancing**, feasting, competitions, shows, **trade** and cultural exchange take place. Usually held in the summer months, pow wows are common in communities all over North America and have become part of an intertribal or multi-tribal expression of Indian identity.

I was told this at one of the White Shield pow wows… this old man came up and he said, 'Do you know how this giveaway came about? Over there in New Town [Fort Berthold Reservation in North Dakota, Mandan and Hidatsa], corn [maize] is sacred to them. One summer when the corn was ripe our [Dakota] scouts were out toward their area and they came to this corn field, so they gathered up all the corn and bundled it and packed it on the horses and they headed back over here. When there got back over here, our leaders said, 'No, those are their sacred things, we never should have taken them. You know we respected each other's religion, that something we never fight over.' And so our people got together and they sent a messenger down there telling them we were coming. So, they were glad, so when we got there we gave gifts to the people showing them that the boys did not know what they were doing. We brought gifts to them and they brought food, and they were thankful.

They got their corn back, so they put on a big pow wow for everybody. The Sioux camped on one side of the river, and during the day they had horse races and games all day and then they had a big feed at supper in the evening. Then after supper everybody danced and had a good time. For three or four days they did that. Then at the end of the pow wow, the get-together – that's what a pow wow is, a gathering – they gave us gifts and showed appreciation that we weren't going to fight or anything, that we respected them.

So then our people said, 'You come down to our place next year, and we'll have a pow wow' and that's how the pow wows and giveaways started here.

*Elmer White, Dakota*

Dances at pow wows are performed in full costume. These include men's and women's, girl's and boy's traditional dances, fancy dances, round dances, straight dances, grass dances and jingle-dress dances. The dances performed vary from region to region, but have their roots in traditional dances. The Grass Dance is developed from a very old Plains tradition. The jingle-dress dance is said by some to have been a gift to the people of Whitefish Bay in Northern Ontario. The Fancy Shawl dance is said to have come from the Plains where the young women would gather to show off their newly painted **buffalo** hides and robes.

Communities now have different reasons for pow wows. Some are **tourist** attractions or for fund raising, others are a gathering of friends and families. Some are used for cultural renewal and have elders' workshops and other teaching sessions. Others are competition pow wows, where dancers come together to compete for prize money. An important part of the pow wow are the singers and the **drums**. Groups of singers, called 'a drum', are invited to participate and provide songs for the dancers. Food and craft booths are also essential parts of pow wows. Dancers and spectators can be found munching on buffalo burgers, Indian tacos, frybread and bacon, maize soup, pies and scones (in Canada), lemonade and ice cream. Crafts and food vendors, dancers and drummers often travel a circuit, the 'pow wow trail', during the summer months, going from one pow wow to another.

184 **Above** Traditional straight dancers at the 1992 Delaware pow wow at Copan, Oklahoma. Unlike 'fancy dancers', traditional **dancers** carry clubs and sticks, wear natural, undyed bird wings and **feathers**. Sometimes they wear large natural feather bustles, animal skins, **headdresses**, and face paint.

## Pueblo Revolt

When the Spaniards came to colonize New Mexico in 1598, they [the Pueblo Indians] tried to get along with them. But like most European powers, the Spaniards tried to dominate the Pueblo people. The Spaniards forced the Pueblos to give them food and to work as free labour. The Spanish tried to make the Pueblos get rid of their religion and accept the Spanish religion. The Pueblos suffered silently until a time in 1675 when the Spanish governor and the Catholic padres realized that the Pueblos were not really accepting the Spanish religion. So the Spaniards arrested 47 Pueblo leaders. Four were condemned to be hung and the others were whipped publicly on the plaza in Santa Fe.

Among those whipped was a person from San Juan by the name of Po'ping. The Spanish called him Popay and that is the way he is recorded in history because the Spanish wrote the history. Anyway, after Popay came home he began to think about the indignity that he had suffered. He decided he should organize other tribal leaders to do something about the Spaniards. Eventually, the Pueblo leaders decided they would go to the Spaniards and the priests to tell them to leave Pueblo land. This would not be a bloody revolt only if the Spaniards did not want to leave would they be killed. Runners took a deerskin strip with knots in it to each Pueblo. They told the Pueblos that each morning as the sun came up, they were to untie a knot. And on the morning that the last knot was untied, the revolt would begin.

On 10 August 1680, the Pueblos began to go to their padres and other Spanish families to ask them to leave or suffer the consequences. As a result, 21 priests were killed and something like 200 Spanish people. Many settlers left their homes and came to Santa Fe for protection inside the Governor's Palace. The Pueblos converged on the Palace and fought against the Spaniards for several days. Finally the Pueblo warriors decided to dam the water that was flowing through Santa Fe. After a few days the Spaniards were suffering from thirst. On 21 August, they began to evacuate Santa Fe. The Pueblo warriors watched them leave and did not attack. The Pueblo Revolt was the only successful revolt by a Native people against the European powers. The Spaniards left New Mexico and the Pueblos had their land again. And it was like this for 12 years.

*Joe Sando, tribal historian, Jemez Pueblo, 1992*

**185 Above** Tommie Montoya, a young Pueblo artist, did a series of pencil drawings in 1980, the 300th anniversary of the Pueblo Revolt. This drawing, called *Catua and Omtua, Pueblo Runners from Tesuque*, shows the runners from Tesuque Pueblo carrying the message (see **calendars**) to all the villages about the planned actions against the Spanish.

### Quillwork

Like most Native craftwork, quillwork – common from the far Northeast to the far West – is not just decorative. The application of porcupine and (less frequently) bird quills onto items of clothing, tipi liners, and **buffalo** or **elk** robes was often a sacred responsibility for the women and their way of praying for someone's good health and welfare. Women on the Plains developed quilling societies and, later, beading societies, whose responsibility it was to protect the process of quilling.

**G**rass Woman, the daughter of Black Coal, was one of the last of the seven medicine women who carried the Quill Society's medicine bundles. The seven medicine women supervised the making of quill ornaments used to decorate tipis, moccasins, buffalo robes and cradles with designs representing prayers for health and long life. The women made gifts of quillwork so that blessings would follow the people as they travelled the four hills of life. The ceremonies of the society have disappeared with other aspects of Arapaho life, and our grandparents say they long for the old ways.

*Debra Calling Thunder, Arapaho, 1993*

In the late 19th century, **beads** were cheaper and easier to acquire than quills, so the quilling societies became dormant for a while. Some quillwork has continued, for example Plains women today are trying to revive the **art** and the spiritual connections it held in Plains life.

**F**or the people who hold to this art form very strongly, quillwork still has strong spiritual and religious overtones that are integral to the art. I have a lot of respect for the people from the Sioux tribes and the respect they hold for that art form. That respect is what I try to introduce to my students… there's a lot more of the artist at work than just making a craft, just making a living. If you can go into it first with an understanding of the spiritual part of it – understanding the animal, understanding the people who put these things together and what the objects were intended for – you will hold the art of quillwork in your heart. I will tell my students – about my experiences hearing porcupines sing, and talking to porcupines and understanding what they have to offer. Porcupines are not just an animal.

*Joanne Bigcrane, Pend d'Oreille, 1994*

### Rabbit

Rabbit, like **Coyote**, Spider, **Raven** and other characters in the origin stories (see **creation stories**) of Indian people, is a so-called trickster hero to Southeastern Indian peoples and to some Southwestern and Northeastern peoples. He is very similar to the character in the **African** tales of Bre'r (Brother) Rabbit, in that he jokes, lies, charms and befriends his way into and out of trouble. For **Cherokee**s, in particular, the Rabbit is a great singer and **dancer**, having taught the people many of their songs and dances. He is also a great storyteller, having invented many of the great lies that humans now believe.

**186 Left** In 1992 Murv Jacob, a **Cherokee** artist, illustrated an old Cherokee story about one of Rabbit's adventures. The **wolves** capture Rabbit who is coming from a **dance**. They tell him that they are going to eat him. However, Rabbit tells the wolves that, before he dies, he wants to teach them a new dance. Mesmerized by his songs, they dance happily. He slips through their legs and escapes, laughing at their gullibility.

THE ART MARKET

MAY 9–31, 1992

TULSA, OKLAHOMA

17th ANNUAL SPRING SHOW

## Rain

For **agricultural** peoples and all those who are dependent on a supply of fresh water, rain is very important. Throughout the centuries, humans have prayed, danced and sung for rain. For most Native people – from the Hidatsa to the **Cherokee** to the Navajo – the **ceremonies** to bring rain are a sacred responsibility. In the dry lands of the Southwest, almost every aspect of life – clothing, **pottery**, **dances**, songs, prayers, and stories of the origins and nature of the world and its plants, animals and humans – reflects a concern about rain. For example, **Zunis** and Pueblos offer cornmeal, which is sacred to them, to the ancestors and spirits who provide all that sustains life. Quite common near the hearths and doorways of Pueblo homes are pottery bowls that hold sacred cornmeal, for the daily prayer offerings. Terraced Pueblo cornmeal bowls represent the world, with steps up to the clouds and ancestors who bring rain (see **clowns**).

**187 Above** A cornmeal bowl made in 1991 by Josephine Nahohai of Zuni Pueblo. The tadpoles and creatures on it are associated with water. As in all things connected with water and with corn, this bowl is also associated with fertility, so it could be given to a newly married couple as a wedding present.

An anthropologist asks a Pueblo man why all Pueblo songs, dances, prayers, and pots are about rain. He replied that people pray, sing, dance about what they don't have enough of, saying to the anthropologist, 'Why, all your songs are about love.'
*A story some Zunis like to tell*

## Rattle

Most Native instruments are percussion instruments. **Drums** and rattles are the most common. Rattles are made from the most local and often the most sacred of materials. They are then filled with stones, seeds or shot, held in the hand and shaken. Many on the Plains were made from rawhide, wood or a gourd (see **squash**). At the turn of the 19th century, deprived of traditional materials with which to make rattles, many people made them out of tin cans and **metal** salt shakers (as in Oklahoma-style Gourd Dance rattles). During the **Second World War** in the Pacific, Southeastern tribal peoples made dance rattles out of hollow coconuts, instead of turtle **shells**, and often continued to make them out of coconuts after they had returned home.

Many Indians wear deer dewclaw rattles tied to leather bands around their legs. Others make them from **recycled** metal pieces (such as tin-lids), shells, bones and hooves, fixed to cloth or hide and worn on the body and used as percussive instruments when the body moves (as in a dance).

For many, the rattle makes a powerful and magical sound. Some Anishinabe even describe the sound of the gourd rattle or shaker as 'the Sound of Creation'.[43] The sound of a rattle can imitate or signal the presence of a supernatural power or spirit. It can also be the sound of **rain**, thunder, lightning, bird call, wind, breath or running water.

Rattles, like drums and bone whistles, are used in curing spiritual and physical illness. They are carved or painted carefully in a ritual way because they are used in a **ceremonial** context. Designs often come from supernatural powers in **dreams**.[44]

The *tsi'ka* is a kind of prayer that things will go well and nothing will go wrong. It is always done with a rattle, never a drum. *Helma Ward, Makah, 1991.*

**188 Above** Dancers from Santa Clara Pueblo in a Corn Dance (*kho'he'je*) held on Santa Clara's Feast Day, 12 August 1991. The men are wearing **bandoliers** of **shells** across their chest and carrying gourd rattles covered with clay from the river. The same clay wash covers parts of their bodies. Their sashes (**rain** belts) and their kilts are covered with symbols of rain and water. The rattles, shells from the ocean and gourds from a relative of the **squash**, imitate and call the thunder and lightning.

## Raven

Raven, like **Coyote**, **Rabbit** and Spider, is a creator and a trickster. According to some **Inuit** and Northwest Coastal peoples, he brought light into the world. On the **Northwest Coast** his image can be found on **rattles** used for healing. The colour black symbolizes the power that Raven brings.

**189 Below** A bird-handled rattle, carved with a frog, a human and other animals, from the **Northwest Coast**.

When Raven reached the pea-vine he found three other men that had just fallen from the pea-pod that gave the first one (first man)…. Raven remained with them a long time, teaching them how to live. He taught them how to make a fire-drill and bow…. He made for each of the men a wife, and also made many plants and birds such as frequent the sea coast…. He taught the men to make bows, arrows, spears, nets and all the implements of the chase and how to use them; also how to capture the seal which had now become plentiful in the sea. After he taught them how to make kayaks, he showed them how to make houses of drift logs and bushes covered with earth.

*An Inuit story*

**190 Below** Some Native people, such as the **Yurok**, Tolowa and Karuk from Northern California, use rattles – **shells**, in this instance – over their whole bodies as the percussion for **dance**. Yuroks connect shells with water, the ocean and the creation of all things.

**191 Below** Indians did not need brass tacks to secure leather to wood, so they used them for decorative grips for war clubs and knives. This **Blackfeet** knife has brass tack decoration on the handle.

**192 Left** The Gourd **Dance**, developed by Comanche and Kiowa men's societies (for example the Comanche Little Ponies and the Kiowa Gourd **Clan**), is often a prelude to a **pow wow** or social gathering. Traditionally, the rattles had **beaded** handles, soft hide fringes and a **horse**hair or soft **quill** top. Today, however, **metal** salt shakers and tins are used more than gourds.

**193 Below** A wooden **war** club associated with Red Jacket.

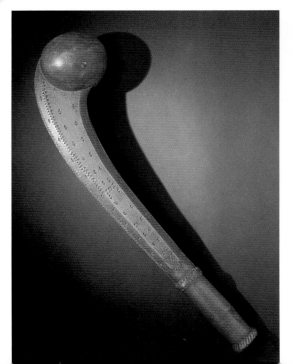

**194 Above** In this 1828 painting of Red Jacket by Robert Weir he carries a **diplomatic** gift, a pipe tomahawk, and wears the Peace Medal given him by George Washington, who betrayed him and his people, not fulfilling the pledges he made to protect his Seneca allies.

## Recycled materials

Indians used and reused materials of all kinds. Native peoples took what was rubbish to Europeans and turned it into things that were of use and importance to them. Natives converted scrap copper and iron of all sorts (from kettles and tools, for example) into **metal** decorations for clothing and weapons.

Captured rifle stocks were transformed into **war** clubs. Gun barrels and metal scythes were made into **awl**s and scrapers for taking the flesh and hair off animal hides. People scavenged shipwrecks and abandoned camps for cast-off, worn out bits and pieces.

Items of considerable value to Europeans, such as gold coins, meant little to Indians not yet in a cash **economy**. They too were turned into distinctive ornaments and tools.

## Red Jacket

Red Jacket (*Sagoyewatha*) (1756–1830), a **Seneca**, was a man of such intellectual and political skills that he was 'raised up' as a non-hereditary chief.

Although he was forced to join the majority of his people in a **British** alliance against the American rebels, he warned the **Iroquois** people against all European alliances.

After the war, he became grudgingly reconciled to the new government and many Seneca felt he had betrayed

them by bowing to Washington's power. However, he always strongly rejected white efforts to wipe out Seneca culture and power.

Our seats were once large and yours were small. You have now become a great people, and we have scarcely a place left to spread our blankets. You have got our country, but are not satisfied; you want to force your religion upon us. We do not wish to destroy your religion or take it from you. We only want to enjoy our own.

*Red Jacket, to a representative of the* US *government,* 1841

## Red Stick Wars

In the history of warfare between the United States and Indian tribes, few battles cost more Indian lives than the one that ended the Red Stick Wars (1813–14). After Britain defaulted on its Native allies in the South during the War of 1812, the struggles between Indians and the new 'Americans' escalated in the Upland South. There was much discontent among the tribes and a series of battles between Anglo-American invaders, Muskogee (**Creek**) Indians and Muskogee rebel warriors (known by whites as 'redsticks' for the red clubs that they carried). The war began on 22 July 1813, when the Muskogee rebels, guided by religious leaders, attacked in a determined and unified effort to remove US agents and the Muskogee chiefs from tribal lands. By the time the battles ended in Tohopeka on 27 March 1814, 80 percent of Red Stick warriors were dead. As a result of this defeat, Creeks gave up 14 million acres of land. This was the largest amount of land ever surrendered by a Native group to the government. The peace **treaty** signed at Fort Jackson ended the wars by re-drawing the boundaries between the United States and the Muskogee Nation.

**195 Right** The **Creek/** Muscogee chief Josiah Francis went to England in 1814, at the end of the Red Stick Wars, to regain **British** support for his people. Unable to return home because of his support of the rebels, he made this Southeastern-style finger-woven **bandolier** pouch of blue worsted wool. Eventually, Andrew Jackson's Navy captured and hung Francis.

196 **Above** A Navajo political activist and relocation resister, Katharine Smith, Big Mountain, Arizona, in 1991.

## Relocation

The policy called 'relocation' involved Indian peoples moving from rural **reservations** to the cities. It came with another new policy called '**termination**', which was designed to remove as many reservations as possible from the list of tribes for whom the government was responsible according to its **treaties**. These policies, together with the collapse of **farming** and **subsistence**, and the **Second World War**, caused the massive resettlement of Native peoples to cities. This pattern of urbanization now has over 50 percent of Indians living off reservations in cities throughout the country. These people are called '**urban Indians**'.

The relocation of the 1950s changed the lives of Natives as much as the **Removal** of the 18th and 19th centuries. The **Navajos** and the other tribes that experienced the most relocation, lost their matrilocal style of residence and their control over their **economies** and distribution of goods. Urban life also put great pressure on all Indians to deny their Indian identity. They often felt rejected by reservation Indians and separated from traditional religious and cultural life. Although relocation traditionally included job placement, training and subsidies, Indians may have traded rural poverty for urban poverty. They had fewer resources than other groups, and Indian families, larger than most, still lived below the poverty line at twice the national rate.

Native peoples all over the United States and Canada have continued to suffer other forms of relocation. **Seneca**, Makah, Colville, **Salish**, Kootenai, **Cherokee** and Mandan-Hidatsa (and in Canada, **Cree** and **Inuit**) were relocated because of hydro-electric power utilities and **dams** sited on their traditional lands. At Colville, for example, even traditional burial grounds were relocated to other sites. In the 1950s, the Canadian government 'relocated' Inuits from Northern Québec to the high **Arctic**. Inuits who lived traditionally in extended family units were often separated in the relocation, and game once hunted in Québec did not exist in the new colonies. In the late 1980s, faced with the massive failure of the programme, the government agreed to send home any Inuit who wished to return. The US government also abandoned the policy of relocation, although over half the reservation population chose to relocate voluntarily in the 1980s as people lost land, searched for work to fit their newly gained skills or moved for military service.

## Removal

**W**e are almost surrounded by the whites and it seems to be their intention to destroy us as a people.... We had hoped that the white man would not be willing to travel beyond the mountains. Now that hope is gone. They have travelled beyond the mountains and settled on Cherokee land. They wish to have that usurpation sanctioned by treaty. When that is gained, the same encroaching spirit will lead them upon other lands of the Cherokees. New cessions will be asked. Finally the whole country, which the Cherokees and their fathers have so long occupied, will be demanded and the remnant of the Ani-Yuni-wiya, 'The Real People', once so great and formidable, will be compelled to seek refuge in some distant wilderness. There they will be permitted to stay only a short while, until they again behold the advancing banners of the same greedy host.
*Dragging Canoe, Cherokee, 1776*

After the Revolutionary War, increasing numbers of settlers moved out of the original colonies toward the West. Although most of the 116 treaties signed before 1820 involved the handover of a great deal of **land**, settlers wanted even more. Treaty promises to protect the tribes from further loss of land faded. Leaders such as the Shawnee *Tecumseh* (1768–1813) and his brother, *Tenskatawa* (the Prophet) (1775–1836), tried to unite tribes in military and religious rebellion against these new invasions, but they failed. The so-called 'opening of the frontier', triggered by the Louisiana Purchase, made westward expansion onto more Indian lands inevitable. Voluntary Removal was encouraged as a way of preventing further violence, but compulsory Removal (enacted by the Indian Removal Act of 1830) was enforced despite much debate and resistance in Congress. Most tribes resisted Removal, and there were enormous, often bloody, inter-tribal disputes

**197 Below** Removal routes of the Cherokee, Choctaw, Chickasaw, Creek and Seminole peoples.

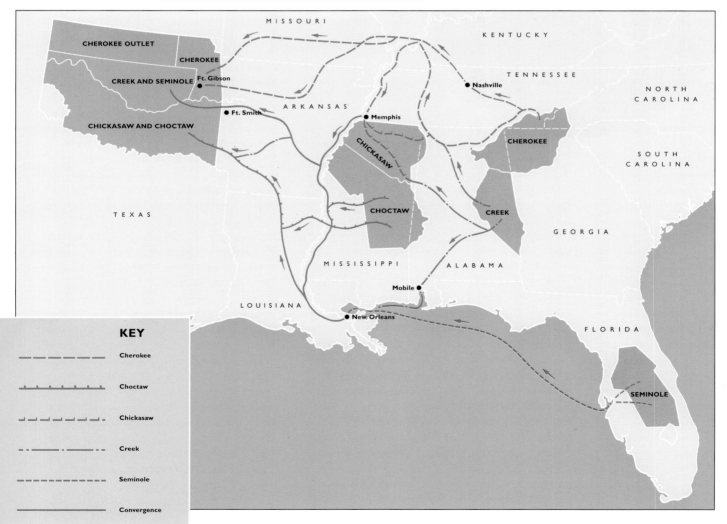

**KEY**

| | |
|---|---|
| – – – – – | Cherokee |
| ·–·–·– | Choctaw |
| — – — – — – | Chickasaw |
| – · — · — · — | Creek |
| – – – – – – | Seminole |
| ———— | Convergence |

between those who would give in to Removal and those who would not.

In the 1820s, the state of Georgia enacted laws to drive the Cherokees from their homelands, land made even more desirable to whites by the recent discovery of gold and by its suitability for farming cotton. The Cherokees took their case to the US Supreme Court, which found the Georgia laws unconstitutional (in *Worcester v. Georgia* and *Cherokee Nation v. Georgia*). The Supreme Court ruled that the Cherokee Nation was a **sovereign** 'domestic dependent nation' and, therefore, exempt from Georgia law. President Andrew Jackson, the 'Father of Democracy' to non-Indians, refused to enforce the Court's ruling. When it became clear that the government would never uphold the decision of the Supreme Court, a few Cherokees (including Major Ridge and **Elias Boudinot**) began to consider negotiating Removal. They felt that they would save Cherokee lives if they went where they were promised no more white men would follow. Although their Treaty Party had little support among Cherokees, US commissioners met with them in 1835 and negotiated the Treaty of New Echota. It provided for the exchange of all Cherokee territory in the Southeast for a piece of land in **Indian Territory** (today Northeast Oklahoma). Most Cherokees in the East (including Principal Chief John Ross) signed a petition protesting that the treaty had been made by an unauthorized minority, but the US Senate approved the document.

In the summer of 1838, government troops began rounding up Cherokees and imprisoning them. Families were separated. Soldiers burned Cherokee cabins and crops. Some groups of Cherokees were forcibly moved west. Chief Ross appealed to President Van Buren to allow the Cherokees to carry out their own Removal. In the winter

**198 Above** John Ross, the **Cherokee** Nation's first Principal Chief, was born in 1790 at Turkeytown, Alabama, to a Scottish father and a Cherokee mother. Ross held the Office of Principal Chief of the Cherokee Nation for 38 years through the stormy periods of Removal and the **Civil War**. In his personal appearance and upper-class lifestyle, John Ross seemed far from traditional, but he remains today a great hero to Cherokees everywhere because of his support for Cherokee **sovereignty**.

of 1838–39 the Cherokee Nation moved west, where they joined a smaller number of so-called Old Settler Cherokees already there. Even the wealthy Cherokees who had embraced the way of life promoted by the government, were forced from their homes by the Georgia Guards. The Cherokee Removal became known as the Trail of Tears (in Cherokee, 'The Place Where We Cried') because of the dreadful suffering they endured. Between 25 and 50 percent of those who began the journey died from **disease**, malnutrition, starvation or execution.

The Cherokees are nearly all prisoners. They have been dragged from their houses and camped at the forts and military posts all over the Nation. Multitudes were not allowed time to take anything with them but the clothes they had on. Well-furnished houses were left a prey to plunderers who, like hungry wolves, follow the progress of the captors and in many cases accompany them. It is a painful sight. The property of many has been taken and sold before their eyes for almost nothing, the sellers and buyers being in many cases combined to cheat the poor Indian. Private purchases, or at least the sham of purchases, have in many instances been made at the instant of arrest and consternation: the soldiers standing with guns and bayonets, impatient to go on with their work, could give but little time to transact business. The poor captive in a state of distressing agitation, his weeping wife almost frantic with terror, surrounded by a group of crying, terrified children, without a friend to speak one consoling word, is in a very unfavourable condition to make advantageous disposition of his property even were suitable and honest purchasers on the spot. Many who a few days ago were in comfortable circumstances are now the victims of abject poverty. Many who have been allowed to return to their homes under passport to inquire after their property have found their houses, cattle, hogs, ploughs, hoes, harness, tables, chairs, earthenware, all gone. It is altogether a faint and feeble representation of the work of barbarity which has been perpetrated on the unoffending, unarmed and unresisting Cherokees. I say nothing yet of several cold-blooded murders and other personal cruelties.

*Evan B. Jones, Baptist missionary and Cherokee supporter*

There was much sickness among the emigrants and a great many little children died of whooping cough.
*Rebecca Neugin, a Cherokee girl removed during the Trail of Tears*

If I could… I would remove every Indian tomorrow beyond the reach of the white men, who like vultures, are watching, ready to pounce upon their prey and strip them of everything they have or expect from the government of the United States.
*General John Ellis Wool, Director of Removal, 1836*

## Repatriation

From the 17th century, the US government urged Indians to put aside their old religion and even to destroy the artefacts associated with that religion. In the meantime, traditional practice was eroded by active policies such as '**civilization**', 'assimilation' (see **acculturation**) and 'allotment'. Native people found it increasingly difficult to keep up their traditional religions, believing that their Gods had abandoned them. Ceremonial objects were sold, taken or given away. Although many later generations would want these objects returned from **museums** and collectors, only a few, such as the Hidatsa in the 1930s, would be successful until the government would take legal action. When the great drought in the late 1930s threatened the survival of the Hidatsa, they succeeded in recovering their sacred Waterbuster Bundle from the Museum of the American Indian in New York. This **medicine bundle** had always brought the Hidatsa **rain**. It had been transferred to the museum

**199 Above** A Spanish soldier made this *bulto* or **sculpture** of the Archangel St Michael in 1779 for the altar screen of the newly built church at Zuni Pueblo. In 1879, the Smithsonian Institution anthropologists removed the statue from the church and sent it back to the **museum** in Washington. In 1992, when Smithsonian scholars discovered that it has been inappropriately and illegally removed, the National Museum of American History returned the *bulto* to Zuni.

by its keeper, Wolf Chief, who believed that when he died no-one would care for it. It was the first object repatriated to Indians by an American museum.

Today, following the Native American Graves and Repatriation Act of 1990, many tribes hope to regain objects once separated from them and to recover and bury once again ancestral remains. They want to practise their religious rituals and to put right hostile relationships. The Act makes it necessary for government-funded museums and institutions to list and return if requested to do so skeletal remains, ceremonial/sacred objects and cultural objects that can be identified with specific **federally recognized** tribes. These repatriations only apply to the United States (not to Canada or to other countries).

The objects most vigorously pursued for repatriation from museums have been Zuni *ahay:uda* (war gods) and **Iroquois wampum** belts. Long before the enactment of the Native American Graves and Repatriation Act, the Grand Council of the *Haudenosaunee* tried to retrieve wampum belts held in museums. Two institutions in the state of New York – the New York Historical Society and the Museum of the American Indian (now the National Museum of the American Indian of the Smithsonian Institution) – held a number of significant belts in their collections. As of 1998, these have been returned, along with other belts from other museums, to Iroquois in Canada and the United States.

The Act and attempts at repatriation have been widely criticized by archaeologists, anthropologists and museum officials who question how such repatriations will affect research, learning and legal notions of property. Indians do not all agree on repatriation, particularly concerning skeletal remains, the handling of ceremonial and sacred objects that have long been out of traditional caretaking, and the spiritual and cultural consequences of repatriating remains and objects. However, most agree on the moral need to repatriate religious objects.

## Reservations

Since the creation of the United States in 1776, the government has forced tribes to give up millions of acres of land. In the 19th century tribes were forced to accept reservations as the price for guarantees of **sovereignty**, personal safety, land, water and other resources as set out in treaties. Rounding up the resistant Plains tribes and putting them on reservations was, for many, the last act of the '**civilization**' campaign begun by the government in the 18th century.

Reservations, however, were not the only models for Indian residence. In the New Mexico Territories, many of the most recent reservations were based on old land grants from Spanish royalty, themselves often based on aboriginal territories occupied for thousands of years. After California was made a separate state, Indians who had no **treaties** with the government were moved to or allowed to stay on **federally recognized** old **mission** farm and ranch lands (*Rancherias*). These were **terminated** in the 1950s and half restored in the 1980s.

**200 Above** In this 1989 photograph, Jake Thomas (a traditional chief of the **Cayuga** and of the Grand Council of the **Iroquois**) and Roland Force (then the Director of the Museum of the American Indian) examine a number of **wampum** belts to be returned.

**201 Above** This ledger drawing (*c.* 1875), *A Cheyenne Warrior Killing a Soldier*, shows a Native version of resistance to land cessions, reservationization and defeat by the government.[45]

| B | E | O | T | H | U | K |
|---|---|---|---|---|---|---|
| M | O | H | I | C | A | N |
| N | A | T | C | H | E | Z |
| N | E | U | T | R | A | L |
| T | I | M | U | C | U | A |
| T | O | B | A | C | C | O |
| Y | A | M | A | S | E | E |

| B | M | N | N | T | T | Y |
|---|---|---|---|---|---|---|
| E | O | A | E | I | O | A |
| O | H | T | U | M | B | M |
| T | I | C | T | U | A | A |
| H | C | H | R | C | C | S |
| U | A | E | A | U | C | E |
| K | N | Z | L | A | O | E |

## Royal Proclamation

The defeat of the French in Canada by the **British** General Wolfe in 1759 ended French domination over the interior and maritime areas of North America. The 1763 Royal Proclamation established Canada as a British colony and was meant to make peace after years of conflict between the French and British. The Proclamation specifically recognized Native control over all unsettled **lands** and developed ways of negotiating these lands. It was decided that all lands would have to be purchased from Native groups once terms had been agreed. Once America gained independence from Britain, the Royal Proclamation no longer applied to the lands of the United States, but the Proclamation continues to form the basis for **land claims** cases in Canada. First Nations in Canada argue that the rights granted in this document are still in force despite all the federal or provincial government policies that followed, including the Indian Act.

**202 Above** This was painted in 1992 by Robert Houle, a Canadian Native artist. It uses a famous painting by the American artist Benjamin West, *The Death of Wolfe*, centred between the tribal names of extinct or nearly extinct groups of Indians. West painted large historic scenes, the most well-known being one of the death of the **British** hero General James Wolfe in the decisive battle for Canada between the French and the British in 1759. Wolfe is shown as a Christ-figure, the Indian represents America, and the painting probably represents the conquest of America.[46] Houle's reinterpretation of West's painting gives a tragic version of how the British Empire advanced.

176622

## Sacred sites, sacred objects

Sacred sites are the places where people's origin and **creation stories** tell them they began or where significant events and moments in the creation of the world took place. Thus, the city of Jerusalem is sacred to Jews, **Christians** and Muslims, because events central to their religion took place there. Often, a sacred site is linked with a natural phenomenon, such as a volcano (Mount St Helen's to the Pomo), a mountain (Mount Taylor to the **Navajos**) or an entire area (the Black Hills to the Lakota **Sioux**), or with a a an astronomical or geological phenomenon (such as rock formations). In some cases, the sacred site is made by humans to commemorate or re-enact a sacred event. For example, a *kiva* to the Pueblos represents the Earth's Navel (*sipapu*) through which they emerged into this world.

People continue to travel to these sacred sites to hold **ceremonies** and protect them from acts that would contaminate or interfere with their special powers. Thus, there are conflicts between Indians and governments, businesses and private individuals who threaten to demolish, build on or alter those sacred sites. Vision quest sites, sites with rock paintings or picture writing, sweat bath sites, ceremonial grounds (such as Sun **Dance** lodges and stomp grounds), areas where sacred plants and other materials are gathered and mythic origin sites remain of great concern to Native peoples.

Sacred objects have a power that comes from their origin as a gift from a supernatural spirit. Most **medicine bundles**, for example, contain that sacred power, which is why so many tribal peoples (including Navajos, Hidatsas, Pawnees and Cheyennes) have tried to get medicine bundles returned to them from **museums**.

## Salish

The Southern coast of British Columbia and south into Washington was the homeland of the Coastal Salish. Six distinct Salish **languages** were spoken, excluding the Northern group at Bella Coola.

Most Coastal Salish groups had typical **Northwest Coastal economies** based mainly on the sea and rivers, which provided **fish** and mammals. The communities had leaders rather than chiefs. The system was flexible

and allowed talented people to move up and gain status. A leader spoke only for his extended family or household. Households were the largest political groups and villages consisted of a group of households.

Unlike other groups near them, the Salish did not have large, dramatic **ceremonial art**. Common were carved **house posts**, grave figures and smaller works of art such as **rattles** and the combs and whorls associated with weaving. The Salish were skilled weavers, making beautiful practical **baskets** of split cedar root decorated with geometric designs in cherry **bark**. They also made loom-woven cedar bark capes and **blankets** for everyday use and 'nobility blankets' from goat or **dog** hair.

**Salmon** was important to the Plateau groups. Their economy was based on the seasonal patterns of the salmon's movement, with people living in small mobile bands from spring to autumn. In the winter, several bands would join together to form a larger village with permanent houses. They lived on mainly stored **food**. Fishing was mostly a men's activity and they **hunted** small game throughout the year. Women spent a great deal of time preparing and preserving the catch along with berries and roots for the winter months.

The US/Canadian border slices through the centre of the lands occupied by the Interior Salish. Four Salishan languages are spoken on the area called the Canadian Plateau, and others exist in the south. The Salish (misnamed Flathead) peoples of the Plateau in the United States live, following the Hellgate Treaty of 1855, in Western Montana. The government forced them there to join with the Kootenai people to whom they are related culturally. They inhabit agricultural land, rich in timber, water and fish. Through education they have tried to re-establish their **self-determination**, including running a very successful and expanding tribal college. They have also tried to maintain their tribal culture by keeping alive their language, art and ceremony.

## Salmon

In the same way as **maize** was important to Northeast, Southwest and Southeast peoples and **wild rice** was to the **Ojibwa**, so salmon was central to Native peoples in the Northwest and Alaska.

Then there's our ceremony for the salmon. We respect the salmon, we call them 'Salmon People'... . The people gather with their ritualist in the Longhouse on the Tulalip Reservation. It's a big wooden structure, oblong, about 100 feet long.... Open fires provide heat and light. The people sing the old songs. Each one carries a hand drum, and they drum to the beat of the song they are singing. Then a young man comes in to announce that... our guest is coming ashore. So the young people bring the King Salmon, the first salmon of the season, to shore on a canoe.... They circle the longhouse four times – that is a magic number in our culture – chanting:

> This is King Salmon,
> Upland it goes,
> Upland it goes.
> King Salmon this is,
> King Salmon this is.

Then we... have a feast honouring the spirit of the salmon. After the feast, the skeleton of the salmon is... returned to the waters, to his people... the spirit informs the Salmon People that it has been treated respectfully in Tulalip so the salmon will return another year to be food for the people.

Vi Hilbert (taqʷšoblu), Lushootseed, 1990

## Schools

In the 15th century there was much debate in Spain over whether Indians had souls and so could be educated and **Christianized**. This resulted in early attempts by **missionaries** in South America and in 'New Spain' to teach Indians to read. In the 17th century, Louis XIV ordered missionaries to educate Indian children in the St Lawrence, Mississippi and Great Lakes regions 'in the French Manner'. They were taught the French language and customs, handicrafts, singing, **agriculture** and traditional academic subjects. The **British** (both Protestant and, in Maryland, Catholic) established schools to educate the 'savages'. Their attempt to educate Native people was really a way to get land grants and funds from colonial rulers. A number of prestigious US institutions – William and Mary, and the Universities of Harvard, Pennsylvania, Dartmouth and Yale – were established on that basis. The numbers of 'savages' educated in these systems was tiny (fewer than 50 via Dartmouth even until 1970).

In some ways, Indians tried to counter the Europeans' schooling. In a story often printed in the late 18th century, some Indians decline a Quaker offer to send children for education.

We know that you highly esteem the kind of learning taught in those colleges, and that the maintenance of our young men while with you would be very expensive to you. We are convinced that you mean to do us good by your proposal and we thank you heartily. But you who are wise must know that different Nations have different conceptions of things, and you will, therefore, not take it amiss if our ideas of this kind of education happen not to be the same with yours.

We have had some experience of it. Several of our young people were formerly brought up at the College of the Northern Provinces. They were instructed in all your sciences. But when they came back to us, they were bad runners, ignorant of every means of living in the woods, unable to bear either Cold or Hunger, knew neither how to build a cabin, take a Deer, kill an Enemy, spoke our language imperfectly. Neither for Hunters, nor Councillors, they were totally good for nothing. We are, however, not the less obliged by your kind offer, tho' we decline accepting it and to show our grateful sense of it, the Gentlemen of Virginia will send us a dozen of their Sons, and we will take great Care of their Education, instruct them in all we know, and make Men of them.

In 1840, the **Cherokees** decided to set up their own free state school system. By 1846, 21 state schools were running alongside 10 missionary schools. In 1847, after **Removal**, the Council wanted to train more Cherokee teachers for the state school system, so it started two secondary schools called seminaries, one for girls and one for boys. These seminaries were approved by both English-speaking and traditionalist Cherokees. The traditionalists hoped this new effort would lead to more instruction in the Cherokee language.

Cherokees had long been believers in universal education for men and women (unlike many white societies). In an age when women generally received only a basic education, students at the Cherokee Female Seminary near Tahlequah had to pass an entrance exam and study geometry, algebra, physiology, geography, Latin, English grammar and history. Students also learned

**203 Above** The **Cherokee** Female Seminary was established in 1850 near Tahlequah, Oklahoma (the Cherokee capital in **Indian Territory**) by Chief John Ross, the Cherokee Council and **missionaries**.

the domestic arts and social skills to prepare them to become 'ladies'. These new schools were deeply **Christian** and European in their approach to education and toward 'Indians'.

School was another way of making Indians change. Indians were sent to school in order for them to become like whites (ironic when **Africans** were forbidden an education by supporters of slavery). They were to change from 'pagan wanderers' to responsible citizens, whether as **farmers**, ministers, seamstresses or millers and sawyers (as set out in the 1794 **treaty** with the **Oneida**, Tuscarora and the Stockbridge). Indians came to expect schooling and later they demanded it as part of the social and political contracts with the invaders. Treaties often guaranteed some form of education. This, along with the

**civilization** policy of the United States, made schools the 'Americanizers' of Indian young people.[47]

Indians became captives of boarding schools. Parents had to send their children to school. The government would even use military force to place children in school, and written and spoken stories tell of children 'kidnapped' from their homes to be put in boarding schools far away. Many ran away repeatedly, never losing their Indian ways of thinking and being. Others, forbidden to speak their l**anguages**, wear Native dress and practise Indian singing and **dancing**, became assimilated (see **acculturation**). Children were even placed with white families after completing school, so that their education in white culture would be complete. In another

**204 Left** Woxie Haury, Carlisle Indian School, in 1897. Photographs from many schools show before and after shots of Indians. The 'before' portrait has the Indians wrapped in **blankets**, with **feathers** in their hair. They look dirty, hungry, perhaps dangerous. The 'after' portrait shows stiff young people, brown faces and new haircuts above the starched collars and shirtwaist dresses.

way, school also fostered a **pan-Indian** identity, as children from many different tribes attended the large boarding schools and the schools encouraged mutual interests and **intermarriage**.

We were now loaded into wagons hired from and driven by our enemies.... We were taken to the schoolhouse... into the big dormitory, lighted with electricity... had never seen so much light at night.... Evenings we would gather... and cry softly so the matron would not hear and scold or spank us.... I can still hear the plaintive little voices saying, 'I want to go home. I want my mother.' We didn't understand a word of English and didn't know what to say or do.
*Helen Sekaquaptewa, Hopi, 1906*

First, I will tell you about the Cherokees.... I think they improve. They have a printing press and print a paper which is called the *Cherokee Phoenix*. They come to meetings on Sabbath Days.... I hope this nation will soon become civilized and enlightened.
*Sally Reece, a 12-year-old Cherokee student, in 1828*

By 1928, however, the government had concluded that the boarding school system had failed to educate Indian students, and to improve their health or their ability to work. Military service during the **Second World War** had a profound effect on Indian education. Veterans returned to communities, often taking advantage of the GI Bill (see page 178) to complete their high school qualifications and go to college. Government programmes were designed to support schools faced with a flood of Indian children. Following **relocation** in the 1950s, many Indians lived in a world of urban

**205 Below** The carpentry shop at Carlisle Indian School, which was the first boarding school. It was started in 1878 by General Richard Pratt, who once wrote 'Hair, scalplock and paint will vanish like a dream before a neat suit of 'Confed' grey... [we must] kill the Indian and Save the Man'.

**141**

**206 Below** Jaune Quick-to-See-Smith, a **Salish** painter, shows her version of an Indian school in this 1992 pastel, *I See Red, One Little, Two Little…* . It refers to the **stereotypes** of Indians often found in schools, as in the common nursery counting song, 'One Little, Two Little, Three Little Indians'. She superimposes the rhyme over a blackboard, setting Indian miseducation to rights by covering the board in the Salish **language** rather than in the English language forced on Indian children in the schools.

**207 Right** Sam Ell studying at Sitting Bull College, Fort Yates, North Dakota.

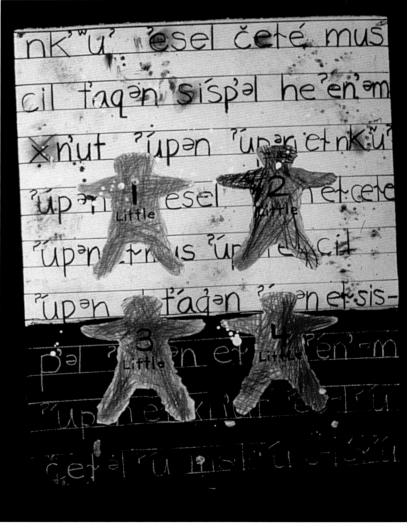

reservations. The Civil Rights Movement was not yet a reality for Indians and relocation took place once again in an atmosphere of racism and discrimination. How Indians were treated in schools which segregated blacks and whites varied from place to place. Often it depended on how 'culturally identifiable' the Indians were. Thus, **Sioux** in Chicago went to 'white' schools, but Pamunkeys in Virginia went to 'black' schools, or, sadly, to no school at all.[48]

The demand for self-government and **self-determination** by Indians changed schooling. By 1998, few government boarding schools remained open. Monies guaranteed in treaties still partially support most Indians in a college education and some professional training. Today, most Indian students go to state schools. Others go to old **Bureau of Indian Affairs** schools, now run by tribes. Some independent, Indian-controlled schools operate in cities and on **reservations**. In the 1970s, tribally controlled community colleges brought higher education to the reservations. The colonial dream of educating Indian children is alive, but today that dream is one shared and often controlled by Indian parents and by tribes.

**208 Below** Bill Reid (1920–97), a **Haida** artist, was one of the best-known sculptors in Indian Country. His huge pieces, carved from stone and cast in **metal**, draw on Haida and other traditional designs of the Queen Charlotte Islands of the **Northwest Coast**. This sculpture, *The Spirit of Haida Gwaii or Black Canoe* (on display at the Canadian Embassy in Washington, D.C.) is an abstract monument to the great seagoing canoes and **whalers** of the Haida past. The canoe carries 13 figures – **Raven**, Mouse Woman, Grizzly **Bear**, Bear Mother, **Beaver**, Dogfish Woman, **Eagle**, Frog, Wolf and a chief. Raven and **Wolf** represent the two **clans** in the Haida world.

## Sculpture

Most indigenous people have some sculptural traditions in wood, stone, clay or **metal** carving and moulding, and even in the moulding of huge mound-like earthworks. In some cultures (among **Northwest Coastal** peoples, for example) those traditions produced monumental sculptures; in others, useful tools, religious artefacts and figurative carvings. With European tools came the possibility of carving and shaping larger and more refined works.

Early sculptors on the Plains, in the Southeast, in the **Arctic** and on the Northwest Coast produced **pipes** and pipe stems, clubs, speaker's staffs, **house posts**, architectural features of houses, eating bowls, spoons and ladles, **rattles**, animal and human figures and faces, bone and ivory carving, **pottery** and stone figures and **dance** sticks. In the early 20th century, artists combined Western/European and Native traditions and began to produce sculptural works of **art** in **metal**, stone, clay and wood.[49]

**209 Right** Bob Haozous is a contemporary **Apache** artist whose work can be a humorous well as a political commentary on Indian history. His father was the distinguished sculptor, Alan Houser, and Haozous puts his own history and that of the Apache people into this 1989 cast metal, painted piece, *Apache Soul House*. The *gaan* dancer on top, a spirit figure that comes during the Crown Dance of the Apache, represents a way of communicating with the spirit world.

## Self-determination, self-government

Along with **land claims**, the other major issue of concern for Native communities in Canada has been self-government. Native groups argue that they never gave up their right to self-government, but no-one agrees as to what is meant by 'self-government'. In the 1980s the Canadian Constitution was rewritten and the existing aboriginal treaty rights of Canada's Native people were recognized. In addition, a large proportion of Native people live in cities away from reserves and the question of how this affects self-government needs to be addressed.

A series of amendments to the Constitution on native self-government were proposed, including naming the aboriginal government as one of the three orders of government in Canada. This amendment in the Charlottetown Accord was rejected in a national referendum. A second agreement, the Meech Lake Accord, was also unsuccessful because Elijah Harper (the Manitoba Native Member of the Legislative Parliament) went against it. The Meech Lake Accord would have allowed amendments to the Canadian Constitution that would have provided special rights and recognition for the province of Québec and for First Nations people. It was worked out at a meeting of provincial and Native leaders, and had to be approved by all the provincial governments within a two-year period. Many Native communities were not satisfied with the agreement because they felt it did not go far enough in recognizing Native rights. Native women felt it gave too much power to band councils, the same councils that supported women being excluded from the Indian Act if they married non-Native men. The province of Manitoba was the last to hold a vote on the issue. Elijah Harper used a little known legal clause to stall the vote until after the time limit ran out.

**W**e're going to create political institutions that will reflect our beliefs and our thinking… . Native people will have much to contribute over the next century. It's our turn.
*Georges Erasmus, former Grand Chief of the Assembly of First Nations*

Elijah Harper was born on a trap line in Northern Manitoba to **Cree-Ojibwa** parents.

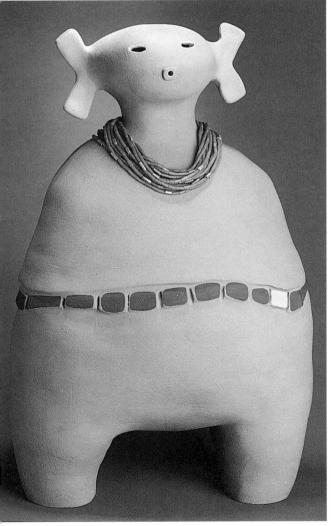

**210 Above** *Emergence of the Clowns*, 1988, by Roxanne Swentzell from Santa Clara Pueblo.

**211 Left** Nora Naranjo Morse, from Santa Clara Pueblo, and her niece, Roxanne Swentzell, have taken their traditional **pottery** toward sculpture in the large ceramic figures they produce. This sculpture, *Mudwoman*, refers to the connection between the origins of Pueblo people and pottery (see **adobe**) and to the mudhead **clowns** that often appear in Pueblo **art**, **dance** and mythology.

212 Left The most famous image of Elijah Harper shows him holding an **eagle** feather for strength and guidance. Harper was unswerving in his opposition to the Meech Lake Accord.

He completed his high-school certificate and spent a year at the University of Manitoba studying anthropology. He was appointed as Chief of the Red Sucker Band and was later elected to the Alberta government. He ran in the federal elections as a Liberal candidate and served one term. Harper is a good example of the efforts of present-day Canadian Indians to achieve self-government.

In the United States, the struggle for what Native people call self-determination can be seen in the call for the return of tribal lands to Native control. The people also want to be able to follow their Native religion, to use and preserve sacred lands and sites, to control education and healthcare, and to develop natural resources. The battles, mostly unsuccessful, for the return of Blue Lake to Taos Pueblo, Pyramid Lake to the Paiutes, the Black Hills to the **Sioux**, and large parts of the state of Maine to the Passamaquoddy and Penobscot, came to stand for Indian struggles for self-determination.

**Tribal governments** in the United States can now set their own priorities and goals for educational and social programmes and use the annual payments set out in **treaties** to operate their own **schools**, hospitals and law enforcement agencies. Most tribal governments, however, are too small, too poor and too dependent on the government to achieve the sort of ideal self-government they might hope for. Some fear that the move for self-determination is simply another way for the government to avoid its responsibilities toward Indians. Others fear that the efforts do not go far enough toward freeing tribal governments to function as **sovereign** nations.

## Seminoles

The word 'Seminole' comes from the Spanish *cimarron*, meaning wild or runaway. Seminoles and Miccosukees are descendants of **Creek** Indians who fled to Florida from the coastal and interior South in the early 18th century. They included groups such as the Apalachi and Yamassee, who fled to North Florida after the Yamassee War in 1715 and the Upper Creeks who joined them in 1814 after the **Red Stick Wars**. The Seminoles followed Creek cultural and **economic** practices, organizing themselves into **matrilineal** villages, governed by chiefs. Living in the Everglade swamps of Florida, they have been and still are **hunters**, **farmers** and **fisherpeople**. The Second Seminole War in 1835–42 was as a result of Seminole resistance to resettlement and **Removal**. The majority of the Seminoles were removed to Oklahoma, although some managed to remain in Florida. They endured various further migrations to **Indian Territory** – one group of so-called Black Seminoles went to Northern Mexico (an area that became part of the state of Texas in 1848).

Florida Seminoles, because of their isolation, remained very traditional; most still speak the Muskogee **language**. They established three reservations in 1911, with an additional area for the Miccosukees who separated into the Everglades in South Florida. Although most Seminoles and Miccosukees remain poor, they pioneered the development of **tourism** in Everglades and swamps and eventually set up successful tribal museums. The Seminole women took up the sewing machine in the early 20th century, and their people are known for their superb ribbonwork, appliqué and patchwork clothing. In the 1980s, they led the way for other tribes in the development of high stakes **gambling** based on their status as a **sovereign** nation.

The Seminoles in Oklahoma (combined of Muskogee- and Hitchiti-speaking peoples) and the Black Seminole Freedmen (see **Africans**) are fairly indistinguishable from Creeks/Muscogees. Many still speak Muskogee, and keep their traditional ceremonial life, although they combine it with **Christian** practice as do most of the Southeastern tribal peoples in Oklahoma. Although they have been paid some money for the lands lost in Florida in the early 19th

**145**

century, they have only 36,000 of the 347,000 acres of land originally set aside in Oklahoma. They lost most of this land through **allotment** and the 'land grab' period in Oklahoma Indian history.

## Seneca

The original name for the Seneca means 'people of the big hill'. During much of the 18th century the Seneca were a powerful and wealthy Indian nation, the westernmost nation of the **Iroquois Confederacy**. Their traditional lands included a large part of present-day Western New York State and ranged into Ohio and Canada. They had acquired much of this territory through alliances and wars in the 17th century. Their vast domain enabled them to become major partners in the **fur trade** with the new European settlers. As the most numerous of the peoples in the Iroquois Confederacy, they were central figures in the territorial and political struggle between nations and cultures – European and Indian.

European **diseases** wiped out entire villages and weakened many Native peoples' trust in their religious leaders. In the 17th century the Senecas increasing involvement in the fur trade had led to **wars** against the Huron, the Erie and their French allies, and these hostilities persisted into the 18th century until a **treaty** was signed with the French and Indian allies in 1710. Other tribes in the Confederacy favoured alliances with the **British** or the rebellious American settlers. Missionaries pressured tribes to become **Christian** and Indian lands were given or sold to acquire European goods or to encourage friendly relations.

The Seneca reluctantly sided with the British in the American Revolution and so fell in defeat with their allies. In 1797 the Treaty of Big Tree established Seneca **reservations** in the state of New York. The Treaty of Fort Stanwix forced the Seneca to give up much of their land. By 1838, the four reservations of Buffalo Creek, Tonawanda, Cattaraugus and Allegheny remained. From the 1830s, many Seneca and other Iroquois were removed from Ohio and New York to reservations in Kansas and Oklahoma. The Tonawanda Seneca later bought back most of their reservation. They restored a government by hereditary chiefs, whereas the Allegheny and Cattaraugus Seneca have elected systems.

In the 1960s the Allegheny Seneca lost one-third of the reservation to the Kinzua **dam** project. They received compensation, but the land was irreplaceable. At Tonawanda, 99-year leases to non-Indians by the **Bureau of Indian Affairs** on the Tonawanda Reservation ran out. The Tonawanda Seneca forced the government to acknowledge that they still retained the lands that they once bought back and that it had violated its trust agreement with the Seneca. Negotiations continue between non-Indian residents and Seneca who want the land back and compensation for territories that should not have been taken.

## Sequoyah

The **Cherokees** became a literate people in the 1820s when Sequoyah (1790–c.1843), whose English name was George Guess, developed a method of writing the Cherokee language. Sequoyan is the only known, widely used written **language** invented by one person alone. By 1830, most Cherokees could read and write in their own language. In those years of turmoil, the creation of a written language gave Cherokees power. Sequoyan was a real form of resistance against white domination and a force for cultural revitalization.

The Cherokee Nation brought a printing press and two sets of type, one in English and one in the syllabary (set of characters) invented by Sequoyah. In 1828 the first issue of a bilingual newspaper, edited by **Elias Boudinot**, rolled off the presses. Cherokee hymnals, New Testaments and other publications soon followed, as did a flood of handwritten official documents, school lessons, correspondence, personal memoirs and record books.

Sequoyah, who had joined the 'Old Settlers' who had voluntarily moved to the Arkansas territory in the 1820s, tried to reunite the tribe in the West in the face of

**213 Above** A painting of 1828, by Charles Bird King, shows Sequoyah with a copy of his **Cherokee** syllabary in his hand. Sequoyah is dressed, like other Cherokee and Southeastern men of his time, in a cloth turban decorated with bird plumes, and a cloth European-style 'hunting jacket'. His clay pipe also speaks of European **trade** influences on Native practices, even though Sequoyah himself opposed the adoption of white ways.

**214 Right** The front page of the newspaper, *Cherokee Advocate*. With its name in computer-generated Sequoyan script, it features the 1994 graduating students from Sequoyah High School in Tahlequah, Oklahoma.

enormous political unrest, violence and separation. When he was in his eighties, he and a band of followers went to the Texas territories and Mexico in order to visit other Indians and see something of the Western country. He died and was buried in Mexico before he could be reached by a messenger sent from the tribe to find him. *Oo-noo-leh*'s letter announcing his death to the Cherokee Council is evidence of the revolution in literacy caused by this extraordinary man.

**215 Above** As the Bible was among the first documents to appear using his invented written language, Sequoyah feared that his invention would be used to undermine **Cherokee** culture. However, his work was immediately used to preserve Cherokeean traditional culture. **Medicine** men and women (*disganawisdi*) began to write down many of their 'prescriptions', in the form of chants, prayers and formulae for plant medicines. This is part of a page with a 'dawn Song' in the Sequoyan script, from the writings of Ayasta, a female *disganawisdi* in the East.

## Shells, shellwork

Molluscs were an important food source for coastal peoples. For centuries, people have also used sea and freshwater shells as currency (see **wampum**), decoration, religious objects, musical instruments and tools. Inland Natives (for example Pueblos) journeyed to the great rivers and to the oceans in order to obtain particular shells. They **traded** hides, **feathers** and other important objects for shells from faraway places. People from the Mississippi delta carved stories in and made gorgets from the whelk and freshwater pink mussel shells of their inland rivers. **Cherokee** people today do the same. Pueblos, from

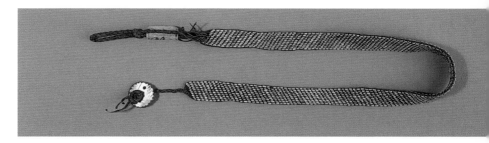

Santo Domingo, mirror the world in shell necklaces with the earth below in seashell and the sky above in turquoise. Plains people, far away from the sea, burn their cedar, sage and sweetgrass for prayers in abalone shells. Shells are used by many as **dance** rattles. They are connected with water, and so with the origin of life.

**216 Above** A shellwork necklace from Northern California.

**217 Below** A necklace of albalone shells made by Native people in California.

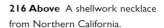

## Sitting Bull

Sitting Bull was an Oglala Lakota holy man who became a war chief embodying all the virtues of his people. Known and feared as a warrior, both by whites and other Indians, he was a skilful political leader as well as a spiritual one. It fell on him to make the last resistance to the whites who wanted the Indians' land. However, neither his leadership nor his sponsorship of resistance could stop the final disaster for the **Sioux** people. Sitting Bull, after his time as a prisoner of war following the battle at the **Little Bighorn**, retired to the reservation to farm, raise cattle, send his children to white schools, and travel with Buffalo Bill Cody's Wild West Show.

Eventually, however, Sitting Bull could not hold back his opposition to land **allotments** under the Dawes Act nor his participation in the **Ghost Dance**. The Ghost Dance was intended to bring back the buffalo and to expel the whites from Indian lands forever. For Indians it was a last resort against assimilation into a non-Indian world. Trying to resist removal from the reservation, Sitting Bull was murdered by an Indian policeman in 1890, but his reputation is known around the world.

## Sioux (Lakota, Dakota, Nakota)

The word 'Sioux', perhaps a mixture of **Ojibwa** and French words that may mean 'little snakes', has been used to describe at least 14 related groups of peoples speaking three different dialects. They occupied territories from Eastern Wisconsin to South Dakota to Montana as well as north to the Canadian plains. They included the Eastern Dakota (Mdewankânton or Santee, Sisseton, Wahpeton and Wahpekute), the middle territory Nakota (Yankton, Yanktonai, Assiniboine) and the Western Lakota (Oglala, Sicangu, Sihasapa, Itazipacola, Minneconjou, Hunkpapa, and Oowenupa). These peoples formed a loose confederacy of members of the Sioux Nation (Ocetai Sakowin or Seven Council Fires). They fished and gathered **wild rice** and other plants in the east, protected pipestone quarries and mined pipestone in the middle territories, and protected the Black Hills and hunted buffalo (*pte*) in the West. Living in small, family-centred groups called *tiyospaye*, they traded with each other and practised shared religious beliefs given to them by *Wakan Tanka* (the Creator) and White Buffalo Calf Woman long ago.

Sioux lives and economies were revolutionized when the Spanish introduced the **horse** to America. The horse enabled them to hunt, travel and trade over vast areas. They were able to develop much more elaborate artistic traditions, especially beadwork, because of the extent of their trade in beads and hides. Later the French **fur trade** brought both peaceful interaction between Sioux and Europeans (including **intermarriage**) and the beginning of territorial disputes that escalated when American soldiers and traders arrived in the mid-nineteenth century. Dakota and Lakota had long-standing territorial arguments with Pawnees and **Ojibwa**, and the missionary intrusions into Sioux country and the seizures of Sioux land by the US army and settlers made the conflicts worse.

The **Treaty** of Fort Laramie in 1851 was meant to define protected territories, but it only split the Sioux into factions that supported or rejected the treaty, and further worsened relations between all Sioux and the government. The 1868 Fort Laramie Treaty confined all Sioux onto the Great Sioux Reservation, and the government forced them to sell the gold-rich Black Hills. (The Lakota never accepted the payments.) Armed resistance followed, leading to the Battle of the **Little Bighorn** when **Sitting Bull** and Crazy Horse defeated General Custer. Minneconjou, Hunkpapa, Oglala and other Lakota bands began to take part in the **Ghost Dance** movement. The murder of Sitting Bull and the massacre of Lakota at **Wounded Knee** in 1980 ended the so-called Indian Wars. The Sioux were confined to a reservation reduced by **allotment** and by new settlement by ranchers and farmers.

For the Seven Council Fires the twentieth century has been a continuing struggle to regain **sovereign** control over their religious practice, **language**, territory and government. The Sioux have continued to press their claims against the US government, trying to regain the resources that would allow them to be independent. In the 1970s they produced a ground-breaking educational system of community-based **schools** and tribal colleges much imitated by other Native nations.[50]

# Sovereignty

We consider ourselves as a free and distinct nation and the government of the United States has no police over us further than a friendly intercourse in trade.
*Cherokee statement, June 1818*

The several Indian nations are distinct political communities, having territorial boundaries, within which their authority is exclusive, and having a right to all lands within those boundaries, which is not only acknowledged, but guaranteed by the United States.
*US Supreme Court Chief Justice John Marshall, in Worcester v. Georgia, 1832*

Indians have always insisted on their existence as sovereign, separable, free and independent governments – as nations. In the 1820s and the 1960s, Indians began to test their sovereignty in the courts, with cases on aboriginal rights and those laid down in **treaties**. Indian claims of sovereignty are involved in movements to regain alienated lands and aboriginal **hunting** and **fishing** territories, and most recently in the tribal development of the sale of **tobacco** products and the establishment of **gambling** activities on **reservations**. Although the courts and the government almost always uphold the legal principle of sovereignty, the actual attempts to practice it cause enormous conflicts both inside Indian communities and in their relationships with the outside world.

---

THE WHITE HOUSE

Office of the Press Secretary
For Immediate Release 29 April 1994
MEMORANDUM FOR THE HEADS OF EXECUTIVE DEPARTMENTS
AND AGENCIES

SUBJECT: Government-to-Government Relations with Native American Tribal Governments

The United States Government has a unique legal relationship with Native American tribal governments as set forth in the Constitution of the United States, treaties, statutes and court decisions. As executive departments and agencies undertake activities affecting Native American tribal rights or trust resources, such activities should be implemented in a knowledgeable, sensitive manner respectful of tribal sovereignty. Today, as part of an historic meeting, I am outlining principles that executive departments and agencies, including every component bureau and office, are to follow in their interactions with Native American tribal governments. The purpose of these principles is to clarify our responsibility to ensure that the Federal Government operates within a government-to-government relationship with federally recognized Native American tribes. I am strongly committed to building a more effective day-to-day working relationship reflecting respect for the rights of self-government due the sovereign tribal governments. In order to ensure that the rights of sovereign tribal governments are fully respected, executive branch activities shall be guided by the following...

WILLIAM J. CLINTON

# Squash

Squash is one of the three major traditional Indian food plants (the 'Three Sisters'). The other two are **beans** and **maize**. The genus *curcurbita* includes all of today's edible and ornamental squashes, as well as pumpkins and gourds. Like most crops cultivated by American Indians before the arrival of Europeans, squash (an **Algonquian** word) is presumed to have originated in Mexico. By the 10th century, most **agriculturally** oriented tribes regarded squash as a staple **food**.

The blossoms, meat and seeds are edible. The seeds also provide an important source of oil. Slices or circular cuts of squash and pumpkin flesh were either sun- or fire-dried, making them ready to eat simply by rehydrating them. In the East, squashes were traditionally grown with beans and maize. This method of interplanting saved space and increased crop yield, and the large-leafed squash kept down weed growth and provided cover to the dry soil.

**218 Left** Many different kinds of native squashes are held for recovery of their seeds at the Native Seeds/SEARCH. This group of biologists and agricultural specialists in Tucson, Arizona, works to restore traditional **agriculture** among native peoples of Mexico and the United States.

**219 Right** Frank Poolheco, a Hopi-Tewa artist from Albuquerque, makes beautiful gourd **rattles**, like this one, for **Buffalo Dances** at Hopi and Zuni. They call the **rain**, so that the crops will grow.

**220 Left** A feast day dance at Santa Clara Pueblo. The man in the foreground wears a **headdress** featuring squash blossom. The women wear *tablitas* with cloud and **rain** designs on them.

**221 Left** An early 19th-century **Cherokee** gourd **rattle**, probably used by **medicine** men (*disganawisdi*) in their prayers, songs and rituals.

Gourds are a type of squash and tribes made use of them in many ways. After removing the inner flesh of a gourd, the tough outer rind was made into objects such as bottles, bowls, cornmeal sifters, cups, funnels, ladles, spoons and strainers. Large gourds were used for storing and carrying water and as **fish** bait containers and fishnet floats. Two dried and hollow gourds around the body of a child learning to swim made a fine life jacket. Southeastern Indians also made gourd birdhouses which were placed on poles located throughout their fields of cultivated crops to attract insect-eating birds. Tribal peoples made hollow gourds into **rattles**, by placing seeds, small stones or shotgun pellets into them to create different sounds.

Squashes are mentioned in sacred songs of Southwestern tribes, such as the Pima and **Navajo**, and they appear in the **creation stories** of many Northeastern tribes such as the **Iroquois** and **Ojibwa**. There are four sacred plants in Navajo origin stories – maize, **tobacco**, beans and squash. The image of the squash plant appears in many Navajo weavings and the squash blossom in silver Navajo jewellery. The Tewa-speaking Northern Pueblo **clans** divide into winter and summer people or turquoise and squash people. The squash blossoms also appear in Pueblo **dance headdresses**, in traditional paintings and in designs on **pottery**.

Truly in the East
The white bean
And the great corn-plant
Are tied with the white lightning.
Listen! Rain approaches!
The voice of the bluebird is heard.
Truly in the East
The white bean
And the great squash
Are tied with the rainbow.
*Navajo chant*

**Status Indians**, see **Federally recognized tribes**

## Stereotypes

Picture these old scenes.

A young Indian woman throws herself into a ravine, because her father has forbidden her love for the young white man.

A handsome, strong warrior, dressed in buckskins, with flowing black hair, and a full war bonnet, raises his bow to the sky as he sings his death song.

An Indian with a raised tomahawk and scalplock, creeps from a grove of trees towards a small cabin in a clearing.

An old man, his long braids hanging forward over his shoulders, is slumped at dusk on a tired pony, his lance dragging the ground. It is the End of the Trail.

A beautiful dark-haired woman, throws her body over the kneeling and bound figure of a white man. Other Indians, fierce and hostile, loom over them.

Picture these new scenes.

On an American football field, a young white man dressed as a Plains war chief dances and shouts every time the team (the 'Braves' or the 'Redskins') scores, while the band plays a loud drumbeat.

Children on a suburban housing estate, dressed in cowboy hats and **feather** headbands, chase each other.

A spiritualist hands out flyers to passers-by advertising her service, which features an Indian spirit guide called Chief Red **Eagle**.

In stores in Santa Fe, white women dressed in turquoise and silver **squash** blossom necklaces buy designer clothes styled in the manner of the Old Indian West.

In a television advert an actor plays an Indian weeping over a polluted stream.

In the Black Forest of Germany, families visit a 'Sioux' encampment, spending the week dancing war dances, tanning hides and taking sweatbaths.

These figures are part of the mythology of Native American people – the Maid of the Mist, The Noble Savage, the Chieftain's Death Song, the Skulking Savage, the Poor Indian at the End of the Trail and the Tragic Half-Breed.

Particularly in New England and the Mid Atlantic, where Indians were no longer common, they were often romanticized in poems, songs, legends, Wild West Shows, medicine shows, circuses, films and artefacts.

Virtually all of these images, stories and stereotypes transferred themselves in a new form into the 20th century – Indian sports mascots dance on sports fields, 'New Age' 'shamans' lead white men and women through expensive healing **ceremonies** and children still play '**cowboys and Indians**'. Americans and Europeans still treasure their old ideas and images of Indians.[51]

## Stickball

Stickball, played by **Cherokees**, is similar in some ways to lacrosse, particularly in its connection with ritual. Unlike lacrosse, it is played with two sticks. Although life among the Eastern Cherokees changed, many traditional beliefs, pastimes and ways of life were preserved as a result of their resistance to Anglo-American pressures. In the 1880s, the anthropologist James Mooney from the Smithsonian's Institution visited the Eastern Cherokees to document surviving traditional aspects of their culture. He found the Cherokee **language** still written and spoken, many ancient religious beliefs and practices still followed, activities of daily life performed in traditional ways, and stickball playing and traditional **dancing as** popular as ever.

**222 Above Cherokee** men and women preparing for a game of stickball, *c.* 1885.

# Stomp dance

Here's the scene. Night. A fire. A circle. Indians dancing around it. But something is wrong. Where are the beads? Only an occasional feather on a man's hat. Hats, jeans, overalls, cowboy boots. Calico dresses, regular clothes.... The music doesn't sound right either. No *dum*-dum-dum-dum drum. Just a high-pitched small drum. One man's voice calls out a line.... A small drum, the water drum, small enough to fit in one hand, makes the beat for this music. Creek songs are fast and crazy Cherokees like Creek singing. But if you don't watch it, the Creek men will charm you with that singing. Moving feet and rattles on the women's legs make the rest of the percussion for the call-and-response of the men's songs. The women make the rattles, called shackles, out of box turtles – sometimes condensed milk tins – sewn onto pieces of leather. Nowadays, they're just as likely to be sewn on the top parts of old cowboy boots.... The shackles are heavy and the people dance all night, but the shell-shakers keep the beat. Linda Hogan, a Chickasaw writer told it this way in a poem called 'Calling Myself Home'.

> There were old women
> who lived on amber. Their dark hands
> laced the shells of turtles
> together, pebbles inside
> and they danced
> with rattles strong on their legs.

In 1889, many [traditional] Cherokees reacted against changes in Cherokee society and resuscitated the Keetoowah Society. A Cherokee named Red Bird Smith formed a group known as the 'Nighthawk Keetoowah'. They not only sought to restore old practices and ceremonies such as the stomp dance, but actively, though unsuccessfully, opposed the allotment of Cherokee tribal lands. Stomp dances and other ceremonies continue today in Oklahoma. The members of the Keetoowah Society keep the stomp grounds because they keep the Sacred Fire. The Keetoowahs help the *Aniyunwiya* remember.

The people who belong to the stomp grounds sit under their seven brush arbors. Things begin when they are all represented, and everybody else rings around that huge circle. At particular celebrations, the people might play stickball and make a speech telling the history of the People and this stomp ground. After playing ball and sharing food, they dance. Some go back and forth to their arbors or trucks and cars and to lawn chairs and benches sitting with friends. People come from the outside rings and inside to join the counter-clockwise movement of a particular dance. The leader and the men turn their heads and hands toward the fire, honouring the fire. The people dance all night. There are lots of stomp dance songs; some are about animals, others about friendship, even love. These are always happy dances. Sometimes the song tells a funny story and laughter rises up in the middle of the dance. You should hear what Rabbit sang when he taught the wolves a new dance.... You will not see this dance at a pow wow, scarcely even when just Indians are gathering with each other, because this music and dance hasn't been widely shared with other people. Only those who know the songs, summer after summer, sing them.... At the end, Cherokees might say '*wado, wado*', 'thank you, thank you', because they have so appreciated the song and the dance.

*Rayna Green, Cherokee folklorist*

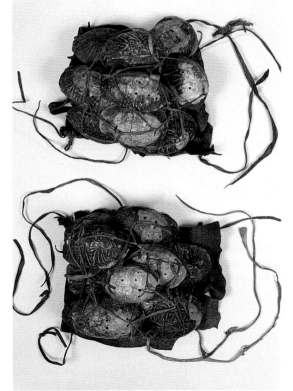

**223 Left** Southeastern Indian women (**Cherokee**, Choctaw, **Seminole** and **Creek**) make the rhythm for the stomp dance with the **turtle shells** they wear on their legs. Cherokees call the women 'shell shakers'.

**224 Above** These young Choctaw women in Washington, D.C., demonstrate a stomp dance. One woman wears shackles or 'turtles' made of tin cans.

For God said, if the Cherokees be destroyed and become extinct, then that will be the destruction of the whole world. This is the word of the forefathers of our own land.
*Keetoowah Society of Cherokee Indians*

## Subsistence

Subsistence (subsistence **economies**), or living off the resources of the land, is a way of life – spiritual and physical. For most Native people in the **Arctic**, in the far Northwest and in Northern Canada, **hunting** and **fishing** are necessities, which have been undermined by sport, trophy and commercial fishing. Subsistence life is threatened by competition for resources, whether industrial, chemical,

legal or human. Thus, Native Alaskans, **Ojibw**a in Michigan, Wisconsin and Minnesota, and Puyallup and others in the state of Washington are now working to restore their hunting and fishing rights because of their physical and spiritual need for the subsistence lifestyle. As before, Native men and women need to know how to hunt, fish, grow and preserve their **food**, and how to grow it, but today they also need to know how to protect it in the courts.

Our subsistence way of life is especially important to us. Among other needs it is our greatest. We are desperate to keep it.
*Paul John, Tununak, 1984*

*Bear's Heart. Cheyenne*

## Sun Dance

To Plains people, the Sun Dance was, and to some still is, their most important ceremonial event. Crow, Cheyenne, **Cree**, Assiniboine, Lakota, **Blackfeet**, Arapaho, Paiute, Shoshone, Bannock, Kiowas and Utes all shared the Sun Dance Religion. The dance was a target for **missionaries** and governments and so was banned (along with the **potlatch** and the **Ghost Dance**) by both Canada and the United States in the latter part of the 19th century. The Sun Dance, which requires that its believers work, pray and sacrifice for the good of all, has been revitalized in a number of places.

> **S**un Dance
> *Wakan tanka*
> when I pray to him, he hears me
> Whatever is good,
> he grants me.
> *Teton Sioux Sun Dance song*

**225 Above** In this ledger drawing made by Bear's Heart, a Cheyenne, c. 1874, men and women gather in front of a Sun Dance Lodge to fulfil their pledge to dance. Sheets of paper from ledgers (large, bound inventory and accounts books used by traders and military men) were used by Indians to make drawings about their lives and histories.

## Sweetgrass

This grass grows from Siberia to the Northern Plains of the United States and Canada and east to Nova Scotia. Many Indians use it to make **baskets** or as a kind of incense, that is a purifying smoke to accompany prayers and songs. Like sage, cedar and, to some extent, **tobacco**, the smoke from burning sweetgrass sends prayers to the spirits.

**S**weetgrass
This sacred medicine, associated with the northern direction,
is made from hair of our mother, the earth.
…
Strength, Courage, Love,
Humbleness, Knowledge, Sharing and Respect,
The sweetgrass teaches us these gifts,
and helps us to embrace them in our prayers… .

*Andrea Johnston*

**S**weetgrass is a link to remembering our past and a process of recovery… . Reclaiming, recovering and honouring the work and knowledge of these grandmothers is at the core of this effort.
*Rebecca Baird*

**226 Left** Barbara Kiyoshk with her sweetgrass **baskets** at the Six Nations **pow wow** in 1994.

**227 Left** In 1993 Rebecca Baird, a Canadian Native artist, produced this work called *A Time Within Memory*, together with traditional **basketmakers** such as Barbara Kiyoshk.

T

## Tekakwitha, Kateri

The Blessed *Kateri Tekakwitha*, the 'Lily of the **Mohawks**' was an **Iroquois** woman who converted to Catholicism in the 1500s. She died of smallpox when nursing others with the **disease**. During the 20th century, she became a focal point of Indian national pride, with non-Catholic and Catholic Indians alike demanding that the Church declare her a saint.

**228 Right** A fringed and embroidered banner for *Kateri Tekakwitha*, from St Joseph's **Apache** Mission in New Mexico.

## Termination

After the reorganization of the **Bureau of Indian Affairs** (BIA) in 1934 and the involvement of Indians in the **Second World War**, many felt there were clear signs of reform and progress for the Indian people. However, a new conservative movement in government demanded cuts to the budget. In 1953 some Congressmen proposed a policy of termination in order to end the government's relationship with Indians and to end their status as 'wards of the government'. Indian Commissioner Dillon Myers, in charge

of Japanese-US imprisonment during the Second World War put forward a plan to stop government Indian programmes. Congress passed a resolution 'freeing' tribes in California, New York, Texas and Florida from government supervision. Other Bills followed, terminating Menominee, Klamath, Siletz, Grande Ronde, some Paiute bands and all California rancherias from their federal **status**. Governments in a number of states took over the control of the administration and legal systems of some tribes. The US government was still responsible nationally for Indian education in the state and reservation **schools** and for Indian healthcare.

Within 10 years, the policy had proved a disaster (as had **relocation** to the cities). The termination policy was eventually rejected and a policy of **self-determination** for tribes was adopted. Many tribes had Acts passed to restore them to federal status. For example, the Menominee Restoration Act of 1973 returned Menominee land to trust status, re-establishing tribal authority and giving the tribe access to government services. A young Menominee woman called Ada Deer, who would 25 years later serve as head of the BIA, led the fight to restore her people. Even though the termination policy of the government was abandoned, some tribal peoples still remain terminated and unrestored.

O ne of the continuing themes that the majority culture never wants to hear is that Indians want to be Indians. Indians want to retain culture, want to retain the land, want to live as Indians live… despite the many policies of the federal government over the years, from Removal to putting people on reservations, to allotment, to assimilation [see acculturation], to termination, the continuing wish and desire of the Indians is to remain Indian, and this never seems to get across.

*Ada Deer, Menominee*

## Tlingit

One of the Tsimshian language family, the Tlingit live along the islands in the archipelago of Southeast Alaska. Famed as seafaring **traders**, they exchanged goods with the **Haida**. They traded copper and mountain-goat wool for slaves and **shell** ornaments. They traded inland, taking European goods to the **Athabaskan**s in exchange for furs.

Their society is highly complex. The community is **matrilineal** and children are born into the mother's clan (either **Eagle** or **Raven**) and live in the mother's house. The **clans** govern social, political and **ceremonial** life. Members of houses joined to **hunt**, **fish** and trade. Today, Tlingit families live as nuclear families but hold ceremonial activities in the clan houses. These houses are filled with their clan symbols, such as the 'crests' that adorn houses, which tell stories of the history of the clans and serve as titles to land, and images carved onto **boxes**.

Land claims and hunting and fishing rights have occupied the Tlingits during the 20th century. Along with the Haida, they pursued their first **land claims** settlement in 1968. They were awarded US$7.5 million by the US Court of Claims, far short of their proposed settlement of US$80 million. This money was put into trust to help social and educational programmes. A second settlement in 1971 transferred large areas of land into communal ownership with other groups under the **Alaska Native Claims Settlement Act of 1971**.

## Tobacco

Native to North America, tobacco is an important plant in the lives of Native North Americans and has been used for centuries for ceremonial and medicinal purposes. There is archaeological evidence of tobacco existing from 200 BC. Plains groups use tobacco in **ceremonies** in elaborately decorated **pipes** or *calumets*, to recognize important events such as **war**, peace, **trade**, death and birth. Among the **Cherokees**, tobacco is called 'grandfather'. Among many other nations, it is considered one of the four sacred **medicines** along with sage, sweetgrass and cedar. **Gifts** of tobacco, as a sign of respect, are given at naming ceremonies, healing ceremonies or special counsel from elders.

> **F**or us Natives, most anything that lives and grows has a purpose and a spirit, for the purpose of communication in times of need and in appreciation in meeting those needs; it could be for food… or… medicine… . The medium we have been given for communicating with any spirit is Indian Tobacco.
> *Reg Henry, Cayuga head faithkeeper, from Six Nations*

## Tourism/tourist market

The enormous pressures that tourism put on Western and Southwestern tribal cultures undoubtedly created many features of Indian life we now regard as normal. Native Americans tried to respond positively to these developments by incorporating tourism into their patterns of living. Many Native women were forced into poverty when they lost access to traditional natural resources, and so converted their traditional skills into an artistry that allowed them to join in the cash **economy**. In the Midwest, Winnebagos and Menominees at Wisconsin Dells and in the Northeast at Niagara Falls, New York, **Iroquois basketmakers** and **beadworkers** developed entirely new **art** forms based on Iroquois traditions. In the Southwest too, women skilled at weaving, **pottery** and basketmaking produce goods for tourists (the new Conquistadors), who have built up a substantial demand for Indian goods. The shapes and sizes of pots and baskets changed and became smaller to suit the tourist market. European-style objects, such as picture frames, hats, ladies purses and parasols are beaded, and it is this beadwork that makes these things 'Indian'.

> **W**e didn't make fancy baskets until we were discovered.
> *Eunice Crowley, Mashpee Wampanoag, 1987*

One of the most important cultural projects of the 1930s was the government's restoration of the ruins throughout the Southwest, especially in the Grand Canyon, Chaco Canyon and Pueblo Bonito. The United States was discovering its ancient Indian heritage. Thousands of Eastern tourists came by train to New Mexico and Arizona to 'see the Indians'. Various institutions, trade and art markets, and even **schools** were developed to capitalize on the beauties of American Indian land, craft and art. In this way, tourism made Pueblos and Hispanics into commodities (just

**229 Below** Fancies' or 'whimsies', such as this **Iroquois** pin cushion, represent an important point in the evolution and persistence of native **art** as it adapts to tourist demands and maintains its Indian style.

**230 Above** The Fred Harvey 'Indian Building' at the Alvarado Hotel in Albuquerque, New Mexico, in 1905.

**231 Above** Gerald Nailor painted this humorous view of wealthy tourists shopping for **Navajo** rugs in 1937, while he was a student at Santa Fe Indian School.

like their crafts). The Pueblos adapted and transformed their production from goods for their own communities to those for the tourist market.

Private enterprise, such as the Fred Harvey Company, joined the government in promoting tourism in Indian Country. The Santa Fe Railroad delivered tourists to Harvey hotels, and tours offered a peaceful, safe, beautiful, exciting and exotic adventure, complete with affordable mementoes to take home. The Harvey Company also provided emerging US cultural institutions, such as fairs, expositions and **museums**,[52] with major collections of Indian artefacts and, sometimes, live Indians.

**232 Left** Little beaded 'Comanche' **dolls** (so-called because Zunis learned **beadwork** from Plains Indians with whom they have always traded), such as this one called 'Tourist Girl', are a way of humorously commenting on the outsiders. They also make objects and symbols from the outside world into a **Zuni** way of thinking.

> **W**ell, I can tell you more about the train because it ran right close back where the road is going down to the two rivers. And according to the thing I have heard my grandparents tell me about was the first time when it was going to run through there was a lot of people from the village that came to see it come, and because they had never see a train, they were relating it to *o'khua*, our *katsinas*. And I suppose of the sound that it made. And many of them came, I suppose all of them came with cornmeal. And when they heard the whistle just before it came into sight, they started throwing their cornmeal and told it to come in peace.
> *Estefanita (Esther) Martinez, San Juan Pueblo/Oke Okweenge, 1996*

Indians in the Southwest and elsewhere developed special songs, dances and new instruments for the performances for tourists. This was partly to protect their religious dances from prying eyes and also to produce things that tourists wanted to see. In fact, *tse va ho*, the Tewa word for tourist, means 'someone not afraid to stare'. In some parts of Indian Country, the people who perform

**233 Right** Mary Adams, a **Mohawk** woman, made this 'wedding cake' fancy **basket** in the early 1990s. Fancy baskets of ash splint, as opposed to practical or work baskets, were first made for the tourist trade at Niagara Falls. With all sorts of amendments to common baskets (for example twists, curls and sweetgrass or paper twine), these baskets were produced in shapes and for uses that Anglo-Americans wanted, such as egg baskets.

for this market by dressing in costumes and posing with tourists for photographs are called 'show Indians'. Others, such as the Pueblos, use **humour** as a means of commenting on and controlling those forces that threaten to take over their land, culture and religion. Through ritual clowning, and verbal and visual joking, they deal with peoples and issues that disturb the order of the Pueblo world. Sacred or ceremonial **clowns**, for example, will often tease tourists attending **ceremonies** and even Pueblo members who have upset the order of things.

Nowadays, all over the United States and Canada, Native craft cooperatives and companies market Indian **art** and performance, just as the Harvey Company and Santa Fe Railway once did. Some cater for tourism, providing plastic tomahawks and photographs of tourists with 'Chiefs' in war bonnets. Others support economic development through the production of traditional art, and strive to manage the negative aspects of tourism.

# Trade

Indian nations have long traded goods, such as **shells**, **feathers**, hides and **baskets**, with each other. They travelled from the Mississippi to the Gulf of Mexico, from the high desert Southwest to the Pacific Ocean, from the Northern Plains to the Pacific Northwest and from the Southern Plains to Central Mexico. Languages, such as Mobilian, Chinook 'jargon' and sign, were developed solely for the intertribal trade. Indian women had societies, such as quilling societies, that traded with each other across the Plains.

Trade with Europeans began with the Dutch in the early 1600s. Each group had products that the other wanted and needed, so their trade was useful for both groups. Whites wanted animal pelts, **food**, clothing and advice about survival in this new world. The **Iroquois** and **Algonquin** peoples in the Northeast and Southeast wanted European-made items, such as bells, mirrors, **metal** tools, thimbles, scissors, **blankets**, metal pots, guns, **horses**, cloth, buttons, horse equipment, **beads**, swords, coffee, sugar and **alcohol**. In the early 1700s, the European desire for Indian land and the Indian desire for European goods encouraged trade. Indians gave up traditional **quillwork**, skin

**234 Above** These knives show both traditional and imported technologies. The 18th-century blades, excavated at the Six Nations Reserve in Brantford, Ontario, are made of European **metal**, the wood and antler handles are **Seneca**.

**235 Above** These 18th-century trade **beads** are from Seneca country.

processing and **pottery** in favour of trade cloth, glass beads, metal pots and tools. Wooden utensils, such as spoons and cups and larger carved sculptural pieces became more common after the introduction of European knives and axes. Many goods used by Indians in the 19th century that came from Europe were adapted by Natives to suit their own needs.

Some day you will meet a people who are white. They will always try to give you things, but do not take them. At last I think that you will take these things that they offer you, and this will bring sickness to you.
*Sweet Medicine, Cheyenne prophet*

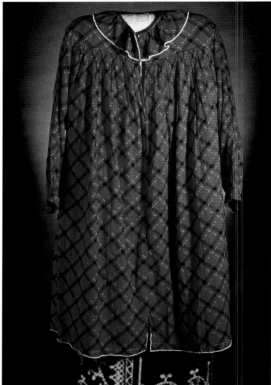

**236 Left** Wendat/Wyandotte women valued Paisley shawls, such as these, from Scottish mills. They also decorated European pouches, made of velvet and cotton, with seed **beads** and Venetian beads in a mix of European and **Iroquoian** floral designs.

**237 Above** Cattaraugus **Seneca** women of the 18th century wore trade cloth dresses, such as this red plaid dress with a white seed-beaded collar, over their tunics and leggings.

## Traders and agents

When the Spanish arrived in the Southwest, they demanded that the Pueblo people give them **food**, **blankets** and **maize**. They forced Indians to make knitted stockings and provide tanned hides. At first, Indians valued most items made of **metal**, then things made of cloth and wool. Many things became valuable for both groups of people, but the balance quickly shifted, making Indians dependent on the European goods.

Commercial trade was often the basis for early **exploration** and **contact** with Indians. Sir Walter Raleigh made **tobacco** the source of a financial empire for England. Captain James Cook went to North America for the **fur trade**. By the mid 1780s, **British**, Spanish, French and Americans all competed for sea otter pelts, which they then took to China to trade. This intensive **hunting** brought about the extinction of the sea otter along the coast of British Columbia. Chiefs in this area built up great wealth due to this trade, redistributing it through the **potlatch**.

Traders were rarely interested in land, only in goods. The next major contact was for land-based fur trade and the Hudson Bay Company set up a trading post in Fort Langley in 1827.

**238 Above** This trading post at Fort Defiance or Camp Apache was established in 1873 before the development of the Southern Apache reservations. A few stores were later operated by Indians as government employees or licensed agents, and they often became the centre for most of the commercial exchange on the reservations.

Commercial agents in private business, often licensed by the British, Spanish, French and later the 'American' governments, entered Indian Country. The government sent agents to supply their troops, then to look after the government's business on **reservations** and in **Indian Territory**. The agents were supposed to fulfil the government's **treaty** obligations in goods and services – the 'annuities' that were guaranteed by treaty to Indians. The first stores and agents, established in forts, delivered flour, ploughs, salt, sugar, coffee, wagons, meat, tools and cloth. Often corrupt agents took the profits, delivered inferior goods or didn't deliver goods at all. Some agents were supposed to teach the Indians **farming** to carry out the government policy of 'civilization'. Later agents, particularly in the Southwest, developed private companies and were extraordinarily influential in the development of Indian crafts, such as **Navajo** weaving and jewellery, Hopi **baskets** and Pueblo **pottery**, for the outside market. Trade items also enabled great leaps in artistic technology – with iron tools, artists could carve large house poles and figures.

# Transport

The **Inuit dog**sled is as famous as the kayak and the canoe. Like its human-propelled cousin, the toboggan, it has largely become a **sport** for non-Indians. A major annual sporting event in Alaska, the Iditarod, is now built around a dogsledding competition.

In addition to the birch**bark** canoes, kayaks and large log canoes of the Northwest, Indians developed many types of vehicle, such as the *travois*, to transport goods.

In the far regions of the **Arctic** and Northwest Territories, Alaska and elsewhere, where distances are great and there is a need to travel quickly, the motorized snowmobile provides a faster and cheaper means of transport than dog teams and sleds. However, this form of transportation has made Inuit and others dependent on imported gasoline and machine parts.

**241 Above  Algonquin** snow shoes. **Ojibwe**, **Cree**, and **Inuit** made different kinds of snow shoes to suit the many kinds of snow conditions.

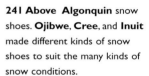

**239 Below**  A Woodlands toboggan.

**240 Above**  An Inupiaq sled.

**242 Above**  A motorized snowmobile used in the Arctic.

## Treaties

Treaties, made between **sovereign** governments, were a main part of European **diplomatic** relations with the new territories. European governments treated Indian governments like those of other states, negotiating treaties with them in order to acquire more land. The treaty was a simple device. Indians gave up certain lands in return for peace, protection from their enemies and one-off or continuous payments. Treaties began the government-to-government relationships between the United States and the tribes and they set out the government's responsibility towards the tribes for 'as long as the grass shall grow and the waters flow' (according to the language of many treaties).

Treaties became the main instruments in the relationship between tribes and Britain France and the new US government. Although treaties are recognized by the US Constitution (the 'supreme law of the land'), there has been much conflict and different interpretations of what they mean for and to tribes, the government and states and what their responsibilities and obligations are to one another.

---

### A Gold Chain

### Chiefs and Warriors of the Choctaw Nation of Indians

The President of the United States takes you by the hand and invites you and all the Nations of Red people within the territory of the United States to look unto him as their father and friend; and to rely in confidence upon his unvarying disposition to lead and protect them in the paths of peace and harmony, and to cultivate friendship with their Brothers of the same colour, and with the Citizens of the United States.

O the chain of friendship is now bright and binds us all together. For your and our sakes and for the sake of your and our children, we must prevent it from becoming rusty. So long as the mountains in our lands shall endure, and our Rivers flow, so long may the Red and White People dwelling in it live in the bonds of brotherhood and friendship.

In order that this friendship may be perpetual and to prevent... every cause which may interrupt it, it is hereby announced... that all lands belonging to you... shall remain the property of your Nation forever, unless you shall voluntarily relinquish or dispose of the same. And all persons Citizens of the United States are hereby strictly forbidden to disturb you or your Nation in the quiet possession of said lands.

The President of the United States sends you by your beloved chiefs, now present, a Chain. It is made of pure gold, which will never rust. And may the Great Spirit assist us in keeping the Chain of Friendship of which this Golden Chain is an emblem bright for a long succession of ages.

H. Dearborn
Indian Office of The United States
War Department
29 December 1803

# Tribal governments

The Yup'iks had their own government for many years before the Indian Reorganization Act was introduced. Yup'iks had their own instructions from way back… that was government… and that whole idea is powerful and can be defined by one word by the white men – sovereignty.
*Mike Albert, Tununak*

Tribal government has existed from time immemorial. It was governing here in 1492 when Columbus supposedly discovered America. The elders say 'Re-establish your own governments, practice self-determination.'
*Willie Kasayulie, Akiachak*

Indians had many forms of government before **contact** with Europeans. These included large, formal and complex multi-tribal confederacies (such as the **Iroquois** and Wabenaki Confederacies). They ranged from governments based in religious structures (the Pueblos) to the loosely organized and leadership-based organizations (Plains tribes). All those forms of government, along with the groups of people themselves, had to change from the moment the European assault began on their old ways of life.

In the mid 19th century, many tribes from the Southwest and Midwest were moved west to **Indian Territory**. They faced tremendous difficulties in merging and existing in these new territories. **Removal** from their old homelands disrupted their traditional forms of government and lifestyles. In 1843, **Cherokee** Principal Chief John Ross called a meeting, a Council of tribes, at Tahlequah, which was the seat of government of the Cherokee Nation. For most tribes, a Council of adult men (and in some cases, women too) was the group that made decisions. Hundreds of representatives from numerous tribes removed to Indian Territory and those whose ancestral homes were in that region and a few US government officials attended the Council.

The Council's purpose was to 'preserve the existence of our race, to revive and cultivate friendly relations between our several communities, to secure to all their respective rights and to promote the general welfare'. The Cherokee Assistant Principal Chief George Lowrey spoke about the

**243 Right** This painting, *The Indian Council of 1843 at Tahlequah, Indian Territory*, is by John Mix Stanley, who was present during the Grand Council in 1843. The figure standing on the podium at the left is probably **Cherokee** Assistant Principal Chief George Lowrey, with John Ross to the far right. The very different forms of dress among the tribal delegates (including Cherokee, **Creek**, Chickasaw, Delaware, Witchita, Potawotomie, Chippewa and **Seminole**) indicates the different peoples who had been removed to Oklahoma. It also shows how important it was to them to wear tribal or 'citizen' clothing at this point in their histories.

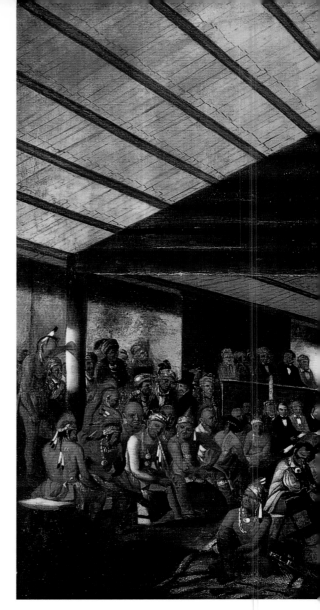

wampum belt given to the Cherokee by the **Seneca** in 1781. He brought it to the Council, where it was used to begin the proceedings. The belt portrayed two men shaking hands at the end of a path, showing the desire that 'the rising generation may travel in peace'. Some of these belts are still used by Cherokees in Oklahoma. The delegates agreed to remain at peace with each other and with the government. In order to please the government, they decided to encourage **agriculture** and education. The Council was one of the first attempts to restore tribal government and to find a way for Indians to speak to Washington and to each other with a unified voice.

Believing that a central government would help them retain control over their lives and their lands, Cherokees in the 1820s recorded

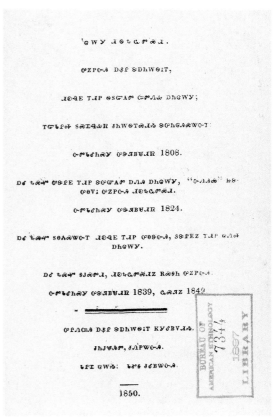

**244 Above** The 1849/1850 Constitution of the **Cherokee** Nation.

We, The Members of the Cherokee Nation in Convention assembled, in order to establish justice, ensure tranquillity, promote the common welfare, and secure to ourselves and our posterity the blessing of liberty: acknowledging with humility and gratitude the goodness of the sovereign Ruler of the Universe, in offering us an opportunity so favourable to the design, and imploring his aid and direction in its accomplishment, do ordain and establish this Constitution for the Government of the Cherokee Nation.
*Preamble to the 1827 Constitution of the Cherokee Nation*

their first formal laws. They also established a national police force and created a Supreme Court. This movement away from local, communal government resulted in the Republican Constitution of 1828. It authorized a government like that of the United States, with a Principal Chief (for administration), a National Council (for laws and regulations) and a Supreme Court. This Constitution was published in Cherokee and in English and tried to unite several groups of Cherokee people and to present a united front to the forces demanding their Removal. Modelled on Southern state constitutions, it went against traditional Cherokee ideas of justice. For example, it legalized slavery and took away the power of Cherokee women who according to traditional law, controlled property and children.

Modern tribes – like nations, states or provinces – adopted Constitutions that set out the principles and methods in which the tribe would be governed and operated, its legal and tax systems, its **citizenship** and its relationships with the US government, states and other political bodies. The Wheeler-Howard or Indian Reorganization Act of 1934 was intended to put tribal governments on an equal footing with other civilian forms of government in the United States. Under this Act, tribes would have their own, standardized Constitutions and elected governments. The **allotment** policy and the handover of land (with the '**civilization**' policy that went with it) were stopped. Enrolled members of tribes had two years in which to accept the Indian Reorganization Act. Some tribes insisted (and still do) that the Act was another way of forcing European ideas onto tribal cultures. However, some tribes were able to incorporate traditional forms of government into the standard Constitution. Although most tribes in the United States have very different forms of government, they do follow practices common to elected, civic governments throughout the world.

The story of Wilma Mankiller, a former Cherokee Principal Chief, demonstrates how tribal governments have developed and evolved in the late 20th century. Raised in Eastern Oklahoma by a **farming** family relocated to California in the 1950s, Mankiller stayed in California and received a better education than that available in rural Oklahoma. In the early 1960s, she became

involved in national politics and the Indian rights movement. As a local Indian community organizer, she participated in the takeover of Alcatraz (see page 121). She returned to Oklahoma and became involved in the development of her own Cherokee community. She was so successful at meeting the needs of rural, traditional communities with the methods of a new, progressive tribal government that Chief Ross Swimmer asked her to run for Deputy Chief of the Cherokee Nation (*Tsalagi Ayili*). Her later election as Principal Chief (*ugu*) of the second largest Indian nation in the country brought her national prominence and she received the Presidential Medal of Freedom.

Some of her opponents for election said women should not serve in public office. However, many Cherokees remembered women's importance in public affairs in the past and Outacitty's words to the **British** delegation: 'Where are your women?'. 'Mankiller' (*Outacitty* or *Asgayadihi*) was a distant relative of Wilma, whose family name still bears his military title. Some in the Cherokee Nation class Wilma Mankiller in the same category as **Nancy Ward** (*Nanyehi*), who

**245 Above** Symbolic of **Cherokee** desire for unity and independence was the 1871 seal. It records the 1839 adoption of the Constitution of the Cherokee Nation in the West. This seal was imprinted on all documents until the Cherokee Nation was dissolved when Oklahoma was made a state in 1906. Today the seal is used once more by the Cherokee Nation of Oklahoma. The seven pointed star symbolizes the seven **clans** of the Cherokees and the seven characters of **Sequoyah**'s syllabary that mean 'Cherokee Nation' (*Tsalagi Ayili*). The wreath of oak leaves stands for the sacred fire of the Cherokee.

**246 Left** A 1994 poster urging the election of an individual for tribal chairman of the **Navajo** Nation.

**247 Above** A 1992 tribal council meeting of the Eastern Band of **Cherokee** Indians, in North Carolina. On the ceiling of the meeting room are carved **masks** representing the seven Cherokee **clans**.

**248 Above** Modern elected tribal governments are responsible for education, economic development, housing, law enforcement and healthcare. The building of the Santa Clara Pueblo government, a combination of a new elected and traditional form of government, has meeting space for residents of Santa Clara, a basketball court, a community library and some offices of the tribal law enforcement.

was one of the last Beloved Women of the Cherokee. This is because they both defended the Cherokee people's **self-determination** so strongly. For many Native people, Mankiller's leadership embodies the old Indian prophecy that that women will lead Indian people into a new era.[53]

**249 Above** The tribal police uniform patches show the **sovereignty** of the nations they are connected with.

**250 Above** The Principal Chief of the **Cherokee** Nation, Wilma Mankiller, giving her inaugural speech in 1987.

Certainly I believe the ancient tribal cultures have important lessons to teach the rest of the world about the interconnectedness of all living things and the simple fact that our existence is dependent upon the natural world we are rapidly destroying. The traditional value systems that have sustained us throughout the past 500 years of trauma are those value systems that will bolster us and help us enter the 21st century on our own terms. Despite the last 500 years, there is much to celebrate. Our languages are still strong, ceremonies that we have been conducting since the beginning of time are still being held, our governments are surviving, and most importantly, we continue to exist as a distinct cultural group in the midst of the most powerful country in the world. Yet we also must recognize that we face a daunting set of problems and issues – continual threats to tribal sovereignty, low educational attainment levels, double digit unemployment, many homes without basic amenities and racism. We are beginning to look more to our own people, communities and history for solutions. We have begun to trust our own thinking again, not the Columbus myth. We look forward to the next 500 years as a time of renewal and revitalization for Native people throughout North America.
*Wilma Mankiller*

## Turtle

According to the **Seneca** creation story, the original beings lived in a world above the sky. At their chief's request, they uprooted a large tree that stood near the chief's lodge. This made a large hole in the sky, revealing green waters in the world below. The chief's pregnant wife fell through the hole and landed on a turtle's back. With the soil she had grasped as she fell she created the earth and gave birth to the beings who became the Seneca people. Thus, for the Seneca and other **Iroquois**, the earth sits on Grandmother Turtle's back.

The Seneca story of how and why their people have a special feeling for the turtle is not uncommon among Native peoples. Iroquois and many Southeastern peoples value and look to the turtle as a creator. Many Indians also tell stories about the persistence, stubbornness and cleverness of the seemingly slow and weak turtle.

**251 Below** A late 19th-century turtle **shell** rattle with an **Iroquois** gourd and hickory **bark rattle** from the Six Nations Reserve in Brantford, Ontario, Canada. The turtle rattle, like this one used in the Cold Spring **Seneca** Longhouse in New York, is central to the most important Iroquois **ceremonies**. Gourd rattles were used in planting and harvesting ceremonies and the hickory bark rattle was used for social **dances**.

I told you I was little and can't run fast, but I can outsmart you. Wolf, wolf, your bones will be quivering, the flies will be quivering, the flies will be buzzing and buzzing around you.
*Turtle's Song to the Wolf when he won the race, a Creek story-song similar to Aesop's fable The Tortoise and the Hare, as sung by Betty Mae Jumper, Seminole traditionalist and former tribal chairman*

## Tuscarora

The original Tuscarora lands are in Virginia and North Carolina, and the people are culturally and linguistically Iroquoian. They were a powerful **trading** nation.

Encroachment by Europeans led to conflict and then **war** in 1711. The British drove them from North Carolina and most fled north to Iroquois Country. A few stayed on a small **reservation** in North Carolina and some were sent into slavery. In 1720, the Tuscarora were officially adopted into the **Iroquois Confederacy** through their sponsoring nation, the **Oneida**.

During the American Revolution, Tuscarora and Oneida allied with the colonists. After the war, the Tuscarora were punished because the rest of the Iroquois nations had sided with the British. Once again without a home, they settled on a reservation near Lewiston, New York, and at Six Nations Reserve on the Grand River, Ontario. Many converted to **Christianity**, but some also retained the Longhouse traditions.

The Tuscarora resisted the construction of a reservoir on their lands by the New York State Power Authority in 1957, but lost that struggle and hundreds of acres of their New York reservation. Like other Iroquois, many have developed work in the construction industries, including high steel.

# U

## Ulu

This crescent shaped knife – similar to the Italian double-bladed knife called a *mezzaluna* (half moon) – is used by **Inuit** peoples in the **Arctic** for eating, cutting skins and cleaning fur and hair. Men make *ulus* from bone, antler, stone, **metal** and wood for their wives, daughters and other female relations. They are so distinctive and important to Inuit cultures that people now make jewellery in the shape of *ulus* and use their design on clothes, official communications and so on. Today, **tourists** and Inuit people buy commercially produced *ulus* made in Alaska and Greenland.

**252 Above** An Inuit *ulu* made from copper in the late 19th century.

Every woman has her own tools made with her own design. When an elder dies, her *ulu* is sometimes buried with her.
*Ulayok Kaviok, Arviat, 1986*

**255 Below** Urban Indians.

## Urban Indians

The Great Depression and the **Second World War** affected Indian Country as deeply as the rest of the United States. During the period of the Dust Bowl on the Prairies, many Indians fled to California and other parts of the United States to escape the devastation. This was followed by forced **relocation** into cities by the **Bureau of Indian Affairs** (BIA) in the 1950s. The great migrations of the 1930s and 1950s created a population of 'urban' Indians living in cities such as Los Angeles, Phoenix, Cleveland, Minneapolis, New York City, Dallas, Buffalo, San Francisco and Chicago. In Canada, too, Indians migrated from 'the bush' to Toronto, Winnipeg and Ottawa. Over half of American Indians and over 30% of Canadian Indians now live in cities. Most of the urban areas developed 'Indian centres' – organizations which bring Indians together to share their cultures, languages and life histories. Many different tribal peoples met and worked together in the cities. This continued to form the characteristics of '**pan-Indian**', intertribal cultures which had begun in Indian **schools**. Furthermore, urban Indians have been at the centre of national Indian political activity. Despite their number, achievements and political influence, urban Indians still struggle for recognition (by Indians and non-Indians alike) as Native people.

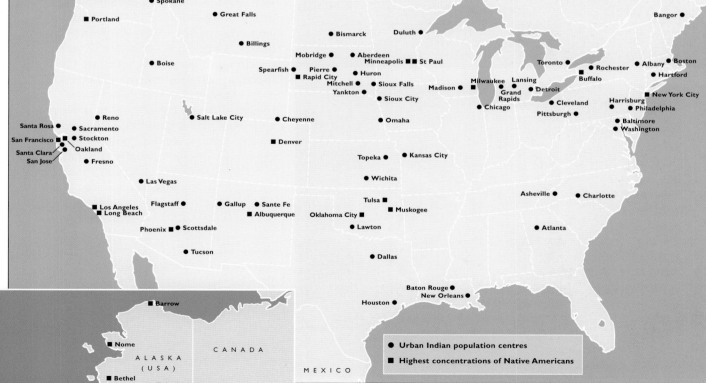

● Urban Indian population centres
■ Highest concentrations of Native Americans

## Wampum

On his way to bring the Great Law of Peace to the Mohawks, the first of the Five Nations to receive it, the Peacemaker came to a small lake. While he was thinking how he would cross the lake, a flock of waterfowl lit on the water. He watched, and as they flew off the lake became dry and the bottom was covered with wampum beads. From these beads the Peacemaker made the first wampum belts to document the creation of the Great Peace – the League of the *Haudenosaunee*
*Reg Henry, Cayuga faithkeeper, 1989*

Wampum beads record important events and appear in a ceremonial context, as decorations and a symbol of status for chiefs and the **clan** mother. When the **Iroquois** confirmed treaties, offered condolences or made important statements, they gave **gifts** to acknowledge the seriousness of the occasion. By the late 18th century, the usual

**254 Below** A late 18th-century wampum belt, with a **turtle**.

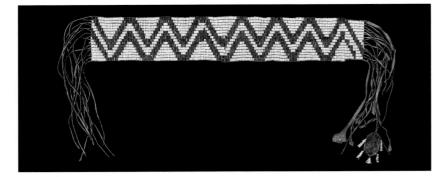

gifts were belts or strings of wampum made of whelk or quahog clam **shells**. The white beads can be carved from many different shells, but only the shell of the quahog clam gives purple beads. The Dutch used the belts and beads as currency, although the Iroquois did not, and they quickly began manufacturing wampum to use in negotiations with the Iroquois. Other Indians in Dutch areas also began to use the wampum as currency.

During the 18th century, wampum was woven into belts with particular designs of mnemonics and pictures to mark **treaties** or agreements. The *Gus-weh-tah* or the Two-Row wampum belt dating from 1664, shows perhaps the most important of these agreements – the **British**, Dutch or French and the Iroquois Confederacy. The two straight lines on the belt represent the peace, friendship and respect between the two nations. The two rows symbolize two boats travelling down the same river, neither interfering with the course of the other but abiding by each other's values.

Modern Iroquois believe that some wampum belts play an important role in how treaties are interpreted in legal cases today, because they symbolize attempts at relationships that failed. Ironically, until recently, these most powerful symbols of the Iroquois Confederacy and its relationships with other peoples were rarely in Iroquois hands. Wampum is symbolically very important to Iroquois leadership, therefore Indian agents removed many belts and chief's strings from reservations and communities and sold them to **museums** and collectors. Some have been the subjects of long disputes over their ownership and others have been loaned to tribal museums or to members of the Iroquois Grand Council for use in ceremonial recountings of the

**255 Left** A late 18th-century purple **shell** wampum belt. Coastal **Algonquian** peoples in the Southeast made and used trade bead shells (*roanoke*) made from mussel shells and peak (*wampumpeak*), the purple part of clam shells, and the other parts of whelk shells.

events where the belts were first given. In recent times, Iroquois have launched legal battles to have these important artefacts returned to communities as they are symbols of nationhood.

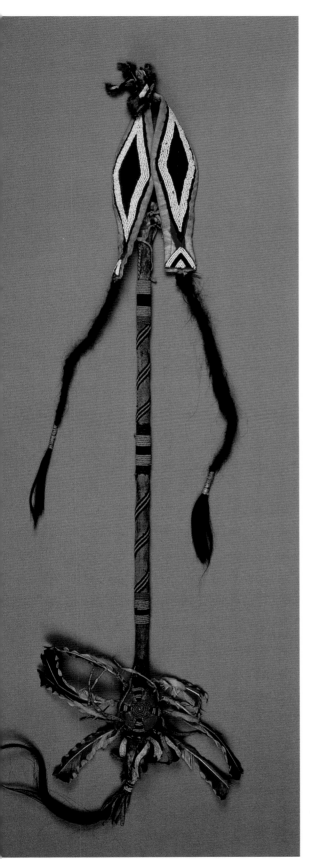

256 **Left** A late 19th-century Blood coup stick, with its wrist straps covering the handle.

257 **Below** This work, *Counting Coup*, by Gerald McMaster (Plains **Cree**) is taken from 'Cowboy and Indian Show' in 1991. McMaster is Curator of Contemporary Indian Art at the Canadian Museum of Civilization. He uses 'humour as a tool, as a weapon. For him, it is 'another way of being serious'.

# War

War was common between Native peoples, but what it actually consisted of and what actually took place varied among different groups, in different places and at different times. War could be short concentrated periods of armed aggression between large groups or periodic outbursts of violence over a longer time.

For some, war consisted of a number of raids over time on one set of people by small groups of others. Acts that caused war included the taking of captives (women and children), acts of violence, the stealing of **horses** and encroachments on **hunting, fishing** and water resources.

For many Plains peoples, acts of bravery by warriors could include striking or touching an enemy with a *coup* (French for 'blow' or 'strike') stick, or killing or wounding with one. An experienced warrior might have a *coup* stick with paintings or carvings of how many times he had struck the enemy, thus giving rise to the notion of 'counting *coup*'.

Until guns and bullets made it useless, men (and **horses**) carried and wore reinforced and painted hide armour for protection against arrows and spears. Often the designs on shields and other hunter's and warrior's equipment came from **dreams** and visions and were meant to be protective.

**171**

**258 Below** The cover for a painted buffalo hide Pawnee shield, c. 1820–25.

## Ward, Nancy

The early Indian **Removal** period before 1830 cannot be characterized better than in the life and actions of Nancy Ward (N*anyehi*). Having earned the title of 'Beloved Woman of the **Cherokees**' and 'War Woman of Chota', she was the governor of the Women's Council during **war** with the **Creeks**. She could speak for the women on matters of peace, war and community life.

At first, N*anyehi* believed that the way to survive was by accommodating the new ways of the whites and trying to live with them. There are many stories of her intervention in the fate of whites who had intruded on the Cherokee people. Others believed that Native peoples could not peacefully co-exist with the intruders.

She married an Irish trader called Brian Ward, after her first husband, a Cherokee named Kingfisher, died. Now known to whites as Nancy Ward, she became wealthy, with land, slaves and some power. When Americans declared war on the **British**, the Cherokees were dragged into armed conflict with them. Although she had often defended British settlers even against the wishes of her own people, she could not prevent the war that followed, which devastated Cherokee lands and resources. Trying to save what remained, the Cherokees were the first tribe to sign a treaty with the new US government. She was present at the Peace Commission in 1785, presenting strings of **wampum** to the Peace Commissioners on behalf of the Women's Council. For a while, peace seemed to come to the Cherokee people, and they adopted many of the ways of the whites that now populated their land.

More settlers came and wanted more Cherokee land. Many Cherokees felt that they should simply go to the proposed **Indian Territory** and give up dealing with these people who were never satisfied. Others, such as Nancy Ward, felt that they could never leave their homelands and their sacred grounds.

Native men also made and carried war clubs for war, hunting and for ceremonial purposes. In the Northeast, traditional war clubs were often 'ball-headed', often with **clan** animals or other symbols of power carved into the handle and ball. Others were carved from roots with the root nodule left intact on the end of the club. On the Plains, the clubs were often carved from or in the shape of a rifle stock or like a tomahawk. They were then etched, carved in designs or (as in the root clubs and Plains dance sticks) shaped into human, animal or bird heads or feet. When the clubs were replaced by rifles, men carried them as part of their ceremonial dress. In the 19th century, some carved them for the **tourist** trade. Men carry them today in the Northwest and the Plains, more often as 'dance sticks' than as war clubs, as part of the ceremonial dress worn by 'straight **dancers**'.

**259 Above** A Woodlands ball-headed club with otter.

Cherokee mothers do not wish to go to an unknown country; we have raised all of you on the land which we now inhabit. We have understood that some of our children wish to govern the Mississippi, but this act would be like destroying your mothers. We beg of you not to part with any more of our land…. The Cherokee ladies now being present at the meeting of the Chiefs and warriors in council have thought it their duties as mothers to address their beloved Chiefs and warriors now assembled…. [W]e know that our country has once been extensive but by repeated sales has become circumscribed to a small tract and never have thought it our duty to interfere in the disposition of it till now, if a father or mother was to sell all their lands which they had to depend on, which their children had to raise their living on, which would be bad indeed and to be removed to another country. We do not wish to go to an unknown country which we have understood some of our children wish to go over the Mississippi but this act of our children would be like destroying your mothers. Your mother and sisters ask and beg of you not to part with any more of our lands. *Nancy Ward's message to the Cherokee National Council, 1817*

Yet no matter what Nancy Ward, the Women's Council and many in the Men's Council felt, things had changed forever. A new form of government had been shaped through a new Constitution and had been adopted by the Cherokees and other tribes. This deposed the Women's Councils and substituted a legal system modelled on white governments. In the **Removal** that followed, as many as 6,000 died on the Trail of Tears, and Nancy Ward's beloved homelands were lost. Moreover, the system which supported government by both men and women was also disbanded. Today, Cherokees often cite Nancy Ward's leadership as a model for restoring of the old ways of government.

**260 Below** An early Coastal **Salish** spindle whorl, used for spinning **dog** and mountain goat hair into wool. The wool was then used to make capes, blankets, and ceremonial dress.

## Water rights

Concern about water rights is common to indigenous peoples everywhere. Access to water is the basis for survival. For economic development, water resources – often from lands previously given or dammed – are essential. Many tribes, particularly those in the dry West, are trying to regain access to valuable waters which have been given over to commercial interests and states. They are challenging the government and corporations in court, quoting **treaty** agreements that promised them access to water 'as long as the grass shall grow and the water flows'.

## Weaving

Weaving is probably one of the oldest of skills among peoples of the world. The **Navajo** weavings have stories of their own about its origin. White Shell Woman came upon a dark hole in the ground, apparently the home of Spider Woman. She was busy creating designs. Spider Woman invited White Shell Woman in and taught her how to weave a Navajo dress.

There is a Navajo phrase, *aashi bi' bohlii*, which means, it's up to you. When my mother uses this term, she says there are no formulas in weaving. Weaving allows us to create and express ourselves with tools, materials, and designs. It is up to you – the weaver.
D.Y. B*egay, weaver*

**261 Above** A Chilkat **blanket**, made of dyed mountain goat wool, with cedar **bark** sewn and woven into it. These woven textiles were the dancing blankets of high-ranking people of the **Northwest Coast** in the 19th century. The designs on the weaving – the same designs and figures that appear on **house posts** and on painted walls, **drums** and **masks** – represent the crest of the wearer. They also tell the stories of the original crest and the way in which it obtained power and position.

The use of reeds and grasses, wood splints and animal hair and fur to make containers, small animal pens, bedding, seating and clothes is an ancient and complex craft. For most Native people, the invention and export/import of mass-produced, machine-weaving in the 18th century marked the end of hand weaving. Indians still weave **baskets** and ceremonial clothing for the **tourist** market and for use in their own communities. The variation and complexity of different kinds weaving, among Pueblos, **Northwest Coastal** peoples and Navajos in wool, cotton and fur is as remarkable as basket weaving in the Northeast, Southeast, California and Plateau regions.

**263 Above** *Beeldléi* (meaning 'wearing **blanket**') **Navajo** woven blank

Oh, Mother the Earth, Oh Father the Sky…
Then weave for us a garment of brightness,
May the warp be the white light of morning,
May the weft be the red light of evening,
May the fringes be the falling rain,
May the border be the standing rainbow.
*Tewa song*

**262 Left** A **Tlingit** woman putting the raised border on the Chilkat **blanket** she has twined, *c.* 1995.

**264 Above** A weaving by the Hopi textile artist Ramona Sakiestewa, from her Katsina Series, No. 11, 1991. The strips of colour represent the *katsinas*, the spirits of ancestors who return annually to bless the people. They are alive and undefeated, not banished to the past, as the conquerors wished. She says: 'I cannot bear one more book or exhibit that calls Indians vanishing, enduring, the last of anything. I'd rather be described as persistent and annoying.' So these *katsinas* 'dance in the homes … of those who wished them gone'.

## Whale

For peoples on the **Northwest Coast** (including the **Inuit** and Makah) the whale provided physical and spiritual sustenance to the people who hunted him.

The whale – the largest mammal – was dangerous to hunt because he was clever and treacherous. It took great skill, bravery and special powers to hunt whales. Thus, a good hunter needed elaborate **ceremony** and ritual clothing.

In the Kwakwaka'wakw story, the hero *Siwidi* (Paddled-to) becomes part killer-whale. He can find and visit the undersea creatures.

Then Born-to-be-Head-Harpooner started, and he told his people to get ready. Then he loaned to Paddled-to a small canoe, and Born-to-be-Head-Harpooner told Paddled-to to try to spout. Paddled-to went aboard the new little canoe. As soon as he went aboard, the small canoe became a killer-whale, and Paddled-to did well with his spouting.
*A Kwakwaka'wakw story about whales and men*

The Kwakwaka'wakw people carve feast dishes shaped like killer-whale. Whale hunters wear hats with references to the stories of great spirit whales and whale hunters. Vancouver Island is full of carved whale figures. The great **Tlingit** whale houses represent the men with the power to hunt whales. The whale shrines of Nuu-chah-nulth, filled with the figures of famous whaling hunters and dedicated to ritual purification of hunters, attract whales to shore.

## Wild rice

'Wild rice' refers to a grass species, possibly from Asia originally (*Zizania*), which grows in the wild in the fresh waters of North America and Asia. The common grass has long been used as **food**. Some lakes are completely covered with rice in season and the harvesting beds are huge. Wild rice stands can be damaged by a few fungi, some competing plants, birds, animals, insects, and hail and floods. Rice failures brought famine to entire groups of **Ojibwa** in the 19th and early 20th centuries.

Wild rice was harvested and eaten by Ojibwa, by Dakota **Sioux** in the Northern Woodlands, and later in the 19th century by the Osage, Omaha, Ponca, Menominee, Potawatomi and Winnebago. It also became a major cash crop in **trade** throughout the world. The nutritional value of wild rice is high – it is rich in carbohydrates, low in fat and contains essential proteins, vitamins and minerals.

Wild rice was an important part of Ojibwa nutrition, being the principle staple, along with hunted meat, maple sugar and gathered fruits. The Ojibwa have many stories that explain the role of wild rice (*manoomin*) in their lives and its ceremonial and medicinal uses. They speak of its discovery by *Wenabozhoo* (Nanabush, Manbozhoo), their cultural hero and spiritual founder, who then gave them sugar, **fish** and other staples of the diet and culture. As well as describing the origin of rice and its gift to the Indian people, the stories tell how to use rice, how to make sure it keeps growing and how to protect it. They also suggest how its abundance or disappearance can be explained. Wild rice is used in child naming, curing and other religious **ceremonies**, such as those of the Midéwiwin (the Grand Medicine Society of the Ojibwa). Ojibwa believed that ceremonies helped preserve the rice beds and rice growth, ensuring good harvests. Even today, **pow wows** have some place for the prayers for and consumption of wild rice.

The rice was harvested traditionally by poling canoes (like punts). Then smaller, flat bottomed wood **boats** were used. The rice is gathered with two long sticks, one to bend the rice and the other to thresh the rice kernels into the canoe. Called 'knocking' the rice, this process caused much of the rice grain to fall in the water, thus providing reseeding for the coming years. Whereas in the 19th century it was an activity for women and younger children, today men are more involved. It is now an entire family enterprise, with men poling boats, women knocking rice and the whole family processing. People go to the rice camps in August and September for two-week periods. These times are great social occasions with entertainment and **games** as well as work.

After harvesting, rice is dried, either in the sun or by fire-drying. It is then scorched or parched and hulled to remove the close-fitting chaff next to the kernel. The old-fashioned way of preparing rice was to place it in a bag of some kind, traditionally deer or mooseskin, in a wood lined pit. Then men and children, wearing moccasins, would

**265 Right** In this 1946 photograph from Minnesota **Ojibwa** country, two women are parching and drying wild rice in birch**bark** trays (*nooshkaachinaagan*) and galvanized tin tubs. They are under a wigwam frame against which a baby in a **baby carrier** leans.

**266 Above** An Ojibwa couple knocking rice from a flat-bottomed skiff canoe in 1987. The canoes or flat-bottomed **boats** used in the Great Lakes don't harm the roots of rice, and the pointed end of the raft hardly bends the stalks.

'dance', 'jig' or tread the rice. Songs often accompanied this part of the process. Some people hulled the rice using a large mortar and pestle. Finally, rice was winnowed to rid the rice of the chaff. This was done by putting it onto a birch**bark** tray and tossing it so that the heavier kernels remained in the tray and the chaff would fly out. The rice was then stored. Although there are now many shortcuts and new techniques, many Ojibwa still like to prepare rice in the old ways.

Rice is cooked by boiling in water or broth. It is sometimes eaten as a sort of porridge or used to thicken meat, vegetable and fish stews. A flour can be made from rice and a type of bread baked from it. Children made popped rice by frying the rice like popcorn, then sweetening it or eating it plain. Gathered berries, animal fats and maple products were often used to flavour rice.

Nothing can equal the aroma of a ricing camp. Wood fires burning, rice drying and the dewy fresh air drifting in from the lake. A contented feeling of well-being filled the camp. The first grain of the season had been offered for blessing from the Great Spirit. The time had come to partake of the gift. Boiled with venison or with ducks or rice hens, it was nourishing and delicious.
*Lolita Taylor, Ojibwe, c.1988*

Although still harvested as an important cash and cultural crop by Ojibwa people and others, it is now considered a gourmet crop throughout the world. Thus, commercial rice production in paddies from Michigan to California is common. As traditional ricing areas are turned to commercial production, the amount of land devoted to traditionally harvested and grown rice is reduced. Competition from non-Indian grown paddy rice has negatively affected the economy of Native people. Nowadays, industrial and agricultural development means there are fewer and more polluted rice beds and **dams** cause variable water levels.

## Wolf

The wolf – related to **dogs** and **Coyote** – is highly esteemed by many Native peoples. Indians called on his protective spirit. There are many wolf **clans** among tribal peoples including the **Cherokee** and **Iroquois**. Indians speak of the wolf in terms of his close relationship to humans, even of his ability to transform into a human.

**267 Above** A **Northwest Coast** wolf **headdress**, probably Nuu-chah-nulth from Vancouver, used in a **dance** which referred to a story or stories involving the wolf.

## World War, Second

The Second World War had a huge impact on American Indians, taking large numbers of volunteers off the **reservations** and out of the boarding **schools** and putting them with other Americans in the war effort. By doing so, for the first time since becoming citizens in 1924, many Indians gained the respect of their fellow Americans for their courage and patriotism. The kind of racism experienced by black soldiers worked in reverse for American Indians. They were not separated into all-Indian units, and stereotypes about their warrior-like capabilities worked to their benefit. They were successful. The **Navajo** Code Talkers who served in the Pacific Theatre – Marines who used the complex Navajo language to communicate – offered the only code unbroken by the Japanese. Ira Hayes (a soldier and Pima hero) raised the US **flag** at Iwo Jima, when the US military recovered a major battle site from the

**268 Above** Horace Poolaw, a Kiowa who served as an aerial **photographer** during the Second World War, took this photograph of himself and Gus Palmer, another Kiowa and a tail gunner, in a B-29 nose cone.

Japanese in the South Pacific.

Many Indian women also participated in the war effort, and the war was a revolutionary moment for Indian people when they became involved in mainstream society. Women from the reservations and rural ranching and **farming** areas worked in the cities in industrial and war-related jobs, such as in aircraft factories, asbestos plants, Army ordinance depots and shipyards. Most, like the white and black women, lost their jobs to returning veterans or when the work finished at the end of the war. Many went to work in Indian schools, as matrons, cooks or caretakers, or in urban areas as semi-skilled labour, home helps or waitresses.

The Second World War also created a growing number of educated and experienced new leaders for tribal nations. The GI Bill of Rights in 1944 offered some the chance for higher education. For others, the skills gained during the war propelled them into different positions. However getting jobs on reservations was not easy, as most had little opportunity for work. So, many Indians who ended their military service in a large city stayed there – in Chicago, Los Angeles, Atlanta, Dallas or San Francisco. This created the first pool of **urban Indians** which was added to by the **relocation** of the 1950s. The mainstreaming Indians experienced after the War was important in promoting the virtues of education and middle-class values in a way that the Indian schools had not. A new generation of tribal leaders was born out of the war.

Curiously, participation in the Second World War also revitalized traditional Indian ways. Warrior and War Mothers' societies returned to Indian Country. All the traditional ceremonial attention once paid to the honouring of veterans and warriors began again and continued in tribes everywhere.

The warriors, they went overseas. The war is over now. They're all coming back, and we're all happy, we're proud and we're honoured that they fought for us, these men and women in uniform, to fight for our freedom and we're singing for joy.
*Anita Anquoe George, a Kiowa woman's War Mothers' song*

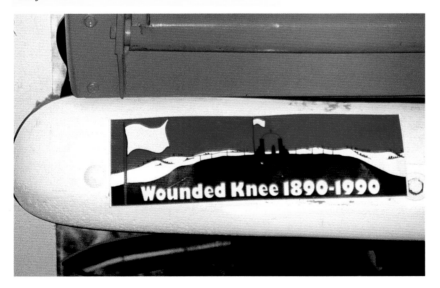

**269 Below** A car sticker, which shows the outline and gate of the graveyard at Wounded Knee, issued during the centennial of the massacre.

## Wounded Knee, 1883 and 1973

One of the most famous and most horrifying **photographs** of the 19th century shows the mass grave into which Army soldiers pushed Indian men, women and children after the deadly battle at Wounded Knee Creek in 1883. The massacre of **Sioux** by the government troops, after the government had assured peace to Red Cloud and his people, occurred because the Sioux continued to hunt in lands the government had closed off to them and opened to white settlement. The Sioux continued the **Ghost Dance** that they believed would defeat the whites and they continued to judge criminal cases in their traditional way. So, in 1883, the government passed the Seven Major Crimes Act in order to gain legal control over the reservations for certain crimes.

According to the Sioux, the government ignored their **treaty** again and again. Their protests ended in the arrest and murder of **Sitting Bull** and the actions at Wounded Knee against virtually unarmed people. Big

## Writing systems

The earliest known written works in a Native language were documents produced by Native **Christians** and town officials and a Bible printed in the **Algonquian** language in Massachusett in 1663. Christian Indian and white collaborators developed most early writing systems to encourage literacy, so that people could read the Bible. Only **Cherokee** has a system invented entirely by an Indian person (the Cherokee **Sequoyah**), and Cherokees have used that writing system to their own benefit. Writing systems were developed for the Mohican, Delaware, **Mi'kmaq**, Maliseet-Passamaquoddy, Western **Abenaki**, Northern **Iroquois**, Fox (Mesquakie), Sauk, Kickapoo, Ottawa, Potawatomi, Winnebago, **Cree**-Montagnais and **Ojibwa**, **Athapaskan** and Eskimo-**Aleut**. Most have made and continue to make limited use of these writing systems.

A number of tribal peoples now use recently developed writing systems (mostly based on the English alphabet) in order to revitalize their language through the schools. Ojibwa, Cree and **Inuit** have developed writing systems to help communication between tribes, for example in school materials and

**270 Above** January 1891, the scene at Wounded Knee, South Dakota, after the massacre of Big Foot and his followers on 20 December 1890.

Foot and his people, about 350 starving, ill and cold Minneconjou Sioux, joined by the now leaderless followers of Sitting Bull (all Ghost Dancers), gathered in late December a short distance from the Pine Ridge Agency. The Army decided to surround and disarm them. Someone fired a shot. Although many of the Sioux tried to resist, the larger and better-armed Army forces killed 153 men, women and children. Twenty-five soldiers died. The dead Indians were buried in a mass grave at Wounded Knee.

In 1973 at Wounded Knee there was a 70-day armed confrontation between activists of the American Indian Movement, residents of the Pine Ridge Reservation community, the tribal officials of the Pine Ridge Reservation and government authorities (the Federal Bureau of Investigation). The confrontation resulted in the death of two Indians and two federal agents, and years of court cases and debate over the incidents. Like the massacre nearly 100 years earlier, the confrontation drew public attention to Native issues previously ignored by the general public.

**271 Above** Steven Ross, Eastern Band **Cherokee**, writes his name using *Tsalagi* characters during a cultural class at the Cherokee Elementary Tribal School in North Carolina, 1992. Cherokee is not a language threatened with extinction. Although the writing system has been useful in teaching and maintaining Cherokee as a spoken language, there are few opportunities to use it as a written language. In classrooms in Oklahoma and North Carolina, however, Cherokees still use the **Sequoyan** system to teach the language.

newspapers. Computer software has been developed so that tribal newspapers and other materials can be printed in the Native language. Additionally, a number of tribal linguists now work in their own communities to develop written materials and other strategies for **language** preservation.

**272 Above** A **Cree** newspaper, *Wawatay News*, 12 March 1998, from Sioux Lookout, Ontario, Canada, in Inuktitut syllabics.

**273 Above** A page from the *Wawatay News*, 12 March 1998, in English and Cree.

## Yurok

The Yurok people live next to their Hupa neighbours in the Redwood forests of Klamath River Valley along the Pacific Coast. They have **fished salmon**, **hunted** and harvested acorns there for centuries. Attempts at **treaties** and land settlements with the US government, following the 1849 Gold Rush into their country, were left unresolved until the 1990s, when at last they established a Yurok **reservation** and enrolled several thousand people. Before that time, their **economies**, lands, rights and interests were combined with those of the Hupa.

Yuroks have been at the forefront of Native political action to restore traditional Native subsistence and hunting methods (such as spearfishing and gillnetting), land management and resource protection, and **ceremonies**. For example, along with Hupa, Karok and other Northern California peoples, they have organized environmental clean-ups of areas where basketmakers would gather materials for ceremonial **baskets** and basket hats.

## Zuni/A:shiwi

By 1,000 AD the ancestors of the present-day Zuni had migrated to the Southwestern river valley they occupy today. They were among the first Native peoples recorded to have **contact** with the Europeans (in 1539). For five centuries, they have struggled to maintain their unique **language**, their **matrilineal clan** and religious government and ceremonial systems. Although they now are part of the US tribal trust system operated by the **Bureau of Indian Affairs**, with an elected civil government, tribally controlled schools and hospital and modern housing, much of their daily and ceremonial life is governed by religion. Most Zunis speak the Zuni language, alongside English and Spanish.

Known for their traditional **pottery** and innovative, distinctive silver-and-stone jewellery, they have maintained the ancient crafts as part of their religion, although the crafts are also the centre of their family based **economy**.

# Information sources

1 For more information on tribal culture areas and specific tribal histories in North America, see *The Handbook of North American Indians*, vols 4 (*History of Indian White Relations*, 1988), 5 (*Arctic*, 1984), 6 (*Subarctic*, 1981), 7 (*Northwest Coast*, 1990), 8 (*California*, 1978), 9 and 10 (*Southwest*, 1979, 1983), 11 (*Great Basin*), 1986), 12 (*Plateau*, 1998), 15 (*Northeast*, 1978), 17 (*Languages*, 1998), Washington, D.C.: Smithsonian Institution Press. See also Taylor, Colin F. and William C. Sturtevant (consultants), *The Native Americans: Indigenous Peoples of North America*, New York: Smithmark Books, 1996; and the series, *Indians of North America*, by Chelsea House Publishers, New York (Abenaki, Crow, Apache, Arapaho, Aztec, Cahuilla, Catawba, Cherokee, Cheyenne, Chickasaw, Chinook, Chipewyan, Choctaw, Chumash, Coast Salish, Comanche, Creek, Crow, Eskimo, Hidatsa, Huron, Iroquois, Kiowa, Kwakiutl, Lenape, Lumbee, Maya, Menominee, Modoc, Montagnais-Naskapi, Nanticoke, Narragansett, Navajo, Nez Perce, Ojibwa, Osage, Paiute, Pima-Maricopa, Potawatomi, Powhatan, Pueblo, Quapaw, Seminole, Tarahumara, Tunica-Biloxi, Wampanoag, Yakima, Yankton Sioux, Yuma, Urban Indians, American Indian Literature, Women in American Indian Society, Archaeology of North America and Federal Indian Policy). For Natives in Canada, see Olive Dickason, *Canada's First Nations: A History of Founding Peoples from Earliest Times*, Norman: University of Oklahoma Press, 1992. On Indians in the twentieth century, see Hirschfelder, Arlene and Martha Kreipe de Montaño, *The Native American Almanac: A Portrait of Native America Today*, New York: Prentice Hall, 1993; and Davis, Mary B., *Native America in the Twentieth Century: An Encyclopedia*, New York and London: Garland Publishing Co., 1996. See also Johansen, Bruce E. and Donald A. Grimble, Jr, *The Encyclopedia of Native American Biography*, New York: DaCapo Press, 1998.

2 For excellent information on African-Americans and Native Americans, see Forbes, Jack D., *Black Africans and Native Americans: Colour, Evolution and Class in the Evolution of Red-Black Peoples*, Oxford, England: Basil Blackwell Publishers, 1988.

3 Hoxie, Frederick E. (ed.), *Encyclopedia of North American Indians*, Boston and New York: Houghton Mifflin Company, 1996, 7–11.

4 For information cited throughout this encyclopaedia and for other references on American Indian women, see Green, Rayna, *Women in American Indian Society*, New York and Philadelphia: Chelsea House Publishers, 1992.

5 Hoxie, 1996, 19–21.

6 For extensive information on Native architecture, see Nabokov, Peter and Robert Easton, *Native American Architecture*, New York and Oxford: Oxford University Press, 1989.

7 For more on contemporary Native art, see Archuleta, Margaret and Rennard Strickland, *Shared Visions: Native American Painters and Sculptors in the Twentieth Century*, Phoenix, A.Z.: The Heard Museum, 1991; McMaster, Gerald and Lee Ann Martin (Mi'kmaq), *Indigena: Contemporary Native Perspectives*, Hull, Quebec: Canadian Museum of Civilization, 1992; Coe, Ralph T., *Lost and Found Traditions: Native American Art, 1965–1985*, New York: American Federation of Arts, 1986; and Nemiroff, Diana, Robert Houle and Charlotte Townsend-Gault, *Land Spirit Power: First Nations at the National Gallery of Canada*, Ottawa: National Gallery of Canada, 1992. On earlier art, see Coe, Ralph T., *Sacred Circles: Two Thousand Years of North American Indian Art*, London: Arts Council of Great Britain, 1976; and King, J.C.H., *Thunderbird and Lightning: Indian Life in Northeastern North America, 1600–1900*, London: British Museum Press, 1982.

8 Northrup, Jim (Anishinabe), 'Fond du Lac Follies', *News From Indian Country*, Mid-August, 1997, 10B.

9 Hassrick, Royal B., *The Sioux: Life and Customs of A Warrior Society*, 1964, xiii, 42.

10 Hill, Tom (Seneca) and Richard Hill Sr (Tuscarora), *Creation's Journey: Native American Identity and Belief*, Washington, D.C.: Smithsonian Institution Press, 1994, 73.

11 Jones, Suzi (ed.), *Pacific Basketmakers: A Living Tradition, Catalogue of the 1981 Pacific Basketmaker's Symposium and Exhibition*, Fairbanks, A.K.: University of Alaska Museum, 1983, 34.

12 Hill and Hill, 1994, 118–119.

13 Hill and Hill, 1994, 138.

14 Fitzhugh, William W. and Susan Kaplan, *Inua: Spirit World of the Bering Sea Eskimo*, Washington, D.C.: Smithsonian Institution Press, 1982, 286.

15 *The Papers of Sir William Johnson*, 16 vols, Albany: State University of New York Press, 1925–1965, III, 707–708.

16 For more on Native calendars and astronomy, see Williamson, Ray, *Living the Sky: The Cosmos of the American Indian*, Boston: Houghton Mifflin, 1984.

17 Gilman, Carolyn and Mary Jane Schneider, *The Way to Independence*, Minneapolis: Minnesota Historical Society Press, 1987, 224.

18 For more on Indians and the Civil War, see Hauptmann, Lawrence M., *Between Two Fires: American Indians in the Civil War*, New York: The Free Press, 1995.

19 For more on Native dolls, see Lenz, Mary Jan, *The Stuff of Dreams: Native American Dolls*, New York: Museum of the American Indian, 1986. On *katsina* dolls, see Secakuku, Alph H., *Following the Sun and Moon: Hopi Kachina Tradition*, Flagstaff, A.Z:. Northland Publishing in co-operation with the Heard Museum, 1995.

20 Diamond, Beverley, M., Sam Cronk and Franziska von Rosen, *Visions of Sound: Musical Instruments of First Nations Communities in Northeastern America*, Chicago and London: University of Chicago Press, 1994, 33.

21 'Lakota Flute Song', Green, Rayna and Howard Bass, producers. *Heartbeat: Voices of First Nations Women*. Smithsonian Folkways SF CD 40415, 1995.

22 Fitzhugh, William W. and Aron Crowell, *Crossroads of Continents: Cultures of Siberia and Alaska*, Washington, D.C.: Smithsonian Institution Press, 1988, 203.

23 Lowie, Robert, 'Plains Indian Age Societies: Historical and Comparative Summary', *American Museum of Natural History, Anthropological Papers* 11, pt 10, 1916, 279.

24 MacDowell, Marsha L. and C. Kurt Dewhurst (eds), *To Honor and Comfort: Native Quilting Traditions*, Santa Fe, N.M.: Museum of New Mexico Press, 1997, 166.

25 Ewers, John C., *The Horse in Blackfoot Indian Culture*, BAE Bulletin 159, Washington, D.C.: Smithsonian Institution, 1955.

26 Ewers, 137.

27 Jonaitis, Aldona (ed.), *Chiefly Feasts: The Enduring Kwakiutl Potlatch*, Seattle: University of Washington, Press, 1991, 25.

28 See Fagg, William (ed.), *Eskimo Art in the British Museum*, London: Trustees of the British Museum, 1972.

29 Hoxie, 1996, 219–220.

30 Golla, in Davis, 1996, 311.

31 Davis, 1996, 311.

32 For more on modern Native literature, see Green, Rayna (ed.), *That's What She Said: Fiction and Poetry by Native American Women*, Bloomington, Indiana: Indiana University Press, 1984; Brown Ruoff, Lavonne, *American Indian Literature*, New York: Chelsea House Publishers, 1991; and read novels by Leslie Silko (*Ceremony, Storyteller*), James Welch (*Winter in the Blood*), N. Scott Momaday (*House Made of Dawn, The Way to Rainy Mountain*), D'arcy McNickle (*The Surrounded, Wind From An Enemy Sky*), Louise Erdrich (*Love Medicine*), Susan Power (*The Grass Dancer*), and poetry by Simon Ortiz (*Going for the Rain, From Sand Creek*), Elizabeth Woody (*Luminaries of the Humble, Seven Hands, Seven Hearts*).

33 For more on Northwest Coast masks, see King, J.C.H., *Portrait Masks From the Northwest Coast of America*, New York: Thames and Hudson, 1979; also Jonaitis, 1991.

34 Wayman, M.L., J.C.H. King and P.T. Craddock, *Aspects of Early North American Metallurgy*, London: Trustees of the British Museum, 1992.

35 For more on the Métis, see Harrison, Julia D., *Métis: People Between Two Worlds*, Vancouver/Toronto: Glenbow-Alberta Institute with Douglas and McIntyre, 1985.

36 For more on Native Americans and museums, see Ames, Michael, *Cannibal Tours and Glass Boxes: The Anthropology of Museums*, Vancouver: University of British Columbia, British Columbia Press, 1992; Cole, Douglas and Ira Chaikin, *An Iron Hand Against the People: The Law Against the Potlatch of the Northwest Coast*, Seattle: University of Washington Press, 1990; and King, J.C.H., *Artificial Curiosities from the Northeast Coast of America: Native American Artefacts in the British Museum Collected on the Third Voyage of Captain James Cook and Acquired Through Sir Joseph Banks*, London: British Museum Publications, 1981.

37 Stine, Jeffrey, 'Oil From the Arctic: Building the Trans-Alaska Pipeline', An Exhibition at the National Museum of American History, Smithsonian Institution, 1998.

38 Fitzhugh, 1982, 221.

39 See Green, Rayna, 'Rosebuds of the Plateau: Frank Matsura and the Fainting Couch Aesthetic' and other Native writers on Indians and photography in Lucy R. Lippard, *Partial Recall: Photographs of Native North Americans*, New York: The New Press, 1992, 47–54; also Richardson Fleming, Paula and Judith Luskey, *The North American Indians in Early Photographs*, New York: Dorset Press, 1988. 160 Neihardt, John G., *Black Elk Speaks: Being the Life Story of a Holy Man of the Oglala Sioux*, Lincoln: University of Nebraska Press, 1961, 3–4.

40 For more on Native pipes, see King, J.C.H., *Smoking Pipes of the North American Indian*, London: British Museum Publications, 1977.

41 Green, Rayna, 'The Pocahontas Perplex: The Image of Indian Women in American Culture', *The Massachusetts Review* XVI, no. 4, 1975, 698–714.

42 A superb account of Indian activism can be found in Warrior, Robert and Paul Chaat Smith, *Like a Hurricane, The Indian Movement from Alcatraz to Wounded Knee*, New York: New Press, 1996.

43 Diamond, 1994, 68.

44 Hill and Hill, 98.

45 A fine source for understanding the Indian history told through ledger drawings is Berlo, Janet Catherine (ed.), *Plains Indian Drawings, 1865–1935: Images From A Visual History*, New York: Harry Abrams, 1996.

46 King, 1991.

47 Green, Rayna, 'Kill the Indian and Save the Man: Indian Education in the United States', in Mary Lou Hultgren and Paulette Fairbanks Molin, *To Lead and To Serve: American Indian Education at Hampton Institute, 1978–1923*, Virginia Beach, V.A.: Virginia Foundation for the Humanities, 9–14.

48 Green, 1989.

49 Davis, 570–574.

50 Hoxie, 590–593.

51 Green, Rayna, 'Poor Lo and Dusky Ramona: Scenes From An Album of Indian America', in Jane S. Becker and Barbara Franco, *Folk Roots, New Roots: Folklore in American Life*, Lexington, Massachusetts: Museum of Our National Heritage, 1989, 77–102. For more on American Indian stereotypes and images in American and European culture, see Doxtator, Deborah, *Fluffs and Feathers: An Exhibit on the Symbols of Indianess: A Resource Guide*, Brantford, Ontario: Woodland Cultural Centre, 1988; and Green, Rayna, *Handbook of North American Indians*, IV, Washington, D.C.: Smithsonian Institution, 1979.

52 An excellent source of information about Indians and tourism can be found in Weigle, Marta and Barbara Babcock (eds), *The Great Southwest of the Fred Harvey Company and the Santa Fe Railway*, Phoenix, A.Z.: The Heard Museum, 1996.

53 Mankiller, Wilma and Michael Wallis, *Mankiller: A Chief and Her People*, New York: St Martin's Press, 1993 (Mankiller's autobiography).

# Picture credits

Introduction maps drawn by James Farrant.

1   (BM 1949 AM 22.141);

2   (BM 1987 AM 9.3);

3   (SI/NAA 14891, photograph by J. Pankratz , neg. #76-14891);

4   (SI/NAA 53.378, photograph by Jesse Hastings Bratley);

5   (Courtesy of National Woman's Christian Temperance Union, photograph by Richard Strauss, SI);

6   (Courtesy of Nebraska State Historical Society, RG 2026.PH: 00067 (L164);

7   (photograph by Annie Sahlin);

8   (photograph by Annie Sahlin);

9   (SI/NAA 1169-A);

10   (SI/NAA 74-3623);

11   (BM 1949 Am 22.13, 1949 Am 22.19);

12   (SI/NMAH Division of Cultural History, neg. #94-202);

13   (photograph by Annie Sahlin);

14   (courtesy of MALAK Photographs, Limited, neg. #240Q-8M-294);

15   (SI/NMNH Department of Anthropology, no #, photograph by Jeff Tinsley and Hugh Tallman, neg. #97-8705A);

16   (BM 5211);

17   (BM 1979 Am 9.1);

18   (BM Sl 2040);

19   (Courtesy of A Poolaw Photo, photograph by Horace Poolaw);

20   (SI/NMAI 2667, photograph by M.R. Harrington);

21   (SI/NMAH Hands on History Room, photograph y Richard Strauss);

22   (RG, photograph by Rayna Green);

23   (SI/NMNH Department of Anthropology 18809, photograph by Eric Long, neg. #87-11773);

24   (BM 6976);

25   (BM Q85 AM 352 (7262);

26   (BM NWC 48);

27   (BM SL 1218);

28   (SI/CFPCS, photograph by Barbara Strong, neg. #FAF 78-18037-8);

29   (SI/CFPCS, photograph by Kim Nielsen, neg. #FAF 85-150-78-5);

30   (BM 1954 W Am 5.947);

31   (RG, photograph by Rick Vargas, SI, neg. #98-164, strip 2 );

32   (RG, courtesy Marjorie Bear Don't Walk, photograph by Rick Vargas, SI, neg. #98-162, strip 1);

33  (BM +5930);

34  (Courtesy of the Maxwell Museum of Anthropology, University of New Mexico, Albuquerque 82.52.1, photograph by Eric Long, SI);

35  (BM 1962 Am 4.1);

36  (BM Sl 758);

37  (BM 2583);

38  (RG, photograph by Richard Strauss, SI);

39  (BM 1859.11-26. 79);

40  (BM +228);

41  (Courtesy of the New York Public Library, neg. #N-124781);

42  (BM 5205);

43  (BM 1944 Am 2.197);

44  (BM Van 190);

45  (BM);

46  (SI/NMAI 15/8002);

47  (BM 1981 Am 17.1);

48  (SI/NMAH Graphic Arts Collections 8116, neg. #97-8319);

49  (SI/NMAA 1979.144.24, neg. #6208135T);

50  (SI/NMAH Hands on History Room, courtesy of Dennis Fox, Jr);

51  (SI/NMAH Hands on History Room, courtesy of Georgianna Old Elk and Anna Old Elk);

52  (SI/NMAI 25951, photograph by Edward H. Davis);

53  (BM 1942 Am 7.2);

54  (Courtesy of Jimmy Dick);

55  (SI/NMAH Division of Cultural History, photograph by Eric Long, neg. #92-5031);

56  (RG, photograph by Richard Strauss, SI);

57  (SI/CFPCS, photograph by Rick Vargas, neg. #FAF 92-7321/2);

58  (SI/NMAH Division of Cultural History Collections 1991.6035.03, photograph by Richard Strauss, neg. #92-5013);

59  (SI/L PM 784 B5 1860);

60  (SI/NMAH Division of Cultural History Collections, photograph by Rick Vargas, neg. #92-5032);

61  (Courtesy of Oren Lyons and M. and T. Bank, Syracuse, New York);

62  (SI/NMAH Division of Cultural History Collections 1991.3192.01, courtesy of Lois Gutierrez de la Cruz, photograph by Eric Long, neg. #92-5037);

63  (photograph by Owen Seumptewa);

64  (RG, photograph by Rick Vargas, SI, neg. #98-168, strip 2);

65  (BM Q86 AM 11);

66  (Permission of the artist, Jaune Quick-to-See-Smith, photograph by Richard Strauss, SI);

67  (Library of Congress, Prints and Photographs Division USZ62-1030);

68  (photograph by Joel Grimes);

69  (SI/NMAA 1979.144.77);

70  (Courtesy of Harry Fonseca and The Heard Museum, Phoenix, Arizona IAC1758);

71  (SI/NMAH Division of Cultural History, photograph by Richard Strauss);

72  (Courtesy of Melanie Fernandez, artwork by Bill Powless, photograph by Richard Strauss, SI);

73  (National Archives of Canada C-092418);

74  (BM Q85 Am 21);

75  (SI/NMAH, National Numismatics Collection 1990.0466.01, photograph by Douglas Mudd);

76  (BM 1921.10-14.84);

77  (SI/NAA 55-664);

78 (BM 78 D.b 2);

79 (BM 1891.6-12-25);

80 (SI/NMAH Hands on History Room, photograph by Dane Penland);

81 (SI/NMNH Department of Anthropology,421274 and 421275, neg. #87-11784);

82 (photograph by Owen Seumptewa);

83 (BM 1949 AM 22.145);

84 (SI/CFPCS, neg. #FAF 78-3483-7);

85 (RG, photograph by Rayna Green);

86 (SI/NMAH Division of Cultural History, photograph by Laurie Minor-Penland);

87 (SI/NMAA 1979.144.2);

88 (BM 1970 Am 9. 4);

89 (SI/NMAI 54496, 108164, 1371, 8847, 2585, 8141);

90 (RG, photograph by Rick Vargas, SI, neg. #98-162, strip 3);

91 (BM 1930.20);

92 (SI/NMAI 15.2393, photograph by David Heald);

93 (BM 1933. 11-29.1);

94 (RG, photograph by Rick Vargas, SI, neg. #98-165, strip 2);

95 (BM 1949 Am 22 35);

96 (SI/NAA);

97 (Courtesy of Great Lakes Indian Fish and Wildlife Commission, photograph by Charlie Otto Rasmussen);

98 (SI/NMAH, Military History Collections 4104, photograph by Hugh Tallman, neg. #98-3869);

99 (SI/NMAI 19.3217, photograph by David Heald);

100 (RG, photograph by Rick Vargas, SI, neg. #98-165, strip 1);

101 (BM 5004);

102 (SI/NMAH, Division of Cultural History, photograph byLaurie Minor-Penland, neg. #87-16622-4);

103 (Courtesy of the Seneca-Iroquois National Museum, Salamanca, NY 81.0001.0003, photograph by Rich Strauss, SI);

104 (Courtesy of Thomas Vennum, photograph by Jim Leary);

105 (Library of Congress, American Folklife Center 22862, photograph by Michael Crommett);

106 (RG, photograph by Richard Hill, Sr);

107 (SI/NMAI 6.8343, 24.1544, 2.7101, 14.3357, 19.7123, 21.1921, 24.3362, 19,6341, 2.5985, 24.4386, 2.2202, 20.5948, 20.5868, 22.8991, 7.1079, 12.2127, 18.2199, 20.5877, 16.2326, 22.9638, 25.2635, 21.994, 21.3539, 20.8703, 8.4686, 2.1312, 2.7386, 24.1092, 15.4471, 10.4450, 19.3690, and 16.4122, photograph by David Heald);

108 (SI/NMAI 23.9267, photograph by David Heald);

109 (RG, photograph by Rick Vargas, SI, neg. #98-166, strip 1);

110 (RG, photograph by Rayna Green);

111 (Courtesy of the Mashantucket Pequot Nation, photograph by Gary Thibault/Tebo Photography);

112 (Courtesy of Tudjaat, photograph by Joseph Kugielski);

113 (BM 5168 and 5169);

114 (Courtesy of the Arizona Historical Society, Tucson, Arizona AHS 8847);

115 (BM 1976 AM 3. 94);

116 (Notman Photographic Archives, McCord Museum of Canadian History, Montreal 1-29099, photograph by William Notman);

117 (BM 1958 AM 4.1 and 2);

118 (SI/CFPCS, photograph by J. Ploskonka, neg. #FAF 84-9104-34A);

119 (SI/NAA);

120 (SI/NMAI 1993.6052, neg. #1/3303, photograph by Pam Dewey);

121 (SI/NMAI 2.1673, photograph by David Heald);

122 (Courtesy of Michigan State University Museum, Lansing, Michigan 02.1997:60.1:4);

123 (SI/NMNH Department of Anthropology 380991, 380992, photograph by Eric Long, neg. #85-11261);

124 (SI/NMA 20.5318);

125 (RG, photograph by Rayna Green);

126 (BM 5216);

127 (BM 1929.12-16.7);

128 (BM 1949 AM 23 1);

129 (BM 1944 AM 2.293 and Q 87 AM 5);

130 (SI/NMAI P13584);

131 (Courtesy of Bob Haozous and The Hood Museum of Art, Dartmouth College, Hanover, New Hampshire, purchased through the Joseph B. Obering '56 Fund);

132 (BM NWC 42);

133 (BM NWC 6);

134 (BM Van 194);

135 (Map drawn by James Farrant);

136 (BM Sl 1842);

137 (SI/NMAI 8.2719);

138 (Courtesy of the Woodland Cultural Centre);

139 (BM 1983 AM 37.1, courtesy of Richard Glazer Danay);

140 (Map drawn by James Farrant, after Francis Paul Prucha, *Atlas of American Indian Affairs*, Lincoln and London: University of Nebraska Press, 1990, maps 14, 17, 20 and 22);

141 (Courtesy of Joy Harjo, photograph by Hulleah Tsinhnahjinnie);

142 (Courtesy of Tomson Highway, photograph by Micheal Cooper);

143 (BM 1980 AM 32.1);

144 (RG, photograph by Rayna Green);

145 (photograph by Joel Grimes);

146 (Courtesy of Pablita Abeyta and RG, photograph by Richard Strauss, SI);

147 (Courtesy of the Seneca-Iroquois National Museum, Salamanca, NY 81.0001-1560-1, photograph by Richard Strauss, SI);

148 (BM 1976 Am 3.79);

149 (Courtesy of Atlatl Inc., National Service Organization for Native American Arts and Kristopher Beck);

150 (Courtesy of Atlatl Inc., National Service Organization for Native American Arts and Lillian Pitt );

151 (BM 1976 Am 3.15);

152 (photograph by Annie Sahlin);

153 (BM 1900.4-11.30);

154 (SI/NMAH, Social History Collections 1981.1030.1. and 1981.1030.2, neg. #82-1456);

155 (BM 1932 3-7.16);

156 (National Library of Canada C-007625);

157 (National Archives of Canada C-079643);

158 (SI/NMAH, Division of Cultural History RSN 81668U00, neg. #8711783);

159 (Courtesy of James Luna);

160 (BM Van 196);

161 (BM Sl 2065);

162 (BM Sl 1730);

163 (Courtesy of James Luna);

164 (RG, photograph by Rick Vargas, SI, neg. #98-168, strip 1);

165 (Map drawn by James Farrant);

166 (Courtesy of Michigan State University Museum, Lansing, Michigan 02.1997: 60.1: 76);

167 (BM 1855.11-26.266);

168 (SI/NMNH Department of Anthropology, no acc. #, photograph by Hugh Tallman and Jeff Tinsley, neg. #97-8706);

169 (BM 1842.12-10.46);

170 (silver print by Greg Staats);

171 (photograph by Shelley Niro);

172 (Courtesy of A Poolaw Photo, photograph by Horace Poolaw);

173 (BM 1921.10.14.07);

174 (BM 1991 Am 9.1);

175 (BM 1924.10-9.7);

176 (SI/NPG, 65.61);

177 (Courtesy of Murv Jacob and RG, photograph by Richard Strauss, SI);

178 (SI/NMAH, Photographic History Collections 69.236.105, photograph by Gertrude Kasebier, neg. #85-7213);

179 (BM 1939 AM 9.1);

180 (BM Q83 Am 330);

181 (BM 1951 Am 8.2);

182 (Courtesy of The Heard Museum, Phoenix, Arizona RC 1312/C, photograph by Edward S. Curtis);

183 (SI/NMAH Division of Cultural History 1991.3029.02, courtesy of Russell Sanchez, photograph by Laurie Minor-Penland, neg. #92-97);

184 (photograph by Shan Goshorn, from the series Challenging Indian Stereotypes);

185 (Courtesy of the Indian Pueblo Cultural Center, Inc., Albuquerque, NM 88.3.6);

186 (Courtesy of Murv Jacob);

187 (SI/NMAH, Division of Cultural History 1991.3123.01, photograph by Richard Strauss, neg. #92-5009);

188 (photograph by Annie Sahlin);

189 (BM 1944 Am 2125);

190 (SI/CFPCS, neg. #FAF 76-142 49-26);

191 (BM 1991 Am 11.2);

192 (RG, photograph by Rick Vargas, SI no neg. number);

193 (SI/NMAI photograph by Eric Long, neg. #85-12395);

194 (Collection of The New-York Historical Society 1893.1);

195 (BM 7479(i));

196 (photograph by Joel Grimes);

197 (Map drawn by James Farrant);

198 (SI/NAA 988-A, neg. #45-876);

199 (Courtesy of Zuni Pueblo, photograph by Diane Nordeck, SI, neg. #92-1240);

200 (Courtesy of the Woodland Cultural Centre, photograph by Tim Johnson);

201 (SI/NMAH, Graphic Arts Collections 8111, neg. #97-8329);

202 (Courtesy of Robert Houle, photograph by Greg Staats);

203 (SI/NAA 1063-0);

204 (unidentified);

205 (Library of Congress, Prints and Photographs Division 45805/262-26790, photograph by Frances Benjamin Johnston);

206 (Permission of the artist, Jaune Quick-to-See-Smith);

207 (Courtesy of Sitting Bull College);

208 (Courtesy of the Canadian Embassy, Washington, D.C., photograph by Bo Polatty);

209 (Courtesy of Bob Haozous);

210 (Courtesy of Roxanne Swentzell and The Heard Museum, Phoenix, Arizona IAC 2344, photograph by Craig Smith);

211 (SI/NMAH Division of Cultural History 1991.3058.01 a-b, courtesy of Nora Naranjo Morse, photograph by Laurie Minor-Penland, neg. #91-19814);

212 (photograph by Ed Prokopchuk);

213 (SI/L, Dibner Library. Thomas A. McKenney. *The Indian Tribes of the United States*);

214 (Courtesy of Cherokee Advocate, photograph by Rick Vargas, SI);

215 (SI/NAA MS2287-b, 4-30a, WW, 8-7-11);

216 (BM Van 209);

217 (BM 2004);

218 (RG, photograph by Rayna Green);

219 (RG, photograph by Rick Vargas, SI, neg. #98-167, strip 1);

220 (photograph by Annie Sahlin);

221 (BM SI 1237);

222 (SI/NAA Cherokee 1044B, photograph by James Mooney);

223 (SI/NMAI 1/8239);

224 (SI/CFPCS, photograph by S. Sweezy, neg. #FAF 75-14251-32);

225 (SI/NMAH Graphic Arts Collections 8118, neg. #97-8321);

226 (Courtesy of Rebecca Baird, photograph by Rebecca Baird);

227 (Courtesy of Rebecca Baird *et al.*, photograph by Rebecca Baird);

228 (SI/NMAH Division of Cultural History 1991.6035.02, Courtesy of St Joseph's Apache Mission, photograph by Jeff Tinsley, neg. #92-5000);

229 (BM 1979 AM 22. 65);

230 (Courtesy of Museum of New Mexico, Santa Fe, New Mexico, photograph by Hance and Nast, neg. #1507);

231 (Courtesy of Courtesy of Museum of New Mexico, Santa Fe, New Mexico, Museum of Indian Arts and Culture/Laboratory of Anthropology, Dorothy Dunn Kramer Collection 5140413, photograph by Blair Clark);

232 (SI/NMAH, Division of Cultural History 1991.3042.02, photograph by Eric Long, neg. #92-5039);

233 (SI/NMAA 1989.30.1 a-e);

234 (Courtesy of Cranbrook Institute of Science CS 2118 and 2117, photograph by Rick Vargas, SI);

235 (Courtesy of the Seneca-Iroquois National Museum, Salamanca, NY 81.0001.1112-1129, 81.0001.0231-40, 81.0001.0260, 81.0001.0391, no. neg. #, photograph by Eric Long, SI);

236 (SI/NMAI 24/7279, 24/1358, 16/9757, photograph by Rick Vargas);

237 (SI/NMAI 14/4989, photograph by Rick Vargas);

238 (SI/NAA Coll. 78, photograph by Timothy H. O'Sullivan);

239 (BM 1944 Am 2.208);

240 (BM 1855.11-26.354);

241 (BM 1988 Am 4.1);

242 (BM 1986 Am 10.107);

243 (SI/NMAA 1985.66. 248, 934B);

244 (SI/NAA BAE 7344, neg. #92-8895);

245 (RG, photograph by Richard Strauss, SI);

246 (RG, photograph by Rayna Green);

247 (photograph by Shan Goshorn);

248 (photograph by Annie Sahlin);

249 (SI/NMAH Division of Cultural History, photograph by Rick Vargas, neg. #98-163);

250 (Courtesy of Wilma Mankiller, photograph by Cherokee Nation Communications Department);

251 (SI/NMNH, Department of Anthropology 380935, 380918, 381395);

252 (BM St 748);

253 (Map drawn by James Farrant);

254 (BM 1931.12);

255 (BM 1949 Am 22.119);

256 (BM 1903.81);

257 (Courtesy of Gerald McMaster);

258 (BM 5202);

259 (BM 1949 Am 22 146);

260 (BM 1861.3-12.62);

261 (BM 1976 Am 3. 28);

262 (SI/CFPCS, neg. #FAF 84-9087-29a);

263 (BM 1948 AM 17 21);

264 (SI/NMAH Division of Cultural History 1991.3195.01, courtesy of Ramona Sakiestewa, photograph by Jeff Tinsley, neg. #98-5005);

265 (Minnesota Historical Society, photograph by Monroe Kelley);

266 (Courtesy of Thomas Vennum);

267 (BM 1939 Am 11 3);

268 (Courtesy of A Poolaw Photo, photograph by Horace Poolaw);

269 (RG, photograph by Rayna Green);

270 (SI/NAA 3200-B-15, photograph by George Trager);

271 (photograph by Shan Goshorn, from the series *Reclaiming Cultural Ownership*);

272 (photograph by Richard Strauss, SI);

273 (photograph by Richard Strauss, SI).

## Quotation acknowledgements

Page 3
Gattuso, John, *Circle of Nations: Voices and Visions of American Indians, North American Native Writers and Photographers*, Hillsboro, O.R.: Beyond Words Publishing Company, 1993, 60. Reprinted by permission of Beyond Words Publishing Company.

Page 4
Trimble, Stephen, The People: Indians of the American Southwest, Santa Fe, N.M.: School of American Research Press, 1993, 44. Reprinted by permission of the School of American Research Press and Steven Trimble.

Page 5
*Between Sacred Mountains: Navajo Stories and Lessons From the Land. Sun Tracks: An American Indian Literary Series*, vol. 11, Tucson, A.Z.: University of Arizona Press, 1984, 23. Copyright *c.* 1984, the Arizona Board of Regents. Reprinted by permission of the University of Arizona Press.

Page 6 top
Smohalla, the Wanapum prophet, *c.* 1880, reported by an army officer. *Fourteenth Annual Report of the Bureau of American Ethnology*, pt 2, 1896, 720–721.

Page 6 bottom
Wilson, Gilbert, Field Report, vol. 13, 1913, in *Wilson Papers*, Minneapolis, M.N.: Minnesota Historical Society, 109–110.

Page 7 top left
In Rayna Green and Rick Tejada Flores (co-directors), *Corn Is Who We Are: The Story of Pueblo Indian Food*, 20-minute colour documentary film, Smithsonian Productions and Alturas Productions, 1995. Printed by permission of the film directors, Smithsonian Productions and Alturas Productions.

Page 7 bottom left
Berger, Thomas R., *Village Journey: The Report of the Alaska Native Review Commission*, New York: Hill and Wang, 1985, 6. For more on land issues in Canada and the Arctic, see Alden Cox, Bruce (ed.), *Native Peoples, Native Land: Canadian Indians, Inuit and Métis*, Ottawa: Carlton University Press, 1988.

Page 7 right
Berger, 1985, 15.

Page 8
Diamond, Beverley, M., Sam Cronk and Franziska von Rosen, *Visions of Sound: Musical Instruments of First Nations Communities in Northeastern America*, Chicago and London: University of Chicago Press, 1994, 164. Reprinted by permission of the University of Chicago Press, *c.* 1984. Reprinted in Canada by permission of Wilfrid Laurier University Press.

Page 10
Karen Loveland, producer and Rayna Green, writer, *We Are Here: 500 Years of Pueblo Sovereignty*, 15-minute colour documentary film, Smithsonian Productions, 1992. Printed by permission of Rayna Green and Smithsonian Productions.

Page 11
Maxidiwiac (Buffalo Bird Woman, Waheenee), *Waheenee: An Indian Girl's Story: Told By Herself to Gilbert Wilson*, illus. by Frederick N. Wilson, St. Paul: Webb Publishing Co., 1921. Reprint: Bison Books. Lincoln, Nebraska: University of Nebraska Press, 1981, 45.

Page 14 top left
Radulovitch, Mary Lou Fox, Ojibwe Cultural Foundation.

Page 14 bottom left
Momaday, N. Scott, *The Names: A Memoir*, New York: Harper and Row, Publishers, 1976, 35.

Page 14 right
Gattuso, 1993, 89. On earlier art, see Information sources, Coe, 1976, and King, 1982

Page 16
Michelson, Truman, 'Narrative of an Arapaho Woman', *American Anthropologist* 35, no. 4, 1933, 595–610.

Page 18
Jones, Suzi (ed.), *Pacific Basketmakers: A Living Tradition, Catalogue of the* 1981 *Pacific Basketmaker's Symposium and Exhibition*, Fairbanks, A.K.: University of Alaska Museum, 1983, 33. Reprinted by permission of the University of Alaska Museum.

Page 20 left
Winch, Terrence (ed.), *All Roads Are Good: Native Voices on Life and Culture*, Washington, D.C.: Smithsonian Institution, 1994, 197. Reprinted by permission of the National Museum of the American Indian and the Smithsonian Institution Press.

Page 20 right
Tewa song, translation by Herman Agoyo, San Juan Pueblo, to Rayna Green, 1995.

Page 21 left
Green, Rayna, 'Red Earth People and Southeastern Basketry', in Linda Mowat, Howard Morphy and Penny Dransart, *Basketmakers: Meaning and Form in*

Native American Baskets, Oxford, England: Pitt Rivers Museum, University Of Oxford, 1992, 11–18. Reprinted by permission of the Pitt-Rivers Museum.

**Page 21 top right**

Teit, James, 'The Salishan Tribes of the Western Plateaus', in Franz Boas (ed.), 45th Annual Report of the Bureau of American Ethnology for the Years, 1927–28, Washington, D.C.: Smithsonian Institution, 1930, 23–396, 392.

**Page 21 bottom right**

Teit, 1930, 328.

**Page 23**

Adapted from 'Tepary Beans and Human Beings at Agriculture's Arid Limits', in Gathering the Desert by Gary Nabhan. Copyright 1985 the Arizona Board of Regents. Reprinted by Permission of the University of Arizona Press.

**Page 24**

Boas, Franz (1858–1992), Kwakiutl Ethnography, in H. Codere (ed.), Chicago: University of Chicago Press, 1966, 100.

**Page 26 top left**

Excerpts from The Native American Perspective on the Trade Blanket: A Woman's Experience by Rain Parrish, is reprinted with the permission of Gibbs Smith, Publisher (Salt Lake City, 1992), from the book Language of the Robe, by Robert Kapoun, with Charles Lohrman, 3.

**Page 26 bottom left**

Excerpts from The Native American Perspective on the Trade Blanket: A Man's Experience by Bob Block, is reprinted with the permission of Gibbs Smith, Publisher (Salt Lake City, 1992), from the book Language of the Robe, by Robert Kapoun, with Charles Lohrman, 3–5.

**Page 26 right**

Pitseolak, Pictures Out of My Life, Seattle: University of Washington Press, 1971.

**Page 27 left**

Boudinot, Elias, An Address to the Whites. Delivered at First Presbyterian Church, May 26, 1826, Philadelphia, printed by William F. Geddes, 1826; see also Perdue, Theda (ed.), Cherokee Editor: The Writings of Elias Boudinot, Knoxville, T.N.: The University of Tennessee Press, 1983.

**Page 27 right**

Boudinot, cited in Walker, Robert Sparks, Torchlights to the Cherokees, New York: The Macmillan Company, 1931.

**Page 29**

Domine Pater or Good Peter, a Seneca-Cayuga orator, 1788. In the Papers of Sir William Johnson 1715–1779, 16 vols, Albany: State University of New York Press, 1921–1965, III.

**Page 33**

Davis, Mary B., Native America in the Twentieth Century: An Encyclopedia: New York and London: Garland Publishing Co., 1996, 84. Reprinted by permission of Garland Publishing Co.

**Page 34**

In Kennedy, Michael S., The Assiniboines, Norman, Oklahoma: University of Oklahoma Press, 1961. Reprinted by permission of the University of Oklahoma Press.

**Page 35**

From an interview with Tessie Naranjo (Santa Clara Pueblo), 1997 for Rayna Green, writer, producer and director and Tessie Naranjo, researcher, From Ritual to Retail: Native Americans, Tourism and the Fred Harvey Company, 20-minute colour documentary video, The Heard Museum, Phoenix, Arizona, 1997. Printed by permission of the Heard Museum, Tessie Naranjo and Rayna Green.

**Page 36**

Waubagesig (ed.), The Only Good Indian: Essays By Canadian Indians, Toronto: New Press, 1970. Reprinted by permission of Stoddard Publishing, North York, Ontario.

**Page 37 top left**

In Keegan, Marcia, Southwest Indian Cookbook, Pueblo and Navajo Images, Quotes and Recipes. Santa Fe: Clearlight Publishers, 1996. Reprinted by permission of Clearlight Publishers.

**Page 37 bottom left**

Truman. Joel, photographs and Betty Reid, text, Navajo: Portrait of a Nation. Eaglewood, Ca: Westcliffe Publishers, 1992. Reprinted by permission of Betty Reid.

**Page 38 top**

Vision experienced by three Cherokees, 1811.

**Page 38 centre**

Resolution of the Georgia Legislature, December 1827.

**Page 38 bottom**

John Ross to Lewis Cass, 14 February 1835, US House of Representatives, Memorial and Protest of the Cherokee Nation, Document 286 (serial 292), 129–133, 1835.

Page 41
Davis, 1996, 84.

Page 42 right
In Perdue, 1980, 7–8, from interviews conducted in the 1930s under the US Works Progress Administration, papers at the University of Oklahoma.

Page 43 top
Trimble, 1993, 122.

Page 43 bottom
Benton-Banai, Eddie, The Mishomis Book, Minneapolis: Indian Country Press and Publications, 1979, 74.

Page 44
Winch, 1994, 78.

Page 48 left
Nabhan, 1982, 83. Adapted from 'Tepary Beans and Human Beings at Agriculture's Arid Limits' in Gathering the Desert by Gary Nabhan. Copyright 1985 The Arizona Board of Regents. Reprinted by Permission of the University of Arizona Press.

Page 48 top right
Rayna Green and Howard Bass, producers, Heartbeat: Voices of First Nations Women, 1995. Smithsonian Folkways SF CD 40415. Printed by permission of the producers and Smithsonian Folkways Recordings.

Page 48 bottom right
Stories of the People, Washington, D.C.: National Museum of the American Indian and Universe Publishing, 1997, 68. Reprinted by permission of National Museum of the American Indian and Universe Publishing.

Page 49
Gilman and Schneider, 1987.

Page 52
Diamond, 1994, 164.

Page 55
Malotki, Ekkehart with Michael Lomatuway'ma, Earth Fire: A Hopi Legend of the Sunset Crater Eruption, Flagstaff, A.Z.: Northland Press, 1987, 154. Reprinted by permission of Ekkehart Malotki and Northland Press.

Page 56 from top left
Vennum, Thomas, Jr, Wild Rice and the Ojibwa People, St Paul, M.N.: Minnesota Historical Society Press, 1988, 58. Reprinted by permission of the Minnesota Historical Society Press. Original quote in Eva Lips, Die Reisernte der Ojibwa-Indianer: Wirtschaft und Recht Eines Erntevolkes, Berlin:

Academie Verlag, 1956, 55, 65.
John Fire Lame Deer and Richard Erdoes, Lame Deer, Seeker of Visions, New York: Simon and Schuster, 1972, 155–160.

Diamond, 1994, 177.

Diamond, 1994, 160.

Diamond, 1994, 35–38.

Green and Bass, 1995.

Page 59
Stung Serpent, c. 1720, cited in Ballentine, Betty and Ian Ballentine (eds), The Native Americans: An Illustrated History, Atlanta, G.A.: Turner Publications, 1993, 274.

Page 60
Densmore, Frances, 'Teton Sioux Music', Bureau of American Ethnology Bulletin, 61, 1918.

Page 61
Hill, Tom and Richard Hill Sr, Creation's Journey: Native American Identity and Belief, Washington, DC: National Museum of the American Indian and the Smithsonian Institution Press, 1994, 89. Reprinted by permission of National Museum of the American Indian and the Smithsonian Institution Press.

Page 63 top
Katz, Jane (ed.), Messengers of the Wind: Native American Women Tell Their Life Stories, New York: One World Books, 1995, 147–169. Reprinted by permission of Ramona Bennett.

Page 63 bottom
United States of America 1837 Treaty with the Chippewa, Article 5.

Page 64
Herbst, Toby and Joel Kopp, The Flag in American Indian Art, New York State Historical Association, University of Washington Press Seattle, University of Washington Press for The New York State Historical Association, 12–13. Reprinted by permission of the New York State Historical Association.

Page 65 left
Reprinted with permission from Native American Dance, Ceremonies and Social Traditions, National Museum of the American Indian and Charlotte Heth, General Editor, c 1992, Fulcrum Publishing, Inc./Starwood Publishing, Golden, Colorado. All Rights Reserved. See also Drumbeat … Heartbeat: A Celebration of the Pow Wow, Minneapolis: Lerner Publications.

Page 65 right
Stories and Legends of the Palm Springs Indians, Los Angeles: Times-Mirror Press, 1943, 25.

Page 66 left
Adapted from 'Tepary Beans and Human Beings at Agriculture's Arid Limits', in Gathering the Desert by Gary Nabhan. Copyright 1985, the Arizona Board of Regents. Reprinted by Permission of the University of Arizona Press, 101.

Page 66 top right
Keegan, Marcia, 8; books for young people on Native food tradition include Clambake: A Tradition; Ininlatig's Gift of Sugar; Traditional Native Sugarmaking; The Sacred Harvest; Wild Rice Gathering, Minneapolis: Lerner Publications.

Page 66 bottom right
Tallmountain, Mary, There is no Word for Goodbye, Marvin, S.D.: Blue Cloud Quarterly Press, 1982.

Page 68
Ackerman, Lillian (ed.), A Song to the Creator: Traditional Arts of Native Women of the Plateau, Norman: University of Oklahoma Press, 1996, ix. Reprinted by permission of the publishers, the editor and Barbara Coddington for the Plateau Project.

Page 70 top
Winch, 1994, 135.

Page 70 bottom
Green and Bass, 1995.

Page 72
Chona, Maria, Papago Woman, Edited by Ruth Underhill, Orlando, FL: Holt, Rinehart and Winston/Harcourt Brace, 1979.

Page 75 top
Ghost Dance Song, believed to be sung by Kicking Bear, the Minneconjou Sioux leader. Oral tradition.

Page 75 bottom
Ghost Dance Song. Oral tradition.

Page 76 left
McDowell, Marsha and C. Kurt Dewhurst (eds), To Honor and Comfort: Native Quilting Traditions, Santa Fe, N.M.: Museum of New Mexico Press and the Michigan State University Museum, 1997. Reprinted by permission of the Michigan State University Museum.

Page 76 top right
Ackerman, 1996, ix.

Page 76 bottom right
Chrystos, Not Vanishing, Vancouver: Press Gang Publishers, 1988.

Page 78 left
Excerpt from an English version of the traditional Thanksgiving address, gawi'yo, given in part by Reg Henry, Cayuga faithkeeper, at the Six Nations Reserve, Canada, in 1996.

Page 78 right
Gattuso, 1993, 88–89.

Page 83
Thomas Jefferson to the Western Indians, 5 May 1808.

Page 85 left
Oakes, Jill and Rick Riewe, Our Boots: An Inuit Women's Art, London: Thames and Hudson, 1996, 17. Reprinted by permission of Thames and Hudson.

Page 85 right
King, J.C.H. (ed.), The Living Arctic: Hunters of the Canadian North-A Report and Catalogue, London: British Museum Press, 1989, 17; see also King, J.C.H., Arctic Hunter: Indians and Inuits of Northern Canada, London: British Museum Press, 1987.

Page 87
A Treaty Between Great Britain and the Iroquois, 1794.

Page 88 top right
Trimble, 1993, 45.

Page 88 from centre left
Attakullakulla, c. 1769 in Davis, K.G. (ed.), Documents of the American Revolution, 1770–1773, 15 vols, Shannon: Irish University Press, 1972.

Oral tradition.

Loveland, 1992.

Stories of the People, Washington, D.C.: National Museum of the American Indian and Universe Publishing, 1997, 68. Reprinted by permission of National Museum of the American Indian and Universe Publishing, 43.

Green and Tejada Flores, 1995.

Page 89
King, J.C.H. (ed.), The Living Arctic: Hunters of the Canadian North – A Report and Catalogue, London: British Museum Press, 1989, 17.

Page 91 top left
Diamond, 1994, 164.

Page 91 bottom left
Indian Education, pt I, US Congress, Special Senate Subcommittee on Indian Education, Hearings, 91st Congress, 1st Session, 1969.

Page 91 bottom left
Trimble, 1993.

Page 92
Joy Harjo and Poetic Justice. *Letter From the End of the Twentieth Century*. Silver Wave Records, SD/SC 914, 1996. Reprinted by permission of Joy Harjo, 1994.

Page 93
Humfreville, J. Leo, *Twenty Years Among Our Savage Indians*, Hartford: Hartford Publishing Co., 1897.

Page 94
Barboncito, 28 May 1868 at a council convened on the subject of Navajo Removal.

Page 95
Keegan, 1977, 14.

Page 96 from top right
Green and Tejada Flores, 1995.

Maxidiwiac (Buffalo Bird Woman, Waheenee), *Waheenee: An Indian Girl's Story: Told By Herself to Gilbert Wilson*, Illus. by Frederick N. Wilson, St Paul: Webb Publishing Co., 1921, 175. Reprint: Bison Books. Lincoln, Nebraska: University of Nebraska Press, 1981, 45.

Green and Tejada Flores, 1995.

Grimes and Reid, 1992.

Page 98
Fitzhugh, William W. and Aron Crowell, *Crossroads of Continents: Cultures of Siberia and Alaska*, Washington, D.C.: Smithsonian Institution Press, 1988, 333. Reprinted by permission of the Smithsonian Institution Press.

Page 99
Hungry Wolf, Beverley, *The Ways of My Grandmothers*, New York: William Morrow and Company, 1980, 140–141. Reprinted by permission of William Morrow and Company.

Page 105 top
Hammond, George P. and Agapito Rey (eds and trans.), *Don Juan de Onate: Colonizer of New Mexico, 1595–1628*, Albuquerque: University of New Mexico Press, 1953, 675–676.

Page 105 bottom left
Oral tradition, Rayna Green.

Page 108 from top left
Gante, Edna (Catalogue ed.), *Circle of Life: Cultural Community in Ojibwe Crafts*, Duluth: St. Louis Historical Society, Chisholm Museum and Duluth Art Institute, 1984, 5. Reprinted by permission of the publishers and Fred Benjamin.

Keegan, 1977, 14.

Green and Bass, 1995.

Oral tradition, Rayna Green.

Page 111 left
Grimes and Reid, 1992, 119.

Page 111 right
Grimes and Reid, 1992, 122.

Page 116
Lewis, Richard, *I Breathe A New Song: Poems of the Eskimo*, New York: Simon and Schuster, 1971.

Page 118 top
Katz, Jane (ed.), *This Song Remembers: Self-Portraits of Native Americans in the Nineties*, N.Y.: Houghton Mifflin, 1980.

Page 118 bottom
Reprinted from *Black Elk Speaks*, by John G. Neihardt, by permission of the University of Nebraska Press. Copyright 1932, 1959, 1972, by John G. Neihardt. Copyright 1961, by the John G. Neihardt Trust, 3–4.

Page 124 top
'Nan Chu Kweejo' (Clay Mother) from *Mudwoman: Poems From the Clay* by Nora Naranjo-Morse. Copyright 1992 Nora Naranjo-Morse. Reprinted by permission of the University of Arizona Press, Tucson.

Page 124 bottom
Cited in Morrison, Howard *et al. American Encounters. An Exhibition Book*. Washington: National Museum of American History, 1992.

Page 125
Martin, Christopher (ed.), *Native Needlework: Contemporary Indian Textiles From North Dakota*, Fargo: North Dakota Council on the Arts, 1988, 13–14. Reprinted by permission of the North Dakota Council on the Arts.

Page 126
Loveland, 1992; for a good history of the Pueblo peoples from a Pueblo perspective, see Sando, Joe S., *Pueblo Nations: Eight Centuries of Pueblo History*, Santa Fe, N.M.: Clear Light Publishers, 1992.

Page 127 left
Gattuso, 1993, 49.

Page 127 right
Ackerman, 1996, 126.

Page 128 left
Oral tradition, Rayna Green.

Page 128 right
Hill and Hill, 1994.

Page 131
In William L. Stone, *The Life and Times of Sa Go Wat Ha*, New York: Wiley and Putnam, 1841.

Page 133
*Colonial Records of North Carolina*, X, 763–785, Henry Stuart, a letter to John Stuart, 25 August 1776.

Page 134
Evan Jones' journal, 16 June 1838, at the Baptist Historical Society, Rochester, New York; see more McLoughlin, William G., *After the Trail of Tears: The Cherokees' Struggle for Sovereignty, 1839–1880*, Chapel Hill: University of North Carolina Press, 1994.

Page 135 top
Foreman, Grant, *Indian Removal: The Emigration of the Five Civilized Tribes of Indians*, Norman: University of Oklahoma Press, 1932, reported from interviews conducted in the 1930s under the Works Progress Administration, papers at the University of Oklahoma.

Page 135 bottom
Gen. John Ellis Wool, Commander of the United States troops in the Cherokee Nation, 1836. Wool to Cass, 10 September 1836, US Senate, *Report From the Secretary of War ... In Relation to the Cherokee Treaty of 1835*, Document 120 (serial 315), 29–30.

Page 139 left
Katz, 1995, 250–251. Reprinted by permission of Vi Hilbert.

Page 139 right
In Smyth, Albert Henry (ed.), *The Writings of Benjamin Franklin*, American History, no. 47, 10 vols, New York: Haskell House, X, 1969, 98–99.

Page 141 top
Sekaquaptewa, Helen, 'School to Keams Canyon', in *Me and Mine: The Life Story of Helen Sekaquaptewa* as told to Louise Udall, 93. Copyright 1969 the Arizona Board of Regents. Reprinted by permission of the University of Arizona Press.

Page 141 bottom
John Howard Payne Papers. Letters from Brainerd Mission, Sally Reece Letter to Reverend Daniel Campbell, 25 July 1828, Newberry Library, Chicago, Illinois.

Page 144
Georges Erasmus, Maclean's Magazine (14 July 1986).

Page 149 top
Cherokee Statement to the Secretary of War, June 1818. Papers of the War Department, US National Archives

Page 149 bottom
US Supreme Court Chief Justice John Marshall, in *Worcester v. State of Georgia*, 1832.

Page 150
Keegan, 1977, 58.

Page 152
Green, Rayna, *Cherokee Stomp Dance: Laughter Rises Up*, Reprinted with permission from Native American Dance, Ceremonies and Social Traditions, National Museum of the American Indian and Charlotte Heth, General Editor, 1992, Fulcrum Publishing, Inc./Starwood Publishing, Golden, Colorado. All Rights Reserved, 177.

Page 153 left
Keetoowah Society of Cherokee Indians.

Page 153 right
Berger, 1985, 5.

Page 154
Densmore, 1918, 140.

Page 155 top
Brant, Beth and Sandra Laronde (eds), *Sweetgrass Grows All Around Her*, Toronto: Native Women in the Arts, 1996, 4. Reprinted by permission of Native Women and the Arts.

Page 155 bottom
Brant and Laronde, 1996. Reprinted by permission of Native Women and the Arts.

Page 156
Berger, 1985, 129.

Page 157 left
Diamond, 1994, 26.

Page 157 right
Lester, Joan A., *We're Still Here: Art of Indian New England*, Boston, M.A.: The Children's Museum, 1987, 25.

Page 158
Green and Naranjo, 1997.

Page 160
Sweet Medicine, Cheyenne Prophet.

Page 164 top
Berger, 1985, 140.

Page 164 bottom
Berger, 1985, 137.

Page 165

Laws of the Cherokee Nation: Adopted at Various
Periods, Printed for the Benefit of the Nation.
Tahlequah, Oklahoma: Cherokee Advocate, 1852.

Page 167

Reprinted by permission of Wilma Mankiller.

Page 168

Green and Bass, 1995.

Page 169

Oakes and Riewe, 1996, 22.

Page 170

*Council Fire: A Resource Guide*, Brantford, Ontario:
Woodland Cultural Centre, 1989, 1. Reprinted by
permission of the Woodland Cultural Centre.

Page 173

Nancy Ward.

Page 174 top

Bonar, Eulalie H., *Woven By The Grandmothers:
Nineteenth Century Navajo Textiles From the National
Museum of the American Indian*, Washington, D.C.:
Smithsonian Institution Press, 1996, 25. Reprinted
by permission of National Museum of the
American Indian and the Smithsonian Institution
Press. See also Roessel, Monty (Navajo), *Songs
from the Loom: A Navajo Girl Learns to Weave*,
Minneapolis: Lerner Pubications.

Page 174 bottom

Keegan, 1977, 39.

Page 175

Boas, Franz and George Hunt, 'Kwakiutl Texts',
Second Series Publications of the Jesup North
Pacific Expedition 10, American Museum of
Natural History, 1906, 63.

Page 176

Lolita Taylor.

Page 178

Green and Bass, 1995.

# Authors' acknowledgements

**Rayna Green** is Director of the American Indian Program, National Museum of American History, Smithsonian Institution. Of Cherokee ancestry, she holds a PhD in Folklore and American Studies, and is the author of several books and many articles and a producer of many museum exhibitions, films and audio recordings on American Indians.

*Abundant thanks and gratitude go especially to Sarah Grogan, Research and Production Assistant, whose fine mind, considerable organization and good company kept Rayna Green productive; to Penny Bateman, whose good idea it was we should produce this book; to Jonathan C.H. King, Keeper, North American Collections, British Museum, Museum of Mankind, who made the museum's collections and his good advice available to us; and to the National Museum of American History and the Smithsonian Institution, for financial, legal and intellectual support for this project.*

*Many thanks for excellent photography go to Rick Strauss, Jeff Tinsley, Eric Long, Alan Hart and Rick Vargas in the Office of Printing and Photographic Services and to Pam Dewey, National Museum of the American Indian, Smithsonian Institution; and to Paula Fleming in the National Anthropological Archives, Bill Yeingst, Helena Wright, Joan Boudreau, Susan Myers, Sue Ostroff, Jennifer Locke, Lisa Graddy, Howard Bass and Doug Mudd at the National Museum of American History, for collegial support as well as object and picture research; to Ann Kidd, Linda Quinn and Michael Lell, research interns; to colleagues at ORBIS Associates for material on Native plant medicine, and to Helene Quick for final production support and extraordinary patience.*

**Melanie Fernandez** is .Community Arts Officer and Acting First Nations Officer at the Ontario Arts Council.

*Over time, I have had the privilege to be supported by many people who assisted me through the writing and research processes. Many thanks go to: Dr Trudy Nicks of the Royal Ontario Musuem (ROM), Ethnology Department, for arranging access to ROM resources and to Judy Rittersorn, of the ROM Library, for her enthusiastic assistance; family and friends, Sheila, Jules, Ian, Sandra, Roma, Anna, Diane, Sue, Penny and Ruth for their encouragement and support through this project and past ones; my colleagues at the Ontario Arts Council, who were understanding while I was trying to juggle projects; and, most importantly, the staff, former and current, of the Woodland Cultural Centre in Brantford, Ontario, Alice, Renee, Winnie, Shiela, Tom, Amos and especially Reg Henry, for helping me to truly understand First Nations culture and perspectives, past and present.*

*Special thanks go to Dave Agar, Mike Rowe and Saul Peckham of The British Museum Photographic Service.*

# General Index

**a**

Abenaki 2, 20, 94, 104
aboriginal title 7, 29, 89, 112
acculturation, *see* assimilation
adaptation 2, 3, 59, 65, 157, 158
Adobe 4, 11, 13
adoption 121
Africans and African-Americans 4, 5, 45, 83, 92, 93, 127, 140, 145
agriculture/ farming 5, 6, 9, 14, 22, 34, 59, 66, 67, 74, 89, 106, 114, 128, 139, 142, 145, 150, 161, 166, 176
Alabama 50, 109
Alaska 7, 8, 9, 13, 14, 15, 69, 112, 116, 156, 162
Alaska Native Claims Settlement Act 7, 15, 157
Alaska pipeline 15
Alaska Purchase 7, 9, 15
Alberta 13, 26, 103, 145
Alcatraz 121, 166
Alcohol/alcohol abuse 7, 8, 69, 77, 85, 159
Aleut/Alutiiq/Alutiit 7, 8, 9, 69, 82, 106, 109, 116, 122
Aleutian Islands 7, 8
Algonquin(people)/Algonquian (language) 2, 5, 8, 18, 68, 72, 79, 104, 110, 119, 159, 162, 170, 179
Alibamu 17
alliances (political/social) 29, 30, 33, 83, 86, 104, 115, 130, 131, 137, 146, 168
Allotment 5, 9, 25, 38, 46, 50, 51, 135, 146, 148, 152, 156, 166
Alutiiq *see* Aleut
Alutiit *see* Aleut
American Fur Company 69
American Indian Movement 45, 121, 122, 179
American Indian Religious Freedom Act 9, 10
American War for Independence/American Revolution 7, 29, 36, 50, 86, 95, 106, 114, 133, 136, 146, 168
ancient people 1, 106, 167
Androscoggin 2
animals 15, 19, 21, 23, 24, 42, 52, 56, 67, 68, 78, 95, 100, 119, 115, 116, 127, 128, 172
Anishinabe *see* Ojibwa
Ant 21
anthropologists 60, 76, 106, 128
Apaches 10, 11, 38, 43, 49, 54, 56, 65, 71, 74, 81, 94, 96, 97, 110, 143, 161
Apalachi 145
Appaloosas 46, 80
Arapaho 14, 16, 69, 82, 112, 127, 154
anthropology/anthropologists and
archaeology/archaeologists 45, 106, 123, 125
architecture 4, 11, 12, 13, 43, 80, 143
Arctic 8, 13, 44, 72, 82, 84, 85, 98, 107, 112, 115, 116, 132, 139, 143, 153, 162, 169, 176
Arikara 6, 49, 97

Arizona 111
art/artist 3, 7, 13, 14, 17, 20, 21, 22, 23, 32, 45, 51, 77, 81, 85, 87, 97, 105, 107, 114, 121, 127, 136, 137, 143, 144, 154, 155, 157, 171
assimilation/acculturation policy 2, 3, 9, 17, 33, 35, 41, 52, 90, 12, 135, 140, 141, 148, 156
Assiniboine 23, 26, 35, 49, 65, 154
astronomical/celestial observation/signs 13, 23, 34, 138
Athabaskan/Athapaskan 11, 14, 15, 156
atlatl 28
awls 15, 131
Aztecs 34

**b**

baby carriers, cradleboards 16, 127, 176
bags/pouches 17, 21, 26, 64, 100, 119, 131, 160
ban (on ceremonies/languages, potlatch, peyote, clothing) 36, 41, 90 97, 111, 112, 123, 140, 154
bandolier bag 17, 64, 131
bark 18, 19, 26, 162, 168
Basket Dance 20
basket hat 78, 82
basket, basketmaking 2, 14, 15, 18, 19, 20, 21, 78, 82, 105, 123, 138, 155, 157, 174, 181
beads, beadwork 7, 14, 15, 16, 17, 21, 22, 23, 59, 64, 70, 77, 78, 79, 100, 101, 102, 118, 130, 157, 158, 160
beans 5, 22, 23, 41, 55, 66, 88, 95
Bear 23, 53, 65, 143
beaver 15, 24, 26, 43, 49, 69, 113, 143
Bella Coola 98, 111, 138
Beothuk 18, 24, 44
Bering Sea 97
Bering Strait Theory 25
bingo 68, 70, 93
birchbark 18, 26, 49, 104, 106, 113, 162
birds 13, 28, 43, 61, 65, 78, 108, 116, 127, 129, 145
Black Hills 90, 93, 145, 138, 148
Blackfeet/Blackfoot 13, 23, 25, 79, 99, 109, 154
Blood 26, 40
blood quantum 36, 40, 41, 84
Blue Corn Woman 49
boats 18, 26, 49, 67, 69, 84
bone/ivory 3, 15, 17, 19, 21, 24, 63, 82, 143
Bosque Redondo *see* Long Walk of the Navajo
bow and arrow 15, 28, 59, 129, 172
Box of treasures 28
'brave' 109
British Columbia 90, 101, 112, 138, 161
British Museum 24, 53, 106, 107
British North America Act (Constitution Act, 1867) 35
British, the/Great Britain 2, 24, 29, 30, 50, 52, 53 60, 64, 69, 86, 95, 102, 106, 114, 120, 131, 135, 137, 139, 146, 161, 170, 172
buffalo 13, 23, 27, 30, 32, 34, 49, 65, 67, 69, 74, 79, 93, 102, 103, 119, 124, 127, 148, 150, 172

Bureau of Indian Affairs (BIA) 15, 30, 33, 51, 89, 107, 156, 169, 181

**c**

Caddo 82, 110
Cahuilla 65, 70
calendars/time 34, 126, 158
California 11, 20, 59, 70, 78, 90, 101, 105, 106, 108, 129, 136, 147, 156, 181
camas root 7, 66, 68
Canada 1, 2, 8, 29, 30, 31, 35, 50, 67, 69, 73, 80, 82, 84, 85, 86, 87, 90–92, 95, 97, 102–104, 106, 109, 112, 115, 123, 132, 137, 144, 145, 146, 153, 155, 169, 180
Canadian Confederation 69, 103, 113
Canadian Constitution 144
Canadian government 6, 85, 97, 103
Canadian Museum of Civilization 106
canoes 18, 26, 49, 67, 77, 84–85, 104, 114, 143, 139, 162, 175, 176
Caribbean 4, 60
caribou 13, 15, 68, 84
Carlisle Indian School 72, 141
carving/carvers 12, 28, 77, 80, 111, 161
Catholic Church/Catholicism 39, 99, 104, 105, 106, 114, 126, 139, 156
cattle 6, 7, 11, 32, 64, 65, 77, 80, 112, 124, 148
Cayuga 29, 30, 36, 52, 78, 85, 115, 136, 170
cedar 68, 111, 138, 147
Central America 95
ceremonies/ ceremonial life 6, 7, 9, 11, 13, 17, 19, 20, 26, 34, 36, 43, 44, 55, 56, 66, 71, 74, 76, 78, 80, 87, 90, 95, 97,100, 101, 108, 111, 118, 127, 128, 136, 138, 139, 152, 154, 155, 157, 158, 166, 168, 170, 172, 174, 175, 181
Changing Woman 23, 101
Cherokee Phoenix/Advocate 27, 141, 146, 147, 151
Cherokees 5, 9, 11, 17, 19, 20, 27, 31, 37, 52, 56, 57, 58, 59, 70, 72, 76, 78, 90, 97, 99, 109, 127, 132, 133, 134, 135, 139, 140, 141, 146, 147, 150, 151, 152, 153, 157, 164, 165, 166, 167, 172, 173, 179
Cheyenne 14, 31, 70, 78, 93, 109, 110, 136, 138, 154
Chickasaw 38, 82, 152
Chilkat 174
Chiltooth 82
Chippewa *see* Ojibwa
Choctaw 5, 9, 17, 38, 70, 76, 82, 109, 152, 153, 163
Christianity/Church 2, 3, 7, 9, 11, 15, 17, 21, 27, 30, 32, 33, 34, 36, 38, 39, 40, 41, 49, 51, 69, 70, 74, 77, 90, 98, 99, 100, 104, 105, 108, 119, 120, 121, 135, 138, 139, 140, 145, 168, 179
Chugatch 29
citizenship 9, 41
Civil War 5, 10, 34, 35, 38, 82
'Civilization'/policy 2, 30, 84, 135, 136, 140, 141, 161, 166
clan mother 29, 86, 170

clans 11, 12, 23, 24, 29, 42, 43, 53, 55, 58, 61, 77, 80, 86, 99, 114, 123, 143, 150, 157, 166, 181
cloth 69, 76, 104
clothing 14, 15, 16, 17, 18, 19, 21, 25, 26, 31, 32, 33, 34, 37, 51, 52, 53, 54, 55, 56, 59, 61, 64, 68, 70, 74, 75, 76, 77, 78, 79, 84, 97, 99, 102, 104, 113, 115, 116, 125, 127, 128, 130, 131, 141, 145, 146, 160, 173, 174
Clowns 10, 43, 44, 81, 88, 99, 144, 159,
Code of Handsome Lake 77, 78
collectors/collecting 60, 100, 106, 135
colonization/colonists 5, 30, 31, 51, 91, 94, 105, 119, 133
colours (sacred) 95, 129
Colville 132
Comanche 14, 33, 69, 79, 82, 110, 130
contact/encounter 4, 24, 44, 45, 60, 69, 82, 84, 87, 106, 108, 122, 123, 181
copper/s 101, 123, 156
Corn Dance 21, 28
Corn Mother 66, 97
cowboys and Indians 46, 47, 81, 151, 171
cowboys, Indian 47, 80
coyote 23, 81, 100, 127, 129, 177
creation/origin stories 19, 25, 36, 80, 94, 96, 97, 99, 104, 110, 118, 120, 127, 138, 147, 150, 175
Cree 8, 13, 16, 51, 108, 113, 132, 144, 154, 162, 171, 180
Creek/Muskogee 5, 9, 11, 14, 17, 38, 56, 65, 76, 82, 92, 97, 131, 145, 152, 168
Crown Dance 11, 39, 143
Crow 52, 57, 70, 79, 80, 154

**d**

Dakota (Sioux) 69, 118, 125, 148, 175
dams/hydro-electric projects 11, 51, 132, 168
dance 5, 7, 10, 14, 17, 32, 33, 36, 52, 55,56, 57, 58, 61, 64, 68, 70, 78, 84, 88, 96, 98, 102, 104, 108, 110, 111, 114, 116, 125, 127, 128, 130, 147, 150, 158, 178
Dawes General Allotment Act 5, 9, 26, 38, 47, 50, 51, 82, 88, 92, 148
deer 24, 33, 58, 69, 79, 99, 128
Deg Het'an 14
Delaware 164
Den 13, 112
Denaina *see* Tanaina
Department of Indian Affairs (Canada) 12, 30, 52
design, designs 3, 18, 19, 21, 56, 64, 79, 85, 102, 138, 173
diplomacy 26, 30, 52, 53, 54, 75, 119, 121, 130, 163
disease 22, 23, 51, 54, 69, 85, 94, 104, 105, 115, 119, 122, 135, 146
distribution of goods/resources 6, 59, 84, 124
dog 54, 55, 81, 85, 173
dogsled racing 55, 85, 162
dolls 55, 77
dreams/visions 56, 74, 77, 111, 171

drums 56, 57, 70, 84, 108, 110, 125, 128, 139, 152
Dutch 31, 106, 159, 170

**e**

eagles and eagle feathers 21, 23, 24, 43, 58, 61, 64, 77, 79, 114, 118, 143, 157
Eastern Woodlands 8, 14, 68
economic development 20, 33, 51, 67, 77, 159, 167, 173
economies and economic change 6, 20, 49, 59, 69, 77, 79, 112, 124, 132, 138, 153, 157, 158, 159, 170, 176
eel 43
elk 16, 59, 60, 69, 127
English language 41, 90, 91, 100, 103, 142, 181
enrolment 36, 38, 40, 165
environment 13, 14, 20, 51, 54, 67, 69, 176, 180, 181
Erie 146
Eskimo *see* Inuit
explorers/exploration 19, 44, 45, 60, 69, 84, 106
extinction (tribes, languages, etc.) 25, 32, 69, 137

**f**

feathers 3, 14, 17, 21, 25, 58, 61, 78, 81–82, 100, 125, 147, 159; *see also* birds, eagles and eagle feathers
'First Nations' 1, 90, 109
fish/fishing 2, 5, 7, 8, 9, 14, 19, 20, 24, 59, 67, 77, 82, 84, 85, 104, 113, 138, 145, 149, 150, 181
fishing rights 51, 63, 123, 149, 157
Five Civilized Tribes 82
flag, American 64
Florida 74, 145, 146
flutes 14, 65, 108
food 4, 5, 6, 7, 8, 9, 10, 13, 17, 18, 19, 22, 23, 24, 26, 30, 32, 33, 35, 55, 59, 60, 61, 65, 66, 68, 69, 72, 75, 76, 81, 95, 97, 115, 125, 127, 138, 139, 150, 157, 161, 169, 175, 176
footgear 21, 37, 53, 68, 70, 77, 99, 102, 109, 110, 127
France/French 2, 24, 52, 60, 69, 79, 102, 103, 104, 106, 108, 113, 137, 139, 148, 170
French and Indian Wars 2
fur trade 7, 24, 26, 27, 69, 82, 84, 102, 104, 113, 146, 148, 156, 161

**g**

gambling/gaming 56, 70, 71, 72, 75, 76, 114, 145, 149
games and sports 3, 17, 37, 50, 70, 71, 72, 73, 84, 86, 126, 151, 162, 167, 175
gathering (plants) 5, 17, 19, 65, 68, 84, 87, 181
gender roles (men/women) 5, 6, 7, 8, 11, 15, 20, 21, 26, 29, 35, 36, 37, 40, 41, 49, 55, 56, 59, 65, 68, 69, 71, 72, 77, 78, 83, 84
Georgia 27, 105, 134
Germany/Germans 60
Ghost Dance 31, 52, 61, 74, 75, 93, 110, 148, 154, 178, 179

gifts/giveaways 26, 30, 59, 70, 75, 125, 127, 157, 170
Gitsan-Wet'suwet'en 29, 90, 112
Glooscap 104
Gold Rush/discovery of gold 69, 92, 134, 181
gorgets *see* silver gorgets
gourds 70, 128, 150, 168
Grandmother Turtle 114, 168
Grande Ronde 156
Great Basin 7, 20, 25, 56, 70
Great Lakes 8, 18, 20, 26, 56, 67
Great Law of Peace 86
Greenland 13, 115
Gros Ventre 25, 109
guns/rifles 28, 50, 59, 69, 81, 101, 131, 159
Gwitch'in *see* Kutchin

**h**

Haida 24, 26, 60, 77, 111, 112, 122, 143, 156
hairstyles 78, 79
Hampton Institute 5
hats *see* headgear
headdresses *see* headgear
headgear 20, 24, 28, 29, 58, 61, 68, 78, 79, 82, 105, 150, 177
health/healing/health care 11, 33, 67, 97, 100, 101, 118, 119, 128, 156, 157, 175,
Hidatsa 6, 11, 26, 32, 54, 76, 96, 125, 128, 132, 135, 138
hide painting 35
hides 24, 26, 35, 60, 69, 72, 124
high steel construction 87, 168
history, oral 29, 89, 90, 112
Hitchiti 145
hogan 11
Holikachuck 14
holy man 148
Home Dance 88
honour 76
hoop dances 52
Hopi 19, 20, 43, 55, 81, 88, 95, 97, 104, 124, 141, 150, 161, 174
horse 3, 7, 14, 16, 26, 31, 34, 46, 47, 54, 59, 60, 70, 75, 76, 79, 80, 123, 148, 159, 171
house poles/posts 12, 61, 80, 138, 143, 157
houses, housing 4, 11, 13, 18, 19, 20, 32, 34, 49, 81, 104, 113, 138, 167, 181
Hudson Bay 84
Hudson's Bay Company 26, 30, 69, 103, 161
humour 10, 43, 44, 51, 72, 81, 87, 93, 143, 158, 171
hunting/fishing rights 17, 51, 54, 104, 112, 153
hunting/hunters 2, 6, 7, 9, 14, 24, 26, 28, 31, 32, 36, 56, 63, 66, 69, 82, 84, 89, 97, 104, 122, 138, 139, 145, 149, 153, 157, 171, 175
Hupa 19, 181
Huron/Wyandotte 60, 82, 86, 106, 109, 147
hydro-electric projects *see* dams

**i**

Ice Age 26, 31
Illini 109
'Indian' 109
Indian Act/s (Canada) 30, 35, 36, 86, 124, 137, 144
Indian agencies/agents 34, 66
Indian Citizenship Act 41
Indian Claims Commission 89
Indian Commissioner 64
Indian Removal Act 33
Indian Reorganization Act 50, 123, 156, 165
Indian Territory 5, 9, 27, 28, 38, 82, 134, 140, 145, 164
Indian Trade and Intercourse (Non-Intercourse) Act 2, 89
Indies 44
'indigenous' 109
Ingalik 14
Innu *see* Montagnais
Institute of American Indian Arts 14, 92
Intermarriage 5, 40, 49, 69, 83, 84, 94, 108, 114, 141, 148
intertribal relationships 57, 69, 70, 81, 94, 108, 126, 159, 164
Inuit/Inupiaq/Eskimo 3, 8, 11, 12, 13, 16, 19, 24, 26, 28, 44, 50, 51, 55, 56, 63, 69, 72, 73, 82, 84, 85, 97, 98, 109, 113, 116, 117, 123, 129, 132, 162, 169, 175
Inuktitut 85
Inupiak *see* Inuit
invention, innovation 3, 18, 82, 85, 146
Iowa 82
Irish 108
Iroquois 6, 11, 14, 22, 24, 29, 30, 31, 36, 37, 41, 43, 49, 52, 55, 56, 58, 59, 60, 61, 69, 72, 73, 77, 86, 87, 90 , 95, 97, 99, 106, 109, 110, 114, 115, 118, 121, 136, 150, 157, 159, 164, 168, 170
Iroquois Confederacy 29, 36, 43, 77, 85, 87, 90, 106, 115, 116, 146, 170
Italy 60

**j**

James Bay 51
Jay Treaty 87
jewellery 101, 102, 110, 111, 124, 147, 150, 161

**k**

Kansas 69
Kansas Territory 82
Karuk 19, 115, 129, 181
*katsina* dolls 55, 88
*katsinas* 43, 81, 88, 174
kayaks 27, 84, 85, 109, 129, 162
Keetoowah Society 9, 152, 153
Kennebec 2
Kiowa 13, 14, 16, 52, 57, 70, 75, 80, 108, 110, 118, 177, 178

Klamath 156
Klikitat 84
Koasati (Coushatta) 17
Kodiak Island 8
Koniaq 28
Kootenai/Kutenai 25, 69, 70, 132, 138
Koyukon 14
Ku Klux Klan 94
Kutchin/Gwitch'in 14
Kutenai *see* Kootenai
Kwakwaka'wakw/Kwakiutl 57, 80, 97, 111, 123, 175

**l**

Labrador 13, 24, 50, 84
lacrosse 37, 72, 73, 86, 120
Lakota 15, 34, 39, 46, 56, 57, 60, 64, 66, 68, 76, 118, 138, 148, 154
land/s 2, 5, 7, 8, 30, 32, 33, 37, 38, 44, 51, 59, 60, 67, 69, 74, 82, 88, 89, 90, 93, 102, 103, 104, 105, 111, 112, 114, 132, 145, 148, 156, 157, 173
land cessions 9, 30, 50, 88, 89, 131, 136, 146, 163
land claims 7, 36, 50, 77, 85, 89, 90, 103, 104, 112, 114, 137, 145, 148, 156, 157
languages (Native, English, written, etc.) 2, 4, 7, 8, 9, 11, 14, 13, 17, 19, 20, 27, 28, 34, 37, 39, 40, 41, 42, 49, 50, 72, 77, 78, 82, 84, 85, 89, 90, 91, 96, 103, 108, 109, 111, 113, 115, 116, 124, 139, 140, 145, 146, 147, 148, 151, 156, 159, 167, 169, 179, 180, 181
League of the Iroquois 86, 170
ledger drawings 14, 22, 136, 154
literature, oral 35, 90, 91
literature, written 14, 45, 91, 92, 93
Little Bighorn, Battle of 93, 148
Long Walk of the Navajo/Bosque Redondo 10, 94, 111
Longest Walk, The 122
longhouse 11, 37, 56, 77, 78, 86, 115, 139, 168
Longhouse religion 77, 78, 86
Loon 43
Louisiana Purchase 82, 133
Lumbee 94
Lushootseed 72, 139

**m**

Maidu 58
Maine 2
maize (corn) 2, 5, 7, 11, 21, 22, 32, 37, 38, 40, 41, 44, 55, 66, 67, 76, 95, 96, 97, 108, 125, 128, 138, 150, 161
Makah 82, 88, 123, 128, 132, 175
Malecite/Maliseet 56, 104
Manabozhoo *see* Wenabozhoo
Mandan 6, 11, 27, 32, 51, 54, 96, 125, 132
Manitoba 8, 50, 103, 144
marriage/weddings 20, 26, 35, 40, 43, 55, 59, 65, 76, 79, 83, 84, 97, 115
masks/masked 31, 39, 61, 97, 98, 174

Massachusetts 94, 109

matriarchal societies 83, 120

matrilineal/matrilocal societies 11, 13, 83, 84, 99, 106, 120, 132, 145, 157, 181

Maya 35

medicine 19, 21, 23, 24, 41, 56, 61, 60, 97, 100, 110, 113, 117, 118, 126, 155, 157, 175

medicine men and women 74, 100, 113, 116, 126, 127, 147, 150

medicine pouch/bag, medicine bundle 100, 101, 119, 127, 138

men (roles/work) 5, 6, 7, 15, 20, 29, 35, 41, 49, 65, 69, 72, 73, 83, 84, 99, 100, 139, 169, 175

Menominee 75, 11, 156, 157, 175

Mesquakie 91

metal/metalwork, minerals/mining 15, 37, 41, 60, 61, 69, 84, 101, 102, 110, 123, 128, 130, 131, 143, 159, 160, 161, 205

Métis 84, 102, 103, 112, 122

Mexico 22, 95, 102, 104, 110, 123, 145, 147, 150, 159

Miami 38

Miccosukee 145

Michigan 63, 109, 153

Mi'kmaq 3, 25, 53, 79, 104, 118

Minnesota 63, 153, 176

missions/missionaries 2, 27, 32, 33, 34, 38, 39, 40, 41, 49, 51, 69, 84, 90, 91, 103, 104, 105, 106, 110, 114, 134, 136, 139, 140, 146, 148, 154

Mississauga 8

Mississipian peoples 17, 147

Missouri River 26

moccasins see footgear

Mohawk 16, 18, 20, 29, 30, 40, 53, 61, 79, 85, 86, 87, 89, 90, 104, 106, 113, 114, 115, 118, 156, 159, 170

Montagnais/Naskapi/Innu 8, 13, 25,

Montana 26, 63, 138

Minnesota 63

Montreal 73, 106

moose 13, 15, 49

Moose Factory 36

Moravian missionaries 84, 104

Mother Clay 124

Mother Earth 49

Moundbuilders/mounds 101, 143; see also Mississipian peoples

movies/films 3, 46, 78, 120, 151

Museum of the American Indian 135, 136

museums 3, 9, 17, 20, 24, 41, 53, 64, 100, 106, 107, 135, 136, 138, 158, 170

music/musical instruments 14, 17, 19, 23, 36, 52, 55, 56, 57, 60, 61, 65, 70, 72, 81, 84, 90, 91, 92, 102, 104, 108, 128, 147, 150, 158

Muskogee see Creek

Myth of the Vanishing Indian 54

**n**

Nakota 108, 148

Names/naming 76, 96, 109

Nanabush 113

Narragansett 5

Naskapi see Montagnais

Natchez 59

National Congress of American Indians 121

National Indian Youth Council 121

'Native' 109

'Native American' 109

Native American Church 56, 102, 110

Native American Graves and Repatriation Act 107, 135, 136

Native newspapers 27, 141, 146, 147, 151, 180; see also Boudinot

natural resources 33, 36, 59, 63, 69, 88, 89, 136 138, 145, 153, 157, 171; see also fish/fishing, fishing rights, land, water rights

Nava 69

Navajo 5, 10, 11, 15, 19, 20, 23, 26, 26, 37, 47, 56, 57, 59, 64, 65, 71, 72, 78, 90, 94, 96, 97, 99, 100, 101, 102, 104, 109, 110, 111, 115, 128, 132, 138, 150, 158, 161, 166, 174, 177

Nebraska 109

New Age 151

New England 100, 151

New Mexico 2, 20, 74, 94, 110, 126, 136; see also Pueblos

New World (New France, New Spain, New England, Nieuw Amsterdam) 44, 60, 139

New York 36, 51, 77, 85, 86, 106, 114, 136, 146

Newfoundland 24, 44, 84, 104

Nez Perce 25, 46, 69, 78, 109

Niña, Pinta or Santa Maria (Columbus' ships) 45

Nipissing 8

Nishga 112

non-federally recognized/non-status tribes 36, 62, 84, 94, 103

non-Indian settlement 81

Nootka see Nuu-chah-nulth

Norridgewock 2

Norse 44, 84

North Carolina 20, 38, 85, 94, 168, 179

Northwest Rebellion 103

Northeast 5, 7, 18, 20, 27, 44, 77, 78, 95, 96, 102, 104, 127; see also Iroquois, Ojibwa, Mi'kmaq

Northern Plains 6, 15, 23, 26, 55, 74, 93, 118, 155; see also Sioux

Northwest 43, 60, 67, 68, 70, 101, 102, 138, 172; see also Aleut, Haida, Nuu-chah-nulth, Tlingit

Northwest Coast 11, 14, 18, 19, 26, 28, 35, 56, 59, 63, 77, 80, 81, 97, 111, 112, 116, 122, 129, 138, 143, 174, 175, 177

Northwest Passage 60

Northwest Territories 13, 51, 81, 89, 112, 115, 162
novels 90
Nunavut 85, 112, 115
Nuu-chah-nulth/Nootka 19, 60, 81, 109, 111, 112, 122, 175, 177

**o**
Office of Indian Trade 33
Ohio 85
Oji-Cree 8, 49, 113, 144
Ojibwa/Ojibwe/Anishinabe/Chippewa/Saulteaux 8, 14, 11, 15, 20, 23, 26, 37, 43, 49, 56, 58, 59, 65, 67, 70, 72, 81, 91, 108, 109, 113, 118, 128, 144, 148, 150, 153, 162, 164, 175, 176, 179
Oka 89, 113, 114
Oklahoma 9, 10, 13, 14, 16, 21, 36, 38, 50, 82, 84, 92, 108, 109, 110, 118, 125, 134, 140, 145, 146, 152, 164, 165, 166, 167; *see also* Cherokees, Choctaw, Indian Territory
Okute 60
Omaha 8, 15, 28, 121, 175
Oneida 69, 85, 114, 140, 168
Onondaga 41, 61, 77, 85, 97, 106, 114
Ontario 90, 106, 114, 117 180
Osage 26, 53, 70, 84, 175
Otoe 15, 41, 78, 109, 115
Ottawa 8, 103, 114

**p**
painting/painters 14, 30, 33, 61, 78, 101, 117, 119, 120, 124, 130, 142, 146
Paiute 20, 32, 74, 154, 156
Palm Springs, California 89
pan-Indian identity 115, 141, 169
Papago 23; *see also* Tohono O'odham
'papoose' 109
parkas 15, 16, 115, 116; *see also* Inuit
Passamaquoddy 2, 88, 104
patrilineal society 83, 84, 99, 113
Pawnees 11, 35, 41, 46, 65, 110, 138, 148
Peace Medals 52, 53, 130; *see also* diplomacy
Pecos 4
Pend d'Oreille 127
Pendleton blanket shawl 26, 37, 99
Pendleton Company 26
Pennacook 2
Pennsylvania 51
Penobscot 2, 56, 88, 100, 104
Pequot 5, 71
Peyote 56, 111
peyote stitch 21, 64
photographs/photographer 14, 44, 16, 55, 116, 117, 121, 177, 179, 121, 125
Piegan 25
pigs 7, 65, 67

Pigunni 25
Pigwacket 2
Pima 35, 150, 177
Pipe tomahawks 30, 52, 130
pipes 34, 53, 55, 118, 143, 146, 148, 157
Plains 3, 10, 21, 25, 30, 31, 32, 34, 35, 46, 47, 54, 56, 57, 58, 59, 60, 61, 64, 65, 70, 78, 81, 111, 113, 116, 119, 127, 143, 154, 157, 171
plants 5, 7, 13, 17, 19, 20, 21, 44, 51, 59, 62, 65, 95, 100, 101, 112, 114, 119, 120, 128, 129, 138, 168, 175
Plateau 7, 21, 22, 138
plays/playwrights 55, 93
poets/poems 66, 76, 88, 91
political activism 63, 89, 90, 113, 114, 121, 132, 169
Pomo 20, 138
Ponca 57, 70, 108, 121, 175
population 54, 104, 122
Portuguese 60
Potawatomie 41, 113, 164, 175
potlatch 12, 24, 29, 35, 59, 77, 97, 101, 111, 122, 154, 161
pottery/potters 2, 14, 19, 23, 44, 45, 51, 80, 101, 123, 124, 128, 143, 144, 150, 157, 161
pouches *see* bags
pow wow 52, 57, 68, 78, 80, 108, 115, 125, 130, 175
prayers/praying 10, 19, 26, 36, 52, 55, 61, 87, 96, 97, 110, 124, 125, 128, 147, 150, 154, 155, 175
pre-contact 35, 88, 101
presentation pieces 22, 30, 52, 53, 55
Prince William Sound 8
'Princesses' 78, 91, 109, 110, 116
property 82, 83, 134
Protestantism 21, 27, 39, 74, 104, 139
puberty ceremonies 11, 43, 71
Pueblo Revolt 34, 45, 105, 126
Pueblos 2, 4, 10, 11, 13, 20, 23, 31, 32, 34, 37, 39, 40, 43, 44, 45, 49, 51, 52, 59, 63, 65, 66, 67, 71, 72, 78, 81, 87, 88, 95, 96, 98, 101, 105, 108, 109, 111, 124, 125, 126, 128, 138, 144, 147, 150, 158, 159, 161, 167, 174
Puyallup 63, 153

**q**
Quakers 139
Quebec 2, 50, 51, 84, 89, 104, 132, 144
Queen Charlotte Islands 143
quills/quillwork 3, 14, 15, 16, 17, 21, 49, 53, 58, 64, 76, 78, 102, 104, 106, 113, 127, 130, 159
quilts 27, 64, 114

**r**
Rabbit 15, 80, 120, 127, 129, 152
railroads 33
rain 43, 55, 88, 96, 111, 128, 135, 150
ranchers/ranching 7, 11, 32
rattles 23, 43, 97, 128, 129, 130, 143, 147, 152, 168
Raven 23, 61, 77, 127, 129, 143

recognition, federal 2, 35, 93, 156, 169

recycled materials 128, 130, 131

Red' Indians 25

Red Stick Wars 50, 131, 145

'redskins' 109

redistribution of wealth 77, 123, 161

religions and religious practice 3, 9, 10, 32, 39, 40, 45, 49, 52, 85, 90, 110, 127, 135, 145, 147, 148, 154, 158, 181

Relocation 51, 104, 111, 115, 132, 156, 169, 178

Removal 5, 9, 11, 17, 20, 27, 37, 38, 50, 51, 52, 54, 82, 86, 87, 105, 114, 115, 122, 132, 133, 139, 146, 164, 165, 172

Removal Party 28

repatriation 97, 100, 107, 135, 136, 138, 170

reservations/rancherias 6, 8, 11, 31, 34, 51, 63, 68, 70, 74, 77, 89, 93, 113, 115, 122, 132, 136, 142, 145, 146, 148, 156, 161, 177, 179, 181

reserve lands (Canada) 8, 30, 31, 36, 77, 112, 144

ritual 36, 37, 52, 61, 81, 88, 118, 124, 128, 151, 175

rodeo 47, 80

Royal Proclamation 31, 35, 90, 104, 137

Royal Ontario Museum 106

running 34, 71, 72, 126

Russia 9, 15, 26, 69

Russian Orthodox Church 9

**S**

Sac and Fox 38, 72, 82

sacred 9, 26, 43, 88, 90, 95, 100, 105, 126, 127, 128, 150, 175

sacred sites, sacred objects 9, 10, 25, 76, 88, 90, 105, 111, 135, 136, 138, 145

Sage 155, 157

Salish 7, 14, 21, 23, 26, 45, 68, 70, 79, 111, 112, 132, 138, 142, 173

salmon 23, 62, 63, 65, 77, 111, 138, 181

Sand Creek 93

Sarcee 26

Saskatchewan 26, 103

Saulteaux 8; see also Ojibwa

'savage' 9, 109, 139

schools/education 2, 5, 6, 11, 25, 31, 32, 33, 35, 38, 39, 40, 41, 49, 50, 52, 72, 85, 90, 111, 115, 116, 134, 139, 140, 141, 142, 145, 146, 147, 148, 156, 157, 158, 167, 178, 179, 181

Scots 67, 78, 102, 108

sculpture/sculptors 12, 14, 61, 77, 82, 97, 124, 135, 143

sea mammals 13, 24, 26, 68, 69, 77, 81, 161

seals 13, 65, 68, 69, 111, 129, 161

Sechelt 112

self-determination, self-government 33, 36, 38, 52, 112, 122, 138, 142, 144, 145, 156

Seminole 5, 11, 37, 38, 81, 95, 145, 146, 152, 164, 168

Seneca 11, 20, 21, 29, 36, 51, 55, 61, 66, 77, 86, 106,

131, 132, 146, 159, 160, 164, 168

settlement/settlers 29, 31, 102, 104, 133, 148

shawls 26, 76, 102, 160

Shawnee 41, 69, 133

sheep 7, 67

shells/shellwork 17, 21, 24, 37, 59, 60, 82, 120, 123, 128, 147, 156, 159, 170

Shinnecocks 5

Shoshone 7, 69, 111

Shoshone-Bannock 3

Siberia 25

Siletz 156

silver/silversmiths 30, 31, 52, 53, 110; see also metals, Navajo

silver gorgets 30, 102

Sioux (Lakota, Dakota, Nakota) 6, 32, 33, 34, 35, 41, 49, 55, 56, 65, 68, 74, 81, 90, 93, 109, 115, 118, 121, 125, 148, 151, 175, 178, 179

Six Nations Reserve 8, 29, 52, 86, 118, 156, 157, 159, 168

slaves/slavery 5, 59, 69, 156, 165, 172

sleds 18, 49, 54, 104, 113, 162

smallpox 2, 35, 44, 54, 122, 156; see also disease

Smithsonian Institution 53, 54, 64, 106, 107, 135, 136, 151; see also museums

Snipe 43

snowmobiles 50, 85, 162

snowshoes 49, 162

snowsnake 73

Society of American Indians 121

Sokokis 2

songs/singing 19, 23, 36, 39, 52, 56, 57, 59, 60, 61, 65, 70, 72, 81, 84, 91, 92, 96, 97, 108, 125, 127, 128, 139, 150, 151, 152, 155, 176

South America 44, 95, 104, 123, 139, 174, 178

South Carolina 19

South Dakota 6

Southeast 5, 6, 7, 17, 38, 24, 44, 50, 58, 67, 76, 82, 96, 97, 101, 102, 127, 131, 134, 146, 164, 168, 170

Southern Plains 10, 11, 56, 74, 102, 159

Southwest 4, 5, 7, 11, 20, 25, 31, 44, 64, 95, 96, 101, 102, 104, 108, 127, 128, 157, 159, 161, 181

sovereignty 38, 41, 50, 71, 86, 88, 104, 109, 112, 134, 136, 145, 149, 156, 163, 164, 167

Spain/Spanish 2, 4, 10, 25, 35, 39, 44, 50, 53, 60, 95, 98, 101, 102, 104, 105, 108, 123, 124, 126, 127, 135, 136, 139, 145, 148, 158, 161

Spider 127, 129, 173

Spider Woman 173

Squamish 36, 92

squash 5, 7, 20, 22, 66, 95, 128, 150; see also beans, maize

'squaw' 109, 110

status 2, 7, 35, 36, 40, 41, 52

stereotype 3, 46, 79, 81, 117, 142, 151, 177; see also names

stickball 17, 37, 50, 71, 72, 73, 151; *see also* games and sports
stomp dances 10, 50, 76, 138, 152, 153, 166; *see also* dance
stories/storytelling 14, 21, 32, 37, 48, 49, 81, 84, 91, 97, 100, 101, 105, 114, 116, 120, 127, 128, 129, 173, 175, 177
Subarctic 13, 9
subsistence 7, 9, 59, 62, 63, 66, 67, 69, 85, 96, 112, 113, 153
sugar 5, 66, 113
Sun Dance 6, 35, 138, 154
sunglasses 85
Supreme Court of Canada 90, 104, 112
Suqpiaq 7, 8
sutures 18
sweathouse/sweatlodge 11
sweetgrass 147, 155, 157, 159
symbols 33, 38, 43, 53, 58, 61, 64, 71, 96, 99, 100, 102, 114, 128, 170, 172

**t**

Tanaina/Denaina 14
technologies 3, 11, 85
Termination 33, 132, 136, 156
Thanksgiving 78
theatre 14, 93; *see also* plays, playwrights
Three Sisters 22, 66, 78, 150
thunder 57, 128, 150
thunderbirds 57, 58, 61, 113
Timuacan 90
tipi 11, 13, 15, 32, 93, 127
Tlingit 11, 12, 24, 28, 77, 111, 122, 156, 174, 175
tobacco 7, 30, 66, 95, 96, 118, 150, 155, 157
toboggans 49, 110, 162
Tohono O'odham/Papago 22, 23, 66, 69, 72, 73
Tolowa 129
tomahawk 31, 46, 53, 151
tools/utensils 15, 17, 18, 19, 21, 29, 43, 69, 82, 100, 101, 102, 104, 129, 143, 150, 159, 169
'totem poles' 80
tourism 2, 11, 20, 21, 38, 49, 51, 77, 145, 157, 158, 159, 174
trade beads/silver 17, 23, 29, 104, 160, 170
trade blankets/cloth 17, 27, 69, 160
trade languages 90, 115
trade/traders 7, 11, 15, 17, 20, 23, 25, 26, 30, 31, 32, 33, 34, 37, 38, 39, 45, 49, 59, 60, 61, 69, 78, 84, 85, 102, 104, 108, 115, 131, 146, 147, 149, 159, 160, 161, 168, 170, 175
trading posts 31, 39, 49, 161
Trail of Tears 38, 39, 134, 135, 173
train 35, 158
transport 18, 26, 49, 50, 54, 67, 77, 84, 104, 113, 139, 143, 162, 175, 176; *see also* canoes, sleds
treaties 6, 25, 27, 30, 34, 35, 36, 38, 40, 41, 47, 50, 51, 63, 82, 86, 90, 93, 104, 114, 123, 131, 132, 133, 134, 136, 140, 144, 145, 146, 148, 149, 161, 163, 170, 173, 178
Treaty Party 27, 134
Tree of Peace 58, 114
tribal colleges 138, 142, 148
tribal government 2, 14, 34, 85, 86, 90, 103, 111, 123 145, 146, 149, 156, 164, 165, 166, 167; *see also* sovereignty, treaties
tribal membership 36, 40
trickster 23, 81, 104, 120, 127, 129
trust relationship 33, 156, 163; *see also* Bureau of Indian Affairs, treaties
Tsimshian 77, 101, 111, 122, 156
tuberculosis 44, 54, 85
Tulalip 139
Turtle 37, 43, 55, 81, 97, 114, 118, 152, 153, 168, 170
Turtle Mountain Chippewa 103
Tuscaroras 5, 69, 85, 86, 114, 140, 168

**u**

United States of America 1, 2, 5, 9, 10, 11, 34, 37, 38, 39, 40, 41, 51, 52, 74, 87, 89, 90, 109, 111, 135, 149
US Cavalry 22, 38, 74, 92, 178, 179
US Constitution 111
US Supreme Court/Constitution 40, 89, 105, 110, 134
ulu 169
umiak 27, 84; *see also* canoes, transport
Unangan 8
Upper Kuskokwim 14
urban Indians 51, 132, 142, 144, 169, 178
Utes 20, 70

**v**

Vancouver Island 2, 79, 175, 177
Vermont 2, 94
veterans 58, 61, 64, 178
Viking 24
Virginia 119, 139, 168
visions *see* dreams

**w**

Wabenaki Confederacy/Alliance 2, 104
walrus 98
Wampanoags 92, 94, 159,
wampum 52, 59, 86, 136, 164, 170, 172
Wanapum 6
War Department of US Government 33, 163
War of 1812 131
war/wars/warfare 2, 14, 23, 24, 25, 29, 30, 31, 36, 37, 38, 46, 50, 54, 69, 71, 74, 86, 93, 104, 105, 108, 112, 113, 114, 116, 122, 130, 131, 133, 136, 141, 145, 146, 148, 168, 171, 172, 178, 179
warriors 14, 22, 30, 35, 58, 61, 64, 126, 131, 148, 151, 171, 173, 177
Wasco/Warm Springs Reservation 7, 14, 57, 68, 70, 76, 78, 98

water 23, 111, 123, 124, 125, 128, 136, 138
water rights 51, 63, 123, 173
watermelons 6, 44, 66, 74; *see also* food
Wawenock 2
weapons 31, 46, 53, 82, 101, 129, 130, 151, 159, 171, 172; *see also* bows and arrows, guns
weaving/weavers 17, 18, 19, 20, 25, 37, 64, 101, 111, 131, 138, 157, 158, 161, 173, 174
Wenabozhoo/Manabozhoo 175
Wet'suwet'en 28
whale/whaling 12, 13, 69, 82, 84, 85, 97, 129, 175; *see also* food
wheat 6, 65, 124
White Buffalo Calf Woman 31, 34, 49, 119, 148
White Corn Maiden 49
White Mountain Apache 11, 44
White Painted Woman 49
White Shell Woman 173
Wichita 54
wild rice 8, 56, 63, 65, 120, 138, 148, 175
Wild West Show 46, 93, 103, 148, 151
Windigo 113
Winnebago 64, 109, 110, 175
Winter Counts 31, 34, 123
Wisconsin 20, 36, 63, 86, 114, 154
wolf/wolves 15, 43, 99, 116, 127, 143, 177
women 5, 6, 7, 8, 11, 15, 20, 21, 25, 29, 35, 36, 37, 40, 41, 44, 49, 56, 59, 65, 68, 69, 72, 77, 78, 79, 83, 84, 95, 97, 99, 100, 101, 108, 114, 120, 121, 125, 127, 144, 145, 172, 173, 175, 177; *see also* gender roles, men
women's suffrage 8
World War, Second 122, 123, 132, 156, 177
Wounded Knee 74, 122, 148, 178, 179
writers 15, 45, 55, 66, 68, 76, 87, 91, 92, 121
written language 85, 91–92, 28, 39, 78, 82, 84, 85, 90, 146, 179
Wyandotte *see* Huron

**Y**
Yakima 63
Yamassee War 145
Yukon 13, 84, 90, 101
Yuma 22
Yup'ik 7, 8, 88, 98
Yuroks 19, 20, 129, 181

**Z**
Zuni 4, 10, 22, 43, 45, 87, 88, 128, 135, 150, 181

# Index of Individuals

**a**

Abeyta, Pablita 97
Abrams, Rovena 55
Adams, Mary 159
Albert, Mike 164
Alexander, Dixie 15
Allagariuk, Madeline 72
American Horse 4
Angaiak, Mike 88
Anne, Queen of England 30, 53
Arnold, Greig 88
Atagotaaluk, Phoebe 72
Awa Tsireh 14, 32, 58

**b**

Baca, Janice 37
Bad Hand, Howard 64
Baird, Rebecca 155
Baker, Dick 57
Baldwin, Susan 91
Barboncito 94
Bear Don't Walk, Marjorie 23, 26
Bear Don't Walk, Scott (i)
Bear's Heart 14, 31, 154
Beck, Larry 98
Begay, D.Y. 174
Benjamin, Fred 108
Bennett, Ramona 63
Bent, Jesse 54
Benton-Banai, Eddie 43
Berger, Justice Thomas 7
Bernal, Paul 10
Biakeddy, Jesse 111
Big Foot 179
Big Horn, Spike 76
Bigcrane, Joanne 127
Billy, Susan 20
Bird Chief, Sr. 54
Black Coal 127
Black Coyote 54
Black Elk 118
Block, Bob 26
Blueeyes, George 5
Bodmer, Karl 60
Bonnin, Gertrude Simmons 121
Boudinot, Elias 27, 40, 91, 134
Brant 53
Brant, Joseph 29, 86, 106
Brant, Mary/Molly 29
Buck, Hubert 70
Buck, John 86
Buck, Sadie and Betsy 70
Buffalo Bird Woman 11, 96

Burns, Robert 54

**c**

Cajete, Gregory 7, 88
Calling Thunder, Debra 127
Cardinal, Douglas 13
Carson, Kit 94
Cartier, Jacques 60, 104
Champagne, Duane 33
Champlain, Samuel 60
Charles II, King of England 69
Chief Joseph 25
Chona, Maria 72
Chrystos 75, 76
Clinton, William J., President 149
Cody, Buffalo Bill 46, 93, 103
Columbus 60, 109, 164, 167
Cook, Captain James 19, 60, 161
Cook, Phillip 54
Coon-Come, Grand Chief Matthew 51
Conklin, Abe 70
Corn Tassel 88
Cornplanter 51, 77
Crazy Horse 93, 148
Crowley, Eunice 159
Curtis, Edward 60, 116
Custer, General George Armstrong 93

**d**

Danay, Richard Glazer 87
Dasheno, Walter 96
de Champlain, Samuel 60
de Zamora, Fray Francisco 105
Deacon, Belle 18
Deer, Ada 156
Deganawida/The Peacemaker 43, 85
DeSoto, Hernando 90
Dick, Jimmy 36
Dill, Agnes 95, 108
Dragging Canoe 133
Dreadfulwater, Louise 39
Dumont, Gabriel 103

**e**

Eastman, Charles 60, 121
Elizabeth I, Queen of England 120
Erasmus, Georges 144
Erdrich, Louise 91
Estevanico/Esteban 4

**f**

Firethunder, Cecelia 68
Fitzpatrick, John 57
Fonseca, Harry
Force, Roland 136

Fourkiller, Joanne 39
Fox, Jr., Dennis 32
Francis, Josiah 131

**g**

George, Anita Anquoe 178
Geronimo (Goyathlay) 10, 74
Gillette, George 51
Glass, Georgia 39
Goodbird 6
Goshorn, Shan 125, 166, 179
Goyathlay *see* Geronimo
Grass Woman 127
Green, Rayna 21, 26
Gutierrez de la Cruz, Lois 44

**h**

Handsome Lake 8, 51, 77, 78, 86, 110
Haozous, Bob 14, 81, 143
Harjo, Eufaula 9
Harjo, Joy 92
Harper, Elijah 144, 145
Haury, Woxie 141
Hayes, Ira 177
Head, Joseph 34
He Bear 54
Henry, Reg 8, 52, 78, 91, 157, 170
Heye, George Gustav 106
Hiawatha 85
Highway, Tomson 93
Hilbert, Vi 72, 139
Hill, Isaac 86
Hill, Jay 57
Hogan, Linda 152
Houle, Robert 137
Humishuma (Chrystal Quintasket) 92

**i**

Ishi 106

**j**

Jackson, Andrew 38, 105, 131, 134
Jackson, Nettie 85
Jacob, Murv 12, 120, 127
Jefferson, Thomas 53, 83
John, Andrew 54
John, Paul 152
Johnson, Bill 56
Johnson, Emily Pauline 91–92
Johnson, George Martin 86
Johnson, James 77
Johnson, John Smoke 86
Johnson, Seneca 86
Johnson, Sir William 29, 30
Johnston, Andrea 155

Jones, Celina 108
Jones, Evan B. 134
Jumper, Betty Mae 168

**k**

Kaniodohora 29
Kimball, Kirby 57
King, Charles Bird 146
King Charles II *see* Charles II
King of France 113
Kingfisher 172
Kiyoshk, Barbara 155
Knife Chief 46

**l**

LaFlesche, Susan, Francis and Suzette 8, 121
Lame Deer, John Fire 56
Lame Man 54
Left Hand, Grant 54
LeJeune 56
Lewis and Clark 53, 60
Little Chief/White Spoon 54
Little Joe, Lizzie 116
Little Man 54
Lomatewama, Ramson 88
Long Wolf 46
Lookout, Chief Henry 53
Lorne, Marquis of 60
Louis XIV 139
Lowrey, Assistant Principal Chief George 164
Luna, James 105, 107
Lyons, Oren 43

**m**

Ma Pe Wi 46
Mankiller, Wilma 166, 167
Marion, Maxim 103
Marshall, Chief Justice John 149
Martinez, Estefanita/Esther 34, 158
Martinez, Maria 124
Mathews, John Joseph 91
Matoaka *see* Pocahontas
McDonald, Peter 156
McGeshick, Mary and George 67
McGillivray, Alexander 50
McLemore, Joanne 39
McMaster, Gerald 171
Membertou 104
Mikkanen, Arvo 79
Mitchell, Matilda 57
Moctezuma 99
Momaday, N. Scott 14, 91
Montezuma, Carlos 121
Montoya, Tommie 126
Mooney, James 151

**n**

Nahohai, Josephine 128
Nailor, Gerald 158
Nampeyo 124
Naranjo Morse, Nora 14, 124, 144
Nerysoo, Richard 88
Neugin, Rebecca 135
Nez Baza 64
Nicolson, Sir Francis 19
Nigiyok 84
Niro, Shelley 14, 117
Northrup, Jim 15

**o**

Old Elk, Anna 33
Orozco, Molly Jim 66
Ortiz, Seferina 51
Ortiz, Simon 88
Otak, Leah 169
Outacitty 166
Owen, Amos 118
Oyenque, Ramos 96

**p**

Paddock, J.P. 47
Palmer, Dixon 13
Palmer, Gus 177
Parker, Ely S. 77
Parrish, Rain 26
Patencio, Francisco 65
Paul, Margaret 56
Perry, Edgar 44
Pitseolak 26
Pitt, Lillian 14, 98
Pitt-Rivers, General 106
Pocahontas/Matoaka 110, 119, 120
Poolaw, Horace 14, 16, 117, 177
Poolheco, Frank 150
Popay/Po'ping 126
Porter, Tom 56
Powhatan 120
Pratt, General Richard 141

**q**

Queen Anne *see* Anne, Queen of England
Queen Elizabeth *see* Elizabeth, Queen of England
Queen Victoria *see* Victoria, Queen of England
Quick-to-See-Smith, Jaune 45, 142

**r**

Radulovitch, Mary Lou Fox 14
Raleigh, Sir Walter 60, 161
Red Cloud 178
Red Jacket 30, 130, 131
Reece, Sally 141

**Reid, Bill 143**
Reil , Louis 103
Rexford-Leavitt, Nora Ann 117
Ridge, John Rollin 91
Ridge, Major John (The Ridge) 27, 34
Rogers, Will 91
Rolfe, John 119, 120
Roman Nose, Henry 54
Ross, Principal Chief John 134, 164

**s**

Sakiestewa, Ramona 174
Sanchez, Russell 125
Sanders, Mose 39
Schweitzer, Herrman 60
Sekaquaptewa, Helen 141
Sequoyah 27, 39, 78, 82, 85, 90, 146, 147, 166, 179
Serra, Fray Junipero 105
Seumptewa, Owen 44, 55
Shanawdithit, Nancy 25
Showaway, Nettie 57
Shunatona, Chief Charles 57, 65
Silko, Leslie 91
Silversmith, Bennie 111
Sitting Bull 93, 148, 178, 179
Siwidi 175
Sloane, Sir Hans 19, 106, 107
Smith, Captain John 60, 120
Smith, Katharine 132
Smith, Red Bird 9, 152
Smohalla 6
Snow, Joseph 64
St Michael 135
Staats, Greg 117, 137
Stamper, Lottie 19
Standing Bear 121
Stanley, John Mix 164
Stung Serpent 59
Sweet Medicine, the Cheyenne Prophet 160
Sweethearts of Navajoland 57
Swentzell, Rina 4
Swentzell, Roxanne 144
Swimmer, Chief Ross 166

**t**

Tafoya, Margaret 23, 124
Talachy, Thelma 44
Tallmountain, Mary 66
Taylor, Ken 17
Tecumseh 133
Tekakwitha, Kateri 40, 156
Tenskatawa, the Shawnee Prophet 133
Thayendanega 30
Thomas, Jake 136
Thorpe, Jim 72

Trahant, Mark 3
Turkey Legs 54
Two Hatchet, Leroy 57
Tyler, Leonard 54

**v**

Van Buren, President Martin 134
Vanderburg. Agnes 68
Velarde, Pablita 66
Victoria, Queen of England 30, 46, 53
Victory, Cleaver Warden 54

**w**

Wallulatum, Sylvia 57
Wanatee, Don 91
Ward, Helma 128
Ward, Nancy 167, 172
Washington, George 30
Waska, Peter 7
Watie, General Stand 27
Watt, Nettie 21
Weir, Robert 130
Welch, James 91
West, Benjamin 137
Wettlin-Larsen, Georgia 65
White, Elmer 125
Whycocomaugh 53
Wied, Prince Maximillian of 60, 106
Wild Horse 54
Williams, Alice Olsen 114
Wolf, Beverley Hungry 99
Wolf Chief 135
Wolfe, General 137
Woody, Elizabeth 14, 76, 68
Wool, Gen. John Ellis 135
Worcester, Reverend Samuel 28, 40, 105
Wovoka/Jack Wilson 32, 74
Wurtemburg, Prince Paul of 60

**y**

Yellow Bear 54
Yellow Eyes 54
Young Chief 46

Green Cathedrals

# Green Cathedrals

*The Ultimate Celebration of Major
League and Negro League Ballparks*

**Philip J. Lowry**

WALKER & COMPANY
NEW YORK

Published by Walker Publishing Company, Inc., New York
Distributed to the trade by Holtzbrinck Publishers

All papers used by Walker & Company are natural, recyclable products made from wood grown in well-managed forests. The manufacturing processes conform to the environmental regulations of the country of origin.

Some funding for the publication of this updated edition of *Green Cathedrals* was provided by HOK Sport, Kansas City, Missouri, and the dues-paying members of the Society for American Baseball Research.

Library of Congress Cataloging-in-Publication Data
has been applied for.

ISBN-10: 0-8027-1562-1          ISBN-10 (SABR EDITION): 0-8027-1608-3
ISBN-13: 978-0-8027-1562-3     ISBN-13 (SABR EDITION): 978-0-8027-1608-8

Visit Walker & Company's Web site at www.walkerbooks.com

First U.S. edition 2006

10  9  8  7  6  5  4  3  2  1

Designed and typeset by Rachel Reiss
Printed in the United States of America by RR Donnelley

This book is dedicated to Richard Clark and Larry Lester, Co-Chairs, and their Negro Leagues Committee of SABR. Its members deserve special thanks for the hundreds of hours they have devoted to helping me identify the many many neutral sites and home parks for all of the Negro League teams, which in this book are treated exactly as the Major League teams they were, no more, no less.

*Green Cathedrals* is also dedicated to the eternal preservation of Wrigley Field in Chicago, Fenway Park in Boston, and Rickwood Field in Birmingham. May the cheers of fans, the crack of the bat, and the aroma of hot dogs never disappear from these three sacred cathedrals and cherished shrines of baseball.

# Contents

**FOREWORD** by Bob Bluthardt     xi

**ACKNOWLEDGMENTS**     xiii

**PREFACE**     xv

**THE BALLPARKS** *(alphabetical by city)*

Akron, Ohio     1

Albany, New York     1
   *(see also* Greenbush, New York)

Altoona, Pennsylvania     2

Anaheim, California     2

Arlington, Texas     4

Asheville, North Carolina     6

Atlanta, Georgia     7

Atlantic City, New Jersey     11

Austin, Texas     11

Baltimore, Maryland     12
   *(see also* Westport, Maryland)

Belleville, Illinois     20

Birmingham, Alabama     20

Bloomfield, New Jersey     21

Bloomington, Minnesota     21

Boston, Massachusetts     23

Broad Ripple, Indiana     33

Brooklyn, New York     33
   *(see also* Jersey City, New Jersey; Newtown, New York;
   Weehawken, New Jersey; West New York, New Jersey)

Buffalo, New York     42

| | | | |
|---|---|---|---|
| Butler, Pennsylvania | 45 | Geddes, New York | 91 |
| Camden, New Jersey | 45 | Gloucester City, New Jersey | 91 |
| Canton, Ohio | 45 | Grand Rapids, Michigan | 91 |
| Charlotte, New York | 45 | Greenbush, New York | 92 |
| Charlotte, North Carolina | 46 | Greensboro, North Carolina | 92 |
| Chattanooga, Tennessee | 46 | Greenville, South Carolina | 93 |
| Chicago, Illinois | 47 | Greenwood, South Carolina | 93 |
| Cincinnati, Ohio | 61 | Hamilton, Ohio | 94 |
| (see also Covington, Kentucky; Hamilton, Ohio; Ludlow, Kentucky) | | Hammond, Indiana | 94 |
| Clarksville, Virginia | 69 | Hampton, Virginia | 94 |
| Cleveland, Ohio | 69 | Hamtramck, Michigan | 94 |
| (see also Collinwood, Ohio; Geauga Lake, Ohio; Newburgh Heights, Ohio) | | Harrisburg, Pennsylvania | 95 |
| | | Harrison, New Jersey | 95 |
| Collinwood, Ohio | 75 | Hartford, Connecticut | 96 |
| Columbus, Georgia | 76 | Havana, Cuba | 96 |
| Columbus, Ohio | 76 | Hoboken, New Jersey | 97 |
| Conway, South Carolina | 78 | Homestead, Pennsylvania | 98 |
| Covington, Kentucky | 78 | Honolulu, Hawaii | 98 |
| Crawfordsville, Indiana | 78 | Houston, Texas | 99 |
| Danville, Virginia | 78 | Indianapolis, Indiana | 104 |
| Dayton, Ohio | 78 | (see also Broad Ripple, Indiana) | |
| Decatur, Alabama | 79 | Irondequoit, New York | 107 |
| Denver, Colorado | 79 | Irvington, New Jersey | 107 |
| Detroit, Michigan | 82 | Jacksonville, Florida | 107 |
| (see also Hamtramck, Michigan; Springwells, Michigan) | | Jersey City, New Jersey | 108 |
| | | Johnstown, Pennsylvania | 109 |
| Dover, Delaware | 86 | Kansas City, Missouri | 110 |
| Durham, North Carolina | 87 | Keokuk, Iowa | 114 |
| East Orange, New Jersey | 88 | Kokomo, Indiana | 114 |
| Edenton, North Carolina | 88 | Lake Charles, Louisiana | 115 |
| Elizabeth, New Jersey | 89 | Lancaster, Pennsylvania | 115 |
| Elmira, New York | 89 | Lansingburgh, New York | 115 |
| Erie, Pennsylvania | 89 | Las Vegas, Nevada | 115 |
| Fort Wayne, Indiana | 90 | Lebanon, Indiana | 116 |
| Geauga Lake, Ohio | 91 | Lima, Ohio | 117 |

Little Rock, Arkansas                          117

Los Angeles, California                        117

Louisville, Kentucky                           122

Ludlow, Kentucky                               124

Lumberton, North Carolina                      124

Macon, Georgia                                 124

McKeesport, Pennsylvania                       125

Meadville, Pennsylvania                        126

Memphis, Tennessee                             126

Miami, Florida                                 127

Middletown, Connecticut                        128

Milwaukee, Wisconsin                           128

Minneapolis, Minnesota                         133
   (*see also* Bloomington, Minnesota)

Mobile, Alabama                                135

Monessen, Pennsylvania                         135

Monroe, Louisiana                              135

Monterrey, Nuevo Leon, Mexico                  136

Montgomery, Alabama                            136

Montreal, Quebec                               137

Mounds, Illinois                               139

Muncie, Indiana                                139

Nashville, Tennessee                           139

Newark, New Jersey                             142
   (*see also* Bloomfield, New Jersey;
   Harrison, New Jersey; Irvington,
   New Jersey)

Newburgh Heights, Ohio                         143

New Haven, Connecticut                         144

New Orleans, Louisiana                         144

Newport, Rhode Island                          145

Newton, North Carolina                         146

Newtown, New York                              146

New York, New York                             147
   (*see also* East Orange, New Jersey;
   Hoboken, New Jersey; Jersey City,
   New Jersey; Newtown, New York;

Paterson, New Jersey; Riverhead,
New York; Weehawken, New Jersey;
West New York, New Jersey)

Oakland, California                            168

Paterson, New Jersey                           170

Petersburg, Virginia                           170

Philadelphia, Pennsylvania                     171
   (*see also* Gloucester City, New
   Jersey; Yeadon, Pennsylvania)

Phoenix, Arizona                               181

Phoenix, New York                              183

Piqua, Illinois                                183

Pittsburgh, Pennsylvania                       183
   (*see also* Homestead, Pennsylvania;
   Johnstown, Pennsylvania;
   McKeesport, Pennsylvania;
   Monessen, Pennsylvania)

Providence, Rhode Island                       193
   (*see also* Warwick, Rhode Island)

Raleigh, North Carolina                        193

Richmond, Virginia                             194

Riverhead, New York                            195

Rochester, New York                            195
   (*see also* Charlotte, New York;
   Irondequoit, New York)

Rockford, Illinois                             196

Rockingham, North Carolina                     197

Rocky Mount, North Carolina                    197

St. Louis, Missouri                            197
   (*see also* Belleville, Illinois)

St. Paul, Minnesota                            206

St. Petersburg, Florida                        206

Salisbury, Maryland                            208

San Diego, California                          208

San Francisco, California                      211

San Juan, Puerto Rico                          215

Savannah, Georgia                              215

Seattle, Washington                            216

Smithfield, North Carolina                     220

Springfield, Illinois                              220

Springfield, Massachusetts                         221

Springfield, Ohio                                  221

Springwells, Michigan                              222

Sumter, South Carolina                             222

Syracuse, New York                                 222
    (*see also* Geddes, New York;
    Phoenix, New York)

Tallahassee, Florida                               224

Tokyo, Japan                                       224

Toledo, Ohio                                       225

Toronto, Ontario, Canada                           228

Trenton, New Jersey                                231

Troy, New York                                     231
    (*see also* Lansingburgh, New York;
    Watervliet, New York)

Wallace, North Carolina                            231

Warwick, Rhode Island                              231

Washington, D.C.                                   231

Watervliet, New York                               240

Weehawken, New Jersey                              240

West New York, New Jersey                          241

Westport, Maryland                                 241

Wheeling, West Virginia                            241

Whiteville, North Carolina                         241

Wilmington, Delaware                               242

Wilmington, North Carolina                         242

Worcester, Massachusetts                           243

Yeadon, Pennsylvania                               244

Zanesville, Ohio                                   245

**BIBLIOGRAPHY**                                   247

**PHOTO CREDITS**                                  249

**INDEX**                                          251

# Foreword

*Bob Bluthardt*

If Phil Lowry had been Captain Ahab and if a ballpark replaced Moby Dick, then the story would have ended several chapters earlier–and, I would suspect, more successfully.

This fractured literary analogy is my way of noting with great admiration that no man has spent more time seeking more data about more ballparks than Phil Lowry. An obsession? Perhaps, but in the Society for American Baseball Research (SABR) there are no obsessions, though many members do spend hours seeking the ultimate truth!

Welcome to *Green Cathedrals*, a book of "all things ballparks," including facts and factoids, dimensions and capacities, locations, occupants, names and nicknames, architects, and "phenomena," where Phil compiles hundreds of stories that will probably make their way into some radio broadcaster's rain delay performance. Beware, there is a little of the whimsical Phil here too as he stretches the occasional fact into an unusual observation.

I first met Phil in 1982 at the society's annual meeting in Towson, Maryland, just outside of Baltimore. SABR affairs in those days were smaller and somewhat chummier, thus a less frantic schedule allowed you to see and do everything, and we all were energized by Phil's ballparks history revival speech. At that point, Phil had been working for years on what would become the first edition of *Green Cathedrals*, published by SABR in 1986. Phil's enthusiasm led to the creation of the Ballparks Research Committee of SABR.

Of course, Phil didn't invent either ballparks or their history, but timing is indeed everything and few writers had given the game's "cathedrals" their due before Phil. In 1975, Bill Shannon and George Kalinsky's *The Ballparks* marked the first of a soon growing line of ballparks histories, but Phil's first version of *Green Cathedrals* provided a unique collection of data about all major league parks since the professional age began in 1871.

Ballparks as a building invention date to the 1860s, when entrepreneurs created a facility to keep the paying faithful inside and everyone else outside. As the club teams of the 1850s became the para-professionals of the 1860s and the full-fledged mercenaries of the 1870s, the business of baseball transformed the crude wooden stands of the late nineteenth century to the brick, concrete, and steel edifices of the twentieth century. When we speak of the "classic" parks, we mourn the passing of Forbes, Ebbets, Crosley, Shibe, Griffith, Sportsman's, and lately, Tiger and Comiskey.

Phil does not limit himself to the twentieth century, nor is he a snob who deals with just the American and National leagues. As a "ballparks progressive" he includes all Negro Leagues, the Players and Federal Leagues, and many more. He also seeks the "neutral" sites used when fire, flood, local ordinance, or other obstacles prevented a game from taking place at a regular site. Read the entire text as you may find a major league game that took place in your backyard.

So, why should you care about all this? Even as a baseball fan, you might consider this material a little arcane and esoteric. You shouldn't! Baseball has two charming aspects that separate it in both style and intensity from other sports: statistics and stories, and *Green Cathedrals* will wash over you with both. And we all know that often-repeated quote that says if we are to understand America, we must first understand baseball. Well, I would suggest we must understand ballparks to understand baseball.

If baseball is a "game of inches," isn't it worthwhile to know how those inches have shaped the game at so many ballparks? A higher wall, a shorter power alley, a screen or not over the bleachers: How many such factors can (and did) change the game and its numbers? Most sports take place in standardized settings, but once you follow the ninety-foot square infield and place the pitcher's mound sixty feet and six inches from home plate, the rest is left to chance or some interesting and purposeful design aspects that continue in this modern era of retro-classics.

Growing up at Fenway Park I assumed that all ballparks were quirky and angular places where batted balls bounced off of walls, ladders, and poles. Imagine my surprise when I first visited Veterans Stadium in Philadelphia!

Regardless of your ballpark past, enjoy this book. It will fill many a rain delay, win you a few trivia contests, and fill you with an appreciation and new perspective of the national pastime and its developing homes for the past 136 years. Read this book and you will never look at a ballpark in the same manner. And if you see a mistake or can suggest an addition, feel free to contact Phil as Captain Ahab sails again soon.

*Robert F. Bluthardt*
Ballparks Committee Chair
Society for American Baseball Research
June 2006

# Acknowledgments

I would like to acknowledge the assistance of the following people in helping me to finish this book: Dallas Adams, Donald Adams, Doug Alford, Priscilla Astifan, Bob Bailey, Evelyn Begley, Phil Bess, Richard Beverage, Peter Bjarkman, Cliff Blau, Robert Bluthardt, Bob Boynton, James Bready, Doug Brei, Chet Brewer, Edward Brown, Dick Burtt, Jack Carlson, Jim Charlton, Richard Clark, Dean Coughenour, Kit Crissey, Ray Dandridge, Bob Davids, Leon Day, Jorge Colon Delgado, Nancy Dickinson, Joe Dittmar, Paul Doherty, Dutch Doyle, David Dyte, Eric Enders, Chris Epting, Wendy Farrell, Edwin Fernandez-Cruz, Scott Flatow, Bruce Foster, Cappy Gagnon, George Gibson, Steve Gietschier, Ralph Graber, Paul Healey, Tom Heitz, Bob Hoie, Ken Holt, John Holway, John Horne, Bill Hugo, Monte Irvin, Bill Jenkinson, Linda Johns, Judy Johnson, W. Lloyd Johnson, Tom Jozwik, Cliff Kachline, Charlie Kagan, Larry Keefe, Pat Kelly, Jim Laughlin, Glen Ledoux, Buck Leonard, Larry Lester, Len Levin, Jack Little, Bertha Lowry, Ellen Lowry, Evan Lowry, John Lowry, Megan Lowry, Larry Lucchino, Bob McConnell, Joe McGillen, John Maher, Steven Mau, Ray Medeiros, Joe Mock, Carrington Montague, Linda Nichols, Skip Nipper, Marty O'Connor, John O'Malley, Buck O'Neil, Tip O'Neill, Marc Okkonen, John Paine, Dan Palubniak, John Pastier, Eric Pastore, Claudia Perry, Alvin Peterjohn, Bob Prince, Rachel Reiss, Greg Rhodes, Ric Roberts, Mark Rucker, John Schleppi, Carl Schoen, Ron Selter, Seymour Siwoff, David Smith, Hilton Smith, Tal Smith, Paul Soyka, Andy Strasberg, Gene Sunnen, Jeff Suntala, John Tattersall, John Thorn, Stew Thornley, Richard Topp, Frank Vaccaro, Mike Veeck, David Vincent, Bill Wagner, Willie Wells, Paul Wendt, Miles Wolff, William Young.

In addition, I have received 5,247 letters or e-mails from authors, ballplayers, curators, fans, groundskeepers, halls of fame, historical societies, leagues, librarians, mayors, researchers, sportswriters, stadium managers, teams, and umpires from all over the world. To all who assisted, thank you very much.

And lastly, a very special thank you to a very special old friend, who is sorely missed. Forbes Field, in your majesty and your beauty, your style and your elegance, your in-play flagpole and in-play monuments, your in-play batting cage and in-play wooden Marine Sergeant, your in-play screen in right and in-play scoreboard in left, your smells of hot dogs and cigars and horse hide and pine tar, none will ever be your equal. When you were opened in 1909, and throughout all the years in which you flourished through 1970, and today as your center field brick wall and flagpole still stand tall, you will always remain, forever and ever, the Jewel of Ballparks, the very best ballpark to ever grace the game of baseball, bar none. Beat 'em, Bucs!

# Preface

*Philip J. Lowry*

Here are the vital statistics for our 30 current major league parks and, more important, for every one of baseball's storied shrines of the past where regular season or post-season championship major league baseball games have ever been played. The saga of major league ballparks dates back to 1871, and includes an incredible variety of playing sites, from cricket grounds, polo fields, and beer taverns to racetracks, fairgrounds, and cow pastures. There were even two palaces in two of America's best baseball towns, Cincinnati and St. Louis. When the third edition of *Green Cathedrals* was published back in 1992, 273 ballparks were cited where major league baseball had been played. After much further research, you will find here descriptions for more than 400 parks.

There have been several ballpark books since mine, but no one else has ever provided a complete listing of every major league park, including Negro League parks. The focus is on ballpark geometry, the oddities in play caused by unique and crazy configurations, and what makes the game fun for fans. All dimensional changes are catalogued and dated in outfield fence distances and heights. This is crucial to understanding the statistical history of baseball. The following leagues are covered:

| | |
|---|---|
| **NA** | National Association, 1871–75 |
| **NL** | National League, 1876 to date |
| **AA** | American Association, 1882–91 |
| **UA** | Union Association, 1884 |
| **NCL** | National Colored League, 1887 |
| **PL** | Players League, 1890 |
| **AL** | American League, 1901 to date |
| **FL** | Federal League, 1914–15 |
| **NNL** | Negro National League, 1920–31, 1933–48 |
| **ECL** | Eastern Colored League, 1923–28 |

ANL    American Negro League, 1929

NSL    Negro Southern League, 1932

NEWL   Negro East–West League, 1932

NAL    Negro American League, 1937–61

I differ from many baseball authors by including the Negro Leagues as major leagues rather than as somehow a different category. I was very fortunate to attend a three-day 1982 conference in Ashland, Kentucky, attended by almost all of the living Negro League veterans, and I interviewed each attendee on the amazing variety of ballparks used for regular season games by barnstorming Negro League teams. Concerning inclusion of the Negro Southern and Negro East-West Leagues in 1932, none of the three other principal Negro Leagues (NNL, ECL, NAL) were operating in 1932. Since the NSL and NEWL were the only Negro Leagues that year, they should be considered as major league.

Before 1900, most ballparks were simple, small, wooden grandstands hastily constructed around recreation fields, in some cases not enclosed by outfield fences. Beginning with the erection of Shibe Park and Forbes Field in 1909, however, almost entirely concrete-and-steel ballparks became the rule. These big palaces signaled the growing prominence of baseball, and the golden era in ballpark design. Beginning in the 1950s, multipurpose stadiums were developed for use by both football and baseball, a marriage definitely not made in heaven. The result was a series of sterile, concrete ashtrays, perhaps better described as a series of cookie-cutter, carpeted toilet bowls. Thankfully, Baltimore's Camden Yards in 1992, like Buffalo's earlier minor league park, Pilot Field, presaged a return to usually asymmetrical, grass-surface, baseball-only parks. For this we have Larry Lucchino, then of the Orioles, now of the Red Sox, to thank. Starting with Camden Yards, HOK Sport has designed the great majority of these new parks, including Jacobs Field in Cleveland, AT&T Park in San Francisco, and PNC Park in Pittsburgh.

Dimensional data are difficult to interpret. There are obvious mistakes, such as typos in team guides,

and incorrect measurements. Then there are other mistakes that are not so obvious, such as when team guides do not keep up-to-date when changes occur, and when some teams or other sources listed power alley for left-center/right-center measurements, or vice versa. In this edition of *Green Cathedrals* the following dimensional definitions are used: left field/right field means at the foul poles; straightaway left/right field means 15 degrees in from the foul line; left field/right field power alley means 22.5 degrees; left-center/right-center means 30 degrees; and center field (as in dead center) means 45 degrees. Where available, center field corner dimensions are also provided. In summary, dimensional data often necessarily reflect the researcher's best judgment.

The categories I use to describe the ballparks deserve some explanation.

AKA (also known as) gives alternate names and nicknames used for the park.

ARCHITECT lists the architect or architects, if known, for classic and post-classic ballparks.

OCCUPANT lists teams using the park in chronological order, with dates of play.

LOCATION cites surrounding streets, with associated fields and bases, and geographical directions. Although Official Baseball Rule 1.04 states, "It is desirable that the line from home base through the pitcher's plate to second base shall run east-northeast," you will see that this has definitely not always been the case.

DIMENSIONS gives the distance in feet from home plate to outfield fences and the backstop, with dates denoting the first time when boundaries stood at that distance. If there is no date next to a dimension, then that figure is the original dimension.

**FENCES** lists outfield fence heights in feet, with dates for the first time fences stood at that height. If there is no date next to a fence height, then that figure is the original fence height.

**FORMER USE** describes how the site was used before park construction, while

**CURRENT USE** chronicles development of the site after the park was abandoned.

**CAPACITY** figures are noted only when they change by more than 1000, but the most recent figure is always given. If there is no date next to a capacity, then that figure is the original capacity.

**PHENOMENA** is a general category for historical data, important changes, and noteworthy events.

What have I learned by immersing myself for 28 years in such details as whether North Avenue West is the south or east boundary of Recreation Park (it's the south), why the distance to center field at the Polo Grounds changed 20 times (I still don't know), and whether there was a 32-foot-high wooden Marine sergeant in play and standing against the left field wall during World War II at Forbes Field (there was)? After going through endless newspaper microfilm and

historical archives, and interviewing hundreds of players, fans, umpires, and sportswriters, three impressions stand out from the rest. First, history delights in shrouding her many precious baseball mysteries in the fog of conflicting sources, and many facts can never be known for certain, especially concerning the Negro Leagues, whose documentation is so scarce.

Second, ballpark geometry really matters when you analyze the game. Before 1931, fly balls down the foul lines were ruled fair or foul by where they landed rather than where they left the field of play. Bill Jenkinson's excellent forthcoming book *The Year Babe Ruth Hit 104 Home Runs* examines in detail the landing spots for every long ball ever hit by Babe Ruth, projecting that had he played in ballparks with 2006 dimensions, he would have had 104 homers in 1921 rather than just 59. Jenkinson also projects that had fly balls been judged to be homers based on where they left the playing field rather than where they landed, Ruth would have had 75 additional homers over his career, so Henry Aaron would have been chasing a Ruthian record of 789 rather than 714. Remember, Yankee Stadium's right field stands were simply 70 rows of wooden bleachers in Ruth's time, before the 1936–38 construction of the upper decks, so when one of his long curving fly balls passed the foul pole way fair, it had another hundred feet or so of wide open bleachers in which to curve foul.

And last, and most importantly, I've found that baseball research is great fun and you meet some wonderful people along the way.

# Green Cathedrals

# The Ballparks

## Akron, Ohio

### *League Park (II)*

**A.K.A.**

St. Mary's Field (1970s)

**OCCUPANTS**

NNL Akron Black Tyrites 1933; neutral site used by NEWL Pittsburgh Crawfords AM game August 8, 1932

**DIMENSIONS**

Left Field: 315 (1928), 300 (1940)
Center Field: 385 (1928), 387 (1940)
Right Field: 345 (1928), 347 (1940)

**FENCES**

All 10 (wood)

**LOCATION**

Left Field (N) West Crozier St; Third Base (W) Lakeside Blvd where the trolley line ended at the Summit Beach Amusement Park, then Summit Lake; First Base (S) West Long St, Right Field (E) alley, then Victory St

**CURRENT USE**

Soccer field

**CAPACITY**

4500 (1933), 3500 (1940)

**PHENOMENA**

Replaced the first League Park at Beaver and Carroll Streets. ♦ This ballpark had one of the strangest outfield fences ever. Because the ground fell off so sharply behind the left field fence, it was built at an angle so that wooden supports would hold it up. The slope ranged from 35 degrees to 60 degrees, and many left fielders literally ran up the wall to catch a long fly ball. There was a ground rule that if a batted ball rolled up and over the wall it was a double.

## Albany, New York

*See also* Greenbush, New York

### *Riverside Park*

**OCCUPANT**

Neutral site used by NL Troy Trojans September 11, 1880; June 15 and September 10, 1881

**LOCATION**

(N) Herkimer St, (W) Broadway, (S) Westerlo St, (E) Quay St

### *Hawkins Stadium*

**OCCUPANT**

Neutral site used by NNL New York Black Yankees on May 22, 1948

**PHENOMENA**

Black Yankees hosted Newark Eagles here. Also hosted minor league teams 1928–60.

# Altoona, Pennsylvania

### *Columbia Park*

**AKA**

4th Ave Grounds, Waverly Field

**OCCUPANT**

UA Altoona Mountain Citys April 30–May 31, 1884

**LOCATION**

(NW) Lower 6th Ave, (SW) 32nd St, (SE) 4th Ave, (NE) Mill Run Rd

**CURRENT USE**

Brightly painted gasoline storage tanks, Pennsylvania RR tracks, houses

**PHENOMENA**

Built in 1884 and used until June 1912.

### *Pennsylvania Railroad Park*

**OCCUPANT**

Neutral site used by NNL Homestead Grays 1930s

**DIMENSIONS**

Right Field: 150

# Anaheim, California

### *Angel Stadium of Anaheim*

**AKA**

Big A, Bigger A 1980, Anaheim Stadium 1966–97, Edison International Field of Anaheim 1998–2003, Angel Stadium 2004 to date

**ARCHITECTS**

Nobel Herzberg (design engineer) 1966, HOK Sport 1997–99 Renovation

**OCCUPANTS**

AL California Angels April 19, 1966–September 25, 1996; AL Anaheim Angels April 2, 1997–2004; AL Los Angeles Angels of Anaheim April 5, 2005, to date

**LOCATION**

Left Field (N) Katella Ave; Third Base (W) 2000 State College Blvd, then Santa Anna Frwy/I-5; First Base (S) Orangewood Ave; Right Field (E) Orange Frwy/CA Route 57; Center Field (NE) Amtrak RR station

**DIMENSIONS**

Foul Lines: 333, 330 (1998), 333 (2003)
Bullpens: 362, 365 (1998)
Left Field 380 (2002)
Left Field Power Alley: 375, 369 (1973), 374 (1974), 370 (1989), 376 (1998), 381 (2000), 387 (2002)
Deep Alleys (right of left-center and left of right-center): 386
Left Center: 386 (1974), 396 (1998), 387 (1999)
Center Field: 406, 402 (1973), 404 (1974), 408 (1998), 400 (1999)
Right Center: 386 (1974), 372 (1989), 375 (1998), 370 (2002)
Right Field Power Alley: 375, 369 (1973), 374 (1974), 364 (1989), 365 (1998), 395 (2002)
Backstop: 55, 60.5 (1973)

Angel Stadium, aka the "Big A" for the giant A with a halo beyond the left-center field wall.

## FENCES

Most of fence: 10 (wire), 7.86 (wire 1973), 7.86 (padded 1981)

Corners between Foul Poles and Bullpens: 4.75 (steel)

Left Center between 386 and 404 marks: 7.5 (padded 1981)

Padded posts at left sides of both Left and Right Field Bullpen gates: 9 (padded 1981)

Bullpen gates: 9.95 (wire)

Left Field to Right Center: 8 (padded 1997)

Right Center to Right Field: 8 (padded 1997), 18 (Scoreboard 1998)

## SURFACE

Santa Ana Bermuda 1966–88, bluegrass 1989 to date

## FORMER USE

Four farms: Camille Allec's 39 acres of orange and eucalyptus trees, Roland Reynolds' 70 acres of alfalfa, John Knutgen's 20 acres of corn, Bill Ross and George Lenney's 19 acres of corn

## CAPACITY

43,204, 44,500 (1967), 43,204 (1968), 64,593 (1980), 67,335 (1981), 65,158 (1984), 64,573 (1986), 33,851 (1997), 45,050 (1998), 45,037 (2005)

## PHENOMENA

First game was April 9, 1966–an exhibition game vs. the San Francisco Giants. ♦ Power hitter's park, the ball carries very well. ♦ Huge 230-foot-high letter A stood behind the fence in left as a scoreboard support until 1980, then it was moved to the parking lot when the stadium was enclosed for the NFL Rams. The letter has a gold halo at its top. ♦ Angels' mascot, the Angel Ape, roamed the stands in 1980. ♦ Sections 69 and 70 in center covered by green-canvas batters background. ♦ Two thin black TV cables used to run in fair territory on the warning track from the left field corner bullpen gate to the foul pole, and then along the wall in foul territory about 50 feet toward third base, then into the stands. ♦ Outfield enclosed and triple-decked in 1980. New owner Disney un-enclosed it October 1996–April 1998, ripped out the outfield structure, and replaced it with the Outfield Extravaganza, which is supposed to look like the rocks along the Pacific Ocean, with a 90-foot-high geyser. ♦ In 1998 the bullpens were moved to a two-tier arrangement in left field. ♦ An 18-foot-high scoreboard was added in right field, with the second deck right field pavilion seats above the scoreboard.

# Arlington, Texas

## *Arlington Stadium*

### AKA
Turnpike Stadium 1965–71

### OCCUPANT
AL Texas Rangers April 21, 1972–October 3, 1993

### LOCATION
Left Field (E) Stadium Dr East, then Arlington Convention Center and Six Flags Over Texas Amusement Park; Third Base (N) Seven Seas Rd, then 1500 South Copeland Rd; First Base (W) Stadium Dr West (later Pennant Dr), then Collins St/State Hwy 157 (later Nolan Ryan Expressway/I-30); Right Field (S) East Randol Mill Rd

### DIMENSIONS
Foul Lines: 330
Power Alleys: 380, 370 (1974), 383 (1981), 380 (1982)
Center Field: 400
Backstop: 60 (1972), 65 (1993)
Foul Territory: small

### FENCES
11, 12 (1981), 11 (1986)

### SURFACE
Tifway 419 Bermuda grass

Arlington Stadium was built in a natural bowl 40 feet below the surrounding land.

Located just a quarter mile from the old Arlington Stadium, Ameriquest Field opened on April 11, 1994. Like its predecessor, the playing field is well below street level.

**FORMER USE**

Minor league ballpark 1965–71

**CAPACITY**

10,500, 20,000 (1970), 35,739 (1972), 41,097 (1979), 43,508 (1985), 43,521 (1992)

**PHENOMENA**

Like Dodger Stadium, the field was far below surrounding parking lots. Before 1978, when the upper deck was added, fans would walk in at the top of the stadium. ♦ Cotton Eye Joe played for the seventh inning stretch so fans could dance in the aisles. ♦ Wind blew in directly from the outfield, but since it was the hottest park in the majors, the ball carried well, since warm, humid air is not as dense as cool, dry air and does not offer as much resistance to the ball in flight. The Lone Ranger on the Texas-shaped scoreboard in left center rooted for the Rangers. ♦ Largest extent of bleachers in the majors, along with Tiger Stadium, from foul pole to foul pole. ♦ Upper deck added in winter of 1978–79.

## *Ameriquest Field in Arlington*

**AKA**

Ballpark in Arlington (1994–May 2004)

**ARCHITECT**

David M. Schwarz, HKS Inc.

**OCCUPANT**

AL Texas Rangers April 11, 1994, to date

**LOCATION**

Left Field (E) 1000 Ballpark Way, Third Base (N) Copeland Rd, Home Plate (NW) location of old Arlington Stadium, First Base (W) Pennant Dr, then Nolan Ryan Expressway/I-30, Right Field (S) East Randol Mill Rd

**DIMENSIONS**

Left Field: 334, 332 (2000)
Left Field kink: 354
Left Field Power Alley: 388, 390 (2000)

Left Center: 397
Deepest Left Center: 404
Center Field: 400
Deepest Right Center: 403, 407 (2001)
Right Center: 388
Right Field Power Alley: 381 (at the back of the kink)
Right Center kink (at the front): 377
Right Field kink: 349
Right Field: 325, 326 (2000)
Backstop: 60
Foul Territory: small

**FENCES**

Left Field: 14 (wood)
Center Field and Right Field: 8 (wood)

**SURFACE**

Tifway 419 Bermuda grass

**CAPACITY**

49,178, 48,100 (1996), 49,166 (1997), 49,115 (2003), 48,911 (2006)

**PHENOMENA**

Covered pavilion porch in right features pillars reminiscent of Tiger Stadium. ♦ Playing field is 22 feet below street level. ♦ Wind helps carry balls hit to right center. ♦ The Rangers' 10th home game here was postponed April 25, 1994, due to a tornado. The next day, wind gusts of 50 mph blew Rangers winning pitcher Rick Helling off the mound in the top of the sixth, and caused a 45-minute delay in the bottom of the sixth. ♦ Outfield has many nooks and crannies reminiscent of Ebbets Field. ♦ Site of first AL/NL interleague game in major league history on June 12, 1997, as Willie Mays and Nolan Ryan threw out ceremonial first pitches to the NL and AL presidents before the Giants beat the Rangers, 4–3. ♦ Tarp stored underground along the third base line.

# Asheville, North Carolina

## *McCormick Field*

**OCCUPANT**

Neutral site used by NAL Birmingham Black Barons 1940s

Built in 1924, McCormick Field is one of the oldest minor league parks in continuous use.

McCormick Field— "America's prettiest ballpark"

**LOCATION**

Valley St, Charlotte St, McCormick Plc

**DIMENSIONS**

Left Field: 328, 365 (1940), 325 (1985), 328 (1988)

Left Center: 360 (1988)

Center Field: 397, 410 (1940), 414 (1985), 404 (1988)

Right Center: 325 (1988)

Right Field: 301, 325 (1940), 301 (1985)

**FENCES**

Left and Center: 18

Right: 18 (1924), 36 (1992)

**CAPACITY**

3500, 3000 (1940), 3500 (1985)

**PHENOMENA**

Beautiful park, with lots of trees all around. ♦ Vines on outfield walls are thicker than at Wrigley Field. ♦ Built in 1924, it is one of the oldest minor league parks in continual use. ♦ Rickwood Field in Birmingham was built in 1910, but is used only once per year for an official Barons game. ♦ Many books incorrectly report that Ebbets Field's clock was moved here when Ebbets Field was torn down. What happened was that some scam artists sold the Tourists ballclub a fake clock that looked like the old Ebbets Field clock. ♦

The park was totally rebuilt in 1992. ♦ Stands for Negro fans behind wall burned down in 1937.

---

# Atlanta, Georgia

## *Ponce De Leon Park (II)*

**AKA**

Spiller Park 1924–32, Poncey

**OCCUPANTS**

NSL Atlanta Black Crackers 1932; NAL Atlanta Black Crackers 1938

**LOCATION**

Left Field (N) parking lot, Third Base (W) North Blvd, First Base (S) 650 Ponce de Leon Blvd, Right Field (E) Southern RR tracks

**DIMENSIONS**

Left Field: 365 (1932), 330 (1951)

Left Center left of Scoreboard: 525

Center Field: 462 (1932), 448 (1938), 410 (1951)

Right Field: 321 (1932), 324 (1938), 321 (1951)

In this game at Ponce De Leon Park on April 10, 1949, the Atlanta Crackers beat the Brooklyn Dodgers, 8–4, in an exhibition game.

## FENCES

Left Field: 2 (hedge April 1949), 4 (cyclone fence May 1949)

Left Center: 25 (scoreboard)

Center Field: 6

Right Center: 75 (magnolia tree in front of a very steep embankment, no fence)

Right Field: 15

## CURRENT USE

Midtown Place Shopping Center just across from City Hall East, Whole Foods restaurant in the outfield, Smoothie King at second base, Pearl Vision store at first base, the huge magnolia tree in right -center is still standing above a bank of kudzu out in back behind the stores.

## CAPACITY

11,000 (1903), 15,000 (1924), 15,500 (1940), 12,500 (1949)

## PHENOMENA

The only two batters to hit the magnolia tree on the fly were Eddie Mathews and Babe Ruth. ◆ First Ponce de Leon Park built 1907, burned down September 9, 1923. Second park built 1924, torn down 1967. ◆ At the end of spring training in 1949, the Brooklyn Dodgers, with Jackie Robinson, played a series of three exhibitions against the minor league Crackers, the first integrated games ever played in Georgia. ◆ A two-foot-high hedge formed the outfield fence from the left field foul line to the right side of the left-center scoreboard in 1949. This reduced the foul line from 365 to 330, and caused many arguments, because a left fielder had to stay within the hedge. If he fell over the hedge, it was a home run. ◆ Behind the hedge in left were the bleachers, the only place where African-American fans could sit. ◆ Train engineers would pause on the tracks high atop the embankment above right field to look down on the game. ◆ In 1954, Bob Montag hit a homer to right that landed in a coal car and traveled 518 miles to Nashville before a train fireman brought it back to get it autographed. ◆ The ashes of longtime Crackers owner, and former peanut vendor, Earl Mann were

scattered around the roots of the magnolia in right-center. ◆ The minor league Crackers left after 1964 and played their last season, 1965, in the new Atlanta-Fulton County Stadium. ◆ Fortunately for baseball history, the magnolia tree is now cared for by horticulturists Don and Chris Hastings.

## *Atlanta-Fulton County Stadium*

### AKA

Atlanta Stadium, Launching Pad

### ARCHITECTS

Heery International Inc., Williams-Russell & Johnson Inc., and Ellerbe Beckett Inc.

### OCCUPANT

NL Atlanta Braves April 12, 1966–October 24, 1996

### LOCATION

Left Field (N/NE) Fulton St; Third Base (W/NW) Washington St, then I-75/85; First Base (S/SW) Georgia Ave (later Pulman St), then I-20; Right Field (E/SE) 521 Eustace (later Capitol) Ave

### DIMENSIONS

Foul Lines: 325, 330 (1967)

Power Alleys: 385, 375 (1969), 385 (1974)

Center Field: 402, 400 (1969), 402 (1973)

Backstop: 59.92 (1973), 50 (1996)

Foul Territory: large (1966), medium (1977)

### FENCES

6 (wire), 10 (4 plexiglass above 6 wire 1983), 10 (plexiglass 1985)

### CURRENT USE

Parking lot for Turner Field

### CAPACITY

50,893, 52,870 (1974), 51,556 (1976), 52,785 (1982), 52,270 (1996)

Fulton County Stadium, with Atlanta's skyline in the distance. Hank Aaron hit his 715th home run here on April 8, 1974, off Al Downing, breaking Babe Ruth's record.

**PHENOMENA**

Called the Launching Pad because of the number of home runs hit here, in part due to the 1050-foot altitude that allows batted balls to travel farther. ♦ A 400-foot fly ball hit at sea-level Yankee Stadium would travel 407 feet here (and 427 feet at 5280-foot "mile-high" Coors Field in Denver). ♦ Big Victor, a large totem-pole-styled figure, stood in the stadium in 1966. His huge head tilted, and his eyes rolled whenever a Brave hit a home run. ♦ Chief Noc-A-Homa's Wigwam replaced Big Victor in 1967. From 1967 to 1971, his teepee stood on a 20-foot-square platform behind the left field fence. In 1972, the teepee was moved to right field. From 1973 to 1977, it returned to left field. From 1978 to August 1982, the teepee was moved to left center, occupying 235 seats between aisles 128 and 130 in rows 18–30. From August to early September 1982, it was removed in anticipation of ad-ditional revenue in the playoffs, "causing" a disas-trous tailspin for the first-place Braves. Its replace-ment coincided with the Braves' comeback to win the 1982 division crown. ♦ Tempting fate again the next year, the teepee's removal on August 11, 1983, saw another losing streak, which could not be over-come by its return on September 16. ♦ Henry Aaron's 715th home run hit here on April 8, 1974. ♦ The 22-foot outfield wall was never in play. ♦ An 80-year-old calliope organ was installed in 1971. ♦ Horrible field conditions, no full-time groundskeepers 1966–89. ♦ Mets defeated Braves here 16–13 in 19 innings, in a game twice delayed by rain, finally ending at 3:55 AM on July 5, 1985. The Fourth of July fireworks show went from 4:01 to 4:12 AM. ♦ Demolished August 2, 1997. ♦ Longest homer ever here sailed into the third deck off the bat of Orestes Kindelan of Cuba during the 1996 Olympics.

## *Turner Field*

**AKA**

Olympic Stadium 1996

**ARCHITECTS**

Heery International Inc., William-Russell & John-son Inc., and Ellerbe Beckett Inc.

**OCCUPANT**

NL Atlanta Braves April 4, 1997, to date

**LOCATION**

Left Field (N/NW) Georgia Ave (later Ralph Abernathy Blvd); Third Base (W/SW) Washington St (later Pollard Ave), then I-75/85; First Base (S/SE) Love St (later Bill Lucas Dr); Right Field (E/NE) Capitol Ave (later 755 Hank Aaron Dr)

**DIMENSIONS**

Left Field: 335
Left Center: 380
Center Field: 401
Right Center: 390, 385 (2001), 390 (2005)
Right Field: 330
Backstop: 53, 60 (2003)
Foul Territory: large

Tom Glavine throws the first pitch in the Braves' 2–0 exhibition-game win against the Yankees to open play at Turner Field on March 29, 1997.

**FENCES**

8

**SURFACE**

Prescription Athletic Turf (PAT) grass

**CAPACITY**

80,000 (1996), 50,528 (1997), 50,091 (2001)

**PHENOMENA**

Hosted 1996 Summer Olympics, with huge temporary bleachers out in what is now the outfield. ♦ Hand-operated scoreboard posts out-of-town scores above left field stands. ♦ Center field scoreboard dominated by 100-foot image of Hank Aaron hitting 715th home run. ♦ Huge Coke bottle sits in upper deck in left. ♦ Monument Grove, a large park area at the north entrance, contains statues of Hank Aaron, Ty Cobb, and Phil Niekro, which had been at Atlanta Stadium. The grove also has the retired number statues of Aaron, Niekro, Warren Spahn, Eddie Mathews, and Dale Murphy.

# Atlantic City, New Jersey

## *Bacharach Park*

**OCCUPANTS**

ECL Atlantic City Bacharach Giants 1923–27, April–May 1928; ANL Atlantic City Bacharach Giants 1929; NNL Atlantic City Bacharach Giants July–September 1934; neutral site used by NNL Baltimore Black Sox August 26, 1933

**LOCATION**

(NW) McKinley Ave; (SW) North New York Ave; (SE) Grant Ave; (NE) South Carolina Ave

**CURRENT USE**

Carver Hall public housing project

## *Atlantic Park Dog Track*

**OCCUPANT**

ECL Atlantic City Bacharach Giants some games 1920s

**LOCATION**

Absecon Blvd, by Municipal Market

**CURRENT USE**

Shop'n Bag Supermarket

# Austin, Texas

## *Clark Field*

**OCCUPANT**

Neutral site use by NAL Houston Eagles 1949–50

**DIMENSIONS**

Bottom of the cliff Left Field: 313
Left Center Scoreboard: 357
Center Field: 341
Right Center: 303
Top of the cliff Left Field: 350
Left Center Scoreboard: 375
Deepest Center Field just left of dead center: 401
Right Center: 363
Right Field: 300

**FENCES**

Left and Right Field: 10
Center Field: 40; complicated measurements courtesy of March 16, 1967, Breazeale-Sims geological survey reveal that the limestone cliff height sloped from zero at the Left Field Foul Pole to 30 in Center Field back to zero in Right Center; majority of the cliff was 12

**CAPACITY**

5000 (1928)

Clark Field in Austin, Texas, one of the most unusual stadiums in history: the limestone cliff across the outfield was in play, and could only be reached via a goat path in left-center.

**PHENOMENA**

This home of the University of Texas Longhorns was the most unique baseball field ever created. There was a 12- to 30-foot-high cliff in left center and center that forced the left fielder and the center fielder to choose whether to play on top of the cliff or in front of it. About half the outfielders chose to play on top, and about half chose to play down below. Either way, they were bound to have an adventure. The cliff could only be climbed on a goat path in left-center. ◆ A typical play occurred in 1973, when the Longhorns got an inside-the-park homer to third base. Both outfielders were playing "down below" when a towering fly ball was hit to deep center. The center fielder went back to the cliff, but the ball landed up on the plateau. The left fielder ran up the goat path to the plateau, but the ball hit some of the rocks on top of the plateau and bounced down toward the left field line. The nearest fielder was the third baseman, who retrieved the ball, but his throw to the plate was no way near getting the batter out at home. ◆ Opened on March 24, 1928. ◆ Legend has it that Lou Gehrig hit a 611-foot homer way over the plateau, and way over the 40-foot-high fence in deep center in March 1929.

---

# Baltimore, Maryland

*See also* Westport, Maryland

## *Madison Avenue Grounds*

**AKA**

Pastime Base Ball Grounds

**OCCUPANT**

Neutral site used by NA Washington Olympics July 8, 1871

**LOCATION**

Center Field (E) Linden Ave, Third Base (N) Bloom St (later Boundary Ave, later North Ave),

Home Plate (W) Madison Ave, First Base (S) an old path between what are now Roberts St and Laurens St

## Newington Park

**OCCUPANTS**

NA Lord Baltimores April 22, 1872–October 14, 1874; NA Baltimore Marylands April 14–July 11, 1873; AA Baltimore Orioles May 9–September 30, 1882; neutral site used by NA Washington Olympics July 8, 1871; June 1 and 9, 1875

**LOCATION**

(N) Baker St, (W) Gold St, (S) Calhoun St, (E) Pennsylvania Ave

## Oriole Park (I)

**AKA**

Union Park (I), Huntingdon Avenue Grounds 1887–88, American Association Park

**OCCUPANTS**

AA Baltimore Orioles May 1, 1883–October 10, 1889; NCL Lord Baltimores 1887; neutral use for the Temple Cup Series NL Detroit Wolverines vs. AA St. Louis Browns afternoon game on October 21, 1887

**LOCATION**

Left Field (W) Barclay St, Third Base (S) 5th (later 24th) St, First Base (E) York Rd (later Greenmount Ave), Right Field (N) Huntingdon Ave (later 6th St, later 25th St); on the SE corner of Barclay and 25th

**PHENOMENA**

Adjacent to an amusement park where fans paid only 25 cents for dining, dancing, and band concerts after the game.

## Belair Lot

**AKA**

Union Park (II)

**OCCUPANTS**

UA Baltimore Monumentals April 17–August 8 and August 28–September 24, 1884; neutral site used by UA Pittsburgh Stogies September 17, 1884

**LOCATION**

(NW) Gay St, (SW) Chestnut (later Colvin) St, (SE) Low St, (NE) Forrest St

**CURRENT USE**

Old Town Mall parking lot, just SW of Belair Market

## Monumental Park

**OCCUPANT**

UA Baltimore Monumentals August 25, 1884

**PHENOMENA**

After the EL team playing at Monumental Park disbanded, the UA team decided to move their last 19 home games of the 1884 season here from tiny Belair Lot, because this park was so much larger. But after defeating Washington here, 12–11, on August 25, and discovering how badly uneven and bumpy the infield was, they moved their last 18 home games back to Belair Lot.

## Oriole Park (II)

**OCCUPANT**

AA Baltimore Orioles August 27, 1890–May 9, 1891

**LOCATION**

Left Field (E) York Rd (later Greenmount Ave), Third Base (N) 10th (later East 29th) St, First Base

(W) Barclay St, Right Field (S) 9th (later East 28th) St; on the SW corner of Greenmount and 29th

## Oriole Park (III)

### AKA

Union Park (III), Baltimore Baseball and Exhibition Grounds

### OCCUPANTS

AA Baltimore Orioles May 11–October 3, 1891; NL Baltimore Orioles April 12, 1892–October 10, 1899

### LOCATION

Left Field (E) Barclay St, Third Base (N) Huntingdon Ave (later 6th St, later 25th St), First Base (W) St. Paul St (later Guilford Ave), Right Field (S) Sumwalt (later 24th) St and Brady's Run; on the SW corner of Barclay and 25th, across street from site of Oriole Park (I)

### DIMENSIONS

Left Field: 300
Right Field: 350

### FENCES

16 (wood)

### CAPACITY

30,000, 11,000 (1897)

### PHENOMENA

Damaged by fire in 1894. ♦ Fly balls to right field were quite an adventure because field sloped steeply down to right field fence, and because the water from a nearby stream (Brady's Run) created a perpetual swamp in right by oozing underneath the outfield fence.

## Oriole Park (IV)

### AKA

American League Park

### OCCUPANT

AL Baltimore Orioles April 26, 1901, to September 29, 1902

### LOCATION

Same as that for Oriole Park (II); Oriole Park (IV)

A crowd of 30,000 Oriole fans watched this 1897 game against the eventual league champion Boston team at Oriole Park III.

Oriole Park V, also known as Terrapin Park, in the late 1930s.

was built on the same site after Oriole Park (II) was torn down, SW corner of Greenmount and 29th

**DIMENSIONS**

Left Field: 360
Left Field Power Alley: 435
Left Center Field: 420
Center Field: 435
Right Center Field: 392
Right Field Power Alley: 411
Right Field: 281
Backstop: 72

**CURRENT USE**

Gas station

**PHENOMENA**

Flag pole in right center. Large tree beyond fence in right. ♦ The outfield fence was angled like the fence at Ebbets Field in Brooklyn–the lower two-thirds of the fence angled back away from the plate, and then the top third of the fence was vertical. ♦ Orioles forfeited to the Browns July 17, 1902, when they failed to show up. ♦ Dimensions based on 1902 Sanborn fire insurance map with right field estimated. ♦ A better than average AL park for hitters: 1901–02 batting park factors were: BA 108, OBP 104, Slugging 108, Home Runs 115.

## Terrapin Park

**AKA**

Federal League Park, Oriole Park (V)

**ARCHITECT**

Otto G. Simonson

**OCCUPANTS**

FL Baltimore Terrapins April 13, 1914–October 2, 1915; NAL Baltimore Elite Giants April 1938–July 3, 1944

**LOCATION**

Left Field (N) 30th St, Third Base (W) Vineyard Ln, First Base (S) 29th St, Right Field (E) Greenmount Ave; on the NW corner of Greenmount and 29th, just across the street from the site of Oriole Parks (II) and (IV)

**DIMENSIONS**

Left Field: 300, 305 (1944)
Left Center: 422, 392 (1915)
Center Field corner: 450, 412 (1944)
Center Field: 384, 347 (1915), 384 (1916)
Right Center: 345, 336 (1915)
Right Field: 335, 310 (1944)
Backstop: 76 (1914)

**FENCES**

Left Field, Left Center: 25 (wood)
Center Field: 8
Right Field: 8 (wood and screen)

**CAPACITY**

16,000 (1914), 14,000 (1940)

**PHENOMENA**

Interior fence in 1915 ran from left edge of right field bleachers to the left field perimeter fence. This made dead center field only 347, which resulted in several home runs over the center field fence in 1915. ♦ Destroyed July 3–4, 1944, by a fire caused by holiday fireworks. ♦ The 1914–15 dimensions were based on 1915 Sanborn fire insurance map and 1914–15 ballpark photos.

## Maryland Baseball Park

**AKA**

Moore's Field

**OCCUPANTS**

ECL Baltimore Black Sox 1923–27, April–May 1928; ANL Baltimore Black Sox 1929; neutral site use for Negro World Series NNL Kansas City Monarchs vs. ECL Darby Hilldales games 3–4 in 1924 and NNL Chicago American Giants vs. ECL Atlantic City Bacharach Giants game three in 1926

## Druid Hill

**OCCUPANT**

ECL Baltimore Black Sox some games 1920s

**LOCATION**

Madison Ave, in Druid Hill Park

## Bugle Field

**AKA**

Miss Snyder's Cow Pasture

**OCCUPANTS**

NEWL Baltimore Black Sox April–June 1932; NNL Baltimore Black Sox 1933, July–September 1934

**LOCATION**

Biddle St, Edison Hwy

**PHENOMENA**

Named for the Bugle Coat and Apron Supply Company, Maryland's largest laundry. Joe Cambria, the chief scout for the Washington Senators, owned the laundry, the park, and the Black Sox with Marty Reinholdt.

## Venable Stadium

**AKA**

Babe Ruth Stadium 1949–50, Baltimore Stadium, Metropolitan Stadium, Municipal Stadium

**OCCUPANTS**

NNL Baltimore Elite Giants July 4–September 1944, 1945–48; NAL Baltimore Elite Giants 1949

**LOCATION**

Same as Memorial Stadium

**DIMENSIONS**

Left Field: 270, 291 (1949)
Right Field: 406, 291 (1949)

**CAPACITY**

78,000 (1923), 60,000 (1940), 80,000 (1941), 30,000 (1944), 76,658 (1947), 58, 917 (1948)

**PHENOMENA**

This was a football stadium which was converted for baseball use after Oriole Park (V) burned down

A capacity crowd of 46,354 at Baltimore's Memorial Stadium, which was originally designed for football.

on July 3–4, 1944, so the minor league Orioles and the Negro League Elite Giants would have a place to play. Later, it was torn down to make way for Memorial Stadium on the same site.

## Memorial Stadium

### ARCHITECT

L. P. Kooken Company

### OCCUPANT

AL Baltimore Orioles April 15, 1954–October 6, 1991

### LOCATION

Center Field (N) East 36th St, Third Base (W) Ellerslie Ave, Home Plate (S) 1000 East 33rd St (later Babe Ruth Plaza), First Base (E) Ednor Rd

### DIMENSIONS

Foul Lines: 309 (1954)

Alleys where 7-foot fence met 14-foot wall: 360 (1954)

Power Alleys: 446 (1954), 447 (1955), 405 (1956), 380 (1958), 370 (1962), 385 (1970), 375 (1976), 378 (1977), 376 (1980), 378 (1990)

Center Field: 445 (1954), 450 (1955), 425 (1956), 410 (1958), 400 (1976), 405 (1977), 410 (1978), 405 (1980)

Backstop: 78 (1954), 58 (1961), 54 (1980), 75 (1987), 65 (1991)

Foul Territory: large

### FENCES

Foul Line corners: 11.33 (concrete 1954), 14 (11 concrete below 3 plywood 1959); these walls bounced balls toward center, reducing triples

Left Center to Right Center: 10 (hedges April–May 1954), 8 (wire June 1954), 7 (wire 1955), 6 (wire 1958), 14 (wire 1961), 6 (wire 1963), 7 (canvas 1977)

**FORMER USE**

When Venable Stadium, a football stadium also used for baseball after the July 4, 1944, fire destroyed Oriole Park (III), was torn down in 1950 to make way for Memorial Stadium, home plate was moved from the north to the south.

**CURRENT USE**

Underwater, Gale's Lump oyster reef, five miles NE of Baltimore, constructed beneath Chesapeake Bay with the concrete from the stadium

**CAPACITY**

31,000 (1950), 47,855 (1953), 49,375 (1961), 52,184 (1965), 53,208 (1970), 54,076 (1986), 53,371 (1991)

**PHENOMENA**

Beautiful trees on an embankment beyond the fence in center. ♦ In April 1954, hedges served as the center field fence. In June 1954, a wire fence was erected which stood right in front of the high hedges. The top six feet of this fence were covered with canvas padding in 1958 after Harvey Kuenn cut his face trying to catch a home run ball by climbing the fence. The walls in the left and right field corners were also padded after Curt Blefary injured his hip chasing a Max Alvis fly. ♦ Fans yelled "O" (for Orioles) in unison when the singing of the "Star-Spangled Banner" reached "Oh, say does that star-spangled banner yet wave." ♦ Famous fan and taxi driver Wild Bill Hagy from Section 34 would twist his body to spell Orioles atop the home dugout. Oriole Landing was a picnic area in the upper deck in the 1960s. ♦ Wind helped hitters. ♦ Best crabcakes in baseball. Scoreboard crab races in bottom of sixth: Wee Willie in orange, Paco in blue, and Mugsy in yellow. ♦ Frank Robinson hit only homer completely out of the park May 8, 1966. ♦ Inscribed into concrete façade Memorial Wall: "Dedicated as a memorial to all who so valiantly fought in the world wars with eternal gratitude to those who made the supreme sacrifice to preserve equality and freedom throughout the world—time will not dim the glory of their deeds." ♦ All but Memorial Wall torn down November 2000–April 21, 2001, Memorial Wall torn down in February 2002.

## Camden Yards

**AKA**

Oriole Park at Camden Yards

**ARCHITECT**

HOK Sport

**OCCUPANT**

AL Baltimore Orioles April 6, 1992, to date

**LOCATION**

Left Field (N/NW) 333 West Camden St; Third Base (W/SW) Russell St; First Base (S/SE) Martin Luther King Blvd, Right Field (E/NE) Eutaw St, then Baltimore and Ohio (B&O) RR Warehouse, then Howard St; only two blocks from Babe Ruth's birthplace

**DIMENSIONS**

Left Field: 333, 340 (2001), 333 (2002)
Left Center: 364, 376 (2001), 364 (2002)
Deepest Left Center: 410, 417 (2001), 410 (2002)
Center Field: 400, 407 (2001), 400 (2002)
Right Center corner: 386
Right Center: 373, 393 (2001), 373 (2002)
Right Field: 318, 325 (2001), 318 (2002)
Backstop: 57.5, 50 (2001), 57 (2002)

**FENCES**

Left Field to Right Center: 7
Right Center to Right Field: 25

**FORMER USE**

Le Comte de Rochambeau, French general, camped his troops here on the way to Yorktown in 1781; Baltimore & Ohio RR Station

**CAPACITY**

48,079, 48,190 (2003), 48,290 (2005)

**PHENOMENA**

While constructing the park, the remains of Ruth's Café, a saloon run by Babe Ruth's father at 406 Conway St and Little Paca, were discovered under the loading docks of the B. Green Warehouse, in what is now center field. ♦ Just behind the fence in right, 432 feet from the plate, is the renovated Baltimore & Ohio (B&O) RR Warehouse, longest building on the East Coast, 1016 feet long, only 51 feet wide, housing Orioles offices. ♦ When this ballpark was just in the earliest infant stages of pre-planning, I was fortunate to spend three days with Larry Lucchino, then president of the Orioles, and his architectural adviser, Janet Marie Smith. I suggested they develop a pane of glass that, when hit by a batted ball from around 330 feet away, would shatter exactly 50% of the time, and would not break exactly 50% of the time. Then I suggested we put that glass into all the windows of the B & O Railroad Warehouse (also known as the Long Building) and use the warehouse as the right field wall for the ballpark, with the ground rule that if the ball broke the window it was a home run, and if it did not break the window it was in play (for a double, triple, inside-the-park homer, or single, or whatever). I reasoned that every newspaper and sports TV show in America would comment every night that the glass was hit about whether the glass had broken. Whim-sical? Yes! Unfair to those who think that the game of baseball should be entirely predictable and rational? Yes! But good for baseball? Yes! They liked the idea, but as you know, the warehouse is not the right field wall, because they needed to have room for the food court in the alleyway between the warehouse and what is now the right field wall. At least the warehouse was not destroyed! ♦ Right field lights are mounted on the roof of the warehouse. ♦ Each aisle seat features 1890s Orioles logo. ♦ Double-decked bullpens in left center. ♦ Three-league triple-header on June 6, 1992, hosted by Hagerstown (morning), Frederick (afternoon), Orioles (evening). ♦ Large Babe Ruth statue has Bambino incorrectly wearing a right-handed fielder's glove. ♦ Sportswriter John Steadman's measurements revealed left-center is only 352 rather than 364, deepest left-center is only 397 rather than 410, and right-center is only 363 rather than 373. ♦ Eutaw Street Walkway has bronze baseballs imprinted into the concrete to honor longest homers. ♦ Home plate moved back seven feet for 2001 season, but moved back the next year because batters' background was adversely affected.

Camden Yards, just two blocks from Babe Ruth's birthplace, opened on April 6, 1992. The first of the new retro parks, it features the huge B & O Railroad warehouse beyond the right field wall.

# Belleville, Illinois

## *Belleville High School Athletic Field*

**OCCUPANT**

Neutral site used by NAL Kansas City Monarchs August 7, 1950

# Birmingham, Alabama

## *Rickwood Field*

**OCCUPANTS**

NNL Birmingham Black Barons 1924–25, 1927–30; NAL Birmingham Black Barons 1937–38, 1940–61; neutral site used for Negro World Series game six in 1943, games one and three in 1944; NAL Raleigh Tigers June 7, 1959

**LOCATION**

Center Field (E) 11th St West; Third Base (N) 1137 West 2nd Ave; Home Plate (W) 12th St West; First Base (S) Seaboard Coast Line RR tracks

**DIMENSIONS**

Left Field: 405; 325 (1985)
Center Field: 470; 393 (1985)
Right Field: 334; 332 (1985)

**FENCES**

Left Field: 5
Left Center Scoreboard: 35
Center to Right Field: 15

**CURRENT USE**

Maintained very well, used for amateur games and for one Barons minor league game every summer

**CAPACITY**

9312 (1910), 15,000 (1940); 10,400 (1985); 10,800 (2006)

**PHENOMENA**

Opened August 18, 1910. Named for owner Richard Woodward. ♦ Patterned exactly after Forbes Field in

Rickwood Field is the oldest surviving professional baseball park in the United States. Built for the Birmingham Barons in 1910 by industrialist and team owner Rick Woodward, it is listed on the National Register of Historic Places.

Pittsburgh. ♦ Nobody ever won $500 by hitting a ball through the basketball net hung from the Mellow Yellow sign in right-center. ♦ Oldest minor league park still in use, since the Barons play one regular season game per year here. ♦ The oldest continually used ballpark is Labatt's Park in London, Ontario, where there have been three grandstands: the first built in 1877, although the field began use 11 years earlier in 1866; grandstand was completely rebuilt after floods in 1883 and 1937.

# Bloomfield, New Jersey

## *Sprague Field*

**AKA**

General Electric Field

**OCCUPANT**

NEWL Newark Browns 1932

**LOCATION**

Left Field (SW) Floyd Ave; Third Base (SE) La France Ave; First Base (NE) Bloomfield Ave; Right Field (NW) Arlington Ave

**DIMENSIONS**

Left Field: 330
Center Field: 385
Right Field: 325

**FENCES**

Left Field: 5
Left Center Scoreboard: 35
Center to Right Field: 15

**PHENOMENA**

Balls hit over the outfield fence in front of the laundry building were only doubles, because the laundry was so close to the plate.

# Bloomington, Minnesota

## *Metropolitan Stadium*

**AKA**

The Met, Metropolitan Area Stadium 1956, Bloomington Stadium 1956

**OCCUPANT**

AL Minnesota Twins April 21, 1961, to September 30, 1981

**LOCATION**

Left Field (E) 24th Ave South, then a cornfield; Third Base (N) West 78th St, then Met Center and I-494; First Base (W) 8001 Cedar Ave South/Hwy 77; Right Field (S) West 84th St (later Killebrew Dr)

**DIMENSIONS**

Left Field: 316, 329 (1961), 330 (1962), 344 (1965), 346 (1967), 330 (1975), 343 (1977)
Short Left Center: 365 (1961), 360 (1966), 373 (1972), 350 (1975), 346 (1976), 360 (1977)
Deep Left Center: 402 (1961), 435 (1965), 430 (1968), 410 (1975), 406 (1976)
Deep Left Center Corner: 430 (1965), 406 (1975)
Center Field: 405, 412 (1961), 430 (1965), 425 (1968), 410 (1975), 402 (1977)
Deep Right Center Corner: 430 (1965)
Deep Right Center: 402 (1961), 435 (1965), 430 (1968), 410 (1977)
Short Right Center: 365 (1961), 373 (1968), 365 (1972), 370 (1977)
Right Field: 316, 329 (1961), 330 (1962)
Backstop: 60

**SURFACE**

Grass

**FENCES**

Left Field: 8 (wire 1961), 12 (1964), 7 (1974), 12 (1977)

Metropolitan Stadium, just south of Minneapolis, was built on a farm in 1956 for the American Association Minneapolis Millers. In 1961, the Washington Senators relocated to Minneapolis and became the Twins, playing in the stadium until 1982, when the Twins and Vikings moved into the Metrodome in downtown Minneapolis. Three years later, Metropolitan Stadium was demolished to make way for the Mall of America.

Center Field: 8 (wire 1961)
Right Field: 8 (wire 1961), 12 (1964), 8 (1970)

**FORMER USE**
Cornfield

**CURRENT USE**
Mall of America shopping mall; home plate is displayed there between two amusement park rides

**CAPACITY**
14,979 (April 24, 1956), 18,200 (July 1956), 21,000 (1957), 30,637 (1961), 40,000 (1964), 45,921 (1973), 45,919 (1975)

**PHENOMENA**
When the Millers opened the stadium on April 24, 1956, a steal of home resulted in four different decisions by home plate ump Bill Phillips in the top of the fifth. When Wichita Brave shortstop Joe Koppe slid home, he was called out. The Braves manager protested the call, saying that Miller catcher Vern Rapp had dropped the ball. Umpire Phillips thought the Braves manager said that third base umpire John Mullen had called a balk, and then thought that he saw Mullen nod his head in agreement, so he called Koppe safe. The Millers manager protested this call, and asked Phillips to walk to third base and ask Mullen whether he had called a balk. Phillips agreed.

Mullen said he had not called a balk, so Phillips called Koppe out for a second time. The Braves manager protested this call, and asked Phillips to walk to third base again and ask Mullen whether Rupp had dropped the ball. Phillips agreed. Mullen said Rupp had indeed dropped the ball, so Phillips called Koppe safe for a second time. The Millers manager protested, but the decision stood. ✦ During the second game of the Junior World Series here on September 28, 1959, the Havana Sugar Kings made a fire in their dugout with paper in a wastebasket to keep themselves warm. ✦ The 330-foot marker from 1962 to 1981 was curiously far from the foul pole in right, raising the distinct possibility that the distance to right was actually significantly less than 330. ✦ In its time, likely the most poorly maintained ballpark ever in the majors. Broken railings on third deck overlooking bleachers in left created a distinct safety hazard in 1981. ✦ Third major league park ever built in a cornfield. The first was Walte's Pasture, home of 1875 NA Keokuk Westerns; second was South Street Park, home of 1878 NL Indianapolis Browns. ✦ Bomb scare delayed August 25, 1970, game as 17,967 fans filed calmly into the outfield and parking lots. ✦ Two fans watched the Opening Day game April 6, 1971, from a huge snowpile in the parking lot just beyond the outfield fence. ✦ Big scoreboard in right-center. ✦ Two decks of bleachers in left added in 1965. ✦ Mascot Twinkie the Loon roamed the stands in the last two years here, 1980–81. ✦ Torn down in 1985.

# Boston, Massachusetts

## South End Grounds (I)

**AKA**

Walpole Street Grounds (I)

**OCCUPANTS**

NA Boston Red Stockings May 16, 1871–October

30, 1875; NL Boston Red Caps April 29, 1876–September 10, 1887; NCL Boston Resolutes 1887; neutral site used by NA Hartford Dark Blues August 12, 1874

**LOCATION**

Center Field (NE) Railroad Roundhouse, then Gainsborough St; Third Base (NW) New York, New Haven, and Hartford (later Boston and Providence) RR tracks, then Huntington Avenue Baseball Grounds; Home Plate (SW) Walpole St; First Base (SE) Columbus Ave

**CAPACITY**

3000

**PHENOMENA**

Torn down in late September 1887 and replaced by South End Grounds (II).

## Dartmouth Grounds

**AKA**

Union Park 1884

**OCCUPANTS**

UA Boston Reds April 30–September 24, 1884; neutral use for Temple Cup Series NL Detroit Wolverines vs. AA St. Louis Browns October 18, 1887

**LOCATION**

Home Plate Irvington St, Third Base Dartmouth St, also Huntington Ave; near Copley Place in the Back Bay

**CURRENT USE**

Neiman-Marcus store at 5 Copley Place

**PHENOMENA**

Built as a bicycle racetrack. ✦ When used for Dauvray Cup game October 18, 1887, it was in horrible shape, having been abandoned for the previous three years.

## *South End Grounds (II)*

**AKA**

Grand Pavilion, Walpole Street Grounds (II), Union Baseball Grounds, Boston Baseball Grounds

**OCCUPANT**

NL Boston Beaneaters May 25, 1888–May 15, 1894

**LOCATION**

Same as South End Grounds (I)

**DIMENSIONS**

Left Field: 250
Left Center: 445
Center Field: 500
Right Center: 440
Right Field: 255

**CAPACITY**

6800 (1888)

**PHENOMENA**

This park and Congress Street Grounds were Boston's only double-deck ballparks ever. ◆ Six spires behind home. ◆ Fans could watch for free from Sullivan's Tower beyond the fence in right. ◆ Destroyed by the Great Roxbury Fire in bottom of third on May 16, 1894, during Beaneaters-Orioles game. The fire started in the right field bleachers and eventually destroyed 177 homes.

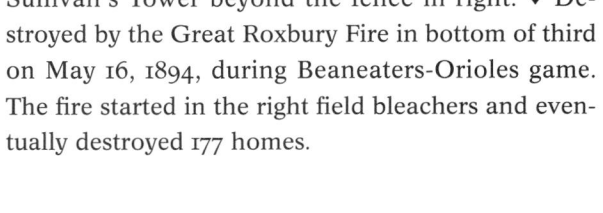

The grand pavilion of South End Grounds II in Boston on a chilly day.

The only known picture of the Congress Street Grounds pavilion shows it nearing completion for the 1890 Players League season, in which the Boston Reds won the short-lived league's lone pennant.

## Congress Street Grounds

**AKA**

Brotherhood Grounds

**OCCUPANTS**

PL Boston Reds April 19–September 10, 1890; AA Boston Reds April 18–October 3, 1891, NL Boston Beaneaters May 16–June 20, 1894

**LOCATION**

(NE) New York, New Haven, and Hartford RR tracks, (W) A St and B St, (S) Congress St; near the waterfront on Boston Harbor, adjacent to Fort Point Channel

**DIMENSIONS**

Left Field: 250
Center Field: 400

**FENCES**

Left Field to Center Field: 22 (wood)
Center Field to Right Field: 3 (wood)

**CURRENT USE**

Two commercial buildings at 368 and 374 Congress Street, built in 1901 and 1903 respectively. In 1910, the building at 374 Congress Street had a sign which read from top to bottom "Iron Steel Metals."

**CAPACITY**

16,500

**PHENOMENA**

The double-deck grandstand design was patterned after South End Grounds (II) because the same architect, John Joseph Deery of Philadelphia, designed them both. He also designed Baker Bowl in Philadelphia and Manhattan Field in New York City before disappearing in 1910. ♦ The entire wall in left and left-center was covered with an ad. The first line read "Read." The second line read "the Boston Herald." The third line read "for the best base ball reports." ♦ There were bleachers from dead center to right field, and a white flagpole was in play in right center, in front of the bleacher seats. ♦ Just as at Fenway Park, the seats down the left field line faced toward home, and came all the way to the foul line for the last 50 feet or so of the foul line.

## South End Grounds (III)

**AKA**

South Side Grounds

**OCCUPANT**

NL Boston Braves July 20, 1894–August 11, 1914

**LOCATION**

Same as South End Grounds (I) and (II)

**DIMENSIONS**

Left Field: 250, 275 (1912)
Left Center: 430, 387 (1908), 394 (1912)
Center Field: 416, 378 (1908), 394 (1912)
Right Center: 392, 382 (1908), 400 (1912)
Right Field: 255, 235 (1912)

**FENCES**

Center Field: 6
Right Field: 14 (1894), 20 (1897)

**CURRENT USE**

Ruggles MBTA subway station on Orange Line; cigar factory that stood behind the fence in right is still standing; twin spires from grandstand now stand on a newer building on Columbus Avenue

**CAPACITY**

5000, 6800 (1895), 10,000 (1908), 11,000 (1912)

**PHENOMENA**

This park was smaller than its predecessor, and the grandstand had only one deck rather than two decks, as did the former park. ♦ When South End Grounds (II) burned down, there wasn't enough insurance money to rebuild it as large as it had been. ♦ Two wings were added to the pavilion after the 1894 season. ♦ Incline in right field. ♦ Dimensions largely based on 1895 Sanborn fire insurance map.

## Huntington Avenue Baseball Grounds

**OCCUPANT**

AL Boston Red Sox May 8, 1901, to October 7, 1911

**LOCATION**

Left Field (NW) 400 Huntington Ave; Third Base

Fans try to see over the wall at the Huntington Avenue Grounds in 1903.

Huntington Avenue Grounds, home of the Red Sox, was built across the New York, New Haven, and Hartford Railroad tracks from the South End Grounds, home of the Boston Braves. It most likely had the deepest center field in the big leagues (530 feet).

(SW) Bryant Ave (later Rogers Ave, then Forsyth St); First Base (SE) New York, New Haven, and Hartford RR tracks; Right Field (NE) New Gravely St, Gainsborough St; just north of South End Grounds (III)

**DIMENSIONS**

Left Field: 350, 305 (1910)

Left Field at Huntington Ave Fence: 376

Left Field at left edge of Left Field Bleachers: 350 (1905)

Left Center: 433, 402 (1905)

Center Field: 530, 456 (1909)

Right Center: 412

Right Field at kink: 353

Right Field: 320

Backstop: 60

**FENCES**

14 (wood)

Scoreboard in Right Field: 28

Left Field-Center Field Bleachers: 6 (1905)

Third Base Bleachers in Left Field: 6 (1910)

**FORMER USE**

Circuses and carnivals

**CURRENT USE**

Cabot Cage (Godfrey Lowell Cabot Physical Education Center) at Northeastern University

**CAPACITY**

9000, 17,000 (1905)

**PHENOMENA**

Scene of first NL-AL World Series in 1903. ♦ Toolshed in deep center was in play. ♦ Bronze statue of Cy Young unveiled in 1993 at home plate where he pitched a perfect game May 5, 1904. ♦ Plaque in World Series Exhibit Room at Cabot Cage was unveiled on May 16, 1956, to commemorate the exact location of the left field foul pole. ♦ Dimensions based on 1901 ballpark diagram in the *Boston Globe* and ballpark photos for 1905 and 1910. ♦ Bleachers built in left field in front of the Huntington Ave fence before the 1905 season. Third base bleachers were extended into far left field in 1910.

The Braves occasionally played in Fenway Park, including the 1914 World Series, above, when they swept the favored Philadelphia Athletics in four games.

## *Fenway Park*

### AKA

American League Park 1912–14

### ARCHITECTS

Charles E. McLaughlin/Osborn Engineering 1912, Osborn Engineering 1934 renovation

### OCCUPANTS

AL Boston Red Sox April 20, 1912, to date; NL Boston Braves April 19, May 30, 1913, August 1 and 8, September 7 and 29, 1914, 1914 World Series, April 14–July 26, 1915, April 17 and 28, 1946

### LOCATION

Left Field (N) Lansdowne St (later Ted Williams Way), then Boston and Albany RR tracks and Mass Turnpike/I-90; Deep Left Field/Third Base Line (NW) Brookline Ave (running from SW to NE), Third Base (W) 24 Jersey St (later 4 Yawkey Way) (running from S/SE to N/NW); First Base (S) Van Ness St (built after ballpark, running from SW to NE); Right Field (E) Fenway Garage Bldg, then Ipswich St (running from S/SW to N/NE)

### DIMENSIONS

Left Field: 324, 320.5 (1926), 320 (1930), 318 (1931), 320 (1933), 308 (actual 1934), 312 (marked 1934), 315 (marked 1936), 310 (marked 1995)

Left Center: 377 (1914), 379 (1934)

Deep Left Center at flagpole: 388 (1934; flagpole removed from field of play in 1970)

Center Field: 458, 488 (1922), 421 (1926), 468 (1930), 388.67 (1934), 389.67 (1936)

Deepest Center corner behind the Center Field Bleachers: 496, 490 (actual 1931–33), 593 (recorded in official Bluebooks 1931–33)

Deepest Right Center corner: 420 (1934)

Right Center just right of deepest corner where bullpen begins: 380 (1939), 383 (1955)

Right of Right Center: 405 (1939), 382 (1940), 381 (1942), 380 (1943)

Right Field: 314, 313.5 (1921), 358.5 (1926), 358 (1930), 325 (1931), 358 (1933), 334 (1934), 332 (1936), 322 (1938), 332 (1939), 304 (1940), 302 (1942)

Backstop: 68, 62 (1914), 60 (1934)

Foul Territory: very small, tiniest in the majors

### FENCES

Left Field: 31 (25 wood on top of 6 inclined slope), 37.17 (tin over wooden railroad ties upper section and over concrete lower section 1934), 37.17 (hard plastic 1976)

Left Field wall to bleacher wall behind flagpole: 18 sloping to 17 (concrete 1934), (padding 1976) crash pad added from 18 inches to 6 feet on left and center field walls (1976)

Center Field: 10 (wood 1917), 8.75 (wood 1940)

Right Center bullpen fence: 5.25 (wood 1940)

Right Field wall and railing from bullpen: 3.42 sloping to 5.37 at foul pole, steel (1940)

Right Field Belly is the name for the low railing and wall that curve out from 302 marker at Right Field foul pole into deep Right Field; many a right fielder has watched helplessly as a 302-foot pop fly falls over the railing for a home run

**FORMER USE**

A swamp in the Fens section of Boston

**CAPACITY**

35,000, 33,368 (1960), 34,218 (1993), 33,993 (2001 evenings), 33,577 (2001 afternoons), 36,298 (2004), 35,095 (2005), 36,108 (2006)

**PHENOMENA**

Fans can sometimes really influence the game. In the eighth and last game of the 1912 World Series, on October 16, a fan threw a pop bottle at Giants left fielder Fred Snodgrass, causing him to drop a fly ball. The next batter's hit won the Series for the Red Sox. ♦ On July 8, 1918, in the first game of a doubleheader vs. the Indians, with one out and a runner on first, in the bottom of the 10th of a scoreless game, Red Sox left fielder Babe Ruth hit a fly ball which landed in the right field bleachers, but he was credited with only a

triple. On April 26, 1969, the Baseball Records Committee ruled that he should have been given a home run, and his career total should be 715 rather than 714, but the ruling has been ignored. ♦ Was it really 593 FEET to deepest center field in 1931–33, as the official Bluebooks for those years state? ♦ The deepest area behind the center field bleachers that was in-play was 490. A ball could theoretically reach this point by bouncing between the center field bleachers and the right field bleachers, and then rolling to the left, from the far right side of the center field bleachers to the far left side of the center field bleachers, along the outside wall behind the center field bleachers. ♦ Players have always assumed the Green Monster was closer than the 315 sign installed in 1936 would indicate. The foul line was measured by Art Keefe and George Sullivan in 1975 at 309 feet five inches. On October 19, 1975, the *Boston Globe*'s aerial photography measured it at 304.779 ft. Osborn Engineering's blueprints document the planned 1912 distance at 308 feet. The sign was finally changed from 315 to 310 in 1995; however, the persistent 315 number still appeared as late as 2003 in the AL Red Book. And underneath the padding, where it says 310 on the wall at the left field foul pole, the old 315 sign is still there, with a 310 spray-painted

The signature Green Monster was born in 1947 when the ads on the left field wall at Fenway Park were covered by green paint.

Watching the Fenway action from deep right field. The right field bullpen was constructed in 1940, one year after Ted Williams arrived, bringing the fences in by 23 feet.

nearby. ♦ There are four drainage pipe screens in fair territory in right field, where the dirt dips down three inches. ♦ Bowling alley at the intersection of Brookline Ave and Yawkey Way is attached to the park. Duffy's Cliff was a five- to six-foot-high incline in front of the left field wall 1912–33, extending from the foul pole to the flag pole in center, frequently and inaccurately reported as 10 feet high. It was named after Sox left fielder Duffy Lewis, who was the acknowledged master of defensive play on the cliff. It was greatly reduced but not completely eliminated in 1934. ♦ The Save Fenway Park organization has done tremendous work to save one of baseball's most cherished sites from the wrecking ball. ♦ The Green Monster in left completely dominates the field. A 23-ft., 7-in. net was placed atop the wall in 1936 to protect windows on Lansdowne St. ♦ Back in the 1930s and 1940s, tin covered the two-by-fours on the Monster. Balls hitting the tin over the two-by-fours had a live bounce, but balls hitting between the two-by-fours were dead and just dropped straight down. ♦ In 1947, the tin was replaced and all advertisements were removed from the Monster. ♦ A ladder starts near the upper-left corner of the score-board, 13 feet above ground, and rises to the top. This allowed groundskeepers to remove batting practice balls from the net, before seats were added to the top of the Monster in 2003. ♦ Balls that have hit uprights above the Wall, which should have been homers, have often been declared in play by the umpires. ♦ Green Monster scoreboard numbers—runs and hits: 16 inches by 16 inches, 3 pounds; errors, innings, pitcher's numbers: 12 inches by 16 inches, 2 pounds. ♦ No ball has ever been hit over the right field roof. ♦ Huge scoreboard added in 1976 above bleachers in center significantly altered wind currents. Wind usually helps batters. New press box built in late 1980s above home plate causes wind to swirl, pushing foul balls back into fair territory. ♦ Tom A. Yawkey's and his wife Jean R. Yawkey's initials, TAY and JRY, appear in Morse code in two vertical stripes on the scoreboard in left. ♦ The screen behind home plate, designed to protect fans and allow foul balls to roll back down onto the field of play, was the first of its kind in the majors. ♦ The low concrete base of the left and center field walls was padded after the 1975 World Series, when Fred Lynn crashed into the concrete wall in center. ♦ Infield grass was transplanted from Huntington Avenue Baseball Grounds to Fenway in 1912. ♦ Wooden bleachers were completed in center and right-center by 1912 World Series. Wooden bleachers stood on the left field line in foul territory, but they burned down, May 8, 1926. Charred remains were removed, increasing the size of foul territory. ♦ During the winter of 1933–34, all wooden grandstands were replaced with concrete and steel. A big fire on January 5, 1934, destroyed much of what had already been built, but all was finished for the 1934 season opener. ♦ In 1940, to help Ted Williams hit home runs, the Red Sox added the right field bullpens, called Williamsburg, reducing the distance to the fence by 23 feet. ♦ Seat 21, Row 37, Section 42 is painted red because Fenway's longest homer ever landed here. It was hit by Ted Williams, traveled 502 feet, and hit Albany construction worker Joe Boucher in the head, breaking his straw hat. ♦ Fenway is "where you can sit for hours and feel a security that does not exist anywhere else in the world."

## *Braves Field*

**AKA**

Bee Hive, Wigwam, National League Field April 17, 1936–April 29, 1941; Nickerson Field 1970s to date

**ARCHITECT**

Osborn Engineering

**OCCUPANTS**

NL Boston Braves August 18, 1915–September 29, 1935; NL Boston Bees April 17, 1936–April 23, 1941; NL Boston Braves April 29, 1941–September 21, 1952; AL Boston Red Sox 1915–16 World Series, October 3, 1916, and Sunday games April 28, 1929–May 29, 1932, because of a law saying no Sunday games could be played within 1000 feet of a church, which eliminated Fenway Park as a possible location for Sunday games during those three and a half years

The entrance to Braves Field in 1933.

## LOCATION

Left Field (N/NE) Boston and Albany RR tracks, then I-90/Mass Pike, Storrow Dr,  and Charles River; Third Base (W/NW) Babcock St; First Base (S/SW) Akimbo Rd, then Commonwealth Ave; Right Field (E/SE) 34 Gaffney St (later Harry Agganis Way)

## DIMENSIONS

Left Field: 402.5, 396 (September 1915), 402.42 (1921), 404 (1922), 402.5 (1926), 320 (April 21, 1928), 353.5 (July 24, 1928), 340 (1930), 353.67 (1931), 359 (1933), 353.67 (1934), 368 (1936), 350 (1940), 337 (1941), 334 (1942), 340 (1943), 337 (1944)

Left Center: 402.5, 396 (1916), 402.42 (1921), 404 (1922), 402.5 (1926), 330 (April 21, 1928), 359 (July 24, 1928), 365 (1942), 355 (1943)

Center Field: 461, 387 (April 21, 1928), 417 (July 24, 1928), 387.17 (1929), 394.5 (1930), 387.25 (1931), 417 (1933), 426 (1936), 407 (1937), 408 (1939), 385 (1940), 401 (1941), 375 (1942), 370 (1943), 390 (1944), 380 (1945), 370 (1946)

Deepest Right Center corner: 542

Right Center: 362 (1942), 355 (1943)

Right Field: 375, 369 (1916), 365 (1921), 310 (April 1928), 297.75 (1929), 297.92 (1931), 364 (1933), 297 (1936), 376 (1937), 378 (1938), 350 (1940), 340 (April 1943), 320 (July 1943), 340 (April 1944), 320 (May 1944), 340 (April 1946), 320 (May 1946), 318 (1947), 320 (1948), 319 (1948)

Backstop: 75, 60 (1936)

## FENCES

Left Field to Right Center: 10 (concrete), 8 (wood 1928), 20 (wood 1946), 25 (wood 1948), 19 (wood 1953)

Left Field scoreboard sides: 64 (1949); middle arch 68 (1949)

Left Center: 1 (gravestones July 1928)

Right Center exit gate: 8 (wire)

Right Field: 10 (6 screen above 4 wood)

## FORMER USE

Allston Golf Club

## CURRENT USE

Nickerson Field, home to Boston University Terriers football and WUSA soccer, some seats from down the right field line; also Myles Standish Dorms, three BU dorm towers built in what had been the seats behind third base and home plate; and the BU hockey rink where the seats down the left field foul line had been. The Gaffney Street first base/right field entrance building is now the headquarters for the BU police. The concrete outer wall in right and center also still exists. The right field foul line bleachers, extending from first base to the right field foul pole, still

When Braves Field opened in 1915 it became the first ballpark with more than 40,000 seats.

stand. Many of the seats now sit in a Rhode Island softball stadium. Plaque written by SABR to mark the site was dedicated August 6, 1988.

**CAPACITY**

40,000, 46,000 (1928), 41,700 (1937), 45,000 (1939), 37,746 (1941), 36,706 (1947), 44,500 (1952)

**PHENOMENA**

Changes in left field and right field dimensions 1915–27 are believed to be only corrections to listed dimensions. Dimensions 1915–27 based on 1924 Sanborn fire insurance map. ♦ The Jury Box was a moderate-sized bleacher section in right with very vocal fans. It got its name when a sportswriter once noticed that there were exactly 12 people sitting in its 2000 seats one day. ♦ A gap existed between the right field Jury Box and the first base pavilion to permit the fans access to the Jury Box bleachers. When the gap was closed off on the field side with a gate, the right field dimension was about 362–370, and if there was no gate, the foul line would have hit the side of the Jury Box and created a right field dimension of about 400 feet. ♦ In the 1940s, fir trees were planted beyond the fence in right-center in an unsuccessful attempt to hide huge clouds of locomotive smoke belching from the Boston and Albany tracks. ♦ Five thousand fans left the April 16, 1946, home opener with green paint on their clothing because that morning's paint job on the seats had not yet dried. The Braves paid $6000 in claims to irate fans, and played the rest of the month's home games at Fenway (April 17 and 28). ♦ Best food was the fried clams. ♦ Outfield fence moved more often than any other in major league history. ♦ Infield grass, transported from South End Grounds (II) in 1915, was kept very long by groundskeepers. ♦ Left field bleachers, installed in April 1928, were removed slowly from mid-June to the end of the season. ♦ Scoreboard moved from left center to right, also in 1928. ♦ The field was rotated slightly in a clockwise direction in the 1940s, resulting at times in the left field foul line being 337 and the right field foul line being 319. ♦ After the Braves moved to Milwaukee, the scoreboard was moved to Kansas City's Municipal Stadium in 1955. ♦ In 1984, under the old

right field bleachers, the author found an old ticket booth, turned on its side and covered with cobwebs, with a 32-year-old 1952 Boston Braves schedule still tacked to its wall. No matter how hard the new tries to cover up the old, the past manages to live on!

# Broad Ripple, Indiana

## *Bruce Grounds*

**AKA**

Fourth Street Grounds

**OCCUPANT**

AA Indianapolis Blues Sundays only May 18–September 21, 1884

**LOCATION**

(N) Bruce (later 23rd) St, (W) College Ave, (S) 21st St, (E) RR tracks; back then it was outside the city of Indianapolis, but today the site is within the city, since Broad Ripple was annexed by Indianapolis

# Brooklyn, New York

*See also* Jersey City, New Jersey; Newtown, New York; Weehawken, New Jersey; West New York, New Jersey

## *Union Grounds*

**AKA**

Union Skating Rink, Union Skating Pond

**OCCUPANTS**

NA Brooklyn Eckfords May 9, 1871–October 22,

1872; NA New York Mutuals May 25, 1871–October 29, 1875; NA Brooklyn Atlantics May 7, 1873–October 9, 1875; NL New York Mutuals April 25–October 17, 1876; NL Hartfords of Brooklyn April 30–September 21, 1877; AA Brooklyn Bridegrooms May 30–June 19, 1889; neutral site used by NA Troy Haymakers July 28, 1871; by NA Philadelphia Athletics October 30, 1871; by NA Elizabeth Resolutes June 12, 1873; by NL Providence Grays July 26, 1878

**LOCATION**

(NW) Hewes St, (SW) Lee Ave, (SE) Rutledge St, (NE) Harrison Ave, Marcy Ave now runs NW-SE through the site; in Williamsburg, just across the East River from lower Manhattan

**DIMENSIONS**

All fences more than 500

**FENCES**

6.5

**FORMER USE**

Union Skating Club's ice rink during the winter throughout the 1870s

**CURRENT USE**

Mosad Keren Hatzole Talmud/Torah store, IS 71 Juan Morel Campos International School, John Wayne Elementary School, New York National Guard 106th Maintenance Battalion armory built in 1883, brownstone housing in a Hasidic neighborhood

**CAPACITY**

2000

**PHENOMENA**

Built by William Cammeyer. Opened May 15, 1862, for baseball. ◆ First enclosed baseball field ever built. ◆ One-story building in right, 350 feet from the plate, was in play. ◆ Entrance was on Rutledge Street.

◆    ◆    ◆

# *Capitoline Grounds*

**AKA**

Capitoline Skating Pond, Union and Capitoline Grounds, Capitoline, Capitoline Skating Lake and Base Ball Ground

**OCCUPANT**

NA Brooklyn Atlantics May 6–October 9, 1872

**LOCATION**

(N/NW) Putnam Ave, (W/SW) Nostrand Ave, (S/SE) Halsey St, (E/NE) Marcy Ave (later Rev. Dr. Gardner C. Taylor Blvd); in Bedford-Stuyvesant, near the old location of 13th Regimental Armory (I), which was torn down in the late 1800s to build a railroad station; 13th Regimental Armory (II) was built ten blocks away to the NE at Sumner Ave and Jefferson Ave

**FORMER USE**

Part of a farm leased from the Lefferts family by Reuben S. Decker's father, Stephen

**CURRENT USE**

Construction on high school building on Putnam between Nostrand and Marcy was begun 1888, completed 1891, and used until 1976 for Boys' High School, then used for alternative high school called the Street Academy; Kingdom Hall of Jehovah's Witnesses; Most Worshipful Enoch Graham Lodge Star of Bethlehem Chapter

**PHENOMENA**

Built in 1862 by Reuben S. Decker as a skating pond. ◆ First used for baseball in 1865, three years after the Union Grounds were used for baseball. ◆ A batter hitting a home run over the top of the cone-shaped roof of a small round brick outhouse in deep right-center received a bottle of champagne. ◆ When Eddie Cuthbert stole second base here in 1865, everybody laughed at him. But when the umpires found nothing in the rulebook saying it was illegal, the laughter ended, and the stolen base had been invented! ♦ The Capitoline Grounds encompassed a huge area, including several ball diamonds. ♦ Entrance was on Nostrand, near Putnam.

## Washington Park (I)

**OCCUPANTS**

AA Brooklyn Bridegrooms May 5, 1884–May 5, 1889; neutral site used by AA New York Mets August 10, 1884 (rained out); by AA Cincinnati Reds October 10, 1884; by AA New York Mets October 8, 1887; for Temple Cup Series October 14 and 22, 1887, NL Detroit Wolverines vs. AA St. Louis Browns; for Temple Cup Series October 19, 1888, NL New York Gothams vs. AA St. Louis Browns

**LOCATION**

Left Field (N) Third St, Third Base (W) Fourth Ave, First Base (S) Fifth St, Right Field (E) Fifth Ave; in the Red Hook (now called Lawn Park Slope) section of Brooklyn, near the Gowanus Canal (beyond left field) and Bay Ridge RR tracks

**FORMER USE**

General George Washington used Gowanus House as his headquarters during the Battle of Long Island during the Revolutionary War, before it was captured by General Cornwallis. The house later served as a baseball clubhouse, but eventually was reduced to rubble by the early 20th century, when it was relocated about 50 yards and rebuilt. It still stands near the site of the ballpark. Facing 2000 English troops, 400 Maryland troops covered the right flank of General Washington's August 27, 1776, retreat during the Battle of Long Island. Of the 400 soldiers, 100 were wounded and 259 were killed in action.

**CURRENT USE**

J. J. Byrne Park, baseball is now played on a concrete field in what used to be right field

**PHENOMENA**

Opened May 12, 1883. ♦ Built down in a hollow. ♦ Destroyed by fire May 19, 1889. ♦ The first game on ice played here on January 12, 1884, between Field and Brooklyn.

## Washington Park (II)

**OCCUPANTS**

AA Brooklyn Bridegrooms June 20–October 5, 1889; NL Brooklyn Bridegrooms April 28–October 3, 1890

**LOCATION**

Same as Washington Park (I)

**CAPACITY**

3000, 8000 (1890)

## Eastern Park

**AKA**

Brotherhood Park 1890, Atlantic Park

**OCCUPANTS**

PL Brooklyn Wonders April 28–September 12, 1890; NL Brooklyn Bridegrooms April 27, 1891–October 2, 1897

**LOCATION**

(N) Eastern Parkway (now Pitkin Ave), (W) Powell St, (S) Sutter Ave, (E) Vesta Ave (later van Sinderen St); also Canarsie RR tracks, City Line and Brownsville Line Elevated RR tracks; in the East New York section of Brooklyn, near Jamaica Bay

**CAPACITY**

12,000

## *Washington Park (III)*

**OCCUPANT**

NL Brooklyn Bridegrooms April 30, 1898, to October 5, 1912

**LOCATION**

Left Field (W) Third Ave, then railyards and Gowanus Canal, Third Base (S) Third St, First Base (E) Fourth Ave, Right Field (N) First St; also Bay Ridge RR tracks; in Red Hook, just across intersection from the location of Washington Parks (I) and (II)

**DIMENSIONS**

Left Field: 335, 376 (1901), 375.95 (1908)
Left Center: 455 (1901), 415 (1908)
Deep Left Center (at the Center Field corner): 500, 443.5 (1908)
Center Field: 417, 424.7 (1908)

Right Center: 300, 340 (1901), 349 (1908)
Right Field: 215, 295 (1899), 301.84 (1908)
Backstop: 90, 15 (1908)
Foul Territory: small by 1908

**FENCES**

Left and Center Fields: 12 (brick)
Center Field Bleachers: 8 (1908)
Right Field: 42 (13 brick, then 29 canvas 1898), 13 (brick 1902), 20 (brick 1905)

**CAPACITY**

18,000 (1898), 16,000 (1912)

**PHENOMENA**

Giants right fielder Archie "Moonlight" Graham made his only major league appearance here on June 29, 1905, with no at-bats and no defensive chances. Dr. Graham was played by Burt Lancaster in the

After the Dodgers moved out of Washington Park, above, for the new Ebbets Field in 1913, it was used by the Brooklyn entry in the Federal League.

movie *Field of Dreams,* but the movie erroneously placed his appearance in 1922 rather than in 1905. ♦ The shape of right field in 1898 was very unusual. The fence abruptly cut directly in toward the plate in right center so as to go around a stone building (Gowanus House), making right center and right field very short, while deep left center and center field were very distant. ♦ The 215 right field dimension for 1898, reported in a newspaper article, is likely in error. ♦ The dimensions for 1901–12 are based on a 1906 Sanborn fire insurance map. ♦ Bleachers added in center field in 1908 and cut the center field corner distance from 500 to 444. ♦ Air was putrid because of the nearby factories and canal. ♦ Fans could watch from apartments called Ginney Flats across the street from the right field wall. ♦ At the top of the 220-foot-high flag pole behind the scoreboard in center was the mast of the America's Cup defender *Reliance.* ♦ Orioles forfeited the first game of doubleheader to the Superbas October 14, 1899, when Oriole right fielder Sheckard attacked the umpire after being called out at second stealing.

## *Washington Park (IV)*

**ARCHITECT**
    Zachary Taylor Davis

**OCCUPANT**
    FL Brooklyn Brook-Feds May 11, 1914, to September 30, 1915

**LOCATION**
    Same as for Washington Park (III), but orientation was different; the diamond was moved a considerable distance north-westward from where it had been, resulting in very different left field dimensions

**DIMENSIONS**
    Left Field: 330
    Left Center: 363
    Center Field: 435
    Right Center: 345
    Right Field: 275

**FENCES**
    Left Field Bleachers: 8
    Left Center to Center: 12 (brick)
    Center to Right: 20 (brick)
    Center Field Scoreboard: 40

**CURRENT USE**
    20-foot brick walls along Third Avenue and 1st Street still stand in Con Ed storage yard used for equipment, cars, and trucks at 222 1st Street. It is likely that the Third Avenue wall was part of the left field wall behind the left field bleachers. The 1st Street wall was part of the right-center field wall. Extensive research by Tom Gilbert and Alan Gottlieb has determined that both walls were part of Washington Park (III) that were saved and incorporated into Washington Park (IV).

**CAPACITY**
    18,800

**PHENOMENA**
    Brook-Feds rebuilt the grandstands in 1914 and put Native American symbols on the outfield walls. ♦ Left field clubhouse started out as a horse stable for fans' horses. It was supposedly once used for a doctor's office after the ballpark was torn down, but there's no proof of that. ♦ A rebuilt Gowanus House stands nearby, where General George Washington directed American forces during the Revolutionary War Battle of Long Island. ♦ The center field scoreboard stood on legs, and a ball hit between the legs was in play in early 1914, so the center fielder had to run under the scoreboard to recover the ball. ♦ The large raised scoreboard, built for the Federal League Tip Tops, was situated diagonally in the center field corner. ♦ In July 1914, a net was hung below the scoreboard. It reached down to the field and was in play. ♦ Dimensions based on 1906 Sanborn fire insurance map, photos, illustrations in Marc Okkonen's *The Federal League of 1914–1915,* and analysis of home run data by field. Torn down in 1926.

Ray Caldwell of the Yankees pitches in the first game played at Ebbets Field, a 3–2 exhibition win by Brooklyn before 30,000 fans on April 5, 1913. Casey Stengel started the Brooklyn scoring with an inside-the-park home run off Caldwell.

## *Ebbets Field*

### ARCHITECT

Clarence Randall Van Buskirk

### OCCUPANTS

NL Brooklyn Dodgers April 9, 1913–September 24, 1957; NNL Brooklyn Eagles 1935

### LOCATION

Left Field (N/NE) Montgomery St, Third Base (W/NW) Franklin Ave (later Cedar Pl, later McKeever Place), First Base (S/SW) 55 Sullivan Place, Right Field (E/SE) Bedford Ave, in the Pigtown/Crown Heights area of Flatbush

### DIMENSIONS

Left Field: 419, 410 (1914), 383 (September 1920), 383.67 (1921), 382.83 (1929), 384 (1930), 353 (1931), 356.33 (1934), 365 (1938), 357 (1939), 365 (1940), 356 (1942), 357 (1947), 343 (1948), 348 (1953), 343 (1955), 348 (1957)

Left Center: 391 (September 1920), 365 (1931), 351 (1948)

Deep Left Center at bend in wall: 407 (1931), 393 (1948), 395 (1954)

Center Field: 508, 500 (1914), 399.42 (1931), 399 (1936), 402 (1938), 400 (1939), 399 (1947), 384 (1948), 393 (1955)

Right side of Center Field grandstand: 390 (1931), 376 (1948)

Right Center's deepest corner: 415 (1931), 403 (1948), 405 (1950), 403 (1955) Right side of Right Center exit gate 399 (1931)

Right Center: 384, 378 (1914)

Scoreboard left side: 344, right side 318 (1931)

Right Field: 301, 300 (1914), 296.17 (1921), 292 (1922), 301 (1926), 296.08 (1930), 295.92 (1931), 296.5 (1934), 297 (1938)

Backstop: 64 (1942), 70.5 (1954), 72 (1957)

### FENCES

Left Field to Left Center: 20 (concrete concave wall, bent at 9.5 midpoint, vertical top half, concave angled bottom half), 2.5 (wood September and 1920 World Series), 9.87 (concrete 1931)

Center Field: 20 (concrete), at 393 marker 9.87 (concrete 1931), 28 (13 screen above 15 sloping concrete 1931)

Right Center: 19 (concrete)

Right Center to Right Field: 19 (concrete concave wall, bent at 9.5 midpoint, vertical top half, concave angled bottom half), 19 (concrete 19 with additional 19 screen above but out of play August 31, 1930, through 1935), 38 (19 top screen, 19 bottom concrete 1936)

Right Field Scoreboard from 344 marker at left side to 318 marker at right side: 34 (1931)

Right Field Scoreboard Clock: 38 (1931)

**FORMER USE**

Pigtown garbage dump

**CURRENT USE**

Gas station behind the right field fence on Bedford is now a combined Kentucky Fried Chicken/Pizza Hut Express. Ebbets Field Apartments housing development was built in 1963. IS 320 Intermediate School is across the road. Apartments were renamed Jackie Robinson Apartments at Ebbets Field in 1972. Jackie Robinson School, previously known as Crown Heights School, houses the Brooklyn Dodger Hall of Fame, just across the street from what was third base. Now in a West Indian neighborhood. Medgar Evers College of City University of New York is nearby.

**CAPACITY**

18,000, 24,000 (June 30, 1913), 30,000 (1914), 26,000 (1924), 28,000 (1926), 32,000 (1932), 35,000 (1937), 32,000 (1938), 34,219 (1940), 32,000 (1946), 31,903 (1957)

**PHENOMENA**

1913–19 dimensions were based on original plans for Ebbets Field. ♦ As an experiment, yellow baseballs were used during the first game of the August 2, 1938, doubleheader here. ♦ Home plate in the visitors bullpen on the first base side was painted yellow, because Cards manager Fred Hutchinson complained that it was always so dirty his pitchers who were warming up could not even see it. ♦ The right field screen was put up on August 27, 1930, when the team was on a road trip. ♦ The first game played with the screen in place was August 31, 1930. ♦ Because the screen was slightly behind the top of the right field wall, it was considered "out of play" through the 1935 season, so balls hitting the screen then were home runs. ♦ The right field scoreboard was put up for the 1931 season, and balls hitting it were "in play." So from 1931–35, a ball hitting the scoreboard was "in play," but a ball hitting the screen on either side of the scoreboard was a home run. Starting in the 1936 season, balls hitting both the screen and the scoreboard were in play. ♦ The scoreboard clock was in play (unlike the scoreboard clock at Forbes Field in Pittsburgh, where a ball hitting the scoreboard was "in play" but one hitting the clock was a home run). ♦ There was also a 13-foot-high green canvas center field screen atop the

The flag-raising ceremony on May 8, 1942, before the first twilight game in 24 years at Ebbets Field. The Dodgers topped the Giants 7–6. With more than 24,000 fans on hand, nearly $60,000 was raised for the Navy Relief Fund.

15-foot high center field wall (total height 28 feet). This was used as a background to help the batters see the ball. This screen, which first appeared in 1930, was taken down to allow extra seating when the Dodgers expected a big crowd. ♦ Babe Herman lost a homer when his drive hit this center field screen on April 30, 1931. During a doubleheader on June 16, 1940, Lonnie Frey's drive hit the right field screen and dropped down onto the top of the wall, bounced several times, and then came to rest atop the wall, so he got an inside-the-park home run. ♦ The Abe Stark sign offered a free suit at 1514 Pitkin Avenue to any batter hitting the 3-foot-by-30-foot sign. Woody English of the Dodgers was the only batter to ever hit it, on June 6, 1937. ♦ When the park was opened in 1913, it was discovered that the flag, a press box, and keys to the bleachers had been forgotten. The press box was finally added in 1929. ♦ In the 1910s, there was a dirt walkway between the mound and the plate, which later disappeared. ♦ Little kids watched the game through a gap under the metal gate in right-center. This was how the term "knothole gang" got started. ♦ There was much confusion about distances to left since the left field foul line and the grandstand wall

were the same in the left field corner. ♦ It was 343 to the front of the grandstand wall and 357 to the foul pole. ♦ The Rotunda was the 27-foot-high domed entrance area, 80 feet in diameter, enclosed in Italian marble, with a floor tiled with stitches of a baseball, and a chandelier with 12 baseball-bat arms holding 12 globe-shaped baseballs. ♦ There were 12 turnstiles and 12 gilded ticket windows. ♦ Braves hitter Bama Rowell hit a blast off Dodger pitcher Hank Behrman in the second inning of the second game of a doubleheader, at 4:25 on May 30, 1946, which broke the right field scoreboard's Bulova clock, raining glass down onto Dodger right fielder Dixie Walker. The ball was "in play" and Rowell got a double, but the clock "kept on ticking" for another hour, not stopping until exactly one hour later, at 5:25. The Bulova Company had promised a free watch to anyone who hit the clock, but Rowell did not receive his free watch until 41 years later, on Bama Rowell Day in his hometown of Citronelle, Alabama. This incident inspired Roy Hobbs' pennant-winning homer in the 1952 novel *The Natural* by Bernard Malamud and the movie starring Robert Redford. ♦ First-ever major league game called due to fog happened here June 6, 1957. The right field wall

Sandy Koufax and Sal Maglie warm up at Ebbets Field on August 25, 1957, during a 6–5 Brooklyn win over St. Louis, nearing the end of the Dodgers' tenure in Brooklyn. The famed Abe Stark sign and the angled right field wall are in full view.

Dexter Park played host to some of baseball's greatest, including Josh Gibson, Joe DiMaggio, Satchel Paige, Jackie Robinson, and Lou Gehrig. In 1935, the recently retired Babe Ruth hit a homer here off 44-year-old Dazzy Vance.

and scoreboard had 289 different angles. ♦ George Cutshaw of Dodgers hit a ground-ball home run in 1916, which bounced crazily up the concave wall in right and over the top of the wall, to the amazement of Phils right fielder Gavvy Cravath. ♦ The scoreboard jutted out five feet from the wall at a 45-degree angle. ♦ Overhang of the center field second deck hung out over the field. ♦ Schaefer Beer sign on the top of the right center scoreboard notified fans of official scorer's decision—the "H" in Schaefer lit up for a hit, the first "E" for an error. ♦ Roger Kahn described the park as "a narrow cockpit of iron and concrete along a steep cobblestone slope." ♦ Cobblestoned Bedford Avenue was hilly, climbing from a low point in right to higher ground in center. ♦ Demolition began on February 23, 1960. Eight light towers were moved to Downing Stadium on Randall's Island. The same wrecking ball was used four years later to demolish the Polo Grounds.

## Dexter Park

**AKA**

Sterling Oval, Bushwick Park

**OCCUPANTS**

ECL Brooklyn Royal Giants 1923–27; neutral site used by NNL New York Cubans and NNL New York Black Yankees 1930s–1940s

**LOCATION**

Left Field (N) Simpson St (later 1 Park Ln South); Third Base (W) Elderts Ln (later Dexter Ct), then Cypress Hills Cemetery, which is where Jackie Robinson is buried; First Base (S) Bushwick (later Jamaica) Ave; Right Field (E) Lott Ave (later 76th St); overlooked by Franklin K. Lane High School; in Woodhaven area of Queens

**DIMENSIONS**

Left Field: 430

Left Center: 418

Center Field: 431

Right Center: 443

Right Field: 310

**CAPACITY**

3000 (1918), 8850 (1922), 15,400 (1937)

**FORMER USE**

Horse stables for racehorses before 1857, Woodruff's Hotel 1857–80

**CURRENT USE**

Elderts Lane subway stop on Jamaica Avenue for the J and Z lines; plaque in the parking lot of the Town Supermarket states, "Home Plate at Dexter Court and Jamaica Avenue 1911–55 Joe DiMaggio, Casey Stengel, Jackie Robinson, Satchel Paige, Phil Rizzuto, Hank Greenberg, Lou Gehrig, Babe Ruth, Josh Gibson all played here

**PHENOMENA**

Most creative outfield wall billboard ever. An optician's ad read: "Don't Kill the Umpire–Maybe It's Your Eyes." ♦ First used for baseball in 1885. ♦ Owners Max Rosner and Nat Strong operated the semipro Brooklyn Bushwicks here, beginning in 1918, and built a new concrete-and-steel grandstand in 1922. ♦ Josh Gibson hit a mammoth homer here over the 30-foot high wall behind the left-center bleachers at the 418 sign. ♦ Big incline in right field was partly caused by horses buried under the grass, including a famous racehorse named Dexter, immortalized in a Currier and Ives 1866 print. ♦ Lights installed here for the first ever night game in the New York area, and the second ever on the East Coast, on July 23, 1930. First night game on East Coast was July 3, 1930, in Buffalo. ♦ Scoreboard in left-center was moved to left field when the racetrack was installed in 1951. ♦ Stock cars raced here 1951–56. ♦ Last game was May 18, 1957, between St.

John's University and City College of New York (CCNY). ♦ Park torn down in June 1957.

---

# Buffalo, New York

## *Riverside Grounds*

**AKA**

Riverside Park

**OCCUPANT**

NL Buffalo Bisons May 1, 1879–September 8, 1883

**LOCATION**

(N) Rhode Island St, (W) Fargo Ave, (S) Vermont St, (E) West Ave

**DIMENSIONS**

Foul Lines: 210

Power Alleys: 400

Left/Right Center: 425

Center Field: 410

Backstop: 37

**CURRENT USE**

Residential area

**CAPACITY**

3000

**PHENOMENA**

A foul ball hit over the left field fence, across West Ave, and into a cottage at 599 West Avenue, broke Lizzie Bluett's collarbone on May 21, 1881. Her cottage is still standing. ♦ Dimensions based on park diagram (by SABR's Howard Henry) derived from two Buffalo city atlases (1884, 1894) and park photos.

♦  ♦  ♦

## Olympic Park (I)

**AKA**

Richmond Ave Grounds

**OCCUPANT**

NL Buffalo Bisons May 21, 1884–October 7, 1885

**LOCATION**

(N) Bryant St, (W) Richmond Ave, (S) Summer St, (E) Howard (later Norwood) Ave

**CAPACITY**

4000

**PHENOMENA**

The diamond faced to the north with home plate located on Summer Street between Richmond and Howard Avenues. ♦ Park consisted of a covered grandstand and bleachers on each end of the grandstand. ♦ Grandstand, in the shape of one half of an octagon, was about 280 feet in length. ♦ Total cost of construction was about $6000. ♦ Scene of record low major league crowd, when a total of 12 fans paid a total gate of $4.50 to see the last National League game ever played in Buffalo. ♦ After use by the NL, the International League played here for three seasons 1886–88. ♦ Stands dismantled and moved to Michigan Avenue near Ferry Street in the fall of 1888 to become Olympic Park (II). ♦ Park configuration data from article by Joseph M. Overfield in Niagara Frontier, a publication of the Niagara Historical Society (Summer 1955).

## Olympic Park (II)

**AKA**

Buffalo Baseball Park

**OCCUPANT**

PL Buffalo Bisons April 19–October 4, 1890

**LOCATION**

Left Field (E) Masten St, Third Base (N) East Ferry St, Home Plate (NW) Covenant Presbyterian Church, First Base (W) 1515 Michigan Ave, Right Field (S) Woodlawn Ave; same site was used later for Offermann Stadium

## International Fair Association Grounds

**AKA**

Federal League Base Ball Park

**ARCHITECT**

Mosler & Summers (Contractors)

**OCCUPANT**

FL Buffalo Buf-Feds May 11, 1914–September 29, 1915

**LOCATION**

(N) Northland Ave, (W) Lonsdale Rd, (S) Boston Ave (later Hamlin Rd)

**DIMENSIONS**

Left Field: 334
Left Center: 344
Center Field: 400
Right Center: 320
Right Field: 312
Backstop: 61

**CAPACITY**

20,000

**PHENOMENA**

A rather small park—the foul line dimensions overstate the apparent size. ♦ The foul lines missed the left field and right field bleachers, creating notches in both the left field and right field corners. ♦ Straightaway left field was 317 while straightaway right field was just 294. ♦ Dimensions based on a 1914 Sanborn fire insurance map.

The Jacobs brothers—Marvin, Charles, and Louis—who made their money selling peanuts at sports parks, were part of a local group that purchased the failing Buffalo Bison franchise and built Offermann Stadium in 1921.

## *Offermann Stadium*

### AKA
Robertson Park 1924, Bison Stadium 1925–34

### OCCUPANTS
Neutral site used by NNL New York Black Yankees 1940s, NAL Indianapolis Clowns 1951–55

### LOCATION
Same as Olympic Park (II)

### DIMENSIONS
Left Field: 321
Left Field Power Alley: 325
Left Center: 334
Right of Left Center: 346
Center Field: 380
Right of Center Field at left edge of Scoreboard: 400
Right Center (about the right edge of Scoreboard): 387
Right of Right Center: 366
Right Field Power Alley: 348
Right Field: 297
Backstop: 60

### FENCES
Left Field: 12 (concrete 1924), 22 (concrete topped with 12 wood in two tiers to block view of spectators in wildcat bleachers across the street on Masten St, 1934), 32 (concrete, wood and wire June 16, 1947)
Left Center: 15 (1924), 26 (wood 1926)
Center Field Scoreboard: 40 (wood 1924), 60 (wood 1934)
Right Center to Right: 12 (concrete 1924)

### CURRENT USE
Torn down in 1960 to make way for a junior high school, then Covenant Presbyterian Church, and now the Bethel Head Start Program. Dimensions based on park diagram, Sanborn map, and original plans researched by Buffalo ballpark expert Howard Henry

### CAPACITY
15,000 (1940)

**PHENOMENA**

First night game on the East Coast played here July 3, 1930. ♦ Henry Aaron, age 18 and a shortstop with the Indianapolis Clowns, was scouted here and signed by the Boston Braves.

# Butler, Pennsylvania

## *Butler Field*

**OCCUPANT**

Neutral site used by NNL Homestead Grays some games 1935–36

**LOCATION**

Center Field (S), Third Base (E), Home Plate (N), First Base (W)

**DIMENSIONS**

Left Field: 356 (1940)
Center Field: 486 (1940)
Right Field: 351

**CAPACITY**

2700 (1940)

# Camden, New Jersey

## *Razzberry Park*

**OCCUPANT**

Neutral site used by ECL Philadelphia Hilldales ten games June–September 1923

**LOCATION**

Third St, Erie St

# Canton, Ohio

## *Mahaffey Park*

**OCCUPANTS**

Neutral site used by NL Pittsburgh Burghers September 18, 1890; by AL Cleveland Blues June 15, 1902, May 10 and June 21, 1903; by NEWL Pittsburgh Crawfords PM game August 8, 1932

**LOCATION**

Center Field (NE), Third Base (NW), Home Plate (SW), First Base (SE)

**DIMENSIONS**

Left Field: 340 (1940)
Center Field: 410 (1940)
Right Field: 266 (1940)

**CAPACITY**

2650 (1902), 4000 (1940)

**PHENOMENA**

Short left field and right field fences. Balls hit over left field fence in 1902 were doubles. ♦ Highest altitude (1125 feet above sea level) ever for an AL game, and for a major league game before Rockies came into being in 1993. ♦ Ticket turnstiles from the St. Louis Exposition were installed here after being obtained from a Chicago wrecking company.

# Charlotte, New York

## *Ontario Beach Grounds*

**OCCUPANT**

Neutral site used by NL Cleveland Spiders August 28, 1898

**LOCATION**

(NW) railroad tracks; (SW) private property; (SE) Genesee River, Lake Ontario; (NE) Charlotte Beach Ave; on Genesee River, near Lake Ontario, one mile NW of Windsor Beach ballpark in Irondequoit, back then in town of Charlotte, New York, but now in Rochester, New York

---

# Charlotte, North Carolina

## *Griffith Park*

**AKA**

Crockett Park, Knights Park

**OCCUPANT**

Neutral site used by NAL Raleigh Tigers May 14, 1961

**LOCATION**

400 Magnolia Ave; Center Field (W), Third Base (S), Home Plate (E), First Base (N)

**DIMENSIONS**

Left Field: 289 (1940), 320 (1987)
Center Field: 410 (1940), 390 (1987)
Right Field: 308 (1940), 320 (1987)

**CAPACITY**

3200 (1940), 6500 (1960), 5500 (1985), 3000 (1988)

**PHENOMENA**

Rebuilt immediately after a fire in March 1987.

---

# Chattanooga, Tennessee

## *Engel Stadium*

**OCCUPANTS**

Neutral site used by NNL Nashville Elite Giants in 1930s; NAL Raleigh Tigers June 6, 1959

**LOCATION**

Center Field (NE), Third Base (NW), Home Plate (SW), First Base (SE)

At Engel Stadium, home park of the Chattanooga Lookouts for more than 30 years, a train would emerge from the scoreboard each time a Lookout player hit a home run.

## DIMENSIONS

Left Field: 377 (1940), 368 (1988)
Left side of the Left Center Scoreboard: 355 (1988)
Center Field: 485 (1940), 471 (1988)
Right Field: 330 (1940), 324 (marked 1988), 318 (actual 1988)

## CURRENT USE

Minor league ballpark

## FENCES

Left Center Scoreboard: 42 in the middle, 32 at the left and right side of the curving top
Rest of the outfield: 22

## CAPACITY

10,000 (1930), 8000 (1988), 7480 (1989)

## PHENOMENA

Built in 1930 to replace Andrews Field, built on the same site in 1909. ♦ Five-foot incline with rose bush garden in center was in play. Only incline in history to not have sloping sides. ♦ Joe Engel ran the minor league Lookouts and had great promotions—free Christmas evening turkey dinners in the outfield, Donald Duck Egg Laying Contest, Great Wild Elephant Hunt, Great Toy Bulldog-Jackrabbit Chase.

---

# Chicago, Illinois

## *White Stocking Grounds*

### AKA

Lake Front Park, Union Base-Ball Grounds, Chicago Base-Ball Grounds (I), Lake Shore Park, Lake Street Dumping Ground, the Dump

### OCCUPANTS

NA Chicago White Stockings May 8–September 29, 1871; neutral site use by NA Rockford Forest Citys August 8, 1871

### LOCATION

Left Field (E) Illinois Central RR tracks, then Lake Michigan; Third Base (N) Randolph St; First Base (W) Michigan Ave; Right Field (S) Madison St

### DIMENSIONS

Foul Lines: 375

### FENCES

6 (wood)

### FORMER USE

Dumping ground

### CURRENT USE

Millennium Park (City of Chicago park)

### CAPACITY

7000

### PHENOMENA

Burned down by Mrs. O'Leary's cow during the Great Chicago Fire of October 8–11, 1871. ♦ Back then Lake Michigan came almost to the Illinois Central RR tracks. Much of the land has now been filled in. ♦ Back then the southern boundary was between what is now Madison and Washington. Although Washington is closer to what was then the boundary than Madison, Washington was then inside the park, so Madison is a better descriptor of the boundary than is Washington.

## *23rd Street Grounds*

### AKA

State Street Grounds, 23rd Street Park, Base Ball Park

### OCCUPANTS

NA Chicago White Stockings May 13, 1874–October

2, 1875; NL Chicago White Stockings May 10, 1876–October 5, 1877; neutral site used by NA Cleveland Forest Citys May 29–30, 1872; by NA Troy Haymakers June 17, 20, 24, July 4, 1872; by NA Philadelphia White Stockings August 16, 1873

**LOCATION**

Home Plate (N) 22nd St (later Cermak Rd), First Base (W) Clark St, Center Field (S) 23rd St, Third Base (E) Burnside St (later Dearborn St)

**CAPACITY**

7000; 11,000 (1877)

**PHENOMENA**

When the park was first built in 1872, a large pavilion seating up to 2000 people was set up on the north side of the ground (along 23rd Street) behind home plate. Additional seating was also constructed on the west side of the park (along Clark Street and adjacent to a side track of the Michigan Southern railroad) which seated up to 5000 persons. ◆ On July 15, 1874 a large fire in downtown Chicago forced the visiting Philadelphia Athletics to change hotels and burned out the lodgings of a number of the White Stockings. ◆ The game played that day on the 23rd Street Grounds drew only 500 to 600 fans (instead of the expected 5000 to 6000). ◆ Batters faced in a southern direction.

## *White Stocking Park*

**AKA**

Lake Front Park, Lake Park, Chicago Base-Ball Grounds (II)

**OCCUPANTS**

NL Chicago White Stockings May 14, 1878–October 11, 1884; UA Chicago Browns some games 1884

**LOCATION**

Left Field (W) Michigan Ave, Third Base (S) Washington St, First Base (E) Illinois Central RR tracks and switchyards, Right Field (N) Randolph St; same site as White Stocking Grounds, but oriented differently

**DIMENSIONS**

Left Field: 186 (1883), 180 (1884)
Left Center: 280
Center Field: 300
Right Center: 252
Right Field: 196

**FENCES**

Left Field to Right Center: 6 (wood)
Right Field: 37.5 (17.5 tarp above 20 wood)

**CAPACITY**

3000, 5000 (1883), 10,000 (1884)

**CURRENT USE**

Old Post Office and a small city park across from Public Library, above the Grant Park underground parking garage

**PHENOMENA**

Infield was bumpy and uneven, littered with stones, boulders, ashes, glass, and broken bottles. ◆ The First Cavalry Band played at the bandstand pagoda overlooking the main entrance. Shortest ever Foul Lines: in the major leagues–186 to left in 1883 and only 180 in 1884, 196 to right. ◆ Hits over the fence in left were doubles in 1883 but homers in 1884 in spite of the fact that it was six feet shorter in 1884. ◆ In 1884, Ned Williamson hit 27 homers (25 at home) to set a ML season record not broken until Babe Ruth hit 29 in 1919.

## *South Side Park (I)*

**AKA**

Union Ball Park, Chicago Cricket Club Grounds (I), 39th Street Grounds (I)

**OCCUPANT**

UA Chicago Browns May 2–August 1, 1884

**LOCATION**

(W) South Wabash Ave, (S) West 39th St (later West Pershing Rd), (E) South Michigan Ave

## West Side Park (I)

**AKA**

Congress Street Grounds, Loomis Race Track, Loomis Street Park

**OCCUPANTS**

NL Chicago White Stockings June 6, 1885–October 6, 1892 (only Mondays, Wednesdays, and Fridays 1891, only half of games 1892); neutral site use for Temple Cup Series NL Detroit Wolverines vs. AA St. Louis Browns October 25, 1887; PL Chicago Pirates 1890 some games

**LOCATION**

Left Field (N) Congress St, Third Base (W) Loomis St, First Base (S) Harrison St, Right Field (E) Throop St

**DIMENSIONS**

Foul Lines: 216

**FENCES**

12 (brick)

**CAPACITY**

10,300

**PHENOMENA**

Originally a bicycle racing track. The bike track surrounded the field. ♦ Bathtub-shaped, narrow and long, just like the Polo Grounds in New York. ♦ The Columbian Exposition in 1893 forced the White Stockings to leave.

♦ ♦ ♦

## South Side Park (II)

**AKA**

Brotherhood Park 1890, 35th Street Grounds (I)

**OCCUPANTS**

PL Chicago Pirates May 5–October 4, 1890; NL Chicago Colts May 5, 1891–September 27, 1893 (only Tuesdays, Thursdays, Saturdays 1891, only half of games 1892)

**LOCATION**

(N) West 34th St, (W) Wentworth Ave, (S) West 35th St; across the street from where Comiskey Park (I) was later built

**FENCES**

10 (wood)

## West Side Grounds

**AKA**

West Side Park (II)

**OCCUPANTS**

NL Chicago Colts May 14–September 17, 1893 (only 14 Sunday games); May 4–August 5, 1894; May 2, 1895–October 3, 1915; neutral site used by NL Cleveland Spiders October 8, 1898

**LOCATION**

Left Field (E) South Wood St, Third Base (N) West Polk St, First Base (W) South Lincoln (later Wolcott) St, Right Field (S) West Taylor St

**DIMENSIONS**

Left Field: 340, 312 (1916)
Left Center: 441, 403 (1916)
Center Field corner: 520 (out of play 1902–15)
Center Field: 475, 442 (1905), 418 (1908), 442 (1913)
Right Center: 365
Right Field: 316, 304.33 (1916)

Foul Territory: large

Backstop: 75

**CURRENT USE**

Illinois State Hospital and Medical School

**CAPACITY**

13,000, 8,000 (September 1894), 14,200 (1905), 16,000 (1915)

**PHENOMENA**

Fire suspended the August 5, 1894, game in the seventh. Players Jimmy Ryan and Walt Wilmot used bats to hack through a barbed-wire fence to rescue 1600 fans by allowing them to escape the fire by moving onto the field. The Cubs, then known as the Colts, finished the season at West Side Grounds, using the undamaged portion of the stands until September 8, when the burnt section was replaced. ♦ Shallow bleachers in both left field and right field—the left field set had nine rows of seats and right field only seven rows of seats. ♦ Center field had a curious history. In 1902–04, and perhaps in earlier seasons as well, there was an elevated walkway in center field connecting the left field and right field bleachers. This walkway was in front of a center field diagonal fence. The new two-story clubhouse, built in center field before the

The ticket booth at West Side Grounds.

1905 season, replaced this ugly walkway. ♦ For the 1908 season the Cubs added a set of very steep bleachers in front of and extending above the front of the roof of the clubhouse. These bleachers reduced the center field dimension to 418. These bleachers in 1913 were replaced by very large raised advertising billboards in center field. The top of the billboards were 40 feet high. These monster billboards were mounted above the center field clubhouse, and extended into

West Side Grounds was home to the most successful Cubs teams ever. From 1906 to 1910, the team won four NL pennants.

(as inside of, not at the back of) both the left field and right field bleachers. The bottom of these huge advertising billboards were set back about 10 ft from the front of left field and right field bleachers and were mounted on poles about 10–12 feet in the air. This strange arrangement meant the fans seated in the back rows of the bleachers had restricted sightlines and could not see many fly balls. ♦ Dimensions 1901–15 based on a 1917 Sanborn fire insurance map and numerous ballpark photos from the Library of Congress.

## South Side Park (III)

### AKA

White Sox Park (I) 1904–10, Chicago Cricket Club Grounds (II), 39th Street Grounds (II), White Stocking Park (IV) 1901–03, Schorling's Park 1920–40, American Giants Park 1911–31

### OCCUPANTS

AL Chicago White Sox April 24, 1901–June 27, 1910; NNL Chicago American Giants 1920–31; NSL Chicago Cole's American Giants 1932; NNL Chicago Cole's American Giants April–May 27, 1933, 1934–35; NAL Chicago American Giants 1937–40; neutral site used by NNL Milwaukee Bears several games in 1923; by NNL Kansas City Monarchs in 1920s; by NNL Cuban Stars West in 1920s

### LOCATION

Left Field (N) West 37th St, Third Base (W) South Princeton Ave, First Base (S) West 39th St (later West Pershing Rd), Right Field (E) South Wentworth Ave

### DIMENSIONS

Left Field: 330
Left Center: 397
Center Field corner (left of dead center): 410
Center Field: 386
Right Center: 360
Right Field: 270, 300 (July 1901), 325 (April 1903)
Backstop: 60

### FORMER USE

Home of Wanderers cricket team; minor league park in 1900

### CURRENT USE

Housing project three blocks from Comiskey Park

### CAPACITY

12,500 (April 1901), 14,000 (June 1901), 15,000 (1910)

### PHENOMENA

Opened in 1900. ♦ Overhanging roof added in 1902. ♦ Luxury boxes added on roof of grandstand in June 1901–removed by order of the City of Chicago Building Commissioner in 1907. ♦ Right field fence cut back sharply around J. F. Kidwell Greenhouse buildings near right-center, making right-center relatively short compared to left-center. ♦ Right field fence moved back for the first time in early July 1901, and for the second time in spring 1903. ♦ Used as a

South Side Park III, aka the 39th Street Grounds, had been the playing field of the Chicago Wanderers cricket team during the 1893 World's Fair. Charles Comiskey built a wooden grandstand on the site in 1900.

dog racing track in summer 1933, forcing NNL Cole's American Giants to move all home games from May 28 through the end of the season to Indianapolis. ♦ Damaged by fire on Christmas Day 1940, and burned down January 3, 1941. ♦ Dimensions based on 1911 Sanborn fire insurance map and numerous ballpark photos (1902–09) from the Library of Congress.

## Comiskey Park (I)

### AKA

White Sox Park (II) 1910–12, Charles A. Comiskey's Baseball Palace 1910, White Sox Park (III) May 1962–September 1975, 35th Street Grounds (II)

### ARCHITECTS

Zachary Taylor Davis; 1927 expansion: Osborn Engineering

### OCCUPANTS

AL Chicago White Sox July 1, 1910–September 30, 1990; NL Chicago Cubs 1918 World Series; NAL Chicago American Giants 1941–52; neutral site used for Negro World Series NNL Kansas City Monarchs vs. ECL Darby Hilldales eighth and tenth games 1926; for NNL Washington-Homestead Grays vs. NAL Birmingham Black Barons third game 1943; for NNL Newark Eagles vs. NAL Kansas City Monarchs fifth game 1946; for NNL New York Cubans vs. NAL Cleveland Buckeye's fourth game 1947

### LOCATION

Left Field (N) West 34th St; Third Base (W) South Portland (later South Shield's) Ave, then Chicago and Western RR tracks; First Base (S) 324 West 35th St, then location of new Comiskey Park (II); Right Field (E) South Wentworth Ave, then Dan Ryan Expressway/I-94

### DIMENSIONS

Foul Lines: 363, 362 (1911), 365 (1927), 362 (1930), 352 (1934), 362 (1936), 332 (April 22, 1949), 352 (May 5, 1949), 335 (1969), 352 (marked 1971), 349 (actual 1971), 341 (1983), 347 (1986)

Power Alleys: 382, 395 (1927), 392 (1930), 370 (1934), 392 (1936), 382 (1942), 359 (April 22, 1949), 381 (May 5, 1949), 362 (1969), 381 (marked 1971), 378 (actual 1971), 369 (1983), 375 (1986)

Left/Right Center: 402, 421 (1927), 418 (1930), 406 (1934), 418 (1936), 383 (April 22, 1949), 406 (May 5, 1949), 387 (1969), 387 (1983), 400 (1986)

Deep Left/Right Center Corners: 425, 409 (1969)

Center Field: 420, 450 (1927), 455 (1927), 450 (1930), 436 (1934), 450 (1936), 422 (1940), 420 (April 22, 1949), 415 (May 5, 1949), 410 (1951), 415 (1952), 400 (1969), 440 (1976), 445 (1977), 402 (marked 1981), 409 (actual 1981), 401 (1983), 409 (1986)

Backstop: 98, 71 (1933), 85 (1934), 86 (1955), 78 (1990)

Foul Territory: large

### FENCES

Foul Lines and Power Alleys: 12 (concrete 1955), 9.83 (concrete 1959), 5 (wire 1969), 9.83 (concrete 1971)

Center Field: 15 (1927), 30 (1948), 17 (1976), 18 (1980)

Left Center to Right Center inner fences: 5 (canvas 1949), 6.5 (24-foot section in front of bullpens 1969), 9 (1974), 7 (canvas 1981), 7.5 (1982), 11 (1984), 7.5 (1986)

### SURFACE

Outfield grass; Infield grass (1910), Sox Sod carpet (1969), grass (1976)

### FORMER USE

Truck garden owned by Signor Scavado and a city dump; South Side Park (II) was almost on the same site, across Wentworth Avenue.

### CURRENT USE

North parking lot for US Cellular Field/Comiskey Park (II)

### CAPACITY

28,800, 52,000 (1927), 50,000 (1938), 51,000 (1939), 50,000 (1940), 46,550 (1942), 50,934 (1953), 44,492 (1969), 43,951 (1990)

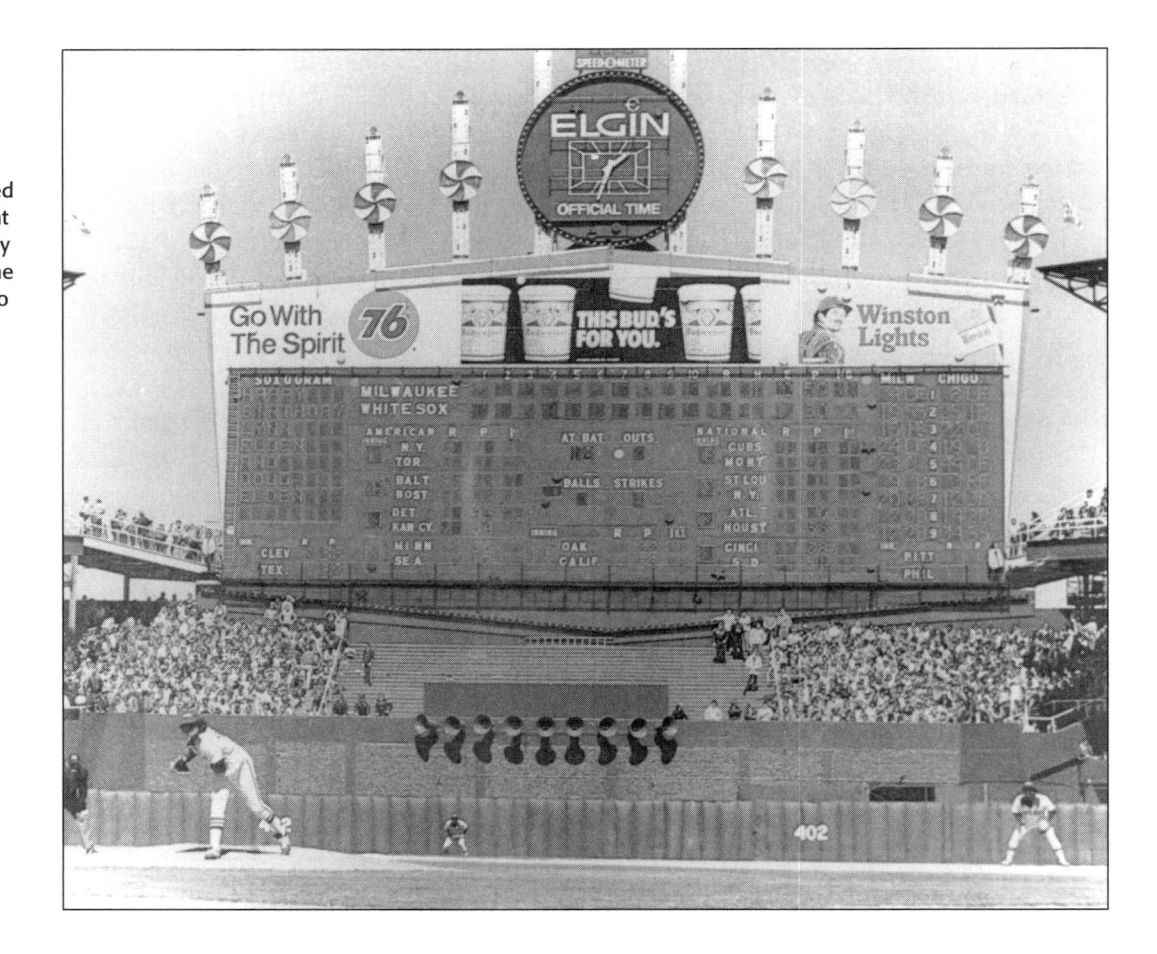

Comiskey Park featured pinwheels on the giant scoreboard installed by Bill Veeck, owner of the White Sox from 1959 to 1961, and again from 1975 to 1981.

**PHENOMENA**

According to an oft-told story, White Sox shortstop Luke Appling once heard his spikes hit metal as he tried to field a bad hop. He asked for time, and the groundskeepers came out and removed a large copper kettle from the infield. From that point forward, infielders here had a ready-made excuse for errors. How did the kettle get there? The site was a city dump before becoming a ballpark. ◆ In 1959, owner Bill Veeck (as in Wreck) had Eddie Gaedel and three other midgets parachute into Comiskey Park, landing at second base just before a game as the White Sox fielders were standing in the field, awaiting the national anthem. The PA announcer then announced that four Martian Midgets had just come to Earth because they had pledged to assist the White Sox Dynamic Duo double-play combination of Luis Aparicio and Nellie Fox, both of whom were fairly small in stature, to combat the Gigantic Earthlings. Gaedel was the midget who Veeck had bat for the St. Louis Browns in 1951. ◆ Sox downed the Brewers here, 8–7, in 25 innings, May 8–9, 1984, the longest game by time in major league history, at 8 hours, 6 minutes. ◆ Scene of longest rain delay in history. The Sox and Rangers waited 7 hours, 23 minutes for the rain to stop on August 12, 1990. It never did, and the game was finally postponed. ◆ Current White Sox groundskeeper Roger Bossard's grandpa first laid out the old squished-flat water hoses on two-by-fours on the Foul Lines beyond first and third bases, and painted them white in the 1930s. He had done the same thing before in Cleveland. ◆ Tradition of playing what later became the official national anthem started spontaneously when the band played it in the home seventh of the first Cubs World Series home game here in 1918. ◆ Part of the grandstand collapsed May 17, 1913. ◆ Special elevator for Lou Comiskey, in use from 1931 to 1982, had an inlaid tile floor. ♦ The 540-foot center field listing in 1931–33 Baseball Guides must have been a misprint. ♦ Used for all 1933–60 Negro League All-Star games with East vs. West; the last one was played in 1961 at Yankee Stadium. ♦ Bullpens moved in 1950 from foul territory down the lines to behind the center field fence. ♦ Green cornerstone laid on St. Patrick's Day 1910 stayed green until 1960, when Bill Veeck painted the exterior all white and installed the first exploding scoreboard in the majors. ♦ Showers in the bleachers in center. ♦ Foul poles bent back to join the top of the roof. ♦ Organist Nancy Faust played "Na-na-na-na, hey-hey, Good bye." ♦ Sox forfeited second game of twi-nighter to Tigers, July 12, 1979, on Disco Demolition Night, when overflow crowd wouldn't leave the field after the between-game disco records dynamite demolition promotion was completed. ♦ Scene of many masterful groundskeeping tricks by Roger, Gene, and Emil Bossard. ♦ Camp Swampy in 1967 referred to the area in front of the plate, dug up and soaked with water when a White Sox sinkerballer was on the mound, but mixed with clay and gasoline and burned to provide hard soil if a sinkerballer were pitching for the visiting team. Opposing team bullpen mounds were lowered or raised from the standard 10-inch height to upset visiting pitchers' rhythm. ♦ Under Eddie Stanky's managerial tenure, the grass in front of shortstop was cut long because the Sox shortstop had limited range, but at second the grass was cut short because the Sox second sacker had very good range. When the Sox had a lousy defensive outfield, the grass was cut long to turn triples into doubles. When the Sox had speedy line-drive hitters, the outfield grass was cut short to turn singles into doubles. When the Sox had good bunters, more paint was added to the foul line to tilt the ball back fair. Veeck said all this gave the Sox an extra 12 wins a year. ♦ In 1949, Frank Lane, having just installed inner fences cutting the Foul Lines from 352 to 332, removed them in the middle of the night just before a series with the Yankees because opposing teams were hitting more homers into the 20-foot space beyond the inner fence than were the Sox. This caused the AL to pass a rule stating that teams could not change dimensions of the field during a season. ♦ Popcorn machine fire caused 4000 fans to come out onto the field during a 70-minute delay in the eighth on June 7, 1974. ♦ White Sox mascots Ribby and Roobarb roamed the stands in the 1980s. ♦ Home plate was moved slightly forward toward second base and center field in 1983, reducing the Foul Lines from 352, which they had been since 1971, when the inner fence was removed, down to 341. When this was done, however, it was discovered that what had been marked as 352 had actually been 349. ♦ Homers into center field bleachers hit only by Jimmie Foxx (May 18, 1934), Hank Greenburg (May 27, 1938), Alex Johnson (September 9, 1970), Dick Allen (August 23, 1972), Richie Zisk (May 22, 1977), Tony Armas (April 28, 1984), and George Bell (August 23, 1985).

## Wrigley Field

### AKA

North Side Ball Park 1914; Weeghman Park 1914–18; Whales Park 1915; Cubs' Park 1919–26; Bobby Dorr's House

### ARCHITECTS

Zachary Taylor Davis; 1937 expansion: Holabird & Root; renovations by HOK Sport in 1989 and 2006

### OCCUPANTS

FL Chicago Whales April 23, 1914–October 3, 1915; NL Chicago Cubs April 20, 1916, to date

### LOCATION

Left Field (N/NW) West Waveland Ave, Third Base (W/SW) North Seminary Ave, Home Plate (SW) North Clark St (running from NW to SE), First Base (S/SE) 1060 West Addison St, Right Field (E/NE) North Sheffield Ave

### DIMENSIONS

Left Field: 302, 327 (April 28, 1914), 325 (1923), 319

Wrigley Field decked out for the 1945 World Series.

(1925), 370 (August 6, 1925), 364 (1928), 341 (June 26–July 26, 1937), 355 (July 27, 1937)

Left Field in the Well: 357 (July 27, 1937)

Left Center: 342, 390 (April 28, 1914), 377 (1915), 361 (1923), 363 (July 27, 1937)

Center Field corner (left of dead center): 406, 455 (April 28, 1914, to end of season)

Center Field: 376, 425 (1915), 420 (1923), 436 (1928), 440 (April 1937), 400 (July 27, 1937)

Deepest Right Center: 447 (1923), 407 (1937)

Right Center: 307, 344 (1915), 383 (1923), 381 (July 27, 1937)

Right Field in the Well: 363 (July 27, 1937)

Right Field: 298, 299 (1922), 318 (1923), 321 (1928), 353 (July 27, 1937)

Backstop: 62, 62.42 (1930), 60.5 (1957), 62.42 (1982), 60 (1986), 60.5 (1993)

Foul Territory: very small

**FENCES**

Left Field and Center Field: 12 (brick April 23, 1914)

Right Center: 6.5 (screen 1914 only)

Right Field: 12 (brick April 23, 1914–July 6, 1916), 22 (12 brick with 10 screen on top July 7, 1916)

Foul Poles and Power Alleys: 6 (screen April 1937)

Left Field corner: 15.92 (11.33 brick with Boston and bittersweet ivy, below 4.59 plywood August 1937), 15.92 (with wire basket 3 added in front but which does not change height of fence 1985), 15 (2003)

Transition between Left Field Corner and Bleachers: 12.5 (screen and yellow railing on top of brick wall August 1937)

Left Center to Right Center: 8 (screen 1914), 11.33 (brick with ivy August 1937), 11.33 (with wire basket 3 added in front but which does not change height of fence May 1970), 11.5 (2003)

Left Field Scoreboard: 30 (April 23–30, 1914), 40 (wood July 9–September 3, 1937)

Left Center Scoreboard: 30 (May 1–October 8, 1914)

Center Field Scoreboard: 30 (1915); 16 (August 1937)

Center Field Batters Eye Screen: 19.33 (8 wire above 11.33 brick June 18, 1963–Sepember 27, 1964)

Right Center Triangle: 17.5 in front of catwalk steps sloping down to 15.5 (screen 1928, plywood 1979, removed 1985)

Right Field Corner: 15.5 (11.33 brick with ivy, below 4.17 plywood August 1937), 3 wire basket in front (1985, does not change height of fence), 15 (2003)

**SURFACE**

Grass, mixture of Merion bluegrass and clover; ivy vines on outfield walls

**FORMER USE**

Seminary

**CAPACITY**

14,000, 18,000 (1915), 20,000 (1922), 32,000 (1923), 38,000 (1926), 38,396 (1927), 40,000 (1928), 36,755 (1951), 37,702 (1972), 39,600 (1989), 39,241 (2003), 39,538 (2005), 41,118 (2006)

**PHENOMENA**

The only remaining Federal League ballpark. ♦ By far the most pronounced un-level areas in fair terri-tory in the major leagues. ♦ A rusted, hollowed-out shell of a grenade was discovered in November 2004 in the right field grass. The areas down both lines in fair territory adjoining the foul territory bullpen pitching mounds slope up two feet from the sur-rounding outfield. ♦ Also, by far the most pro-nounced un-level areas in foul territory. Foul territory surrounding home plate slopes down drastically in three directions: toward both dugouts and toward the screen behind home plate. When chasing a foul pop fly, the catcher can be noticed running downhill. ♦ After the first three-game home series against the KC Packers, in the inaugural 1914 season, resulted in nine home runs, the left field wall was moved back 25 feet at the foul line and 48 feet in left-center to prevent so many home runs. ♦ Bleachers in right-center field re-

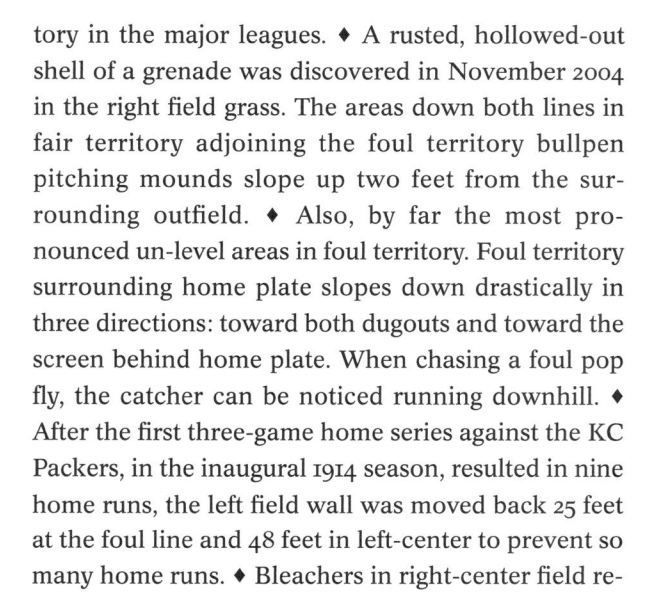

Wrigley Field in the late 1920s, with stands jutting into the outfield in left, and before the trademark ivy was introduced on the out-field wall. Zachary Taylor Davis, the architect who designed Comiskey Park on the South Side, also designed Wrigley Field on the North Side. Each is approximately 35 blocks from Madison Avenue, the North-South dividing line of the city.

Groundskeepers installing the ivy vines at Wrigley Field in 1937.

moved after the 1914 season. New wooden bleachers built in left field for the 1915 season. Home plate was moved 60 feet to the west, away from right field, after the 1922 season. ♦ Much of the dimensional data for 1914–23 was based on a 1923 Sanborn fire insurance map. ♦ Again to prevent too many home runs from being hit, the bleachers in left field were removed midway through the 1925 season, but the left-center bleachers, called the "Jury Box," remained through

The old scoreboard at Wrigley Field before an electric scoreboard was installed in 1937.

July 1937. ♦ Starting in the winter of 1926–27, a second deck was built. The second deck on the left field side was opened April 1927; the second deck on the right field side was opened April 1928. ♦ Bill Veeck Jr. purchased and planted 350 beautiful Japanese bittersweet ivy and 200 Boston ivy vines on the outfield walls in September 1937. ♦ The outfield bleachers as they exist today were built during the 1937 season. ♦ The center field 400 sign is actually to the right of dead center. ♦ Only park where it's more difficult to hit a homer down the foul line than to hit one 50 or so feet out in fair territory, because the bleachers protrude out into the outfield, creating what are called "wells." ♦ From 1923 through the 1930s, Bobby Dorr, the grounds superintendent, lived in a six-room apartment at the ballpark, adjacent to the left field corner gate. The apartment is still there. ♦ Ernie Banks' #14 flies on left field foul pole flag; Billy Williams' #26 flies on right field foul pole flag. ♦ No home run has ever hit the center field scoreboard. Those that came the closest were Bill Nicholson in 1948 onto Sheffield and Roberto Clemente in 1959 onto Waveland. ♦ An eight-foot high batters background, 64 feet wide, stood on top of the wall in

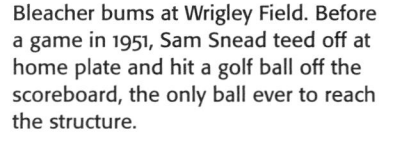
Bleacher bums at Wrigley Field. Before a game in 1951, Sam Snead teed off at home plate and hit a golf ball off the scoreboard, the only ball ever to reach the structure.

center from June 18, 1963, through the end of the 1964 season. Called the Whitlow Wall because Cubs athletic director Robert Whitlow put it up, the screen prevented 10 homers, by Cubs and by visitors, one each by 500+ homer hitters Ernie Banks and Willie McCovey. ♦ Ugly Astroturf cover on seats in center, used for a second batters background, debuted May 18, 1967, and was replaced by beautiful vines in 1990s. ♦ Outfield wall distances before 1981 were marked on plywood markers screwed into the brick. Since then they have been painted directly on the brick. ♦ In 1937, six gates in the brick wall were installed as the bleachers were finished in the outfield. They were painted red, then repainted blue in 1981, then green in the mid-1980s. ♦ The famous Bleacher Bums were formed in 1966 by 10 bleacher fans. ♦ On April 14, 1976, Mets slugger Dave "King Kong" Kingman hit a homer 550 feet over Waveland and up against a frame house three doors down on the east side of Kenmore Avenue, which runs north-south, and dead ends into the left field wall. If the ball had carried three more feet, it would have crashed through a window and smashed the TV on which Naomi Martinez was watching Kingman round the bases. ♦ The William F. Wrigley Jr. Water Fountain is in the Cubs Hall of Fame under the first base stands, near the Friendly Confines café. It was originally dedicated by a Tinker-Evers handshake after they had feuded. ♦ After a game, a blue flag with a white W flying from the center field flag pole signifies a win, a white flag with a blue L a Cubs loss. ♦ Lights were inside the park, ready to be installed, but owner Phil Wrigley donated them to the war effort instead on December 8, 1941, keeping Wrigley Field in the dark until August 8, 1988. ♦ The expansion of the bleachers after the 2005 season added 1700 seats by extending the structure over the sidewalks on Waveland and Sheffield Avenues. This bleacher rework added depth to the preexisting seating areas—principally in the right field and left field bleacher sections.

## *67th and Langley*

**OCCUPANT**
NNL Chicago Giants 1920–21

**LOCATION**
67th St, Langley St

## Normal Park

**OCCUPANT**
NNL Chicago American Giants 1920–21

**LOCATION**
(N) WEST 61st St; (S) West 63rd St; Normal Street; South Racine Ave; on the South Side

## Leland Giants Park

**OCCUPANT**
NNL Chicago American Giants 1922–23

**LOCATION**
West 69th St, 6221 South Halsted St

**PHENOMENA**
Opened in 1910.

## Soldier Field

**OCCUPANT**
NNL Chicago American Giants 1924

**LOCATION**
(N) 425 East McFetridge Pl, then Grant Park; (W) South Lake Shore Dr; (S) East Waldron Dr, then Burnham Park; (E) Lake Michigan

## Asbury Ball Park

**OCCUPANT**
NNL Chicago American Giants 1925–26

◆   ◆   ◆

## Pyott's Park

**OCCUPANT**
NNL Chicago American Giants 1928–30

**LOCATION**
West 48th; South Kilpatrick Ave; West Lake St; on the West Side

**PHENOMENA**
Very short left field fence.

## 37th and Butler

**OCCUPANT**
NNL Chicago American Giants 1931

**LOCATION**
37th St, Butler St

## Shewbridge Park

**OCCUPANT**
NNL Chicago American Giants May 5, 1935

**LOCATION**
74th St, Aberdeen St

## Mills Stadium

**OCCUPANT**
NNL Chicago American Giants one game August 6, 1935

**LOCATION**
Kilpatrick Ave, 4700 West Lake St, on the North Side

**PHENOMENA**

A high school football field, it was used for a regular season NFL game when the Bears hosted the Brooklyn Dodgers here, September 21, 1930.

## Spencer Field

**OCCUPANT**

NNL Chicago American Giants one game August 7, 1935

**LOCATION**

North Central Ave

## Comiskey Park (II)

**AKA**

US Cellular Field January 31, 2003, to date

**ARCHITECTS**

HOK Sport; HKS, Inc. (Dallas; 2001–2005 renovations)

**OCCUPANTS**

AL Chicago White Sox April 18, 1991, to date; neutral site used by NL Florida Marlins September 13 and 14, 2004, because of Hurricane Ivan in Miami

**LOCATION**

Left Field (E) South Wentworth Ave, then Dan Ryan Expressway/I-94; Third Base (N) 333 West 35th St, then location of old Comiskey Park (I); First Base (W) South Portland (later South Shields) Ave, then Chicago and Western RR tracks; Right Field (S) West 37th St

**DIMENSIONS**

Left Field: 347, 330 (2001)
Left Center: 383, 375 (1992), 377 (2001)
Center Field: 400
Right Center: 383, 375 (1992), 372 (2001)

Comiskey Park II featured an incredibly steep upper deck when it was built in 1991, just as the retro parks began to appear. You were closer to home plate in the last row of the upper deck at Comiskey Park I than you are in the first row of the upper deck at Comiskey Park II.

The two Comiskey Parks. The old park, in the foreground, was demolished in January 1991 and is now a parking lot.

Right Field: 347, 335 (2001)
Backstop: 60

**FENCES**
  8

**FORMER USE**
  80 privately owned residential buildings

**CAPACITY**
  44,702, 44,321 (1993), 45,936 (2001), 47,098 (2003), 41,000 (2004), 40,615 (2005)

**PHENOMENA**
  Along with the Rogers Centre, formerly SkyDome, one of the worst modern ballparks ever built. ♦ Seats in the front row of the upper deck are farther from home plate than those in last row at old Comiskey were. ♦ Park improved in recent years by taking out the upper deck rows and making it a little more fan friendly/old style type park. ♦ Organist Nancy Faust plays "Na-na-na-na, hey-hey, Good bye," which is a song called "Na Na Hey Hey Kiss Him Goodbye" by a group called Steam. ♦ Twenty-two dump trucks brought 550 tons of infield dirt from old Comiskey to new Comiskey.

---

# Cincinnati, Ohio

*See also* Covington, Kentucky; Hamilton, Ohio; Ludlow, Kentucky

## *Lincoln Park Grounds*

**AKA**
  Union Cricket Club Grounds, Union Grounds

**OCCUPANTS**
  Neutral site used by NA Cleveland Forest Citys

May 13, 1871; by NA Washington Olympics July 4, 1871; by NA Cleveland Forest Citys July 22, 1871

**LOCATION**

In Lincoln Park, next to the Union Railroad Terminal

**PHENOMENA**

Built in 1867, it served as the home of the Cincinnati Baseball Club (the Reds who were the first pro baseball team) until 1870. First Ladies Day in the major leagues here in 1876.

## Avenue Grounds

**OCCUPANT**

NL Cincinnati Reds April 25, 1876–August 27, 1879

**LOCATION**

(N) Monmouth St, (W) Mill Creek, (S) Alabama Ave, (E) Baltimore and Ohio RR tracks

**CURRENT USE**

Chester Park

**CAPACITY**

7500

**PHENOMENA**

Park opened in September 1875. ♦ Park built by the club owners, George and Josiah Keck, for use in the 1876 season. ♦ Infield was grass, while the outfield was hard clay. Left field fence deeper than right field fence, and center field had a semicircular fence with an entrance for carriages. ♦ Home plate was in the southeastern corner of the park. ♦ Grandstand behind home plate seated about 3000, while covered stands down both Foul Lines seated an additional 4,500. ♦ Innovative marketing-regular admission was 50 cents, but after the fifth inning a special price of 10 cents was in force.

## Bank Street Grounds

**AKA**

Union Athletic Park 1884

**OCCUPANTS**

NL Cincinnati Reds May 1 to September 30, 1880; AA Cincinnati Reds May 21, 1882–September 29, 1883; UA Cincinnati Outlaw Reds April 17–October 15, 1884

**LOCATION**

(N) Cross St, (W) Duck St, (S) Bank St, (E) Western Ave; three blocks north of where Crosley Field was later built

**FORMER USE**

Vacant lot used for circus and wild west shows

**CAPACITY**

2000

**PHENOMENA**

In 1884 the Reds were slow to renew their park lease and the UA used the park for the 1884 season. As a result, the Reds moved to League Park (I) for the 1884 season. During the 1884 season the outfield fence blew down.

## League Park (I)

**AKA**

Cincinnati Base Ball Grounds 1884–89, Western Avenue Grounds 1890

**OCCUPANTS**

AA Cincinnati Reds May 1, 1884–October 15, 1889; NL Cincinnati Reds April 19, 1890–September 29, 1893; neutral site used for Temple Cup Series NL Chicago White Stockings vs. AA St. Louis Browns October 23–24, 1885

**LOCATION**

Left Field (W) McLean Ave, Third Base (S) Findlay St, First Base (E) Western Ave, Right Field (N) York St; same site as Crosley Field but different orientation

**PRIOR USE**

Abandoned brickyard

**CAPACITY**

6000

**PHENOMENA**

A report that when the stands collapsed on Opening Day 1884, one fan was killed, was a myth that persists to this day. ◆ The two principal Cincinnati newspapers supported opposite teams—the *Enquirer* supported the Union Association and the *Commercial Gazette* the American Association. ◆ The *Enquirer* ran a sensational (and erroneous) story about the Opening Day fatality. Actually, the collapse of the stands did injure many, but no fans were killed. ◆ Because of the orientation of the field the afternoon sun shined directly in the batter's eyes. The only major league game ever called because of the sun occurred in 1892 against Boston.

## *Pendleton Park*

**AKA**

East End Park, East End Grounds, Cincinnati Gym Grounds

**OCCUPANT**

AA Cincinnati Porkers April 25–August 13, 1891

**LOCATION**

(W) Ridgley St, (S) Ohio River, (E) Watson St, then Tacoma Park; in the eastern part of Cincinnati

**DIMENSIONS**

Right Field: 400

**CURRENT USE**

Cincinnati Gym Grounds

**PHENOMENA**

Most people, and most books, mistakenly state that this park was in Pendleton, Ohio. Actually, it was in Cincinnati and got its name from the fact that the original owner of the property was named Mr. Pendleton. ◆ When the Porkers were organized hurriedly in the spring of 1891, the team passed up a better ballpark in Covington, Kentucky, because they thought that fans from Cincinnati would not attend if the ballpark were not in Cincinnati. But this park, although in Cincinnati, was remotely located in the less populated East End of the city, and the team would have drawn more fans had they played in Covington. ◆ There was a huge hole in left center. ◆ Many fans arrived by Ohio River steamboat. ◆ Both teams were arrested for playing on Sundays here on April 26, May 24, and June 7, 1891. ◆ In August 1891, the AA Porkers decided to pack it in, and went out of business, in part because of the park's disadvantageous location, resulting in the city losing its American Association franchise.

## *League Park (II)*

**OCCUPANT**

NL Cincinnati Reds April 20, 1894–October 2, 1901

**LOCATION**

April 20, 1894–May 28, 1900: Left Field (N/NE) York St, Third Base (W/NW) McLean Ave, First Base (S/SW) Findlay St, Right Field (E/SE) Western Ave; same site as League Park (I) but different orientation through May 27, 1900; same site as Crosley Field with different orientation May 28, 1900–October 2, 1901; Left Field (W) McLean Ave, Third Base (S) Findlay St, First Base (E) Western Ave, Right Field (N) York St; same site and same orientation as League Park (I) 1884–93

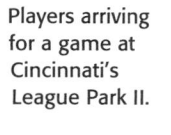

Players arriving for a game at Cincinnati's League Park II.

**DIMENSIONS**

Left Field: 253 (1894–old configuration), 387 (May 28, 1901–new configuration)

Left Center: 384 (1901)

Center Field: 414 (1901)

Right Center: 426 (1901)

Right Field: 340 (1901)

**PHENOMENA**

First batters background in 1895, when the Reds painted the center field wall black to help the hitters see the ball. ◆ The old grandstand behind home plate of League Park (I) was not torn down, but rather used as seats in the right field corner. ◆ After the large fire on May 28, 1900, the park was returned to the same orientation as League Park (I) because the new grandstand behind home plate built for League Park (II) had burned down. ◆ Bleachers built in left field during the 1901 season. ◆ Then another fire burned down the entire ballpark in the fall of 1901, after the end of the season. ◆ 1901 dimensions based on a 1891 Sanborn fire insurance map.

## *Palace of the Fans*

**AKA**

League Park (III)

**ARCHITECT**

John G. Thurtle

**OCCUPANT**

NL Cincinnati Reds April 17, 1902–October 12, 1911

**LOCATION**

Same as League Park (II), but with different orientation

**DIMENSIONS**

Left Field: 360
Left Center: 418
Center Field: 400
Right Center: 375
Right Field: 450

**CAPACITY**

12,000

**PHENOMENA**

Pillars and columns patterned after 1893 Columbian Exposition in Chicago. ♦ Second park (Baker Bowl was the first) to use steel-and-concrete for the major portion of its foundation and superstructure. ♦ Rooters Row was a beer drinking area down both foul lines. ♦ Diamond in southwest corner. ♦ Grandstand from League Park (II) used as pavilion in right field corner. ♦ Dimensions based on a 1904 Sanborn fire insurance map. ♦ Park replaced by Redland Field due to its limited capacity, especially box seats.

## *Crosley Field*

**AKA**

Redland Field 1912–33

**ARCHITECT**

Harry Hake of Hake and Hake

**OCCUPANTS**

NL Cincinnati Reds April 11, 1912–June 24, 1970; NAL Cincinnati Tigers 1937; NAL Cincinnati Buckeyes 1942; NAL Cincinnati Clowns 1943; NAL Indianapolis-Cincinnati Clowns half of the home games 1944; NAL Cincinnati Clowns 1945

**LOCATION**

Left Field (N/NE) York St, Third Base (W/NW) McLean Ave, First Base (S/SW) Findlay St, Right Field (E/SE) Western Ave (running from NW to SE); same as League Park (I) and Palace of the Fans; same site but different orientation from League Park (II)

**DIMENSIONS**

Left Field: 352, 339 (1927), 328 (1938)
Left Center at left side of Scoreboard: 380 (1938)

Palace of the Fans in Cincinnati, one of the most elegant of the old ballparks.

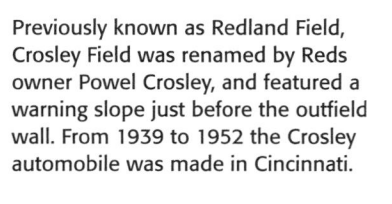

Previously known as Redland Field, Crosley Field was renamed by Reds owner Powel Crosley, and featured a warning slope just before the outfield wall. From 1939 to 1952 the Crosley automobile was made in Cincinnati.

Left Center at right side of Scoreboard: 383 (1938)

Center Field: 420, 400 (1927), 387 (1938), 380 (1939), 387 (1940), 390 (1944), 387 (1955)

Deepest Right Center corner: 387 (1944)

Right Center: 383 (1955)

Right Field: 400, 377, 366 (1938), 342 (1942), 366 (June 30, 1950), 342 (1953), 366 (1958)

Backstop: 38, 58 (1927), 66 (1943), 78 (1953)

### FENCES

Center Field: canvas shield above fence to protect against streetlight glare (April 16, 1935–June 7, 1940)

Left Field: 18 (1938), 12 (1957), 14 (1962), 18 (1963)

Clock on top of Scoreboard: 58 (1957), 45 (1967)

Left Center to Right Center: 18 (1954), 14 (1962), 13.5 (1963), 23 (9.5 plywood over 13.5 concrete 1965)

Right Field: 7.5 (4.5 wire above 3 concrete 1938), 7.5 (4.5 wire above 3 wood 1942), 10 (7 wire above 3 wood 1949), 12 (9 wire above 3 concrete (June 30, 1950), 10 (7 wire above 3 wood 1953), 10 (7 wire above 3 concrete 1958), 9 (6 wire above 3 concrete 1959)

Flag pole in left-center in play: 82

### FORMER USE

League Park (I), (II), Palace of the Fans

### CURRENT USE

Used to impound cars 1970–72; reconstructed on farm near Union, Kentucky; replica constructed with left-center scoreboard at 11540 Grooms Road in Blue Ash, Ohio; site is now an industrial park; plaque placed at Findlay and Western in 1998

### CAPACITY

25,000, 30,000 (1927), 33,000 (1938), 30,000 (1948), 29,488 (1970)

### PHENOMENA

Embankment in front of the fence in left field from 1912 extended all around the outfield late in the 1935 season. ♦ In January 1937, Mill Creek flooded, covering the playing field with 21 feet of water. Pitcher Lee Grissom and Reds traveling secretary John McDonald rowed a boat over the center field fence. ♦ Both home and visitor clubhouses were located behind left field stands. ♦ The right field bleachers were called the Sun Deck for day games and the Moon Deck for night games. ♦ Mislabeled as being in Cleveland in 1942 movie *Pride of the Yankees*. ♦ To reduce noise from a new highway behind the fence in center in 1963, a nine-foot section of plywood was added on top of the

13-foot high center field wall. The plywood was out of play; a ball hitting it was supposed to be a homer. But all during 1963–64, there were controversies about whether balls were home runs that hit near the plywood. Finally, in 1965, the plywood was made part of the wall and was put in play. ♦ The words "Batted ball hitting concrete wall on fly to right of white line—home run" was the only time in major league history that a ground rule was painted on an outfield wall. ♦ A sign on the laundry building beyond the left field wall said Siebler Suits. ♦ Dimensions for 1912–1938 based on a 1904 Sanborn fire insurance map of Palace of the Fans. ♦ Torn down in 1972.

## Northside Park

### OCCUPANT
NNL Cincinnati Cuban Stars 1921

## Riverfront Stadium

### AKA
Cinergy Field September 9, 1996–December 29, 2002

### ARCHITECTS
Heery & Heery, and Finch, Alexander, Barnes, Rothschild & Paschal

### OCCUPANT
NL Cincinnati Reds June 30, 1970–September 22, 2002

### LOCATION
Center Field (E/NE) Broadway, then Riverfront Coliseum (later FirstStar Center); Third Base (N/NW) 201 East Second St (later Pete Rose Way); Home Plate (W/SW) I-71 Central Suspension (later Roebling Suspension) Bridge approach ramp; first Base (S/SE) Mehring Way, then RR tracks and Ohio River

### DIMENSIONS
Foul Lines: 330, 325 (2001)
Left Center: 375, 371 (2001), 370 (2002)
Center Field: 404, 393 (2001)
Right Center: 375, 373 (2001)
Backstop: 51, 41 (2001)
Foul Territory: small

### FENCES
Foul Lines: 12 (wood, 1970), 8 (wood, 1984)

A sellout crowd of 51,050 was on hand June 30, 1970 for the dedication of Cincinnati's Riverfront Stadium, rushed to completion so the Reds could host the All-Star Game. Hank Aaron hit the park's first home run.

Power Alleys: 12 (wood, 1970), 8 (wood, 1984), 14 (wood, 2001)

Center Field: 12 (wood, 1970), 8 (wood, 1984), 40 (wood, 2001)

### SURFACE

AstroTurf-8 1970–2000 hard, balls bounced very high off it; grass 2001–02

### FORMER USE

Singing cowboy Roy Rogers grew up in a house located at what became second base in the park

### CURRENT USE

Rose garden at Great American Ball Park commemorates Pete Rose's 4192nd hit

### CAPACITY

51,050, 52,392 (1979), 39,000 (2001)

### PHENOMENA

First to paint metric distances on outfield walls—100.58 down the lines, 114.30 to the alleys, 123.13 to center. ♦ Circle in left center commemorated Pete Rose's 4192nd hit; it was erased after Rose was expelled from baseball for gambling. ♦ Used Crosley Field's home plate 1970–96. ♦ Parking garage beneath stadium. ♦ Reds and Pirates played slowest game ever here August 30, 1978: 81 minutes per inning, called off after 3½ innings and 3½ hours of rain delays at 12:47 AM. ♦ Winds helped drives to left-center. ♦ Bees attacked the field April 17, 1976, and delayed the game. ♦ Torn down December 29, 2002.

## *Great American Ball Park*

### OCCUPANT

NL Cincinnati Reds March 31, 2003, to date

### ARCHITECTS

HOK Sport

### LOCATION

Left Field (E/NE) Broadway; Third Base (N/NW) Pete Rose Way, then I-71; First Base (W/SW) Johnny Bench Blvd, then Riverfront Sta-

The Reds' first game at Great American Ball Park was a March 28, 2003, exhibition game against the Indians. The stadium's western concourse is on the site where Riverfront Stadium used to sit.

dium; Right Field (S/SE) Mehring Way, railroad tracks, and Ohio River

**DIMENSIONS**

Left Field: 328
Left Field Power Alley: 379
Center Field: 404
Right Field Power Alley: 370
Right Field: 325
Backstop: 51.42
Foul Territory: small

**FENCES**

Left Field to Left Center: 12
Center Field to Right Field: 8

**CAPACITY**

42,053, 42,271 (2005)

**PHENOMENA**

Crosley Terrace features statues, benches, and landscaped grass built at same incline as at old Crosley Field, whose Longines clock is on top of the scoreboard, and whose Sun/Moon Deck is recreated in right.

---

# Clarksville, Virginia

## *Clarksville Stadium*

**OCCUPANT**

Neutral site used by NAL Raleigh Tigers May 1961

---

# Cleveland, Ohio

*See also* Collinwood, Ohio; Geauga Lake, Ohio; Newburgh Heights, Ohio

## *National Association Grounds*

**OCCUPANT**

NA Cleveland Forest Citys May 11, 1871–August 19, 1872

**LOCATION**

(N) Ensign St; (W) East Willson Ave (later East 55th St; (S) Sheridan (later Grand) Ave and railroad tracks; (E) Warrensville (later Kinsman) Rd

## *League Park (I)*

**AKA**

Kennard Street Park, National League Park (I)

**OCCUPANT**

NL Cleveland Spiders May 1, 1879–October 11, 1884

**LOCATION**

(N) Silby (later Carnegie) Ave, (W) Kennard (later East 46th) St, (S) Cedar Ave, (E) East 49th St

**PHENOMENA**

Trees in the outfield in 1879. The distance to the fence in left in 1880–81 was so short that balls hit over the fence were doubles.

## *League Park (II)*

**AKA**

American Association Park 1887–88, National League Park (II)

**OCCUPANTS**

AA Cleveland Spiders May 4, 1887–September 15, 1888; NL Cleveland Spiders May 3, 1889–October 4, 1890

League Park IV was home to both Cleveland's Negro League and American League teams.

**LOCATION**

(W) East 39th St, (E) East 35th St; (S) Euclid Ave, (N) Payne Ave, Robison Trolley Line

**DIMENSIONS**

Foul Poles: 410
Center Field: 420

**PHENOMENA**

The Spiders were so bad and drew so few fans at home that huge numbers of their home games were played on the road. ♦ Large fire caused by lightning in June 1890. ♦ Lights were never installed, making night games impossible.

## *Cedar Avenue Driving Park*

**OCCUPANT**

AA Cleveland Spiders August 21, 1887

**LOCATION**

Cedar Avenue

**PHENOMENA**

This was a racetrack where the Spiders played one Sunday home game vs. the Mets. The fans parked their horse carriages on the track and in the outfield. Several balls were hit out into the carriages in the outfield, and they were "in play," so the outfielders had to crawl under the carriages to retrieve the balls and get the ball back to the infield as the batter ran the bases. McKean's hit went over the carriages for a triple, and Reipschlager's double also went over the carriages.

## *Brotherhood Park*

**AKA**

Players League Park

**OCCUPANT**

PL Cleveland Infants April 30–October 4, 1890

**LOCATION**

First Base New York, Chicago, St. Louis RR (also called Nickel Plate RR, now used by Cleveland RTA) tracks; Willson Ave (later East 55th St)

## League Park (III)

**AKA**

National League Park (III)

**OCCUPANTS**

NL Cleveland Spiders May 1, 1891–September 24, 1899; AL Cleveland Blues April 29, 1901–September 6, 1909

**LOCATION**

Left Field (E) East 70th St, Third Base (N) Linwood Ave, First Base (W) Dunham (later East 66th) St, Right Field (S) Lexington Ave NE; between Hough Ave and Wade Park, on the Robison Trolley Line

**DIMENSIONS**

Left Field: 353
Left Field Power Alley: 352
Left Center: 362
Center Field: 409
Center Field corner (right of dead center field): 445, 429 (1903), 445 (1908)
Right Center: 390, 352 (1903), 390 (1909)
Right Field Power Alley: 348, 310 (1903), 348 (1909)
Right Field: 290

**FENCES**

Left Field: 10
Center Field: 10–20, 6–20 (1908)
Right Field: 20 (wood), 6 (1903), 20 (1909)

**CAPACITY**

9000, 11,200 (1903), 12,200 (1908) 11,200 (1909)

**PHENOMENA**

1892 game vs. Colts cancelled when lightning struck during the game. ◆ On May 24, 1901, the Blues trailed the Washington Senators, 13–5, in the bottom of the ninth, with two out and nobody on base. Then the Blues proceeded to score nine runs to win 14–13. McCarthy singled home Pickering for the winning run. ◆ Grandstand and infield located in the Northwest corner of the park site. ◆ Bleachers built in front of most of the right field fence for the 1903 season. Center field portion of the right field bleachers removed at start of the 1908 season, the remainder were removed after the 1908 season. Unlike the right field bleachers, the left-center bleachers (1908–09) were built behind the left field-center field fence. ◆ Dimensions based on 1896 Sanborn fire insurance map and 1909 panoramic park photo.

## League Park (IV)

**AKA**

Somers Park 1910–15, Dunn Field 1916–27

**ARCHITECT**

Osborn Engineering

**OCCUPANTS**

AL Cleveland Indians April 21, 1910–July 30, 1932; April 17, 1934–September 21, 1946; NAL Cleveland Buckeyes 1943–48, April–June 1950

**LOCATION**

Left Field (E) East 70th St, Third Base (N) Linwood Ave, First Base (W) Dunham (later East 66th) St, Right Field (S) Lexington Ave NE; between Hough Ave and Wade Park, on the Robison Trolley Line; same as League Park (III)

**DIMENSIONS**

Left Field: 375, 376 (August 1920), 374 (1930), 373 (1934) 374 (1938), 375 (1942)
Left Field Power Alley: 387, 408 (August 1920)
Left Center: 413, 431 (August 1920)
Center Field Scoreboard (left of dead center): 460, 420 (World Series 1920) 450 (1926), 467 (1930), 465 (1938), 460 (1939)
Center Field: 420
Deep Right Center (right of dead denter): 400 (1942)
Right Center: 340
Right Field Power Alley: 319
Right Field: 290, 240 (when roped off for overflow crowds)

Backstop: 76, 60 (1942)

**FENCES**

Left Field: 5 (concrete)

Left Center: 10 (7 screen above 3 concrete)

Center Field Scoreboard: 35

Right Center Clock: 20 (left and right sides), 22 (center of clock)

Right Field: 45 (20 concrete topped by 25 screen), 40 (20 concrete topped by 20 screen 1934)

**CURRENT USE**

Ticket booths and part of first base stands remain as League Park Community Center; rest of the park was torn down in 1951; swimming pool where left field was; historical marker put here in 1979

**CAPACITY**

21,414, 22,500 (1939)

**PHENOMENA**

Steel beams protruded from the wall in right, causing balls to bounce at crazy angles. Only here did left fielders handle doubles to right field. Also one of the only two places where a ball could be a home run, but another ball hit higher and farther to almost the exact same point was in play; the other was the Polo Grounds (IV) in New York. The steel supports for the wall in right were like goal posts, so that if a ball missed the goal post it was a homer, but if it were hit higher and further but hit the goal post, then it was in play. ♦ Megaphone speakers on left center wall. ♦ Joe DiMaggio set his 56-game consecutive hitting streak here July 16, 1941. ♦ Also scene of first World Series unassisted triple play and Babe Ruth's 500th home run. ♦ Teepees erected in 1946. ♦ There are plans to rebuild the park. ♦ Grandstand and infield located in the northwest corner of the park site. ♦ Original set of wooden bleachers in left field replaced in August 1920 with a set that was recessed (relative to the left field fence) rather than protruding as did the original bleachers. This change increased the left field power alley and left-center dimensions by about 20 feet. ♦ Temporary seating added in front of center field scoreboard and in right-

center for the 1920 World Series. ♦ Dimensions for 1910–19 based on 1911 Sanborn fire insurance map.

## Cubs Stadium

**OCCUPANT**

NNL Cleveland Cubs 1931

**LOCATION**

Across the street from League Park (IV), home of the Indians

**PHENOMENA**

So small that it literally stood in the shadows of League Park (IV).

## Hardware Field

**OCCUPANTS**

NNL Cleveland Cubs some games 1931; NAL Cleveland Bears 1939–40

**LOCATION**

East 79th St, Kinsman Rd

## Luna Bowl

**AKA**

Luna Park, Luna Stadium, City Park

**OCCUPANTS**

NEWL Cleveland Stars April–June 1932; NNL Cleveland Giants August–September 1933; NNL Cleveland Red Sox 1934

**LOCATION**

(N) Mount Carmel Rd, (W) Woodhill Rd, (S) Woodland Ave, (E) East 110th St

Cleveland's Municipal Stadium empties after the New York Giants won the 3rd game of the 1954 World Series. The stadium was built in a failed attempt to lure the 1932 Olympic Games to Cleveland. Over time, it became jocularly known as "The Mistake by the Lake."

**CURRENT USE**

Amusement park

## Cleveland Stadium

**AKA**

Lake Front Stadium 1930s, Cleveland Public Municipal Stadium 1930s, Municipal Stadium 1940s–50s, Mistake by the Lake

**ARCHITECT**

F. R. Walker of Walker & Weeks

**OCCUPANT**

AL Cleveland Indians July 31, 1932–September 24, 1933 all games; August 2, 1936; May 30–September 6, 1937 Sundays/holidays only Memorial Day to Labor Day; April 19, 1938–June 26, 1939 most Sundays/holidays/selected important games only; June 27, 1939–September 25, 1946 nights/Sundays/holidays/selected important games only (a majority of home games in 1940 and 1942–46); April 15, 1947–October 3, 1993 all games

**LOCATION**

Center Field (NE) East Ninth St; Third Base (NW) Erieside Ave, then Donald Gray Lakefront Gardens Port Authority Dock 28 and Lake Erie; Home Plate (SW) West Third St; First Base (SE) Cleveland Memorial Shoreway, then Amtrak/Conrail RR tracks; Boudreau Boulevard encircled the park

**DIMENSIONS**

Foul Lines: 322, 320 (1933), 321 (1948), 320 (1953)

Corners where inner fence met stadium wall: 362 (1947), 370 (1980)

Power Alleys: 435, 365 (1947), 362 (1948), 385 (1949), 380 (1954), 400 (1965), 390 (1967), 395 (1968), 385 (1970), 395 (1991)

Left Center: 377 (1980)

Deep Left Center: 387 (1980)

Grandstand corners: 435

Bleacher corners: 463

Center Field: 470, 467 (1938), 450 (1939), 410 (April 27, 1947), 408 (1966), 407 (1967), 410 (1968), 400 (1970), 415 (1990), 404 (1992)

Deep Right Center: 395 (1980)

Right Center: 385 (1980)

Backstop: 60

Foul Territory: large

**FENCES**

Left and Right Field: 5.25 (concrete), 5.5 (wire April 27, 1947), 5.25 (concrete June 6, 1947), 6 (1955), 9 (1976), 8 (1977), 8 (canvas 1984)

**CAPACITY**

78,000 (1931), 73,811 (1954), 76,977 (1968), 74,208 (1982), 74,483 (1989)

**PHENOMENA**

Opened July 1, 1931. ♦ Groundskeepers' tools kept in foul territory in 1930s and 1940s. ♦ Teepees erected in 1946 in center. ♦ No ball ever hit into the center field bleachers. Longest homer ever was hit by Luke Easter on June 23, 1950 to right center. ♦ Wind blew out toward the lake. ♦ Cleveland Stadium/League Park ratio of home games 1936–46: 1/77, 15/63, 18/58, 30/47, 49/33, 32/45, 46/34, 48/29, 44/34, 46/31, 41/36. ♦ Largest regular season crowd ever was here, 86,563 (84,587 paid) for doubleheader vs. the Yankees on September 12, 1954. ♦ Indians forfeited to Rangers on Beer Night June 4, 1974. Trailing 5–3 entering the bottom of the ninth, the Indians had scored two to tie the game and had two on with two out when fans stormed the field and attacked Rangers right fielder Jeff Burroughs. ♦ Before inner fence was installed, April 27, 1947, there was a steep incline in front of the center field bleacher wall, and a strange shape in the power alleys caused by the end of the double-deck grandstand, with the fence jumping abruptly deeper to the bleachers in center. ♦ The April 27 inner fence curved all the way to the foul poles. On June 6, it was moved so the inner fence just stretched across center field, hitting the permanent wall at the 362 mark. ♦ Bill Veeck buried their 1948 pennant before the September 23, 1949, game after the Tribe had been mathematically eliminated from the 1949 pennant race. ♦ Torn down in November 1996 after the NFL Browns left for Baltimore.

## *Jacobs Field*

**AKA**

The Jake, Indians Park at Gateway 1994

**ARCHITECT**

HOK Sport

**OCCUPANT**

AL Cleveland Indians April 4, 1994, to date

**LOCATION**

Left Field (NW) East Huron Rd, then Arena at Gateway (later Gund Center); Third Base (SW) 2401

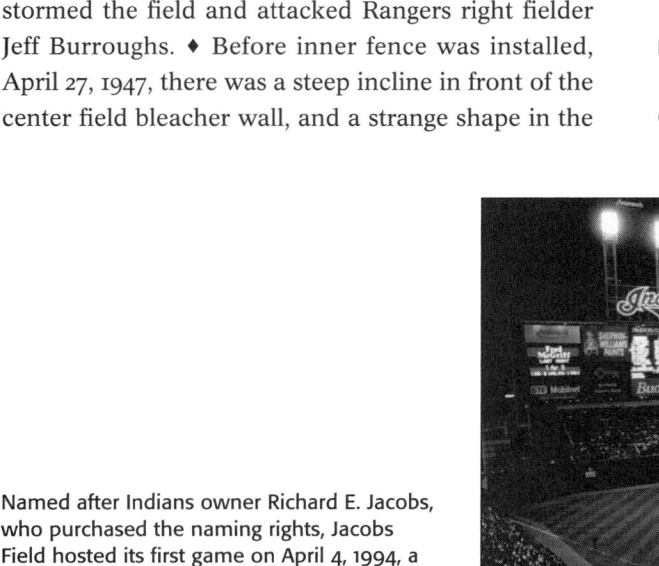

Named after Indians owner Richard E. Jacobs, who purchased the naming rights, Jacobs Field hosted its first game on April 4, 1994, a 4–3 Indians loss to the Mariners. Seattle's Eric Anthony hit the park's first home run.

Baseball Grounds at Euclid Beach Park, Cleveland, Ohio.

Euclid Beach Park in Collinwood, Ohio, occasional home of the Cleveland Spiders in 1898.

Ontario St; First Base (SE) Carnegie Ave; Right Field (NE) East 9th St

**DIMENSIONS**

Foul Lines: 325

Left Center: 368, 370 (2001)

Left of Center Field (at the kink): 410

Center Field: 405

Right Center: 375

Backstop: 59, 65 (2003)

Foul Territory: small

**FENCES**

Left Field: 19

Center and Right Field: 8, 9 (2003)

Right Field corner at foul line: 14

**CAPACITY**

42,865, 43,863 (1997), 43,389 (2003), 43,405 (2005), 43,415 (2006)

**PHENOMENA**

Original plan was for a downtown domed stadium, but local voters fortunately rejected it. ♦ Scoreboard in left field. ♦ Home plate from Cleveland Stadium. ♦ Hosted major league record 455 consecutive sellouts June 12, 1995–April 2, 2001.

# Collinwood, Ohio

## *Euclid Beach Park*

**OCCUPANT**

NL Cleveland Spiders Sunday games on June 12 and 19, 1898

**LOCATION**

Lakeshore Blvd, then nine miles outside the city limits of Cleveland, but this is now in Cleveland, as Collinwood was annexed to Cleveland in 1910

**CURRENT USE**

Apartment building

**PHENOMENA**

Amusement park built in 1895. ♦ Sunday baseball here ended with a bang on June 19, 1898, when the Collinwood police arrested the entire Cleveland team in the bottom of the eighth inning, just after they had taken a 4–3 lead. The Spiders had to celebrate their victory in jail.

AT THE BALL PARK, COLUMBUS, GA.

Golden Park in Columbus, Georgia, used as a neutral site for several years by the Negro League's Kansas City Monarchs.

# Columbus, Georgia

## *Golden Park*

**OCCUPANT**

Neutral site used by NAL Kansas City Monarchs 1957–61

**LOCATION**

(N) 100 Fourth St (later Victory Dr), (W) Broadway, (S) Chattahoochee River, (E) Second Ave

**DIMENSIONS**

Foul Lines: 315
Center Field: 415

**CAPACITY**

6000 (1975), 5700 (1985)

**PHENOMENA**

Built in 1951. ♦ During the 1960s the Confederate flag and the New York Yankees emblem were painted side by side on the exterior wall behind home plate.

# Columbus, Ohio

## *Recreation Park (I)*

**OCCUPANT**

AA Columbus Senators May 1, 1883–September 22, 1884

**LOCATION**

(N) West Mound St, (W) Parsons Ave, (E) Meadow Ln (later Monroe St)

## *Recreation Park (II)*

**OCCUPANT**

AA Columbus Solons April 28, 1889–September 22, 1891

**LOCATION**

(N) Kossuth St, (W) Jaeger (later Fifth) St, (S) East Schiller St (later East Whittier Ave), (E) Ebner St

**DIMENSIONS**

Right Field: 400

## Neil Park (I)

**OCCUPANTS**

Neutral site use by AL Cleveland Blues August 3, 1902; AL Cleveland Naps May 17, 1903

**LOCATION**

(S) Buckingham St, (E) 551 Cleveland Ave

**DIMENSIONS**

Right Field: 240

## Neil Park (II)

**OCCUPANTS**

NNL Columbus Buckeyes 1921; NSL Columbus Turfs August–September 1932: neutral site used by Detroit Tigers July 23–24, 1905

**LOCATION**

Same as Neil Park (I)

## Red Bird Stadium

**AKA**

Jet Stadium, Franklin County Stadium, Cooper Stadium

**OCCUPANTS**

NNL Columbus Bluebirds April–August 1933; NNL Columbus Elite Giants 1935; neutral site used for Negro World Series NNL Washington-Homestead Grays vs. NAL Birmingham Black Barons game four in 1943

**LOCATION**

Center Field (E) South Glenwood Ave; Third Base (N) 1155 West Mound St, then I-70; Home Plate (W) South Princeton Ave; First Base (S) Green Lawn Cemetary

**DIMENSIONS**

Left Field: 415 (1938), 457 (1940), 336 (1960), 350 (1978), 355 (1984)

Center Field: 450 (1938), 430 (1940), 400 (1978)

Right Center: 337

Right Field: 315 (1938), 316 (1940), 345 (1960), 330 (1978)

**FENCES**

Left Field: 6

Branch Rickey built Red Bird Stadium, which opened in June 1932. It was home to various Negro League teams in the 1930s.

Center Field: 10
Right Field: 8

**CURRENT USE**
Minor league baseball

**CAPACITY**
17,500 (1938), 12,000 (1960), 15,000 (1978)

**PHENOMENA**
Opened June 3, 1932.

# Conway, South Carolina

## *Whittemore Athletic Field*

**OCCUPANT**
Neutral site used by NAL Raleigh Tigers May 6, 1961

# Covington, Kentucky

## *Star Baseball Park*

**AKA**
Covington Base Ball Park, Star Grounds

**OCCUPANT**
Neutral site used by NA Philadelphia Pearls September 21, 1875

**LOCATION**
Just across the river from Cincinnati, Ohio

**PHENOMENA**
Home of the Covington Stars.

# Crawfordsville, Indiana

## *Dean Park*

**OCCUPANT**
Neutral site used by NNL Indianapolis ABCs August 23, 1923

# Danville, Virginia

## *Peters' Park*

**OCCUPANT**
Neutral site used by NNL Homestead Grays one game in 1930s

**CURRENT USE**
Only the light towers and a "Peters' Park" sign remain

# Dayton, Ohio

## *Fairview Park*

**OCCUPANT**
Neutral site used by AL Cleveland Blues June 8, 1902

**LOCATION**
(N) 48 West Parkwood Dr, (W) Willowwood Dr, (S) West Fairview Ave, (E) North Main St

**CURRENT USE**
Brown Elementary School

## Ducks Park

**AKA**
Westwood Field

**OCCUPANT**
NNL Dayton Marcos 1920; 1926

**LOCATION**
Center Field (SE), Third Base (NE), Home Plate (NW), First Base (SW)

**DIMENSIONS**
Foul Lines: 360
Power Alleys: 360
Center Field: 360

**CAPACITY**
5000

**PHENOMENA**
Very high brick wall in right field.

# Decatur, Alabama

## Lakeside Park

**OCCUPANT**
Neutral site used by NAL Kansas City Monarchs 1957–61

**LOCATION**
Cherry St Northwest; Washington St Northwest, next to Dry Branch Creek Canal (later Wheeler Lake), adjacent to the Decatur Negro High School,

which in 1948 became Cherry Street Elementary School

## Legion Field

**OCCUPANT**
Neutral site used by NAL Kansas City Monarchs 1957–61

**LOCATION**
Highway 31 (later 6th Ave NE)

**CURRENT USE**
Gateway Shopping Center

# Denver, Colorado

## Mile High Stadium

**AKA**
Bears Stadium August 14, 1948–December 14, 1968

**OCCUPANT**
NL Colorado Rockies April 9, 1993–August 11, 1994

**LOCATION**
Left Field (E) Clay St, Third Base (N) West 20th Ave, First Base (W) Elliot St; Right Field (S) West 17th Ave, then McNichols Arena and I-25

**DIMENSIONS**
Left Field: 348, 335 (1993)
Left Center: 395, 375 (1993)
Center Field: 420, 423 (1993)
Right Center: 400
Right Field: 365, 370 (1993)
Backstop: 65

Den of the Denver Bears

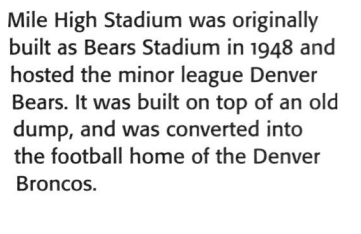

Mile High Stadium was originally built as Bears Stadium in 1948 and hosted the minor league Denver Bears. It was built on top of an old dump, and was converted into the football home of the Denver Broncos.

**FENCES**

Left Field: 12
Center Field: 30
Right Field: 14

**CAPACITY**

16,000, 19,000 (1960), 43,103 (1975), 75,123 (1985), 76,037 (1993), 76,100 (1994)

**PHENOMENA**

Built in 1948, home of minor league Bears/Zephyrs from August 14, 1948, through 1992. ◆ Left field stands moved for football. ◆ Playing field heated electrically to prevent freezing. ◆ Rockies drew largest season attendance ever of 4,483,350 here in 1993. ◆ The author was present here at largest NL regular season paid crowd ever—80,227 vs. Expos April 9, 1993. This was one of only 20 baseball crowds ever to exceed 80,000: AL regular season paid crowds at Cleveland Stadium (84,587 September 12, 1954; 82,781 paid, 83,434 total June 20, 1948); Yankee Stadium (82,437 paid May 30, 1940; 81,841 paid, 84,041 total May 30, 1938; 81,622 paid, 85,265 total September 9, 1928); Melbourne Olympics in Australia (114,000 December 1, 1956), Berlin Olympics in Germany (108,000 August 12, 1936), Meiji Stadium in Tokyo during MLB All-Star tour of Japan (100,000 November 1934), Yankee-Dodger game at LA Coliseum honoring Roy Campanella (93,103 May 7, 1959); World Series games at LA Coliseum (92,294; 92,550; 92,706 October 4–6, 1959) and Cleveland Stadium (81,897; 86,288 Oct 9–10, 1948); total (rather than paid) regular season crowds at LA Coliseum (90,751 August 8, 1959; 82,794 August 31, 1959), Yankee Stadium (80,403 April 19, 1931), and Cleveland Stadium (80,285 July 31, 1932); and lastly a semipro national semifinal between the Omaha Panhandlers and Cleveland White Auto at Brookside Park in Cleveland (100,000 October 10, 1915).

## Coors Field

**ARCHITECT**

HOK Sport

**OCCUPANT**

NL Colorado Rockies April 26, 1995, to date

**LOCATION**

Left Field (NW) Union Pacific RR tracks, then I-25; Third Base (SW) 20th St; First Base (SE) 2001 Blake St; Right Field (NE) Park Ave; in LoDo (lower downtown)

## DIMENSIONS

Left Field: 347
Left Center: 390
Deepest Left Center: 420
Center Field: 415
Deepest Right Center: 424
Right Center: 375
Right Field corner: 358
Right Field: 350
Backstop: 56.33, 50.33 (2003)

## FENCES

Left Field to Right Center: 8
Right Field (Manual Scoreboard): 14, 17 (2000), 14 (2003)

## FORMER USE

Railyards

## CAPACITY

50,200, 50,449 (2003)

## PHENOMENA

By far the most hitter-friendly park in the majors because of the thin air nearly a mile above sea level. Because the Rockies knew the ball would carry 7-8% farther here than at sea level, they tried to make sure the fences were far enough away to reduce home runs. ♦ What they did instead was to create a ballpark where, not only are there the most home runs in any ballpark, but there are the most number of doubles and triples too. ♦ A ball hit 400 feet at Yankee Stadium would travel 407 feet at Turner Field and 426 feet here. ♦ The field holds the record for most home runs in a season: 303 in 1999, which was 3.7 per game. ♦ The first 1–0 game took place July 8, 2005, in the park's 11th year, and there have only been two 2-0 games there through 2005. ♦ A much lesser known factor involving the weather here is the low humidity. Because it is so low, commonly between 5% and 20%, a curveball won't break nearly as much. ♦ Since 2002, the Rockies have kept all game balls in a special storeroom at 40% humidity to give pitchers a better chance to throw the breaking ball. ♦ Features a spectacular view of the Rocky Mountains from first base and right field seats. ♦ Garden in home dugout is maintained by Rockies pitchers. ♦ Originally designed for only 43,800 capacity, but seating was increased due to the huge crowds at Mile High Stadium. ♦ Upper-deck center field bleachers is known as the Rockpile. ♦ The 21st row of the upper deck is painted purple to indicate that it is 5280 feet above sea level, or a "mile high."

Coors Field, built on 76 acres, is a convenient walk from downtown Denver. Most of the seats are green; however, the 20th row in the upper deck is painted purple to show that it is exactly one mile above sea level.

# Detroit, Michigan

*See also* Hamtramck, Michigan; Springwells, Michigan

## *Recreation Park*

**OCCUPANTS**

NL Detroit Wolverines May 2, 1881–September 22, 1888; neutral site use by NL Cleveland Spiders September 23, 1890

**LOCATION**

(N) Willis St, (W) John R St, (S) Brady St, (E) Beaubien St; current Brush St would intersect the site; Brady St no longer exists in this area, but back then it was one block south of what is now Mack St

**FENCES**

All: 9

**PHENOMENA**

Cricket played on the north end of the field. ♦ The NL Spiders transferred a postponed game vs. Boston here on September 23, 1890. ♦ Torn down in 1894 and converted to residential lots.

## *Bennett Park*

**AKA**

Woodbridge Grove, the Haymarket

**OCCUPANT**

AL Detroit Tigers April 25, 1901–September 10, 1911

**LOCATION**

Left Field (W) National (later Cochrane) Ave, Third Base (S) Michigan Ave, First Base (E) Trumbull Ave, Right Field (N) lumberyard, then Cherry St (later Kaline Dr); same as Tiger Stadium but different orientation, in Corktown

**FORMER USE**

Haymarket in 1890s, minor league ballpark 1896–1900

In their first game at Bennett Field, on April 25, 1901, the Tigers pulled off one of the greatest comebacks in baseball history. Down 13–4 to Milwaukee going into the ninth inning, they rallied for 10 runs to win 14–13.

## DIMENSIONS

Left Field: 341, 345 (1901), 330 (1908), 298 (1909 World Series), 295 (1910)

Left Center: 362, 456 (1901) 420 (1910)

Center Field: 467, 432 (1901), 480 (1908)

Right Center: 349, 384 (1901), 325 (1907 World Series), 412 (1908)

Right Field: 371, 370 (1901), 440 (1908)

## FENCES

Left Field and Left Center: 10, 4 (1910)

Center Field: 8, 12 (1901), 16 (1910)

Right Center and Right Field: 10, 4 (1908)

## CAPACITY

5000, 7000 (1901), 10,500 (1908), 14,000 (1910)

## PHENOMENA

Opened in 1896. ◆ Infield was laid over a bunch of cobblestones, which worked their way up through the soil and caused many bad bounces, giving all infielders a ready excuse for any errors. ◆ The left field fence and right field fence met in deepest left center, where there was a clubhouse. To the left of the clubhouse was a small scoreboard, and to the right of the clubhouse was a groundskeepers shed, all of which were in play. The clubhouse was removed in 1908, and the small scoreboard was replaced by a larger one in 1910, left of dead center. ◆ Temporary bleachers in right were built for the 1907 World Series. After the Tigers purchased the lumberyard, behind the fence in right, over the winter of 1907–08, they moved home plate 40 feet toward the outfield, added seats behind the plate, and added permanent bleachers in right. ◆ Temporary bleachers in left for the 1909 World Series were replaced in 1910 by permanent bleachers, built specifically to block the view from wildcat bleachers which sat on top of barns along National Avenue behind left field. ◆ Named for Charlie Bennett, Wolverines catcher, whose legs were amputated after a 1894 train accident. He threw out the first ball every opening day from 1896 to 1927. ◆ Dimensions 1901–11 based on 1897 Sanborn fire insurance map. ◆ Torn down October 1911.

## Tiger Stadium

### AKA

Navin Field 1912–37, Briggs Stadium 1938–60

### ARCHITECT

Osborn Engineering

### OCCUPANTS

AL Detroit Tigers April 20, 1912–September 27, 1999; NAL Detroit Stars June 28, 1957

### LOCATION

Left Field (NW) Cherry St (later Kaline Dr), then Fisher Freeway/I-75; Third Base (SW) National (later Cochrane) Ave; First Base (SE) Michigan Ave (running W to E); Right Field: (NE) 2121 Trumbull Ave; same site as Bennett Park but turned around 90 degrees, in Corktown section of Detroit

### DIMENSIONS

Left Field: 345 (1921), 340.58 (1926), 339 (1930), 339 (1934), 340 (1938), 342 (1939), 340 (1942)

Left Field Power Alley: 368 (1942)

Left Center: 392 (1942)

Center Field: 467 (1927), 455 (1930), 464 (1931), 459 (1936), 450 (1937), 440 (1938), 415 (1954), 440 (marked 1955), 425 (actual 1955),

Right Center: 375 (1942), 349 (1954), 375 (1955)

Right Field: 370 (1921), 370.91 (1926), 372 (1930), 367 (1931), 325 (1936), 302 (1954), 325 (1955)

Backstop: 54.35 (1954), 66 (1955)

Foul Territory: small

### SURFACE

Bluegrass

### FENCES

All Fences: 5 concrete topped by screen

Left Field: 20 (1935), 30 (1937), 10 (1938), 12 (1940), 15 (1946), 12 (1953), 14 (1954), 12 (1955), 11 (1958), 9 (1962)

Center Field: 9 (1940), 15 (1946), 11 (1950), 9 (1953), 14 (1954), 9 (1955)

Briggs Stadium, formerly known as Navin Field. Walter Briggs, a Detroit manufacturer, renamed the park in 1938, two years after he bought a controlling interest in the team.

Flag Pole in play: 125 (5 feet in front of fence in center field, just left of dead center)

Right of Flag Pole: 7 (1946)

Right Field: 8 (1940), 30 (1944), 10 (1945), 20 (1950), 8 (1953), 9 (1958), 30 (1961), 9 (1962)

**FORMER USE**

Bennett Park 1896–1911

**CAPACITY**

23,000, 29,000 (1923), 36,000 (1936), 58,000 (1938), 54,000 (1953), 52,904 (1961), 54,220 (1969), 52,687 (1981), 46,846 (1997), 52,416 (1999)

**PHENOMENA**

When opened in 1912, park was on larger site than 1911 Bennett Park, as this park (called Navin Field in 1912) extended all the way to National Ave. ♦ The 125-foot-high flag pole in play in deep center, just to the left of the 440 mark, was the highest outfield obstacle ever in play in baseball history. ♦ Right field second deck overhung the lower deck by 10 feet. ♦ Spotlights mounted under the overhang illuminated the right field warning track, which was shadowed from the normal light standards. ♦ Second decks added behind home plate in 1923, in right in 1935, and in left and center in 1936. ♦ Screen in right in 1944 and in 1961 required balls to be hit into the second deck to be home runs. ♦ Only double-deck bleachers in the majors, upper deck from left center to center, lower deck from center to right center. ♦ The scoreboard in left was originally at the 440 mark in dead center (that was actually 425), but was moved in 1961 when Norm Cash, Al Kaline, and Charlie Maxwell complained that it hindered the batters' view of the pitch. ♦ First homer at Navin Field, on May 5, 1912, came on a fluke bounce which hopped through the side door of the left-center scoreboard. ♦ Cobb's Lake was the area in front of plate, which was always soaked with water by groundskeepers to slow down Ty Cobb's bunts. ♦ When slugging teams came to visit, manager Ty Cobb had the groundskeepers put in temporary bleachers in the outfield, turning long drives into ground-rule doubles. ♦ Sign above entrance to visitors clubhouse: "Visitors' Clubhouse—No Visitors Allowed." ♦ In the 1930s and 1940s, there was a 315 marker on the second deck in right field. ♦ Home plate and

In June 1956 Mickey Mantle poled two Billy Hoeft pitches into the right-center bleachers at Tiger Stadium, something no other player had done since the bleachers were built in the late 1930s. Two years later, he hit a Jim Bunning pitch over the right field roof onto Trumbull Avenue, some 500 feet away. Al Kaline once said, "Tiger Stadium's strengths lie not in its dazzling architecture or creature comforts but in its character and charm."

batters boxes were oriented toward right-center rather than straight out to the mound. This tended to give right-handed pitchers more outside corner strike calls and disoriented visiting batters. ♦ Mickey Mantle's reported 634-foot homer here on September 10, 1960, is the longest ever claimed. ♦ Saved in 1974 when owner John Fetzer told the Pontiac Silverdome committee, "This franchise belongs to the inner city of Detroit; I'm just the caretaker." That mantle of caretaker passed on to Frank Rashid's Tiger Stadium Fan Club, which managed to stave off the abandonment of the ballpark for almost a decade.

## Mack Park

**OCCUPANTS**

NNL Detroit Stars 1920–29; NAL Detroit Stars 1954–57; NAL Detroit Clowns 1958; NAL Detroit Stars 1959; NAL Detroit-New Orleans Stars (half of the home games) 1960–61

**LOCATION**

Mack Ave, Fairview St

**CURRENT USE**

Fairview Greens Apartments

**PHENOMENA**

Fire halted July 6, 1929, game vs. the Monarchs, injuring 103 people.

## De Quindre Park

**AKA**

Linton Field, Cubs Park

**OCCUPANT**

NAL Detroit Stars 1937

**LOCATION**

(N) McNichols Rd East; (W) Riopelle St, then I-70; (S) RR tracks, then Modern St; (E) De Quindre St

## Sportsman's Park

**OCCUPANT**

NAL Detroit Stars one game 1937

**LOCATION**

Livernois Ave, Burkhouse St

## *Comerica Park*

**ARCHITECTS**

HOK Sport, SHG Inc.

**OCCUPANT**

AL Detroit Tigers April 11, 2000, to date

**LOCATION**

Center Field (S/SE) Adams St, Third Base (E/NE) Brush St, Home Plate (N/NW) Montcalm St, First Base (W/SW) Witherell St

**DIMENSIONS**

Left Field: 345
Left Field Power Alley: 398, 395 (2001), 370 (2003)
Left Center: 418, 398 (2003)
Center Field: 420
Right Center: 403
Right Field Power Alley: 356
Right Field: 330
Foul Territory: small

**FENCES**

Left Field: 8, 6.83 (2003)
Left Center and Center Field: 8, 8.5 (2003)
Right Center: 11, 11.5 (2003)
Right Field: 8, 8.5 (2003)

**CAPACITY**

40,120

**PHENOMENA**

Center field flag pole was in play 2000-02. ♦ When the Tigers hit a home run, the fountain in center spouts and the two big tigers above the huge scoreboard in left roar. ♦ Carousel and Ferris wheel in the stands.

---

# Dover, Delaware

## *Fairview Park Fair Grounds*

**AKA**

Dover Grounds

**OCCUPANT**

Neutral site used by NA Philadelphia Athletics June 24, 1875

When a Tiger player hits a home run at Comerica Park, nestled in downtown Detroit, the two tigers atop the scoreboard roar and the fountain in center field shoots water in the air.

When the original Athletic Park burned down in 1939, a new version was completed just two weeks later. The park is most famous for its role in the film *Bull Durham*.

**LOCATION**

(N) Ross St, (W) Pear St, then Delaware (now PW and B) Railroad, (S) Williams St, (E) Queen (later Kirkwood) St

**FORMER USE**

Delaware State Fair starting in September 1878

**CURRENT USE**

Delaware Public Warehouse since 1929 on the west side of the park

---

# Durham, North Carolina

## *Athletic Park*

**OCCUPANTS**

Neutral site used by NAL Birmingham Black Barons 1940s; NAL Raleigh Tigers May 22, 1961

**LOCATION**

Left Field (N) West Geer St, Third Base (W) Washington St, First Base (S) West Corporation St, Right Field (E) Foster St

**DIMENSIONS**

Left Field: 360 (1939), 361 (1940), 330 (1965)
Center Field: 460 (1939), 440 (1940), 410 (1965)
Right Field: 290 (1939), 301 (1940), 307 (1965)

**FENCES**

Left Field: 24 (12 wood above 12 embankment 1939), 8 (wood 1965)

Center Field: 27 (12 wood above 15 embankment 1939), 8 (wood 1965)

Right Center: 20 (8 wooden bull above 12 Durham Technical Institute brick wall), 8 (wood 1965)

Right Field: 50 (35 brick above 15 embankment 1939), 16 (wood 1965)

**CAPACITY**

4000 (1940)

**PHENOMENA**

Before the inner fence was added in 1965, center field had a unique large triangular ledge on top of the embankment which was in play, with a flag pole,

12 bushes, a tree, and eight telephone poles that buttressed the fence.

---

# East Orange, New Jersey

## Grove Street Oval (II)

**AKA**

Grove Street Senior Ball Diamond, Monte Irvin Field, East Orange Oval

**OCCUPANT**

NNL New York Cubans 1941–47

**LOCATION**

Left Field (E) Greenwood Ave, Third Base (N) Grove Pl, First Base (W) Grove St North, Right Field (S) Eaton Pl

**DIMENSIONS**

Left Field: 240
Center Field: 360 to water fountain
Right Field: 280

**FENCES**

Left Field: 25 (garage walls)
Center Field: 4 (water fountain)
Right Field: none

**CURRENT USE**

Community ball diamond

**PHENOMENA**

No fence in center field, but there were hedges. ◆ The four-foot high water fountain in deepest center was in play. ◆ Trees and tennis courts in right were in play, as there was no fence in right field either. ◆ Scoreboard in left, as well as poplar trees. ◆ Clubhouse down right field line in foul territory. ◆ "Boojum" Jud Wilson hit longest ball ever hit here, over water fountain in center. ◆ Oval (I) dedicated Labor Day 1908 in New Jersey State Senate vs. New Jersey State General Assembly game. ◆ Fire destroyed that park at 4 AM on May 3, 1925. ◆ Oval (II) dedicated May 1, 1926, and renamed Monte Irvin Field June 6, 1986, in ceremony culminating four-year effort initiated by the author and SABR Negro Leagues Committee, which designed the plaque marking the site.

---

# Edenton, North Carolina

## Hicks Field

**OCCUPANT**

Neutral site used by NAL Raleigh Tigers May 20, 1961

**LOCATION**

Left Field (NE Park Ave; Third Base (NW) 600 Woodard St; First Base (SW) East Freemason St; Right Field (SE) North Oakum St; adjacent to John A. Holmes High School

**CAPACITY**

2500

**FORMER USE**

Edenton Agricultural and Fish Fair

**CURRENT USE**

Home of the Edenton Steamers of the Coastal Plain League and the Holmes High School baseball team

**PHENOMENA**

Built in 1939 by FDR's WPA.

◆    ◆    ◆

# Elizabeth, New Jersey

## *Waverly Fairgrounds*

**AKA**

Domestic Field, Waverly Park, Weequahic Park

**OCCUPANT**

NA Elizabeth Resolutes April 28–July 23, 1873

**LOCATION**

Frelinghuysen Ave; Haynes Ave; (E) Conrail RR tracks, then 1/9 Expressway, then Newark Liberty Airport; in Weequahic Park; on Elizabeth side of current Elizabeth/Newark border; back then was in town of Waverly, which no longer exists

**CURRENT USE**

B'nai Jeshuron Cemetery, Weequahic City Park

◆ ◆ ◆

# Elmira, New York

## *Maple Avenue Driving Park*

**AKA**

Elmira Grounds

**OCCUPANT**

Neutral site used by NL Buffalo Bisons morning and afternoon games October 10, 1885

# Erie, Pennsylvania

## *Ainsworth Field*

**AKA**

Athletic Park before 1939

Ainsworth Field in Erie, Pennsylvania, was another neutral site used by the NAL Kansas City Monarchs.

**OCCUPANT**

Neutral site used by NAL Kansas City Monarchs 1940s

**LOCATION**

Center Field (NE), Third Base (NW), Home Plate (SW), First Base (SE)

**DIMENSIONS**

Left Field: 390 (1940)
Center Field: 500 (1940)
Right Field: 356 (1940)

**CAPACITY**

5000 (1940)

---

# Fort Wayne, Indiana

## *Grand Duchess*

**AKA**

Kekionga Base Ball Grounds

**OCCUPANT**

NA Fort Wayne Kekiongas May 4–August 29, 1871

**LOCATION**

Center Field (N) canal, later Nickel Plate RR tracks; Third Base (W) Cherry St; Home Plate (S) West Main St; First Base (E) Frederick St, then West Main St Bridge across the "ever-present menace" of the St. Mary's River (there were many floods back then); in the Nebraska neighborhood, north of Camp Allen and west of downtown

**CURRENT USE**

Catholic elementary school, homes, churches, riverfront park which hosts Fort Wayne's 10-day Three Rivers Festival every year in July

**PHENOMENA**

Scene of the very first major league game ever played. The Kekiongas defeated the Cleveland Forest Citys 2–0, in two hours exactly, on May 4, 1871, before 200 fans. ♦ According to the local newspaper, the *Old Fort News,* the park was christened the "Grand Duchess" because her grandstand ornamentation was so lavish. ♦ At first the unique name applied just to the grandstand, but it gradually came to be used for the entire ballpark. ♦ Burned down November 5, 1871. ♦ Beginning on April 23, 1862, the Summit City Club played baseball at Hamilton Field. Sometime between 1866 and 1871, Hamilton Field was abandoned and baseball in Fort Wayne moved here to Kekionga Base Ball Grounds. ♦ The first major league game ever played is widely reported, albeit inaccurately, to have been played at Hamilton Field.

## *Jailhouse Flats (I)*

**AKA**

League Park (I), Swinney Park

**OCCUPANT**

Neutral site used by AL Cleveland Blues June 22 and August 31, 1902

**LOCATION**

(N) St. Mary's River, (W) Calhoun St, (S) North Clinton St, (E) Duck St; on the near north side of downtown

**PHENOMENA**

The ballpark got its name because it was across the street from the old jailhouse. ♦ Used for a postseason October 24, 1882, game that was part of a series between the champions of the NL and AA, but this is not recognized as anything more than a series of exhibition games, since no championship was at stake. ♦ The park burned down on July 12, 1930, and was rebuilt as League Park (II).

# Geauga Lake, Ohio

## *Geauga Lake Grounds*

**OCCUPANT**

Neutral site used by AA Cleveland Spiders July 22, 29, August 26, 1888

**LOCATION**

On the shores of Geauga Lake, some 20 miles southeast of downtown Cleveland; in 1888 in the city of Aurora. Park located close to railroad station that was used by Cleveland fans attending Sunday games

**CURRENT USE**

Six Flags at Geauga Lake amusement park

**PHENOMENA**

Created in 1883 as a huge amusement park. ◆ Lake was formed by a dam on Burke Brook. ◆ In 1893, 100,000 paying customers visited the rides, boathouse, dance pavilion, skating rink, and zoo. ◆ Torn down in early 1930s and used by Cleveland Building Supply Company as a clay quarry. ◆ The site used to be in the town of Aurora.

# Geddes, New York

## *Lake-Side Park*

**OCCUPANT**

Neutral site used by NL Syracuse Stars 1879

**LOCATION**

(NE) New York Central RR tracks, (N) Bridge St, (SW) Delaware, Lackawanna, and Western RR

tracks, called the West Shore Railroad embankment, (SE) Marsh Rd (later Hiawatha Blvd), (E) Onondaga Lake

**PHENOMENA**

Outfield was a marshy swamp with many weeds growing in it.

# Gloucester City, New Jersey

## *Gloucester Point Grounds*

**OCCUPANT**

Neutral site used by AA Philadelphia Athletics for 31 Sunday games June 10, 1888–October 12, 1890

**LOCATION**

Just behind Thompson's Hotel, along a creek

**PHENOMENA**

A total of four official games were played here in 1888, 14 in 1889, and 13 in 1890. ◆ Although the June 10, 1888, game was later thrown out and not counted in the standings, it was an official game when it was played, and therefore is counted here.

# Grand Rapids, Michigan

## *Ramona Park*

**AKA**

Ramona Athletic Park

**OCCUPANT**

Neutral site used by AL Detroit Tigers May 24, 1903

Ramona Park was part of a large amusement park in Grand Rapids, Michigan. The Tigers avoided Detroit's ban on Sunday baseball by playing Washington in a 1903 game that drew 6,000. Detroit won, 5–4.

**PHENOMENA**

Grass infield but the entire outfield was dirt. ♦ Hosted first minor league night game July 7, 1909, in Central League as Grand Rapids defeated Zanesville 11–10 in seven innings before 4500 fans.

## *Valley Field*

**OCCUPANT**

Neutral site used by NAL Kansas City Monarchs 1956–61

**PHENOMENA**

Kansas City Monarchs' owner Ted Rasberry lived in Grand Rapids, so he moved many of the team's games here.

# Greenbush, New York

## *Greenbush Grounds*

**OCCUPANT**

Neutral site used by NL Troy Trojans May 16–18 and morning game May 30, 1882

**LOCATION**

Just across the Hudson River from Albany; the site was then in the town of Greenbush but is now within the city limits of Rensselaer

# Greensboro, North Carolina

## *War Memorial Stadium*

**OCCUPANT**

Neutral site used by NAL Raleigh Tigers May 13, 1961

**LOCATION**

(NW) Homeland Ave, (SW) 510 Yanceyville St, (SE) East Lindsay St, (NE) Dewey St

**DIMENSIONS**

Foul Lines: 327
Center Field: 401

**CAPACITY**

10,000

**PHENOMENA**

Originally built as a half-mile dirt racing track. ♦

War Memorial Stadium in Greensboro, North Carolina, was a neutral site used by the NAL Raleigh Tigers in 1961. Note the unusual shape of the stands.

The stands are shaped like a big *J*, with the long stem of the *J* along the left field line, extending beyond the left field fence. The short end of the *J* is along the first base side, with very few seats on the first base side of the plate. ♦ The field was featured briefly in the movie *Bull Durham*.

Center Field: 420 (1940), 405 (1950)
Right Field: 315 (1940), 335 (1950)

**CAPACITY**

6500 (1940), 7023 (1950)

# Greenville, South Carolina

## *Municipal Stadium*

**OCCUPANT**

Neutral site used by NAL Memphis Red Sox 1940s

**LOCATION**

(NW) Martin Rd, (SW) Marrowbone Creek, (SE) Ridge Rd (later One Braves Ave), (NE) Mauldin Rd

**DIMENSIONS**

Left Field: 340 (1940), 335 (1950)

## *Meadowbrook Park*

**OCCUPANT**

Neutral site used by NAL Raleigh Tigers May 8, 1961

# Greenwood, South Carolina

## *Brewer High School Field*

**OCCUPANT**

Neutral site used by NAL Raleigh Tigers May 9, 1961

# Hamilton, Ohio

## *Hamilton Grounds*

**OCCUPANT**

Neutral site used by AA Cincinnati Reds August 25, 1889

**PHENOMENA**

The Cincinnati Law and Order Society forced the AA Reds to abandon Sunday play at home after August 11, 1889. The Reds rescheduled their four remaining Sunday home games (August 18, 25, October 6, 13) in Ludlow, Kentucky. However, Kentucky authorities prevented them from doing so. So they moved the August 25 game against Brooklyn here, having been assured by Hamilton authorities it would be OK. But then the Hamilton Law and Order League complained. So in the top of the fourth of a 2–2 game, with Joe Visner on first and Bridegrooms batter Bob Caruthers stepping up to the plate, Hamilton Police Chief Lindsey marched onto the diamond to arrest both teams. The players scattered to avoid arrest, but six or seven were caught and taken off to jail, where the Reds' owner had to pay Mayor Dick $149.40, or $8.30 for each of the 18 players who were in the game in the top of the fourth. The game was never finished, and the Reds played no more Sunday home games that season.

# Hammond, Indiana

## *Turner Field*

**OCCUPANT**

Neutral site used by NAL Chicago American Giants vs. Jacksonville July 6, 1941

# Hampton, Virginia

## *Hampton Institute Field*

**OCCUPANT**

Neutral site used by NNL Chicago American Giants 1920s

# Hamtramck, Michigan

## *Hamtramck Stadium*

**AKA**

Veterans Park

**OCCUPANTS**

NNL Detroit Stars May 11, 1930–September 1931; NEWL Detroit Wolves 1932; NNL Detroit Stars 1933

**LOCATION**

Left Field (NW) Goodson St; Third Base (SW) Joseph Campau St; First Base (SE) Dan St, then railroad tracks; Right Field (NE) Gallagher St; just southwest of Keyworth Stadium, the home of the Hamtramck High School Cosmos football team; just north of GM Cadillac Assembly Plant

**DIMENSIONS**

Left Field: 315
Center Field: 528
Right Field: 407
Back Stop: 55

**CURRENT USE**

High school football

**PHENOMENA**

Opened May 11, 1930, with a game between the Stars and the New York Cubans, with Ty Cobb throwing out the first ball. ♦ Detroit's first major league night game was here, June 28, 1930, vs. the Kansas City Monarchs.

# Harrisburg, Pennsylvania

## *West End Grounds*

**OCCUPANT**

ECL Harrisburg Giants 1924–27

## *Island Stadium*

**AKA**

Forsters Island Park

**OCCUPANT**

NNL Harrisburg-St. Louis Stars April–May 1943 (all home games in Harrisburg, none in St. Louis)

**LOCATION**

On Forsters Island, now called City Island, in the middle of the Susquehanna River; Center Field (SW), Third Base (SE), Home Plate (NE), First Base (NW)

**DIMENSIONS**

Left Field: 320 (1940)
Center Field: 415 (1940)
Right Field: 325 (1940)

**CURRENT USE**

Commerce Bank Park, used for Eastern League games

**CAPACITY**

5000 (1940)

**PHENOMENA**

Frequently flooded by the Susquehanna River. Reached by the Market Street Bridge.

# Harrison, New Jersey

## *Harrison Field*

**AKA**

Federal League Park, Harrison Park, Peppers Park 1915

**ARCHITECT**

C.B. Comstock

**OCCUPANT**

FL Newark Peppers April 16–October 3, 1915

**LOCATION**

(N) Middlesex St, (W) Second St, then Passaic River, (S) Burlington St, (E) Third St; between Hudson and Manhattan RR tracks and Pennsylvania RR tracks; just across the Passaic River from Newark

**DIMENSIONS**

Foul Lines: 375
Center Field: 450

**CAPACITY**

21,000 (1915)

**FORMER USE**

West Hudson football field

**PHENOMENA**

The NL Giants discussed playing Sunday games here in 1918, but never actually did so. ♦ The FL Peppers combined bicycle races here with their baseball games to raise attendance. ♦ Used in summer of 1917 as an army camp by the First Regiment of Anniston and by a company of African-American soldiers from New York. ♦ Fire on August 18, 1923. ♦ Completely destroyed by second fire on August 23, 1924. ♦ Plaque to mark the site dedicated June 3, 1995

# Hartford, Connecticut

## *Hartford Trotting Park*

**OCCUPANT**
Neutral use by NA Middletown Mansfields June 21, July 3, August 9, 1872

## *Hartford Ball Club Grounds*

**OCCUPANTS**
NA Hartford Dark Blues May 1, 1874–October 29, 1875; NL Hartford Dark Blues May 1–September 30, 1876; neutral site used by NL Hartfords of Brooklyn one game in 1877

**LOCATION**
Center Field (W) Father Jerzy Popleluszko Court, Third Base (S) Hendricksen Ave, Home Plate (E) Wyllys St, First Base (N) Charter Oak Ave

**CURRENT USE**
The Church of the Good Shepherd still stands at 155 Wyllys Avenue

**PHENOMENA**
Three large apple trees, one in left, one in center, and one in right. The largest tree by far was the one in center, and the center fielder played right under it.

♦   ♦   ♦

# Havana, Cuba

## *Estadio Gran (I)*

**AKA**
Grand Stadium

**OCCUPANT**
NNL Havana Cuban Stars 1920

**PHENOMENA**
Although this was their home park, the Cuban Stars actually played all their games on the road during 1920. Before they could ever play a home game, they moved to Cincinnati in 1921 and then to New York in 1922. ♦ The 1884 UA St. Paul Saints and the 1920 NNL Havana Cuban Stars are the only major league teams to never play a home game. ♦ The park was replaced in the 1940s with Estadio Gran (II), also called Estadio Latino Americano, where a famous incident happened on July 25, 1959. Cuban soldiers, among 2572 fans watching a Havana Sugar Kings-Rochester Red Wings game, celebrated the Cuban Revolution's 26th of July Celebration as the game went past midnight, tied 4–4 in the 11th, by firing machine guns into the air. This Cuban holiday celebrates the July 26, 1953, attack led by Castro on Batista's Moncada army garrison in Santiago de Cuba, now seen as the birth of Cuban Revolution. After four gunfire delays, bullets struck and injured Red Wings third base Coach Frank Verdi and Sugar Kings shortstop Leo Cardenas. The game was finally postponed at 1:30 AM. It was never finished.

## *Estadio Cerveza Tropicale*

**AKA**
Tropical Stadium, Estadio Pepe Marrero

Havana's La Tropicale, home to years of Cuban baseball, hosted a memorable seven-game series in October 1930 between two teams of traveling all-stars which featured nine future Hall of Famers, including Rabbit Maranville, Paul Waner, Pie Traynor, Carl Hubbell, and Bill Terry.

**OCCUPANT**

NNL Cubans neutral site games 1930s and 1940s

**DIMENSIONS**

Left Field: 498 (1930), 350 (1941)
Center Field: 505 (1930), 494 (1941)
Right Field: 398 (1930), 350 (1941)
Foul Territory: huge down the right field line

**CURRENT USE**

Lacrosse, soccer, track, and field events

**PHENOMENA**

Built in 1930 for the Pan American Games. ◆ Site of seven-game major league all-star series in October 1930, won 5–2 by Jewel Ens' team over Davey Bancroft's team. ◆ Also scene of the Second World Baseball Championships August 12–26, 1939. ◆ When the Brooklyn Dodgers had spring training here in 1941, a wire fence was built around the field which reduced its dimensions. ◆ Cubaball 2001 tour resulted in polishing of the four bronze tablets in the stadium.

# Hoboken, New Jersey

## *Elysian Fields*

**OCCUPANT**

Neutral site used by NA New York Mutuals July 4, 1873

**LOCATION**

(NW) Hudson St; (SW) 10th St; (SE) Hoboken Shore Blvd (later Frank Sinatra Dr), then campus of Stevens Institute of Technology and the Hudson River; (NE) 11th St

**FENCES**

None

**CURRENT USE**

Plaque at 11th St and Washington St shows where

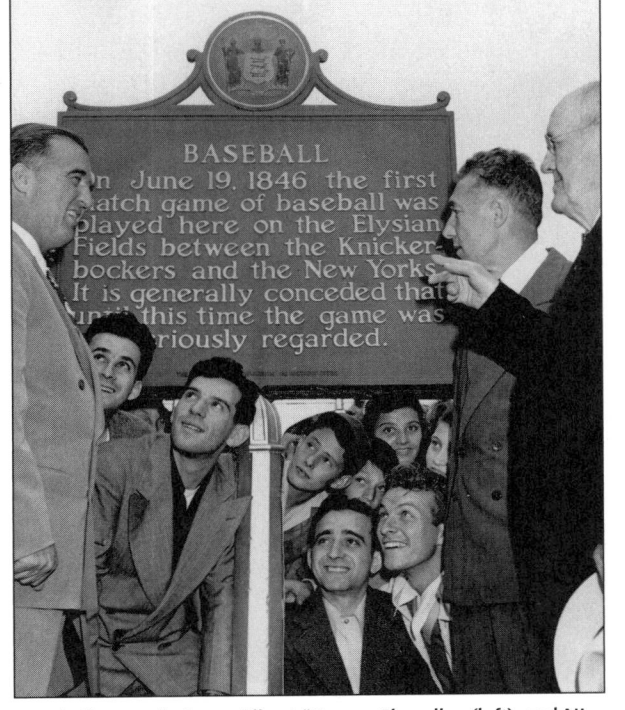

Baseball commissioner Albert "Happy Chandler (left) and NL president Ford Frick at the June 19, 1946 dedication of a plaque in Hoboken, NJ, commemorating baseball's first organized game 100 years earlier.

the park used to be; now an industrial site and a public park occupy the site

**PHENOMENA**

First prearranged baseball game between two organized teams under the Alexander Cartwright rules was played here on June 19, 1846. The New York Base Ball Club defeated the New York Knickerbockers Second Team 23–1. ♦ Two New York Knickerbocker Club teams had played an earlier game here on October 6, 1845. ♦ The field was along the water so that New York teams could get off the ferry boat from Manhattan and start to play ball immediately. ♦ Along the Foul Lines there were trees and taverns. ♦ Earlier games had been played in New York City at Retreat in Broadway (Jones) on April 26, 1823, and at Madison Square in 1832 with the 1st Ward Team of Lower Manhattan playing the 9th/15th Wards Team of Upper Manhattan.

# Homestead, Pennsylvania

## *Municipal Field*

**OCCUPANT**

Neutral site used by NNL Homestead Grays 1930s

**PHENOMENA**

The Grays played rarely in their hometown of Homestead, playing almost all of their games during the 1930s and 1940s in nearby Pittsburgh.

# Honolulu, Hawaii

## *Aloha Stadium*

**AKA**

Halawa Stadium 1975

**OCCUPANT**

Neutral site used by NL San Diego Padres April 19–20, 1997

**LOCATION**

(NW) Kamehameha Hwy, then Pearl Harbor; (SW) 99-500 Salt Lake Blvd; (SE) Halawa Stream, then H1 Expressway; (NE) Moanalua Rd

**DIMENSIONS**

Foul Lines: 325
Power Alleys: 375
Center Field: 400

**SURFACE**

Monsanto AstroTurf

Officially opened on September 12, 1975, Aloha Stadium features a unique air film cushion movement system that makes it possible to move four 7,000-seat sections of the stands into three different configurations: a traditional diamond for baseball (doubling as a wide rectangle for soccer), an oval for football, and a triangle for concerts.

**CAPACITY**

50,000

**PHENOMENA**

Padres moved April 19 doubleheader and April 20 three-game series vs. the Cards here because of construction preparing Qualcomm Stadium to host the Super Bowl. ♦ Opened in 1975 to replace old Honolulu Stadium, an ancient rickety wooden ballpark known as the Termite Palace.

# Houston, Texas

## *Buff Stadium*

**AKA**

Buffalo Stadium, Busch Stadium

**OCCUPANT**

NAL Houston Eagles 1949–50

**LOCATION**

Left Field (NE) 4000 Harby St, Third Base (NW) Cattle St, First Base (SW) 4001 Gulf Freeway/I-45, Right Field (SE) Cullen Blvd, then Southern Pacific RR tracks

**DIMENSIONS**

Left Field: 344, 345 (1938)
Center Field: 430, 440 (1938)
Right Field: 344, 325 (1938)

**FENCES**

Left Field and Right Field: 12
Left Center Scoreboard: 24
Center Field: 18

**CAPACITY**

12,000, 14,000 (1938)

**CURRENT USE**

Home plate's exact location is commemorated by a plaque in the Houston Sports Hall of Fame, which forms part of the Fingers Furniture Store

**PHENOMENA**

Opened in April 1928. ♦ Named for Buffalo Bayou, which bisects Houston. ♦ Two huge black buffaloes stood on either side of the left-center field scoreboard. The one on the left looked right toward the scoreboard, and the one on the right looked left toward the scoreboard. There were also huge pictures of buffaloes on the adobe wall by the Spanish-style entrance.

## *Colt Stadium*

**AKA**

Mosquito Heaven

**OCCUPANT**

NL Houston Colt .45s April 10, 1962–September 27, 1964

**LOCATION**

Left Field (N) East-West Utility Rd, Third Base (W) 8400 Kirby Dr, First Base (S) Murworth St, (SE) construction site for the Astrodome, Right Field (E) North Stadium Dr

**DIMENSIONS**

Foul Lines: 360

Power Alleys: 395
Center Field: 420
Deepest corners in center just left and right of dead center: 427
Backstop: 60

**FENCES**

Left and Right: 8
Center Field Screen: 30

**CURRENT USE**

Site is now the Astrodome's northwestern parking lot, but the stadium itself is used in Gomez Palacio, Mexico, as a Mexican League stadium

**CAPACITY**

25,000, 32,601 (June 29, 1962), 33,010 (1964)

**PHENOMENA**

Home of largest and peskiest mosquitoes in major league history, and the most popular MLB saloon ever–the Fast Draw Saloon. ♦ Park had to be regularly sprayed by the ground crew between innings. ♦ Groundbreaking ceremony used .45-caliber blanks

Bobby Shantz throws the first pitch to Lou Brock on April 10, 1962, to inaugurate Colt Stadium and the Houston Colt .45s' first season. Shantz pitched a complete-game victory, beating the Cubs 11–2.

President Lyndon B. Johnson joined 47,878 fans for the opening of Houston's Astrodome on April 9, 1965. The team, renamed the Astros, won an exhibition with the Yankees 2–1 in 12 innings on a Nellie Fox single. Mickey Mantle hit the first homer in the new park.

rather than shovels. ♦ Scoreboards in center on both sides of a 30-foot-high batters background. ♦ Stiff wind blew in from right toward home. ♦ Power alley measurements not marked on the wall. ♦ Lay in decay until early 1970s, when it was moved to Torreon, Mexico's twin city of Gomez Palacio by the Mexican League Torreon Cotton Growers.

## Astrodome

### AKA

Harris County Domed Stadium 1965, Eighth Wonder of the World

### ARCHITECTS

Herman Lloyd & W. B. Morgan & Wilson, Morris, Crain, & Anderson

### OCCUPANT

NL Houston Astros April 12, 1965–October 9, 1999

### LOCATION

Center Field (E) Fannin St (later Holly Hall St); Third Base (N) Old Spanish Trail (later North Stadium St); (NW) Colt Stadium; Home Plate (W) 8400 Kirby Dr; First Base (S) Astrohall, Astrorena, Six Flags Astroworld, and Exhibit Center, then South Loop Freeway/I-610; domed roof of 4796 lucite panels and steel girders; right next to Reliant Stadium

### DIMENSIONS

Foul Lines: 340, 330 (1972), 340 (1977), 330 (1985), 325 (1992), 330 (1993), 325 (1994)

Power Alleys: 375, 390 (1966), 378 (1972), 390 (1977), 378 (1985), 375 (1992), 380 (1993), 375 (1994)

Center Field: 406, 400 (1972), 406 (1977), 400 (1985)

Dome apex: 208

Backstop: 60.5, 67 (1990), 52 (1993)

### FENCES

Left and Right Field: 16 (9 concrete below 3 wire, 2 concrete, and 2 wire plus railing), 12 (concrete, 1969), 10 (concrete, 1977), 10 (canvas, 1990), 19.5 (concrete, 1991), 10 canvas (1992) Between foul poles and scoreboards 8 (canvas, 1994)

Scoreboards in left and right: 16 (steel, 1994)

Center Field: 12 (concrete), 10 (concrete, 1977), 10 (canvas 1990)

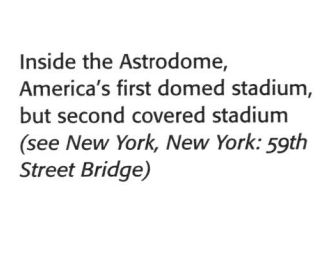

Inside the Astrodome, America's first domed stadium, but second covered stadium (*see New York, New York: 59th Street Bridge*)

**SURFACE**

Infield grass (1965) Tifway 419 Bermuda grass specially selected for indoor play, but it died. AstroTurf on all but the part normally dirt April 18, 1966, through 1970; on all the infield except for sliding pits 1971–99; Outfield grass April 12, 1965–July 18, 1966, but it died too; AstroTurf (July 19, 1966–October 9, 1999)

**CURRENT USE**

Adult league softball games

**CAPACITY**

46,217, 44,500 (1968), 47,690 (1982), 54,816 (1990), 53,821 (1993), 54,370 (1999)

**PHENOMENA**

The second major league covered stadium, the first being the field under the Queensboro/59th Street Bridge in New York City, used by the New York Cubans of the Negro National League in 1939. ♦ The roof had 4796 clear panes of glass, but they caused a glare, preventing fielders from seeing the ball, so two of the eight roof sections were painted white on April 25, 1965. This killed the grass and, many say unfortunately, introduced the world to AstroTurf. ♦ Infielders could legally catch foul flies in the dugout, either by jumping a fence or by entering the dugout through a gap in the middle of the fence. ♦ In its inaugural season of 1965, the Astrodome was the scene of a unique groundskeeping argument. The Mets claimed the groundskeepers were roof-keeping as well by manipulating the air conditioning system so air currents helped Astro long balls and hindered visitors' long balls. The Astros never admitted to doing so, but three decades later the Twins admitted they had done so in the Hubert Humphrey Metrodome. ♦ On April 28, 1965, Mets announcer Lindsey Nelson broadcast a game from a gondola suspended from the apex of the dome. ♦ On June 10, 1974, Phillies third baseman Mike Schmidt hit the public address speaker 117 feet up and 329 feet from home, and what would have been a 500-plus-foot homer ended up as a single as the ball dropped in center. ♦ On June 15, 1976, the game against the Pirates was rained out when seven inches of rain caused flooding in the streets around the Astrodome. Although the players and about 20 fans made it to the game, the umpires did not. ♦ The huge exploding scoreboard was removed in 1988 to increase seating capacity. ♦ Astros owner Judge Roy Hofheinz lived inside in a luxurious apartment.

## *Minute Maid Park*

**AKA**

Enron Field April 7, 2000–February 27, 2002, Astros Park February 27–June 5, 2002

**ARCHITECT**

HOK Sport

**OCCUPANT**

NL Houston Astros April 7, 2000, to date

**LOCATION**

Left Field (NW/W) 501 Crawford St; Third Base (SW/S) Texas Ave, then Union Station; First Base (SE/E) Hamilton St/US Hwy 59; Right Field (NE/N) Congress Ave; adjacent to George Brown Convention Center

**DIMENSIONS**

Left Field: 315
Left Field Power Alley: 362
Left Center: 390
Center Field: 435
Deepest Center Field (right of dead center): 436
Right Center: 397
Right Field Power Alley: 373
Right Field: 326
Roof apex: 242 but much less than that down the LF line
Backstop: 49

**FENCES**

Left Field: 21
Left Center: 10, 25 (2001)
Center Field Flagpole: 80
Center Field and Right Center: 9
Right Field: 7

**SURFACE**

Bermuda grass (April 2000), Seashore Paspalum grass (August 2001)

**FORMER USE**

Parking lots

**CAPACITY**

40,950, 40,976 (2006)

**PHENOMENA**

Just like the 125-foot high flag pole at Tiger Stadium in Detroit, the 80-foot high flag pole in center field here is in-play. ♦ On July 1, 2003, in the top of the fourth, Richie Sexson's deep drive bounced high

Dubbed the "9th wonder of the world," Minute Maid Park has arches, a train above the left field wall, a huge scoreboard, a retractable roof and . . . grass! A warning ramp in center field is reminiscent of stadiums of old.

off the pole and he got only a triple to left, since the left fielder fielded the carom off the pole. ◆ Huge train, built specifically for this park, chugs back and forth on track above the wall in left. ◆ Jeff Bagwell once got a double rather than an out when his fly ball down the left field line hit a girder. ◆ Bull's-eyes on top of both foul poles, patterned after those atop foul poles at Rice Owls' ballpark. So far the bull's-eyes have never been hit by a batted ball in a game, but if this ever happens, the Astros will immediately pick a seat at random, and that seat holder will win a Hummer. ◆ Retractable roof moves to right field when opened, moves back to third base when closed. ◆ The 30-degree incline in deep center is called Tal's Hill, after Tal Smith, Astros GM, who patterned it after previous ballpark inclines at Crosley Field and Fenway Park. ◆ Astroturf from the Astrodome is used in the visitors bullpen under the left field seats. ◆ Enron name removed after Enron became embroiled in scandal.

---

# Indianapolis, Indiana

*See also* Broad Ripple, Indiana

## South Street Park

**AKA**

National League Park 1878, Athletic Park (I)

**OCCUPANTS**

NL Indianapolis Browns May 1–September 14, 1878; neutral site used by AA St. Louis Browns one game in 1885

**LOCATION**

(W) Delaware St, (S) South St; (E) Alabama St

**FORMER USE**

Cornfield

## Seventh Street Park (I)

**AKA**

Athletic Park (II)

**OCCUPANTS**

AA Indianapolis Blues May 14–September 20, 1884; neutral site used by NL St. Louis Maroons September 15, 1885

**LOCATION**

Same as Seventh Street Park (II)

## Seventh Street Park (II)

**AKA**

Athletic Park (III)

**OCCUPANT**

NL Indianapolis Hoosiers April 28–October 8, 1887

**LOCATION**

Left Field (W) Mississippi St (later Boulevard St, later Senate Ave), Third Base (S) Tinker St and 7th (later 16th) St, First Base (E) Tennessee St (later Capitol Ave), Right Field (N) 9th (later 18th) St

**DIMENSIONS**

Left Field: 286
Right Field: 261

**PHENOMENA**

Tall screen in right.

## Seventh Street Park (III)

**AKA**

Athletic Park (IV)

**OCCUPANT**

NL Indianapolis Hoosiers April 20, 1888–October 5, 1889

**LOCATION**

Left Field (N) 9th (later 18th) St, Third Base (W) Mississippi St (later Boulevard St, later Senate Ave), First Base (S) Tinker St and 7th (later 16th) St, Right Field (E) Tennessee St (later Capitol Ave); same site as Seventh Street Park (I) and (II) but turned around so that home plate was in the SW rather than in the SE

**DIMENSIONS**

Left Field: 286
Right Field: 261

**CURRENT USE**

Methodist Hospital

**PHENOMENA**

Ten-foot screen was added in left on June 24, 1889.

## Indianapolis Park

**OCCUPANT**

Neutral site used by NL Cleveland Spiders July 28–August 2, 1890

**LOCATION**

(N) New York St, (W) Hanna (later Oriental) St, (S) East Ohio St, (E) Arsenal Ave

## Federal League Park

**AKA**

Greenlawn Park

**OCCUPANT**

FL Indianapolis Hoosier-Feds April 23–October 8, 1914

**LOCATION**

Left Field (E) South Kentucky Ave (running from SW to NE), then intersection of South West St (running from north to south) and West South St (dead-ending into the cemetery just north of the park and running from west to east); Third Base (N) Greenlawn Cemetery, then Gardner Ln and RR tracks; Home Plate (NW) slaughterhouse and roundhouse; First Base (W) White River; Right Field (S) Oliver St

**DIMENSIONS**

Left Field: 365
Left Center: 421
Center Field: 428
Right Center: 351
Right Field: 304
Backstop: 62

**FENCES**

Right Field: 15

**FORMER USE**

Greenlawn Cemetery

**CURRENT USE**

Diamond Chain Company factory

**CAPACITY**

20,000

**PHENOMENA**

Dimensions based on 1914 Sanborn fire insurance map.

## Riverside Park

**AKA**

Washington Park

**OCCUPANT**

NNL Indianapolis ABCs 1920–23, April–June 1924, 1925–26

**LOCATION**

First Base 1235 West Washington St, in White River State Park just a few blocks west of the White River Bridge

**PHENOMENA**

Wooden park opened in 1904. ♦ Scene of the very first Negro National League game ever played. The ABCs defeated the Chicago Giants, 4–2, on May 2, 1920.

## Northwestern Avenue Ballpark

**OCCUPANT**

NNL Indianapolis ABCs some games 1920–26

**LOCATION**

(N) West 18th St, (W) Northwestern Ave (later Martin Luther King St), (S) West 17th St, (E) Holton Plc (later Mill St), then Central Canal (later I-65)

## Speedway Park

**OCCUPANT**

NNL Indianapolis ABCs some games 1920–26

**LOCATION**

Near the Indianapolis Speedway

## Victory Field (I)

**AKA**

Perry Stadium 1931–42, Owen J. Bush Stadium August 30, 1967, through 1995

**OCCUPANTS**

NNL Indianapolis ABCs 1931; NSL Indianapolis ABCs 1932; NAL Indianapolis Athletics 1937; NAL Indianapolis ABCs 1938, April–May 1939; NAL Indianapolis Crawfords 1940; NAL Indianapolis-Cincinnati

Bush Stadium was named for Indianapolis native Owen "Donie" Bush, who played and managed in the majors during four decades. In a patriotic gesture, the park was renamed Victory Field in 1942.

Clowns half of the home games 1944; NAL Indianapolis Clowns 1946–55; neutral site used by NNL Chicago Cole's American Giants May 28–September 1933, for Negro World Series NNL Washington-Homestead Grays vs. NAL Birmingham Black Barons game five in 1943, NAL Kansas City Monarchs 1957–61

**LOCATION**

Left Field (N) 1501 West 16th St; Third Base (W) East Riverside Dr; First Base (S) Waterway Blvd, then White River (both running from NW to SE); Right Field (E) North Harding St

**DIMENSIONS**

Left Field: 350 (1934), 350 (1938), 335 (1950)
Center Field: 500 (1934), 497 (1938), 500 (1940), 480 (1950), 395 (1985)
Right Field: 350 (1934)

**CAPACITY**

15,000 (1938), 13,254 (1947), 12,934 (1985)

**CURRENT USE**

16th Street Speedway

**PHENOMENA**

Replaced by Victory Field (II) in 1996. Scene of the movie *Eight Men Out*.

# Irondequoit, New York

## *Windsor Beach Grounds*

**OCCUPANT**

AA Rochester Hop Bitters six Sunday games May 11–July 20, 1890

**LOCATION**

(N) Wabash Ave (later Rock Beach Rd), (W)

Mouth-of-the-River Rd (later Point Rd, then Washington Ave), (S) railroad tracks, (E) Rock Beach Rd; one mile SE of ballpark at Ontario Beach in Rochester

**CURRENT USE**

Housing development along Norcrest Drive

**PHENOMENA**

Scheduled Sunday games here on July 27 and August 3, 1890, were stopped by the police.

# Irvington, New Jersey

## *Olemar Field*

**OCCUPANT**

Neutral site used by NNL Newark Dodgers May 5, 1935

# Jacksonville, Florida

## *Durkee Field*

**AKA**

Jacksonville Baseball Park, Douglas Field, Barr's Field, Red Cap Stadium

**OCCUPANT**

NAL Jacksonville Red Caps April–June 1938, 1941, April–July 1942

**LOCATION**

(N) Davis (later West 8th) St; (W) 1701 Myrtle Ave; (S) C (later Hopkins, then West 7th) St; (E) Durkee Ave (later Wilcox St); in James P. Small Park

**DIMENSIONS**

Left Field: 350 (1940)
Center Field: 375 (1940), 400 (1950)
Right Field: 300 (1940), 309 (1950)

**CAPACITY**

5000 (1940), 4564 (1950)

---

# Jersey City, New Jersey

## *Oakdale Park*

**AKA**

Oakland Athletic Association Field

**OCCUPANT**

NL New York Giants April 24–25, 1889

**LOCATION**

(NW) Oakland Ave; (SW) Hoboken Ave, later 1/9

Expressway; (SE) Concord St, then a wagon works and a coal yard which are now I-78; (NE) Fleet St

**PHENOMENA**

When the Giants played these two home games here, it was not neutral site use, since they were anticipating that their entire home schedule for 1889 would be played here. But then owner John Day changed his mind, and they played the rest of the season's schedule on Staten Island at St. George Cricket Grounds.

## *Roosevelt Stadium*

**OCCUPANTS**

NNL New York Black Yankees some games in 1940s; NL Brooklyn Dodgers seven 1956 games and eight 1957 games April 19, 1956–September 3, 1957

**LOCATION**

Center Field (E) State Hwy 440, Third Base (N) Hackensack River, Home Plate (W) Newark Bay, First Base (S) Danforth Ave, Droyers Point

In a game against the Dodgers at Roosevelt Stadium on August 15, 1956, Willie Mays homered off Don Newcombe to give the Giants a 1–0 win. It was the only ball ever hit completely out of the park, which was occasionally used by the NNL New York Black Yankees and the NL Brooklyn Dodgers.

**DIMENSIONS**

Foul Lines: 330
Power Alleys: 397
Center Field: 411
Backstop: 60

**FENCES**

Foul Line corners: 11
Left to Center: 4
Center to Right: 7

**CAPACITY**

20,000 (1937), 26,000 (1938), 30,000 (1939), 25,000 (1940), 24,500 (1957)

**FORMER USE**

Landfill for dirt excavated from Holland Tunnel under the Hudson River

**PHENOMENA**

Built as WPA project in 1937 and named for Franklin D. Roosevelt. ♦ Newark Bay brought mosquitoes and mist into the outfield. ♦ Willie Mays hit the only ball ever completely out of the park here on August 15, 1956,

to beat the Dodgers, 1–0. ♦ Jackie Robinson homered here for the Montreal Royals April 18, 1946, as he broke the color barrier that had racially segregated baseball for more than 50 years. ♦ Torn down in 1984.

# Johnstown, Pennsylvania

## *Point Stadium*

**OCCUPANTS**

Neutral site used by NNL Homestead Grays and NNL Pittsburgh Crawfords 1930s

**LOCATION**

Left Field (SE) Johns St; Third Base (NE) Conemaugh (now Washington) St, then Little Conemaugh River; Home Plate (N) the Point, where the Little Conemaugh River and Stony Creek meet to form the Conemaugh River; First Base (NW) Stony Creek; Right Field (SW) Main St

The left field screen at Point Stadium was, at 70 feet, the highest in Major League history, almost double the height of the Green Monster at Fenway Park. The park was used as a neutral site by the NNL Homestead Grays and Pittsburgh Crawfords.

**DIMENSIONS**

Left Field: 260 (1940), 270 (1980)

Center Field: 405 (1940)

Right Center: 475 (1940)

Right Field: 200 (1940)

**FENCES**

Left Field: 70 (screen)

**CURRENT USE**

Community ball field

**CAPACITY**

16,000 (1940)

**PHENOMENA**

The 70-foot-high screen in left was the highest ever major league outfield fence. Built in 1926 to replace Point Grounds ballpark.

---

# Kansas City, Missouri

## *Athletic Park*

**OCCUPANT**

UA Kansas City Unions June 7–October 19, 1884

**LOCATION**

Summit St, Southwest Blvd

**PHENOMENA**

Fly balls over short fence in right were only doubles.

## *Association Park (I)*

**AKA**

The Hole, League Park

**OCCUPANTS**

NL Kansas City Cowboys April 30–September 18, 1886; AA Kansas City Blues April 18–September 29, 1888; neutral site used by NL St. Louis Browns August 23 morning and afternoon games, October 15, 1892

**LOCATION**

(N) Missouri Ave; (W) Lydia Ave and Tracy Ave; (S) Independence Ave; (E) The Paseo

**PHENOMENA**

Called the Hole because it was down in a huge hole created when highway crews dug up dirt to be used for the roadbed for Independence Avenue. ♦ Outfield sign stated, "Please don't shoot the ump, he's doing the best he can."

## *Exposition Park*

**OCCUPANT**

AA Kansas City Blues September 30, 1888–September 30, 1889

**LOCATION**

(N) 20th St, (W) Prospect Ave, (S) 15th St (later East Truman Rd)

**PHENOMENA**

Opened up again on May 11, 1902, after having burned down.

## *Gordon and Koppel Field*

**AKA**

Federal League Park

**OCCUPANT**

FL Kansas City Packers April 16, 1914–September 28, 1915

**LOCATION**

Left Field (E) The Paseo, then Brush Creek; Third Base (N) East 47th St (later Brush Creek Blvd); First Base (W) Tracy Ave; Right Field (S) East 48th St

**DIMENSIONS**

Left Field: 270
Left Field Power Alley: 302
Left Center: 320
Center Field: 400
Right Center: 360
Right Field Power Alley: 348
Right Field: 350
Foul Territory: normal down third base/LF, very small down first base/RF

**FENCES**

All: 10 (wood) except for 25-foot-high scoreboard added in the LF corner in 1915

**FORMER USE**

Built in 1910 as an amateur athletic field (football and baseball)

**CURRENT USE**

Commercial development

**CAPACITY**

12,000 (1915)

**PHENOMENA**

Park owned by and named after Kansas City merchants Gordon and Koppel. ♦ Dimensions are estimates provided by SABR member Patrick Rock based on his research using land plats and game descriptions. ♦ Home plate was in the northwest corner of the park site. ♦ Brush Creek—located behind the left field fence—flooded in September 1914 and swept away the fence. ♦ Timely repairs to the park were made after the flood to prevent transfer of the FL franchise to Newark—instead the Indianapolis franchise was transferred.

♦    ♦    ♦

## Association Park (II)

**OCCUPANT**

NNL Kansas City Monarchs 1920–22

**LOCATION**

Center Field (S) East 21st St; Third Base (E) RR tracks, then Prospect Ave; Home Plate (N) East 19th St; First Base (W) Olive St

**FENCES**

Right Field: 30 (screen)

**CURRENT USE**

Blues Park covers half of the site, from 19th to 20th St

**PHENOMENA**

During Negro League games, African-American fans were allowed to sit in only the top 14 rows of seats.

## Paradeway Park

**OCCUPANT**

NNL Kansas City Monarchs 1923–30

**LOCATION**

(N) East Truman Rd; (W) The Paseo; (S) John "Buck" O'Neil Way; (E) Woodland Ave; in what is now Parade Park

## Municipal Stadium

**AKA**

Muehlebach Field 1923–37, Ruppert Stadium 1938–42, Blues Stadium 1943–54

**ARCHITECT**

Osborn Engineering

A's owner Charlie Finley tried to shorten the right field fence at Municipal Stadium by creating a 296-foot Pennant Porch, fronting a tiny bleacher section. When the move was vetoed by the league, Finley rebuilt the fence to the bare legal minimum of 325 feet, and repainted it to say One-Half Pennant Porch.

## OCCUPANTS

NAL Kansas City Monarchs 1937–61; AL Kansas City Athletics April 12, 1955–September 27, 1967; AL Kansas City Royals April 8, 1969–October 4, 1972; Negro World Series games 5–7 in 1924, 1–4 in 1925; 4 in 1942, 3–4 in 1946; Negro All-Star Game in 1962

## LOCATION

Left Field (N) 21st St, Third Base (W) Euclid Ave, First Base (S) 22nd St, Right Field (E) 2128 Brooklyn Ave

## DIMENSIONS

Left Field: 363 (1934), 312 (1955), 330 (1956), 370 (1961), 353 (1962), 331 (1963), 370 (1965), 369 (1967)

Left Center: 382 (1955), 375 (1957), 390 (1961), 364 (1963), 392 (1964), 409 (1965), 408 (1969)

Center Field: 559 (1934), 432 (1950), 430 (1955), 421 (1956), 410 (1964), 421 (1965)

Right Center: 382 (1955), 387 (1957), 364 (1962), 360 (1963), 392 (1964), 360 (1965), 382 (1969)

Right Field: 390 (1934), 347 (1955), 352 (1956), 353 (1957), 338 (1963), 325 (1965), 338 (1966)

Backstop: 60 (1955), 70 (1963)

## FENCES

Left Field: 24 (screen 1956), 18.5 (concrete 1958), 38.5 (20 screen over 18.5 concrete 1959), 10 (1961), 13.5 (1962), 10 (1963), 22 (1967), 13 (1969)

Center Field: 12 (1958), 14 (1959), 12 (1961), 13.5 (1962), 10 (1963), 22 (screen 1966), 40 (screen 1969), 22 (screen 1970)

Right Field: 12 (1956), 14 (1959), 12 (1961), 13.5 (1962), 10 (1963), 4.5 (plywood 1965), 40 (screen 1966), 13 (1969), 12 (screen 1970)

## FORMER USE

Swimming hole, frog pond, and ash heap

## CURRENT USE

Community garden

## CAPACITY

17,476, 30,296 (1955), 32,241 (1961), 34,165 (1969), 35,561 (1971)

## PHENOMENA

Opened July 23, 1923. ♦ When rebuilt for the 1955 AL season, home plate was moved 25 feet toward the outfield, and the old Braves Field scoreboard was placed in right-center. ♦ The bottom of the left-center light tower was in play, with the warning track detouring around it. ♦ The right field embankment zoo included the mule named Charlie O (who often traveled with the team to away games), sheep, China golden pheasants, Capuchin monkeys, German checker rabbits, peafowl, and a German short-haired pointer dog. ♦ Little Blowhard was a subterranean device that blew compressed air through the middle of the plate so that the umpire didn't have to brush it off. ♦ Harvey the Mechanical Rabbit rose out of the ground to the right of the plate to offer the umpire new baseballs from a basket between his ears. ♦ Charles O. Finley believed one reason the Yankees won so many pennants was their 296-ft right field porch. So in April 1965, he created his own 296-foot "Pennant Porch" in right field here, but the league forced him to remove it after it was used in only two preseason games. ♦ Torn down in 1976.

♦    ♦    ♦

## Kauffman Stadium

### AKA
Royals Stadium April 10, 1973–July 2, 1993; Harry S. Truman Sports Complex

### ARCHITECT
Charles Deaton; Kivett and Meyers

### OCCUPANT
AL Kansas City Royals April 10, 1973, to date

### LOCATION
Center Field (NE) Spectacular Dr, then I-70; Third Base (NW) Lancer Ln, then Dutton Brookfield Dr; Home Plate (SW) Royal Way, then Chiefs Way, Arrowhead Stadium, Raytown Rd, and CRI&P RR tracks; First Base (SE) Red Coat Dr, then Blue Ridge Cut-Off

### DIMENSIONS
Foul Lines: 330, 320 (1995), 330 (2001)

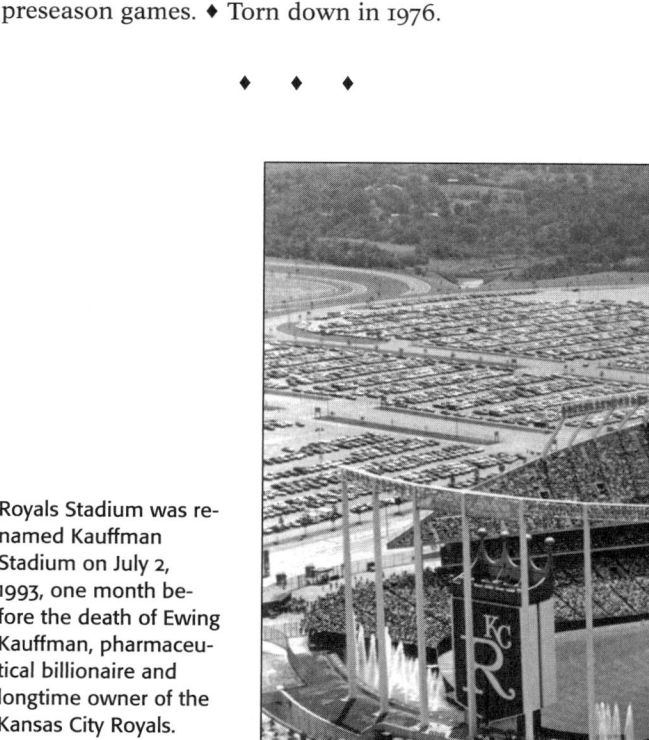

Royals Stadium was renamed Kauffman Stadium on July 2, 1993, one month before the death of Ewing Kauffman, pharmaceutical billionaire and longtime owner of the Kansas City Royals.

Power Alleys: 375, 385 (1990), 375 (1995), 385 (2004)
Center Field: 405, 410 (1980), 400 (1995), 410 (2004)
Backstop: 60, 50 (1999)
Foul Territory: small

**FENCES**

12 (canvas), 9 (canvas, 1995), 8 (canvas, 2004)

**SURFACE**

AstroTurf carpet, very fast 1973–94; grass 1995 to date

**CAPACITY**

40,613, 40,793 (2003), 40,785 (2005)

**PHENOMENA**

Waterfalls and fountains run for 322 feet on embankment overlooking right-center. ♦ Best visibility for hitters in the majors, but homers are few here because alleys are so deep and the fence cuts away sharply from the foul poles. ♦ During rain delays, thousands of sawed webworm moths appear. ♦ Great park for hitting triples. ♦ Kenny Pippin, in his frogman suit, cleans the pond periodically in right-center. ♦ Upper-deck fans near foul poles are in relative darkness. ♦ Before 1995, when grass replaced the hated carpet, the best groundskeeper in baseball had the ironic job of maintaining an ugly plastic carpet. He kept busy maintaining the Runway and the Baja, the grassy running area and the 125-tree forest beyond the fence in left-center.

---

# Keokuk, Iowa

## *Walte's Pasture*

**AKA**

Perry Park

**OCCUPANT**

NA Keokuk Westerns May 4–June 14, 1875

**LOCATION**

Center Field (E) Pleasant Lake, Third Base (N) Plane Rd, First Base (W) U.S. Routes 61/218, (S) Rand Park

**CURRENT USE**

Municipal swimming pool

**PHENOMENA**

Two lakes sat out in center. Outfielders often fell in, chasing fly balls.

---

# Kokomo, Indiana

## *Highland Park Stadium*

**OCCUPANT**

Neutral site used by NAL Kansas City Monarchs 1957–61

**DIMENSIONS**

Left Field: 310
Left Center: 385
Deepest Left Center corner: 490
Center Field: 480
Right Center: 370
Right Field: 265

**CAPACITY**

700 (1980), 4000 (1985)

**CURRENT USE**

American Legion baseball

♦    ♦    ♦

# Lake Charles, Louisiana

## *Legion Field*

**OCCUPANT**

Neutral site used by NAL Kansas City Monarchs 1957–61

**LOCATION**

Left Field (W) 1st Ave; Third Base (S) 5th St; First Base (E) 2nd Ave; Right Field (N) 3rd St

**DIMENSIONS**

Left Field: 307 (1940)
Center Field: 415 (1940)
Right Field: 304 (1940)

**CURRENT USE**

Lake Charles Boston High School athletic field

**CAPACITY**

1500 (1940)

# Lancaster, Pennsylvania

## *Rosemore Park*

**OCCUPANT**

Neutral site used by ECL Hilldale June 19, 1925

**PHENOMENA**

Game vs. Harrisburg was a regularly scheduled league game, but was called off after a few innings due to rain.

# Lansingburgh, New York

*See also* Troy, New York

## *Haymakers' Grounds*

**OCCUPANTS**

NA Troy Haymakers May 9, 1871–June 6, 1872; NL Troy Trojans May 18, 1880–September 30, 1881

**LOCATION**

(N) 104th St, (W) Second Ave, (S) 103rd St, (E) Fifth Ave; on Center Island, in the Hudson River near its junction with the south branch of the Mohawk River; used to be called Lansingburgh but is now in the northern part of the city of Troy

**CURRENT USE**

Twelve large pink, blue, and white oil tanks

**PHENOMENA**

The highest-scoring game in the history of major league baseball was played here on June 28, 1871, as the NA Philadelphia Athletics defeated the Haymakers 49–33. ◆ The NL Trojans game on September 27, 1881, vs. the Chicago White Stockings drew only 12 fans in a driving rainstorm.

# Las Vegas, Nevada

## *Cashman Field*

**AKA**

Cashman Field Center

On April 1, 1996, the Athletics opened their season in Las Vegas in a night game with the Blue Jays at Cashman Field. The game drew just 7,294 fans and the Jays took advantage of a 25-mile-an hour wind to hit three homers and win, 9–6.

**OCCUPANT**

Neutral site used by AL Oakland Athletics April 1–7, 1996

**LOCATION**

Left Field (N) Washington Ave; Third Base (W) Convention Hall, then 850 Las Vegas Blvd North; First Base (S) Maryland Pkwy; Right Field (E) Bruce St

**DIMENSIONS**

Foul Lines: 328
Power Alleys: 364
Center Field: 433
Backstop: 43

**FENCES**

Left and Right Field: 20
Center Field: 22

**CAPACITY**

9353 (1996), 9500 (2004)

**PHENOMENA**

A's played here because Oakland Coliseum was torn up by construction to accommodate NFL Raiders. ♦ Opened in 1983. ♦ Grassy embankment on hill down in left field corner filled with picnicking fans. Usherettes danced the polka in the aisles between innings. ♦ Most billboards ever at a major league park–47 in fair territory, nine in foul territory–including Caesar's Palace Magical Empire, Anderson Dairy, 92.3 KOMP Rocks Vegas, "Since 1907 Arizona Charlie's–Hit Charlie $ Win Dinner for 2."

# Lebanon, Indiana

## *Lebanon Memorial Park*

**OCCUPANT**

Neutral site used by NNL Indianapolis ABCs in early 1920s

♦    ♦    ♦

# Lima, Ohio

## *Halloran Park*

**OCCUPANT**

Neutral site used by NNL Washington-Homestead Grays August 28, 1942

# Little Rock, Arkansas

## *Travelers Field*

**AKA**

Kavanaugh Field, Southern Association Park, Ray Winder Field August 26, 1966 onward

**OCCUPANTS**

NSL Little Rock Grays 1932; neutral site used by NAL Birmingham Black Barons 1940s, by NAL Kansas City Monarchs 1957–61

**LOCATION**

Left Field (E) Jonesboro Dr; Third Base (N) Zoo Dr, then Memorial Park; First Base (W) South Monroe St; Right Field (S) West 8th St, then East-West Expressway/I-630

**DIMENSIONS**

Left Field: 325 (1925), 345 (1934), 320 (1983)
Center Field: 405 (1925), 450 (1934), 390 (1983)
Right Field: 300 (1925), 395 (1934), 340 (1983)

**CAPACITY**

10,500 (1925), 7000 (1938), 6100 (1983)

◆　◆　◆

# Los Angeles, California

*See also* Anaheim, California

## *Memorial Coliseum*

**AKA**

Los Angeles Coliseum, Los Angeles Memorial Coliseum, O'Malley's Chinese Theatre, O'Malley's Alley

**ARCHITECTS**

John and Donald Parkinson

**OCCUPANT**

NL Los Angeles Dodgers April 18, 1958–September 20, 1961

**LOCATION**

Left Field (N/NE) North Coliseum Dr, then Exposition Blvd and University of Southern California (USC) campus; Third Base (W/NW) Menlo Ave; First Base (S/SW) Los Angeles Olympic Swimming Stadium, then Santa Barbara Ave (later Martin Luther King, Jr. Blvd); Right Field (E/SE) South Coliseum Dr, then Los Angeles Memorial Sports Arena, 3911 South Figueroa St, and I-110

**DIMENSIONS**

Left Field: 250, 251.6 (1959)
Left Center at end of screen rectangle: 320
Left Center where fence met wall: 425, 417 (1959)
Center Field: 425, 420 (1959)
Right Center: 440, 375 (1959), 394 (1960), 380 (1961)
Right Field where fence met wall: 390, 333 (1959), 340 (1960)
Right Field: 301, 300 (1959)
Backstop: 60, 66 (1959)
Foul Territory: very strange—tremendously large area on 3rd base line, but almost none on 1st base line

When the Dodgers first played in cavernous Memorial Coliseum in 1958, left-handed-hitting Wally Moon captured the fans' fancy by slicing "moon shots" over the 40-foot fence just 250 feet down the left field line with his inside-out swing.

### FENCES

Left Field: 40 (screen), 42 (screen 1959); 60 (2 support towers for screen 1958)

Left Center: 40 (fence); from Foul Pole 140 feet into Left Center, sloping to ground at 30 degree angle from 320 mark to 348 mark for distance of 24 feet (1958); 4 steps down from 42 to 8–1st step left corner 42 sloping to 41, 2nd step 31, 3rd step 20, 4th step 12 (1961)

Right of Screen in Left Center: 8 (wire)
Center to Right Field corner: 6 (wire)
Right Field corner: 4 (concrete)

### FORMER USE

Gravel pit; agriculture park in 1890s, fairs, livestock shows, amusement park booths, horseracing track and barns, saloons; Exposition Park in 1910s–armory, museum, gardens; Summer Olympics in 1932 and 1984; college and pro football

### CAPACITY

74,000 (1923), 75,000 (1928), 105,000 (1932), 103,000 (1941), 101,528 (1956), 93,000 (1958), 94,600 (1959), 70,000 (1965), 76,000 (1968), 78,000 (1972), 71,432 (1977), 73,999 (1979), 92,488 (1982)

### PHENOMENA

Opened for football October 6, 1923. ♦ Cables, towers, girders, and wires above the screen in left field were in play. This directly caused the Dodgers to win the 1959 pennant. In the top of the fifth, on September 15, 1959, Joe Adcock of the Braves hit a ball which cleared the screen but did not land in the seats because it hit a steel girder behind the screen and got caught in the mesh supporting the screen. According to the rulebook, this should have been a homer. The umps gave him only a double, then changed their minds when fans shook the screen and the ball fell into the seats, then changed their minds again and pulled Adcock out of the dugout and put him back on second base. Adcock never scored, the Dodgers won in extra innings, the Dodgers and Braves ended the regular season in a tie, and the Dodgers won in a playoff. Had Adcock's hit been correctly ruled a home run, the Braves would have finished alone in first place, there never would have been a playoff, and the largest World Series crowd ever–92,706 against White Sox here on October 6, 1959 - would never have happened. ♦ The 42-foot screen in left was meant to prevent 251-foot popups from being homers. ♦ Commissioner

Ford Frick ordered the Dodgers to construct a second screen in left, in the seats, 333 feet from the plate, and a ball clearing both screens would be a homer, but a ball clearing just the shorter screen would be only a double. However, after the lawyers got into the act, they found that the California Earthquake Law made construction of such a screen illegal. ◆ The wall in left-center jutted out twice, going from chest to thigh level, jutting out to ankle level, jutting out to thigh level, then back again to chest level. ◆ Concrete wall in right field corner was the wall surrounding the football field. It sloped sharply away, creating a Fenway-like belly. A long drive to straight-away right field would be an out, but a short fly down the line would be a homer. ◆ Huge tunnel behind home plate. ◆ O'Malley considered using the Rose Bowl in Pasadena for the first years after the move from Brooklyn and before Dodger Stadium opened. It would have been laid out much differently from the Coliseum. Ten rows would have been removed in right and left to deepen the Foul Lines to 300 feet, and center field would have been 460. The field would have been symmetrical, because home plate would have been in one end zone and center field in the other. ◆ It was 700 feet to farthest seats under Peristylum in right-center. Two stones are on exhibit there—the one on the left is from Altis, Olympia, Greece; the one on the right is from the Colosseum, Rome, Italy. ◆ After 182 homers were hit to left, but only three to center and eight to right in 1958, the fence in right field was shortened in 1959, resulting in more homers to right field—in 1959, 132 to left, one to center, 39 to right; in 1960, 155 to left, three to center, 28 to right; in 1961, 147 to left, seven to center, 38 to right. ◆ A small green light pole was in field of play in right field. ◆ Stadium patterned after the Roman Colosseum, built in 82 AD, seating 50,000. ◆ Largest crowds here were 105,236 for college football Southern Cal vs. Notre Dame 11/10/57; 104,022 for the Olympics 8/9/84; 102,368 for pro football Rams vs. 49ers 12/6/47; and 93,103 for baseball Dodgers vs. Yankees 5/7/59 exhibition honoring Roy Campanella.

## Wrigley Field

**ARCHITECT**

Zachary Taylor Davis

**OCCUPANT**

AL Los Angeles Angels April 27–October 1, 1961

**LOCATION**

Left Field (N/NW) East 41st St, Third Base (W/SW) San Pedro St, First Base (S/SE) 435 East 42nd Pl, Right Field (E/NE) Avalon Blvd

**DIMENSIONS**

Left Field: 340
Power Alleys: 345
Center Field: 412
Right Field: 338.5
Backstop: 56

**FENCES**

Left Field to Center Field: 14.5 (concrete)
Center Field to Right Field: 9 (6 wire above 3 concrete)

**CAPACITY**

22,000, 20,457 (1961)

**CURRENT USE**

Gilbert Lindsay Park, a public playground, and City Center Community Mental Health Facility

**PHENOMENA**

Dedicated January 25, 1926; first PCL game was on September 29, 1925. ◆ Tall office tower stood just to first base side of home plate. ◆ Bottom of light tower in left-center was in play. ◆ In 1957, the Dodgers considered double-decking the field in a plan that would have made it look much like the Polo Grounds. ◆ In 1961, Wrigley Field set a then record for most homers (248) in one park in one season because the power alleys were only five feet farther than the foul poles. ◆ Scene of 1950s TV show *Home Run Derby; Munsters* TV episode; movies *It*

With its location near Hollywood, Wrigley Field became the site of many movies, including *The Pride of the Yankees* and a movie version of *Damn Yankees.* It was also the site for the *Home Run Derby* series in 1959, a popular television show. The park was actually the first Wrigley Field, preceding the renaming of Cubs Park in Chicago by several months.

*Happens Every Spring* with Ray Milland, *Pride of the Yankees* (in part), *Damn Yankees* (along with Griffith Stadium) in 1958, *Mighty Casey* in 1960, *Twilight Zone* TV episode about the Hoboken Zephyrs. ♦ Torn down in March 1969.

## *Dodger Stadium*

### AKA

Chavez Ravine during AL use 1962–65 by Los Angeles Angels and by California Angels, Taj O'Malley, O'Malley's Golden Gulch

### ARCHITECT

Praeger-Kavanagh-Waterbury

### OCCUPANTS

NL Los Angeles Dodgers April 10, 1962, to date; AL Los Angeles Angels April 17, 1962–September 1, 1965; AL California Angels September 2–22, 1965

### LOCATION

Left Field (N/NW) Glendale Blvd; Third Base (W/SW) Sunset Blvd; Home Plate (S/SW) 1000 Elysian Park Ave; First Base (S/SE) Stadium Dr, then Pasadena Freeway/I-110; Right Field (E/NE) Los Angeles Police Academy, then Elysian Park, Golden State Freeway/I-5; in Chavez Ravine, on a hill overlooking downtown Los Angeles

### SURFACE

Santa Ana Bermuda grass, Prescription Athletic Turf (PAT)

### DIMENSIONS

Foul Lines: 330
Power Alleys: 380, 370 (1969)
Left/Right Center: 385 (1983)

Center Field: 410, 400 (1969), not 395 (to date)

Backstop: 65, 68.19 (1963), 75 (1969), 57 (2000)

Foul Territory: large 1962–1999, medium 2000–2004, small 2005 to date

## FENCES

Left Center to Right Center: 10 (wood), 8 (1973)

Foul Poles to Bullpens in Left and Right Field corners: 3.75 (steel), 3.83 (1969); the "Dip" where low corner steel wall and screen bullpen fence meet 3.42, 3.5 (1969)

## FORMER USE

Used by squatters and goats

## CAPACITY

56,000—unchanged 1962 to date—*see* PHENOMENA

## PHENOMENA

A classic pitchers park. ♦ Dugout-level box seats behind the plate patterned after Tokyo's Korakuen Stadium. ♦ Designed to be expandable to 85,000 seats. ♦ Only major league park whose capacity has never changed. ♦ Painted every off-season, cleanest ballpark by far. ♦ Palm trees beyond the fence down the foul lines. ♦ Although the center field 400 sign came down in 1980, the distance is still 400 to center; the two 395 signs are to the left and right of dead center. Many references say it is 395 to center; they are incorrect. ♦ No drinking water fountains when stadium was first built. ♦ The original design had a huge fountain in center field, like that in right-center at Royals Stadium. ♦ When the foul poles were installed in 1962, it was discovered that they had been positioned completely in foul territory. Special dispensation was received from the league, but the next year the plate had to be moved so the poles would be in fair territory. Why must foul poles be in fair territory? That's baseball! ♦ Every time in the last four decades that the Dodgers have added seats they have also removed an equal number in the outfield pavilions or in the fourth deck—this due to the original conditional use permit for the park which specifies a limit of 56,000 seats. ♦ Before the 2005 season the Dodgers added 1200 luxury field-level box seats between the dugouts. However, fan complaints about poor sightlines led the Dodgers to redo the area after the end of the 2005 season—adding tables and reducing the number of seats to 700. All this led to no change in overall capacity—still 56,000.

With 52,564 fans on hand, the Dodgers inaugurated Dodger Stadium with a 6–3 loss to the Reds on April 10, 1962. Wally Post hit the first homer in the new stadium, a 3-run shot over the center field fence.

# Louisville, Kentucky

## *St. James Court*

**AKA**

Louisville Baseball Park

**OCCUPANT**

NL Louisville Grays April 25, 1876–September 29, 1877

**LOCATION**

Left Field (W) 6th St, Third Base (S) Hill St, First Base (E) 4th St, Right Field (N) Magnolia St

**CURRENT USE**

Residential area of Victorian homes built in the 1890s

## *Eclipse Park (I)*

**OCCUPANTS**

AA Louisville Colonels May 5, 1882–September 27, 1891; NCL Louisville Falls Citys 1887; NL Louisville Colonels April 12, 1892–September 26, 1892

**LOCATION**

(N) Magazine St, (W) South 29th St, (S) Elliott Ave, (E) South 28th St; in Elliott Park

**DIMENSIONS**

Left Field: 360
Left Center: 405
Center Field: 495
Right Center: 360
Right Field: 320

**FENCES**

8, 12 (1884)

**FORMER USE**

Elliott Estate

**PHENOMENA**

Balls hit over the right field fence in 1882 were only doubles. ♦ Tower behind the grandstands by home plate was built in the spring of 1884 and housed the first luxury skybox, holding 60 guests. ♦ Burned down in the morning of September 27, 1892, but the grandstand was rebuilt in a day, so that it was ready for a doubleheader the next day on September 28.

## *Eclipse Park (II)*

**OCCUPANT**

NL Louisville Colonels September 28, 1892–May 4, 1893

**LOCATION**

Same as Eclipse Park (I)

## *Eclipse Park (III)*

**AKA**

League Park

**OCCUPANT**

NL Louisville Colonels May 22, 1893–August 2, 1899

**LOCATION**

(N) West Broadway, (W) South 30th St, (S) Howard St, (E) South 28th St; across the street from Eclipse Parks (I) and (II)

**FORMER USE**

Kentucky and Indiana Company railroad switching yard and stockyard

The University of Louisville bought Parkway Field in December 1953, and leased it back to the American Association's Louisville Colonels, who subsequently moved to Fairground Stadium in 1956. The field was used by the university for football in 1952–1954 when the Cardinal quarterback was Johnny Unitas.

**PHENOMENA**

Burned down at 2:00 AM on August 12, 1899.

## *Eclipse Park (IV)*

**OCCUPANT**

NL Louisville Colonels August 22–October 7, 1899

**LOCATION**

Same as Eclipse Park (III)

## *Parkway Field*

**AKA**

Colonels Field

**OCCUPANTS**

NNL Louisville White Sox 1931; NSL Louisville Black Caps April–August 1932; NAL Louisville Buckeyes 1949; NAL Louisville Black Colonels 1954

**LOCATION**

Left Field (N) Eastern Parkway, Third Base (W) South 3rd St, First Base (S) Southern RR tracks, Right Field (E) South Brook St; on the University of Louisville campus

**DIMENSIONS**

Left Field: 331 (1923), 326 (1940), 329 (1949)
Deepest Left Center: 512 (1923), 507 (1940), 504 (1949)
Center Field: 467
Right Field: 350 (1923), 345 (1940)

**CURRENT USE**

Grandstand demolished in 1961, but wall in deepest left center still has the 504 marker

**CAPACITY**

13,198 (1938), 13,000 (1940), 13,496 (1952)

**PHENOMENA**

Opened May 1, 1923. Scoreboard in left-center.

---

# Ludlow, Kentucky

## *Ludlow Base-Ball Park*

**OCCUPANTS**

Neutral site used by NA Philadelphia Pearls September 22, 1875; by AA Cincinnati Reds August 18, 1889 (cancelled)

**LOCATION**

(S) River bluffs high on a hill; near the landing point of the Fifth Street Ferry (also called the Ludlow Ferry) just across Ohio River from Cincinnati

**CAPACITY**

200

**PHENOMENA**

Opened May 28, 1875. ♦ There was a big hill on the field behind the catcher on the third base side. ♦ Forced to abandon Sunday play at home in Cincinnati by the Cincinnati Law and Order Society after August 11, 1889, the AA Reds scheduled their Sunday home games for August 18, 25, October 6, 13 here, but local Kentucky authorities prevented them from doing so. They moved the August 18 game to Hamilton, Ohio. However, the Hamilton Law and Order League complained, and the police there moved onto the field in the top of the fourth inning and stopped the game. ♦ Fans paid only a dime to take the Fifth Street Ferry round-trip from Cincinnati to see the games. ♦ The fences were very short. The fence was so short in right that it was a double when you hit the

ball over the fence. The fence in left was also short, but the ground rules allowed a home run if the ball was hit over it. This caused a controversy once when Charlie Jones hit a homer to left, and the visiting team argued unsuccessfully that the fence was so short that it had to be ruled only a double.

---

# Lumberton, North Carolina

## *Old Armory Field*

**OCCUPANT**

Neutral site used by NAL Raleigh Tigers May 1961

**LOCATION**

Behind the present-day Bill Sapp Recreation Center

---

# Macon, Georgia

## *Luther Williams Field*

**OCCUPANT**

Neutral site used by NAL Birmingham Black Barons 1940s

**LOCATION**

(W) Riverside (later Willie Smokie Glover) Dr, then Georgia Central RR tracks; (E) Ocmulgee River

**DIMENSIONS**

Foul Lines: 350 (1938), 330 (1983), 338 (1994)
Power Alleys: 370 (1994)
Center Field: 450 (1938), 405 (1983), 402 (1994)

Built in 1929, Luther Williams Field is the centerpiece of Central City Park in Macon, Georgia. The original covered grandstand is still in place, though a tin roof has replaced the former wooden one.

**CAPACITY**

6000 (1938), 5000 (1960), 3000 (1983), 4000 (1994), 3750 (1999)

**PHENOMENA**

Built in 1929.

---

# McKeesport, Pennsylvania

## Cycler Park

**OCCUPANT**

Neutral site used by NEWL Homestead Grays May 30, 1932

**LOCATION**

Left Field (E), Third Base (N), First Base (W), Right Field (S)

**DIMENSIONS**

Left Field: 393

Center Field: 440
Right Field: 325

## Renziehausen Park

**OCCUPANT**

Neutral site used by NNL Homestead Grays some games 1935–36

**LOCATION**

Center Field (NW) Tulip Dr; Third Base (SW) Allison St; Home Plate (SE) Palm St; First Base (NE) Pinoak Dr

**DIMENSIONS**

Left Field: 485 (1940)
Center Field: 430 (1940)
Right Field: 310 (1940)

**CAPACITY**

4800 (1940)

◆  ◆  ◆

# Meadville, Pennsylvania

## *Meadville Grounds*

**OCCUPANT**

Neutral site used by NA New York Mutuals July 22, 1871

**PHENOMENA**

The Brooklyn Eckfords defeated the Mutuals, 13–5.

# Memphis, Tennessee

## *Martin Park*

**OCCUPANTS**

NNL Memphis Red Sox June–September 1924, 1925, 1927, 1929–30; NSL Memphis Red Sox 1932; NAL Memphis Red Sox 1937–41, 1943–59; neutral site used by NAL Kansas City Monarchs 1960–61

**LOCATION**

East Crump Blvd, Danny Thomas Blvd

**CURRENT USE**

Truck terminal

## *Russwood Park*

**OCCUPANT**

NAL Memphis Red Sox some games 1940s

**LOCATION**

Center Field (N) Jefferson Ave, Third Base (W) North Dunlap St, Home Plate (S) Madison Ave, First Base (E) Edgeway St

**DIMENSIONS**

Left Field: 424
Center Field: 366
Right Field: 301

A sultan and a king played at Russwood Park. In 1930, the Memphis Chicks beat the Yankees in an exhibition game, 3–1, as the Sultan of Swat, Babe Ruth, hit a homer for the only Yankee score. A soon-to-be King of Rock 'n' Roll, Elvis Presley, performed in a concert there on July 4, 1956.

**CURRENT USE**

Medical center built on site after ballpark burned down April 17, 1960

**CAPACITY**

11,500

---

# Miami, Florida

## *Dolphin Stadium*

**AKA**

Joe Robbie Stadium August 16, 1987–August 26, 1996, Pro Player Stadium August 26, 1996–January 9, 2005

**ARCHITECT**

HOK Sport

**OCCUPANT**

NL Florida Marlins April 5, 1993, to date

**LOCATION**

Center Field (E/NE) Florida Turnpike; Third Base (N/NW) Northwest 203rd St, then Snake Creek Canal; Home Plate (W/SW), Northwest 27th Ave (later University Ave, then Carl F. Barger Blvd); First Base (S/SE) 2267 Northwest 199th St (later Dan Marino Blvd)

**DIMENSIONS**

Left Field: 335 (1993), 330 (1994)
Power Alleys: 380 (1993), 385 (1994)
Deepest Left Center corner: 434
Center Field: 410 (1993), 404 (1994)
Right Field: 345
Backstop: 58 (1993), 60 (2003)

**SURFACE**

Tifway 419 Bermuda grass

**FENCES**

Left Center Scoreboard: 33
Everywhere else: 8

**CAPACITY**

75,000 (1987), 43,909 (1993), 46,238 (1995), 41,855 (1996), 42,531 (1999), 36,331 (2001)

The Florida Marlins made their NL debut at Joe Robbie Stadium, later renamed Dolphin Stadium, on April 5, 1993 with a 6–3 win over the Dodgers. Joe DiMaggio threw out the first ball.

**PHENOMENA**

Opened for football August 16, 1987. ♦ First preseason baseball game March 11, 1988. ♦ Many nooks and crannies create crazy bounces and angles. ♦ Helipad site in the parking lot. ♦ Second-deck outfield seats covered by canvas unless a big crowd attends. ♦ Many fans speak Spanish, with Cuban-American accent. ♦ Thirty-three-foot high left field wall is called the "Teal Monster."

# Middletown, Connecticut

## *Mansfield Club Grounds*

**OCCUPANT**

NA Middletown Mansfields May 2–July 27, 1872

**LOCATION**

(N) River Rd, (W) Eastern Dr, (S) Silver St, (E) State Terrace; along the Connecticut River

**CURRENT USE**

Maplewood Terrace public housing project, formerly the Connecticut Hospital for the Insane

# Milwaukee, Wisconsin

## *Milwaukee Base-Ball Grounds*

**OCCUPANT**

NL Milwaukee Cream Citys May 14–September 14, 1878

**LOCATION**

(N) West Michigan Ave, (W) North 12th St, (S) West Clybourn Ave, (E) North 10th St

**PHENOMENA**

Hits over short fence in right were doubles. Trees down the first base line.

## *Wright Street Grounds*

**AKA**

Milwaukee Baseball Park (I)

**OCCUPANTS**

UA Milwaukee Grays September 27–October 12, 1884; neutral site used by NL Chicago White Stockings September 4 and 25, 1885

**LOCATION**

(N) West Clarke St, (W) North 12th St, (S) West Wright St, (E) North 11th St

## *Borchert Field*

**AKA**

Brewer Field, Milwaukee Athletic Park, Athletic Field

**OCCUPANTS**

AA Milwaukee Brewers August 14–October 4, 1891; NNL Milwaukee Bears July–August 1923; NNL Chicago American Giants one game 1935

**LOCATION**

Center Field (N) West Burleigh St, Third Base (W) 3000 North 8th St, Home Plate (S) West Chambers St, First Base (E) West 7th St; in 2006 Interstate 43 runs through the block where Borchert Field stood.

**DIMENSIONS**

Left Field: 267 (1940), 266 (1941)
Center Field: 392 (1940), 395 (1941)

In the 7th inning of a tie game at Borchert Field on June 15, 1945, a sudden thunderstorm erupted, blowing off a 100-ft section of the grandstand roof, knocking down part of the fence, and damaging cars. Thirty fans were injured, some seriously.

Right Field: 268 (1940), 266 (1941)

**CURRENT USE**

Playground from demolition in 1954 until construction of I-43 in 1963

**CAPACITY**

10,000 (1891), 14,000 (1940)

**PHENOMENA**

Opened in 1888 as Athletic Park. ♦ Larger than the prior park (Wright Street Grounds) in both length and width. ♦ Pitcher Ralph Cutting's goat grazed on the grass between games. ♦ Bill Veeck owned the minor league Brewers here in 1941, and allegedly erected a 60-foot-high chicken wire fence in right because he knew his team could not hit 266-foot homers, so he didn't want the other team to be able to either. The next year, he went one step further and rigged the fence so that a hydraulic motor could move the fence along a rail on top of the right

field wall into foul territory when the Brewers were up, and back into fair territory when the Brewers were in the field. He got away with this for one game, but the next day the league passed a rule against it. The above story concerning the Veeck movable fence is, in all probability, an urban legend. Two independent SABR researchers found no evidence to support the story: (1) ballparks author and researcher John Pastier could find no evidence in 1941 of the pulley, cables, and hydraulic motor necessary to make a movable fence work; (2) Milwaukee baseball expert Jim Nitz conducted extensive newspaper research on Borchert Field, and found no references to any movable fence.

## *Lloyd Street Grounds*

**AKA**

Milwaukee Baseball Park (II)

**OCCUPANT**

AL Milwaukee Brewers May 3–September 12, 1901

**LOCATION**

Center Field (N) West North St, Third Base (W) North 18th St, Home Plate (S) West Lloyd St, First Base (E) North 16th St

**DIMENSIONS**

Foul Lines: 295
Straightaway Left/Right Field: 413
Left/Right Center: 384
Center Field: 380
Foul Area: very large

**FENCES**

Left Field: 20 (canvas screen)
Center Field and Right Field: 10 (wood)

**FORMER USE**

Minor league ballpark 1895–1900

Lloyd Street Grounds was home to the AL Milwaukee Brewers during the 1901 season. The franchise was transferred to St. Louis after the season.

### PHENOMENA

Built in 1894 and used by the American League (then a minor league) for the 1900 season. ♦ Playing field orientation was like the Polo Grounds with left and right field fences parallel to each other. ♦ Both Foul Lines intersected the fences at an estimated 135 degrees. Center field fence ran about perpendicular to home plate-center field, and extended from left of left-center to the right of right-center. ♦ Only newspaper writers were allowed in the huge tower behind home plate. ♦ Fans could watch the game for free from behind the center field fence by looking through the hole in the R in the STREISSGUT sign. ♦ After the 1901 season the American League franchise was shifted to St. Louis (becoming the Browns), and the park was then used for the next two years by the Milwaukee Creams of the Western League. ♦ Dimensions estimated on the basis of an 1894 Sanborn fire insurance map that shows only the park site and 1901 photos of the park. ♦ Home/road batting data for 1901 showed the park to be moderately below average in every offensive category, as batting park factors ranged from 90 to 97.

♦    ♦    ♦

## *County Stadium*

### ARCHITECT

Skidmore, Owing, & Merrill

### OCCUPANTS

NL Milwaukee Braves April 14, 1953–September 22, 1965; AL Milwaukee Brewers April 7, 1970–September 28, 1997, NL Milwaukee Brewers April 7, 1998–September 28, 2000; neutral site used by AL Chicago White Sox May 15, 1968–September 26, 1969, for nine games in 1968 and 11 in 1969

### LOCATION

Left Field (E) South 44th St (later US-41/Stadium Freeway), then Menominee River; Third Base (N) Story Pkwy (later East-West Frwy/I-94); First Base (W) General Mitchell Blvd; Right Field (S) West National Ave, then Soldiers Home VA Hospital on Mockingbird Hill

### DIMENSIONS

Left Field: 320, 315 (1975)
Left of straightaway Left Field: 355, 362 (1962)

Power Alleys: 376, 377 (1962)
Deep Center Field Alleys: 397, 392 (1955)
Center Field: 404, 410 (1954), 402 (1955)
Right of straightaway Right Field: 355, 362 (1962)
Right Field: 320, 315.37 (1954)
Backstop: 60

**FENCES**

Left Field: 4, 8 (1955), 8.33 (1959), 10 (1985)
Center Field: 4, 8 (1955), 8.33 (1959), 10 (1985)
Right Field: 4, 10 (1955)

**FORMER USE**

Stone quarry

**CURRENT USE**

Site of Miller Park

**CAPACITY**

36,011, 43,091 (1954), 44,091 (1965), 47,611 (1970), 54,187 (1973), 53,192 (1975)

**PHENOMENA**

In 1953, before the park was expanded, hospital patients at the National Soldiers Home VA Hospital sat outside their rooms on Mockingbird Hill overlooking right field and watched the game for free. ◆ Perini's Woods, spruce and fir trees behind center field fence, planted in 1954, replaced by bleachers in 1961. ◆ Braves Reservation, a picnic area down the left field line, was inaugurated in 1961. ◆ Best bratwurst and best tailgating parties in the majors. ◆ Bernie Brewer slid into a huge beer stein in right center when a Brewer hit a homer. ◆ Cecil Fielder hit the only homer ever hit over the left field roof. ◆ Braves

Though County Stadium was built to house the minor league Brewers, the team never played there. Just three weeks before the start of the 1953 season, the Boston Braves relocated to Milwaukee, blocking a similar attempt by the St. Louis Browns.

hosted both Reds and Cards on September 24, 1954. The first game was the finish of a game two days earlier whose ending on a disputed double play was successfully protested by the Reds. The Reds tied the game after the protested game's resumption, but the Braves won, 4–3, in the bottom of the ninth, and then beat the Cards, 4–2. ♦ Torn down February 21, 2001.

## Miller Park

### AKA

The Sauna on rainy days when the roof is closed

### OCCUPANT

AL Milwaukee Brewers April 6, 2001, to date

### ARCHITECTS

HKS Inc., Eppstein Uhen Associates

### LOCATION

Left Field (E) South 44th St, then Menominee River and Stadium Freeway/US 41; Third Base (N) Story Parkway and I-94; First Base (W) General Mitchell Blvd; Right Field (S) West National Ave, then National Soldiers Home; also One Brewers Way; in what used to be the center field parking lot of County Stadium

### DIMENSIONS

Left Field: 344, 342 (2002), 344 (2005)
Left Field Power Alley: 371, 374 (2002), 371 (2005)
Left Center: 382
Center Field: 400
Right Field Power Alley: 378, 374 (2002), 371 (2005)
Right Center: 383
Right Field: 355, 345 (2002)
Roof apex: 330
Backstop: 56

### FENCES

Left Field and Center Field: 8
Right Field: 6

### CAPACITY

42,885, 41,900 (2003)

### PHENOMENA

Three construction workers were killed and tons of debris were spilled over the site by a crane accident in July 1999, causing a one-year delay in its opening. ♦ Opening day was moved back to April 6, 2001. ♦ Warning track is by far the widest in the history of the major

The first game in Milwaukee's Miller Park, with its butterfly-shaped retractable dome, was on April 6, 2001, as the Brewers beat the Reds 5–4. George W. Bush threw out the first pitch, Sean Casey had the first hit, and the bratwurst won the sausage race.

leagues. It is 27 feet wide in the left field corner and 20 feet wide everywhere else in fair territory. By comparison, the warning track at Ebbets Field in Brooklyn was 10 feet wide, and there weren't even any warning tracks at all in left field at Cleveland's League Park, or in center field or right field at the LA Coliseum. ♦ There is no air conditioning, so when the roof is closed when it rains on warm days, it is like a very warm sauna inside. ♦ Heaters in the top deck increase the temperature by 20 degrees on cold days. ♦ In the bottom of the seventh, they play Kate Smith's rendition of *America the Beautiful,* then the *Star Spangled Banner,* and finally *Roll out the Barrel* (a beer song).

---

# Minneapolis, Minnesota

*See also* Bloomington, Minnesota

## Athletic Park (II)

**OCCUPANT**

Neutral site used by AA Milwaukee Brewers October 2, 1891

**LOCATION**

Left Field (NE) 5th St North, Third Base (NW) 2nd Ave North; First Base (SW) 6th St North, Right Field (SE) 1st Ave North; behind the West Hotel back then; just across the street rom and just northeast of Target Center, home of the NBA Timberwolves

**DIMENSIONS**

Left Field: 275
Right Field: 250

**CURRENT USE**

Butler Square and Butler North

**CAPACITY**

4600

**PHENOMENA**

Minor league Millers opened here on May 15, 1889, and their last game here was May 23, 1896. ♦ The entire Milwaukee Brewers series against the Columbus Colts was to have been played here, but after being rained out October 1, playing here October 2 in a very cold drizzle, and having the October 3 game postponed due to the cold, the two teams returned to Milwaukee for their final game of the season on October 4. ♦ Right field was so short that what would normally have been a single to right was often a groundout to right field. ♦ The first Athletic Park, capacity 600 at 23rd St and 24th Ave opposite the Milwaukee Junction, opened August 1, 1885, and was surrounded by a 12-foot-high wire screen on top of a 12-foot-high wooden wall.

## Hubert H. Humphrey Metrodome

**AKA**

Minnedome, Bounce Dome, Hump Dome, Homer Dome, Hubie Dome, Thunderdome, Sweat Box (before June 28, 1983, when air conditioning arrived)

**ARCHITECT**

Skidmore, Owing, & Merrill

**OCCUPANT**

AL Minnesota Twins April 6, 1982, to date

**LOCATION**

Left Field (NE) Third St South, Third Base (NW) 501 Chicago Ave South (later 34 Kirby Puckett Pl), First Base (SW) Sixth St South; Right Field (SE) Eleventh Ave South

**DIMENSIONS**

Left Field: 344, 343 (1983)
Left of Left Center: 385
Center Field: 407, 408 (1983)
Right of Right Center: 367
Right Field: 327
Backstop: 60

Foul Territory: small

Dome apex: 186

### FENCES

Left Field: 7 (canvas), 13 (6 plexiglass above 7 canvas 1983), 7 (canvas 1994)

Center Field: 7 (canvas)

Right Field: 7 (canvas), 13 (canvas early in 1983), 23 (canvas later in 1983)

### SURFACE

SporTurf 1982–86, liveliest bounce ever on a major league turf, AstroTurf 1987–2003, FieldTurf 2004 to date

### CAPACITY

54,711, 55,883 (1989), 44,457 (1996), 48,678 (1997), 46,564 (2005)

### PHENOMENA

More home runs were hit before the air conditioning system was installed in midseason 1983. The Metrodome superintendent has admitted to manipulating the ventilation system (forces air out of the park) to assist Twins hits. ♦ The curvature of the wall behind plate causes wild pitches and passed balls to bounce directly to first base rather than right back to the plate. ♦ Right field wall called the Hefty Bag, or the Trash Bag. ♦ Almost an exact duplicate of domed stadiums in Seattle, Pontiac, and Vancouver. ♦ White air-supported fabric Teflon roof makes it difficult to see the ball when hit high in the air. ♦ Only postponement happened when a bad storm prevented the scheduled opponent (the Angels) from reaching Minneapolis. That same storm (very wet snow) caused a portion of the roof to collapse April 14, 1983, during the night after the time of the now-postponed scheduled game. ♦ Foul balls hit off the speakers were in play 1982–2004. ♦ Twins batter Randy Bush hit a ball off the roof in 1983, but the ball was caught in foul territory for an out by Blue Jays catcher Buck Martinez. ♦ On May 4, 1984, in the top of the fourth, A's batter Dave Kingman hit a ball through the roof. It should have been a homer, but Kingman got only a double. ♦ Fair balls hit off the speakers are judgment

The Twins used the Metrodome advantage—difficult lighting, the "baggie" in right field—in two World Series: in 1987 against the Cardinals and in 1991 against the Braves. The Twins won each Fall Classic in seven games, losing all their games on the road and winning all their games at home.

calls for the umpires, but will in most cases be ruled home runs, according to Twins GM Terry Ryan. Some exceptions: Tiger Carlos Pena hit a right field speaker and got a ground-rule double in 2003, Angel Mo Vaughn hit a right-center speaker and was ruled out after it was caught by the second baseman in 2000, Twin Chili Davis hit a speaker and was ruled out in 1992. ♦ World Series of 1991 set new decibel records for sound in the Thunderdome. ♦ Rob Deer hit two fly-ball outs off the speakers to shortstop on consecutive at-bats on May 30, 1992. ♦ Game on May 31, 1998, played with a temporary white 10-foot left field foul pole after a violent rainstorm the previous evening snapped the cable connecting the normal 45-foot pole to the roof, causing it to fall over.

## *New Twins Ballpark*

### PROJECTED OPENING

April 2010

**OCCUPANT**

AL Minnesota Twins April 2010 onwards

**LOCATION**

(NW) Burlington Northern Santa Fe Railroad tracks; (SW) 7th St North and Mary's Place; (SE) North 3rd Ave, then I-394, then Target Center; (NE) 5th St North; in Warehouse District, across the street from Mary Jo Copeland's Mary's Place, a transitional housing complex for poor women and children and the home for Caring and Sharing Hands which has been feeding the homeless in Minneapolis since 1985

**DIMENSIONS**

Left Field: TBD
Power Alleys: TBD
Center Field: TBD
Right Field: TBD

**CAPACITY**

42,000

# Mobile, Alabama

## *Hartwell Field*

**AKA**

Monroe Park, League Park

**OCCUPANT**

NAL Mobile Havana Cuban Giants 1957

**LOCATION**

Center Field (E) Owens St, Third Base (N) Virginia St, Home Plate (W) South Ann St, First Base (S) Tennessee St

**DIMENSIONS**

Foul Lines: 335 (1940)
Center Field: 385 (1940), 406 (1950)

**CAPACITY**

8000 (1940)

**PHENOMENA**

Huge scoreboard in left destroyed by lightning during a hurricane.

# Monessen, Pennsylvania

## *Page Park*

**OCCUPANT**

Neutral site used by NNL Homestead Grays 1930s

**LOCATION**

Center Field (SE), Third Base (NE), Home Plate (NW), First Base (SW)

**DIMENSIONS**

Left Field: 455 (1940)
Center Field: 395 (1940)
Right Field: 299 (1940)

**PHENOMENA**

Josh Gibson of the Homestead Grays hit a 513-foot homer here.

# Monroe, Louisiana

## *Casino Park*

**AKA**

Stovall Park, Ramona Park

**OCCUPANT**

NSL Monroe Monarchs 1932

## LOCATION

(N) Prospect St; (W) Missouri Pacific RR tracks, then De Siard St; (S) Renwick St; (E) South 29th St

## DIMENSIONS

Left Field: 337 (1940), 360 (1950)
Center Field: 410 (1940), 450 (1950)
Right Field: 266 (1940), 330 (1950)

## CAPACITY

3500 (1940)

# Monterrey, Nuevo Leon, Mexico

## *Estadio Monterrey*

## OCCUPANT

Neutral site used by NL San Diego Padres August 16–18, 1996; April 4, 1999

## DIMENSIONS

Foul Lines: 310
Center Field: 400

## CAPACITY

25,644 (1996), 26,000 (1999), 30,000 (2003)

## LOCATION

Next to Monterrey's soccer stadium

## PHENOMENA

Site of first major league game played outside the US or Canada. ♦ Mexico's Fernando Valenzuela pitched and won the first game of "La Primera Serie." ♦ Home of the Monterrey Sultans of the Mexican League. ♦ Fireworks after every homer. Harp music over P.A. after every strikeout. ♦ Estadio Monterrey means Stadium of King's Mountain in English.

# Montgomery, Alabama

## *Cramton Bowl*

## OCCUPANTS

NSL Montgomery Grey Sox 1932; neutral site used for Negro World Series NNL Washington-Homestead Grays vs. NAL Birmingham Black Barons game seven in 1943

## LOCATION

(N) 1201 Madison Ave; (W) North Hilliard St; (S) Pelham St; (E) Hall St; just across Madison Avenue from and southwest of Paterson Field

## DIMENSIONS

Left Field: 420
Center Field: 600
Right Field: 600

## CAPACITY

18,000

## PHENOMENA

Scene of Blue-Grey football all-star game for many years.

## *College Hill Park*

## OCCUPANT

NSL Montgomery Grey Sox some games in 1932

## LOCATION

On campus of Alabama State University

♦    ♦    ♦

# Montréal, Québec, Canada

## *Parc Jarry*

**AKA**

Jarry Park, Stade du Maurier, Stade Uniprix

**ARCHITECT**

HOK Sport

**OCCUPANT**

NL Expos de Montreal April 14, 1969–September 26, 1976

**LOCATION**

Left Field (W/NW) rue Jarry, Third Base (S/SW) Canadian Pacific RR tracks, First Base (E/SE) 285 ouest rue Faillon, Right Field (N/NE) swimming pool, then rue St. Laurent

**DIMENSIONS**

Foul Lines: 340

Left Center: 368
Center Field: 415, 417 (1971), 420 (1974)
Right Center: 365
Backstop: 62

**FENCES**

8 (wire 1969), 5 (wire 1970), 8 (wire 1976)

**FORMER USE**

Amateur recreational ballpark

**CURRENT USE**

Tennis complex named Stade Uniprix (Uniprix Stadium)

**CAPACITY**

3000 (1968), 28,000 (April 14, 1969), 28,456 (June 24, 1969)

**PHENOMENA**

Still under construction April-May 1969. ♦ On April 13, 1971, Opening Day fans stood on snow plowed high in mounds behind the 8½-foot wall that stood behind the five-foot wire screen fence in right field and viewed the game for free, just as other fans

Before 1969 Parc Jarry was a public facility with a seating of just 3,000. When Montreal was granted a Major League franchise in 1968 the city expanded the seating capacity to nearly 28,500 in time for the Expos' 1969 inaugural season. Parc Jarry is still standing and is used regularly for social and civic events, professional tennis, and other large outdoor gatherings.

had done seven days before at the Twins opener at Met Stadium in Bloomington, Minnesota. ♦ Wind helped drives to left-center. Homers to right landed in the swimming pool. ♦ Remnants of grandstands used as part of renovated tennis complex called du Maurier Stadium. ♦ In 2004, the stadium, which has had a further refurbishing, was named Stade Uniprix, after a discount drugstore chain.

## Stade Olympique

**AKA**

Olympic Stadium, Big O, Big Owe

**ARCHITECT**

Roger Taillibert

**OCCUPANT**

NL Expos de Montreal April 15, 1977–September 29, 2004

**LOCATION**

Left Field (NW) rue Sherbrooke (running from S/SW to N/NE), Third Base (SW) boulevard Pie-IX, First Base (SE) 4545 avenue Pierre-de-Coubertin, Right Field (NE) Biodome, then boulevard Viau

**SURFACE**

AstroTurf

**DIMENSIONS**

Foul Lines: 325 (1977), 330 (1981), 325 (1983)
Power Alleys: 375
Center Field: 404 (1977), 405 (1979), 404 (1980), 400 (1981), 404 (1983)
Dome apex: 180 above second base, 171 above outfield walls
Backstop: 62 (1977), 65 (1983), 53 (1989)
Foul Territory: large

**FENCES**

12 (wood 1977), 12 (foam 1989)

**CAPACITY**

60,000 (1976), 58,838 (1977), 60,476 (1979), 58,838 (1982), 60,011 (1990), 43,739 (1992), 46,500 (1993), 43,739 (1996), 46,500 (1999)

**PHENOMENA**

First used for the Olympic opening ceremony, July

On April 15, 1977, the Expos left Parc Jarry after eight years to play their first game at Olympic Stadium, losing to Steve Carlton and the Phillies 7–2, in front of 57,592 fans. Not until April 16, 1987 was the Kevlar roof at last put in place.

17, 1976. ♦ All announcements were in French and English. ♦ Plaque inside and statue at main entrance of Jackie Robinson, who starred at Delorimier Downs for the minor league Royals in 1946. ♦ Labatt's Noise-Meter high above right field was baseball's answer to the NBA Sacramento Kings' Arco Arena Noise-Meter. ♦ The huge 623-foot-high umbrella tower in center field from section 766 in left-center to section 767 in right center stood half finished 1976–87. It was finally finished in 1987, but the supposedly retractable umbrella roof was not actually retractable until 1988 because of generator problems. ♦ When the roof continued to cause difficulties, the decision was made to keep it closed, so the O became a fixed-dome stadium in 1989. When it was finally finished, the umbrella roof improved offense by keeping out the cold. ♦ The dome was silver on top and orange on the bottom, with 26 white cones linking the roof to the tower. ♦ On July 13, 1991, the roof ripped during a rainstorm and rained out the Dodgers-Expos game. ♦ A 55-ton concrete beam came crashing down from the upper deck in September 1991, forcing the Expos to reschedule their last three home series on the road. ♦ The O became open-air again in 1998 when the dilapidated orange Kevlar roof was removed in midseason. A new blue non-retractable roof was installed before the 1999 season. ♦ Fans arrived via the Pie IX and Viau Metro (subway) stops. ♦ After Dave Kingman hit the technical ring, which surrounds the stadium on the inside of the roof, but his ball was ruled foul, an orange line was painted on it so umpires could allow a home run for a ball hitting the ring in fair territory. Darryl Strawberry and Henry Rodriguez later got homers by hitting the ring. ♦ A distant seat (painted yellow), where a Willie Stargell home run landed in center field 535 feet from home plate, is now in the Canadian Baseball Hall of Fame in St. Mary's, Ontario. ♦ Expos mascot Youppi cheered on the Expos here for 27 years through all the ups and downs, mostly downs, from 1978 through 2004, but in his first year, 1978, he was named Souki.

♦    ♦    ♦

# Mounds, Illinois

## *Mounds Ballfield*

**OCCUPANT**

Neutral site used by NAL New Orleans-St. Louis Stars August–September 1939

# Muncie, Indiana

## *Walnut Park*

**OCCUPANT**

Neutral site used by NNL Indianapolis ABCs September 11, 1920

# Nashville, Tennessee

## *Sulphur Dell (I)*

**OCCUPANT**

Neutral site used by NNL Memphis Red Sox 1924–25

**LOCATION**

Left Field (S) Tennessee Central RR tracks, Third Base (E) Cherry St (later Fourth Ave North), First Base (N) Jackson St, Right Field (W) Summer St (later 900 Fifth Ave North); same site as Sulphur Dell (II) but different orientation

**FORMER USE**

Trading post and watering hole at Sulphur Springs

Nashville's Sulphur Dell I in 1908.

used often for picnics; first used for baseball right after the Civil War

**DIMENSIONS**

Left Field: 334
Center Field: 421
Right Field: 262
Right Field Shelf when fans sat behind ropes on the bank in right: 235
Backstop: 40

**PHENOMENA**

Sulphur Dell (I) grandstand was built in 1885 and torn down in the winter of 1926–27 to make way for Sulphur Dell (II).

## *Wilson Park*

**OCCUPANTS**

NNL Nashville Elite Giants 1930; NSL Nashville Elite Giants 1932

**LOCATION**

South of Meharry Medical College in the Trimble Bottom neighborhood

**CAPACITY**

8000

**PHENOMENA**

Built by Thomas Wilson, owner of the Elite Giants and president of the NNL for many years. ♦ One of the few parks owned and operated by a Negro League club. ♦ Other than Dyckman Oval, Gus Greenlee Field, and this one, the Negro Leagues were forced into using booking agents, who knew the major league park owners, as middlemen to schedule their games.

## *Sulphur Dell (II)*

**AKA**

Sulphur Springs Bottom, Sulphur Dell Park, Athletic Park, the Dump, Suffer Hell

**OCCUPANTS**

NNL Nashville Elite Giants 1930; NSL Nashville Elite Giants 1932; NNL Nashville Elite Giants 1933–34

**LOCATION**

Left Field (N) Jackson St, Third Base (W) Summer St (later 900 Fifth Ave North), First Base (S) Tennessee Central RR tracks; Right Field (E) Cherry St (later Fourth Ave North)

**DIMENSIONS**

Left Field: 334), 364 (1940)

Center Field: 421

Right Field: 262, 282 (1940)

Right Field Shelf when fans sat behind ropes on the bank in right: 235

Backstop: 40

**FENCES**

Left and Center: 16 (wood 1931)

Right Field: 16, 38.5 to 46 (16 wood below 22.5 to 30 screen from foul line to a point 186 feet from the foul line 1931)

**CAPACITY**

7000, 8000 (1932), 8500 (1938), 10,000 (1940)

**PHENOMENA**

Only a quarter mile from the Cumberland River, park was often flooded. ♦ Nicknamed "the Dump" in honor of the exceptional fragrance that drifted over from the nearby smoldering city dump—and lent a unique character to Sulphur Dell hot dogs! ♦ Craziest right field in history—right fielders were called mountain goats because they had to go up and down the irregular hills in right-center and right. The incline in right rose 25 feet, beginning gradually behind first base, then rising sharply at a 45-degree angle, then leveling off at a 10-foot-wide "Shelf" one-third of the way up the incline, then continuing at a 45-degree angle to the fence. Fielders used to play on the Shelf, 235 feet from the plate. ♦ With overflow crowds, a rope was extended in front of the Shelf, and fans sat on the upper two-thirds of the incline, reducing right field to 235 rather than 262. ♦ There was an incline in front of the left and center field fences as well. ♦ Huge scoreboard with a clock on top stood in left-center. ♦ Stands were very close to the pancake-shaped diamond. First base was only 42 feet from the seats; third base only 26 feet. ♦ Embankments began in left at 301 and in right at 224. Casey Stengel once joked he could bunt a home run down the first base line. ♦ Dismantled in 1969.

Sulphur Dell II contained one of the most unusual features in any stadium—a long and steep incline before the fence, running from right field to center. For many years, a level "shelf" divided the incline, where right fielders positioned themselves.

# Newark, New Jersey

*See also* Bloomfield, New Jersey; Harrison, New Jersey

## *Wiedenmeyer's Park*

**OCCUPANT**

Neutral site used by AL New York Highlanders July 17, 1904

**LOCATION**

(NE) Hamburg Pl (later 262 Wilson Ave), (NW) Ave K

**PHENOMENA**

Built 1902, burned down 1914. Rebuilt in 1926 as Ruppert Stadium.

## *Newark Schools Stadium*

**OCCUPANT**

ECL Newark Stars April–June 1926

**LOCATION**

(NW) North 10th St; (SW) 1st Ave West; (SE) Roseville Ave; (NE) Bloomfield Ave

**PHENOMENA**

Built in 1925 as a football stadium. ◆ The Foul Lines were so short in 1926 that balls hit over the fences down the lines were ruled doubles.

## *Meadowbrook Oval*

**AKA**

Meadowbrook Field

**OCCUPANTS**

NEWL Newark Browns April–June 1932; NNL Newark Dodgers 1934–35

**LOCATION**

Left Field (NE) I-280, then Orange St; Third Base (NW) Steuben St; First Base (SW) Central Ave, then Fairmont Cemetery; Right Field (SE) South 12th St

**DIMENSIONS**

Foul Lines: 300
Center Field: 380

**FENCES**

All: 12

## *Ruppert Stadium*

**AKA**

Davids' Stadium 1926–31, Bears Stadium 1932–33, Davids' Folly

**OCCUPANTS**

NNL Newark Eagles 1936–48; NAL Newark Indians 1959

**LOCATION**

Left Field (SE) Ave L; Third Base (NE) Hamburg Pl (later 262 Wilson Ave); First Base (NW) Ave K, then 1/9 Expressway; Right Field (SW) Delancy St; on the eastern edge of Newark, in lowlands between the Passaic River to the north, Newark Bay to the east, and Newark Liberty Airport to the south

**DIMENSIONS**

Foul Lines: 305 (1936)
Center Field: 410 (1936)

**FORMER USE**

Wiedenmeyer's Park 1902–14

Designed by Charles A. Davids, Ruppert Stadium was built in 1926 by beer baron Jacob Ruppert, who also owned the New York Yankees. While seating was just 12,000, it sometimes hosted crowds as large as 22,000 for Negro League games.

**CURRENT USE**

Industrial park

**CAPACITY**

12,000 (listed), 19,000 (actual)

**PHENOMENA**

Nearby garbage dump caused horrible smell and smoke which could delay games. Sportswriter Randy Dixon wrote that fans needed gas masks to enjoy the ambience of toxic wastes in Newark. Dump fires could often be seen burning outside the park. ♦ Huge smokestack beyond the left field foul pole. ♦ Lights installed in 1932. ♦ Bleachers in left and left-center kept left-center power alley relatively short, but power alley in right-center was much more distant. ♦ The fence in right curved quickly away from the plate, much like Fenway and the LA Coliseum. ♦ Torn down in 1967.

# Newburgh Heights, Ohio

## Beyerle's Park

**AKA**

Forest City Park 1894–1911, Washington Park 1912, Hooper's Field 1913–22, Tate Field 1922–30

**OCCUPANTS**

NNL Cleveland Tate Stars 1922; NNL Cleveland Browns 1924; NNL Cleveland Elites 1926; NNL Cleveland Hornets 1927; neutral site used by AA Cleveland Spiders September 2, 1888

**LOCATION**

Left Field (SE) Sykora St, Third Base (NE) Independence Rd (running from NW to SE) and Hugo Ave Southeast (running from SW to NE), Home Plate (N) Beyerle St, First Base (NW) Hugo Brick Plant, Right Field (SW); just outside the city limits of Cleveland

**PHENOMENA**

A small park according to game accounts–in the only American Association game played here, there were two over-the-fence home runs. ♦ Rough infield with lots of large pebbles.

---

# New Haven, Connecticut

### Brewster Race Track

**AKA**

Hamilton Park

**OCCUPANT**

NA New Haven Elm Citys April 21, 1875

♦   ♦   ♦

Welcome to New Orleans, home of the Pelicans

### Howard Avenue Grounds

**OCCUPANTS**

NA New Haven Elm Citys April 26–October 28, 1875; neutral site used by NL Hartford Dark Blues September 22, 1877

**LOCATION**

(NE) Whalley Ave; (NW) West Park Ave, then West River; (SW) Elm St; (SE) Pendleton St; there must have been a Howard Avenue nearby that it was named after, but its location has been lost in the fog of history; just across the West River from and just northeast of the campus of Yale University

---

# New Orleans, Louisiana

### Pelican Stadium

**AKA**

Heinemann Park

**OCCUPANTS**

NAL New Orleans-St. Louis Stars (half of their games) 1941; NAL New Orleans Eagles 1951; NAL

Pelican Stadium in New Orleans served as a spring training site for many major league teams, and was used by various Negro League teams.

New Orleans Bears 1957; neutral site used for Negro World Series NNL Washington-Homestead Grays vs. NAL Birmingham Black Barons game two in 1944

**LOCATION**

Left Field (NE) Tulane Ave, Third Base (NW) South Carrollton St, First Base (SW) Gravier St, Right Field (SE) Pierce St

**DIMENSIONS**

Left Field: 427 (1915), 292 (1940), 427 (1941)
Center Field: 405
Right Field: 418 (1915), 294 (1940), 418 (1941)

**CURRENT USE**

Fountain Bay Motor Hotel

**CAPACITY**

9500 (1940)

**PHENOMENA**

Unique configuration, in which both Foul Lines were more distant than straightaway center. However, in 1940, they put in an inner fence which made the fences down the lines very short, 292 in left and 294 in right. ♦ Dismantled at former location of Banks and Carrollton Streets. Reassembled here in winter of 1914–15. Opened April 13, 1915. ♦ Torn down October 1957 after ban on black players and civil rights protests drove minor league Pelicans out of town.

## Stars Field

**OCCUPANT**

NAL Detroit-New Orleans Stars (half of the home games) 1960–61

♦　♦　♦

# Newport, Rhode Island

## Cardines Field

**OCCUPANT**

Neutral site used by NAL teams 1930s and 1940s

**LOCATION**

(N) Bridge St; (W) America's Cup Ave, then Narragansett Bay; (S) Marlborough St; (E) Thames St

**DIMENSIONS**

Left Field: 315
Left Center: 365
Center Field: 395
Right Center: 315
Right Field: 295

**FENCES**

20

**CAPACITY**

3000

**FORMER USE**

Called "the Basin" because it was a lake whose water was used to supply railroad steam locomotives with the water they needed to make steam in the 1800s

**PHENOMENA**

Built in 1889, this is the oldest U.S. baseball field still in existence, older than Bisbee, Arizona's field, built in 1909 and older than Birmingham, Alabama's Rickwood Field, built in 1910. ♦ Although London, Ontario, claims its park was built in 1877, that park has been completely rebuilt and turned around since it was originally built. ♦ Home of the Newport Colts of the New England League 1897–99; Newport Ponies of the Atlantic Association 1908, and currently the Newport Gulls of the New England Collegiate Baseball League.

# Newton, North Carolina

## *American Legion Park*

**OCCUPANT**

Neutral site used by NAL Raleigh Tigers June 5, 1959

**LOCATION**

Center Field (SE), Third Base (NE), Home Plate (NW), First Base (SW)

**DIMENSIONS**

Left Field: 340 (1940)
Center Field: 360 (1940)
Right Field: 380 (1940)

**CAPACITY**

2500 (1940)

# Newtown, New York

## *Grauer's Ridgewood Park*

**AKA**

Ridgewood Park (I), Horse Market

**OCCUPANT**

AA Brooklyn Trolley Dodgers on 15 Sundays May 2–September 19, 1886

**LOCATION**

(N) Myrtle Ave, (NW) Weirfield St, (SW) Wyckoff Ave, (SE) Decatur St, (NE) Seneca Ave; the entrance was at Myrtle Ave and Covert St; back then the site was in the village of Ridgewood, in the town of Newtown, in Queens County, which allowed Sunday games, whereas Kings County (where Brooklyn is) did not; the site is now on the Queens-Brooklyn border, the Ridgewood neighborhood name has moved through the years, what was then the Ridgewood neighborhood is now called the Wyckoff Heights neighborhood

**CAPACITY**

7200 (1886)

**CURRENT USE**

Houses, Food Dynasty supermarket

**PHENOMENA**

The Myrtle Avenue horse car went directly to the park. Grauer's Ridgewood Hotel was at Seneca and Myrtle. ◆ After the 1886 season, this park became part of the Ridgewood Picnic Park because Mr. Grauer, the owner, decided he could make more money by transforming it into a dance pavilion. So the Trolley Dodgers moved across Wyckoff to the southwest to Wallace's Ridgewood Park, a much smaller area. ◆ The area bounded by Grauer's Ridgewood Park is more than three times the size of the area bounded by Wallace's Ridgewood Park. ◆ SABR member David Dyte gets credit for discovering that there were two Ridgewood Parks.

## *Wallace's Ridgewood Park*

**AKA**

Ridgewood Park (II), Wallace's Grounds

**OCCUPANTS**

AA Brooklyn Tolley Dodgers Sundays April 24, 1887–October 6, 1889; AA Brooklyn Gladiators April 17–June 8, 1890

**LOCATION**

Left Field (E/NE) New York Manhattan Beach branch Long Island RR tracks, the Wyckoff Ave; 3rd

Base (N/NW) Halsey St; 1st Base (W/SW) Irving Ave; Right Field (S/SE) Covert St.

**CAPACITY**

6000 (1887); 10,000 (1905); 14,000 (1912)

**PHENOMENA**

The AL Highlanders signed an agreement to play Sunday games here in 1904, but never actually did so. ♦ Burned down in September 1917.

## Long Island Grounds

**AKA**

Maspeth Ball Grounds, Long Island Recreation Grounds

**OCCUPANT**

AA Brooklyn Gladiators Sundays on July 27 and August 3, 1890

**LOCATION**

Maspeth Ave, back then in the unincorporated hamlet of Maspeth, which was part of Newtown on Long Island; today this is the Maspeth section of Queens

---

# New York, New York

*See also* East Orange, New Jersey; Hoboken, New Jersey; Jersey City, New Jersey; Newtown, New York; Paterson, New Jersey; Riverhead, New York; Weehawken, New Jersey; West New York, New Jersey

## Polo Grounds (I) Southeast Diamond

**AKA**

Polo Field East

**OCCUPANTS**

NL New York Gothams May 1, 1883–October 13, 1888; AA New York Mets May 12–29, 1883; AA New York Mets June 13–September 6, 1883, for 24 games because they preferred playing here to playing at the Southwest Diamond and did so whenever the NL Gothams were not playing here that day (June 13, July 23, 30, 31, August 1, 3, 4, 6, 7, 9, 10, 16, 17, 18, 20, 21, 22, 23, 25, 27, 29, September 3, 5, 6); AA New York Mets July 17–22, 1884; AA New York Mets July 26–August 23, 1884 only when NL Gothams did not have a home game here that day (August 11 and 12); AA New York Mets September 24–October 15, 1884; AA New York Mets April 24–October 1, 1885–when NL Gothams also had a home game that day, the Mets would play earlier in the day; NCL New York Gothams 1887; neutral site used for Temple Cup Series NL Detroit Wolverines vs. AA St. Louis Browns October 15, 1887

**LOCATION**

Left Field (W) Southwest Diamond, then Sixth (later Lenox) Ave, Third Base (S) West 110th St, First Base (E) Fifth Ave, Right Field (N) West 112th St; just north of Central Park at Douglas Circle

**DIMENSIONS**

Prior to Opening Day of 1886 there were no fences; 180 ft. to small flags marking the foul lines, but this did not mean that it was 180 ft. to where you needed to hit it over for a home run since there was no fence.

**FENCES**

None at first when it was the only diamond May 1–29, 1883; none for the first day when games were played at both Southeast and Southwest Diamonds on May 30, 1883, but beginning May 31 there was a short fence in front of the right field bleachers, and a 10-foot-high canvas barrier between the two outfields; balls rolling under the canvas fence were in play, so outfielders crawled under the fence and then threw the ball over the fence back to the infield; starting in 1886 there was a seven-foot-high fence in center field and right field.

**FORMER USE**

Polo field, owned by James Gordon Bennett, publisher of the *New York Herald,* and used by the Westchester Polo Association

**CURRENT USE**

Public School No. 170

**CAPACITY**

12,000

**PHENOMENA**

Opened for baseball use on September 29, 1880. ♦ The second deck of seats was added before the 1883 season. ♦ There was a large flagpole in short center field, with a flag saying NEW YORK. ♦ There were two diamonds here. The NL Gothams and AA Mets both used the Southeast Diamond, until the Southwest Diamond was completed on May 30, 1883. However, the Southwest Diamond, built on top of stinky garbage, was so smelly that the Mets always preferred playing on the Southeast Diamond, and would do so whenever they could. In 1883, the AA Mets played 13 home games over at the Southwest Diamond on days when the NL Gothams were playing here, and played 34 games here on days when the NL Gothams were not scheduled. ♦ In 1884, the AA Mets played 33 home games over at Metropolitan Park on the East River, also built on top of stinky garbage, on days when the NL Gothams were playing here, and played 22 games here on days when the NL Gothams were not scheduled. ♦ In 1885, both teams played all their home games here; on the six days when both teams were scheduled, on August 26, 28, September 10, 23, 24, and 26, they played a doubleheader, with the Mets hosting the first game and the Gothams hosting the second. ♦ Baseball ended when the city built 111th Street through center and right fields in the fall of 1888. ♦ The ballpark burned down in the spring of 1889.

♦    ♦    ♦

## *Polo Grounds (II) Southwest Diamond*

**AKA**

Polo Field West, Metropolitan Field

**OCCUPANT**

AA New York Mets May 30–September 4, 1883, for 13 games, only on those days when the NL Gothams were playing at the Southeast Diamond (May 30 doubleheader, May 31, June 2, 4, 5, 7, 8, 12, 14, August 30, 31, September 4)

**LOCATION**

Left Field (N) West 112th St, Third Base (W) Sixth (later Lenox) Ave, First Base (S) West 110th St, Right Field (E) Southeast Diamond, then Fifth Ave

**PHENOMENA**

Raw garbage was used as landfill in making the infield, so the players hated this diamond. The Mets would play at Polo Grounds (I) Southeast Diamond whenever they could to avoid playing here. So the AA Mets played 13 home games here in 1883, while playing 34 home games at the Southeast Diamond.

## *Metropolitan Park*

**AKA**

East River Ballpark

**OCCUPANT**

AA New York Mets May 13–June 18, 1884; AA New York Mets July 26–August 23, 1884, only when the NL Gothams had a home game that day at Polo Grounds Southeast Diamond (July 26 and 28, August 7 (rained out), 8, 19–21, 23)

**LOCATION**

Left Field (E) East River, Third Base (N) East 109th St, First Base (W) First Ave, Right Field (S) East 107th St

**PHENOMENA**

As had been the case with Polo Grounds (II) Southwest Diamond, raw garbage was used as landfill to make the infield. Players also hated this diamond, so on June 19 the Mets again decided to play at Polo Grounds (I) Southeast Diamond whenever they could to avoid playing here. The AA Mets played 33 home games here in 1884, while playing 22 home games at the Southeast Diamond. ♦ Mets pitcher Jack Lynch said you could get malaria just by fielding a ground ball here.

## St. George Cricket Grounds

**AKA**

Mutrie's Dump, Mutrie's Dumping Grounds

**OCCUPANTS**

AA New York Mets April 22, 1886–October 7, 1887; NL New York Giants April 29–June 14, 1889

**LOCATION**

Left Field (E) Upper Bay, Third Base (N) Kill van Kull and Bedloe's (later Liberty) Island with the Statue of Liberty on it, First Base (W), Right Field (S); at St. George on Staten Island, just up the shoreline from the Staten Island Ferry dock

**FENCES**

None

**CURRENT USE**

Richmond County Bank Ballpark at St. George, home of the NY-Penn League Staten Island Yankees, since 1999; before that the area was a train yard and a parking lot for most of the 20th century

**PHENOMENA**

First used for baseball in 1853 in a game between the Washington Club (later known as the Gotham Club) and the New York Knickerbockers. ♦ Illuminated geysers here, almost a full century before they reappeared at Kansas City's Royals Stadium. ♦ The field sloped sharply down from third base toward left field. ♦ Your ticket included free admission to the Staten Island Ferry boat ride to and from Manhattan. ♦ While watching Mets games in 1886, fans along the first base line could watch the Statue of Liberty being erected out in the harbor behind third base. ♦ The stage play *The Fall of Babylon* was staged here in 1887, forcing the diamond to be moved to the west. ♦ A huge structure sat in right field, and any balls hit into Babylon (right field) were singles. ♦ One day two warriors held their polished shields so as to reflect sunlight into the eyes of Orioles batters. ♦ One day elephants and camels, on their way to the zoo, paraded through the outfield while the Athletics were taking infield practice. ♦ When used by the Giants in 1889, the field was bare and stony in center field due to the 1888 stage production of *Nero, The Fall of Rome,* by the Kiraltys. The Nero scaffolding remained in place, surrounding the outfield, and the swampy outfield was covered with boards, forcing the outfielders to wear rubber-soled shoes to get any traction.

## Wild West Grounds

**OCCUPANT**

AA New York Mets some games in 1887 when St. George Cricket Grounds was flooded or booked with other events

**LOCATION**

Tomkinsville on Staten Island

## Polo Grounds (III)

**AKA**

Manhattan Field, New Polo Grounds (I) 1889–90

**OCCUPANTS**

NL New York Giants July 8, 1889–September 13,

1890; AA Brooklyn Gladiators June 9, July 23–August 2, 1890

**LOCATION**

Left Field (N) West 157th St, Third Base (W) Harlem River Speedway, Coogan's Bluff, First Base (S) West 155th St, Right Field (E) 8th Ave, Harlem River; on the southern part of Coogan's Hollow

**CAPACITY**

15,000

**PHENOMENA**

Steepest and largest embankment ever in a major league park, in center and right fields, dwarfing even the Dodgers spring training embankment at Holman Stadium in Vero Beach. On September 14, 1889, Cap Anson got an inside-the-park homer when the Giant center fielder George Gore could not climb the muddy embankment. ♦ Separated only by a canvas fence in 1890, the NL Giants in this park and the PL Giants in Polo Grounds (IV) frequently had games under way at the same time. On May 12, 1890, Mike Tiernan hit a 13th-inning home run that fans in both parks cheered. Accounts differ as to whether Tiernan's home run landed in the outfield of the other ballpark, or whether it landed in a narrow alleyway between the two ballparks and bounced up against the other park's outfield canvas fence. If the latter, then there would have been two canvas fences separating the two ballparks. ♦ Used for cricket throughout the 1890s, and as a parking lot for Polo Grounds (V) after it was built in 1911.

## *Polo Grounds (IV)*

**AKA**

Brotherhood Park 1890, New Polo Grounds (II) 1891

**OCCUPANTS**

PL New York Giants April 19–September 18, 1890; NL New York Giants April 22, 1891–April 13, 1911

**LOCATION**

Center Field (SE) Eighth Ave, then IRT elevated

A huge standing crowd rings the outfield of Polo Grounds IV, while luckier fans sit in horse drawn carriages. Coogan's Bluff looms over the stadium.

RR tracks and Harlem River; Third Base (NE) West 159th St, then IRT RR repair yards; Home Plate (NW) Bridge Park, then Harlem River Speedway (later Dr), Coogan's Bluff, and Croton Aqueduct; First Base (SW) West 157th St, then Manhattan Field; on the northern part of Coogan's Hollow, 115 feet below Coogan's Bluff; just N of Polo Grounds (III)

### DIMENSIONS

Left Field: 335, 277 (July 1, 1890)
Center Field: 500, 433 (1909)
Right Field: 335, 258 (July 1, 1890)

Note that the foul pole distances on July 1, 1890, are the exact same distances as left field at Polo Grounds (V) when it opened (277 feet) and as right field at Polo Grounds (V) when it closed (258 feet)

### FENCES

Foul Lines: 4
Bullpens: 25 sloping down to 15
Power Alleys: 15 sloping down to 5
Center Field: 0–3 (rope strung between posts 1891–1908), 8 (1909)

### FORMER USE

Farm granted to John Lion Gardiner by King of England in 17th century; big mystery here is that other sources indicate that Yankee Stadium also sits on land given to Mr. Gardiner by the King of England—could he possibly have owned both?

### CAPACITY

16,000 (1891), 30,000 (1911)

### PHENOMENA

Because balls hit to center field that rolled under the ropes strung between posts were bounce home runs, the effective height of the fence was zero. ♦ Dimensions 1909-10 based on 1909 Sanborn fire insurance map. ♦ One of the only two places where a ball could be a home run, but another ball hit higher and farther to almost the exact same point was in play; the other was League Park (IV) in Cleveland. ♦ The stands here curved about ten feet into fair territory down the left field line, but only the corner of the stands protruded out into fair territory. Behind these seats were the bullpens, which were in play. ♦ There was a sharp incline in the bullpens in front of the left field wall. ♦ One day in April 1901, Tad Dorgan, a *New York Journal* sports cartoonist, couldn't remember how to spell the word "dachshund" in describing the "red hot dachshund sausages" here, so he invented the term "hot dogs." ♦ Giants forfeited to the Phillies on Opening Day, April 11, 1907. The Phillies were leading 3–0 when Giants fans behind the ropes in the outfield rebelled and stormed the field in the ninth inning. ♦ Police estimated that 250,000 people showed up to see the Giants lose to the Cubs in the pennant playoff game, October 8, 1908, necessitated by the Cubs' successful protest of the September 23, 1908, "Merkle's Boner" game, when Fred Merkle forgot to touch second base on what should have been Al Bridwell's game-winning single. Forty thousand people watched the game from Coogan's Bluff because they could not get into the ballpark. ♦ Largely destroyed by fire April 14–15, 1911. Only the left field, center field, and most of the right field bleachers survived.

## *Hilltop Park*

### AKA

Highlanders Park, American League Ballpark, the Rockpile, the Hilltop

### OCCUPANTS

AL New York Yankees April 30, 1903–October 5, 1912; NL New York Giants April 15–May 30, 1911

### LOCATION

Left Field (N) West 168th St; Third Base (W) Fort Washington Ave, then Hudson River; (SW) Deaf and Dumb Asylum; First Base (S) West 165th St; Right Field (E) Broadway; on a rockpile overlooking Washington Heights, near West Side Subway

BATTING CAGE, AM'N LEAGUE PARK, N.Y.

When the Polo Grounds grandstand and left field bleachers ignited in a mysterious fire in April 1911, President Frank Farrell of the AL Highlanders invited the Giants to use Hilltop Park; in return, the Giants invited the Highlanders to use the Polo Grounds when the Hilltop Park lease expired after the 1912 season.

**DIMENSIONS**

Left Field: 365

Left Center: 378

Center Field: 432, 380 (June 1, 1903), 420 (1904), 412 (1907), 370 (1911)

Deepest Right Center: 542, 390 (June 1, 1903)

Right Center: 533, 335 (June 1, 1903), 424 (1904), 412 (1907), 372 (1911)

Right Field: 400, 290 (June 1, 1903), 385 (1904), 365 (1907)

Backstop: 91.5

**CAPACITY**

15,000, 17,000 (1911), with standing room 25,000

**FENCES**

Left Field: 12, sloping from 12 to 15 (1908)

Center Field: sloping from 12 to 20, 12 (June 1, 1903), sloping from 12 to 20 (1904), 3 (1911)

Right Field: 12, 8 (June 1, 1903), 12 (1904)

**CURRENT USE**

Columbia-Presbyterian Medical Center, built in the 1920s

**PHENOMENA**

Shortest post-1900 center field dimensions in the major leagues in 1911–12: only 370 feet. ♦ Excellent view of Hudson River and New Jersey Palisades behind upper seats in the third base portion of the grandstand. ♦ Scoreboard in left. ♦ Large exit gate in right. ♦ Clubhouse behind the fence in center. ♦ Bull Durham sign shaped like a bull in right-center in 1909, twice the height of the rest of the fence. ♦ When the first homestand (only six games) began April 30, 1903, there was a huge hollow in right field, which was roped off and balls hit past the ropes were doubles. When the second homestand began June 1, there was a fence in front of the hollow and balls hit over the short fence were home runs. ♦ Bleachers added in center field in 1911. ♦ Dimensions largely based on

1907 Sanborn fire insurance map. ♦ Torn down in 1914. ♦ Memorial dedicated at site of home plate in 1993 with cooperation of SABR, the Yankees, and Columbia-Presbyterian Medical Center; is located in Medical Center Garden, near Fort Washington Avenue entrance, next to Harkness Pavilion.

## Polo Grounds (V)

### AKA
Brush Stadium 1912–19, Coogan's Bluff, Coogan's Hollow, Matty Schwab's House, Harlem Meadow

### ARCHITECTS
Harry B. Herts and Osborn Engineering

### OCCUPANTS
NL New York Giants June 28, 1911–September 29, 1957; AL New York Yankees May 30, 1912; April 17, 1913–October 7, 1922; NNL New York Cubans 1948; NAL New York Cubans 1949–50; NL New York Mets April 13, 1962–September 18, 1963; neutral use for Negro World Series NNL Newark Eagles vs. NAL Kansas City Monarchs first game 1946

### LOCATION
Center Field (SE) Eighth Ave, then IRT elevated RR tracks, and Harlem River; Third Base (NE) West 159th St, then IRT RR repair yards and high-rise apartments; Home Plate (NW) Bridge Park, then Harlem River Speedway (later Dr), Coogan's Bluff, and Croton Aqueduct; First Base (SW) West 157th St, then Manhattan Field parking lot; on the northern part of Coogan's Hollow, 115 feet below Coogan's Bluff; just north of Polo Grounds (III); same as Polo Grounds (IV)

### DIMENSIONS
Left Field: 277, 286.67 (1921), 279.67 (1923), 279 (1930), 280 (1943), 279 (1955)

Left Field Second Deck: 257.17 (1922), 250.17 (1923), 249.5 (1930), 250.5 (1943), 249.5 (1955)

Left Center left of Bullpen: 447

Left Center right of Bullpen: 455

Left Center side of 1920–22 Green Curtain Batters' Background: 440

Center of 1920–22 Curtain in Dead Center Field: 460

Right Center side of 1920–22 Curtain: 475

Clubhouse front steps: 460

Center Field: 433, 475 (1921), 483 (1923), 484.75 (1927), 505 (1930), 430 (1931), 480 (1934), 430 (1938), 505 (1940), 490 (1943), 505 (1944), 480 (1945), 490 (1946), 484 (1947), 505 (1949), 483 (1952), 480 (1953), 483 (1954), 480 (1955), 475 (1962), 483 (1963)

Bleacher corners: 425 when Center Field was 475, 432 when Center Field was 483, and 451 when Center Field was 505

Right Center left of Bullpen: 449

Right Center right of Bullpen: 440

Right Center exit gate: 433 (1920)

Right Field: 258, 256 (1921), 257.67 (1923), 257.5 (1931), 257.67 (1942), 259 (1943), 257.67 (1944)

Right Field photographers' perch: 249

Backstop: 65 (1942), 70 (1943), 65 (1944), 70 (1946), 74 (1949), 65 (1954), 74 (1955), 65 (1962)

Foul Territory: very large.

Under the Giants, reading from left to right, the markers read 315, 360, 414, 447, 455, 483, 455, 449, 395, 338, and 294. Under the Mets, they read 306, 405, 475, 405, and 281.

The Foul Lines: were never marked. The 29.5-foot overhang of the second deck along the foul line in left reduced the distance to the second deck from 279 to 250.

### FENCES

#### 1911–22:
Left to Center: 10 (concrete)

Center: 20 (tarp)

Right Center: 10 (concrete)

Right Field: 12 sloping down to 11 at pole (concrete)

#### 1923–63:
Left Field: 16.81 (concrete)

Left Center: 18 (concrete)

Left Center wall where it ended at bleachers: 12 (concrete)

Center Field bleachers wall: 8.5 (4.25 wire on top of 4.25 concrete) on both sides of clubhouse runway

Center Field low wall in front of clubhouse alcove: 3 (1931–33 and 1938–39) Center Field hitters background 16.5 on both sides of clubhouse runway

Center Field clubhouse: 60 high and 60 wide, 50 high in 1963

Center Field top of Longine Clock: 80

Center Field top of right side of scoreboard: 71

Center Field top of left side of scoreboard: 68

Center Field top of middle of scoreboard: 64

Center Field top of 5 right scoreboard windows: 57

Center Field top of 4 left scoreboard windows: 55

Center Field bottom of 5 right scoreboard windows: 53

Center Field bottom of 4 left scoreboard windows: 48

Center Field bottom of clubhouse scoreboard: 31

Center Field top of rear clubhouse wall: 28

Center Field top of front clubhouse wall: 19

Center Field top of 14 lower clubhouse windows: 16

Center Field bottom of 14 lower clubhouse windows: 11

Center Field clubhouse floor overhang: 8

Center Field top of Eddie Grant Memorial: 5

Center Field width of little office on top of lower clubhouse: 10

Right Center: 12 (concrete)

Right Field: 10.64 (concrete)

**FORMER USE**

Underneath the Harlem River, until filled in with dirt in the late 1870s. Field was raised 4½ feet in 1949 to help with drainage. In 1609 and 1874 maps, the location is shown as underneath the Harlem River. The water table was only two to six feet below the playing surface, and drainage was complicated by rainwater cascading off the 115-foot-high Coogan's Bluff down onto the site.

**CURRENT USE**

Polo Grounds Towers, four 30-story apartment buildings; Willie Mays Field, an asphalt playground with six basketball backboards where center field used to be; brass historical marker

**CAPACITY**

16,000, 30,000 (August 11, 1911), 34,000 (October 14, 1911), 39,000 (1917), 38,000 (1919), 37,000 (1921), 43,000 (1922), 54,000 (1923), 55,000 (1926), 56,000 (1930), 51,856 (1937), 56,000 (1940), 54,500 (1947), 56,000 (1953), 55,137 (1957), 55,000 (1962)

**PHENOMENA**

Confusion reigns concerning the center field distance and why it changed so frequently. What is important to remember is that when the center field distance was listed as X feet, it was really only (X minus 52 feet) to exact dead center at the imaginary line connecting the first row of the bleachers to the left of the center field alcove and the first row of the bleachers to the right of the center field alcove. In other words, the center field clubhouse alcove added 52 feet to the distance from the plate to the clubhouse wall. But when thinking about how hard it was to hit a home run at the Polo Grounds, this extra 52 feet is meaningless for balls hit into the bleachers. It is only meaningful for balls hit into the alcove in exact dead center. This enables one to more accurately understand power performance statistics, such as home runs hit in various ballparks. Ron Selter's extensive research indicates that when center field was listed as 483 feet, it was 431 to the imaginary line across dead center where the alcove began, and another 52 back to the clubhouse wall, or 483 to the clubhouse wall. Similarly, when center field was listed as 475, it was 423 to that imaginary line in dead center where the alcove began, and 52 more to the clubhouse wall, or 475 to the clubhouse wall. This corresponds nicely with the distance of 430 to center field during the five years when the alcove was not "in play": 1931–33, when there were bleachers in the alcove, and 1938–39, when there was a low fence across the alcove. One could extrapolate that when center field was listed as 505, it was 453 to the imaginary line across dead center where the alcove began, plus 52

*Spacious Polo Grounds*

To this day, nobody knows what would have happened if someone had hit a blast off the wall of the clubhouse, above the monument, in straight-away center at the Polo Grounds. Since it was deemed impossible, the Giants had no ground rule to determine whether it was a home run or in play. Theoretically, one could have hit the longest ball in the history of baseball, off the Longines clock 80 feet above the 505 foot sign, and gotten just a double.

back to the clubhouse wall, which would be 505 to the clubhouse wall. ♦ Because of the geometry of the front of the bleacher wall cutting straight across the outfield, rather than curving around the outfield like most outfield walls, the corners of the bleachers where the alcove began were more distant by a couple of feet than the imaginary line in exact dead center. ♦ Discussions with the ground crew have revealed that the plate was definitely moved forward and backward from season to season, which explains why the center field distance changed so frequently. The groundskeepers state that when home plate was moved forward or backward, the locations of the foul poles and the distances to the foul poles would not change but the center field distance would change; however if that were the case, then the Foul Lines would no longer be perpendicular to each other. Home plate movements also explain the fact that in 1934, when center field was 480, photos show that the right field foul line seats were far from the foul line, whereas photos in 1942, when center field was 505, show that in the exact same place the right field foul line seats were right up against the foul line,

which indicates that, in this case at least, the location of the foul pole did change at least once. ♦ After much of the all-wooden Polo Grounds (IV) burned down April 14–15, 1911, Polo Grounds (V) was built during the rest of the 1911 season. The bleachers in left, left-center, and center did not burn. The old grandstand and part of the right field bleachers were lost in the fire. ♦ This park is frequently viewed as a hitters ballpark, but it was really a home run ballpark. The Giants and other teams averaged .020 points less in batting average than elsewhere. ♦ Ron Selter and Bill Deane have estimated that it was 417–420 feet to where Willie Mays made "the Catch" against the Indians in the 1954 World Series. ♦ Coats of arms of NL teams displayed with Roman Colosseum facade frescoes in 1910s. ♦ There was no line on the 60-foot-high center field clubhouse above which a ball would be a home run. There is no documentation of a ball ever hitting the clubhouse wall on the fly, much less going over it. The mystery remains—what if someone had managed to hit one 505 feet to dead center, and 80 feet high off the Longines clock, or even 60 feet high off the top of the clubhouse wall? It would definitely have been the longest home run ever hit anywhere, anytime, probably traveling over 700 feet were it not for the obstruction provided by the clubhouse. But it would have bounced back into center field. Could it have been a home run? Everyone would assume so, but actually nobody in the world knows, because the Polo Grounds had no ground rule to decide if a ball hitting the clubhouse wall, or the clock above the clubhouse wall, would have been in play or a home run. ♦ Only four home runs were ever hit into the bleachers in center—Luke Easter in a Negro League game in 1948, Joe Adcock of the Braves on April 29, 1953, and then amazingly two were hit on successive days—Lou Brock on June

17, 1962, and Henry Aaron the next day on June 18. ♦ The odds of only four homers into the center field bleachers in 52 years and two of those being on consecutive days are astronomical. ♦ Bullpens in fair territory in left-center and right-center. ♦ Second deck in right had nine-foot photographer's perch overhang 60 feet from foul pole out into right-center. The left field second-deck overhang meant that a homer to left was easier than a homer to right, even though the wall in left was 279 and the wall in right was 258. The overhang down the left field line was 29.5 feet, shortening the distance required for a homer to the second deck in left by 29.5 feet, from 279 to 249.5 feet. ♦ Overhangs here, at Tiger Stadium and Shibe Park,

This remarkable photo shows Yankee Stadium on the right in the Bronx and its neighbor, the horse shoe-shaped Polo Grounds, across the river in northern Manhattan.

and currently at PETCO Park in San Diego, have more significance than one might suspect, according to research published by the American Physical Society. The batted ball's trajectory consists of two component vectors, horizontal and vertical. The vertical deceleration is constant over time due to gravity, but the horizontal deceleration increases dramatically over time due to wind resistance and atmospheric drag. Near the end of its flight, the ball is coming down sharply, rather than arcing down as it arched up, as would occur in a vacuum, so many outfielders watched helplessly as a ball they could have caught dropped into the second deck. ♦ Bobby Thomson's homer "Heard Around the World" which won the 1951 pennant for the Giants over the Dodgers landed in the lower deck in left field. Would it have been a home run only at the Polo Grounds? This is a difficult question. It was not a lazy pop fly, because a lazy pop fly would have landed in the overhanging upper deck. Thomson's hit traveled 285 feet and then went under the second deck overhang, which was 34 feet high. Then it went into the second or third row of seats at the 315 mark. This means that when it left the bat it had to have been struck with a takeoff angle of between 15 degrees and 23 degrees, and therefore would have traveled somewhere between 338 and 363 feet, or 23 to 48 feet beyond the wall at the 315 mark. So the answer to whether the ball might have been a home run elsewhere depends on how hard a line drive it was. Probably the only other 1951 major league ballpark where it might have been a homer is Yankee Stadium, where it would have had to go perhaps another 25 to 40 feet but would only have had to clear a wall which was 12 feet 11 inches shorter in height. ♦ The outfield was sunken. A manager standing in his dugout could see only the top half of his outfielders. The field sloped in a "turtle back" just beyond the infield dirt. It sloped down 1.5 feet to drains about 20 feet out into the outfield, then back up again, then down again to the outfield walls, where it was eight feet below the infield. Left-center wall sloped from 16 feet, 9.75 inches at the pole to 18 feet in left center, then abruptly fell to 16 feet and then to 14 feet and sloped gradually to 12 feet at the bleachers. ♦ When ad signs were removed in the 1940s, abrupt changes in height in left-center disappeared. ♦ Dedicated on May 30, 1921, to a former Giant killed in World War I, the Eddie Grant Memorial stood in center at the base of the clubhouse wall. Five feet high, and in play, it read: "In Memory of Capt. Edward Leslie Grant 307th Infantry–77th Division A.E.F. Soldier–Scholar–Athlete Killed in Action Argonne Forest October 5, 1918 Philadelphia Nationals 1907–1908–1909–1910 Cincinnati Reds 1911–1912–1913 New York Giants 1913–1914–1915 Erected by Friends in Baseball, Journalism, and the Service." ♦ During the 1950s, groundskeeper Matty Schwab and his family lived in an apartment under Section 3 of the left field stands built for him by owner Horace Stoneham. The apartment was the main bait in Stoneham's successful offer to grab Schwab away from the hated Dodgers in 1950. ♦ During the Mets stay in 1962–63, Johnny McCarthy and his crew of groundskeepers painted Schwab's four rooms pink, installed a shower and plywood on the floor and lockers, and called it their Pink Room. ♦ A two-foot-square section of sod from center field was removed and taken to San Francisco in the fall of 1957. ♦ In 1962, the Mets mascot dog, Homer the Beagle, did back flips here. ♦ Home plate was moved out toward center several feet by the Mets in the winter of 1961–62. ♦ In 1962–63, the Howard Clothes sign on the outfield wall promised a boat to any player hitting it, but nobody ever did. ♦ Demolition started on April 10, 1964, with the same wrecking ball that demolished Ebbets Field. ♦ From 1920 to 1922, there was a green curtain in dead center used as a batters' background. The Giants and Yankees would both gain advantage by raising it when they were in the field and lowering it when they were at bat.

## Dyckman Oval

**OCCUPANTS**

NNL Havana Cuban Stars 1920; NNL New York Cuban Stars 1922; ECL New York Cuban Stars East

1923–27, April–May 1928; ANL New York Cuban Stars East 1929; NEWL Cuban Stars 1932; NNL Cubans 1935–36; neutral site used by NNL Washington Elite Giants some games 1937

**LOCATION**

Left Field (NE) West 204th St, then Henry Hudson Bridge crossing Spuyten Duyvil Creek; Third Base (NW) Nagle Ave; First Base (SW) Academy St; Right Field (SE) Tenth Ave, in upper Manhattan, 8 blocks E of Henry Hudson Pkwy, 5 blocks E of Inwood Hill Park, S of Harlem Ship Canal, 4 blocks N of Dyckman St, in the Dyckman neighborhood

**CURRENT USE**

Dyckman Houses apartment buildings, along with three ball diamonds

**CAPACITY**

4500

**PHENOMENA**

Lights installed in 1930 by Cuban Stars owner Alex Pompez. ♦ Second major league park in the New York area to have lights for evening games; the first was Dexter Park in Brooklyn. ♦ Famous fans included Cab Calloway, Louis Armstrong, Count Basie. ♦ The Negro Leagues' nicest ballpark. ♦ Torn down in late 1930s, after Pompez lost his lease for the park during legal troubles with his numbers racket business in 1935–37, and spent part of 1937 in a Mexico City jail as a result of DA Thomas Dewey's campaign against Tammany Hall corruption.

## *Catholic Protectory Oval*

**AKA**

Capital Texture, Catholic Protection, Society for the Protection of Destitute Roman Catholic Children

**OCCUPANT**

NNL New York Cuban Stars West 1923–30

**LOCATION**

Left Field (E) Hoguet Ave, Third Base (N) East Tremont Ave, First Base (W) White Plains Rd, Right Field (S) McGraw Ave; also Jerome Ave, 156th St; in the Parkchester section of the East Bronx, five miles NE of Yankee Stadium

**CURRENT USE**

Parkchester Apartments, which provide housing for 45,000 people, built by Metropolitan Life Insurance in 1938; Unionport Road now crosses the site from home plate to center field; Metropolitan Avenue now runs from right field in to second base and then curves out to left field.

**CAPACITY**

3500 (1923)

**PHENOMENA**

Very tiny ballfield, with shade trees surrounding the entire field. ♦ It was said the fences were so close to the plate that the only person who could hit a triple was Cool Papa Bell. ♦ The Protectory was a Catholic home and school for impoverished boys, whose 50-piece marching band was much in demand and played before each game. ♦ One of their students, Hank Greenberg, is now enshrined in Cooperstown. ♦ No grass in the infield. ♦ Leveled in 1938 to build the Parkchester Apartments.

## *Olympic Field*

**OCCUPANTS**

ECL New York Lincoln Giants 1923–26, April–May 1928; ANL New York Lincoln Giants 1929

**LOCATION**

(N) West 138th St, (W) Fifth Ave, (S) West 135th St, (E) Madison Ave; in central Harlem

**CURRENT USE**

Riverton Houses (14-story apartments) built in 1947

## PHENOMENA

After the game, Lincoln Giants pitcher/manager Smokey Joe Williams would go to his "other" job, bartending nearby at Lenox Avenue and 134th Street. ♦ Frequent fans included such famous entertainers as Bill "Bojangles" Robinson, Nat King Cole, Lena Horne, and Louis Armstrong.

## *Yankee Stadium*

### AKA

House That Ruth Built

### ARCHITECTS

Osborn Engineering, Praeger-Kavanagh-Waterbury 1973–75 Renovation

### OCCUPANTS

AL New York Yankees April 18, 1923–September 30, 1973; NNL New York Black Yankees some games 1940s; neutral site used for Negro World Series NNL Washington-Homestead Grays vs. NAL Kansas City Monarchs third game 1942, for NNL New York Cubans vs. NAL Cleveland Buckeyes first game 1947; AL New York Yankees April 15, 1976, to date

### LOCATION

Left Field (NE) East 161st St; Third Base (NW) Doughty St (later Ruppert Plc); Home Plate (W) Major Deegan Expressway/I-87, then Harlem River; First Base (SW) East 157th St; Right Field (SE) River Ave, then IRT elevated tracks; in the southwest Bronx

### DIMENSIONS

Left Field: 255, 280.58 (1924), 301 (1928), 312 (1976), 318 (1988)

Left Field: left side of bullpen gate in short left field 395, 402 (1928); right side of bullpen gate 415 (1937)

Left Center: 474, 461 (1924), 451 (1937), 419 (1976), 402 (1985), 392 (1988)

The spacious outfield in Yankee Stadium, 1923: 500 feet to deepest left center beyond the "in-play" flag pole. The track was used for running events at track meets.

Deepest Left Center (left of dead center): 500, 490 (1924), 461 (1937), 430 (1976), 411 (1985), 399 (1988)

Center Field left side of screen: 466 (1937)

Center Field: 487, 470 (1924), 449 (1937), 417 (1976), 410 (1985), 408 (1988)

Left of Right Center: 429

Right Center: 423, 417 (1924), 407 (1937), 385 (1976)

Right Field: left side of bullpen gate 367 (1937); right side of bullpen gate 344 (1937), 353 (1976)

Right Field: 255, 295 (1924), 296 (1930), 310 (1976), 314 (1988)

Backstop: 82 (1942), 80 (1953), 84 (1976)

Foul Territory: large for catcher behind home plate, but small for fielders down the foul lines

### FENCES

Left Field Foul Line: 3.92 (3 wire above 0.92 concrete), 8 (canvas 1976)

Left Field left of visitors bullpen: 3.58 (3 wire above 0.58 concrete)

Right of visitors bullpen: 7.83 (3 wire above 4.83 concrete)

Left Center to Right Center: 7 (canvas 1976)

Center Field left side of screen when up for hitters background: 20 (1953), 22.25 (1959), 22.42 (1954); screen when background was down 13.83 (1953), 7 (canvas 1976)

Right Center right side of screen: 14.5 (3 wire above 11.5 concrete)

Left of home bullpen: 7.83 (3 wire above 4.83 concrete)

Right side of home bullpen: 3.58 (3 wire above 0.58 concrete)

Right Center: 8 (canvas 1976), 9 (canvas 1979)

Right Field Foul Line: 12 (wood), 3.75 (3 wire above 0.75 concrete 1924), 10 (canvas 1976)

### SURFACE

Merion Bluegrass

### FORMER USE

City plot 2106, lot 100, farm granted to John Lion Gardiner before the Revolutionary War, purchased by Yankees from William Waldorf Astor

### CAPACITY

58,000, 62,000 (1926), 82,000 (1927), 67,113 (1928), 62,000 (1929), 71,699 (1937), 70,000 (1942), 67,000 (1948), 65,010 (1971), 54,028 (1976), 57,145 (1977), 57,478 (2003)

### PHENOMENA

Fans arrive by C, D, and #4 trains; subway tracks just behind the bleachers in right-center. ♦ Creek mud from a creek in nearby Burlington County, New Jersey, is used by umpires to rub off the gloss of all baseballs used in major league baseball. ♦ The extra grass, which used to be kept near the monuments in center, was in play. ♦ The current Yankee Stadium is a glass of water that is half-full, half-empty. On the positive, half-full side, the 1974-75 renovation saved the ballpark from the wrecking ball and preserved these sacred grounds where Babe Ruth, Lou Gehrig, Josh Gibson, Joe DiMaggio, and so many other greats have roamed. On the other hand, the negative half-empty side, the field has been downsized in a futile effort to give fans more home runs, with the fences having been pulled in a total of five times now. As Yogi Berra has stated, "The bullpens used to be in the bullpens." Left of dead center field was first 500, then 490, then 457, then 430, then 411, and now only 399. Message to Major League Baseball—triples are far more interesting for fans than home runs. ♦ First regular season Negro League game played here July 5, 1930; as well as the last Negro League All-Star Game ever played, in 1961, at which Governor Nelson Rockefeller threw out the first ball. Although no Negro League team was ever based here, many four-team doubleheaders were played here, beginning in 1934. ♦ Before the 1974–75 renovations, the left-center monuments were in play—Lou Gehrig on left, Miller Huggins in middle, Babe Ruth on right. Now the monuments are beyond the fence (Mickey Mantle was added in 1996). Plaques include Ed Barrow, Jacob Ruppert, Joe DiMaggio, Mickey Mantle, Casey Stengel, Joe McCarthy, Pope Paul VI, Pope John Paul II, Billy Martin, Whitey Ford, Lefty Gomez, Roger Maris, Allie Reynolds, Elston Howard, Phil Rizzuto, Bill Dickey, Thurman Munson, and Yogi Berra. ♦ A

On a balmy inauguration day in 1923 at the "House that Ruth Built," the crowd was announced at 74,217, while another 25,000 were turned away. Police arrested two for scalping: one man tried to sell a $1.10 grandstand ticket for $1.25, while another asked $1.50. Babe Ruth hit the first home run in the stadium and also made the first error.

ball hitting the foul pole in the 1930s was ruled to be in play, not a homer. ♦ Until Rule 48 was changed by major league baseball in December 1930, with the exception of several months in 1920, balls leaving the field fair but which hooked foul before they landed were foul. This definitely prevented some extra homers by Babe Ruth. ♦ As originally constructed May 5, 1922–April 18, 1923, there were three concrete decks extending from home plate to each corner, with a single deck in left-center and wooden bleachers around the rest of the outfield. ♦ The Bloody Angle, between the bleachers and the right field foul line in 1923, was very asymmetric and caused crazy bounces. Eliminating this in 1924 caused the plate to be moved 13 feet, and the deepest point, left of dead center, changed from 500 to 490. ♦ Underneath second base there was a 15-foot-deep brick-lined vault with electri-

cal, telephone, and telegraphic connections, which was used for boxing events. ♦ In the winter of 1927–28, second and third decks were added into left field, and several rows of box seats were removed in left, extending the foul pole from 281 to 301. ♦ During the 1936 season, the winter of 1936–37, and continuing through the 1937 season, the wooden bleachers were replaced with concrete ones. During the 1937 season, second and third decks were extended into right-center. The bleacher changes shortened left of dead center from 490 to 461, and reduced seating capacity from the 80,000s to the 70,000s. As outfield bench seats were gradually replaced with chair seats in the 1930s and 1940s, seating capacity gradually dropped from more than 70,000 to about 67,000. ♦ Green curtain in center during the 1940s–1960s was sometimes raised and lowered like a window shade to force visiting batters to face a background of white-shirted bleacher fans, but allow Yankee hitters to face a dark green background. It was removed during World Series to sell more seats. ♦ Home dugout switched from third base to first base on April 19, 1946. ♦ Auxiliary scoreboards were built in the late 1940s, which covered up the 367 right-center sign and the 415 left-center sign. ♦ Minor modifications were made in the winter of 1966–67. During this work, a new 463 sign and a 433 sign appeared in center field, and the exterior was painted blue and white. ♦ During 1974–75 renovation, iron third deck distinctive facades were removed, and portions placed in the bleachers. ♦ The Yankees played their April 15, 1998, home game at Shea after a 500-pound steel joint in the upper deck fell off. ♦ Has hosted crowds of over 80,000 three times (81,841 paid May 30, 1938; 81,622 paid September 9, 1928; 80,403 total April 19, 1931). ♦ Has a fair ball ever been hit out of Yankee Stadium? There have

been three possible. Frank Howard once hit a ball deep down the left field foul line that was hit so hard and so high that as Yankee left fielder Roy White turned to watch it, he did not even bother to run toward the fence. It happened in the late innings of a foggy rainy September game that was meaningless to both the Senators and the Yankees. The third base umpire could not see whether it had gone foul or fair, and waited to see where the kids would find the ball in the upper deck before he signaled fair or foul. No kids looked for it, so he signaled foul ball, and made a signal indicating that it had been foul by four inches. Since he was 10 feet behind third base when he made that call, and the roof was 50 feet behind the 301 mark at the left field foul pole, the umpire was roughly 251 feet in front of, and 118 feet underneath the roof. From that distance, how could he tell it was four inches foul? Howard returned to the plate without any protest. But White, Yankee third baseman

A bird's-eye view from the upper right field deck at Yankee Stadium after the second and third levels were added in 1937. The trademark frieze hangs from the roof.

Clete Boyer, and Senators pitchers Jim Hannan and Dick Bosman all insist that the ball left the park fair. The second possibility is a ball that Howard hit during the first game of the 1963 World Series as a Dodger. This one was also ruled foul, but Yankee shortstop Tony Kubek and second baseman Bobby Richardson think it was really fair. The third possibility is that Josh Gibson may have hit one over the roof in left-center, above the bullpen, during a September 1930 or September 1934 Negro League doubleheader. This would be a much longer hit than down the foul line, like Howard's ball. Three Negro League veterans interviewed at the Ashland Oil Company Negro Leagues Reunion in Ashland, Kentucky, in 1982 stated that Gibson had indeed done this. Gibson himself, when asked by reporters whether the stories were true that he had hit a fair ball out of Yankee Stadium, replied no, that he thought that the ball had only gone far up into the bleachers, beyond a 460 sign in left-center. Mickey Mantle's homer on May 22, 1963, came within inches of leaving the park in right field. It struck the green copper roof frieze facing. Joseph Durso estimated that it would have traveled 620 feet if it had cleared the roof.

## Bronx Oval

**OCCUPANT**

Neutral site used by ECL Atlantic City Bacharach Giants 1920s

**LOCATION**

163rd St, Southern Blvd

## Lewisohn Stadium

**OCCUPANT**

Neutral site used by ECL Atlantic City Bacharach Giants 1920s

**LOCATION**

Near Hebrew Orphan Asylum Oval, on Amsterdam Ave

**CAPACITY**

16,000

**PHENOMENA**

Served as City College of New York's baseball and football stadium. Built in 1915, demolished in 1973. Used for 100 concerts a year.

## Recreation Park (III)

**OCCUPANT**

NNL New York Cubans Monday nights in 1935

**LOCATION**

Left Field: 10th St, Third Base Bridge Plaza North and Queensboro/59th St Bridge, First Base 21st St, Right Field 41st Ave; in the Long Island City area of Queens, on the east side of the Queensboro/59th Street Bridge

**CURRENT USE**

Queensbridge Houses, 24 six-story apartment buildings, which when built were the largest public housing project in the world

**CAPACITY**

3000 (1927), 11,000 (1938)

**PHENOMENA**

Built in 1927, torn down in 1938.

## Hebrew Orphan Asylum Oval

**AKA**

Jasper Oval, Asylum Oval, CCNY Playground

**OCCUPANT**

NNL New York Black Yankees July–September 1936

**LOCATION**

(N) West 138th St and City College of New York (CCNY), (W) Convent Ave, (S) West 136th St, (E) St. Nicholas Terrace and St. Nicholas Park

**CURRENT USE**

CCNY Indoor Athletic Complex and paved playground for Schiff School (formerly known as PS 192)

## Triborough Stadium

**AKA**

Randall's Island Stadium, JJ Downing Memorial Stadium, Icahn Stadium (2005–present)

**OCCUPANT**

NNL New York Black Yankees 1937–38

**LOCATION**

(N) Bronx Kills and Harlem River, Eastern Pkwy and Triborough Bridge; (W) House of Refuge, Vesta Ave; (S) Little Hell Gate, East River, and Ward's Island, Sutter Ave; (E) Sunken Meadow, Powell St, Triborough Bridge

**PHENOMENA**

Eight old light towers moved here when Ebbets Field got new lights. ♦ NASL New York Cosmos with Pele and WFL New York Stars played here in the 1970s.

## 59th Street Bridge

**OCCUPANT**

NNL New York Cubans 1939

**LOCATION**

(N) East 60th St, (W) First Ave, (S) East 59th St, (SE) Sutton Pl, (E) Queensboro/59th St Bridge foundations and East River; overhead were the approach ramps to the Bridge, in Manhattan, on the west side of the Queensboro/59th Street Bridge; on the other side of the bridge from Recreation Park (III), where Negro League games were also played

**PHENOMENA**

The first covered major league ballpark; the Astrodome was the second. ♦ Closest the major leagues have ever come to playing on a real "sandlot"; the infield was covered with small dark gray cinders and ash.

## Queens Park

**OCCUPANT**

NNL New York Cubans 1940

**LOCATION**

Left Field (W) 30th Ave, Third Base (S) 58th St, First Base (E) 31st Ave, Right Field (N) 61st St; in the Woodside area of Queens

**CAPACITY**

2500

**PHENOMENA**

Built in 1938. Torn down in 1951.

## Shea Stadium

**AKA**

Flushing Meadow Stadium 1964

**ARCHITECT**

Praeger-Kavanagh-Waterbury

Shea Stadium was named for William Shea, a lawyer best known for his part in the return of National League baseball to New York City after the departure of the Brooklyn Dodgers and New York Giants.

**OCCUPANTS**

NL New York Mets April 17, 1964 to date; AL New York Yankees April 6, 1974–September 28, 1975; April 15, 1998

**LOCATION**

Center Field (E/NE) 126th St; Third Base (N/NW) Northern (later Willets Point) Blvd, then Whitestone Expressway/I-678 and Flushing Bay; Home Plate (W/SW) Grand Central Pkwy; First Base (S/SE) 123-01 Roosevelt Ave; in Queens, near Flushing Meadow Park, site of 1939 and 1964 World's Fairs, SE of La-Guardia Airport

**DIMENSIONS**

Foul Lines: 330 (marked), 341 (actual), 341 (1965), 338 (1978)

Power Alleys: 371, 378 (2001)

Center Field: 410

Backstop: 80, 48 (2003)

Foul Territory: large in 1964, then smaller over the years as more seats were added in foul territory

**FENCES**

Foul Lines: 16.33 (4 wire and railing above 12.33 brick), 12.33 (brick 1965), 8 (wood 1979)

Power Alleys: 8 (wood); Bullpens 8 (wood), 8 (plexiglass 1967)

Center Field: small section 8.75 (wood), most 8 (wood)

**CAPACITY**

55,000, 56,000 (1968), 56,521 (2001), 57,393 (2003), 57,369 (2005)

**PHENOMENA**

Designed to be expandable to 90,000 seats. ♦ Noisiest ballpark in the majors by far, due to frequent LaGuardia Airport aircraft noise overhead. ♦ Right-center scoreboard 86 feet high with clock (first Bulova, then Longines, then Elgin, now Armitron) on top, 25 feet behind the outfield fence, and 175 feet long. ♦ Mets Magician's Top Hat installed in 1981 behind the fence in center, just to the right of the 410 mark. ♦ When a Met hits a homer, a red Big Apple rises out of the black top hat, which actually looks more like a big kettle. At first the hat said "Mets Magic"; now it says "Home Run." ♦ In 1964, the Foul Lines were marked 330, but when measured before the 1965 season they were discovered to be actually 341. ♦ In 1964, there were controversies about whether a ball hitting the railing at the top of the four-foot wire fence above the brick wall at the Foul Lines was in play or a home run. So to avoid further controversy, the Foul Lines from 1965 to 1978 had the infamous "Orange Line," an orange home run line painted at the top of the 12-foot, 4-inch brick wall, which instead of reducing controversy, just added to it. ♦ Above the orange line was the four-foot wire screen and railing. A ball was a homer if it hit above the line. Like a similar ground rule in Crosley Field's center field, this caused so many controversies that finally, at the suggestion of Mets manager Joe Torre, an inner eight-foot wooden fence was installed in 1978 that reduced the Foul Lines from 341 to 330. ♦ Worst visibility for hitters in the majors. ♦ Church-like spire beyond center field fence formerly graced "Serval Zippers" sign. ♦ In 1973–79, there were distance markers outside the field of play on the rear bullpen walls at 428, base of left-center light tower at 442, and on bottom edge of right-center scoreboard, at 405 on right field end and 420 on center field end. ♦ 1964 Mets Banner Day signs included Mongolia Loves the Mets (in Mongolian) banner carried by the author. Other banners included E=mc² (Errors = Mets times customers squared), Eamus Metropoli (Let's go Mets in Latin). ♦ Christened April 16, 1964, with Dodger holy water from the Gowanus Canal in Brooklyn and Giant holy water from the Harlem River at the exact location where it passed the old Polo Grounds. ♦ Fans arrive on the #7 train into the Willets Point subway station. ♦ After a beam collapsed at Yankee Stadium, Yanks played here during the afternoon of April 15, 1998, even though the Mets had a game scheduled that night. It marked the first time in the 20th century that one ballpark housed two games for four different AL/NL teams in one day. ♦ NFL Jets left in 1984 because cold winds from right-center are so strong. ♦ Longest homer ever here, by Tommie Agee on April 10, 1969, is commemorated by a red and white circle painted on the facing of the upper deck in left at Section 48. ♦ First stadium to ever have two movable seating sections to convert from baseball to football and back again (RFK Stadium has only one movable section). ♦ First stadium to have a light ring around the roof rather than light towers. ♦ Most seats face short center (the 50-yard line) rather than the plate. ♦ When the Beatles played here in 1964, they used the umpires' dressing room, entered the field from the third base dugout, and began with "Twist and Shout." ♦ On Opening Day of 1967, on April 11, the outfield wall was painted an olive shade of white, with dark green distance numbers. By May 2, after only seven home games with that ugly paint scheme, the walls were repainted with the familiar green. ♦ Scene from Walter Matthau's *Odd Couple* movie filmed here before Mets-Pirates game June 27, 1967. ♦ Original 1964 General Indicator scoreboard replaced with new White Way scoreboard in 1988; only remaining portion of old scoreboard is the OUT sign, which now sits in Dennis D'Agostino's garage wrapped in bubble wrap.

Architect's drawing for the new Mets Stadium.

## *New Mets Ballpark*

**PROJECTED OPENING**

April 2009

**ARCHITECT**

HOK Sport

**OCCUPANT**

NL New York Mets April 2009 onwards

**LOCATION**

Shea Stadium's parking lot in Flushing Meadows-Corona Park; just northeast of Shea Stadium; in Queens; Left Field (N) Stadium Rd; Third Base (W) Grand Central Parkway West; First Base (S) Casey Stengel Plc, then Roosevelt Ave; Right Field (E) 126th St

**DIMENSIONS**

Left Field: 335
Left Center: 381
Center Field: 408
Right Center: 391
Right Field: 330

**CAPACITY**

45,000

**PHENOMENA**

The park is being built in the outfield parking lot between Shea Stadium and 126th Street. ♦ Using Ebbets Field as its architectural inspiration, the ballpark tries to blend the past with a modern day sports venue. Limestone, brick and precast concrete comprise the exterior building materials, while exposed structural steel pays tribute to the bridges connecting the city's five boroughs. A 65-foot-tall entry rotunda greets fans. In right field there will be a singular deck situated to extend into and over fair territory with an 8-foot overhang, dedicated to the memory of the famous overhang in left field at the Polo Grounds. Fan gathering areas throughout the park pay tribute to the city, such as the Ebbets Club, Coogan's Landing, East Side Stands, and the Orchard picnic area. ♦ Once complete in 2009, the new Mets ballpark will be completely and uniquely New York. The main entry rotunda is adjacent to the Flushing 7 line subway station. There will be a 14% increase in the number of toilets over Shea (646; 305 for women; 327 for men; 14 for family).

## *New Yankee Stadium*

**PROJECTED OPENING**

April 2009

**ARCHITECT**

HOK Sport

**OCCUPANT**

AL New York Yankees April 2009 onwards

**LOCATION**

Just north of Yankee Stadium, in John Mullaly Park, in the Bronx; (NW) Jerome Ave; (SW) East 161st St, then Yankee Stadium; (SE) River Ave; (NE) East 164th St

Architect's drawing for the new Yankee Stadium.

**DIMENSIONS**

Expected to be the same as the current Yankee Stadium.

**CAPACITY**

50,800

**PHENOMENA**

It will hopefully be as similar to the old Yankee Stadium as possible. One good piece of news is that the distinctive frieze, which surrounded the entire top deck of old Yankee Stadium before 1974, will be brought back in its entirety. ♦ As home to America's most successful sports franchise, Yankee Stadium is an emotional icon, a symbol of excellence, and a reflection of our country in the 1920s. Replacing the "House That Ruth Built" truly requires a national monument, a new home with a blend of tradition and technology. The ballpark's skin will be highlighted by a four-story limestone and granite facade inspired by Yankee Stadium as it opened in 1923. The same field geometry that served as a framework for yesterday's legends will challenge tomorrow's players.

♦   ♦   ♦

# Oakland, California

## *McAfee Coliseum*

**AKA**

Oakland-Alameda County Coliseum April 1968–September 1997; UMAX Coliseum September 1997–June 1998; Oakland-Alameda County Coliseum June–September 1998; Networks Associates Coliseum September 1998–June 2004, the Mausoleum in the 1980s, the Net

**ARCHITECTS**

Skidmore, Owing, & Merrill; 1966 renovation: 1996

**OCCUPANT**

AL Oakland Athletics April 17, 1968, to date

**LOCATION**

Center Field (N/NE) San Leandro St, then Southern Pacific RR tracks; Third Base (W/NW) 66th Ave; Home Plate (S/SW) Oakland-Alameda County Coliseum Arena (also called the Jewel Box), then Nimitz Frwy/I-880 and San Leandro Bay; First Base (E/SE) 77th Ave (later Hegenberger Dr)

**DIMENSIONS**

Foul Lines: 330
Between Foul Lines and Power Alleys: 367 (1996)
Power Alleys: 378, 375 (1969), 372 (1981), 362 (1996)
Deep Power Alleys: 388 (1996)
Center Field: 410, 400 (1969), 396 (1981), 397 (1982), 400 (1990)
Backstop: 90, 60 (1969)
Foul Territory: huge, largest by far in the majors

**FENCES**

Foul Lines: 8 (plywood), 10 (canvas over plywood and plexiglass 1981), 8 (1986)
Power Alleys and Center Field: 8 (plywood), 10

(canvas over plywood and plexiglass 1981), 8 (1986), 18 (1996), 15 (2003)

**CAPACITY**

50,000, 48,219 (1990), 42,219 (1996), 45,177 (1997), 43,662 (2001), 34,007 (2006)

**PHENOMENA**

Backstop was a notch cut in stands. When they added in seats there, the distance to the backstop was reduced from 90 feet to 60. ♦ Steel shell of pitcher's mound was exposed on Opening Day April 17, 1968, and had to keep being covered between innings. ♦ Re-ferred to as the Mausoleum in the late 1970s when the scoreboard didn't work, the entire concrete stadium was depressingly gray in color, and the A's were terrible. ♦ Huge foul area reduces batting averages by five to seven points, making this among the best AL pitchers'-parks. ♦ Winds favor left-handed batters. ♦ Scoreboard shows upcoming home stands, with the Athletics annihilating the opposition. ♦ Fans sitting at the foul poles can catch home run fair balls by reaching in front of the foul pole screens. ♦ Huge ugly center field addition built for the NFL Raiders November 1995–September 1996 is called Mount Davis. ♦ Upper deck closed for the 2006 season reducing capacity to 34,007.

While several football stadiums also host baseball, Oakland's Alameda County Coliseum is the only multi-use stadium still left in major league baseball, having been designed for both sports.

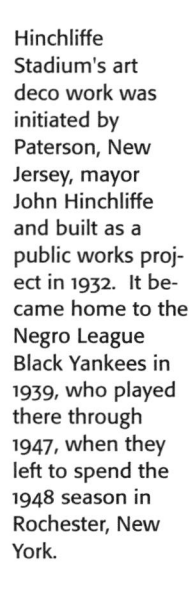

Hinchliffe Stadium's art deco work was initiated by Paterson, New Jersey, mayor John Hinchliffe and built as a public works project in 1932. It became home to the Negro League Black Yankees in 1939, who played there through 1947, when they left to spend the 1948 season in Rochester, New York.

## Paterson, New Jersey

### *Hinchliffe Stadium*

**OCCUPANT**
NNL New York Black Yankees 1939–47

**LOCATION**
Center Field (SE) Passaic River, Third Base (NE) Redwood Avenue, Home Plate (NW) Liberty Street, First Base (SW) Maple Street; also Walnut St, Spruce St

**CURRENT USE**
Community baseball park

## Petersburg, Virginia

### *Petersburg Ballfield*

**OCCUPANT**
Neutral site used by AA Richmond Virginias October 7, 1884

**PHENOMENA**
The game between the Virginias and the Columbus Buckeyes was cut short after five innings to allow both teams to catch the last train of the day back to Richmond.

◆   ◆   ◆

# Philadelphia, Pennsylvania

*See also* Gloucester City, New Jersey; Yeadon, Pennsylvania

## *Jefferson Street Grounds (I)*

**AKA**

Athletic Base Ball Grounds (I)

**OCCUPANTS**

NA Philadelphia Athletics May 15, 1871–October 28, 1875; NA Philadelphia White Stockings May 1, 1873–October 25, 1875; NL Philadelphia Athletics April 22–September 16, 1876

**LOCATION**

(N) Jefferson Ave, (W) 27th St, (S) Master St, (E) 25th St

**CAPACITY**

3000

**PHENOMENA**

Scene of the very first NL game ever played. The Boston Red Caps defeated the Athletics, 6–5, on April 22, 1876.

## *Columbia Park (I)*

**AKA**

Centennial Park

**OCCUPANTS**

NA Philadelphia Centennials April 21–May 24, 1875; neutral site used by NA Philadelphia Athletics June 4, 1875

**LOCATION**

Left Field (W) 25th St, Third Base (S) Columbia Ave, First Base (E) 24th St, Right Field (N) Ridge Ave, Center Field (N) Montgomery St

**FENCES**

10 (wood)

## *Oakdale Park*

**AKA**

Oakland Park

**OCCUPANT**

AA Philadelphia Athletics May 2–September 21, 1882

**LOCATION**

Huntingdon St, 11th St

## *Jefferson Street Grounds (II)*

**AKA**

Athletic Baseball Grounds (II)

**OCCUPANT**

AA Philadelphia Athletics May 10, 1883–October 11, 1890

**LOCATION**

Same as Jefferson Street Grounds (I)

**DIMENSIONS**

Center Field: 500

**FENCES**

9

**CAPACITY**

3000

**PHENOMENA**

Very short distances to foul lines. Swimming pool behind fence in right.

## Recreation Park

**OCCUPANT**

NL Philadelphia Quakers May 1, 1883–October 9, 1886

**LOCATION**

Same as Columbia Park (I)

**DIMENSIONS**

Left Field: 300
Center Field: 410
Right Field: 247
Backstop: 79

**FENCES** ·

10

**CAPACITY**

2000

## Keystone Park

**OCCUPANT**

UA Philadelphia Keystones April 17–August 7, 1884

**LOCATION**

(N) Moore St, (E) Broad St, also Wharton St, 11th St

## Huntingdon Grounds (I)

**AKA**

Philadelphia Baseball Grounds (I), National League Park (I)

**OCCUPANTS**

NL Philadelphia Phillies April 30, 1887–August 6, 1894; NCL Philadelphia Pythians 1887; neutral use for the Temple Cup Series October 17 and 19, 1887, NL Detroit Wolverines vs. AA St. Louis Browns; Temple Cup Series October 22, 1888, NL New York Gothams vs. AA St. Louis Browns

**LOCATION**

Same as Huntingdon Grounds (II) and Baker Bowl

**DIMENSIONS**

Left Field: 500
Center Field: 410
Right Field: 310

**FENCES**

25 (brick)

**CAPACITY**

12,500, 15,000 (1894)

**PHENOMENA**

Pavilion flanked by five turrets. The one at Huntingdon and 15th was 122 feet high; the other four were 75 feet high. ◆ Was the worst infield in the league in 1888, full of ruts. ◆ There was a 15-foot-wide bicycle track around the field, causing a large embankment in front of all the outfield fences. ◆ Burned down August 6, 1894, in a fire started by a plumber's stove.

## Forepaugh Park

**AKA**

Brotherhood Park 1890, Athletic Park 1891

**OCCUPANTS**

PL Philadelphia Quakers April 30–September 17, 1890; AA Philadelphia Athletics April 8–October 5, 1891

**LOCATION**

(N) York St, (W) 14th (later Broad) St, (S) Dauphin St, (E) Park Ave

**DIMENSIONS**

Left Field: 345
Center Field: 450, 420 (1891)
Right Field: 380

## *University of Pennsylvania Athletic Field*

**OCCUPANT**

NL Philadelphia Phillies August 14–August 17, 1894

**LOCATION**

(N) Spruce St; (W) South 39th St; (S) Pine St; (E) South 37th St; on the Penn campus northeast of Woodlands Cemetary

## *Huntingdon Grounds (II)*

**AKA**

Philadelphia Baseball Grounds (II), National League Park (II)

**OCCUPANT**

NL Philadelphia Phillies August 18–September 6, 1894

**PHENOMENA**

Temporary structure built for the rest of the season after the August 6, 1894, fire. ◆ Replaced during the winter by Baker Bowl.

◆  ◆  ◆

## *Baker Bowl*

**AKA**

Huntingdon Grounds (III) 1895–July 1913, National League Park (III) 1895–1938, the Hump, Cigar Box, Band Box, Philadelphia Baseball Grounds (III)

**OCCUPANTS**

NL Philadelphia Phillies May 2, 1895–August 8, 1903; April 14, 1904–May 14, 1927; June 24, 1927–June 30, 1938; also neutral use by NL Cleveland Spiders nine games July 29–30, August 5–6, 8, and 11, 1898; neutral site used for Negro World Series NNL Kansas City Monarchs vs. ECL Darby Hilldales games five and six in 1925

**ARCHITECT**

John Joseph Deery

**LOCATION**

Left Field (N/NE) West Lehigh Ave, Third Base (W/NW) North 15th St, First Base (S/SW) West Huntingdon St, Right Field (E/SE) North Broad St; field was above Philadelphia and Reading RR tracks whose tracks ran through a tunnel beneath center field

**DIMENSIONS**

Left Field: 390, 335 (1910), 341 (1922), 341.5 (1926), 341 (1930), 341.5 (1931)
Left Center: 410, 379 (1910)
Center Field: 408, 388 (1914) 408 (1918), 412 (1922)
Right Center: 325, 324 (1922), 325 (1925)
Right Field: 273 (1910), 272 (1921), 279.5 (1922), 280.5 (1925)
Backstop: 60

**FENCES**

Left Field: 12, 3 (1910), 12 (July 1929)
Left Center Field to right side of front of clubhouse: 35, 3 (1914), 35 (1918)
Right side of front of clubhouse to right field-center field wall: 35, 3 (1914), 35 (1918)

Tiny Baker Bowl in Philadelphia was the site of many hitting records. The Phillies' Gavvy Cravath led the NL with 19 homers in 1914, hitting all of them at Baker Bowl. Chuck Klein, an expert at handling the rebounds off the right field wall, had 44 assists in 1930, and hit .439 at home. The batting average for the entire NL at Baker Bowl that year was .352.

Center Field to Right Center: 47 (35-ft wall with 12 wood on top 1915), 35 (1922)

Right Field: 40 (tin over brick), 55 (40 tin over brick topped by 15 screen July 1929)

**CAPACITY**

18,000, 20,000 (1929), 18,800 (1930)

**CURRENT USE**

Parking lot and car wash in right center, gas station in center, bus garage from home down the right field foul line

**PHENOMENA**

Named the Hump because it was on an elevated piece of ground with a railroad tunnel underneath the outfield. ♦ Swimming pool in basement of the center field clubhouse prior to World War I. ♦ Part of the grandstand collapsed with deadly effect on August 8, 1903, killing 12, injuring 282. As a result, the Phillies did not play at all, August 9–19, and then moved their home games to the Athletics' Columbia Park (II). In order to "catch up," seven of the nine home dates played there August 20–September 10 were doubleheaders. ♦ Another problem with the grandstand happened 24 years later, when 10 rows of seats in the first base section of the grandstand collapsed May 14, 1927, causing the Phillies to play at Shibe Park, May 16–28. ♦ Coke and "Health Soap Stops B.O. Lifebuoy" signs on the high right field wall. ♦ On June 8, 1914, Fred Luderus of the Phillies hit a truly unique home run when his drive stuck in the wall in deep center field. A brick was missing, and the ball lodged in the hole between two jagged edges of broken brick, while Pirates center fielder Kelly "danced frantically underneath but the ball would not fall." ♦ Extra seats added in front of fence in center for 1915 World Series led directly to Phillies losing the Series' last game. ♦ During Prohibition, outfield wall liquor ads were boarded over with grimy blank boards. ♦ Left field bleachers built for the 1910 season extended from junction with third base bleachers to left edge of center field clubhouse. ♦ Center field bleachers sections were added that extended to right-center in 1914, cutting center field dimensions and masking all of center field clubhouse. ♦ Section of center field bleachers in front of about rightmost one-third of clubhouse removed after 1917 season. ♦

Home plate moved back seven feet in 1922, making right field foul pole 279.5. Playing field also reoriented that season about three degrees toward right field to allow left field foul line to avoid the third base bleachers. ♦ Home plate moved back a foot in 1925, making right field foul pole 280.5 rather than 279.5. ♦ Only homers hit completely out of the park to left field hit by Cliff Lee, Wally Berger, Jimmie Foxx, Hal Lee, and Joe Medwick. ♦ Nobody ever hit a ball over the center field clubhouse, but Rogers Hornsby did hit one through a clubhouse window. ♦ Dimensions 1910–21 based on 1921 Sanborn fire insurance map. ♦ Torn down in 1950.

## Columbia Park (II)

**OCCUPANTS**

AL Philadelphia Athletics April 26, 1901–October 3, 1908; NL Philadelphia Phillies August 20–September 10, 1903

**LOCATION**

(N/NE) Columbia Ave, (W/NW) 30th St, (S/SW) Oxford St, (E/SE) 29th St

**DIMENSIONS**

Left Field: 340
Left Center: 392
Center Field corner (left of Dead Center): 440
Center Field: 396
Right Center: 323
Right Field: 280
Backstop: 75
Foul Area: large

**FENCES**

Left Field: 10
Left Center Field to Right Center: 10
Right Field: 30 (10 wood, 20 screen)

**FORMER USE**

Vacant lot

**CURRENT USE**

Kenny's Tires store, pizza shop, houses

**CAPACITY**

9500, 13,600 (1905)

**PHENOMENA**

No dugouts, the players sat on benches. ♦ In

When the Philadelphia Athletics began in 1901 as one of the clubs in the newly formed American League, Columbia Park was quickly built, but the meager seating prompted owner Ben Shibe to move to spacious Shibe Park after the 1908 season.

Brewerytown section of Philadelphia, so the air smelled heavily of hops, yeast, and beer. ♦ Foul area large as Foul Lines and first base and third base bleachers did not converge except in deep left field. ♦ Dimensions based on detailed map of park in 1907 Philadelphia city atlas.

## Shibe Park

### AKA
Connie Mack Stadium 1953–70

### ARCHITECT
William Steele and Sons

### OCCUPANTS
AL Philadelphia Athletics April 12, 1909–September 19, 1954; NL Philadelphia Phillies May 16–28, 1927; July 4, 1938–September 27, 1942; NL Philadelphia Blue Jays April 27, 1943–October 1, 1944; NL Philadelphia Phillies April 20, 1945–October 1, 1970; neutral site used for Negro World Series NNL Chicago American Giants vs. ECL Atlantic City Bacharach Giants first, fourth, and fifth games in 1926; for NNL Washington-Homestead Grays vs. NAL Kansas City Monarchs fifth game in 1942; for NNL Washington-Homestead Grays vs. NAL Cleveland Buckeyes fourth game in 1945; for NNL New York Cubans vs. NAL Cleveland Buckeyes third game in 1947

### LOCATION
Left Field (N/NE) West Somerset St, Third Base (W/NW) North 21st St, First Base (S/SW) West Lehigh Ave, Right Field (E/SE) North 20th St

### DIMENSIONS
Left Field: 378, 334 (1917), 380 (1921), 334 (1922), 349 (1923), 312 (1926), 334 (1930)

Left Center: 436, 384 (1913), 387 (1922), 403 (1923), 360 (1926), 385 (1930), 387 (1969)

Center Field corner: 509, 529 (1923), 438 (1926), 468 (1930), 440 (1951), 460 (1953), 468 (1954), 447 (1956), 410 (1969)

Right Center: 393, 410 (1923), 354 (1926), 382 (1930), 390 (1969)

Right Center left of Scoreboard: 400 (1942)

Right Field: 340, 355 (1923), 307 (1926), 331 (1931), 331 (to lower part of the wall 1934), 329 (to upper iron fence 1934)

Backstop: 85, 64 (1923), 105 (1926), 98 (1930), 90 (1942), 86 (1943), 78 (1956), 64 (1960)

### FENCES
Left Field to Left Center: 12 (4 screen above 8 concrete 1949)

Center Field small section: 20 (1955), 8 (wood 1956), 3 (canvas 1969)

Right Center Scoreboard: 50 (top of black scoreboard 1956), 60 (top of Ballantine Beer sign 1956)

Right Field: 12 (concrete), 34 (22 corrugated iron above 12 concrete 1935)

### FORMER USE
City dog pound, also brickyard in Swampoodle neighborhood nearby

### CURRENT USE
Deliverance Evangelistic Church, seating 5100 worshippers. Top of its cross is 108 feet high, and the entrance is at first base. Several hundred of the seats were moved to Duncan Park, former home of the Sally League Phillies in Spartanburg, SC, and to War Memorial Stadium, Greensboro, NC.

### CAPACITY
20,000, 23,000 (June 1909), 33,500 (1925), 27,500 (1926), 28,250 (1928), 30,000 (April 1929), 31,750 (June 1930), 33,000 (1930), 33,509 (1970)

### PHENOMENA
Usually described as the first all concrete-and-steel ballpark in the majors. Actually, the upper deck of the grandstand was built of wood on steel girders. ♦ Only 23 fans watched as the A's beat the Yankees, 8–2, after a 45-minute rain delay September 8, 1916. ♦

Aerial view of Shibe Park, which opened in 1909, the first of a series of classic 20th-century ballparks. Renamed Connie Mack Stadium in 1953, it served as home to the AL Athletics until their move to Kansas City in 1955, and to the NL Phillies from 1938 until it closed in 1970.

French Renaissance church-like dome on exterior roof behind the plate housed Connie Mack's office. ◆ Sod transplanted here from Columbia Park (II). ◆ At 20 inches, park had the highest pitchers mound. ◆ Batting cage sat behind short fence in center when measurement was only 447. ◆ Balls bounced at crazy angles off the fence in right. Corrugated iron formed the top 22 feet of the 34-foot-high fence. The fence was a two-foot deep frame. It was 329 to the front of the frame and 331 to the rear where the iron sheets were. Reinforcement of the right field wall in 1934 reduced the distance to front of the frame from 331 to 329, but the sign wasn't changed until 1956. ◆ Conduit on right field wall was in play. ◆ Slopes in front of outfield fences in early years. ◆ Ladder in front of raised left field scoreboard in 1909 went all the way to the top. Scoreboard was in play and was located about 15–20 feet in from the left field foul line. ◆

When left field bleachers were built before the 1913 season, they extended from near the center field corner to within about 15 ft of the left field foul line. Thus left field distance was unchanged at 378, but 15 ft to right of foul line it was 334. ◆ Many bounce home runs hit into the left field bleachers starting with the 1913 season. For the 1923 season, manager/owner Connie Mack decided to go with speed vs. power and home plate was moved an estimated 21 ft back—this move increased left field and right field dimensions by 15 ft each. Home runs dropped about 50% in 1923–25. ◆ Double-decked after the 1925 season down the Foul Lines. New left field stands replaced the left field bleachers. ◆ Upper deck in left field overhung the lower deck by a few feet. Mezzanine added in 1929. ◆ Before 1935, 20th Street residents could sit in their front bedrooms or on their roofs and see the game free over the 12-foot right field fence. ◆ Fans could see the lines of laundry on the roof of 20th Street houses. Connie Mack lost a suit to prevent this, so he built the high right field fence. ♦ 1948 plans to add 18,000 seats in right field and reduce foul line to 315 feet never materialized. ♦ Many books have incorrectly stated that the old Yankee Stadium electric scoreboard was installed in front of the right-center wall here in 1957. Although the two scoreboards looked alike, the Yankee Stadium scoreboard was much larger, and it was not replaced by the "tower" scoreboard until 1959, two years after the electric scoreboard was installed here. ♦ Later a clock was added, and balls hitting the clock were homers. The top of the clock was 75 feet high. ♦ Richie Allen was the only batter to hit a homer over the 60-foot-high Ballantine Beer sign above the scoreboard in right-center. ♦ Ashburn's Ridge was a specially tailored region along third base to help his bunts stay fair. ♦ In 1956 the normal screen was replaced by see-through plexiglass, protecting the fans behind the plate from foul balls. ♦ Fire damaged it August 20, 1971. ♦ Dimensions 1909–25 based on 1921 Sanborn fire insurance map. ♦ Torn down in June 1976.

## Chessline Park

### OCCUPANT
ECL Philadelphia Tigers April–May 1928

### LOCATION
In the southern part of the city

## Passon Field

### AKA
48th and Spruce

### OCCUPANTS
NNL Philadelphia Stars 1934–35; NNL Philadelphia Bacharach Giants 1934

### LOCATION
48th St, Spruce St, 49th St, Locust St

## Penmar Park

### AKA
44th and Parkside, Bolden Bowl, Pennsylvania Railroad Park, Pennsylvania YMCA

### OCCUPANTS
NNL Philadelphia Stars 1936–48; NAL Philadelphia Stars 1949–52

### LOCATION
44th St, Parkside Ave, First Base Pennsylvania RR roundhouse

### DIMENSIONS
Left Field: 330
Center Field: 410
Right Field: 310

### PHENOMENA
They rarely cut the grass here, so it was very tall. ♦ Built by the Pennsylvania Railroad in the mid-1920s for the company YMCA. ♦ Dense coal smoke from the locomotives going in and out of the roundhouse behind first base often interfered with fielders and delayed games. ♦ Fans arrived at the game via the #15 trolley along first base at the stop for the Stephen Smith Home for the Aged and Infirm Colored Persons. ♦ In 1947, Satchel Paige had a perfect game here through eight innings. In the ninth inning, he gave up three intentional walks, then he told his seven fielders to lie down and struck out the side on nine pitches. ♦ Amazingly, the ballpark never fell down, despite the fact that Miss Hattie Williams used a hatchet most days to chop some wood from the grandstand as firewood for the blaze that heated her washtub where she cooked the hot dogs for her concession stand behind home plate. ♦ Lights installed 1933.

## Veterans Stadium

**AKA**

The Vet, Veterans Memorial Stadium

**ARCHITECT**

George Ewing of Hugh Stubbins & Associates

**OCCUPANT**

NL Philadelphia Phillies April 10, 1971–September 28, 2003

**LOCATION**

Left Field (N/NE) Packer St, then I-76; Third Base (W/NW) Broad St, then Philadelphia Naval Hospital; First Base (S/SW) Pattison Ave, then Spectrum and John F. Kennedy Stadium (later replaced by First Union Center, now known as Wachovia Center); Right Field (E/SE) Tenth St

**DIMENSIONS**

Foul Lines: 330

Power Alleys: 371

Center Field: 408

Backstop: 60

Foul Territory: large

**FENCES**

8 (wood), 6 (wood 1972), 12 (6 plexiglass above 6 wood 1972)

**SURFACE**

AstroTurf, 1971–2000, slower since 1977; NeXturf 2001–03

**CURRENT USE**

Citizens Bank Park's western parking lot

**CAPACITY**

56,371, 58,651 (1977), 65,454 (1981), 66,507 (1983), 64,538 (1987), 62,382 (1990), 61,831 (2003)

**PHENOMENA**

Park's rounded rectangular shape was called an

As early as 1953, city officials discussed a multi-purpose sports stadium with the Phillies and Eagles, but the talks didn't bear fruit until Veterans Stadium was at long last finished in 1971. Perfectly symmetrical, the stadium was the largest in the National League.

octorad. ◆ Connie Mack Stadium's home plate transplanted here. ◆ Plastic tarp covered unfinished right field wall in April 1971. ◆ Liberty Bell used to hang from center field roof on fourth level, hit only by Greg Luzinski May 16, 1972. ◆ First ball dropped from helicopter April 10, 1971. ◆ Smallest hot dogs and loudest boos in baseball. ◆ Statues of Connie Mack and a sliding runner outside the park. ◆ Phils downed Padres, 6–5, in 10 innings here on July 3, 1993 in the nightcap of a thrice rain-delayed twinbill that ended at 4:40 AM. ◆ Richie Hebner once said, "I stand at the plate in Philadelphia, and I don't honestly know whether I'm in Pittsburgh, Cincinnati, St. Louis, or Philly. They all look alike." This is the best description ever of the disgusting sameness of the "Toilet Bowl" era of cookie-cutter, sterile concrete Ash Tray ballpark architecture that threatened to destroy the soul of baseball in the 1960s and 1970s, before it was rescued by Camden Yards in Baltimore and the new generation of classic ballparks in the 1990s and 2000s. ◆ Imploded March 21, 2004.

## Citizens Bank Park

### OCCUPANT
NL Philadelphia Phillies April 12, 2004, to date

### ARCHITECTS
Ewing, Cole, Cherry, Brott and HOK Sport

### LOCATION
Center Field (N) Phillies Dr (formerly Hartranft St); Third Base (W) Citizens Bank Way (formerly 11th St); Home Plate (S) Pattison Ave, then Lincoln Financial Field, then I-95; First Base (E) Darien St; just east of Veterans Stadium in South Philly

### DIMENSIONS
Left Field (at 0°): 329
Left Field 5 feet in from foul line: 329, 334 (2006)
Left Field Power Alley (at 22.5°): 356 (actual), 369 (marked), 361 (actual 2006)
Left Field deeper Power Alley (at 25°): 369 (2006)

Philadelphia's beautiful and idiosyncratic Citizens Bank Park features a split-level bullpen in right-center. On June 20, 2006 Ryan Howard hit a home run that traveled an estimated 461 feet and reached the third deck; to commemorate the event the Phillies painted a white "H" there.

Left Center (at 30°): 380, 385 (2006)

Left Center corner left side: 385, 390 (2006)

Left Center corner right side: 381

Deepest Left Center: 409

Center Field (at 45°): 401

Deepest Right Center: 398

Right Center (at 30°): 381

Right Field deeper Power Alley (at 26.5°): 369 (marked)

Right Field Power Alley (at 22.5°): 357

Right Field (at 0°): 330

Backstop: 49.5

**SURFACE**

Kentucky Bluegrass

**FENCES**

Left Field: 8, 10.5 (2006)

Left Center: 8, 10.5 (2006)

Left Center corners in "the Angle": 12.67 sloping up to 19

Center Field: 6 (3 plus 3 screen on top)

Right Center: 6 sloping up to 13.25

Right Center and Right Field: 13.25

**CAPACITY**

43,500, 43,826 (2005), 43,630 (2006)

**PHENOMENA**

At the end of the third inning of every game, third base is pulled up out of the field and given to a lucky fan. ♦ A ledge of flowers sits between the wall in left and the seats. ♦ Video boards on the wall in right are the first-ever which are in play. ♦ Fifty-foot-high lanterns outside the park at first, home, and third, along with statues of Mike Schmidt, Robin Roberts, and Steve Carlton. ♦ Ashburn Alley center field concourse area has statue of Richie Ashburn and Bull's Barbeque hosted by Greg "the Bull" Luzinski. ♦ Fans arrive via Broad Street Subway. ♦ Huge scoreboard in left-center above second-deck bleachers. ♦ Huge 35 ft by 50 ft Liberty Bell atop 100-foot-high light tower on the right field roof swings and tolls after every Phillie home run. ♦ Also in right are rooftop bleachers, in-

spired by those across North 20th Street from Shibe Park's right field wall. ♦ Phillie Phanatic roams the stands. ♦ Two-tiered bullpens result in one being much more preferable because it is much quieter and more removed from the insults of angry fans. The Phillies started out in the one closest to the fans, but soon discovered their mistake, so the visiting team now has to use that one. ♦ In 2004 it was discovered that the left field and right field power alleys were mismarked. The markings had been placed in the wrong locations. ♦ After the 2005 season, left field was made larger by moving the left field fence back five feet, starting a few feet to the right of the left field foul line and extending until the left-center field corner. This involved cutting out 196 seats in left field and resulted in raising the height of the left field fence by 2.5 feet.

# Phoenix, Arizona

## *Chase Field*

**AKA**

Bank One Ballpark March 31, 1998–September 23, 2005, the BOB

**ARCHITECT**

Ellerbe Becket

**OCCUPANT**

NL Arizona Diamondbacks March 31, 1998, to date

**LOCATION**

Center Field (N) 401 East Jefferson St, Third Base (W) Fourth St (later Diamondbacks Way), Home Plate (S) Southern Pacific RR tracks, First Base (E) Seventh St

**DIMENSIONS**

Left Field: 330, 328 (2005)

Power Alleys: 374, 376 (1999)

With an elevation 1,100 feet above sea level, Chase Field is the second-highest stadium in the major leagues, trailing only Coors Field in Denver. Originally called Bank One Ballpark, the stadium's name was changed to Chase Field on September 23, 2005, following Bank One's merger with J.P. Morgan Chase.

Deepest corner in Left Center: 413, 412 (2005)
Center Field: 407
Deepest corner in Right Center: 413, 414 (2005)
Right Field: 334, 335 (2005)
Backstop: 55
Dome apex: 200 (above second base), 180 (above outfield walls)

### FENCES

Left and Right Field: 7.5
Center Field: 25

### SURFACE

Shade-tolerant DeAnza zoysia grass 1998; Bull's Eye Bermuda grass 1999; mixture of Perennial rye grass, Kentucky bluegrass, and Bull's Eye Bermuda grass 2000 to date

### CAPACITY

48,700, 49,033 (2001)

### PHENOMENA

Dirt path between pitchers mound and plate was the first in five decades. ♦ Sun Pool Pavilion in Section 101 features pool and jacuzzi holding 35 people, 415 feet from home plate, behind fence in right-center field. ♦ Mark Grace was first batter to "splash" a homer here. ♦ There were two warning tracks here, 1998–2000, with a strip of grass in between the two warning tracks. ♦ The reason was that Diamondbacks manager Buck Showalter wanted to confuse opposing outfielders. ♦ For a while the Diamondbacks allowed their own starting pitchers to make the decision as to whether the roof would be open or closed. Curt Schilling would always choose to keep it closed because he believed the opposing team hit more home runs with the roof open. After fans complained, the Diamondbacks decided to make the open/closed roof decision based on weather and expected temperature. ♦ With an elevation of 1100 feet, Bank One Ballpark is the second highest park in majors, trailing only Coors Field. Eighty percent of seats are in foul territory. ♦ A new statue, nearly 20 feet high, called the Triple Play Tower, stands near the main northeast stadium entrance. It was installed before the home opener April 11, 2006.

# Phoenix, New York

## Three Rivers Park

**OCCUPANT**

Neutral site used by AA Syracuse Stars Sundays May 18–July 20, 1890

**LOCATION**

Twelve miles north of Syracuse, adjacent to the town of Phoenix; on the Rome, Ogdersburg, and Watertown Railroad; at Three Rivers Point where the Oneida and Seneca Rivers join to form the Oswego River

# Piqua, Illinois

## Piqua Park

**OCCUPANT**

Neutral site used for NNL Chicago American Giants game in 1920

♦    ♦    ♦

# Pittsburgh, Pennsylvania

*See also* Homestead, Pennsylvania; McKeesport, Pennsylvania

## Union Park

**OCCUPANT**

Neutral site used by NL Indianapolis Browns August 22–24, 1878

## Exposition Park (I) Lower Field

**OCCUPANTS**

AA Pittsburg Alleghenys May 10–September 23, 1882; June 12–September 6, 1883; UA Pittsburg Stogies August 25–30, 1884 (back then Pittsburgh was spelled Pittsburg, without the h; the h was added later on, in the 1900s)

**LOCATION**

(N) South Ave (later Shore St), (W) Grant (later Galveston) Ave, (S) Pennsylvania and Western (later Baltimore and Ohio) RR tracks, then Allegheny River, (E) School (later Scotland) St (an extension of Bank St); on the North Side; back then the park was in the city of Allegheny, but now the site is in Pittsburgh; same site as Three Rivers Stadium

**PHENOMENA**

Left and center field fences so distant that no ball ever cleared them.

## Exposition Park (II) Upper Field

**OCCUPANT**

AA Pittsburgh Alleghenys May 1–June 9, 1883

**LOCATION**

Same as Exposition Park (I) and Three Rivers Stadium

**PHENOMENA**

Opening games of 1883 season were moved to this hastily constructed field because of flooding on the Lower Field. Although the fields overlapped, because the land sloped considerably, this field did not flood whereas the Lower Field did.

## Recreation Park

**AKA**

Coliseum Bike Track 1890s, Union Park

**OCCUPANTS**

AA Pittsburgh Alleghenys May 1, 1884–October 12, 1886; NL Pittsburgh Alleghenys April 30, 1887–September 30, 1890; NCL Pittsburgh Keystones 1887; neutral site used for Temple Cup Series AA St. Louis Browns vs. NL Chicago White Stockings October 22, 1885; and AA St. Louis Browns vs. NL Detroit Wolverines October 13, 1887

**LOCATION**

(NE) Pittsburgh, Fort Wayne, and Chicago RR tracks and railyard, (N) Pennsylvania Ave, (W) Allegheny Ave, (S) North Ave West, (E) Grant (later Galveston) Ave

**CAPACITY**

17,000, 9000 (1887)

**PHENOMENA**

Catcher Fred Carroll's pet monkey was buried under home plate with full honors in 1887 pre-game ceremony. Infield was hard-packed clay. ♦ Outfield was mostly dirt, with only small patches of grass. ♦ Record low major league paid attendance of only six (with total crowd of only 17), on April 23, 1890.

## Exposition Park (III)

**AKA**

New Expo

**OCCUPANTS**

PL Pittsburgh Burghers April 19–October 4, 1890;

The Allegheny River flooded on the 4th of July 1902 during a doubleheader between Brooklyn and Pittsburgh at Exposition Park. The water was about thigh level in center and right fields, and about head level in deep center field, where any ball hit was a single per a special ground rule. Players occasionally caught a ball and dove under the water. The Pirates won, 4–0 and 3–0.

NL Pittsburgh Pirates April 22, 1891–June 29, 1909; FL Pittsburgh Rebels April 14, 1914–October 2, 1915

## LOCATION

Left Field (S) Pennsylvania and Western (later Baltimore and Ohio) RR tracks, then Allegheny River; Third Base (E) School (later Scotland) St (an extension of Bank St); First Base (N) South Ave (later Shore St); Right Field (W) Grant (later Galveston) St; on the North Side; back then the park was in the city of Allegheny but now the site is in Pittsburgh; same site as Three Rivers Stadium

## DIMENSIONS

Left Field: 400
Left Center: 461
Center Field: 515
Right Center: 439
Right Field: 380
Backstop: 65

## CAPACITY

6500 (1889), 16,000 (1914)

## PHENOMENA

Twin spires behind home plate on the roof. ♦ With the Allegheny River flooding on July 4, 1902, and over a foot of water in the outfield, Pirates swept a doubleheader from Dodgers with special ground rules—all balls hit into the water in the outfield were singles. ♦

Only home run to clear the fences in the 20th century was hit by Tim Jordan of Brooklyn on July 22, 1908, over the right field fence. This titanic home run was first-page news in the Pittsburgh newspapers. ♦ Dimensions based on 1906 Sanborn fire insurance map.

## *Forbes Field*

### AKA

Oakland Orchard, Dreyfuss' Folly

### ARCHITECT

Charles W. Leavitt Jr.

### OCCUPANTS

NL Pittsburgh Pirates June 30, 1909–June 28, 1970; ANL Homestead Grays some games 1929; NEWL Homestead Grays April–June 1932; NNL Homestead Grays some games 1935–38; NNL Washington-Homestead Grays a few home games 1939–48

### LOCATION

Left Field (NE) Schenley Park, then Bigelow Blvd; Third Base (NW) 3940 Sennott (often misspelled "Sonnett") St, then Forbes Ave and the Cathedral of Learning; First Base (SW) Boquet (often misspelled "Bouquet") St; Right Field (SE) Joncaire St, then Pierre Ravine, Junction Hollow, Junction RR tracks

Pictured here on its inauguration day, June 30, 1909, Forbes Field was the site of the only major league tripleheader since the 19th century. On October 2, 1920, the Reds beat the Pirates two out of three games to clinch third place in the NL. Forbes was also the setting for the 1951 movie *Angels in the Outfield,* which at one point was to be called *The Angels and the Pirates.*

Babe Ruth is shown here circling the bases at Forbes Field after hitting one of his last three career homers, on May 25, 1935, while a member of the Boston Braves. His last homer, #714, was the first to clear the right field grandstand. The Babe retired a few days later.

## DIMENSIONS

Left Field: 306, 360 (May 26, 1911), 356.5 (1921), 356 (1922), 360 (1925), 365 (1930), 335 (1947), 365 (1954)

Left Center: 340, 403 (May 26, 1911), 406 (1942), 355 (1947), 406 (1954)

Deepest Left Center corner near dead center at Flag Pole: 438 (1909), 462 (May 26, 1911), 457 (1930)

Center Field: 417, 409 (May 26, 1911), 442 (1925), 435 (1930)

Right Center: right side of exit gate 416 (1955)

Right Center: 363, 375 (May 26, 1911), 408 (1921),

Right Field at the left end of the double-deck stands: 375 (1925)

Right Field: 359, 376 (May 26, 1911), 376.5 (1921), 376 (1922), 300 (1925)

Backstop: 110, 84 (May 26, 1911), 80 (1947), 84 (1953), 75 (1959)

## FENCES

Left Field and Left Center: 14 (wood), 12 (brick and ivy 1946)

Left Field scoreboard: 25.42 (steel left and right sides), 27 (middle)

Marine Sergeant at parade rest to right of scoreboard: 32 (wood June 26, 1943, to end of season)

Greenberg Gardens/Kiner's Korner Left Field front fence: 8 (5 screen above 3 wood 1947), 12 (9 screen on top of 3 wood 1949), 14 (screen 1950), side wall angling back to connect inner Greenberg Gardens/Kiner's Korner fence with outer brick wall 12 (wood)

Light Tower cages just right of scoreboard and in power alleys: 16.5

Center Field: 14 (wood), 12 (brick and ivy 1946)

Right Center: 18 (wood), 9 (wood 1911), 9.5 (concrete 1925)

Right Field screen in front of bleachers: (1909–14)

Right Field where there were no bleachers: 18 (wood), 9 (wood 1911)

Right Field screen at left side at 375 mark: 24 (14.5 wire above 9.5 concrete 1932)

Right Field screen at right side at foul pole: 27.67 (18.17 wire above 9.5 concrete 1930)

## FORMER USE

Schenley Farms hothouse and livery stable, cow

grazing, ravine in right field, rocky football field for Carnegie Tech vs. Penn, October 31, 1908

**CURRENT USE**

University of Pittsburgh's Mervis Hall in right, Forbes Quadrangle and Posvar Hall in infield. Center field and right-center brick walls still stand, along with base of flagpole and Mazeroski Field, a Little League diamond beyond the brick wall in left-center. Roberto Clemente Drive now bisects the site, running 10 feet below what used to be the playing surface.

**CAPACITY**

23,000, 24,000 (July 26, 1909), 25,000 (1915), 41,000 (1925), 40,000 (1938), 33,537 (1939), 35,000 (1960)

**PHENOMENA**

On June 30, 2005, exactly 96 years after the first pitch here, a new monument to Barney Dreyfuss, Pirates owner 1900–32, was dedicated near the remaining left-center field wall. The original granite Barney Dreyfuss Monument, just to the left of the exit gate where fans exited the ballpark into Schenley Park after a game, was installed June 30, 1934, on the park's 25th anniversary. ♦ Just over a month into the park's gloried history, on August 3, 1909, Ed Abbaticchio hit an inside-the-park home run to right. The ball rolled to the "corner tank where horses dive," apparently a water tank for horses that was in play in front of the right field fence. ♦ During 1909–24, there were bleachers in right-center. Back then you could get a bounce home run by bouncing a ball over the outfield wall. One bounce homer was hit over the screen in front of the right-center field bleachers in 1911; one in 1912; one in 1913; none in 1914. ♦ There were also temporary bleachers in right field during the 1925 World Series. ♦ During World War II, from June 26 through the end of the 1943 season, a huge United States Marine made of wood stood against the left field wall, just to the right of the scoreboard. Standing at parade rest, the Marine sergeant was 32 feet high, 15 feet wide across his feet, and in play. ♦ First base by a misspelled street. Boquet Street was named for General Henry Bouquet, a Swiss soldier who fought for the British in the French and Indian War battle at Fort Duquesne. Two mistakes were made. Whoever named the street for General Bouquet did not know how to spell his name, because they got it wrong. And second, people would

The Pirates celebrate after the last out of the last game at Forbes Field, a doubleheader sweep of the Chicago Cubs on June 28, 1970.

always misspell it as Bouquet because they thought it was named after a bouquet of flowers. ♦ Ballpark named for General John Forbes, a British general in the French and Indian War, who captured Fort Duquesne and renamed it Fort Pitt in 1758. ♦ Ivy-covered brick wall in left and left-center. ♦ Fourteen-foot Longines clock and speaker horns on top of left field scoreboard were out of play; balls hitting them were a home run. ♦ Fans in upper left corner of the left field bleachers could not see the plate because the third base grandstand stood between them and the plate. ♦ Babe Ruth hit three home runs here on May 25, 1935. The last one, his 714th and last homer, was the first of 18 home runs to clear the 86-foot-high right field roof. ♦ For many seasons Forbes Field was a good park for triples, with Chief Wilson of the 1912 Pirates setting the all-time record with 36 (24 at Forbes Field). ♦ During World War II, the right field screen could not be replaced due to the priority given to the war effort. It deteriorated badly. ♦ No no-hitter was ever pitched here. ♦ Home plate remains in its exact original location, but it is now encased in glass on the first-floor walkway of the University of Pittsburgh's Forbes Quadrangle. ♦ Bottoms of light tower cages in left-center, center, and right-center were in play, as was bottom of center field flag pole. ♦ Just to the left of the flag pole stood the batting cage, also in play. Before being placed in left-center, it stood behind home plate during batting practice. ♦ Very hard infield surface, just ask Tony Kubek! ♦ Back in the 1910s, there was a small scoreboard on the center field wall. ♦ In the 1920s, cars and trucks were repaired and sold beneath the left field bleachers. ♦ Right field stands built in 1925, reducing distance to right field foul pole by 76.5 feet. ♦ Right field screen added in 1930. It was taken down for a short period once, then put right back up again. ♦ Greenberg Gardens, also called Kiner's Korner, was the area between the scoreboard and a chicken coop wire short fence in left put there to increase home run production 1947–53. It was called Greenberg Gardens 1947, Kiner's Korner 1948-53. ♦ When Greenberg Gardens were in place, a Western Union clock stood on top of the scoreboard, to the right of the familiar Gruen clock. ♦ In 1938 with

the Bucs apparently on their way to the World Series, they built a third deck of seats behind the plate called the Crow's Nest, with the major leagues' first elevator. Buccos finally made the Series 22 years later. ♦ Honus Wagner statue in Schenley Park erected 1955. It stood 18 feet high and weighed 1800 pounds, moved to Three Rivers with Bucs in 1970. ♦ Green foam rubber crash pads placed on concrete wall in right and right-center, first in majors. ♦ Wooden walls installed in left and center in 1909, replaced with brick and ivy in 1946. ♦ Street dead-ending into Sennott Street by third base variously called Pennant Place and Forbes Field Avenue. ♦ Fires damaged park on December 24, 1970, and July 17, 1971. ♦ A plaque today marks the spot where Bill Mazeroski's World Series-winning homer left the park in the bottom of the ninth inning on October 13, 1960, and flew into the trees above Yogi Berra's head. ♦ Torn down July 28, 1971.

## *Central Park*

### AKA
Keystone Field

### OCCUPANT
NNL Pittsburgh Keystones 1922

### LOCATION
Above Centre Ave, near Herron St and Chauncey St, in the Hill District

### PHENOMENA
Although Greenlee Field, built in Pittsburgh in 1932, is always referred to as the first ballpark built for a Negro League baseball team, this park was built 12 years earlier for that specific purpose by A. D. Williams in the late summer of 1920. ♦ Unfortunately, a 1922 game between the Keystones and the Homestead Grays ended in a riot, which caused the fans to stop coming out in great numbers. Things went downhill from that point on, and the park was torn down in June 1925 to make way for a dance pavilion.

## Grays Field

**OCCUPANT**

ANL Homestead Grays 1929

**LOCATION**

(N) Pennsylvania RR tracks, (W) Long Ave, (E) Homewood Ave, in the Homewood section of the city

## Ammon Field

**OCCUPANTS**

ANL Homestead Grays some games 1929; NNL Pittsburgh Craws some games 1933–38

**LOCATION**

Overlooking Bigelow Blvd, off Webster Ave, in the Hill District

**CURRENT USE**

Ammon Playground

**PHENOMENA**

Historical marker, dedicated September 23, 1996, commemorates Josh Gibson's career achievement of 800-plus home runs.

## Washington Park

**OCCUPANT**

ANL Homestead Grays some games 1929

**LOCATION**

On the lower Hill, near where the Civic Arena and Connelly Vocational High School are today, in the Hill District

## Gus Greenlee Field

**OCCUPANTS**

NNL Pittsburgh Crawfords 1933–38; NNL Homestead Grays 1935–38

**LOCATION**

Left Field (N) Ridgeway St; Third Base (W) Junilia St, then Lincoln Cemetery; First Base (S) 2500 Bed-

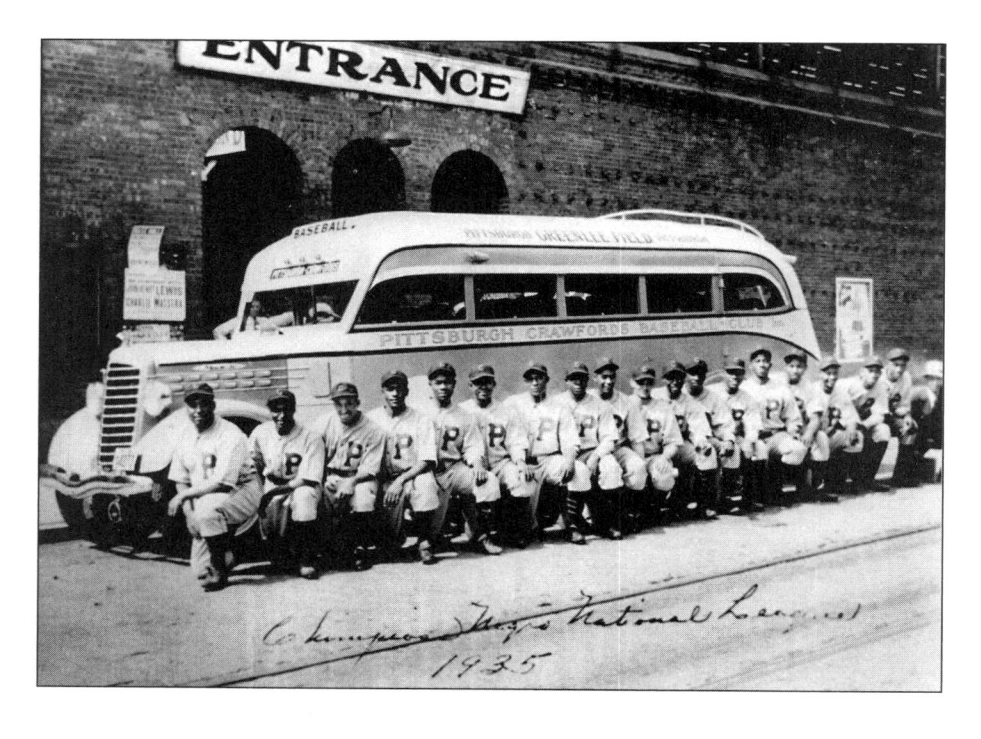

The 1935 Negro League champion Pittsburgh Crawfords, in front of Greenlee Field. The team included five future Hall of Famers: Oscar Charleston (far left); Satchel Paige (second from the right); Josh Gibson (fourth from the right); Cool Papa Bell (seventh from the right); and Judy Johnson (eighth from the right).

*Champs — 1937*

The Homestead Grays inside Greenlee Field. They shared the stadium with the Crawfords. Note the one-foot-tall cinder-block wall in front of the right field bleachers, the lowest outfield wall in major league history.

ford Ave; Right Field (E) Francis St, then Municipal Hospital; in the Hill District

## DIMENSIONS

Left Field: more than 365

## FENCES

Left and Center Fields: (unknown height, made of tin)

Right Field: 1 (cinder block)

## FORMER USE

Entress Brick Company factory

## CURRENT USE

Pittsburgh Housing Authority projects called the Bedford Dwellings

## CAPACITY

7500

## PHENOMENA

The demise of Greenlee Field due to racism is examined in great detail by John Clark in an article in the *Pittsburgh Courier* dated December 9, 1938. Clark describes how the African-American community of Pittsburgh finally turned their backs on the ballpark and the Craws because the owner, Gus Greenlee, an African-American, allegedly allowed Caucasians on his board to freeze out African-Americans from ball-park jobs such as vendors, ushers, and ticket sellers. ♦ Opened on April 29, 1932, with the Craws facing Vandergrift in an exhibition game. The next day, April 30, the official opening came with the Craws facing the New York Black Yankees. ♦ Josh Gibson once hit a home run here so far out of the park that the next day, in Philadelphia, with Gibson catching, when a ball came flying out of the crowds and was caught by one of the players, the umpire said to Josh, "You're out yesterday in Pittsburgh." ♦ Crawfords owner Gus Greenlee scheduled a Craws-Grays game for 12:01 AM on a Monday morning to protest the Sunday blue law that prevented Sunday night games; the game was a sellout. ♦ Greenlee allowed Grays owner Cumberland (Cum) Posey to have his team use the park also. ♦ On July 4, 1934, Satchel Paige pitched a no-hitter here in a morning game, and then somehow got to Chicago in time to pitch a 12-inning shutout there on the same day against the American Giants. ♦ Embankment in play in front of a very low one-foot-high concrete wall in front of the bleachers in right, which were up on a hill. ♦ Tin fence in left and center. Left field foul line was longer than at Forbes Field, where it was 365. ♦ Torn down December 10, 1938.

## *Three Rivers Stadium*

**AKA**

House That Clemente Built

**ARCHITECTS**

Deeter, Ritchey, Sipple; Michael Baker and Osborn Engineering

**OCCUPANT**

NL Pittsburgh Pirates July 16, 1970–October 1, 2000

**LOCATION**

Left Field (E/NE) West General Robinson St (running W/SW to E/NE), then I-279 Fort Duquesne Bridge approach ramp; Third Base (N/NW) Lacock (later Reesdale) St, then Ohio River Blvd; First Base (W/SW) Stadium Dr West, then Manchester (later Allegheny) Ave and Ohio River; Right Field (S/SE) North Shore Dr, then Roberto Clemente Memorial Park and Allegheny River; on the other side of the river beyond right field is the Point, where the Monongahela River joins the Allegheny River to form the Ohio River

**SURFACE**

Tartanturf 1970–82, AstroTurf 1983–2000

**DIMENSIONS**

Foul Lines: 340, 335 (1975)
Power Alleys: 385, 375 (1975)
Center Field: 410, 400 (1975)
Backstop: 60
Foul Territory: large

**FENCES**

10 (wood)

**CAPACITY**

50,500, 54,499 (1981), 58,727 (1988), 47,687 (2000)

**PHENOMENA**

Fan drove his car into the stadium and overturned a 70-gallon jug of cheese dip on December 3, 1987. ♦ Roberto Clemente statue dedicated here in 1994. ♦ On a site that was an island during the French and Indian War. It had been an Indian burial ground, a fact discovered when the Big Flood of 1763 uncovered many graves. Named Kilbuck Island after a friendly Delaware Indian chief. Back channels were

No no-hitters were pitched in 61 years at Forbes Field, but John Candelaria fired one against the Dodgers on August 9, 1976, just the Bucs' seventh year at Three Rivers Stadium. Another memorable game took place on September 30, 1972, when Roberto Clemente made his 3,000th and last career hit.

filled with silt, and it was no longer an island by 1852. ♦ Numbers painted on seats in right field upper deck where Willie Stargell's homers landed. ♦ Without the inner fence, the outfield would have been 342 down the lines and 434 to center. ♦ Honus Wagner statue, which used to stand outside Forbes Field, was moved to stand outside Three Rivers. ♦ Eight-foot by 12-foot area of 406 marker section of Forbes Field brick wall, 12 Romanesque window frames, and Babe Ruth plaque showing where his 714th home run landed, were moved to Allegheny Club at Three Rivers. ♦ Original design by Erik Sirko was for a "Stadium Over the Monongahela," with stadium above two parking lot levels, all constructed above the Monongahela River with plenty of room for boats to pass beneath on the river. ♦ Torn down February 11, 2001.

## *PNC Park*

### ARCHITECTS
HOK Sport

### OCCUPANT
NL Pittsburgh Pirates April 9, 2001, to date

### LOCATION
Left Field (E/NE) 115 Federal St, Third Base (N/NW) East General Robinson St, First Base (W/SW) Mazeroski Way (formerly North Shore Dr, then Ave of the Pirates), Right Field (S/SE) Allegheny River, between the Fort Duquesne and Roberto Clemente (6th St) Bridges

The antithesis of Three Rivers, the Pirates' beautiful new home, PNC Park, is the smallest in the major leagues, just a few hundred seats short of Fenway Park. Pittsburgh native Sean Casey had the first hit in the new park, a two-run homer on April 9, 2001. Three days earlier he had the first hit at Miller Park in Milwaukee.

## DIMENSIONS

Left Field: 325
Left Center: 386, 389 (2003)
Deepest Left Center: 410
Center Field: 399
Right Center: 375
Right Field: 320
Backstop: 52, 51 (2003)
Foul Territory: small

## FENCES

Left Field: 6
Left Center, Center Field, and Right Center: 10
Right Field: 21

## CAPACITY

38,365; 38,496 (2004)

## PHENOMENA

Fans can arrive via ferryboat on the Allegheny River behind right field. ♦ On July 28, 2001, the Pirates trailed the Astros, 8–2, in the bottom of the ninth, with two out and nobody on base. Then the Bucs proceeded to score seven runs to win 9–8 on Brian Giles' home run–a grand slam. ♦ It is 455 feet to the edge of the Allegheny River. During games, boats and kayaks wait anxiously for homers to reach the water. In the 2006 All-Star Game Home Run Derby, 19 homers bounced into the river, and one made it there on the fly. Along with the Giants park, whose name seems to change evey year, this is the best of the new ballparks.

# Providence, Rhode Island

*See also* Warwick, Rhode Island

## Adelaide Avenue Grounds

### AKA

Providence Base Ball Grounds, Adelaide Park

## OCCUPANTS

Neutral site used by NA Hartford Dark Blues June 12, 1875; by NA Boston Red Stockings June 22, 1875

## LOCATION

Adelaide Ave, Broad St, Hamilton St, Sackett St, Elwood Ave

## Messer Street Grounds

### AKA

Messer Park

### OCCUPANT

NL Providence Grays May 1, 1878–September 9, 1885

### LOCATION

(N) Hudson (later Willow) St, (W) Ropes (later Ellery) St, (S) Wood St, (E) Messer St; opposite the Messer School

### DIMENSIONS

Backstop: 40

### PHENOMENA

Just as at Wrigley Field today, fans would watch the games from atop the Tourtellot House, which was behind the very short left field fence.

# Raleigh, North Carolina

## Devereaux Meadow

### OCCUPANT

Neutral site used by NAL Birmingham Black Barons 1940s

**LOCATION**

Downtown Blvd, West St, Peace St

**DIMENSIONS**

Left Field: 310
Center Field: 400
Right Field: 370

**FENCES**

40 everywhere

**CAPACITY**

4000

**PHENOMENA**

Built as a WPA project in 1939, torn down in 1979.

## *Chavis Park*

**OCCUPANT**

NAL Raleigh Tigers 1959–61

**PHENOMENA**

With the team barnstorming so frequently, two of its few "home" games at Chavis Park were June 4, 1959, vs. the Detroit Stars and May 15, 1961, vs. the Kansas City Monarchs.

---

# Richmond, Virginia

## *Virginia State Agricultural Society Fair Grounds*

**AKA**

Richmond Fair Grounds

**OCCUPANT**

Neutral site used by NA Washington Nationals April 29 and May 1, 1875

**LOCATION**

Franklin St, Belvedere St, Main St, Laurel St

**FENCES**

None

**CURRENT USE**

Union RR Station, later Science Museum of Richmond, Monroe Park

## *Allen's Pasture*

**AKA**

Virginia Base-Ball Park

**OCCUPANT**

AA Richmond Virginias August 5–October 15, 1884

**LOCATION**

(NE) Broad St, (NW) Allen Ave, (SW) Scuffletown Rd (later Park Ave), (SE) Lombardy St; opposite the Richmond Fredericksburg and Potomac RR yards; in the Lee district near Joseph Bryan Park

**FENCES**

None

**CURRENT USE**

Monuments to Generals Robert E. Lee and Jeb Stuart at third base

**PHENOMENA**

No fences. Surrounding farmland was owned by Otway S. Allen.

♦   ♦   ♦

# Riverhead, New York

## *Wivchar Stadium*

**AKA**

Riverhead Stadium

**OCCUPANT**

Neutral site used by ECL New York Lincoln Giants 1920s

**LOCATION**

Harrison Ave, School St, Roanoke Ave, Old Country Rd (later Route 58); on Long Island

**DIMENSIONS**

Foul Lines: 325
Power Alleys: 410
Center Field: 500

**FENCES**

10

# Rochester, New York

*See also* Charlotte, New York; Irondequoit, New York

## *Culver Field (I)*

**OCCUPANT**

AA Rochester Hop Bitters April 28–October 6, 1890

**PHENOMENA**

Burned down in 1892.

## *Culver Field (II)*

**OCCUPANT**

Neutral site used by NL Cleveland Spiders August 27 and 29, 1898

**LOCATION**

(N) University (later Atlantic) Ave, (NW) Jersey (later Russell) St, (SW)Culver Park (later 1000 University Ave), (E) Culver Rd; same as Culver Field (I)

**CURRENT USE**

Gleason Works, New York Central/Conrail RR tracks

## *Red Wing Stadium*

**AKA**

Silver Stadium August 19, 1968, onward

**OCCUPANT**

NNL New York Black Yankees May 25–September 1948

**LOCATION**

Left Field (N) Bastian St, Third Base (W) Clinton Ave, First Base (S) 500 Norton St, Right Field (E) Joseph Ave

**DIMENSIONS**

Left Field: 322
Left Center: 445
Center Field: 410
Right Center: 360
Right Field: 315

**FENCES**

Left Field: 6 (wire)
Center to Right: 11 (wood above concrete)

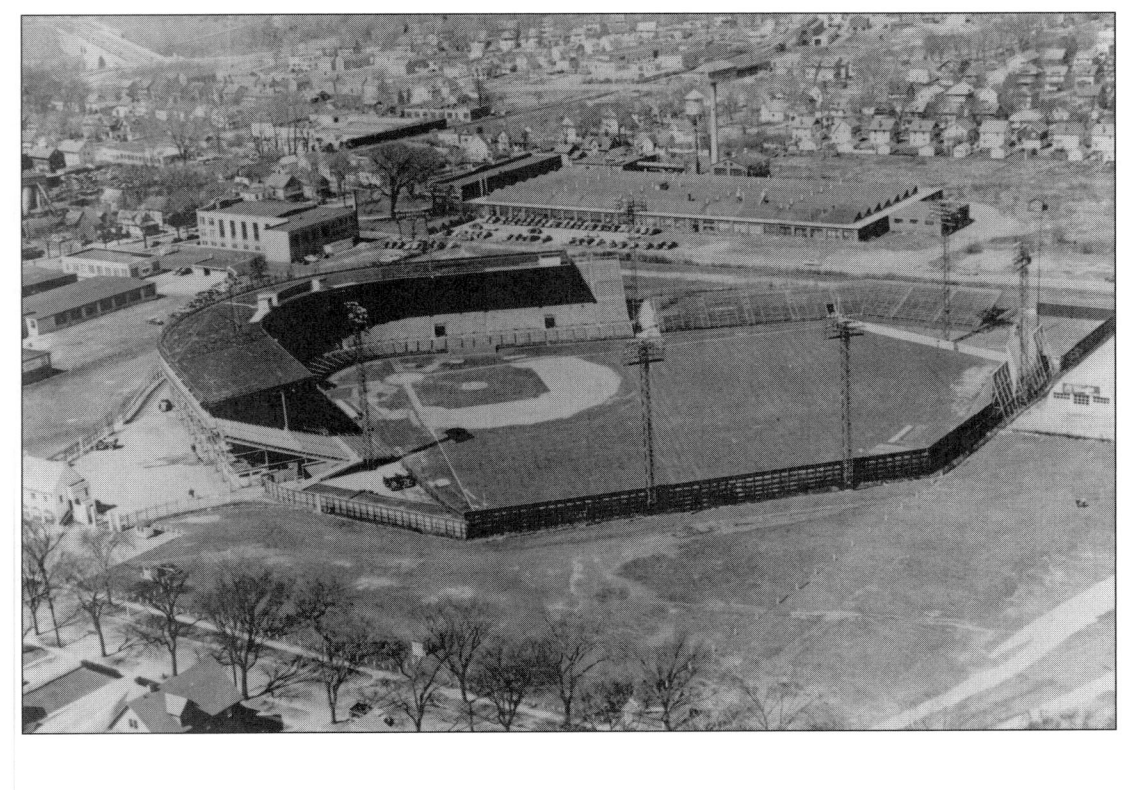

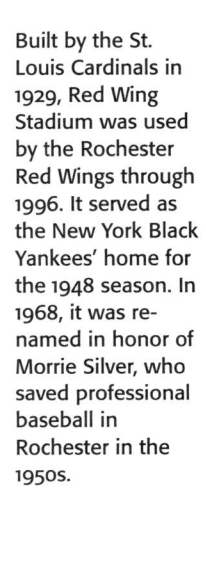

Built by the St. Louis Cardinals in 1929, Red Wing Stadium was used by the Rochester Red Wings through 1996. It served as the New York Black Yankees' home for the 1948 season. In 1968, it was re-named in honor of Morrie Silver, who saved professional baseball in Rochester in the 1950s.

**CAPACITY**

15,222 (1940)

**PHENOMENA**

Opened May 2, 1929. ♦ SABR member Doug Brei of Rochester recently unearthed documents which prove that this was not just a neutral site for many Black Yankee games in 1948, but rather the full-time home base of the Black Yankees for that entire season.

# Rockford, Illinois

## *Agricultural Society Fair Grounds*

**OCCUPANTS**

NA Rockford Forest Citys May 5–September 26, 1871; neutral site used by NA Philadelphia White Stockings August 18, 1873

**LOCATION**

(N) Acorn St; (W) Kent Creek, then railroad tracks, then Ogden Ave; (S) West Jefferson St; (E) Kilburn Ave

**DIMENSIONS**

Foul Territory: almost none because trees completely surrounded the park

**CURRENT USE**

Fairground Park, Kilburn Community Center, Harkins Aquatic Center, Salvation Army Center

**PHENOMENA**

Most interesting and strangest major league ballpark in history. ♦ Numerous trees behind the catcher and along both Foul Lines made catching foul pop-ups impossible. ♦ Third base was up on a hill; home plate was in a deep depression so that when tagging up from third to home, a runner was running downhill the whole way! ♦ All the way around the outfield, there was the first warning track ever. It was a deep gutter providing drainage from the adjacent quarter-mile horseracing track.

---

# Rockingham, North Carolina

## *Rockingham Stadium*

**OCCUPANT**

Neutral site used by NAL Raleigh Tigers May 12, 1961

---

# Rocky Mount, North Carolina

## *Municipal Stadium*

**OCCUPANT**

Neutral site used by NAL Raleigh Tigers May 19, 1961

**LOCATION**

Center Field (SE), Third Base (NE), Home Plate (NW), First Base (SW)

**DIMENSIONS**

Left Field: 300 (1940), 350 (1950)
Center Field: 430 (1940), 350 (1950)
Right Field: 350 (1940), 346 (1950)

**CAPACITY**

3200 (1940), 4500 (1950)

**PHENOMENA**

Built in 1936. Torn down December 1987. ♦ A football stadium which served for many years as the home of the Rocky Mount High School Gryphons.

## *Talbert Park*

**OCCUPANT**

Neutral site used by NAL Raleigh Tigers May 21, 1961

**DIMENSIONS**

Much larger than Municipal Stadium, where the Tigers also played the Monarchs, just two days before in the same city

---

# St. Louis, Missouri

## *Red Stocking Base-Ball Park*

**AKA**

Compton Avenue Base Ball Park 1885–98

**OCCUPANT**

NL St. Louis Red Stockings May 4–July 4, 1875

**LOCATION**

Left Field (W) Theresa Ave; Third Base (S) Larned (later Atlantic) St, then Missouri Pacific RR railyards; Home Plate (SE) Gratiot St; First Base (E) 701 South Compton Ave; Right Field (N) Scott (later Market) St

**CURRENT USE**

Railroad yards and Bi-State bus repair shops

**PHENOMENA**

Built in 1874, torn down in 1898.

## *Sportsman's Park (I)*

**AKA**

Grand Avenue Park, Grand Avenue Grounds

**OCCUPANTS**

NA St. Louis Brown Stockings May 6–October 8, 1875; NL St. Louis Brown Stockings May 5, 1876–October 6, 1877; neutral site used by NL Indianapolis Browns July 9, 11, and 13, 1878

**LOCATION**

Left Field (W) Spring St, Third Base (S) St. Louis Ave (later 3623 Dodier St), Home Plate (SE), First Base (E) 2709 North Grand Ave (later Blvd), Right Field (N) Sullivan Ave; same site as for Sportsman's Parks (II), (III), and (IV), but with home plate in the Southeast

**CAPACITY**

3000 (1875)

**PHENOMENA**

First used for baseball in 1866.

## *Sportsman's Park (II)*

**AKA**

Athletic Park 1901; Solari's Beer Garden

**OCCUPANTS**

AA St. Louis Browns May 2, 1882–October 4, 1891; NL St. Louis Browns April 12–October 13, 1892; NL St. Louis Cardinals May 5, 1901

**LOCATION**

Left Field (S) 3623 Dodier St, Third Base (E) 2907 North Grand Ave (later Blvd), Home Plate (NE), First Base (N) Sullivan Ave, Right Field (W) Spring St; same site as for Sportsman's Park (I), (III), and (IV); same orientation as Sportsman's Park (III), with home plate in the northeast corner

**DIMENSIONS**

Left Field: 350
Left Center: 400
Center Field: 460
Right Center: 330
Right Field: 285
Backstop: 70

**CAPACITY**

6000 (1882), 12,000 (1886), 3000 (1901)

**PHENOMENA**

Browns owner Chris von der Ahe converted Augustus Solari's two-story house in the right field corner into a beer garden for the 1882 season. In accordance with pre-1888 World Series rules, the beer garden was in play. Right fielders charged up into the beer gardens to retrieve balls hit there, and then relay the ball back to the pitchers box, after which the ball was eligible to be used to put out a runner. Imagine, a beer garden, with customers eating and drinking at their picnic tables, in play in a major league ballpark! ◆ During the 1882 season, there was also a Japanese fireworks cannon in the ballpark, made out of bamboo and wrapped with steel wire. ◆ The clubhouse was in the right field corner, behind the beer gardens. ◆ When used by the NL Cards in 1901 for one game due to a fire the previous day at Robison Field, the field was in horrible shape with bicycle racing ruts everywhere because it was being used as a bicycle oval then. The crowd of 6000 swarmed all over the outfield, and there were ten ground-rule doubles hit into the crowd.

## *Palace Park of America*

**AKA**

Union Grounds

**OCCUPANTS**

UA St. Louis Maroons April 20–October 19, 1884; NL St. Louis Maroons April 30, 1885–September 23, 1886

**LOCATION**

Left Field (E) West 25th St, Third Base (N) Mullanphy (later Madison) St, First Base (W) Jefferson Ave, Right Field (S) Cass Ave

**DIMENSIONS**

Foul Lines: 285

Backstop: 25

**CURRENT USE**

Vacant commercial buildings

**CAPACITY**

10,000

**PHENOMENA**

Numerous cages throughout the park with canaries chirping away inside. Torn down in 1888. Wire screen on top of outfield fence.

## *Robison Field*

**AKA**

Vandeventer Lot (I), League Park 1898–1911, Cardinal Field 1918–20, Coney Island of the West, Shoot the Chutes

**OCCUPANTS**

NL St. Louis Cardinals April 27, 1893–June 6, 1920; neutral site used by NL Cleveland Spiders September 28–29, 1898, and on September 24, 1899

**LOCATION**

Left Field (SE) Prairie Ave; Third Base (NE) 3852 Natural Bridge Ave, then Fairground Park; First Base (NW) Vandeventer Ave; Right Field (SW) Ashland (later Lexington) Ave

**DIMENSIONS**

Left Field: 470, 350 (1898), 410 (1901)

Left Center: 470 (1898) 458 (1901)

Deepest Left Center: 520, 475 (1901)

Center Field: 500, 441 (1901)

Right Center: 330, 360 (1901)

Right Field: 290, 312 (1901)

Backstop: 120, 72 (1901)

Foul Territory: huge

**FENCES**

Shoot the Chutes at Left Field Foul Pole and in Right Field: none

Left Field: ropes often strung in front of fence for fans to stand behind

Center Field: picket fence and bulletin board (scoreboard)

**CAPACITY**

10,300, 14,500 (1894), 15,200 (1899), 21,000 (1901)

**CURRENT USE**

Beaumont High School

**PHENOMENA**

Shoot the Chutes was the name given to two areas added in 1896 and 1897 where the ball could roll as far as 500 feet, between bleacher sections, and still be in play. One area was at the left field foul pole, where the ball could roll to Prairie Avenue, and the other area was in right field, where the ball could roll to a lake. ♦ Fire destroyed grandstand, April 16, 1898, and again during game on May 4, 1901. ♦ Balls that rolled underneath the center field scoreboard could not be reached, and were home runs. ♦ A short picket fence was put across left field in 1896–97. ♦ The 1901–20 dimensions come from measurements using a 1916 Sanborn fire insurance map of the park and 1901 photos. ♦ In later years the right field pavilion had a low screen in the front.

## *Sportsman's Park (III)*

**OCCUPANT**

AL St. Louis Browns April 23, 1902–October 6, 1908

**LOCATION**

Left Field (E) 2907 North Grand Ave (later Blvd), Third Base (N) Sullivan Ave, First Base (W) Spring St, Right Field (S) 3623 Dodier St; same site as for Sportsman's Parks (I), (II), and (IV); same orientation as Sportsman's Park (II), with home plate in the northwest corner of the site

Sportsman's Park III, home of the AL Browns from 1909 to 1953 and of the NL Cardinals from 1920 to 1966, was host to the 1944 all-St. Louis World Series, dubbed the "Streetcar Series," which the Browns and Cardinals played on continuous days.

**DIMENSIONS**

Left Field: 342

Left Center: 350

Center Field: 390

Center Field at the Scoreboard: 430

Right Center: 400

Right Field: 300

Backstop: 60

**FENCES**

Left Field: 8

Center Field Scoreboard: 15

Right Field: 10

**CAPACITY**

15,000, 18,000 (1907)

**PHENOMENA**

Home plate was in northwest corner of field. ♦ Field oriented such that left field foul line hit the left field bleachers at less than 90 degrees, and right field foul line hit the right field fence at more than 90 degrees. ♦ Short fence connected the left field and third base bleachers, 1902–06. Fence eliminated when gap between third base and left field bleachers filled with additional seats for 1907 season. ♦ Clubhouse located in center field behind scoreboard at right end of left field bleachers. ♦ An entrance, called the carriage entrance, was also located at the right end of the left field bleachers in front of the clubhouse. ♦ Behind right field fence was a peach orchard. ♦ Left field bleachers of Sportsman's (III) became the right field bleachers of Sportsman's (IV). ♦ Dimensions based on 1909 Sanborn fire insurance map, 1902 Opening Day left field and right field dimensions from the St. Louis Star, and ballpark photos from 1902–07.

## Sportsman's Park (IV)

**AKA**

Busch Stadium (I) 1954–66, Bill Veeck's House

**OCCUPANTS**

AL St. Louis Browns April 14, 1909–September 27,

1953; NL St. Louis Cardinals July 1, 1920–May 8, 1966; neutral site used by NAL Kansas City Monarchs July 4, 1941; by NAL New Orleans-St. Louis Stars one game in 1941

**LOCATION**

Left Field (NE) Sullivan Ave, Third Base (NW) North Spring Ave, Home Plate (W/SW), First Base (SW) 3623 Dodier St, Right Field (SE) 2907 North Grand Ave (later Blvd); same as the earlier Sportsman's Parks, but first and only park with home plate in the southwest corner of the site

**DIMENSIONS**

Left Field: 368, 350 (May 1909) 340 (1921), 356 (1923), 355 (1926), 360 (1930), 351.1 (1931)

Left Center: 435, 414 (May 1909), 404 (1911)

Deepest corner left of dead center: 426 (1938)

Center Field: 445, 430 (1926), 450 (1930), 445 (1931), 420 (1938), 422 (1939)

Center Field corner: 492, 475 (May 1909)

Deepest corner right of dead center: 422 (1938)

Right Center: 354 (1942)

Right Field: 315, 270 (1911), 315 (1921), 320 (1925), 310 (marked 1926), 309.5 (actual 1926), 310 (1931), 309.5 (1939)

Backstop: 80, 90 (May 1909), 75 (1942), 67 (1953)

**FENCES**

Left to Center: 11.5 (concrete)

354 mark in Right Center to Right: 11.5, 33 (11.5 concrete below 21.5 wire July 5, 1929), 11.5 (1955), 36.67 (11.5 concrete below 25.17 wire 1956)

**CURRENT USE**

Herbert Hoover Boys' Club, with baseball diamond in the same spot

When August Busch purchased Sportsman's Park IV from Bill Veeck in 1953, he added box seats, renovated the clubhouses, and renamed the park Busch Stadium. He also placed a Budweiser eagle atop the scoreboard.

**CAPACITY**

17,600, 24,040 (June 1909), 34,023 (1926), 31,250 (1947), 34,000 (1948), 30,500 (1953)

**PHENOMENA**

Local newspaper, the *Globe-Democrat,* had an ad on the right-center wall which showed the star of the previous game. Just to the right of this ad, league standings for both leagues were listed. ♦ Bill Veeck gave Satchel Paige a rocking chair to rock in while in the bullpen when Paige pitched for the Browns here in 1951–53. ♦ Busch eagle flapped its wings after a Cardinal home run. It sat on top of the left-center scoreboard. During World War II there was a War Chest sign there. ♦ Cards office was at 3623 Dodier, Browns office was at 2911 North Grand. ♦ Pavilion seats in right field after 1925. ♦ New double-deck grandstand from first to third built in the southwest corner of the park in early 1909. Second deck expanded to foul poles in 1925–26. Concrete bleachers also replaced the wooden left field bleachers and a new covered pavilion replaced the old right field bleaches in 1925–26. ♦ Beginning in 1940s, the outfield signs were 351, 358, 379, 400, 426, 425, 422, 422, 405, 354, 322, and 310. In 1950s, the 426 and the right 422 signs that marked the corners just left and right of straightaway center were removed. ♦ Midget Eddie Gaedel batted here for the Browns on August 19, 1951, and drew a walk. ♦ Flag pole in fair territory until removed in the 1950s. ♦ Bill Veeck's family lived in an apartment under the stands in the 1950s. ♦ When Cardinals owner Gussie Busch bought the stadium from the Browns in 1953, he almost named it Budweiser Stadium, but was prevented from doing so by league pressure. ♦ The wire screen in front of the right field pavilion was removed for the entire 1955 season. It had been installed on July 5, 1929, by the St. Louis Browns after the Tigers hit eight home runs in a four-game series. ♦ Helicopter carried home plate to Busch Memorial Stadium after the last game May 8, 1966. ♦ Old grandstand behind home plate, 1902–08, became pavilion in the left field corner of this park, 1909–10. ♦ Dimensions for 1909–20 based on 1909 Sanborn fire insurance map. ♦ Park torn down in 1966.

## *Handlan's Park*

**AKA**

Federal Field, Federal League Park, Laclede Street Field, Grand and Market, Steininger Field

**OCCUPANTS**

FL St. Louis Terriers April 16, 1914–October 3, 1915; NNL St. Louis Giants some games 1920–21; NNL St. Louis Stars some games 1920s

**LOCATION**

Left Field (W) Theresa Ave, Third Base (N) Laclede Ave, First Base (W) Grand Ave, Right Field (S) Clark (later Market) St

**DIMENSIONS**

Left Field: 325
Left Center: 375
Center Field: 375
Right Center: 346
Right Field: 285

**FENCES**

Left Field: 8

**CURRENT USE**

Grand Forest Apartments

**CAPACITY**

12,000 (1914), 15,000 (1915)

**PHENOMENA**

Dimensions based on 1908 Sanborn fire insurance map of the park site and 1914 ballpark diagram from the *St. Louis Globe Democrat.* ♦ Much shorter distance to right field than to left field. ♦ Odd-shaped park. East end of grandstand ended at about third base, and there were no stands at all down the left field line as other properties along Laclede Ave extended almost to the foul line. These properties, in combination with similar ones on the south along Clark St, limited the depth of right field.

## Giants Park

**AKA**

Tigers Park after June 15, 1922

**OCCUPANTS**

NL St. Louis Giants May 9, 1920–August 30, 1921; NNL St. Louis Stars May 30–June 15, 1922

**LOCATION**

(N) Pope Ave, (W) Prescott Ave, (S) Clarence Ave; also North Broadway, East Taylor St, Hall St, one block from Kuebler's Park, which was abandoned in 1917

## Stars Park

**AKA**

Dick Kent's Ballyard, Compton Park

**OCCUPANT**

NNL St. Louis Stars July 9, 1922–August 11, 1931

**LOCATION**

Compton St, Laclede St, Market St

**DIMENSIONS**

Left Field: 250
Left Center: 425

**CAPACITY**

10,000 (1922)

## Vandeventer Lot (II)

**OCCUPANT**

NNL St. Louis Stars some games 1920s

**LOCATION**

Grand Ave, Vandeventer St, Franklin St, Spring St, Belle St

## Easton Street Park

**OCCUPANT**

NNL St. Louis Stars some games 1920s

**LOCATION**

Easton St, Vandeventer St, stockyards

## Market Street Park

**OCCUPANT**

NNL St. Louis Stars some games 1920s

**LOCATION**

North Market St, Broadway, Elephants St

## Metropolitan Park

**OCCUPANT**

NAL St. Louis Stars 1937

**LOCATION**

Same as Giants Park

## South End Park

**AKA**

National Nite Baseball Park

**OCCUPANTS**

NAL St. Louis Stars 1939; NAL New Orleans-St. Louis Stars (half of the home games) 1941

**CURRENT USE**

American Can Company plant

◆  ◆  ◆

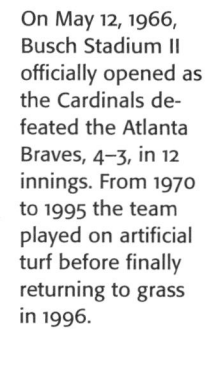

On May 12, 1966, Busch Stadium II officially opened as the Cardinals defeated the Atlanta Braves, 4–3, in 12 innings. From 1970 to 1995 the team played on artificial turf before finally returning to grass in 1996.

## *Busch Stadium (II)*

### AKA

Civic Center Stadium 1966, Busch Memorial Stadium 1966–83

### ARCHITECT

Sverdrup, Parcel & Associates; HOK Sport (1995 renovations)

### OCCUPANT

NL St. Louis Cardinals May 12, 1966–October 19, 2005

### LOCATION

Left Field (E/NE) Broadway, I-70, Gateway Arch, and Mississippi River are a few blocks farther away; Third Base (N/NW) Walnut St; First Base (W/SW) Seventh St (later McGwire Way); Right Field (S/SE) Spruce St

### DIMENSIONS

Foul Lines: 330

Power Alleys: 386, 376 (1973), 386 (1977), 383 (July 1983), 375 (1992), 372 (1996)

Center Field: 414, 410 (1971), 414 (1972), 404 (1973), 414 (1977), 402 (1992)

Backstop: 64–Vin Scully's unofficial measurement during 1985 World Series showed this was 50 rather than 64

Foul Territory: large

### FENCES

Left and Right Fields: 10.5 (padded concrete), 8 (padded canvas 1992)

Center Field: 10.5 (padded concrete), 8 (wood 1973), 10.5 (padded concrete 1977), 8 (padded canvas 1992)

### SURFACE

Grass 1966–69; carpet (very fast) 1970–95; grass 1996 to 2005. From 1970 to 1976, the entire field was carpeted except for the part of the infield that is normally dirt on a grass field. In 1977 this was carpeted except for the sliding pits. This was one of only four instances where there was a full dirt infield, with an otherwise fully carpeted field, the others being Astrodome 1966–70, Candlestick 1971, and Tropicana Field 1998 to date.

### CAPACITY

49,275, 53,138 (1987), 54,224 (1988), 54,727 plus 1500 standing room equals 56,227 (1990, from this time forward the Cards included standing room in their capacity statistics, the only major league team to do so), 52,244 (1996), 49,676 (1997), 50,354 (2001), 50,345 (2005)

**PHENOMENA**

A line drive park, because of deep power alleys, deep center field, and quick surface. ◆ Ninety-six open arches surrounded the field just below the roof. ◆ From 1966 to 1982, right field scoreboard lights showed a cardinal in flight when a Cardinal hit a home run; same show was put on each time Lou Brock set a new base-stealing record. ◆ Home plate transplanted from old Busch Stadium at opening game. ◆ Next to the Gateway Arch and the Mississippi River; you could see the Arch from the top deck behind first base. ◆ Statue of Stan "the Man" Musial outside the stadium unveiled in 1968. ◆ Small sections of bleachers in the outfield. ◆ Chicken wire basket (à la Wrigley Field in Chicago) installed in front of left-center and right-center bleacher sections, July 1983, was two feet high and reduced distance to fence by three feet (386 to 383 in power alleys). It did not raise the height of the 10½ foot wall. ◆ At league direction, site designated for any Cubs playoffs or World Series home games from 1986 to 1987, after which Wrigley Field got lights. ◆ Most fans seemed to wear Cardinal red, to match the seats,

which were all painted red in 1987. ◆ Manual scoreboard in center since 1997. ◆ Seventh inning brought Clydesdale horses to the scoreboard. ◆ They used to play the Anheuser-Busch "King of Beers" theme song on the organ during the seventh inning stretch instead of "Take Me Out to the Ballgame," then they played the "Beer Song" at the end of the seventh.

## *Busch Stadium (III)*

**ARCHITECT**

HOK Sport

**OCCUPANT**

NL St. Louis Cardinals April 10, 2006, to date

**LOCATION**

Left Field (N) Clark St; Third Base (W) Eighth St; First Base (S) Poplar St, then US-40/I-64; Right Field (E) Broadway

**DIMENSIONS**

Left Field: 336

Busch Stadium III occupies a portion of Busch II's former footprint. It opened on April 4, 2006 with an exhibition between the Memphis Redbirds and Springfield Cardinals, both minor league affiliates of the Cardinals.

Left/Right Field Power Alleys: 391
Left/Right Center: 396
Center Field: 400
Right Field: 335
Backstop: 52

**FENCES**

8

**SURFACE**

Grass

**CAPACITY**

40,713, 46,861 (July 13, 2006)

**PHENOMENA**

The new park is just south of Busch Stadium (II), with the new left-center field wall where the old right field foul pole was. ♦ The Gateway Arch, hidden behind left field in the old park, in this new park is visible above the center field seats and Coca-Cola scoreboard. ♦ Cardinal first baseman Albert Pujols posted the ballpark's first three-homer game on April 16, 2006.

---

# St. Paul, Minnesota

## *Fort Street Grounds*

**AKA**

West Seventh Street Park

**OCCUPANT**

UA St. Paul Saints 1884

**LOCATION**

Left Field (W) Oneida St, Third Base (S) Short Line (later Chicago, Minneapolis, St. Paul, and Peoria RR) tracks, First Base (E) Duke St, Right Field (N) St. Clair Ave, (NW) Fort St (later West Seventh St); across the Mississippi River from downtown St. Paul, on what is called the West Side, even though it is south, not west of downtown.

**CAPACITY**

1200, plus standing room for another 1200

**PHENOMENA**

Although this was their home park, the Saints actually played all their games on the road during their brief September 27–October 13, 1884, stay in the major leagues. Opened June 9, 1884.

---

# St. Petersburg, Florida

## *Tropicana Field*

**AKA**

Florida Suncoast Dome March 3, 1990–August 5, 1993; Thunderdome August 5, 1993–October 4, 1996; the Trop

**ARCHITECT**

HOK Sport

**OCCUPANT**

AL Tampa Bay Devil Rays March 31, 1998, to date

**LOCATION**

Left Field (N) Central (later First) Ave South, Third Base (W) 16th St North, First Base (S) Dunmore (later Fourth) Ave South, Right Field (E) 10th St South

**DIMENSIONS**

Left Field: 315
Power Alleys: 359.5 (1998 actual), 370 (1998 marked), 370 (1999 actual and marked)
Deepest Left Center: 415 (1998), 410 (1999)
Center Field: 407 (1998), 404 (1999)
Deepest Right Center: 409 (1998), 404 (1999)

"The Trop" is the first park in more than 20 years to have artificial turf and all-dirt base paths. The dome is tilted toward the outfield, resulting in the catwalks being lower there. The upper catwalks, rings A and B, are in play and balls bouncing off them can be caught for outs or drop for base hits. Rings C and D are out of play.

Right Field: 322

Backstop: 50

Dome apex: 225 (above Second Base), 85 (above Center Field wall)

Foul Territory: small

### FENCES

Left and Right Fields: 9.5 (1998), 11.42 (1999)

Center Field: 9.5 (1998), 9.33 (1999)

### SURFACE

AstroTurf-12 with dirt infield 1998–99; FieldTurf with dirt infield 2000 to date

### FORMER USE

NHL hockey rink hosting the Tampa Bay Lightning

### CAPACITY

45,000 (1998), 43,772 (2003), 41,315 (2005)

### PHENOMENA

Opened March 3, 1990, in attempt to lure a major league team. White Sox nearly came in 1990. Giants announced in September 1992 press conference they would move here; the deal later fell through. Several other teams used the threat of a move to St. Petersburg as leverage with their own hometown to get new stadiums. ♦ Patterned after Ebbets Field's outfield dimensions. ♦ Main entrance on east side of stadium features an Ebbets Field–style rotunda. ♦ Scene of furious rhubarbs over ground rules concerning whether balls which hit the four catwalks which hang over the outfield were homers or in play. On May 27, 1998, the league approved a ground rule change making balls hitting the two lower catwalks automatic home runs. On September 19, 2000, in the top of the ninth, Mariner Jay Buhner hit a ball that hit the catwalk in the "B" ring, 250 feet from the plate and 150 feet high. It never came down, and Buhner was given a double. ♦ Restaurant in straightaway center field features a specially designed dark film that gives batters an ideal background for seeing a pitch coming off the mound. ♦ Translucent roof is illuminated orange on nights when Devil Rays win. ♦ Has hosted NHL Lightning ice hockey 1993–96, as well as 5-K runs, basketball, equestrian events, figure skating, football, gymnastics, karate, monster truck, motorcycle, and mud bog racing, ping pong, soccer, sprint car racing, tennis, and weightlifting.

# Salisbury, Maryland

## *Gordy Park*

### OCCUPANT
Neutral site used by NNL Baltimore Elite Giants July 15, 1941

### PHENOMENA
Philadelphia Stars were the opposing team.

# San Diego, California

## *Qualcomm Stadium*

### AKA
San Diego Stadium 1967–79, San Diego-Jack Murphy Stadium 1980, Jack Murphy Stadium 1981–May 20, 1997, Qualcomm Stadium at Jack Murphy Field May 20, 1997, to date, the Murph, the Q

### ARCHITECT
Gary Allen of Frank L. Hope & Associates

### OCCUPANT
NL San Diego Padres April 8, 1969–September 28, 2003

### LOCATION
Left Field (NE/N) 9449 Friars Rd (running from W/SW to E/NE) and Village Dr (running from S/SE to N/NW); Third Base (NW/W) Stadium Way, then

San Diego's Qualcomm Stadium was previously named for sports editor Jack Murphy, who campaigned in the 1960s for a new facility to house the NFL Chargers and a baseball expansion team. Murphy was the brother of Bob Murphy, announcer for the Mets from 1962 to 2003.

a rock quarry; First Base (SW/S) San Diego River, then Camino del Rio North and I-8; Right Field (SE/E) I-15; in Mission Valley

## DIMENSIONS

Left Field: 330 (1969), 327 (fence 1982), 329 (foul poles 1982)

Power Alleys: 375 (1969), 370 (1982)

Center Field: 420 (1969) 410 (1973), 420 (1978), 405 (1982)

Right Field: 330 (1969), 327 (fence 1982), 329 (foul poles 1982); 330 (1996)

Backstop: 80 (1969), 75 (1982)

## FENCES

Left and Right Fields: 17.5 (concrete 1969), 9 (line painted on concrete 1973), 18 (concrete 1974), 8.5 (canvas 1982)

Center Field: 17.5 (concrete 1969), 10 (wood 1973), 18 (concrete 1978), 8.5 (canvas 1982), one section in right center 9 (canvas 1982)

Right Field: 17.5 (scoreboard 1996)

## FORMER USE

San Diego River and marshy swampland

## CAPACITY

50,000, 47,634 (1969), 44,790 (1973), 47,634 (1974), 51,362 (1979), 48,443 (1980), 51,362 (1981), 58,671 (1984), 59,700 (1992), 47,750 (1995), 49,639 (1996), 59,772 (1997), 67,544 (1998), 66,307 (1999), 63,890 (2003)

## PHENOMENA

Opened for football August 20, 1967. ♦ Author organized first-ever night to honor a Negro Leagues veteran here in 1988. ♦ Chet Brewer of the Kansas City Brewers was wheeled to home plate by his wife, Tina, to accept the cheers of the crowd in July 1989 shortly before he passed away at the age of 89. ♦ Named for Jack Murphy, local sports editor who campaigned to bring major league baseball to San Diego. ♦ Noticeable lack of Spanish-speaking fans and Spanish-language ads in only major league ball-

park close to Mexican border was reversed in late 1990s. ♦ Foul poles sit two feet behind the fence, and one foot in front of the wall. ♦ Right-center scoreboard sits directly behind right center seats, and used to be so hot that fans there could feel the heat on their backs. ♦ Only park where bullpen dirt area touched the foul lines. ♦ Only park where a foul ball could be caught out of sight of all umpires and most players, in either bullpen near the foul poles. ♦ After 1981 season, plate was moved five feet back toward the backstop. ♦ Expanded during 1983 football season by adding seats in right and right-center, and then again during 1997 baseball season by completing upper decks in right and right-center in preparation for hosting the Super Bowl. ♦ Ivy put on center field fence in 1980 was removed in 1997. ♦ Twenty-foot-wide black batter's eye section on both center field wall and fence July–October 1982.

## *PETCO Park*

## ARCHITECTS

HOK Sport, Antoine Predock

## OCCUPANT

NL San Diego Padres April 8, 2004, to date

## LOCATION

Center Field (N) J St; Third Base (W) 7th Ave; Home Plate (S) Park Blvd, railroad tracks; First Base (E) 10th Ave; adjacent to San Diego Convention Center

## SURFACE

Bull's Eye Bermuda grass

## DIMENSIONS

Left Field: 334
Left Field Power Alley: 367
Left Center: 390
Left Center corner (just right of left center): 402
Center Field: 396

The official address of PETCO Park is 19 Tony Gwynn Way, in honor of the eight-time National League batting champion who wore that uniform number during his career with the Padres. In the first game there, March 11, 2004, the San Diego State Aztec baseball team, coached by Gwynn, set a new college attendance record of 40,106. In March 2006, Japan beat Cuba 10–6 at Petco to win the inaugural World Baseball Classic.

Right Center (at the kink): 411, 400 (2006 no longer any kink)

Right Field Power Alley: 394

Right Field notch: (front 358) (back 378)

Right Field: 322

Backstop: 44.58

## FENCES

Left Field to Center Field: 7.5

Right Center Scoreboard: 10

Right Field: 10 sloping down to 7.5 on first trapezoid, then 7.5, then 7.5 sloping up to 10 at the foul pole on second trapezoid

## CAPACITY

46,000, 42,445 (2005)

## PHENOMENA

Voters approved park funding in November 1998, but tax protesters managed to delay construction in October 2000, pushing back the park's opening from 2002 to 2004. ♦ Lawn seating for 2500 fans at Park at the Park, an elevated area behind center field fence. ♦ Design meant to recall Spanish missions, with jacaranda trees, palm court, water walls. ♦ The southeastern corner of a former iron and steel foundry, the 80-foot high Western Metals Supply Building (WMSB), built in 1909, constitutes the left field foul pole. ♦ The Padres deserve great credit and a thumbs up for including bleachers atop the WMSB and three levels of balconies for 500 fans who hover above the left fielder with an overhang of 10 feet. This is the only current overhang in a major league park, reminiscent of the Polo Grounds in left and Tiger Stadium in right. ◆ When opened for its first exhibition games on April 6, 2004, the right field foul line wall caused problems. It was just higher than knee-high and not clearly visible to right fielders going after foul fly balls. Two right fielders were injured running into the low wall and toppling over it into the stands. Before the opener on April 8, concrete and padding was added to make the wall two feet higher. ◆ Sandstone on the outside Spanish facade comes from India, and is meant to look like the Torrey Pines seaside bluffs. ◆ Home Plate Plaza has a waterfall, jacaranda and palm trees, and a coral tree. ◆ The Beach is located in right-center, where a playground of sand for kids sits between the fence and the bleachers. ◆ After criticism from left-handed batters—some of them Padres—the right-center dimension was reduced from 411 to 400 for the 2006 season.

# San Francisco, California

## *Seals Stadium*

**AKA**

Home Plate Mine

**OCCUPANT**

NL San Francisco Giants April 15, 1958–September 20, 1959

**LOCATION**

Left Field (E) Potrero Ave, Third Base (N) Alameda St, First Base (W) Bryant St; Right Field (S) 16th St, then Franklin Square Park

Seals Stadium was home to the Giants in their first two seasons in San Francisco. It was built in 1931 as the home park of two Pacific Coast League teams, the Seals and Missions. The Missions moved to Hollywood in 1938 and became the Stars. Joe DiMaggio played for the Seals from 1932–1935 before joining the Yankees in 1936.

## DIMENSIONS

Left Field: 340, 365 (1958), 361 (1959)

Left Center: 375 (1958), 364 (1959)

Deepest Left Center corner: 404

Center Field: 400, 410 (1958), 400 (1959)

Deepest Right Center corner: 415

Right Center just right of 415 mark where seats jutted out: 397

Right Center: 365

Right Field: 385, 365 (1940), 355 (1958), 350 (1959)

Backstop: 55.42

## FENCES

Left Field: 15 (5 concrete below 10 wire)

Center Field Scoreboard: 30.5

Right Field: 16 (5 concrete below 11 wire)

## CURRENT USE

San Francisco Auto Center and Safeway store; seats and lights are being used at Cheney Stadium in Tacoma, Washington

## CAPACITY

16,000, 18,600 (1932), 20,700 (1933), 25,000 (1938), 23,601 (1939), 20,700 (1941), 18,500 (1946), 22,500 (1947), 22,900 (1958), 23,750 (1959)

## PHENOMENA

Opened April 7, 1931. ♦ Original deed for the land under the park was listed as "Home Plate Mine." ♦ Stiff winds blew from right to left. ♦ Nearby Hamms Brewery still standing. ♦ Torn down November 1959. ♦ Had no warning track.

# Candlestick Park

## AKA

3Com Park April 12, 1996–January 1, 2002, 49ers Stadium January 1, 2002–2004, Monster Park 2004–2008, Candlestick Park from 2008 as long as it stands by vote of the citizens of San Francisco, the Stick, Maury's Lake, Cave of the Winds, Wind Tunnel, Croix de Candlestick, North Pole

## ARCHITECT

John Bolles

## OCCUPANT

NL San Francisco Giants April 12, 1960–September 30, 1999

## LOCATION

Left Field (NW) Gilman Ave (later Giants Dr); Third Base (SW) Harney Way (running from SW to NE) and Jamestown Ave (running from N/NW to S/SE), then Bay View Hill; First Base (SE) Jamestown Ave (running from W to E), then Candlestick Point and Candlestick Cove, which is part of San Francisco Bay; Right Field (NE) Hunters Point, then Hunters Point Expressway/State Route 1 and San Francisco Bay; Candlestick Point's rock outcroppings were leveled to fill in water for parking lots

## DIMENSIONS

Left Field: 330, 335 (1968)

Left Center: 397, 365 (1961)

Center Field: 420, 410 (1961), 400 (1982)

Right Center: 397, 365 (1961)

Right Field: 330, 335 (1968), 330 (1991), 328 (1993)

Backstop: 73, 70 (1961), 55 (1975), 65 (1982), 66 (1985)

Foul Territory: very large

## FENCES

10 (wire); 8 (wire 1972); 12 (6 canvas below 6 plexiglass 1975); 9 (6 canvas below 3 plexiglass 1982); 9 (wire 1984), 9.5 (fence posts 1984); 8 (canvas 1993)

## SURFACE

Grass 1960–69, carpet 1970–78, bluegrass 1979 to date

## CURRENT USE

NFL 49ers football

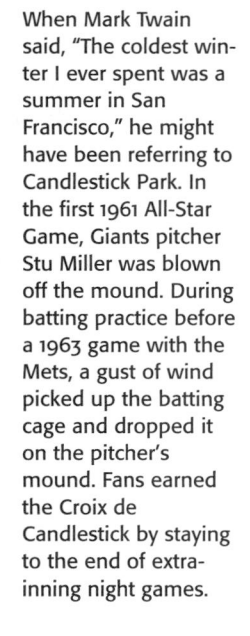

When Mark Twain said, "The coldest winter I ever spent was a summer in San Francisco," he might have been referring to Candlestick Park. In the first 1961 All-Star Game, Giants pitcher Stu Miller was blown off the mound. During batting practice before a 1963 game with the Mets, a gust of wind picked up the batting cage and dropped it on the pitcher's mound. Fans earned the Croix de Candlestick by staying to the end of extra-inning night games.

## CAPACITY

43,765, 42,553 (1961), 58,000 (1972), 59,080 (1975), 58,000 (1976), 62,000 (1989), 58,000 (1993), 63,000 (1995), 62,000 (1997), 63,000 (1999)

## PHENOMENA

Named for the candlestick bird, a curlew wader that was hunted almost to extinction, according to ornithologist Henry Betten, and for jagged rocks and trees rising from tidelands like giant candlesticks. ♦ Many fans arrived by boat in 1960s. ♦ Was the only hot-water-heated open-air stadium in the majors. ♦ Bay View Hill overlooked park from behind third base. ♦ Before bleachers were enclosed, so many fans would stream out of bleachers in right-center when Mays and McCovey batted and crowd up against flimsy cyclone fence that a white line was painted on the asphalt 20 feet behind the fence. Fans had to stand behind this line. ♦ In 1984, the San Francisco Crab, major league baseball's craziest-ever mascot, roamed the stands here. According to then Astros GM Al Rosen, who served on Okinawa during World War II, "the beaches on Okinawa were safer than Candlestick when the Crab was around." ♦ Earthquake on October 17, 1989, postponed World Series game. ♦ Fifty-nine posts every 20 feet or so on the outfield fence caused strange bounces, their tips extended six inches above the nine foot wire fence. ♦ Wind, wind, and more wind! Before stadium was enclosed, wind roared in from left-center and out toward right-center. After being enclosed, wind became a swirling monster, just as strong as before. ♦ Giants' retired numbers on white baseballs on right field fence. ♦ Maury's Lake was the basepath between first and second. It was drenched before the game to make it very difficult for Dodger Maury Wills to steal second in the early 1960s. ♦ Umps protested location of foul poles being completely in fair territory in third inning of opening game April 12, 1960. ♦ Stu Miller was blown off the mound by the wind in the 1961 All-Star Game. ♦ Stadium was enlarged and fully enclosed in the winter of 1971–72 to house the 49ers. Architect John Bolles' boomerang-shaped concrete shell baffle behind the upper tier's last row of seats was intended to protect the park from wind; it didn't work. ♦ In the winter of 1978–79, the Giants ripped up their carpet and replaced it with grass. ♦ By far the coldest park in the majors, resulting in fewer home runs. ♦ Croix de Candlestick pin awarded to fans at conclusion of night extra-inning games because of extreme wind chill conditions. ♦ Beatles' last concert was here August 29, 1966.

## AT&T Park

### AKA

Pac Bell Park April 11, 2000–January 1, 2004; SBC Park January 2 2004–February 28, 2006

### ARCHITECT

HOK Sport

### OCCUPANT

NL San Francisco Giants April 11, 2000, to date

### LOCATION

Left Field (NE) Second St, Third Base (NW) King St, First Base (SW) Third St, Right Field (SE) McCovey Cove in China Basin, which is part of San Francisco Bay; the entire site is known as 24 Willie Mays Plaza

### DIMENSIONS

Left Field: 339
Left of Left Center: 364
Left Center: 378
Left of Dead Center Field: 404
Center Field: 399
Deepest Right Center: 421
Right Field at kink in wall—just left of straightaway RF: 365
Right Field: 309
Backstop: 48

### FENCES

Left Field: 8
Left Center: 8 sloping up to 11

Before the 2006 season, a replica of the Eddie Grant memorial was placed near an elevator on the left field side of AT&T Park, previously Pac Bell Park. The original granite monument, honoring the only major league player killed in WWI, had stood in center field at the Polo Grounds. McCovey Cove, landing spot of many home runs, is beyond the right field wall.

Center Field: 8
Right Field: 25

**SURFACE**

Sports Turf hybrid bluegrass

**CAPACITY**

40,930, 41,503 (2003), 41,584 (2005), 41,606 (2006)

**PHENOMENA**

Fans arrive via ferry boat, Muni Metro trolleys, Caltrain, and BART subway, and can watch for free from above the right field wall. ♦ High above the left field seats, there is a big baseball glove, 501 feet from the plate. ♦ Homers over the right field seats splash in McCovey Cove, setting off feverish rush by boaters to recover "splash" home run balls.

# San Juan, Puerto Rico

## *Estadio Hiram Bithorn*

**OCCUPANTS**

Neutral site used by AL Toronto Blue Jays April 1, 2001; Montreal Expos 22 games April 11–September 11, 2003; 22 games April 9–July 11, 2004

**DIMENSIONS**

Left Field: 315 (2001), 318 (2004)
Left Field Power Alley: 341 (2001), 375 (2004)
Left Center: 364 (2001), 388 (2004)
Center Field: 399 (2001), 404 (2004)
Right Center: 361 (2001), 386 (2004)
Right Field Power Alley: 339 (2001), 375 (2004)
Right Field: 313 (2001), 318 (2004)
Foul Territory: huge

**FENCES**

10 to 12

**SURFACE**

Grass (1962), Astro Turf (1995), Field Turf (2004)

**CAPACITY**

18,000

**PHENOMENA**

The first major league game played here, with the Blue Jays hosting the Rangers on April 1, 2001, was chaotic, as many fans that had purchased tickets were not allowed in when the police determined that the safe capacity of the ballpark had already been vastly exceeded. Apparently, way more than the official number of 19,891 fans somehow got into the park. The author and his son were two of the 4000 or so fans who never got in. ♦ Home of the Santurce Cangrejeros (Crabbers) of the Puerto Rican Winter League 1962 to date; also home to San Juan Senadores (Senators) some years. ♦ Opened in October 1962, replacing Estadio Sixto Escobar. ♦ Four flags above batters-eye background–Puerto Rico, USA, Canada, and San Juan. ♦ Scoreboard above the bleachers in right. ♦ Three national anthems–Canada, USA, then Puerto Rico. ♦ Food from Pizza Hut, KFC, Taco Bell. ♦ Fans dance to salsa music. ♦ Drinks are pina coladas and rum. ♦ Named for first Puerto Rican to play in the majors. Bithorn pitched four years for the Cubs and White Sox, beginning in 1942. ♦ Dimensions of the outfield were modified over the 2003–04 winter to approximate those in Montreal.

# Savannah, Georgia

## *Grayson Stadium*

**OCCUPANT**

Neutral site used by NAL Birmingham Black Barons 1940s

**LOCATION**

Center Field (S), Third Base (E), Home Plate (N), First Base (W)

**DIMENSIONS**

Left Field: 249 (1940), 290 (1950)
Center Field: 500 (1940), 415 (1950)
Right Field: 249 (1940), 320 (1950)

**FENCES**

Left Field Light Tower: 90

**CAPACITY**

7500 (1940)

**PHENOMENA**

The in-play 90-foot-tall light tower in left field was the second highest outfield obstruction ever. The highest was the 125-foot-high flag pole at Tiger Stadium.

# Seattle, Washington

## *Sicks' Stadium*

**AKA**

Sick's Stadium 1938–49 when it belonged to Mr. Sick; Sicks' Stadium after 1949, when it belonged to the entire Sick family; Sicks' Seattle Stadium

**OCCUPANT**

AL Seattle Pilots April 11–October 2, 1969

**LOCATION**

Left Field (E/NE) Empire (later Martin L. King Jr.) Way South, Third Base (N/NW) South Bayview St, First Base (W/SW) 2700 Rainier Ave South (running from NW to SE), Right Field (S/SE) South McClellan St

The first South Atlantic League game played with both black and white players took place at Grayson Stadium in Savannah, Georgia, on April 14, 1953, when the Savannah Indians hosted the Jacksonville Braves, a team that included a young Hank Aaron. The stadium was a neutral site for the NAL Birmingham Black Barons.

Sicks' Stadium opened in 1938 and was the second ballpark built on the site in Seattle. Dugdale Park, built there in 1913, burned down after a 4th of July celebration in 1932.

**DIMENSIONS**

Left Field: 325, 305 (1969)

Power Alleys: 345 (1969)

Corners just right and left of center: 405 (1969)

Center Field: 400, 402 (1969)

Right Field: 325, 320 (1969)

Backstop: 54

Foul Territory: very small

**FENCES**

Left Field and Right Field: 8 (3 concrete below 5 wire)

Center Field: 12.55 (3 concrete below 9.55 wire)

**FORMER USE**

Dugdale Park, minor league ballpark from 1913 until it burned down July 4, 1932

**CURRENT USE**

Lowe's Home Improvement, glass display case inside the store shows Rainiers' and Pilots' memorabilia

**CAPACITY**

11,000, 18,000 (April 11, 1969), 25,420 (June 20, 1969), 28,500 (August 15, 1969)

**PHENOMENA**

Opened June 15, 1938. ♦ Bleachers down left field line, just as at Forbes Field. Fans could see Mt. Rainier in the distance. ♦ On April 11, 1969, fans got a free view of the Pilots' Opening Day game by looking through numerous openings in the unfinished left field fence. Seven thousand seats were unfinished and 700 fans had to wait an hour before they could take their seats while the carpenters finished their work. ♦ Insufficient water pressure if crowd was large. ♦ When demolished in 1979, after minor league play in the 1970s, the lights were moved to Washington State University's Buck Bailey Field in Pullman.

## *Kingdome*

**AKA**

King County Stadium, the Tomb, Puget Puke

**ARCHITECTS**

Naramore Bain Brady & Johanson; Skilling Engineers; Osborn Engineering; Praeger Kavanaugh Waterbury

**OCCUPANT**

AL Seattle Mariners April 6, 1977–June 27, 1999

**LOCATION**

Left Field (N) 201 South King St, Third Base (W) 589 Occidental Ave South (running from N to S) and Railroad Way South (running from NW to SE), First

Base (S) South Royal Brougham Way; Right Field (E) Burlington Northern RR/Amtrak RR tracks, then Fourth Ave South and I-5

### DIMENSIONS

Left Field: 315, 316 (marked 1978), 314 (actual 1978), 324 (1990), 331 (1991)

Left Field Power Alley: 357 (1981)

Left Center: 375, 365 (1978), 372 (1990), 376 (1991)

Deep Left Center: 385 (1990), 389 (1991)

Center Field: 405, 410 (1978), 405 (1981), 410 (1986), 405 (1991)

Deep Right Center: 375 (1990), 380 (1991)

Right Center: 375, 365 (1978), 362 (1990)

Right Field Power Alley: 357 (1981)

Right Field: 315, 316 (1978), 314 (1990), 312 (1991)

Speakers in Left (3), Left Center, and Center 110, 133.5 (1981); 11 other speakers 130

Backstop: 63

Apex of dome: 250

Foul Territory: large

### FENCES

Left Field: 11.5 (wood), 17.5 (6 plexiglass over wood 1988), 11.5 (wood 1990), 8.5 (wood 1994)

Center Field: 11.5 (wood)

Right Field: 11.5 (wood), 23.25 (wood 1982), 11.5 (wood 1988)

### SURFACE

AstroTurf

### CAPACITY

59,059, 57,748 (1991), 59,702 (1992), 58,100 (1996), 59,084 (1999)

### PHENOMENA

Large American flag flew above concrete dome. ◆

The first baseball sellout in Kingdome history didn't come until opening night, 1990, in the team's 14th season. That year, on August 31, Mariners' fans turned out to see Ken Griffey and Ken Griffey, Jr. start their first game together.

23-foot mini-Green Monster in right and right-center called the Walla Walla. ♦ Carpet was rolled out by the Rhinoceros machine, and smoothed by the Grasshopper machine after it had been zipped together. ♦ Domed roof looked from below as if it were made of thousands of bricks. ♦ Sicks' Stadium home plate on display in Royal Brougham trophy case. ♦ In winter of 1980–81, the three speakers above left, left-center, and center were raised from 102 to 133.5 feet to reduce chances of their being hit again. ♦ Two foul balls went up but never came down. Ruppert Jones of Mariners hit a foul ball, August 4, 1979, that stuck in the speaker above the first base dugout, thus disproving the old adage of physics that what goes up must come down. On May 20, 1983, Ricky Nelson of the Brewers did the same. By some arcane logic, both fly balls were ruled strikes. ♦ Four foul balls bounced off speakers and were caught for outs: August 3, 1979, caught by A's pitcher Matt Keough; September 3, 1979, caught by Mariners' first baseman; May 19, 1980, caught by Mariners' first baseman; April 25, 1985, caught by Mariners' pitcher Mark Langston. ♦ Other foul balls bounced off Supersonics basketball speakers above first base and the basketball scoreboard above and behind home plate, without being caught. One fair ball bounced off a roof support wire and remained in play on April 11, 1985. A ball hit by Dave Kingman of the A's was caught for an out in deep left: it would have been a home run. One fair ball struck the right field speaker. Ken Phelps of the Mariners hit a tape-measure blast on August 13, 1987, but the ball landed foul. Seven fair balls bounced off speakers and remained in play. ♦ Called the Tomb by visiting sportswriters because it was sickeningly gray concrete and quiet in the 1980s. ♦ Roof's hanging red, white, and blue streamers tangled up infield flies and deflected them. ♦ U.S.S. *Mariner* was a huge yellow sailing ship behind the center-field fence which fired a cannon after every Mariner homer. ♦ Forty-two air-conditioning units (16 in fair territory, 26 in foul territory, eight ducts in each unit) blew air in toward the field, which meant fewer home runs in what would have normally been a "Homer Dome" because of the

short 357-foot power alleys. ♦ Outfield distances marked on fences in both feet and fathoms 1977–80 (1 fathom equals 6 feet). ♦ Third deck highest at third base and in right field. ♦ AL East and AL West standings posted on right field third-deck facade. ♦ Plate moved 10 feet toward first base dugout in 1990 in a change that altered outfield distances. ♦ New classic "in-play" 123-foot by 11½-foot scoreboard placed on right field wall in 1990 in dramatic face-lift. It matched the Metrodome's right field wall as the second-highest wall in the major leagues (23 feet) after Boston's Green Monster at Fenway Park (37 feet). ♦ Scene of Funny Nose-Eye Glasses night and Buhner Buzz Night. ♦ Two and a half hours before an Orioles vs. Mariners game on July 19, 1994, four 26-pound pieces of acoustic ceiling tile crashed down into the seats between third base and home plate, very near where Cal Ripken Jr. was being interviewed. Nobody was injured, but the Mariners were forced to play all their home games on the road through August 11, when the players strike wiped out the rest of the season. ♦ Imploded March 26, 2000.

## Safeco Field

**ARCHITECT**
NBBJ

**OCCUPANT**
AL Seattle Mariners July 15, 1999, to date

**LOCATION**
Left Field (N) Royal Brougham Way, then Kingdome; Third Base (W) 1250 First Ave South; First Base (S) South Atlantic St; Right Field (E) Third Ave South

**DIMENSIONS**
Left Field: 331
Left Field Power Alley: 373 (2003)
Left Center: 390, 388 (2003)
Center Field: 405

A typical game at Safeco Field is interrupted by several loud train whistles from passing locomotives on the tracks beyond the right field wall. Safeco is unique among domed stadiums in that its sides are open; thus, during a rainstorm, though the field stays dry since the roof is covered, wind and rain blow through the open sides.

Right Center: 386, 387 (2000), 385 (2003)
Right Field Power Alley: 371 (2003)
Right Field: 326
Roof apex: 215

**FENCES**

All: 8

**CAPACITY**

46,621, 47,772 (2003), 47,447 (2005)

**PHENOMENA**

Along with the BOB in Phoenix, Minute Maid Park in Houston, Miller Park in Milwaukee, and Sky-Dome in Toronto, Safeco has a retractable roof. ♦ Hand-operated scoreboard in left. ♦ Even when the roof covers the field, the sides of the park are refreshingly open. ♦ If there is a rainstorm occurring while the game is in progress, players and fans are very aware of the storm because the winds and the sound of rain come right in since the sides are open, even while the field is being protected from the rain. ♦ When it is rainy, the ball carries very well to right-center, but not to left-center.

## Smithfield, North Carolina

### *Smithfield Stadium*

**OCCUPANT**

Neutral site used by NAL Raleigh Tigers May 1961

## Springfield, Illinois

### *Lanphier Park*

**AKA**

Robin Roberts Stadium

**OCCUPANT**

Neutral site used by NAL Cincinnati Clowns one game in May 1943

For many years Lanphier Park hosted Frontier League and Midwest League games, and it was the neutral site for one game played by the NAL Cincinnati Clowns in 1943. The park was renamed for native son, Robin Roberts, a Hall-of-Fame pitcher.

**LOCATION**

Left Field (N) Converse Ave, Third Base (W) Lanphier High School Football Stadium, First Base (S) Grand Ave, Right Field (E) 15th St

**DIMENSIONS**

Foul Lines: 320 (1940)
Center Field: 400 (1940), 410 (1950)

**CAPACITY**

4500

# Springfield, Massachusetts

## *Hampden Park Race Track*

**AKA**

Springfield Track

**OCCUPANTS**

Neutral site used by NA Middletown Mansfields July 23, 1872; by NA Boston Red Stockings July 16, 1873, and May 14, 1875

**LOCATION**

South end of mile-long oval bicycle race track, running along NW-SE axis

# Springfield, Ohio

## *Municipal Stadium*

**OCCUPANT**

Neutral site used by NNL Cincinnati Clowns May 25, 1943

**LOCATION**

Center Field (N), Third Base (W), Home Plate (S), First Base (E)

**DIMENSIONS**

Foul Lines: 340 (1940)
Center Field: 340 (1940)

**CAPACITY**

3500 (1940)

# Springwells, Michigan

## *Burns Park*

**AKA**

West End Park

**OCCUPANT**

AL Detroit Tigers Sundays only for 23 games April 28, 1901–September 7, 1902

**LOCATION**

(N) RR tracks, (S) Dix Ave; also Vernon St, Waterman St, Livernois Ave; near the stockyards, just outside what was then the western city limits of Detroit; today Waterman St and Springwells St intersect the site in Springwells Township

**CAPACITY**

6000

**CURRENT USE**

Shipping container storage area

**PHENOMENA**

Built before the 1900 season and used only for Sunday games. ♦ Park was owned by and named after the Tigers owner (1900–01) James D. Burns. ♦ Infield reported to be very rough. ♦ A good hitters' park, especially for home runs. In 1901–02 the Tigers hit .354 and .322 at Burns Park vs. .270 and .245 at all other (home and road) parks. In the 23 games played here in 1901–02, the Tigers and their opponents accounted for 19 home runs—a rate of 0.83 home runs per game. In contrast, at Bennett Park in the same two seasons, the Tigers and their opponents hit home runs at less than one-third that rate (0.24 per game). Based on the home run data (all but one of the known home runs were over the left field fence), left field was likely not more than 300 ft down the line—similar to Washington's American League Park (I) in the same time period.

# Sumter, South Carolina

## *Riley Park*

**OCCUPANT**

Neutral site used by NAL Raleigh Tigers April 30, 1961

**LOCATION**

615 Church St, a half mile north of Broad St/US Route 521

**DIMENSIONS**

Left Field: 337
Center Field: 372
Right Field: 338

**CAPACITY**

4000

# Syracuse, New York

*See also* Geddes, New York; Phoenix, New York

## *Star Park (I)*

**AKA**

Newell Park

**OCCUPANTS**

NL Syracuse Stars May 28–September 10, 1879; neutral site used by NL Buffalo Bisons June 27, 1885, October 8, 1885 (but rained out)

**LOCATION**

(N) Croton St (later East Raynor Ave), (W) South Salina St

## Star Park (II)

**OCCUPANT**

AA Syracuse Stars April 28–October 6, 1890

**LOCATION**

(N) Temple St, (W) Oneida St, (S) West Taylor St, (E) Delaware, Lackawanna, and Western RR tracks, (NE) South Salina St; also South Clinton St

**CURRENT USE**

Mann and Hunter Lumber Company plant, now vacant

**PHENOMENA**

Built in 1886.

## Iron Pier

**OCCUPANT**

AA Syracuse Stars August 3, 1890

**LOCATION**

On the shores of Onondaga Lake, within the Syracuse city limits

**PHENOMENA**

After police banned Sunday baseball at Three Rivers Park, the Stars scheduled their Sunday, August 3, 1890, game here. The other team, the Louisville Colonels, did not show up because the police had stated they would not allow the game to be played. But the umpires and the Stars did show up, so the Stars won by forfeit. ♦ Iron Pier was an amusement park resort.

## MacArthur Stadium

**AKA**

Municipal Stadium 1934–June 10, 1942

**OCCUPANT**

Neutral site used by NNL New York Black Yankees 1940s

On June 6, 1996 the Syracuse Chiefs paid tribute to the Negro Baseball Leagues at MacArthur Stadium before a Chiefs game with the Rochester Red Wings, as both teams wore old Negro League uniforms. The stadium was a neutral site for the NNL New York Black Yankees in the 1940s.

**LOCATION**

Left Field (N), Third Base (W), First Base (S) East Hiawatha Blvd; Right Field (E); also Second St North, LeMoyne Park

**DIMENSIONS**

Foul Lines: 335 (1934), 320 (1946)
Center Field: 464 (1934), 455 (1940), 434 (1946)

**FENCES**

Right Center Scoreboard: 24, rest of fence 8 (metal over wood)

**CAPACITY**

10,100 (1940), 8000 (1975), 10,500 (1985)

**PHENOMENA**

Built in 1934. ♦ Renamed June 11, 1942, for General Douglas MacArthur. ♦ Fire on May 15, 1969, destroyed the seats behind home plate, and the park existed for several years with no seats behind the plate until the grandstand was finally rebuilt.

# Tallahassee, Florida

## *Centennial Field*

**OCCUPANT**

Neutral site used by NAL Kansas City Monarchs 1957–61

**LOCATION**

Center Field (SE), Third Base (NE), Home Plate (NW), First Base (SW)

**DIMENSIONS**

Left Field: 353 (1940)
Center Field: 450 (1940)
Right Field: 382 (1940)

**CAPACITY**

1800 (1940)

**PHENOMENA**

Opened in 1924. ♦ It was enclosed with a high wooden fence in 1928, and the grandstand was built in 1935 by the WPA. ♦ The grandstand started at first base and wrapped around home plate, but then stopped about 20 feet up the third base line. Behind third base, instead of a grandstand, there was a flagpole and then a large wooden barracks-like building, also built by the WPA.

# Tokyo, Japan

## *Big Egg*

**AKA**

Tokyo Dome, Tokyo Kyujyo

**OCCUPANTS**

Neutral site used by NL New York Mets March 29, 2000; by NL Chicago Cubs March 30, 2000; by AL Tampa Bay Devil Rays March 30–31, 2004

**LOCATION**

Left Field (W) Koishikawa Korakuen Park, JR Railroad Suidobashi Station; Third Base (S) Sotobori Street, Toei-Mita Subway Suidobashi Station, Tokyo Dome Hotel; First Base (E) Hakusan Street, Marunouchi Subway Korakuen Station; Right Field (N) Route 434; 1-3-61 Koraku 1-chome Bunkyo-ku

**DIMENSIONS**

Foul Lines: 328
Power Alleys: 361
Center Field: 400
Dome: above second base 202.34; above outfield walls 184.3

The Big Egg was the first domed stadium in Japan. The multi-purpose facility was modeled after the Metrodome in Minneapolis, and like it, the roof is supported by air.

**FENCES**

13

**SURFACE**

Ugly Astroturf

**CAPACITY**

56,000, 55,000 (1995)

**PHENOMENA**

Opened March 17, 1988. ♦ Best ballpark name in baseball. Name of this domed stadium comes from the fact that it appears from overhead and from a distance to look like a big egg. ♦ Crowds led by the *oendan* or cheerleaders, who wave flags and bang drums and sing songs, just as at American football games. ♦ Used during the regular season by the Yomiuri Giants for all their home games in the Central League, and by the Nippon Ham Fighters for about ten of their home games in the Pacific League. ♦ Just to the right of Gate 21 is the entrance to the Japan Baseball Hall of Fame. ♦ Horrible multiuse facility; you always see soccer or football lines painted on the carpet.

---

# Toledo, Ohio

## *League Park*

**OCCUPANT**

AA Toledo Blue Stockings May 14–September 23, 1884

**LOCATION**

(NE) Jefferson Ave, (NW) 15th St, (SW) Monroe St, (SE) 13th St

**PHENOMENA**

Cap Anson threatened to pull his Chicago team

from the field one day here if Blue Stockings player Fleet Walker was not removed by the Blue Stockings, yelling, "Get that nigger off the field." Toledo's management replied that if Anson refused to play with Walker on the field, then the Blue Stockings would pull nine fans out of the stands to play against, and that regardless, the game would go on. Anson backed down and played, but he was influential later in activities leading to the racial segregation of baseball.

## Tri-State Fair Grounds

**OCCUPANTS**

AA Toledo Blue Stockings September 13, 1884; neutral site used by NL Detroit October 5, 1885

**LOCATION**

(N) Frazier St (later Oakwood Ave), (W) Woodstock Ave (later Addington St), (S) Dorr St, (E) Ravensburg (later Upton) Ave

## Speranza Park

**OCCUPANT**

AA Toledo Maumees May 1–October 2, 1890

**FORMER USE**

Armory

**LOCATION**

(NE) Cherry St, (W) Franklin Ave, (S) Frederick St

## Armory Park

**AKA**

Military Park

**OCCUPANT**

Neutral site used by AL Detroit Tigers June 28 and August 16, 1903

**LOCATION**

Left Field (NE) Armory and Gas Tank, then Orange St; Third Base (NW) Speilbusch Ave; First Base (SW) Beech St, later called Jackson St; Right Field (SE) Ontario St; several blocks west of the Maumee River

**DIMENSIONS**

Left Field: 350
Center Field: 450
Right Field: 230
Backstop: 32

**FENCES**

Left Field: 60 (stone Armory wall)
Center Field and Right Field: 12 (wood)

**CURRENT USE**

Federal District Court House, Civic Center Mall

**CAPACITY**

330 (1897), 4500 (1898), 6900 (1906)

**PHENOMENA**

The 60-foot-high gothic brick Armory formed the left field wall, complete with hexagonal towers topped by turrets reminiscent of a medieval castle. This could have been called the Gray Monster, and was 23 feet taller than the Green Monster at Fenway Park. ♦ There was a steep five-foot incline extending for 75 feet in front of the center field wall. ♦ Because it was only 230 to right, balls hit over the fence in right field were doubles. ♦ Fire destroyed the third base grandstand July 9, 1903. ♦ Right field wall had this sign: Buckeye Paints, Colors, Varnishes. ♦ The fence in left-center detoured around the Gas Tank, which contained natural gas. ♦ Opened May 29, 1897.

♦    ♦    ♦

This photo is from opening day at Swayne Field, July 3, 1909, then a minor league park. It was used by several Negro League teams in the 1920s and 1930s.

## Swayne Field

**AKA**

Mud Hen Park

**OCCUPANTS**

NNL Toledo Tigers April–July 15, 1923; NAL Toledo Crawfords July–September 1939; neutral site used by NNL Pittsburgh Crawfords 1937

**LOCATION**

Left Field (NE) Council St, then Red Man Tobacco factory, coal piles; Third Base (NW) New York Central RR tracks; First Base (SW) Monroe St; Right Field (SE) Detroit Ave

**DIMENSIONS**

Left Field: 382, 354 (1940), 347 (1946)
Center Field: 505, 482 (1923), 448 (1938)
Right Field: 326, 327 (1923), 306 (1946)
Backstop: 72

**FENCES**

12 (concrete)

**CURRENT USE**

Shopping center

**CAPACITY**

11,800, 10,000 (1923), 14,800 (1928), 12,500 (1938)

**PHENOMENA**

Opened July 3, 1909, with an 18-inning game, the Mud Hens losing to Columbus, 12–11. ♦ Art Deco scoreboard topped by a white clock in left-center. ♦ Nicknamed Mud Hen Park for the coot birds that live in the swamps and marshes surrounding the ballpark. The mud hens have short wings and long legs, and were frequently mentioned in the TV show *M.A.S.H.* ♦ Sam Jethroe of the Negro Leagues was the only batter to ever hit a ball into the coal piles far beyond the left field fence. ♦ Any child returning a batting practice ball could receive a free bleacher seat to a future game.

♦ Fans could see the Red Man Tobacco factory and the Edison smokestack reading "Heat Light Power" beyond the fence in left-center. ♦ Torn down January 3, 1956, to make room for a Kroger grocery store.

---

# Toronto, Ontario, Canada

## *Exhibition Stadium*

### AKA

Prohibition Stadium April 7, 1977–July 30, 1982, Canadian National Exhibition (CNE), CNE Stadium

### ARCHITECTS

Marini & Morris

### OCCUPANT

AL Toronto Blue Jays April 7, 1977–May 28, 1989

### LOCATION

Center Field (N) Prince's Blvd, then Gardiner Expressway; Third Base (W) Ontario Blvd; Home Plate (S) Lake Shore Blvd, then Exhibition Plc and Lake Ontario; First Base (NE) New Brunswick Way, then CNE Amusement Park; across the street from the Hockey Hall of Fame

### DIMENSIONS

Foul Lines: 330

On a snowy opening day on April 7, 1977, Doug Ault hit two home runs in a 9–5 win over the Chicago White Sox before 44,649 freezing fans. Al Woods hit a pinch homer on the first pitch of his first major league at bat, just the 11th player in history to do so.

Power Alleys: 375
Center Field: 400
Backstop: 60, 65 (1989)

**FENCES**

12 (8 canvas below 4 wire)

**SURFACE**

Carpet

**CAPACITY**

25,303 (1959), 38,522 (1977), 43,737 (1978)

**PHENOMENA**

Opened in 1879 as the Canadian Exposition. ♦ Rebuilt in 1959 as a football stadium. ♦ First baseball game here, on April 7, 1977, vs. the White Sox, was the only major league game ever played with snow covering the entire field. The snow covered the field for the first three innings; for the rest of the game snow covered only the outfield carpet. The Zamboni machine, borrowed from Maple Leaf Gardens for this -10 degrees F. wind-chill day, ran over the infield between innings, but still could not keep the field free from snow during the first three innings. ♦ Half the football gridiron lay beyond the fence in right and right-center, just as it had at LA Memorial Coliseum. ♦ Nicknamed Prohibition Stadium from opening until July 30, 1982, first day beer sales were allowed. ♦ Sections J through T in distant left center, and Sections 1 through 5 far down the right field foul line were sold only for playoffs because they were such bad seats. ♦ Orioles forfeited to the Jays here on September 15, 1977, because a tarpaulin in the windy Orioles bullpen was being held down with bricks. ♦ Only game ever postponed for high winds was here. After six pitches, and then a 30-minute wind delay on April 30, 1984, the game was called off. ♦ Torn down February 1, 1999. ♦ The farthest most seat at the far right side of the football bleachers that ran from left to behind right-center, in the last row, was 820 feet from home plate, which is the farthest ever in a major league park. The farthest seat at the LA Coliseum was 710 feet. ♦ From the very beginning of Blue Jays home games here, Mascot B. J. Birdie roamed the stands. He continued at SkyDome through 2000.

## Rogers Centre

**AKA**

SkyDome June 5, 1989–February 2, 2005

**ARCHITECTS**

Rod Robbie and Michael Allen

**OCCUPANT**

AL Toronto Blue Jays June 5, 1989, to date

**LOCATION**

Center Field (NW) Canadian National (CN) RR tracks, then Front St West; Third Base (SW) Spadina Ave; Home Plate (SE) Bremner Blvd, then Lake Shore Blvd West and Gardiner Expressway; First Base (NE) CN Tower, then John St

**DIMENSIONS**

Foul Lines: 330, 328 (1990)
Power Alleys: 375
Left/Right Center: 390
Center Field: 400
Backstop: 60
Dome apex: 310

**FENCES**

All: 10 (canvas)

**FORMER USE**

Water-supply pumping station at second base

**SURFACE**

AstroTurf June 8, 1989–2004; FieldTurf 2005 to date. Toronto is the only major league city which has never seen a major league game played the way it was intended to be played—on grass

**CAPACITY**

50,516, 45,100 (2001), 50,516 (2003), 50,598 (2005)

**PHENOMENA**

Second highest dome. Fixed domes: Seattle's Kingdome 250, St. Pete's Tropicana Field 225, Houston's

The Rogers Centre, previously the SkyDome, has the world's first fully retractable roof, which is made up of four sections.

Astrodome 208, Tokyo's Big Egg 202.34; Minneapolis' Metrodome 186, Montreal's Stade Olympique 180. Retractable roofs: Milwaukee's Miller Park 330, Toronto's Rogers Centre 310, Houston's Minute Maid Park 242, Seattle's Safeco Field 215, Phoenix's Chase Field 200. ♦ The 400-foot sign in center is actually right of dead center. ♦ Stands 31 stories high (Astrodome was just 18). ♦ Jumbotron scoreboard is world's biggest video display board (115 by 33 feet). ♦ Hotel has 348 rooms, 70 with a view of (and by) the stadium. ♦ Fitness club boasts the world's largest indoor running track (2.2 laps per mile circuit) at the top of the stadium. ♦ First park to draw more than four million fans in a season (1991–93). ♦ When roof is opened, 91% of all seats are exposed to sky. ♦ Hard Rock Cafe in right-center. ♦ Jose Canseco became first player to hit a home run into the stadium's fifth deck with a memorable blast in game four of the 1989 ALCS. ♦ Site of first World Series games played outside United States. ♦ Two 30-pound roof tiles fell during a game on June 22, 1995, injuring seven fans. ♦ When they open up the roof, the home plate end is open, while the roof slides back into center field. ♦ The closed end of the stadium in center field serves as a wind scoop, causing downdrafts in the outfield which prevent home runs. ♦ April 12, 2001, game postponed when two of the three roof panels collided, sending roof siding and insulation debris crashing down into left field. Visiting Royals were taking batting practice, but nobody was hurt. ♦ August 29, 2004, game vs. Yankees delayed one hour 25 minutes by power failure. ♦ On three occasions spectators were provided auxiliary entertainment by patrons inside the hotel during a game.

# Trenton, New Jersey

## *Dunn Field*

**OCCUPANT**

Neutral site used by NNL Newark Eagles six games 1946

**DIMENSIONS**

Left Field: 385 (1940)
Center Field: 420 (1940)
Right Field: 375 (1940)

**CURRENT USE**

Abandoned supermarket

**CAPACITY**

5500 (1940), 3500 (1950)

**PHENOMENA**

Extremely poor lighting.

# Troy, New York

*See also* Lansingburgh, New York; Watervliet, New York

## *Putnam Grounds*

**AKA**

The Puts

**OCCUPANT**

NL Troy Trojans May 28–September 20, 1879

**LOCATION**

(N) Peoples Ave, (W) 15th St

# Wallace, North Carolina

## *American Legion Field*

**OCCUPANT**

Neutral site used by NAL Raleigh Tigers June 3, 1959, and May 21, 1961

# Warwick, Rhode Island

## *Rocky Point Park*

**OCCUPANT**

Neutral site used by NL Boston Beaneaters September 6, 1903

**LOCATION**

Just outside of Providence

# Washington, D.C.

## *Olympic Grounds*

**OCCUPANTS**

NA Washington Olympics May 4, 1871–May 24, 1872; NA Washington Nationals April 15–October 23, 1873; NA Washington Olympics April 26–June 8, 1875; neutral site used by NA Lord Baltimores May 14, 1873

**LOCATION**

(W) 17th St NW, (S) S St NW, (E) 16th St NW

**CAPACITY**

500

This early photograph shows Athletic Park in Washington, D.C., home of the Washington Nationals in 1884.

**PHENOMENA**

Restaurant under the grandstand. ♦ At the time they were played, the five NA games played by the 1871 NA Washington Nationals were official league games, and all were played here. The first game, on April 22, vs. the Olympics, was an away game for the Nationals. The last four, however, were Nationals home games, on April 29 vs. the Olympics, May 2 vs. Boston, June 1 vs. Troy, and June 27 vs. Cleveland. However, after they failed to pay their $10 league dues, the Nationals were thrown out of the league, and their games were removed from the standings in the middle of July 1871. The reason this is interesting is that if one views these five games as official league games, then the first major league baseball game ever played would be here on April 22, 1871, Washington Nationals at Washington Olympics-with the Olympics winning 36–12, rather than the Cleveland Forest Citys at Fort Wayne Kekiongas, May 4, 1871.

## National Grounds

**OCCUPANT**

NA Washington Nationals April 20–May 25, 1872

**LOCATION**

16th St, R St

## Athletic Park

**OCCUPANT**

AA Washington Nationals May 1–August 5, 1884

**LOCATION**

(N) S St NW, (S) T St NW, (E) Ninth St NW

## Capitol Grounds

**AKA**

Union Association Park

**OCCUPANT**

UA Washington Nationals April 18–September 25, 1884

**LOCATION**

Center field grounds of the US Capitol Building; (N) C St NE; (W) Delaware Ave NE; (S) B St (later Constitution Ave) NE (E) First St NE

**CURRENT USE**

US Senate underground garage, R. A. Taft Memorial Building

**CAPACITY**

6000

**PHENOMENA**

Right field very short, left field very distant.

## Swampoodle Grounds

**AKA**

Capital Park Grounds

**OCCUPANTS**

NL Washington Statesmen April 29, 1886–September 21, 1889; Temple Cup Series NL Detroit Wolverines vs. AA St. Louis Browns, October 21, 1887

**LOCATION**

Left Field (W) North Capitol St NE, then Baltimore and Ohio RR side track; Third Base (S) F St NE; First Base (E) Delaware Ave NE; Right Field (N) G St NE; also Massachusetts Ave; in the Swampoodle section of town

**CURRENT USE**

Infield and right field used to be the western section of the old Union Station National Visitors Center, which is now the Shops at Union Station (a shopping mall); left field used to be the old City Post Office, which is now a brewery/cafe

**CAPACITY**

6000

**PHENOMENA**

Distance to the left field wall was very short. Outfield walls were high, perhaps 20 feet or so.

## Boundary Field

**AKA**

National Park (I), Beyer's Seventh Street Park

**OCCUPANTS**

AA Washington Nationals April 13–October 5, 1891; NL Washington Senators April 16, 1892–October 14, 1899

**LOCATION**

(N) W St NW; (W) Georgia Ave Northwest; (S) U St NW; (E) Fifth St NW; also Seventh St NW; Florida Ave NW; the Boundary; same site as American League Park (II) and Griffith Stadium

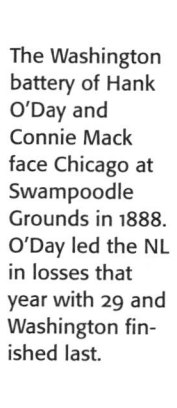

The Washington battery of Hank O'Day and Connie Mack face Chicago at Swampoodle Grounds in 1888. O'Day led the NL in losses that year with 29 and Washington finished last.

Standing room only for a Washington Senators game at American League Park I.

**CAPACITY**

6500

**PHENOMENA**

Built in the spring of 1891 by felling 125 large oak trees and filling in the 125 stump holes to make the infield; during the 1891 season some oak trees hung over the outfield fences. The trees interfered with outfielders' attempts to catch long fly balls, and some apparent home runs hit the trees and bounced back into play.

## *American League Park (I)*

**AKA**

National Park (II)

**OCCUPANT**

AL Washington Senators April 29, 1901–September 29, 1903

**LOCATION**

Left Field (NE) Neal St NE; Third Base (NW) Trinidad Ave NE; First Base (SW) Florida Ave NE; Right Field (SE) Bladensburg Rd (later H St) NE; also 12th (later 13th) St NE, 13 1/2th St (later 14th) St NE; near the old toll gate on Bladensburg Rd

**DIMENSIONS**

Left Field: 290

Left Center: 338
Center Field: 424
Center Field corner: 440
Right Center: 378
Right Field: 338
Backstop: 55

**PHENOMENA**

Home plate near center (north-south) of western edge of field; home plate-center field axis faced about due east. ♦ Behind short left field fence was a small pond–this led to the first AL splash home runs. ♦ Baseball's first public address announcer, E. Lawrence Phillips, gave the lineups by megaphone for the first time in 1902. ♦ Dimensions derived from newspaper stories of the left field dimension, the dimensions of the park site, and analysis of home run data. ♦ Grandstands were literally moved to American League Park (II) at Florida and Seventh for the 1904 season.

## *American League Park (II)*

**AKA**

National Park (III)

**OCCUPANT**

AL Washington Senators April 14, 1904–October 6, 1910

**LOCATION**

Same as Boundary Field and Griffith Stadium

**DIMENSIONS**

Left Field: 356
Left Center: 410
Center Field: 442
Right Center: 449
Right Field: 328
Backstop: 60

**PHENOMENA**

Diamond located in southwest corner of the field. ♦ The grounds crew had a dog house in the outfield near the flagpole where they stored the flag between games. One day they forgot to close the dog house door, and it just so happened that a Senator hit a ball over A's center fielder Socks Seybold's head and the ball rolled into the dog house. Socks got his head stuck in the house trying to recover the ball. Three minutes later, the Athletics got Socks out, but the batter had long crossed the plate with the first and only inside-the-dog-house-home run in major league history. ♦ First presidential opener in April 1910, with President William Howard Taft throwing out the first ball. ♦ In-play clubhouse located in right field. ♦ Dimensions based on a 1910 Sanborn fire insurance map. ♦ Burned down during spring training on March 17, 1911, in a fire caused by a plumber's blow lamp.

## *Griffith Stadium*

**AKA**

National Park (IV) 1911–21, Clark Griffith Park 1922

**ARCHITECT**

Osborn Engineering

**OCCUPANTS**

AL Washington Senators (I—now the Minnesota Twins) April 12, 1911–October 2, 1960; NEWL Washington Pilots 1932; NNL Washington Elite Giants 1936–37; NNL Washington Black Senators April–August 1938; NNL Washington-Homestead Grays (most home games) 1939–48; AL Washington

In 1945, the Washington Senators hit just one home run in cavernous Griffith Stadium, and that was an inside-the-park homer by Joe Kuhel. The center field wall detoured around three houses, making for crazy bounces in the outfield.

Senators (II—now the Texas Rangers) April 10–September 21, 1961; Negro World Series first game 1942, first and second games 1943, third game 1945

**LOCATION**

Left Field (E/NE) Larch St (later Fifth St NW); Third Base (N/NW) Howard University Medical Center, then W St NW; First Base (W/SW) J. Frank Kelley Lumber and Mill Works, then Georgia Ave (later Brightwood St, then Seventh St) NW; Right Field (S/SE) Spruce St (later U St NW); Florida Ave NW is nearby

**DIMENSIONS**

Left Field: 407, 424 (1921), 407 (1924), 358 (1926), 407 (1931), 402 (1936), 405 (1942), 375 (Opening Day 1947), 405 (remainder 1947), 402 (1948), 386 (1950), 408 (1951), 405 (1952), 388 (1954), 386 (1956), 350 (1957), 388 (1961)

Left of Left Center at corner: 383 (1931), 366 (1954), 360 (1956)

Left Center: 393, 372 (1950), 380 (1951)

Right of Left Center at bend in bleachers: 411, 409 (1942), 398 (1954), 383 (1955), 380 (1956)

Center Field: 421

Center Field corner to left of building protection wall: 423 (1926), 441 (1930), 422 (1931), 426 (1936), 420 (1942), 426 (1948), 420 (1950), 394 (1951), 420 (1952) 421 (1953), 426 (1954), 421 (1955), 426 (1961); inner tip of building protection wall 409 (1943), 408 (1953)

Deepest corner at right end of building protection wall: 457 (1953), 438 (1955), 401 (1956)

Right Center: 405, 419 (1914), 378 (1954), 372 (1955), 373 (1956)

Right Field: 280, 320 (1914), 326 (1921), 320 (actual 1924), 328 (marked 1924), 320 (1955)

Backstop: 61

**FENCES**

Left Field: 11.25 (foul pole to 408 mark concrete 1953), 12 (from 410 corner near left field foul pole to 408 mark just right of dead center 1954), 6.5 (wire and plywood in front of bullpen 1954—extended for 90 feet toward center field)

Center Field: 30 (concrete 408 mark to 457 mark 1953), 31 (concrete 408 mark to 457 mark 1954), 6 (wire and plywood 1956)

Right Center to left of scoreboard in front of bullpen: 4 (wood from 457 mark to 435 mark 1953), 10 (wood 1955), 4 (wood 1959)

Right Center Scoreboard: 41 (1946)

Right Field: 11 (wood 1911), 20 (concrete 1914), 31 (1925), 31 (concrete 1954)

**CURRENT USE**

Howard University Medical Center and College of Dentistry, 909 seats moved to Tinker Field in Orlando

**CAPACITY**

32,000 (1921), 30,171 (1936), 31,500 (1939), 29,473 (1940), 25,048 (1948), 35,000 (1952), 28,669 (1960), 27,550 (1961)

**PHENOMENA**

Diamond located in northwest corner of site. ♦ Ballpark property in 1911–13 did not include strip of land used for a warehouse behind the short right field fence. During the 1913 season, the Nationals purchased the land and built a high right field wall along Spruce St (later U St). ♦ Loudspeaker horn high on wall in center. Center field wall detoured around five houses and a huge tree in center, jutting into the field of play. ♦ For many years right field foul line was the grandstand wall for last 15 feet in front of foul pole, so there was no way to catch a foul ball there. ♦ It was downhill from the plate to first base, supposedly to help save a step for slow Washington batters. ♦ Senators owner Clark Griffith once said that Josh Gibson of the Negro Leagues hit more homers into the distant left field bleachers than the entire American League. ♦ The field was reoriented two degrees towards right field in 1921, with home plate moving 16 feet toward first base and two feet toward right field, resulting in the left field foul pole distance changing from 407 to 424. In 1924, the field was reoriented back the way it was in the first place. ♦ Josh Gibson (twice) and Mickey Mantle were the only batters to ever

Negro League Hall of Famer Josh Gibson rounds third base in a game at Griffith Stadium.

clear the left field bleachers. Yankees PR director Red Patterson promptly paced off Mantle's drive as having rolled to a stop 565 feet from the plate in Perry L. Cool's backyard at 434 Oakdale Street. It is often incorrectly stated that Mantle's ball traveled 565 feet in the air. ♦ Ballpark expert Ron Selter has done meticulous research on home runs hit at Griffith Stadium that seriously calls into question (there is no record of any home run hit over any interior fence in the 1920s) whether there was ever really an interior fence in left field that reduced the left field foul line distance from over 400 feet to 358 feet from 1926 to 1930, regardless of what the 1926 Spalding Guide says. ♦ Right field clock out of play. ♦ Ball rolling between top of scoreboard and bottom of the clock was in play; if it didn't come out, it was a homer; if it did, the outfielder could throw it back into play. ♦ Presidents

traditionally opened each season here by throwing out the first ball. ♦ Memorials honoring Walter Johnson and Clark Griffith stood outside the main entrance to the first base grandstand. The former now stands at Walter Johnson High School in Bethesda, Maryland; the latter at RFK Stadium. ♦ Height of National Bohemian beer bottle, above right-center scoreboard was 56 feet. ♦ Built after March 17, 1911, fire destroyed American League Park (II) on the same site. The park was ready for use only 26 days later on April 12, but was not completed until July 24. ♦ Double-decked in 1920 from the bases down to the foul poles with a roof higher than the original grandstand's second-deck roof. ♦ Temporary seats placed in front of left field bleachers for 1924 World Series. ♦ Senators forfeited to Red Sox when the grounds crew was too slow in putting on the tarp when it began to rain August 15, 1941. ◆ In 1954 the visitors bullpen was enclosed behind screen fence in left field corner in fair territory. ◆ Clark Calvin Griffith Memorial, dedicated by Vice President Nixon on August 8, 1956, was later moved to RFK Stadium. ◆ In 1956 all distances to outfield fences were remeasured, and it was discovered right field had lost eight feet over the years! ◆ Also in 1956, 10 rows of temporary seats were added in front of the left field bleacher section. ◆ Scene (along with Wrigley Field in LA) of 1958 *Damn Yankees* movie. ◆ Dimensions 1911–1925 based on 1911 Sanborn fire insurance map. ◆ Park demolished January 26–August 14, 1965.

### Standpipe Park

**OCCUPANT**

ECL Washington Potomacs 1924

**LOCATION**

16th St NW, Euclid St NW

### Robert F. Kennedy Stadium

**AKA**

DC Stadium 1962–68; RFK Stadium

**ARCHITECTS**

George A. Dahl, Osborn Engineering

**OCCUPANTS**

AL Washington Senators (II—now the Texas Rangers) April 9, 1962–September 30, 1971; NL Washington Nationals April 14, 2005, to date

**LOCATION**

Center Field (E) East Capitol St Bridge, then Anacostia River; Third Base (N) C St NE; Home Plate

Opening day in 1962 at District of Columbia Stadium, later renamed RFK Stadium. President John F. Kennedy threw out the first ball as a record Washington crowd of 42,143 saw Bennie Daniels stop Detroit with a 5-hit, 4–1 win.

(W) 22nd St NE (running north to south) and East Capitol St (running east to west); First Base (S) East Independence Ave

### DIMENSIONS

Left Field: 335, 260 (1982), 335 (2005)

Left Field Power Alley: 385, 381 (1963), 295 (1982), 380 (marked 2005) 395 (actual 2005)

Center Field: 410, 410 (marked 2005) 408 (actual 2005)

Right Field Power Alley: 385, 378 (1963), 380 (marked 2005) 395 (actual 2005)

Right Field: 335, 335 (2005)

Backstop: 60, 53.17 (2005)

### FENCES

7 (wire screen)

Left Field and Left Center: 24 (wood, only in 1987), 10 (canvas, 2005)

### CAPACITY

43,500, 45,016 (1971), 45,250 (2005)

### PHENOMENA

Looks like a wet straw hat or a waffle whose center stuck to the griddle because of its curved dipping roof. ♦ Many center field seats painted to indicate where Frank Howard's gigantic homers landed. ♦ During the 1962 season, parts of left field and left-center sank six feet due to leveling after the recent construction of the stadium. ♦ On September 30, 1971, in the last game played here before they moved to Texas, the Senators led the Yankees, 7–5, with two out in the ninth. The security guards had all left early in the game, and non-paying fans had been walking in all during the game, increasing the crowd from the paid of 14,460 to perhaps 25,000. After the second out in the top of the ninth, a very obese teenager ran out on the field, picked up first base, and ran off the field. As more and more fans poured out onto the field, without a first base, and with no security guards anywhere to be seen, the umpires forfeited the game to the Yankees, 9–0. ♦ Luke Appling homered over the short 260-foot left field fence off

Warren Spahn in the 1982 Old-timers Game here, the day Tony Gwynn debuted. ♦ Blue Monster (24-foot-high left field fence) used for preseason game April 5, 1987. ♦ Park is planned to be used for three years from 2005 through 2007 before a new stadium is ready for the 2008 season. ♦ Fly balls carry well down the lines, but not to the power alleys and center field.

## *New Nationals Ballpark*

### PROJECTED OPENING

April 2008

### ARCHITECTS

HOK Sport; Devrouax & Purnell Architects-Planners

### OCCUPANT

NL Washington Nationals April 2008 onwards

### LOCATION

Left Field (N) N St Southeast; Third Base (W) South Capitol St Southeast; First Base (S) Potomac Ave Southeast; Right Field (E) First St Southeast; by the Anacostia River in the southeast part of the city, a mile south of the U.S. Capitol Building

### DIMENSIONS

Left Field: 332

Left Center: 377

Center Field: 409

Right Center: 370

Right Field: 335

### FENCES

Left Field: 8

Center Field: 12

Right Field: 8

### CAPACITY

41,000

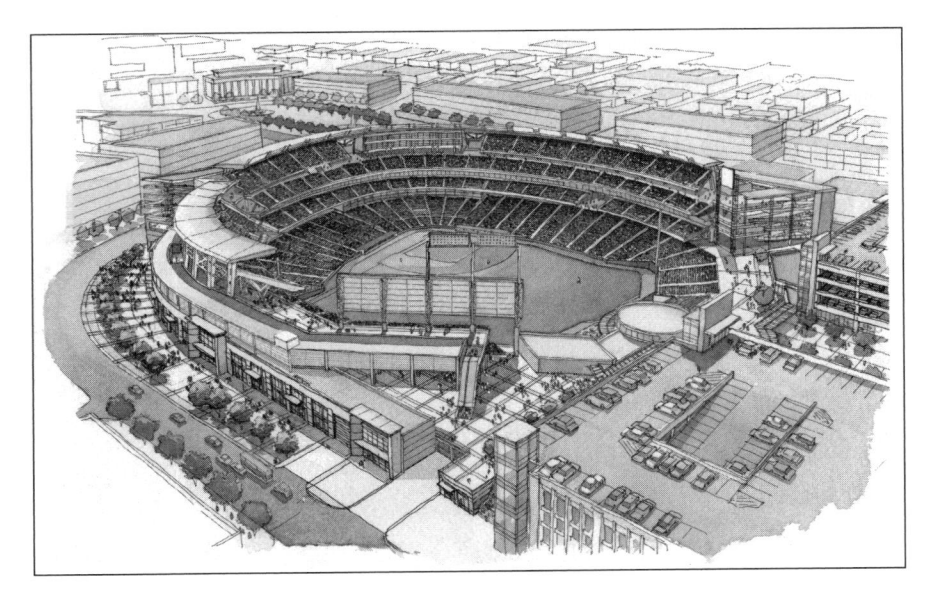

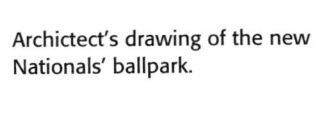

Archictect's drawing of the new Nationals' ballpark.

### PHENOMENA

Groundbreaking took place on May 4, 2006. ♦ Fans in the upper seating bowl will be able to see the U.S. Capitol building only a mile away. Seating decks are arranged to create a variety of distinct seating neighborhoods, each with its own identity and viewing experience. ♦ With a beautiful setting along the Anacostia River in Southeast Washington, the new park will be reflective of its surroundings. The glass, concrete, and steel structure allows both views from street level into the playing field, and also views from inside the park looking out to the monuments and river beyond. The structure will be crowned by a blade-like sunscreen structure, which will be visible from all across the city, and when illuminated at night will signal the ballpark's drama.

---

# Watervliet, New York

## *Troy Ball Club Grounds*

### AKA

West Troy Grounds

### OCCUPANT

NL Troy Trojans May 20–August 26, 1882

### LOCATION

(W) D and H RR tracks, (S) Genesee (later 19th) St

---

# Weehawken, New Jersey

## *Monitor Grounds*

### AKA

Monitor Park

### OCCUPANTS

Neutral site used by AA Brooklyn Trolley Dodgers September 4, 1887; by AA New York Mets September 11, 1887

### LOCATION

Three blocks from where Miller Stadium stands now in Hudson County

♦   ♦   ♦

## West New York, New Jersey

### *West New York Field Club Grounds*

**AKA**

Weehawken Cricket Grounds

**OCCUPANTS**

Neutral site used by NL New York Giants September 11, 1898; June 4, July 16, August 13, and September 17, 1899; by NL Brooklyn Bridegrooms September 18 and October 2, 1898

## Westport, Maryland

### *Westport Stadium*

**AKA**

Westport Race Track, Westport Park

**OCCUPANT**

NAL Baltimore Elite Giants 1950–51

**LOCATION**

Westport Blvd, Russell St, Bush St

**CURRENT USE**

The concrete foundation for the stock car racetrack can still be seen in a field behind a shopping center on the site

◆   ◆   ◆

## Wheeling, West Virginia

### *Island Grounds*

**AKA**

Wheeling Grounds

**OCCUPANT**

Neutral site used by NL Pittsburg Alleghenies September 22, 1890 (no h in Pittsburg back then, it was added later, in the 1900s)

**LOCATION**

Wheeling Island, in Ohio River between Wheeling, West Virginia, and Bridgeport, Ohio

**PHENOMENA**

The grass was so high on September 22, 1890, that Mike Tiernan's hit was lost in the outfield and he got an inside-the-park homer. The Giants defeated the Alleghenies, with 1500 fans in attendance. Game was moved here because Giants captain Jack Glasscock was born (and died) in Wheeling.

## Whiteville, North Carolina

### *Legion Field*

**AKA**

League Field

**OCCUPANT**

Neutral site used by NAL Raleigh Tigers June 1, 1959

**DIMENSIONS**

Left Field: 340

Left Center: 350
Center Field: 340
Right Center: 365
Right Field: 350

**FENCES**

10 (wood)

**CAPACITY**

2750 (1959), 700 (2004)

# Wilmington, Delaware

### *Union Street Park*

**AKA**

Union Street Ball Grounds, Union Park, Wilmington Grounds, Quickstep Park

**OCCUPANT**

UA Wilmington Quicksteps September 2–15, 1884

**LOCATION**

Left Field (NW) Bayard Ave, Third Base (SW), First Base (SE) Union St, Right Field (N) Front St (later Lancaster Ave), then cemetery

**PHENOMENA**

The game on September 15, 1884, drew just a handful of fans. Faced with the prospect of a game between his last-place 2-15 Quicksteps and the next-to-last-place 7-54 Kansas City Unions, Wilmington manager Joe Simmons called his team off the field, forfeited the game, and disbanded the team.

◆  ◆  ◆

# Wilmington, North Carolina

### *Hilton Park*

**OCCUPANT**

Neutral site used by NAL Birmingham Black Barons 1930s

**LOCATION**

(N) railroad tracks, (W) Clarendon Water Works Pipe Line, then Cape Fear River, (S) Cape Fear St, (E) Hilton St Pond

### *Thirteenth and Ann Streets Park*

**OCCUPANT**

Neutral site used by NAL Raleigh Tigers May 31, 1959

**LOCATION**

(N) Thirteenth St, (W) Ann St, (S) Eleventh St, (E) Castle St

### *American Legion Stadium*

**OCCUPANT**

Neutral site used by NAL Raleigh Tigers May 7, 1961

**LOCATION**

Left Field (S) Carolina Beach Blvd, Third Base (E) Southern Blvd Extension, First Base (N) Greenfield Lake, Right Field (W) Morningside Ave

**DIMENSIONS**

Left Field: 335 (1940)
Center Field: 430 (1940)

Right Field: 370 (1940)

**CAPACITY**

7000 (1940)

---

# Worcester, Massachusetts

## *Agricultural County Fair Grounds Race Track (I)*

**AKA**

Worcester Driving Park (I)

**OCCUPANTS**

NL Worcester Brown Stockings May 1, 1880–September 29, 1882; neutral site used by NA Boston Red Stockings October 30, 1874

**LOCATION**

(N) Highland St, (W) Agricultural (later Russell) St, (S) Williams St, Cedar St, (E) Sever St

**PHENOMENA**

Site of the first "real" doubleheader on September 25, 1882, vs. the Providence Grays, where one ticket admitted fans to two games. All previous "doubleheaders" were separate-admission events. Brown Stockings were trying to increase attendance; they had drawn only 54 on May 15, and later that week would draw only 25 on September 28, and 18 on September 29, the last major league game ever in Worcester. ♦ NA Boston Red Stockings played neutral site game here, October 30, 1874, vs. Hartford, with 500 fans in attendance, many of them sitting in trees or on fences.

The last-place Worcester Brown Stockings played their final game at the Agricultural County Fair Grounds Race Track in 1882 before a crowd of just 25 fans, an improvement over the day before when they drew just 6. Worcester was dropped and replaced by Philadelphia in 1883.

### *Agricultural County Fair Grounds Race Track (II)*

**AKA**

Worcester Driving Park (II)

**OCCUPANT**

Neutral site used by NL Washington August 17, 1887

**CAPACITY**

1500

**PHENOMENA**

This field was built near where the first park had been. ♦ The neutral site game between Boston and Washington drew 4600 fans, which included 1500 in the grandstand plus "standing room only" for more than 3000 more. ♦ There is a dispute as to which was the home team in this game. It was probably Washington, for it was moved here to honor "Honest John" Gaffney, a Worcester resident then managing Washington, who later went on to become the greatest umpire of the 19th century. ♦ Boston hosted nine other games with Washington that year, while Washington hosted only eight other games with Boston that year. Boston batted last, which caused many to list Boston as the home team. However, this is probably a case in which the home team, Washington, batted first.

---

# Yeadon, Pennsylvania

### *Hilldale Park*

**AKA**

Darby Catholic High School Stadium

**OCCUPANTS**

ECL Darby Hilldales 1923–27; ANL Darby Hilldales 1929; NEWL Darby Hilldales April–June 1932

**LOCATION**

Left Field (N) Bunting Ln (later MacDade Blvd); Third Base (W) Cedar Ave, then greenhouses; First Base (S) Chester Ave; Right Field (E) Darby Catholic High School (also called Yeadon School); in suburbs of Philadelphia on the Darby-Yeadon borderline, mostly in Yeadon

At Hilldale Park, home of the Negro League Hilldales, the branches of a huge tree in right center were in play. In February 2006, three men who played for Hilldale were inducted into baseball's Hall of Fame in Cooperstown: Biz Mackey, Louis Santop, and Ben Taylor. The Hilldales won the Negro League championship in 1925.

**DIMENSIONS**

Left Field: 315
Right Center: 400
Right Field: 370

**CURRENT USE**

Acme Super Saver supermarket and drive-in bank

**PHENOMENA**

Huge tree rose beyond fence in right-center; branches hung out over the fence and were in play.

---

# Zanesville, Ohio

## *Mark Grey Athletic Park*

**AKA**

Mark Park, Farm Diamond

**OCCUPANT**

Neutral site used by NNL Homestead Grays one game in 1938

**LOCATION**

Putnam Ave; Left Field (N), Third Base (W), First Base (S), Right Field (E)

**DIMENSIONS**

Left Field: 304 (1940)
Center Field: 386 (1940)
Right Field: 265 (1940)

**CAPACITY**

2000 (1940)

**PHENOMENA**

Built in 1918.

◆   ◆   ◆

# Bibliography

Benson, Michael. *Ballparks of North America: A Comprehensive Historical Reference to Baseball Grounds, Yards, and Stadiums.* Jefferson, North Carolina: McFarland & Co., 1989.

Bess, Philip. *City Baseball Magic: Plain Talk & Uncommon Sense About Cities and Baseball Parks.* Minneapolis, Minnesota: Minneapolis Review of Baseball, 1989.

_____. *City Baseball Magic: Plain Talk & Uncommon Sense About Cities and Baseball Parks.* Saint Paul, Minnesota: Knothole Press, 1999.

Enders, Eric. *Ballparks: Then and Now.* San Diego, California: Thunder Bay Press, 2002.

Gershman, Michael. *Diamonds: The Evolution of the Ballpark–From Elysian Fields to Camden Yards.* Boston, Massachusetts: Houghton Mifflin, 1993.

Gmelch, George, and J.J. Weiner. *In The Ballpark: The Working Lives of Baseball People.* Herndon, Virginia: Smithsonian Institution Press, 1998.

Hogan, Kenneth. *America's Ballparks: 76 Major League Stadiums, Past, Present, Future.* Vancouver, Washington: Pediment Publishing, 2003.

Jaspersohn, William. *The Ballpark: One Day Behind the Scenes at a Major League Game.* Boston/Toronto: Little, Brown & Co., 1980.

Kammer, David John. *Take Me Out to the Ballgame: The Architectural Evolution of the Modern Baseball Stadium.* Albuquerque: University of New Mexico Press, 1982.

Leventhal, Josh. *Take Me Out to the Ballpark: An Illustrated Tour of Baseball Parks Past and Present.* New York, New York: Black Dog & Leventhal Publishers, 2000.

Lowry, Philip J. *Green Cathedrals.* Cleveland, Ohio: Society for American Baseball Research, 1986.

_____. *Green Cathedrals: The Ultimate Celebration of All 271 Major League & Negro League Ballparks Past and Present.* Reading, Massachusetts: Addison-Wesley, 1992.

Palacios, Oscar, Eric Robin, and STATS Staff. *Ballpark Sourcebook: Diamond Diagrams.* Skokie, Illinois: STATS, 1998.

Pietrusza, David. *Lights On!: The Wild Century-Long Saga of Night Baseball.* Lanham, Maryland: The Scarecrow Press, 1997.

Reidenbaugh, Lowell, and Amadee. *Take Me Out to the Ball Park.* St. Louis, Missouri: The Sporting News, 1983.

Richmond, Peter. *Ballpark: Camden Yards and the Building of an American Dream.* New York, New York: Simon & Schuster, 1992.

Ritter, Lawrence S. *Lost Ballparks: A Celebration of Baseball's Legendary Fields.* New York, New York: Viking Studio Books, 1992.

Rosen, Ira. Blue Skies, *Green Fields: A Celebration of 50 Major League Baseball Stadiums.* New York, New York: Clarkson N. Potter/Publishers, 2001.

Sandalow, Marc, and Jim Sutton. *Ballparks: A Panoramic History.* Edison, New Jersey: Chartwell Books, 2004.

Serby, Myron W. *The Stadium: A Treatise on the Design of Stadiums and Their Equipment.* New York, New York: American Institute of Steel Construction, 1930.

Shannon, Bill, and George Kalinsky. *The Ballparks.* New York, New York: Hawthorn Books, 1975.

Smith, Curt. *Storied Stadiums: Baseball's History Through Its Ballparks.* New York, New York: Carroll & Graf, 2001.

Smith, Ron. *The Ballpark Book: A Journey Through the Fields of Baseball Magic.* St. Louis, Missouri: The Sporting News, 2000.

Staten, Vince. *Why Is the Foul Pole Fair? Secrets of the Ballpark.* New York, New York: Simon & Schuster, 2003.

Tackach, James, and Joshua B. Stein. *The Fields of Summer: America's Great Ballparks and the Players Who Triumphed in Them.* New York, New York: Crescent Books, 1992.

Vincent, David W., ed. *Home Runs in the Old Ballparks: Who Hit the First, the Last, & the Most Round-Trippers in our Former Major League Parks, 1876–1994.* Cleveland, Ohio: Society for American Baseball Research, 1995.

von Goeben, Robert. *Ballparks: Major League Stadiums Past and Present.* New York, New York: Metro Books, 2000.

_____. *Ballparks: Major League Stadiums Past and Present.* New York, New York: Metro Books, 2004.

Woodbury, William N. *Grandstand and Stadium Design.* New York, New York: American Institute of Steel Construction, 1947.

# Photo Credits

Photographs identified by page number are reproduced with the kind permission of the following:

Boston Public Library/Boston Wharf Collection: 25

George Brace: 57 (top)

Chicago Historical Society: 50 (bottom), 57 (bottom)

Jim Charlton: 220

Ebbets Field Color Photos, Inc.: 40

Chris Epting: 118

Paul Healey: 170

HOK Sport: 167, 168, 205

HOK Sport/Devrouax and Purnell Architects: 240

Library of Congress: 38, 152

Maryland Historical Society: 15

Joe Mock, BASEBALLPARKS.COM: 210

National Baseball Hall of Fame: 3, 4, 5, 7, 9, 14, 19, 22, 24, 26, 29, 30, 31, 32, 36, 39, 44, 46, 51, 53, 55, 56, 60, 61, 64, 66, 67, 73, 74, 77, 82, 84, 85, 86, 92, 97, 98, 100, 101, 102, 112, 113, 120, 121, 123, 126, 127, 129, 131, 134, 138, 140, 143, 156, 161, 162, 165, 174, 177, 179, 185, 186, 187, 189, 190, 196, 207, 211, 213, 214, 218, 221, 223, 228, 230, 232, 235, 237, 238, 243

NBL: David Barrett: 125, 216; David Beir: 137; Jonathan Busser: 89, 106, 224; Eric Enders: 191; Barry Gossage: 184; Mark Hertzberg: 81, 182; Jerome Kelly: 208; Fred Kraft: 17; Scott O'Neill: 10; John Pardon: 108; Robert Runyan: 70; Mike Smith: 86; Tom Ulhlman: 68

Skip Nipper: 141

St. Louis Sports Hall of Fame: 204

# Index

23rd Street Grounds 47-48

23rd Street Park, see 23rd Street Grounds

3Com Park, see Candlestick Park

35th Street Grounds (I), see South Side Park (II)

35th Street Grounds (II), see Comiskey Park (I)

37th and Butler 59

39th Street Grounds (I), see South Side Park (I)

39th Street Grounds (II), see South Side Park (III)

4th Avenue Grounds, see Hawkins Stadium

44th and Parkside, see Penmar Park

49ers Stadium, see Candlestick Park

59th Street Bridge 102, 163-164

67th and Langley 58

9th Wonder of the World, see Minute Maid Park

Aaron, Hank xvii, 9, 11, 45, 67, 156, 216

Abbaticchio, Ed 187

Adcock, Joe 118, 156

Adelaide Avenue Grounds 193

Adelaide Park, see Adelaide Avenue Grounds

Agee, Tommy 166

Agricultural County Fair Grounds Race Track (I) 243

Agricultural County Fair Grounds Race Track (II) 244

Agricultural Society Fair Grounds 196

Ainsworth Field 89

Alabama

    Birmingham 7, 20

        Barons 7, 20, 21

        Black Barons 6, 7, 20, 52, 77, 87, 107, 117, 124, 136, 145, 193, 215, 216, 242

        Rickwood Field 7

Citronelle 40

Decatur 79

Mobile 135

    Havana Cuban Giants 135

Montgomery 136

    Gray Sox 136

    State University 136

Alexander Cartwright rules 98

Allec, Camille 3

Allen, Dick 54

Allen, Gary 208

Allen, Michael 229

Allen, Otway S. 194

Allen, Richie 178

Allen's Pasture 194

All-Star Game 67, 193, 213

Aloha Stadium 98-99

Altoona Mountain Citys 2

Alvis, Max 18

American

    Association Park (Baltimore), see Oriole Park (I)

    Association Park (Cleveland), see League Park (II) (Cleveland)

    Giants Park, see South Side Park (III)

    League Ballpark, see Hilltop Park

    League Park (Baltimore), see Oriole Park (IV)

    League Park (Boston), see Fenway Park

    League Park (I) (Washington, D.C.) 222, 234

    League Park (II) (Washington, D.C.) 233, 234-235, 237

    Legion Baseball 114

    Legion Field 231

    Legion Park 146

    Legion Stadium 242

Ameriquest Field in Arlington 5-6

Ammon Field 189

Anaheim Stadium, see Angel Stadium of Anaheim

Andrews Field 47

Angel Stadium, see Angel Stadium of Anaheim

Angel Stadium of Anaheim 2-3

*Angels and the Pirates* 185

*Angels in the Outfield* 185

Anson, Cap 150, 225-226

Anthony, Eric 74

Aparicio, Luis 53

Appling, Luke 53, 239

Arizona

    Bisbee 145

    Diamondbacks 181-183

    Phoenix 181-183, 220, 230

Arkansas

    Little Rock 117

        Grays 117

Arlington Stadium 4-5

Armas, Tony 54

Armory Park 226

Armstrong, Louis 158, 159

Asbury Ball Park 59

Ashburn, Richie 178, 181

Association Park (I) 110

Association Park (II) 111

Astor, William Waldorf 160

Astrodome 100, 101-102, 104, 164, 204, 230

Astros Park, see Minute Maid Park

Asylum Oval, see Hebrew Orphan Asylum Oval

AT&T Park 214-215

Athletic Base Ball Grounds (I) 171

Athletic Base Ball Grounds (II) 171

Athletic Field 128

Athletic Park (Durham, North Carolina) 87

Athletic Park (Kansas City) 110

Athletic Park (Milwaukee), see Borchert Field

Athletic Park (Erie, Pennsylvania), see Ainsworth Field

Athletic Park (Nashville), see Sulphur Dell (II)

Athletic Park (Philadelphia), see
    Forepaugh Park
Athletic Park (St. Louis), see
    Sportsman's Park (II)
Athletic Park (Washington, D.C.)
    232
Athletic Park (I) (Indianapolis), see
    South Street Park
Athletic Park (II) (Indianapolis), see
    Seventh Street Park (I)
Athletic Park (III) (Indianapolis), see
    Seventh Street Park (II)
Athletic Park (IV) (Indianapolis), see
    Seventh Street Park (III)
Athletic Park (I) (Minneapolis)    133
Athletic Park (II) (Minneapolis)    133
Athletics    149
Atlantic Park    35
Atlantic Park Dog Track    11
Ault, Doug    228
Avenue Grounds    62
Babe Ruth Stadium, see
    Venable Stadium
Bacharach Park    11
Bagwell, Jeff    104
Baker Bowl    25, 65, 172, 173-174
Baker, Michael    191
Ballpark in Arlington, see Ameriquest
    Field in Arlington
Bancroft, Davey    97
Band Box, see Baker Bowl
Bank One Ballpark, see Chase Field
Bank Street Grounds    62
Banks, Ernie    57, 58
Barrow, Ed    160
Barr's Field, see Durkee Field
Base Ball Park, see 23rd Street
    Grounds
Bears Stadium (Denver), see Mile
    High Stadium
Bears Stadium (Newark), see Ruppert
    Stadium (Newark)
Beatles    166, 214
Bee Hive, see Braves Field
Behrman, Hank    40
Belair Lot    13
Bell, Cool Papa    158, 189
Bell, George    54
Bennett, Charlie    83
Bennett, James Gordon    148
Bennett Park    82-83, 84, 222
Berger, Wally    175
Berra, Yogi    160, 188
Betten, Henry    213
Beyer's Seventh Street Park, see
    Boundary Field
Beyerle's Park    143
Big A, see Angel Stadium of Anaheim
Big Egg    224-225, 230
Big O, see Stade Olympique
Big Owe, see Stade Olympique

Bigger A, see Angel Stadium of
    Anaheim
Bill Veeck's House, see Sportsman's
    Park (IV)
Bison Stadium, see Offermann
    Stadium
Bithorn, Hiram    215
Blefary, Curt    18
Blue-Gray football all-star game    136
Bluebooks    29
Bluett, Lizzie    42
Blues Stadium, see Municipal Sta-
    dium (Kansas City)
BOB, The, see Chase Field
Bobby Dorr's House, see Wrigley
    Field (Chicago)
Bolden Bowl, see Penmar Park
Bolles, John    212, 213
Borchert Field    128-129
Bossard, Emil and Gene    54
Bossard, Roger    53, 54
Bosman, Dick    163
Boucher, Joe    31
Bounce Dome, see Hubert H.
    Humphrey Metrodome
Boundary Field    233-234, 235
Boyer, Clete    163
Braves Field    31, 113
Brei, Doug    196
Brewer, Chet    209
Brewer Field, see Borchert Field
Brewer High School Field    93
Brewster Race Track    144
Bridwell, Al    151
Briggs Stadium, see Tiger Stadium
Briggs, Walter    84
Brock, Lou    100, 156, 204
Bronx Oval    163
Brookside Park    80
Brotherhood Grounds, see Congress
    Street Grounds
Brotherhood Park (Brooklyn), see
    Eastern Park
Brotherhood Park (Chicago), see
    South Side Park (II)
Brotherhood Park (Cleveland)    70
Brotherhood Park (New York City),
    see Polo Grounds (IV)
Brotherhood Park (Philadelphia), see
    Forepaugh Park
Bruce Grounds    33
Brush Stadium, see Polo Grounds (V)
Buck Bailey Field    217
Buff Stadium    99
Buffalo Stadium (Houston), see Buff
    Stadium
Bugle Field    16
Buhner, Jay    207
*Bull Durham*    87, 93
Bunning, Jim    85
Burns, James D.    222

Burns Park    222
Burroughs, Jeff    74
Busch, August    201, 202
Busch Memorial Stadium, see Busch
    Stadium (II)
Busch Stadium (Houston), see Buff
    Stadium
Busch Stadium (I) (St. Louis)    201,
    205, see Sportsman's Park (IV)
Busch Stadium (II) (St. Louis)
    204-205, 206
Busch Stadium (III) (St. Louis)
    205-206
Bush, George W.    132
Bush, Randy    134
Bushwick Park, see Dexter Park
Butler Field    45
Caldwell, Ray    38
California
    Anaheim    2, 117
        Angels    2
    Angels    2, 120, 134
    Earthquake Law    119
    Hollywood    120
        Stars    211
    Los Angeles    117-121
        Angels    119, 120
        Angels of Anaheim    2
        Coliseum    80, 133, 143,
            see Memorial
            Coliseum
        Dodgers    80, 117-121, 127,
            139, 150, 163,
            191, 213
        Memorial Coliseum, see
            Memorial
            Coliseum
        Rams (NFL)    3, 119
    Oakland    168-169
        Alameda County Coliseum,
            see McAfee
            Coliseum
        Athletics    116, 134, 168-
            169, 219
        Coliseum    116
        Raiders (NFL)    116, 169
    Pasadena    119
    San Diego    157, 208-211
        Chargers (NFL)    208
        Jack Murphy Stadium, see
            Qualcomm
            Stadium
        Padres    98-99, 136, 180,
            208-211
        Stadium, see Qualcomm
            Stadium
    San Francisco    157, 211-215
        49ers (NFL)    119, 212, 213
        Giants    3, 6, 193, 207, 211,
            212-215
Calloway, Cab    158

Cambria, Joe 16
Camden Yards xvi, 18-19, 180
Campanella, Roy 80, 119
Canada 215
  British Columbia
    Vancouver 134
  Ontario
    London 21, 145
    St. Mary's 139
    Toronto 220, 228-230
      Blue Jays 116,
        134, 215, 228-230
  Quebec
    Montreal 137-139, 215,
      230
      Expos 80, 137-
        139, 215
      Royals 109, 139
Canadian
  Baseball Hall of Fame 139
  Exposition 229
  National Exhibition (CNE), see
    Exhibition Stadium
Candelaria, John 191
Candlestick Park 204, 212-214
Canmeyer, William 34
Canseco, Jose 230
Capital Park Grounds, see
  Swampoodle Grounds
Capital Texture, see Catholic
  Protectory Oval
Capitol Grounds 232
Capitoline, see Capitoline Grounds
Capitoline Grounds 34-35
Capitoline Skating Lake and Base
  Ball Ground, see Capitoline
  Grounds
Capitoline Skating Pond, see
  Capitoline Grounds
Cardenas, Leo 96
Cardinal Field, see Robison Field
Cardines Field 145
Carlton, Steve 138, 181
Carroll, Fred 184
Caruthers, Bob 94
Casey, Sean 132, 192
Cash, Norm 84
Cashman Field 115, 116
Cashman Field Center, see Cashman
  Field
Casino Park 135
Catholic Protection, see Catholic
  Protectory Oval
Catholic Protectory Oval 158
Cave of the Winds, see Candlestick Park
CCNY Playground, see Hebrew
  Orphan Asylum Oval
Cedar Avenue Driving Park 70
Centennial Field 224
Centennial Park, see Columbia Park
  (I) (Philadelphia)

Central Park 188
Charles A. Comiskey's Baseball
  Palace, see Comiskey Park (I)
Charleston, Oscar 189
Chase Field 181-183
Chavez Ravine, see Dodger Stadium
Chavis Park 194
Cheney Stadium 212
Chesapeake Bay 18
Chessline Park 178
Cigar Box, see Baker Bowl
Cinergy Field, see Riverfront Stadium
Citizens Bank Park 180
City Park, see Luna Bowl
Civic Center Stadium, see Busch
  Stadium (II)
Civil War 140
Clark, Dick v
Clark Field 11-12
Clark Griffith Park, see Griffith
  Stadium
Clark, John 190
Clarksville Stadium 69
Clemente, Roberto 57, 191
CNE Stadium, see Exhibition
  Stadium
Cobb, Ty 11, 84, 95
Cole, Nat King 159
Coliseum Bike Track, see Recreation
  Park (Pittsburgh)
College Hill Park 136
Colonels Field, see Parkway Field
Colorado
  Denver 9, 79-81, 182
    Bears 80
    Broncos (NFL) 80
    Zephyrs 80
  Rockies 45, 79-81
Colt Stadium 100
Columbia Park 2
Columbia Park (I) (Philadelphia)
  171, 172
Columbia Park (II) (Philadelphia)
  174, 175, 177
Columbian Exposition 49, 65
Comerica Park 86
Comiskey, Charles 51, 52
Comiskey, Lou 54
Comiskey Park (I) xii, 49, 52-53, 56,
  60, 61
Comiskey Park (II) 51, 52-53, 60-61
Commerce Bank Park 95
Compton Avenue Base Ball Park, see
  Red Stocking Base-Ball Park
Compton Park, see Stars Park
Coney Island of the West, see Robison
  Field
Congress Street Grounds (Boston)
  24, 25
Congress Street Grounds (Chicago),
  see West Side Park (I)

Connecticut
  Hartford 96, 243
    Ball Club Grounds 96
    Dark Blues 23, 96, 144,
      193
    Trotting Park 96
  Middletown 128
    Mansfields 96, 128, 221
  New Haven 144
    Elm Citys 144
Connie Mack Stadium, see Shibe Park
Coogan's Bluff, see Polo Grounds (V)
Coogan's Hollow, see Polo
  Grounds (V)
Cool, Perry L. 237
Cooper Stadium, see Red Bird
  Stadium
Coors Field 9, 80-81, 182, 183
Count Basie 158
County Stadium 130-132
Covington Base Ball Park, see Star
  Baseball Park
Covington Stars 78
Cramton Bowl 136
Cravath, Gavvy 41, 174
Crockett Park, see Griffith Park
Croix de Candlestick, see Candlestick
  Park
Crosley Field xii, 62, 63, 65-66, 68,
  69, 104, 166
Crosley, Powel 66
Cuba 9, 96-97
  Cubaball 2001 97
  Havana 96-97
    Cuban Stars 96, 157
    Sugar Kings 23, 96
Cubs' Park (Chicago) 120, see also
  Wrigley Field (Chicago)
Cubs Park (Detroit), see De Quindre
  Park
Cubs Stadium 72
Culver Field (I) 195
Culver Field (II) 195
Cuthbert, Eddie 34
Cutshaw, George 41
Cutting, Ralph 129
Cycler Park 125
Dahl, George A. 238
D'Agostino, Dennis 166
Daniels, Bennie 238
*Damn Yankees* 120, 238
Dartmouth Grounds 23
Dauvray Cup Game 23
Davids, Charles A. 143
Davids' Folly, see Ruppert Stadium
  (Newark)
Davids' Stadium, see Ruppert
  Stadium (Newark)
Davis, Chili 134
Davis, Zachary Taylor 37, 52, 54, 56,
  119

Day, John   108
DC Stadium, see Robert F. Kennedy
    Stadium
De Quindre Park   85
Dean Park   78
Deane, Bill   155
Decker, Reuben S. and Stephen   34
Deer, Rob   134
Deery, John Joseph   25, 173
Deeter, Ritchey, Sipple   191
Delaware
    Dover   86
        Grounds, see Fairview Park
            Fair Grounds
    Wilmington   242
        Quicksteps   242
Delorimier Downs   139
Devereaux Meadow   193
Devrouax & Purnell Architects-
    Planners   239
Dewey, Thomas   158
Dexter Park   41, 158
Dick Kent's Ballyard, see Stars Park
Dickey, Bill   160
DiMaggio, Joe   41, 42, 72, 127, 160, 211
Disney   3
District of Columbia Stadium, see
    Robert F. Kennedy Stadium
Dixon, Randy   143
Dodger Stadium   5, 119, 120-121
Dolphin Stadium   127
Domestic Field, see Waverly
    Fairgrounds
Dorgan, Tad   151
Dorr, Bobby   57
Douglas Field, see Durkee Field
Downing Stadium   41
Dreyfuss, Barney   187
Dreyfuss' Folly, see Forbes Field
Druid Hill   16
Ducks Park   79
Dugdale Park   217
Dump, The (Chicago), see White
    Stocking Grounds
Dump, The (Nashville), see Sulphur
    Dell (II)
Duncan Park   176
Dunn Field (Cleveland), see League
    Park (IV) (Cleveland)
Dunn Field (Trenton)   231
Durkee Field   107
Durso, Joseph   163
Dyckman Oval   140, 157
Dyte, David   146
East End Grounds, see Pendleton Park
East End Park, see Pendleton Park
East Orange Oval, see Grove Street
    Oval (II)
East River Ballpark, see Metropolitan
    Park (New York City)
Easter, Luke   74, 156

Eastern Park   35
Easton Street Park   203
Ebbets Field   xii, 6, 7, 15, 36, 38-41,
    133, 157, 164, 167, 207
Eclipse Park (I)   122
Eclipse Park (II)   122
Eclipse Park (III)   122-123
Eclipse Park (IV)   123
Edenton Steamers   88
Edison International Field of
    Anaheim, see Angel Stadium of
    Anaheim
Eight Men Out   107
Eighth Wonder of the World, see
    Astrodome
Elizabeth Resolutes   34, 89
Ellerbe Beckett Inc.   8, 10, 181
Elmira Grounds, see Maple Avenue
    Driving Park
Elysian Fields   97-98
Engel, Joe   47
Engel Stadium   46
English, Woody   40
Enron Field, see Minute Maid Park
Ens, Jewel   97
Eppstein Uhen Associates   132
Estadio Cerveza Tropicale   96
Estadio Gran (I)   96
Estadio Gran (II)   96
Estadio Hiram Bithorn   215
Estadio Latino Americano, see
    Estadio Gran (II)
Estadio Monterrey   136
Estadio Pepe Marrero, see Estadio
    Cerveza Tropicale
Estadio Sixto Escobar   215
Euclid Beach Park   75
Evers, Johnny   58
Ewing, Cole, Cherry, Brott   180
Exhibition Stadium   228-229
Expos de Montreal   137, 138
Exposition Park   110
Exposition Park (I) Lower Field
    183, 184
Exposition Park (I) Upper Field
    183-184
Exposition Park (III)   184-185
Fairground Stadium   123
Fairview Park   78
Fairview Park Fair Grounds   86
Fall of Babylon, The   149
Farm Diamond, see Mark Grey
    Athletic Park
Farrell, Frank   152
Faust, Nancy   54, 61
Federal Field, see Handlan's Park
Federal League Base Ball Park, see
    International Fair Association
    Grounds
Federal League Park (Baltimore), see
    Terrapin Park

Federal League Park (Harrison, New
    Jersey)   95
Federal League Park (Indianapolis)
    105
Federal League Park (Kansas City),
    see Gordon and Koppel Field
Federal League Park (St. Louis), see
    Handlan's Park
Fenway Park   xii, 25, 28-31, 104,
    109, 119, 143, 192, 219, 226
Fetzer, John   85
Field of Dreams   37
Fielder, Cecil   131
Finch, Alexander, Barnes, Rothschild
    & Paschal   67
Finley, Charlie   112, 113
First Union Center   179
Florida
    Jacksonville   107
        Braves   216
        Red Caps   107
    Marlins   60, 127-128
    Miami   60, 127
    St. Petersburg   206-208, 229
    Suncoast Dome, see Tropicana
        Field
    Tallahassee   224
    Tampa Bay
        Devil Rays   206-208, 224
    Vero Beach   150
Flushing Meadow Stadium, see Shea
    Stadium
Forbes Field   xii, xiii, xvi, xvii, 20,
    39, 185-188, 190, 191, 192, 217
Forbes, John   188
Ford, Whitey   160
Forepaugh Park   172
Forest City Park, see Beyerle's Park
Forsters Island Park, see Island
    Stadium
Fort Street Grounds   206
Fourth Street Grounds, see Bruce
    Grounds
Fox, Nellie   53, 101
Foxx, Jimmie   54, 175
Frank L. Hope & Associates   208
Franklin County Stadium, see Red
    Bird Stadium
Frey, Lonnie   40
Frick, Ford   119
Gaedel, Eddie   53, 202
Gaffney, "Honest John"   244
Gardiner, John Lion   151, 160
Geauga Lake Grounds   91
Gehrig, Lou   12, 41, 42, 160
General Electric Field, see Sprague
    Field
Georgia
    Atlanta   7-9
        Black Crackers   7
        Braves   8-10, 134, 204

Crackers   7, 8
  Fulton County Stadium   8,
    9, 11
  Stadium, see Fulton County
    Stadium
Columbus   76
Macon   124
Savannah   215
  Indians   216
  Stadium, see Atlanta-Fulton
    County Stadium
Giants Park   203
Gibson, Josh   41, 42, 135, 160, 163,
  189, 190, 236, 237
Gilbert, Tom   37
Giles, Brian   193
Glasscock, Jack   241
Glavine, Tom   10
Gloucester Point Grounds   91
Golden Park   76
Gomez, Lefty   160
Gordon and Koppel Field   110
Gordy Park   208
Gore, George   150
Gottlieb, Alan   37
Grace, Mark   182
Graham, Archie "Moonlight"   36
Grand and Market, see Handlan's
  Park
Grand Avenue Grounds, see
  Sportsman's Park (I)
Grand Avenue Park (I), see
  Sportsman's Park (I)
Grand Duchess   90
Grand Pavilion, see South End
  Grounds (II)
Grand Stadium, see Estadio Gran (I)
Grant, Eddie   157, 214
Grauer's Ridgewood Park   146
Grays Field   189
Grayson Stadium   215
Great American Ball Park   68-69
Greenberg, Hank   42, 54, 158
Greenbush Grounds   92
Greenlawn Park, see Federal League
  Park (Indianapolis)
Greenlee Field   140, 188, 189-190
Greenlee, Gus   190
Griffey, Ken   218
Griffey, Jr., Ken   218
Griffith, Clark   236, 237, 238
Griffith Park   46
Griffith Stadium   xii, 120, 233,
  235-236
Grissom, Lee   66
Grove Street Oval (I)   88
Grove Street Oval (II)   88
Grove Street Senior Ball Diamond,
  see Grove Street Oval (II)
Gwynn, Tony   210
Hagy, Wild Bill   18

Hake and Hake   65
Hake, Harry   65
Halawa Stadium, see Aloha
  Stadium
Halloran Park   117
Hamilton Field   90
Hamilton Grounds   94
Hamilton Park, see Brewster Race
  Track
Hampden Park Race Track   221
Hampton Institute Field   94
Hamtramck Stadium   94
Handlan's Park   202
Hannan, Jim   163
Hardware Field   72
Harlem Meadow, see Polo
  Grounds (V)
Harris County Domed Stadium, see
  Astrodome
Harrison Field   95
Harrison Park, see Harrison Field
Harry S. Truman Sports Complex, see
  Kauffman Stadium
Hartfords of Brooklyn   34, 96
Hartwell Field   135
Hastings, Don and Chris   8
Hawaii
  Honolulu   98
    Stadium   99
Hawkins Stadium   2
Haymakers' Grounds   115
Haymarket, The, see Bennett Park
Hebner, Richie   180
Hebrew Orphan Asylum Oval   163
Heery & Heery   67
Heery International Inc.   8
Heinemann Park, see Pelican
  Stadium
Helling, Rick   6
Henry, Howard   42, 44
Herman, Babe   40
Herts, Harry B.   153
Hicks Field   88
Highland Park Stadium   114
Highlanders Park, see Hilltop Park
Hilltop, The, see Hilltop Park
Hilltop Park   151-152
Hilton Park   242
Hinchliffe, John   170
Hinchliffe Stadium   170
HKS Inc.   5, 60, 132
HNTB   113, 168
Hoeft, Billy   85
Hoffheinz, Roy   102
HOK Sport Facilities Group   2, 18,
  54, 68, 74, 80, 86, 103, 127, 137,
  167, 180, 192, 204, 205, 206,
  209, 214, 219, 239
Holabird & Root   54
Hole, The, see Association Park (I)
Holman Stadium   150

Home Plate Mine, see Seals Stadium
Home Run Derby   119, 120
Homer Dome, see Hubert H.
  Humphrey Metrodome
Hooper's Field, see Beyerle's Park
Horne, Lena   159
Hornsby, Rogers   175
Horse Market, see Grauer's
  Ridgewood Park
House That Clemente Built, see Three
  Rivers Stadium
House That Ruth Built, see Yankee
  Stadium
Howard Avenue Grounds   144
Howard, Elston   160
Howard, Frank   162-163, 239
Howard, Ryan   180
Hubbell, Carl   97
Hubert H. Humphrey Metrodome
  22, 102, 133-134, 219, 224, 230
Hubie Dome, see Hubert H.
  Humphrey Metrodome
Huggins, Miller   160
Hugh Stubbins & Associates   179
Hump, The, see Baker Bowl
Hump Dome, see Hubert H.
  Humphrey Metrodome
Huntingdon Avenue Grounds, see
  Oriole Park (I)
Huntingdon Grounds (I)   172
Huntingdon Grounds (II)   172, 173
Huntingdon Grounds (III), see Baker
  Bowl
Huntington Avenue Baseball Grounds
  26-27, 31
Hutchinson, Fred   39
Icahn Stadium, see Triborough
  Stadium
Illinois
  Belleville   20
    High School Athletic Field
      20
  Chicago   45, 47-61, 65, 120,
    190, 225, 233
    American Giants   16, 51,
      52, 59, 60, 94,
      128, 176, 183, 190
    Base-Ball Grounds (I), see
      White Stocking
      Grounds
    Base-Ball Grounds (II), see
      White Stocking
      Park
    Bears (NFL)   60
    Browns   48, 49, 130
    Cole's American Giants
      51, 52, 107
    Colts   49, 50
    Cricket Club Grounds (I),
      see South Side
      Park (I)

Cricket Club Grounds (II),
    see South Side
    Park (III)
Cubs    50, 52, 53, 54-58,
    100, 151, 187, 205,
    215, 224, 225-226
    Giants    58, 106
    Pirates    49
    Wanderers    51
    Whales    54
    White Sox    51, 52, 53, 54,
        60-61, 118, 130,
        207, 215, 228, 229
    White Stockings    47-48,
        49, 62, 115, 128,
        184
    Mounds    139
    Piqua    183
    Rockford    196
        Forest Citys    47, 196
    Springfield    220
Indiana
    Broad Ripple    33, 104
    Crawfordsville    78
    Fort Wayne    90
        Kekiongas    90, 232
    Hammond    94
    Indianapolis    33, 52, 104-107,
        111
        ABCs    78, 105, 106, 116,
            139
        Athletics    106
        Blues    33, 104
        Browns    23, 104, 183,
            198
        Cincinnati Clowns    65,
            106-107
        Clowns    44, 45, 107
        Crawfords    106
        Hoosier-Feds    105
        Hoosiers    104, 105
        Park    105
    Kokomo    114
    Lebanon    116
        Memorial Park    116
    Muncie    139
    Summit City    90
Indians Park at Gateway, see Jacobs
    Field
International Fair Association
    Grounds    43
Iowa
    Keokuk    114
        Westerns    23, 114
Iron Pier    223
Island Grounds    241
Island Stadium    95
It Happens Every Spring    119-120
Jack Murphy Stadium, see Qualcomm
    Stadium
Jacksonville    94

Jacksonville Baseball Park, see
    Durkee Field
Jacksonville Red Caps    107
Jacobs, Marvin, Charles, and Louis
    44
Jacobs Field    74
Jacobs, Richard E.    74
Jailhouse Flats (I)    90
Jake, The, see Jacobs Field
Japan
    Baseball Hall of Fame    225
    Tokyo    80, 121, 224-225,
        230
        Dome, see Big Egg
        Kyujyo, see Big Egg
    Yomiuri Giants    225
Jarry Park, see Parc Jarry
Jasper Oval, see Hebrew Orphan
    Asylum Oval
Jefferson Street Grounds (I)    171
Jefferson Street Grounds (II)    171
Jenkinson, Bill    xvii
Jet Stadium, see Red Bird Stadium
Jethroe, Sam    227
JJ Downing Memorial Stadium, see
    Triborough Stadium
Joe Robbie Stadium, see Dolphin
    Stadium
John F. Kennedy Stadium    179
Johnson, Alex    54
Johnson, Judy    189
Johnson, Lyndon B.    101
Johnson, Walter    237
Jones, Charlie    124
Jones, Ruppert    219
Jordan, Tim    185
Junior World Series    23
Kahn, Roger    41
Kaline, Al    84, 85
Kalinski, George    xi
Kansas
    Wichita Braves    22-23
Kauffman, Ewing    113
Kauffman Stadium    113
Kavanaugh Field, see Travelers Field
Keck, George and Josiah    62
Keefe, Art    29
Kekionga Base Ball Grounds, see
    Grand Duchess
Kelly, Joe    174
Kennard Street Park, see League Park
    (I) (Cleveland)
Kennedy, John F.    238
Kentucky
    Ashland    xvi, 163
    Covington    61, 63, 78
        Stars    78
    Louisville    122-124
        Baseball Park, see St. James
Court
        Black Caps    123

        Black Colonels    123
        Buckeyes    123
        Colonels    122-123, 223
        Falls City    122
        Grays    122
        White Sox    123
    Ludlow    61, 94, 124
        Base-Ball Park    124
    Union    66
    University of    122
Keough, Matt    219
Keystone Field, see Central Park
Keystone Park    172
Keyworth Stadium, see Hamtramck
    Stadium
Kindelan, Orestes    9
King County Stadium, see Kingdome
Kingdome    217-219, 229
Kingman, Dave    58, 134, 139, 219
Kivett and Meyers    113
Klein, Chuck    174
Knights Park, see Griffith Park
Knutgen, John    3
Koppe, Joe    22-23
Korakuen Stadium    121
Koufax, Sandy    40
Kubek, Tony    163, 188
Kuhel, Joe    235
Kuenn, Harvey    18
L. P. Kooken Company    17
Labatt's Park    21
Laclede Street Field, see Handlan's
    Park
Lake Front Park, see White Stocking
    Grounds, White Stocking Park
Lake Front Stadium, see Cleveland
    Stadium
Lake Park, see White Stocking Park
Lake Shore Park, see White Stocking
    Grounds
Lake-Side Park    91
Lake Street Dumping Ground, see
    White Stocking Grounds
Lakeside Park    79
Lancaster, Burt    36
Lane, Frank    54
Langston, Mark    219
Lanphier Park    220-221
Launching Pad, see Atlanta-Fulton
    County Stadium
L. D. Astorino & Associates    192
League Field    241
League Park (Kansas City), see
    Association Park (I)
League Park (Louisville), see Eclipse
    Park (III)
League Park (Mobile), see Hartwell
    Field
League Park (St. Louis), see Robison
    Field
League Park (Toledo)    225

League Park (I) (Cincinnati) 62-63, 64, 65, 66
League Park (I) (Cleveland) 69
League Park (I) (Fort Wayne), see Jailhouse Flats (I)
League Park (II) (Akron) 1
League Park (II) (Cincinnati) 1, 63-64, 65, 66
League Park (II) (Cleveland) 69-70
League Park (II) (Fort Wayne) 90
League Park (III) (Cincinnati), see Palace of the Fans
League Park (III) (Cleveland) 71
League Park (IV) (Cleveland) 71-72, 74, 151
Leavitt, Jr., Charles W. 185
Lebanon Memorial Park 116
Lee, Cliff 175
Lee, Hal 175
Lee, Robert E. 194
Lefferts family 34
Legion Field (Decatur, Alabama) 79
Legion Field (Lake Charles) 115
Legion Field (Whiteville, North Carolina) 241
Leland Giants Park 59
Lenney, George 3
Lester, Larry v
Lewis, Duffy 30
Lewisohn Stadium 163
Lincoln Park Grounds 61
Linton Field, see De Quindre Park
Lloyd, Herman 101
Lloyd Street Grounds 129-130
Loomis Race Track, see West Side Park (I)
Loomis Street Park, see West Side Park (I)
Long Island Grounds 147
Long Island Recreation Grounds, see Long Island Grounds
Lord Baltimores 13, 14, 231
Louisiana
    Lake Charles 115
    Monroe 135
        Monarchs 135
    New Orleans 144-145
        Bears 145
        Eagles 144
        Pelicans 145
        St. Louis Stars 139, 144, 201, 203
L. P. Kooken Company 17
Lucchino, Larry xvi, 19
Luderus, Fred 174
Luna Bowl 72
Luna Park, see Luna Bowl
Luna Stadium, see Luna Bowl
Luther Williams Field 124-125
Luzinski, Greg 180, 181
Lynch, Jack 149

Lynn, Fred 30
MacArthur, Douglas 224
MacArthur Stadium 223
Mack, Connie 177, 178, 180, 233
Mack Park 85
Mackey, Biz 244
Madison Avenue Grounds 12
Maglie, Sal 40
Mahaffey Park 45
Malamud, Bernard 40
Mall of America 22
Manhattan Field, see Polo Grounds (III)
Mann, Earl 8
Mansfield Club Grounds 128
Mantle, Mickey 85, 101, 160, 163, 236-237
Maple Avenue Driving Park 89
Maranville, Rabbit 97
Maris, Roger 160
Mark Grey Athletic Park 245
Mark Park, see Mark Grey Athletic Park
Market Street Park 203
Martin, Billy 160
Martin Park 126
Martinez, Buck 134
Martinez, Naomi 58
Maryland
    Baltimore xvi, 12-19, 74
        Baseball and Exhibition Grounds, see Oriole Park (III)
        Black Sox 11, 16
        Elite Giants 15, 16, 17, 208, 241
        Lord Baltimores 231
        Marylands 13
        Memorial Stadium 16-17
        Monumentals 13
        Orioles xvi, 13, 14, 17-19, 24, 37, 149, 219, 229
        Stadium, see Venable Stadium
        Terrapins 15
    Baseball Park 16
    Bethesda 237
    Frederick 19
    Hagerstown 19
    Salisbury 208
    Westport 12, 241
Maspeth Ball Grounds, see Long Island Grounds
Massachusetts
    Boston 14, 23, 63, 82, 219, 232, 244
        Baseball Grounds, see South End Grounds (II)
        Beaneaters 24, 25, 231
        Bees 31

        Braves 26, 27, 28, 31, 33, 45, 131, 174, 186
        Red Caps 23, 28, 171
        Red Sox xvi, 26, 27, 28, 31, 237
        Red Stockings 23, 193, 221, 243
        Reds 23, 25
        Resolutes 23
    Springfield 221
    Worcester 243-244
        Brown Stockings 243
        Driving Park (I) 243
        Driving Park (II) 244
Mathews, Eddie 8, 11
Matthau, Walter 166
Matty Schwab's House, see Polo Grounds (V)
Maury's Lake, see Candlestick Park
Mausoleum, The, see McAfee Coliseum
Maxwell, Charlie 84
Mays, Willie 6, 108, 109, 155, 213
Mazeroski, Bill 188
McAfee Coliseum 168
McCarthy, Jack 71
McCarthy, Joe 160
McCarthy, Johnny 157
McCormick Field 6
McCovey, Willie 58, 213
McDonald, John 66
McKean 70
McLaughlin, Charles E. 28
Meadowbrook Field, see Meadowbrook Oval
Meadowbrook Oval 142
Meadowbrook Park 93
Medwick, Joe 175
Meiji Stadium 80
Memorial Coliseum 117-119, 133, 143, 229
Memorial Stadium 16, 17, 18
Merkle, Fred 151
Messer Park, see Messer Street Grounds
Messer Street Grounds 193
Met, The, see Metropolitan Stadium (Bloomington)
Metropolitan Area Stadium, see Metropolitan Stadium (Bloomington)
Metropolitan Field, see Polo Grounds (II) Southeast Diamond
Metropolitan Park (New York City) 148
Metropolitan Park (St. Louis) 203
Metropolitan Stadium (Baltimore), see Venable Stadium
Metropolitan Stadium (Bloomington, Minnesota) 21-23, 138
Mexico
    Gomez Palacio 100

Monterrey, Nuevo Leon   136
        Sultans   136
Torreon Cotton Growers   101
Michigan
    Detroit   82-86, 103, 226, 238
        Clowns   85
        Corktown   82, 83
        New Orleans Stars   85, 145
        Stars   83, 85, 94-95, 194
        Tigers   54, 77, 82-86, 91-92,
            134, 202, 222, 226
        Wolverines   13, 23, 35, 49,
            82, 83, 147, 172,
            184, 233
        Wolves   94
    Grand Rapids   91-92
    Hamtramck   82, 94
    Pontiac   134
    Springwells   82, 222
Mighty Casey   120
Mile High Stadium   79-80, 81
Military Park, see Armory Park
Milland, Ray   120
Miller Park   131, 132-133, 192, 220,
    230
Miller Stadium   240
Miller, Stu   213
Mills Stadium   59
Minnedome, see Hubert H.
    Humphrey Metrodome
Minnesota
    Bloomington   21, 133, 137
        Stadium, see Metropolitan
            Stadium
            (Bloomington)
    Minneapolis   22, 133, 225, 230
        Millers   22, 133
    St. Paul   206
        Saints   96, 206
    Twins   21, 102, 133-135, 138,
        235
    Vikings (NFL)   22
Minute Maid Park   103-104, 220,
    230
Miss Snyder's Cow Pasture, see Bugle
    Field
Missions   211
Missouri
    Kansas City   110-113
        Athletics   33, 112, 177
        Blues   110
        Brewers   209
        Cowboys   110
        Monarchs   16, 20, 51, 52,
            76, 79, 85, 89-90,
            92, 95, 107, 111,
            112, 114, 115, 117,
            126, 153, 159, 173,
            176, 194, 197, 201,
            224
        Municipal Stadium   33

Packers   56, 110
Royals   112, 113, 230
Unions   110, 242
St. Louis   xv, 40, 45, 95, 130,
    180, 197-206
    Browns   13, 15, 23, 35, 49,
        53, 62, 104, 110,
        131, 147, 172, 184,
        198, 199, 200,
        201, 202, 233
    Brown Stockings   198
    Cardinals   99, 132, 134,
        196, 198, 199,
        200, 201, 202,
        204-206
    Giants   202, 203
    Maroons   104, 198
    Red Stockings   197
    Stars   202, 203
    Terriers   202
    Springfield Cardinals   205
Mistake by the Lake, see Municipal
    Stadium (Cleveland)
Monitor Grounds   240
Monitor Park, see Monitor Grounds
Monroe Park, see Hartwell Field
Monster Park, see Candlestick Park
Monte Irvin Field, see Grove Street
    Oval (II)
Montag, Bob   8
Monumental Park   13
Moon, Wally   118
Moore's Field, see Maryland Baseball
    Park
Morgan, W. B.   101
Mosler & Summers   43
Mosquito Heaven, see Colt Stadium
Mounds Ballfield   139
Mrs. O'Leary's cow   47
Mud Hen Park, see Swayne Field
Muehlebach Field, see Municipal
    Stadium (Kansas City)
Mullen, John   22-23
Municipal
    Field   98
    Stadium (Baltimore), see Venable
        Stadium
    Stadium (Cleveland), see
        Cleveland Stadium
    Stadium (Kansas City)   33,
        111-112
    Stadium (Greenville, South
        Carolina)   93
    Stadium (Rockingham, North
        Carolina)   197
    Stadium (Springfield, Ohio)
        221
    Stadium (Syracuse)   223
Munson, Thurman   160
Munsters   119
Murph, The, see Qualcomm, Stadium

Murphy, Bob   208
Murphy, Dale   11
Murphy, Jack   208, 209
Musial, Stan   205
Mutrie's Dump, see St. George
    Cricket Grounds
Mutrie's Dumping Grounds, see St.
    George Cricket Grounds
Naramore, Skilling, & Praeger   217
National
    anthem   53, 215
    Association Grounds   69
    Grounds   232
    League Field, see Braves Field
    League Park (Indianapolis)
        104
    League Park (I), see League Park
        (I) (Cleveland)
    League Park (I) (Philadelphia),
        see Huntingdon Grounds
        (I)
    League Park (II), see League
        Park (II) (Cleveland)
    League Park (II) (Philadelphia),
        see Huntingdon Grounds
        (II)
    League Park (III) (Cleveland),
        see League Park (III)
        (Cleveland)
    League Park (III) (Philadelphia),
        see Baker Bowl
    Nite Baseball Park, see South
        End Park
    Park (I), see Boundary Field
    Park (II), see American League
        Park (I) (Washington, D.C.)
    Park (III), see American League
        Park (II) (Washington, D.C.)
    Park (IV), see Griffith Stadium
Natural, The   40
Navin Field, see Tiger Stadium
Nebraska
    Omaha Panhandlers   80
Negro League All-Star Game   54,
    160
Negro World Series   16, 20, 52, 77,
    107, 112, 136, 145, 153, 159, 173,
    176, 236
Neil Park (I)   77
Neil Park (II)   77
Nelson, Lindsey   102
Nelson, Ricky   219
Nero, The Fall of Rome   149
Net, The, see McAfee Coliseum
Networks Associates Coliseum, see
    McAfee Coliseum
Nevada
    Las Vegas   115-116
New Expo, see Exposition Park (III)
New Jersey
    Atlantic City   11

Bacharach Giants 11, 16, 163, 176
Bloomfield 21, 142
Burlington County 160
Camden 45
East Orange 88, 147
Elizabeth 88
  Resolutes 34, 89
Gloucester City 91, 171
Harrison 95, 142
Hoboken 97, 147
  Zephyrs 120
Irvington 107
Jersey City 33, 108, 147
Newark 111, 142-143
  Browns 21, 142
  Dodgers 107, 142
  Eagles 2, 52, 142, 153, 231
  Indians 142
  Peppers 95
  Schools Stadium 142
  Stars 142
Paterson 147, 170
Trenton 231
Weehawken 33, 147, 240
  Cricket Grounds, see West New York Field Club Grounds
West New York 33, 147, 241
  Field Club Grounds 241
New Mets Ballpark 167
New Nationals Ballpark 239-240
New Polo Grounds (I), see Polo Grounds (III)
New Polo Grounds (II), see Polo Grounds (IV)
New Twins Ballpark 134-135
New Yankee Stadium 167-168
New York
  Albany 1, 92
  Base Ball Club 98
  Black Yankees 2, 41, 44, 108, 159, 164, 170, 190, 195, 196, 223
  Brooklyn 33-42, 119, 133, 158, 166, 184, 185
    Atlantics 34
    Bridegrooms 34, 35, 36, 94, 241
    Brook-Feds 37
    Bushwicks 42
    Dodgers 7, 8, 36, 38-41, 97, 108, 109, 157, 163, 165, 166, 185
    Dodgers (NFL) 60
    Eagles 38
    Ebbets Field xii, 6, 7, 15, 38-41
    Eckfords 33, 126
    Gladiators 146, 147, 150
    Hartfords 34, 96

  Royal Giants 41
  Trolley Dodgers 146, 240
  Wonders 35
Buffalo xvi, 42-45
  Baseball Park, see Olympic Park (II)
  Bisons 42-43, 89, 222
  Buf-Feds 43
Charlotte 45, 46, 195
Cooperstown 158
Cosmos (NASL) 164
Cuban Stars 96, 157, 158
Cuban Stars East 157-158
Cuban Stars West 158
Cubans 41, 52, 88, 95, 96, 97, 102, 153, 158, 159, 163, 164, 176
Elmira 89
Geddes 91, 222
Giants 29, 39, 72, 95, 108, 149, 150, 151, 152, 153, 155, 157, 165, 166, 240, 241
Gothams 35, 147, 147, 148, 149, 172
Greenbush 1, 92
Harrison 95
Highlanders 142, 147, 152
Irondequoit 46, 107, 195
Jets (NFL) 166
Knickerbockers 97, 149
Lansingburgh 115, 231
Lincoln Giants 158-159, 195
Manhattan 98, 149, 156
  Field 25, 149, see Polo Grounds (III)
Mets 9, 35, 70, 102, 147, 148, 149, 153, 157, 165-167, 208, 213, 224, 240
Mutuals 34, 97, 126
Newtown 33, 146-147
New York City 25, 98, 147-168
New Yorks 98
Phoenix 183, 222
Rensselaer 92
Riverhead 147, 195
Rochester 46, 170, 195
  Hop Bitters 107, 195
  Red Wings 96, 196, 223
Staten Island Yankees 149
Stars (WFL) 164
Syracuse 222-224
  Chiefs 223
  Stars 91, 183, 222, 223
Troy 115, 231, 232
  Ball Club Grounds 240
  Haymakers 34, 48, 115
  Trojans 1, 92, 115, 231, 240
Watervliet 231, 240
Yankees 10, 38, 54, 74, 76, 80, 101, 113, 119, 126, 143, 151,

  153, 157, 159-163, 165, 166, 167, 176, 178, 211, 230, 239
Newcombe, Don 108
Newell Park, see Star Park (I)
Newington Park 13
Nickerson Field, see Braves Field
Nicholson, Bill 57
Niekro, Phil 11
Nippon Ham Fighters 225
Nitz, Jim 129
Nixon, Richard M. 238
Nobel Herzberg 2
Normal Park 59
North Carolina
  Asheville 6
  Charlotte 46
  Durham 87
  Edenton 88
    Steamers 88
  Greensboro 92-93, 176
  Lumberton 124
  Newton 146
  Raleigh 193
    Tigers 20, 46, 69, 78, 87, 88, 92-93, 124, 146, 194, 197, 220, 222, 231, 241, 242
  Rockingham 197
    Stadium 197
  Rocky Mount 197
  Smithfield 220
  Wallace 231
  Whiteville 241
  Wilmington 242
North Pole, see Candlestick Park
North Side Ball Park, see Wrigley Field (Chicago)
Northside Park 66
Northwestern Avenue Ballpark 106
Oakdale Park 108
Oakdale Park (Philadelphia) 171
Oakland Athletic Association Field, see Oakdale Park
Oakland Park, see Oakdale Park (Philadelphia)
Oakland Orchard, see Forbes Field
O'Day, Hank 233
Odd Couple 166
Offermann Stadium 44
Ohio
  Akron 1
    Black Tyrites 1
  Aurora 91
  Blue Ash 66
  Bridgeport 241
  Canton 45
  Cincinnati xv, 61-69, 78, 124, 180
    Base Ball Club 62
    Base Ball Grounds, see League Park (I)
    Buckeyes 65

Clowns   65, 220, 221
Cuban Stars   67, 96
Gym Grounds, see
        Pendleton Park
Outlaw Reds   62
Porkers   63
Reds   35, 62-68, 94, 124,
        132, 157, 185
Tigers   65
Cleveland   53, 66, 69-75, 80,
        133, 232
Bears   72
Blues   45, 71, 77, 78, 90
Browns   143
Browns (NFL)   74
Buckeyes   52, 71, 159, 176
Cubs   72
Elites   143
Forest Cities   48, 61, 62, 69,
        90, 232
Giants   72
Hornets   143
Indians   29, 68, 71, 72,
        73-75, 155
Infants   70
Naps   77
Public Municipal Stadium,
        see Cleveland
        Stadium
Red Sox   72
Spiders   45, 49, 69-70, 71,
        75, 82, 91, 105,
        143, 173, 195, 199
Stadium   73-74, 75, 80
Stars   72
Tate Stars   143
White Auto   80
Collinwood   69, 75
Columbus   76-77, 227
Bluebirds   77
Buckeyes   77, 170
Colts   71, 133
Elite Giants   77
Senators   76
Solons   76
Turfs   77
Cuban Stars West   51
Dayton   78
Marcos   79
Geauga Lake   69, 90
Hamilton   61, 94, 124
Lima   117
Newburgh Heights   69, 143
Pendleton   63
Springfield   221
Toledo   225-227
Crawfords   227
Maumees   226
Mud Hens   227
Blue Stockings   225-226
Tigers   227

Zanesville   92, 245
Okkonen, Marc   37, 96
Old Armory Field   124
Olemar Field   107
Olympic
Berlin   80
Field   158
Games   9, 11, 118, 119, 138
Grounds   231
Melbourne   80
Park (I)   43
Park (II)   43, 44
Stadium   10
Stadium (Montreal), see Stade
        Olympique
Tokyo   80
O'Malley, Walter   119
O'Malley's Alley, see Memorial
        Coliseum
O'Malley's Chinese Theatre, see
        Memorial Coliseum
O'Malley's Golden Gulch, see Dodger
        Stadium
Ontario Beach Grounds   45
Oriole Park (I)   13, 14
Oriole Park (II)   13
Oriole Park (III)   14, 18
Oriole Park (IV)   14-15
Oriole Park (V), see Terrapin Park
Oriole Park at Camden Yards, see
        Camden Yards
Osborn Engineering   28, 29, 31, 52,
        71, 83, 111, 153, 159, 191, 235,
        238
Overfield, Joseph M.   43
Owen J. Bush Stadium, see Victory
        Field (I)
Pac Bell Park, see AT&T Park
Page Park   135
Paige, Satchel   41, 42, 178, 189, 190,
        202
Palace of the Fans   64-65, 66, 67
Palace Park of America   198
Pan American Games   97
Paradeway Park   111
Parc Jarry   137, 138
Parkinson, John and Donald   117
Parkway Field   123
Passon Field   178
Pastier, John   129
Pastime Base Ball Grounds, see
        Madison Avenue Grounds
Patterson, Red   237
Pele   164
Pelican Stadium   144
Pena, Carlos   134
Pendleton Park   63
Penmar Park   178
Pennsylvania
Altoona   2
        Mountain Citys   2, 242

Butler   45
Erie   89
Darby
Catholic High School
        Stadium, see
        Hilldale Park
Hilldales   16, 52, 173, 244
Harrisburg   95, 115
Giants   95
St. Louis Stars   95
Giants   95
Hilldale   115
Hilldale Park   244
Homestead   98, 183
Grays   2, 45, 78, 98, 109,
        125, 135, 183,
        185, 188, 189,
        190, 245
Johnstown   109
Lancaster   115
McKeesport   125, 183
Meadville   126
Grounds   126
Monessen   135
Philadelphia   xii, 25, 171-181,
        190, 243
Athletics   28, 34, 48, 86,
        91, 115, 149, 171,
        172, 174, 175,
        176-178, 235
Bacharach Giants   178
Baseball Grounds (I), see
        Huntingdon
        Grounds (I)
Baseball Grounds (II), see
        Huntingdon
        Grounds (II)
Baseball Grounds (III), see
        Baker Bowl
Blue Jays   176
Centennials   171
Eagles (NFL)   179
Hilldales   45
Keystones   172, 184
Nationals   157
Pearls   78, 124
Phillies   102, 138, 151, 172,
        173, 174, 175, 176-
        181, 243
Pythians   172
Quakers   172
Stars   178, 208
Tigers   178
White Stockings   48, 171, 196
Pittsburg
Alleghenys   183, 184, 241
Stogies   13, 183
Pittsburgh   39, 98, 180, 183-193
Burghers   45, 184
Crawfords   1, 45, 109, 189,
        190, 227

Keystones 184, 188
Pirates 68, 102, 166, 185-188, 191-193, 241
Railroad Park 2
Rebels 185
Railroad Park (Altoona) 2
Railroad Park (Philadelphia), see Penmar Park
University of Pennsylvania Athletic Field 173
University of Pittsburgh 187, 188
Vandergrift 190
Yeadon 171, 244
YMCA, see Penmar Park
Peppers Park, see Harrison Field
Perry Park, see Walte's Pasture
Perry Stadium, see Victory Field (I)
PETCO Park 157, 209-210
Peters' Park 78
Petersburg Ballfield 170
Phelps, Ken 219
Phillips, Bill 22-23
Phillips, E. Lawrence 234
Pickering, Ollie 71
Pilot Field xvi
Pippin, Kenny 114
Piqua Park 183
Players League Park, see Brotherhood Park (Cleveland)
PNC Park 192-193
Point Grounds Ballpark 110
Point Stadium 109
Polo Field East, see Polo Grounds (I) Southeast Diamond
Polo Field West, see Polo Grounds (II) Southwest Diamond
Polo Grounds (I) Southeast Diamond 147-148, 149
Polo Grounds (II) Southwest Diamond 147, 148, 149
Polo Grounds (III) 149-150, 151
Polo Grounds (IV) 72, 150-151, 152, 155
Polo Grounds (V) xvi, xvii, 41, 49, 119, 130, 150, 151, 153-157, 166, 167, 211, 214
Pompez, Alex 158
Ponce de Leon Park 7-8
Poncey, see Ponce de Leon Park
Pope John Paul II 160
Pope Paul VI 160
Posey, Cumberland 190
Post, Wally 121
Praeger-Kavanagh-Waterbury 120, 159, 164
Predock, Antoine 209
Presley, Elvis 126
Pride of the Yankees 66, 120
Pro Player Stadium, see Dolphin Stadium

Prohibition Stadium, see Exhibition Stadium
Puerto Rico
San Juan 215
Senadores 215
Santurce Cangrejeros 215
Puget Puke, see Kingdome
Pujols, Albert 206
Putnam Grounds 231
Puts, The, see Putnam Grounds
Pyott's Park 59
Q, The, see Qualcomm Stadium
Qualcomm Stadium 99, 208-209
Qualcomm Stadium at Jack Murphy Field, see Qualcomm Stadium
Queens Park 164
Quickstep Park, see Union Street Park
Ramona Athletic Park, see Ramona Park
Ramona Park (Grand Rapids) 91
Ramona Park (Monroe, Louisiana), see Casino Park
Randall's Island Stadium, see Triborough Stadium
Rapp, Vern 22-23
Rashid, Frank 85
Rasberry, Ted 92
Ray Winder Field, see Travelers Field
Razzberry Park 45
Recreation Park (Detroit) 82
Recreation Park (Philadelphia) 172
Recreation Park (Pittsburgh) 184
Recreation Park (I) 76
Recreation Park (II) 76
Recreation Park (III) 163, 164
Red Bird Stadium 77
Red Book 29
Red Cap Stadium, see Durkee Field
Red Stocking Base-Ball Park 197
Red Wing Stadium 195-196
Redford, Robert 40
Redland Field, see Crosley Field
Reinholdt, Marty 16
Reipschlager, Charlie 70
Reliant Stadium 101
Renzieshausen Park 125
Reynolds, Allie 160
Reynolds, Roland 3
RFK Stadium, see Robert F. Kennedy Stadium
Rhode Island 33
Newport 145
Colts 145
Gulls 145
Ponies 145
Providence 193, 231
Base Ball Grounds, see Adelaide Avenue Grounds
Grays 34, 193, 243

Warwick 193, 231
Richardson, Bobby 163
Richmond Ave Grounds, see Olympic Park (I)
Rickey, Branch 77
Rickwood Field v, 7, 20, 145
Ridgewood Park (I), see Grauer's Ridgewood Park
Ridgewood Park (II), see Wallace's Ridgewood Park
Riley Park 222
Ripken, Jr., Cal 219
Riverfront Stadium 67-68
Riverhead Stadium, see Wivchar Stadium
Riverside Grounds 42
Riverside Park (Albany) 1
Riverside Park (Buffalo), see Riverside Grounds
Riverside Park (Indianapolis) 105
Rizzuto, Phil 42, 160
Robbie, Rod 229
Robert A. M. Stern Architects 2
Robert F. Kennedy Stadium 166, 237, 238-239
Roberts, Robin 181
Robertson Park, see Offermann Stadium
Robin Roberts Stadium, see Lanphier Park
Robinson, Bill "Bojangles" 159
Robinson, Frank 18
Robinson, Jackie 8, 41, 42, 109, 139
Robison Field 198, 199
Rochambeau, Le Comte de 18
Rock, Patrick 111
Rockefeller, Nelson 160
Rockpile, The, see Hilltop Park
Rocky Point Park 231
Rodriguez, Henry 139
Rogers Centre 61, 229-230
Rogers, Roy 68
Roosevelt, Franklin D. 109
Roosevelt Stadium 108
Rose Bowl 119
Rose, Pete 68
Rosemore Park 115
Rosen, Al 213
Rosner, Max 42
Ross, Bill 3
Rowell, Bama 40
Royals Stadium 121, 149
see Kauffman Stadium
Ruppert, Jacob 143, 160
Ruppert Stadium, see Municipal Stadium (Kansas City)
Ruppert Stadium (Newark) 142-143
Russwood Park 126
Ruth, Babe xvii, 8, 9, 18, 19, 29, 42, 48, 72, 126, 160, 161, 186, 188, 192

Ryan, Jimmy    50
Ryan, Nolan    6
Ryan, Terry    134
Safeco Field    219-220, 230
St. George Cricket Grounds    108, 149
St. James Court    122
St. Mary's Field, see League Park (II)
    (Akron)
St. Paul Saints    96
Santop, Louis    244
Sauna, The, see Miller Park
SBC Park, see AT&T Park
Scavado, Signor    52
Schantz, Bobby    100
Schilling, Curt    182
Schmidt, Mike    102, 181
Schorling's Park, see South Side Park
    (III)
Schwab, Matty    157
Schwarz, Davis M.    5
Scully, Vin    204
Seals    211
Seals Stadium    211-212
Selter, Ron    154, 155, 237
Seventh Street Park (I)    104
Seventh Street Park (II)    104
Seventh Street Park (III)    104-105
Seybold, Socks    235
Shannon, Bill    xi
Sexson, Richie    103
Shea Stadium    162, 164-166, 167
Shea, William    165
Sheckard, Jimmy    37
Shewbridge Park    59
SHG, Inc.    68, 86
Shibe, Ben    175
Shibe Park    xii, xvi, 156, 174, 175,
    176-178, 181
Shoot the Chutes, see Robison Field
Showalter, Buck    182
Sick's Stadium, see Sicks' Stadium
Sicks' Stadium    216, 219
Silver, Morrie    196
Silver Stadium, see Red Wing
    Stadium
Simmons, Joe    242
Simonson, Otto G.    15
Sirko, Erik    192
Skidmore, Owing & Merrill    130,
    133, 168
SkyDome    61, 220, 229-230, see
    Rogers Centre
Smith, Janet Marie    19
Smith, Kate    133
Smith, Tal    104
Smithfield Stadium    220
Snead, Sam    58
Snodgrass, Fred    29
Society for the Protection of Destitute
    Roman Catholic Children, see
    Catholic Protectory Oval

Solari, Augustus    198
Solari's Beer Garden, see Sportsman's
    Park (II)
Soldier Field    59
Somers Park, see League Park (IV)
    (Cleveland)
South Carolina
    Conway    78
    Greenville    93
    Greenwood    93
    Spartanburg Phillies    176
    Sumter    222
South End Grounds (I)    23, 24, 26
South End Grounds (II)    23, 24, 25,
    26
South End Grounds (III)    26, 27
South End Park    203
South Side Grounds, see South End
    Grounds (III)
South Side Park (I)    48
South Side Park (II)    49, 52
South Side Park (III)    51-52
South Street Park    23, 104
Southern Association Park, see
    Travelers Field
Spahn, Warren    11, 239
Spectrum, The    179
Speedway Park    106
Spencer Field    60
Speranza Park    226
Spiller Park, see Ponce de Leon Park
Sportsman's Park    xii, 85
Sportsman's Park (I)    197, 199
Sportsman's Park (II)    198, 199
Sportsman's Park (III)    198, 199-200
Sportsman's Park (IV)    xii, 198, 199,
    200-201
Sprague Field    21
Springfield Track, see Hampden Park
    Race Track
Stade Olympique    138, 230
Stadium Over the Monongahela
    192
Standpipe Park    238
Stanky, Eddie    54
Star Baseball Park    78
Star Grounds, see Star Baseball Park
Star Park (I)    222
Star Park (II)    223
Stargell, Willie    139, 191
Stars Field    145
Stars Park    203
State Street Grounds, see 23rd Street
    Grounds
Steadman, John    19
Steam    61
Steininger Field, see Handlan's Park
Stengel, Casey    38, 42, 141, 160
Sterling Oval, see Dexter Park
Stick, The, see Candlestick Park
Stoneham, Horace    157

Stovall Park, see Casino Park
Strawberry, Darryl    139
Strong, Nat    42
Stuart, Jeb    194
Suffer Hell, see Sulphur Dell (II)
Sullivan, George    29
Sulphur Dell (I)    139, 140
Sulphur Dell (II)    139, 140-141
Sulphur Dell Park, see Sulphur Dell (II)
Sulphur Springs Bottom, see Sulphur
    Dell (II)
Summit City Club    90
Super Bowl    99, 209
Superbas    37
Sverdrup, Parcel & Associates    204
Swampoodle Grounds    233
Swayne Field    227
Sweat Box, see Hubert H. Humphrey
    Metrodome
Swinney Park, see Jailhouse Flats (I)
Taft, William Howard    235
Taillbert, Roger    138
Taj O'Malley, see Dodger Stadium
Talbert Park    197
Tate Field, see Beyerle's Park
Taylor, Ben    244
Temple Cup Series    13 23, 35, 49, 62,
    147, 172, 184, 233
Tennessee
    Chattanooga    46
        Lookouts    46-47
    Memphis    126
        Chicks    126
        Red Sox    93, 126, 139
        Redbirds    205
    Nashville    8, 139
        Elite Giants    46, 140-141
Termite Palace, see Honolulu Stadium
Terrapin Park    15
Terry, Bill    97
Texas    239
    Arlington    4-7
    Austin    11-12
    Houston    99-104, 220, 230
        Astros    101-104, 193, 213
        Colt .45's    100
        Eagles    11, 99
        Rangers    4-6, 53, 74, 215, 235,
            238
    University of    11-12
Thirteenth and Ann Streets Park
    242
Thomson, Bobby    157
Three Rivers Park    183, 223
Three Rivers Stadium    183, 184, 185,
    188, 191-192
Thunderdome (Minneapolis), see
    Hubert H. Humphrey
    Metrodome
Thunderdome (St. Petersburg), see
    Tropicana Field

Thurtle, John G.   64
Tiernan, Mike   150, 241
Tiger Stadium   xii, 5, 6, 82, 83-85, 103, 156, 211, 216
Tigers Park, see Giants Park
Tinker, Joe   58
Tip Tops   37
Tomb, The, see Kingdome
Torre, Joe   166
Travelers Field   117
Traynor, Pie   97
Triborough Stadium   164
Tri-State Fair Grounds   226
Tropical, La, see Estadio Cerveza Tropicale
Tropical Stadium, see Estadio Cerveza Tropicale
Tropicana Field   204, 206-208, 229
Turner Field (Atlanta)   8, 10-11, 81
Turner Field (Hammond, Indiana)   94
Turnpike Stadium. See Arlington Stadium
Twain, Mark   213
Twilight Zone   120
UMAX Coliseum, see McAfee Coliseum
Union
    and Capitoline Grounds, see Capitoline Grounds
    Association Park, see Capitol Grounds
    Athletic Park, see Bank Street Grounds
    Ball Park, see South Side Park (I)
    Base-Ball Grounds, see White Stocking Grounds
    Baseball Grounds (Boston), see South End Grounds (II)
    Cricket Club Grounds, see Lincoln Park Grounds
    Grounds (Brooklyn)   33, 34
    Grounds (Cincinnati), see Lincoln Park Grounds
    Grounds (St. Louis), see Palace Park of America
    Park (Boston), see Dartmouth Grounds
    Park (Pittsburgh), see Recreation Park (Pittsburgh)
    Park (I) (Baltimore), see Oriole Park (I)
    Park (II) (Baltimore), see Belair Lot
    Park (III) (Baltimore), see Oriole Park (III)
    Park (Pittsburgh)   183
    Park (Wilmington, Delaware), see Union Street Park
    Skating Pond, see Union Grounds (Brooklyn)
    Skating Rink, see Union Grounds (Brooklyn)
    Street Ball Grounds, see Union Street Park
    Street Park   242
Unitas, Johnny   123
US Cellular Field, see Comiskey Park (II)
Valenzuela, Fernando   136
Valley Field   92
Van Buskirk, Charles Randall   38
Vandeventer Lot (I), see Robison Field
Vandeventer Lot (II)   203
Vaughn, Mo   134
Veeck, Bill   53, 54, 57, 43, 74, 129, 201, 202
Venable Stadium   16-17, 18
Verdi, Frank   96
Vet, The, see Veterans Stadium
Veterans Memorial Stadium, see Veterans Stadium
Veterans Park, see Hamtramck Stadium
Veterans Stadium   xii, 179-180
Victory Field (I)   106
Victory Field (II)   107
Virginia
    Base-Ball Park, see Allen's Pasture
    Clarksville   69
    Danville   78
    Hampton   94
    Petersburg   170
    Richmond   194
        Fair Grounds, see Virginia State Agricultural Society Fair Grounds
        Virginias   170, 194
    State Agricultural Society Fair Grounds   194
Visner, Joe   94
Von der Ahe, Chris   198
Wachovia Center   179
Wagner, Honus   188, 191
Walker & Weeks   73
Walker, Dixie   40
Walker, F. R.   73
Walker, Fleet   226
Wallace's Grounds, see Wallace's Ridgewood Park
Wallace's Ridgewood Park   146
Walnut Park   139
Walpole Street Grounds (I), see South End Grounds (I)
Walpole Street Grounds (II), see South End Grounds (II)
Walte's Pasture   23, 114
Waner, Paul   97
War Memorial Stadium   92-93, 176
Washington   13, 92
    Black Senators   235
    Club   149
    D.C.   231-240, 244
    Elite Giants   158, 235
    George   35, 37
    Homestead Grays   52, 77, 107, 117, 136, 145, 159, 176, 185, 235
    Nationals   194, 231, 232, 233, 238, 239, 244
    Olympics   12, 13, 62, 231, 232
    Park (Indianapolis), see Riverside Park
    Park (Newburgh Heights, Ohio), see Beyerle's Park
    Park (Pittsburgh)   189
    Park (I)   35, 36
    Park (II)   35, 36
    Park (III)   36-37
    Park (IV)   37
    Pilots   235
    Potomacs   238
    Pullman   217
    Seattle   134, 216-220, 229, 230
        Mariners   74, 217-220
        Pilots   216-217
        Supersonics (NBA)   219
    Senators   15, 16, 22, 71, 92, 162-163, 233, 234-239
    State University   217
    Statesmen   233
    Tacoma   212
Waverly Fairgrounds   89
Waverly Field, see Hawkins Stadium
Waverly Park, see Waverly Fairgrounds
Weeghman Park, see Wrigley Field (Chicago)
Weequahic Park, see Waverly Fairgrounds
West End Grounds (Harrisburg, Pennsylvania)   95
West End Park, see Burns Park
West Seventh Street Park, see Fort Street Grounds
West Side Grounds   49-51
West Side Park (I)   49
West Side Park (II), see West Side Grounds
West Troy Grounds, see Troy Ball Club Grounds
West Virginia
    Wheeling   241
Western Avenue Grounds, see League Park (I)
Westport Park, see Westport Stadium
Westport Race Track, see Westport Stadium
Westport Stadium   241
Westwood Field, see Ducks Park

Whales Park, see Wrigley Field

Wheeling Grounds, see Island Grounds

White, Roy   162

White Sox Park (I), see South Side Park (III)

White Sox Park (II), see Comiskey Park (I)

White Sox Park (III), see Comiskey Park (I)

White Stocking Grounds   47, 48

White Stocking Park   48

White Stocking Park (IV), see South Side Park (III)

Whitlow, Robert   58

Whittemore Athletic Field   78

Wiedenmeyer's Park   142

Wigwam, see Braves Field

Wild West Grounds   149

William-Russell & Johnson Inc.   8

William Steele and Sons   176

Williams, A. D.   188

Williams, Billy   57

Williams, Hattie   178

Williams, Smokey Joe   159

Williams, Ted   30, 31

Williamson, Ned   48

Wills, Maury   213

Wilmington Grounds, see Union Street Park

Wilmot, Walt   50

Wilson, "Boojum" Jud   88

Wilson, Chief   188

Wilson, Morris, Crain & Anderson   101

Wilson Park   140

Wilson, Thomas   140

Wind Tunnel, see Candlestick Park

Windsor Beach Grounds   107

Wisconsin

    Milwaukee   33, 82, 128-133, 192, 220, 230

        Athletic Park, see Borchert Field

        Base-Ball Grounds   128

        Baseball Park (I), see Wright Street Grounds

        Baseball Park (II), see Lloyd Street Grounds

        Bears   51, 128

        Braves   33, 118, 130-132, 156

        Brewers   53, 128-129, 130-132, 133, 219

        Cream Citys   128

        Creams   130

        Grays   128

        Millers   133

Wivchar Stadium   195

Woodbridge Grove, see Bennett Park

Woods, Al   228

Woodward, Rick   20

World Baseball Championships   97

World Baseball Classic   210

World Series   27, 28, 29, 30, 31, 52, 53, 55, 72, 73, 80, 83, 118, 134, 162, 163, 174, 187, 188, 198, 200, 204, 205, 213, 230, 237

WPA   88, 109, 194, 224

Wright Street Grounds   128, 129

Wrigley Field (Chicago)   v, 7, 54-58, 120, 193, 205

Wrigley Field (Los Angeles)   119-120, 238

Wrigley, Phil   58

Wrigley, Jr., William F.   58

Yankee Stadium   xvii, 9, 54, 80, 81, 156, 157, 158, 159-163, 166, 167-168

Yawkey, Tom A. and Jean R.   30

Yellow baseballs   39

Young, Cy   27

Zisk, Richie   54